SAGE
vantage

SAGE Outcomes:
Measure Results, Track Success

FOR STUDENTS, understanding the objectives for each chapter and the goals for the course is essential for getting the grade you deserve!

FOR INSTRUCTORS, being able to track your students' progress allows you to more easily pinpoint areas of improvement and report on success.

This title was crafted around specific chapter objectives and course outcomes, vetted by experts, and adapted from renowned syllabi. Tracking student progress can be challenging. Promoting and achieving success should never be. We are here for you.

COURSE **OUTCOMES** FOR AMERICAN GOVERNMENT:

ARTICULATE the foundations of American government, including its history, critical concepts, and important documents and achievements.

EXAMINE the main institutions of American government, including their roles and interrelationships.

DESCRIBE the roles and relative importance of major entities and influences in American political life.

ANALYZE the development and impact of important governmental policies.

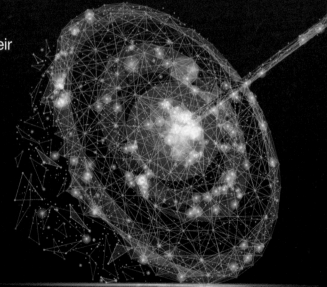

Want to see how these outcomes tie in with this book's chapter-level objectives? Visit us at edge.sagepub.com/dautrich6e for complete outcome-to-objective mapping.

Praise for

"I find the writing style to be **PERFECT.** I believe this book is a well-researched and well-written survey on the federal government. The book provides nice historical context and covers topics in a thoughtful and thorough manner."

—Tracy Cook
Central Texas College

"In my post-lecture survey of students, one comment students make all the time is that they enjoy the way this textbook explores demographic changes in the country, and how it **HELPS THEM UNDERSTAND** political changes in the country."

—Augustine Ayuk
Clayton State University

"In general, I find the book to be well researched and well written. In my opinion, the main strength of the book is the writing style. Concepts are described and explained in a manner that is similar to how I explain them to students. This provides my students with an **EASY TRANSITION** from reading to lecture. This book does a nice job of balancing readability with content. It feels up-to-date and the visual elements are **ENGAGING.** My students don't have to be harassed to get them to read it. They like having the learning objectives right up front."

—Bo Wood
University of North Dakota

"This is an excellent core textbook for American Government. It is a clear presentation of the basic information with an emphasis on institutions and context. This text has been **WELL-LIKED** by my students. I like the strong institutionalist elements of the book, which pair well with its emphasis on **ACCESSIBILITY** for students. The balance between understanding the institutions, how they shape political behavior, and the influence of historical context is good. Further, it avoids the overly technical elements of some institutionalist texts. Students see the impact of institutions without getting deterred by the technical elements."

—Gregory Dixon
University of West Georgia

The Enduring Democracy

Sixth Edition

Sara Miller McCune founded SAGE Publishing in 1965 to support the dissemination of usable knowledge and educate a global community. SAGE publishes more than 1000 journals and over 800 new books each year, spanning a wide range of subject areas. Our growing selection of library products includes archives, data, case studies and video. SAGE remains majority owned by our founder and after her lifetime will become owned by a charitable trust that secures the company's continued independence.

Los Angeles | London | New Delhi | Singapore | Washington DC | Melbourne

The Enduring Democracy

Sixth Edition

Kenneth J. Dautrich
University of Connecticut

David A. Yalof
University of Connecticut

Christina E. Bejarano
Texas Woman's University

FOR INFORMATION:

CQ Press
An imprint of SAGE Publications, Inc.
2455 Teller Road
Thousand Oaks, California 91320
E-mail: order@sagepub.com

SAGE Publications Ltd.
1 Oliver's Yard
55 City Road
London, EC1Y 1SP
United Kingdom

SAGE Publications India Pvt. Ltd.
B 1/I 1 Mohan Cooperative Industrial Area
Mathura Road, New Delhi 110 044
India

SAGE Publications Asia-Pacific Pte. Ltd.
18 Cross Street #10-10/11/12
China Square Central
Singapore 048423

Printed in Canada

Library of Congress Cataloging-in-Publication Data

Names: Dautrich, Kenneth J., author.
Title: The enduring democracy / Kenneth J. Dautrich - University of Connecticut, David A. Yalof - University of Connecticut, Christina E. Bejarano - Texas Woman's University.
Description: 6th Edition. | Thousand Oaks : CQ Press, 2020. | Includes bibliographical references and index.
Identifiers: LCCN 2019025924 | ISBN 978-1-5443-6447-6 (paperback) | ISBN 978-1-5443-6445-2 (epub) | ISBN 978-1-5443-6444-5 (epub) | ISBN 978-1-5443-6446-9 (adobe pdf)
Subjects: LCSH: Representative government and representation—United States—History. | United States—Politics and government.
Classification: LCC JK2484 .D38 2020 | DDC 320.473—dc23
LC record available at https://lccn.loc.gov/2019025924

Acquisitions Editor: Scott Greenan
Editorial Assistant: Sam Rosenberg
Content Development Editor: Scott Harris
Production Editor: Rebecca Lee
Copy Editor: Colleen Brennan
Typesetter: Hurix Digital
Proofreader: Eleni Maria Georgiou
Indexer: Celia McCoy
Cover Designer: Candice Harman
Marketing Manager: Erica DeLuca

This book is printed on acid-free paper.

20 21 22 23 24 10 9 8 7 6 5 4 3 2 1

BRIEF CONTENTS

DETAILED CONTENTS

LETTER TO INSTRUCTORS

This is a textbook about American government, the success of which depends upon a responsible citizenry willing to ask tough questions of its leaders and demand reasonable answers in return. This book encourages student readers to hone their critical thinking skills, ask the tough questions, and become responsible citizens. We encourage students to become educated citizens through two paths: (1) by learning how the problems and controversies characterizing American government today have been successfully tackled in America's past, and (2) by examining how the changing demographics of America have affected its political landscape.

The first path to understanding focuses on history. Certainly history tends to repeat itself, and we can learn important lessons from history to better address the problems we face today. American government and politics have changed dramatically in the more than two centuries of the nation's existence, yet certain issues persist. The challenge facing instructors of American government is how to take adequate account of all these changes while never losing sight of the issues and events from the nation's past and their significance today. We thus offer in this sixth edition of *The Enduring Democracy* all the nuts and bolts of the U.S. government and how it works, but we also seek to educate students about American politics in ways that go beyond the essentials by **placing current political issues and debates in historical perspective**. This theme runs throughout the book's narrative and is reflected in its organization. The book begins with a discussion of how the road map of history provides a guide to the future, how the use of a historical perspective on American politics can add to and help shape our understanding of contemporary problems and the creation and evolution of its institutions and processes, before diving into the foundations of U.S. government, the institutions of government formed under the Constitution, and then later to political behavior and public policy.

The second path examines diversity by considering the changing demographics of our polity and the various ways in which those changes have an impact on our politics. Over and over during the 2016 presidential campaign and the 2018 midterm elections, America's diverse character became a focal point for discussion, as both major parties' candidates faced an electorate more diverse than ever before. These changing demographics also have a sizeable impact on governing political institutions, their public policy formulation, and nearly all types of informal political behavior as well, including media coverage and interest-group dynamics. Accordingly, this textbook considers American politics in ways that are informed by these fundamental changes in the political landscape. Throughout the book's narrative, we take note of the ways in which traditional institutions and entities have successfully (or in some cases, not so successfully) taken account of this changing political reality.

Many of the book's past features support these themes, and several of them return in the sixth edition. For example, **Then & Now** boxes continue to give ample attention to the premise that American political history has a habit of repeating itself through examples of contemporary problems and controversies that have been identified, tackled, and in some cases resolved in earlier years. We also continue to offer a fully updated and revised civil rights, equality, and social movements chapter that more comprehensively considers racial/ethnic politics, especially Latino politics, and the evolution of discrimination against disadvantaged groups in the political arena as well as in the courts. *The Enduring Democracy* has also been updated to include complete coverage of the Trump administration's first three years in office, the 2018 midterm election results, and the 2020 presidential election contest.

We also offer **Debates over Diversity** boxes within every chapter that offer examples and illustrations of how America's changing demographics and increased diversity have altered the political landscape. This feature touches on many contemporary political debates across the broad range of American politics. Our ever-changing population poses significant challenges that must be addressed by local institutions such as schools and by national institutions, including Congress, executive agencies, and the U.S. Supreme Court. Students will consider these debates and then address questions that seek students' reflections on how we as a society should most effectively address the challenges and opportunities presented with our diversity.

Additionally, this new edition has been shortened to 15 chapters to better accommodate the length of a typical semester. The domestic and foreign policy chapters have been combined into a single chapter to provide succinct, well-rounded coverage of major policy concepts.

By examining the current state of American politics through the lens of American history and the nation's changing demographics, we encourage students to think critically about the significance of certain persons, places, and events in American politics and consider all the different ways in which they might be viewed and interpreted. The historical perspective and the materials that address American politics from students' own perspectives do not interfere with the description of essential foundations. Rather, they spark student interest in revisiting what they learned in high school, from the media, and elsewhere about American politics with a more discerning and critical eye. Perhaps many students will take this critical approach beyond the course itself and become actual participants in the process. If they do so with a more critical and skeptical eye, our democratic system can only benefit.

Sincerely,

Kenneth J. Dautrich
k.dautrich@uconn.edu

David A. Yalof
david.yalof@uconn.edu

Christina E. Bejarano
cbejarano@twu.edu

The idea that "history repeats itself" is not merely a piece of conventional wisdom. Looking back provides important lessons applicable to today's challenges. In examining the past we find that some of our new and "unprecedented" political controversies are neither new nor unprecedented. By the same token, changes in the demographics of our population should force a reconsideration of many aspects of American political behavior, past and present. The faces may have changed and the policies may have been modernized, but the challenges the nation faces today are often newer versions of past dilemmas and problems.

In *The Enduring Democracy*, you will learn the essentials of American government with a dual focus on placing current issues and controversies into historical perspective, as well as on considering how the changing face of the American public influences those issues and controversies. By adopting these perspectives, you'll gain a greater appreciation for American government— both its flaws and its successes—as well as its challenges. At the conclusion of each chapter we frame contemporary problems from the perspective of what they mean to college students like you, so that you can see the relevance of American government in your life.

- **Learning Objectives** open each chapter and serve as a road map to the key concepts and major sections you'll find within, helping you focus on the most important points and assess your comprehension as you read. We conclude each chapter with a review of those objectives to help you master the chapter's material. Additionally, within each chapter **key terms** are highlighted in boldface type and defined in the margins of the pages. These key terms are also listed at the end of the chapter, and the terms and definitions are repeated in a **glossary** at the end of the book.
- **Debates over Diversity** boxes found within every chapter offer examples and illustrations of how America's changing demographics and increased diversity change the American political landscape. The feature touches on many contemporary political debates, such as voting rights and immigration policy, across the broad range of American politics. Our ever-changing population poses significant challenges that must be addressed by local institutions such as schools and by national institutions, including Congress, executive agencies, and the U.S. Supreme Court itself. You will have the opportunity to consider these debates and then address questions that seek your reflections on how we as a society should most effectively address the challenges and opportunities presented by our diversity.
- **Then & Now** boxes show that although the specific names and details change, most contemporary problems and controversies have been identified, tackled, and in some cases outright resolved over and over at different points in the past. It is thus no wonder that "those who cannot remember the past are condemned to repeat it."
- **From Your Perspective** features consider contemporary political issues from the unique perspective of college students like yourself, tapping into the experiences you bring to the table when studying American government. They'll help you consider your own views and find opportunities to get involved in your community and American politics.
- **Critical Thinking** questions at the end of every thematic box help you think about the material in new and interesting ways and may spark discussions with your classmates.

A thorough examination of past problems, issues, and conflicts does not negate the uniqueness of the current American condition, but it does offer a better understanding of contemporary issues. In some cases, studying the past assures us that the political process does work in a positive way; in other cases, it reminds us that we are not the first to face certain difficulties, and it suggests that we may want to seek more direction from the past about what works and what does not. We hope that this exploration encourages you not only to succeed in your intro class but also to join the conversation on a larger scale and become an active participant in your community and *your* American government.

Sincerely,

Kenneth J. Dautrich
k.dautrich@uconn.edu

David A. Yalof
david.yalof@uconn.edu

Christina E. Bejarano
cbejarano@twu.edu

⑤SAGE vantage™

Engage, Learn, Soar with **SAGE vantage**, an intuitive digital platform that delivers *The Enduring Democracy* textbook content in a learning experience carefully designed to ignite student engagement and drive critical thinking. With evidence-based instructional design at the core, SAGE vantage creates more time for engaged learning and empowered teaching, keeping the classroom where it belongs—in your hands.

Easy to access across mobile, desktop, and tablet devices, SAGE vantage enables students to engage with the material you choose, learn by applying knowledge, and soar with confidence by performing better in your course.

HIGHLIGHTS INCLUDE:

- **eReading Experience.** Makes it easy for students to study wherever they are—students can take notes, highlight content, look up definitions, and more!
- **Pedagogical Scaffolding.** Builds on core concepts, moving students from basic understanding to mastery.
- **Confidence Builder.** Offers frequent knowledge checks, applied-learning multimedia tools, and chapter tests with focused feedback to assure students know key concepts.
- **Time-saving Flexibility.** Feeds auto-graded assignments to your gradebook, with real-time insight into student and class performance.
- **Quality Content.** Written by expert authors and teachers, content is not sacrificed for technical features.
- **Honest Value.** Affordable access to easy-to-use, quality learning tools students will appreciate.

FAVORITE SAGE VANTAGE FEATURES

- **3-step course setup** is so fast you can complete it in minutes!
- **Control over assignments**, content selection, due dates, and grading empowers you to teach your way.
- **Quality content** authored by the experts you trust.
- **eReading experience** makes it easy to learn and study by presenting content in easy-to-digest segments featuring note-taking, highlighting, definition look-up, and more.
- **LMS integration provides single sign-on** with streamlined grading capabilities and course management tools.
- **Auto-graded assignments** include:

  - formative **knowledge checks** for each major section of the text that quickly reinforce what students have read and ensure they stay on track;
  - dynamic, hands-on **multimedia activities** that tie real-world examples and motivate students to read, prepare for class;
  - summative **chapter tests** that reinforce important themes; and
  - **helpful hints and feedback** (provided with all assignments) that offer context and explain why an answer is correct or incorrect, allowing students to study more effectively.

- **Compelling polling questions** bring concepts to life and drive meaningful comprehension and classroom discussion.
- **Short-answer questions** provide application and reflection opportunities connected to key concepts.
- **Instructor reports** track student activity and provide analytics so you can adapt instruction as needed.
- **A student dashboard** offers easy access to grades, so students know exactly where they stand in your course and where they might improve.
- **Honest value** gives students access to quality content and learning tools at a price they will appreciate.

⑤SAGE coursepacks

SAGE COURSEPACKS FOR INSTRUCTORS

The **SAGE coursepack** for *The Enduring Democracy* makes it easy to import our quality instructor materials and student resources into your school's learning management system (LMS), such as Blackboard, Canvas, Brightspace by D2L, or Moodle. Intuitive and simple to use, **SAGE coursepack** allows you to integrate only the content you need, with minimal effort, and requires no access code. Don't use an LMS platform? You can still access many of the online resources for *The Enduring Democracy* via the **SAGE edge** site.

Available SAGE content through the coursepack includes:

- Pedagogically robust **assessment tools** that foster review, practice, and critical thinking and offer a more complete way to measure student engagement, including:
  - Diagnostic **coursepack chapter quizzes** that identify opportunities for improvement, track student progress, and ensure mastery of key learning objectives.
  - **Test banks** built on Bloom's taxonomy that provide a diverse range of test items.
  - **Activity and quiz options** that allow you to choose only the assignments and tests you want.
- Editable, chapter-specific **PowerPoint®** slides that offer flexibility when creating multimedia lectures so you don't have to start from scratch but can customize to your exact needs.
- **Instructions** on how to use and integrate the comprehensive assessments and resources provided.

⑤SAGE edge™

SAGE edge is a robust online environment featuring an impressive array of tools and resources for review, study, and further exploration, keeping both instructors and students on the cutting edge of teaching and learning. SAGE edge content is open access and available on demand. Learning and teaching has never been easier!

SAGE edge for Students at **http://edge.sagepub.com/dautrich6e** provides a personalized approach to help students accomplish their coursework goals in an easy-to-use learning environment.

- **Learning objectives** reinforce the most important material.
- Mobile-friendly **Flashcards** strengthen understanding of key terms and concepts, and make it easy to maximize your study time, anywhere, anytime.
- Mobile-friendly practice **quizzes** allow you to assess how much you've learned and where you need to focus your attention.

SAGE edge for Instructors at **http://edge.sagepub.com/dautrich6e** supports teaching by making it easy to integrate quality content and create a rich learning environment for students.

- The **Test bank**, built on Bloom's taxonomy (with Bloom's cognitive domain and difficulty level noted for each question), is created specifically for this text.
- **Sample course syllabi** provide suggested models for structuring your course.
- Editable, chapter-specific **PowerPoint® slides** offer complete flexibility for creating a multimedia presentation for the course, so you don't have to start from scratch but can customize to your exact needs.
- An **instructor's manual** for each chapter includes a chapter summary, outline, multimedia links, discussion questions, and in-class activities.
- A set of all the **graphics from the text**, including all the maps, tables, and figures in PowerPoint formats are provided for class presentations.

SAGE PREMIUM VIDEO

The Enduring Democracy offers premium video, available exclusively in the **SAGE vantage** digital option, produced and curated specifically for this text, to boost comprehension and bolster analysis.

SAGE COURSE OUTCOMES

Outlined in your text and mapped to chapter learning objectives, SAGE course outcomes are crafted with specific course outcomes in mind and vetted by advisers in the field. See how SAGE course outcomes tie in with this book's chapter-level objectives at **http://edge.sagepub.com/dautrich6e.**

ACKNOWLEDGMENTS

The sixth edition of *The Enduring Democracy* is the product of the hard work of many, many people. Though she moved on to other creative challenges after our fifth edition was in production, we continue to owe much to our original product team manager at Cengage, Carolyn Merrill, for this and all previous editions. At Cengage she was the prime mover of this project, just as she was for each of our earlier editions. It is impossible to imagine pulling off a project like this without the management skills, temperament, and good humor that Carolyn provided.

Thankfully, our move to CQ Press and SAGE Publications for this sixth edition has been seamless thanks to some extremely talented individuals at SAGE who have stepped in to supervise this new edition's production and marketing. The one-time executive publisher and now director of editorial, Monica Eckman, believed in us and this project from the very outset, and her passionate advocacy of the book laid the foundation for what has been a model transition from one major publisher to another. Our content development manager at SAGE, Scott Harris, has kept the sixth edition moving forward and on schedule; his quick turnaround of our chapters made this schedule manageable. The editorial assistant, Sam Rosenberg, helped with photo selections and captions. Scott Greenan's contributions on the editorial and marketing side have been invaluable.

The many sales representatives at SAGE do a terrific job of getting the word out on our book; we are grateful for their many efforts. Appreciation also goes to our colleagues at the University of Connecticut, the University of Kansas, and Texas Woman's University, especially those in the Department of Political Science and the Department of Public Policy, of which there are too many to list by name. Their patience, support, and advice in our writing of this sixth edition have not gone unnoticed, nor has the input we have received from our graduate students and undergraduate users of the text.

The many professionals, colleagues, and students who provide support and advice are not the only ones who influence the writing of a textbook. Our families must live with us through the writing and production cycles. Not only do they tolerate the fact that we often bring our work home, but they also give us strong motivation to get the job done. We cannot thank our families enough, especially two of our better halves Andrea and Mary Beth, and the Bejarano family: Benita, Ray, Chris, and Jessica. Our children are never shy about offering their ideas. As always, the book benefits from their youthful perspectives and advice.

Finally, there are many members of our profession and many practitioners in American politics who put in countless hours and intellectual energy aiding in the writing of this manuscript and the book's supplements. Special thanks goes to Tracy Cook of Central Texas College for working with us on past editions. Some participated in focus groups, others in informal conversations with us, and still others spent much time marking up chapters. We are indebted to all those who have generously given time to this effort. These contributors' names appear in the list of reviewers. Please note, however, that any errors that remain are entirely our own.

REVIEWERS

We would also like to thank the instructors who have contributed their valuable feedback through reviews of this text:

Tracy Cook, Central Texas College

Bo Wood, University of North Dakota

Cherry Rain, Redlands Community College

Augustine E. Ayuk, Clayton State University

Gregory C. Dixon, University of West Georgia

Meena Bose, Hofstra University

Daphne M. Cooper, Indian River State College

W. R. Mack, Central Texas College

William Lee Jackson, Central Texas College

Kim Seckler, New Mexico State University

Amanda Friesen, Indiana University–Purdue University Indianapolis

Nicholas Pyeatt, Penn State Altoona

Amy Colon, SUNY Sullivan

Abbylin Sellers, Azusa Pacific University

ABOUT THE AUTHORS

Kenneth J. Dautrich (PhD, Rutgers, 1995) is an associate professor of public policy at the University of Connecticut. He is also the founder and former director of the Center for Survey Research & Analysis at the University of Connecticut. Previously, Dr. Dautrich was a research fellow at the Media Studies Center in New York and has served as a senior faculty fellow at the Heldrich Center at Rutgers. His first book, *How the News Media Fail American Voters* (Columbia University Press, 1999), received scholarly praise in numerous political science circles. He also coauthored *The First Amendment and the Media in the Court of Public Opinion* (Cambridge University Press, 2002) and *The Future of the First Amendment* (Rowman & Littlefield, 2008). Dr. Dautrich's research and teaching focus on public opinion and American elections. For the past six years he has directed a set of national surveys on civic literacy in the American public and the role of higher education in advancing knowledge about American government. He directs an annual national survey on the state of the First Amendment for the Freedom Forum's Newseum Institute and a biannual survey of the millennial generation on the future of the First Amendment for the Knight Foundation.

David A. Yalof (PhD, Johns Hopkins University, 1997; JD, University of Virginia, 1991) is department head and professor of political science at the University of Connecticut in Storrs. His first book, *Pursuit of Justices: Presidential Politics and the Selection of Supreme Court Nominees* (University of Chicago Press, 1999), was awarded the American Political Science Association's Richard E. Neustadt Award as the best book published on presidential studies in 1999. His most recent book is *Prosecution among Friends: Presidents, Attorneys General, and Executive Branch Wrongdoing* (Texas A&M University Press, 2012). He is also the coauthor of *The First Amendment and the Media in the Court of Public Opinion* (Cambridge University Press, 2002), *The Future of the First Amendment* (Rowman & Littlefield, 2008), and *Constitutional Law: Civil Liberty and Individual Rights* (Foundation Press, 2007). Dr. Yalof has written extensively on issues in constitutional law and Supreme Court appointment politics. His work has been published in *Political Research Quarterly*, *Judicature*, *Constitutional Commentary*, and various other journals.

Christina E. Bejarano (PhD and MA, University of Iowa; BA, University of North Texas) is department chair and professor of Multicultural Women's and Gender Studies at Texas Woman's University. Her research and teaching interests are in American gender politics, in particular the areas of gender, race/ethnicity, and political behavior. Her interest in the conditions under which racial/ethnic minorities and women successfully compete for U.S. electoral office is reflected in her book, *The Latina Advantage: Gender, Race, and Political Success* (University of Texas Press, 2013). Her work also focuses on how racial/ethnic minorities and women can shape or influence the current electoral environment, which is reflected in her book, *The Latino Gender Gap in U.S. Politics* (Routledge, 2014). Professor Bejarano has also written journal articles for publication in *Political Research Quarterly* and *Politics & Gender*.

CAREER OPPORTUNITIES: POLITICAL SCIENCE

INTRODUCTION

It is no secret that college graduates are facing one of the toughest job markets in the past fifty years. Despite this challenge, those with a college degree have done much better than those without since the 2008 recession. One of the most important decisions a student has to make is the choice of a major; many consider future job possibilities when making that call. A political science degree is incredibly useful for a successful career in many different fields, from lawyer to policy advocate, pollster to humanitarian worker. Employer surveys reveal that the skills that most employers value in successful employees—critical thinking, analytical reasoning, and clarity of verbal and written communication—are precisely the tools that political science courses should be helping you develop. This brief guide is intended to help spark ideas for what kinds of careers you might pursue with a political science degree and the types of activities you can engage in now to help you secure one of those positions after graduation.

CAREERS IN POLITICAL SCIENCE

LAW AND CRIMINAL JUSTICE

Do you find that your favorite parts of your political science classes are those that deal with the Constitution, the legal system, and the courts? Then a career in law and criminal justice might be right for you. Traditional jobs in the field range from lawyer or judge to police or parole officer. Since 9/11, there has also been tremendous growth in the area of homeland security, which includes jobs in mission support, immigration, travel security, and prevention and response.

PUBLIC ADMINISTRATION

The many offices of the federal government combined represent one of the largest employers in the United States. Flip to the bureaucracy chapter of this textbook and consider that each federal department, agency, and bureau you see looks to political science majors for future employees. A partial list of such agencies includes the Department of Education, the Department of Health and Human Services, and the Federal Trade Commission. There are also thousands of staffers who work for members of Congress or the Congressional Budget Office, many of whom were political science majors in college. This does not even begin to account for the multitude of similar jobs in state and local governments that you might consider as well.

CAMPAIGNS, ELECTIONS, AND POLLING

Are campaigns and elections the most exciting part of political science for you? Then you might consider a career in the growing industry based around political campaigns. From volunteering and interning to consulting, marketing, and fund-raising, there are many opportunities for those who enjoy the competitive and high-stakes electoral arena. For those looking for careers that combine political knowledge with statistical skills, there are careers in public opinion polling. Pollsters work for independent national organizations such as Gallup and YouGov or as part of news operations and campaigns. For those who are interested in survey methodology, there are many nonpolitical career opportunities in marketing and survey design.

INTEREST GROUPS, INTERNATIONAL ORGANIZATIONS, AND NONGOVERNMENTAL ORGANIZATIONS

Is there a cause that you are especially passionate about? If so, there is a good chance that there are interest groups out there that are working hard to see some progress made on similar issues. Many of the positions that one might find in for-profit companies also exist in their nonprofit interest-group and nongovernmental organization counterparts, including lobbying and high-level strategizing. Do not forget that there are also quite a few major international organizations—such as the United Nations, the World Health Organization, and the International Monetary Fund—where a degree in political science could be put to good use. Although competition for those jobs tends to be fierce, your interest and knowledge about politics and policy will give you an advantage.

FOREIGN SERVICE

Does a career in diplomacy and foreign affairs, complete with the opportunity to live and work abroad, sound exciting for you? Tens of thousands of people work for the State Department, both in Washington, DC, and in consulates throughout the world. They represent the diplomatic interests of the United States abroad. Entrance into the Foreign Service follows a very specific process, starting with the Foreign Service Officers Test (FSOT), an exam given three times a year that includes sections on American government, history, economics, and world affairs. Being a political science major is a significant help in taking the FSOT.

GRADUATE SCHOOL

Although not a career, graduate school may be the appropriate next step for you after completing your undergraduate degree. Following the academic route, being awarded a PhD or master's degree in political science could open additional doors to a career in academia, as well as many of the professions mentioned earlier. If a career as a researcher in political science interests you, you should speak with your advisors about continuing your education.

PREPARING WHILE STILL ON CAMPUS

INTERNSHIPS

One of the most useful steps you can take while still on campus is to seek information from your college's career center about an internship in your field of interest. Not only does it give you a chance to experience life in the political science realm, it can lead to job opportunities later and add experience to your résumé.

SKILLS

In addition to your political science classes, the following additional skills will complement your degree:

Writing: Like anything else, writing improves with practice. Writing is one of those skills that is applicable regardless of where your career might take you. Virtually every occupation relies on an ability to write cleanly, concisely, and persuasively.

Public Speaking: An oft-quoted 1977 survey showed that public speaking was the most commonly cited fear among respondents. And yet oral communication is a vital tool in the modern economy. You can practice this skill in a formal class setting or through extracurricular activities that get you in front of a group.

Quantitative Analysis: As the internet aids in the collection of massive amounts of information, the nation is facing a drastic shortage of people with basic statistical skills to interpret and use these data. A political science degree can go hand-in-hand with courses in introductory statistics.

Foreign Language: The ability to communicate in a language other than English can help you stand out in a crowded job market. Solidify or set the foundation for your verbal and written foreign language communication skills while in school.

STUDENT LEADERSHIP

One attribute that many employers look for is "leadership potential," which can be tricky to indicate on a résumé or cover letter. What can help is a demonstrated record of involvement in clubs and organizations, preferably in a leadership role. While many people think immediately of student government, most student clubs allow you the opportunity to demonstrate your leadership skills.

CONCLUSION

Hopefully reading this has sparked some ideas on potential future careers. As a next step, visit your college's career placement office, which is a great place to further explore what you have read here. You might also visit your college's alumni office to connect with graduates who are working in your field of interest. Political science opens the door to a lot of exciting careers. Have fun exploring the possibilities!

Part I
FOUNDATIONS

1

INTRODUCTION TO *THE ENDURING DEMOCRACY*

Democratic socialist candidates are not new to American politics. George McGovern's 1972 campaign and Bernie Sanders' 2016 and 2020 campaigns appealed to Democratic voters on the far left.

ON NOVEMBER 3, 2020, tens of millions of Americans will cast their votes in the 59th presidential election. Since the first election in 1788, the United States has chosen its leader in this way like clockwork. Few events have eclipsed these quadrennial elections in the level of attention, fanfare, scrutiny, and contentiousness that they attract. Certainly, the 2020 campaign has been no different. Indeed, it has been accompanied by hotly contested congressional elections, which occur every two years as has been the case for more than two centuries. Like so many other institutions in American politics, the U.S. system of elections has endured.

The level of attention given to these elections is warranted by the stakes involved. Election outcomes have significant consequences, determining the direction of policymaking in Washington, DC. The 2020 outcomes will determine whether the Democrats or Republicans occupy the White House and control Congress. The 2008 election of President Barack Obama and the return of a Democrat-controlled Congress that year resulted in a new system of healthcare insurance in 2010 (the Affordable Care Act, or Obamacare) and two new liberal voices on the Supreme Court. The 2016 election of President Donald Trump has so far delivered one of the largest income and corporate tax cuts in American history, as well as the appointment of two conservative Supreme Court justices.

In this book, we explore how the patterns of history can inform us about present debates and controversies in American politics. We also discuss how many of these controversies are rooted in the great diversity of the American people. In all of this, we inquire into how the U.S. system of government, through all its recurring tensions, has endured.

Learning Objectives

1-1 Presidential Campaigns, History, Diversity, and American Politics

- Analyze the 2020 presidential campaign in historical context.

1-2 Forms and Functions of Government

- Explain the philosophical underpinnings of the American political system through the exploration of important theories such as the "social contract" theory and the concept of the "natural law."

1-3 American Government and Politics

- Assess the importance of the value of popular sovereignty and how that value is realized through "representative democracy" in the United States.

1-4 American Political Culture

- Define *political culture* and describe the unique combination of political beliefs and values that form the American political culture.

1-5 Is American Democracy in Decline?

- Assess the health of American democracy and evaluate whether the American system is in decline by applying a historical perspective on contemporary politics.

1-1 PRESIDENTIAL CAMPAIGNS, HISTORY, DIVERSITY, AND AMERICAN POLITICS

THE 2020 PRESIDENTIAL ELECTION CAMPAIGN

All presidential elections occur in an environment of unique circumstances, and 2020 is no exception. Incumbent President Donald Trump has been a polarizing figure, loved by his base voters and despised by his detractors. Trump supporters point to a strong economy that is the product of tax cuts and business deregulation as a key reason for their loyalty, along with an enhanced military and two conservative Supreme Court appointments. Trump's detractors argue that the president's rhetoric has fanned the flames of racism and that his economic policies have not helped lower- and working-class people. Moreover, the very legitimacy of Trump's 2016 victory was tainted by accusations that his campaign conspired with the Russian government to help defeat Hillary Clinton. Compounding this is the fact that despite winning the electoral vote, Trump lost the popular vote.

All this has whetted the appetite for a possible Democratic resurgence in 2020. A record 25 hopefuls formally announced their candidacy for the Democratic nomination by spring 2019. Many endorsed the idea that Trump should be impeached and the electoral college should be eliminated. Additionally, the seeds sown by democratic socialist Bernie Sanders in 2016 helped elect a small contingent of like-minded representatives to Congress in 2018, who in turn have moved the 2020 Democratic presidential candidates to the left on many issues. All told, the 2020 campaign is characterized by deep divisions between Democrats and Republicans, unease about the future of the Supreme Court, increased racial tensions, and heated debate over immigration and economic policy.

While partisan polarization is significant in 2020, this environment is not new to American elections. Highly-charged partisanship led to the impeachment of Presidents Andrew Johnson in 1867 and Bill Clinton in 1998. Trump's 2016 electoral college victory, despite his popular vote loss, was actually the fifth time in the history of presidential elections that a president was elected without securing the popular vote. Candidates espousing democratic socialist ideals have risen to national prominence a number of times, including Democratic nominee George McGovern in 1972. Unfortunately, accusations of racism and racist policies have often taken center stage in American presidential campaigns, most notably in the 1860 contest between Abraham Lincoln and Stephen Douglas over the issue of slavery. Concerns about the ideological makeup of the Supreme Court have often been important, including in 1936 when President Roosevelt proposed increasing the number of seats on the Court to create a liberal majority (as some Democratic candidates have endorsed in 2020).

The actors, particulars, and specific situations of elections change. However, the broad context of the debates and the polarization often recur. This idea holds true not only for elections, but for governing as well.

HISTORY REPEATS ITSELF

The patterns of history provide a powerful tool for understanding American government today. In recent years, for example, the internet and social media have revolutionized American politics. In 2016, presidential candidate Donald Trump used Twitter daily to communicate with voters, and he continues to use this medium to communicate as president. In 2008 and 2012, presidential candidate Barack Obama used Facebook to build extensive volunteer networks and campaign donations to the tune of more than $1 billion. These successful candidates utilized social networking to mobilize voters to their cause. Other politicians have tried to duplicate their use of social media; in the 2020 presidential contest, social media dominated the campaign process. Voters of all political persuasions use social media to connect with their favorite campaigns. Consider the possibilities: in 2019 Facebook subscribed 240 million users in the United States, and Twitter had 126 million users. Not only is this a massive audience, but it is an active audience, as social networks allow users to trade and share information and opinions with their friends and families. In the past, political strategists were forced to rely on the paid TV spot as the primary way to communicate with voters. Today, however, there is a noticeable shift toward using social media to send messages, raise money, and mobilize voters. Why? A message from a friend is

Image of mushroom cloud from Lyndon Johnson's controversial "Daisy Girl" commercial from the 1964 presidential campaign.

considered much more personal, powerful, and effective than an impersonal TV spot.

Of course, social network sites like Facebook are not the only type of breakthrough technology to revolutionize political campaigns. Barack Obama was the first candidate to win the presidency by making extensive use of social media; nearly a half-century earlier, John F. Kennedy pioneered the use of television to win the White House. When he ran for the presidency in 1960, TV was dramatically changing American society, just as social media are changing it today. As a relatively new medium with a mass audience in Kennedy's time, TV provided prospective voters with what no communications platform had offered ever before—the chance to see the candidates' campaign on a daily basis. Television audiences could tune in to watch TV spots, and they could see the candidates debate each other live in their own living rooms; voters saw the candidates in action. Kennedy's youth and enthusiasm made effective use of television commercials touting his candidacy. His ability to "out-charisma" Richard Nixon in the 1960 debates led to a surge in turnout and helped to pave the way for a Kennedy victory. Kennedy's use of this new medium provided a model for how presidents would interact with voters over the next four decades. By 1964, candidates had mastered the art of the 30-second spot, as evidenced by Lyndon Johnson and his now-famous "Daisy Girl" commercial, which suggested that the election of his opponent could result in a nuclear war.

Although revolutionary, TV was not the first communications medium to transform political campaigns. Radio, which by 1932 had reached most U.S. households, enabled voters to listen to the candidates' voices instead of just reading their speeches or statements. Both President Franklin Delano Roosevelt (FDR) and President Herbert Hoover used radio addresses and advertising extensively during the 1932 campaign. Whereas Roosevelt's voice on the radio inspired confidence and enthusiasm for tackling the ills of the Great Depression, Hoover's logical and monotone monologue was far less effective. From that point forward, candidates could not just focus on the words that they used; they also had to excel in articulating those words with passion. FDR's use of radio eventually mobilized voters, particularly those who were most negatively affected by the economic doldrums of the Great Depression. After winning the 1932 election, FDR continued to use radio to personally connect with voters and inspire them through his "fireside chats," which he broadcast for the next 12 years.

One hundred years earlier, yet another communications revolution occurred that had a lasting impact on political campaigns. By the 1830s, newspapers were changing in a number of ways. The invention of the "rotary press" in 1815 facilitated the mass production of affordable newspapers and eventually gave way to the so-called penny press. A decade later, the invention of the telegraph enabled penny-press papers to quickly produce stories on breaking news events. Further, the laying of railroads to all parts of the country to accommodate rapid westward expansion paved the way for mass distribution of newspapers. Americans gobbled up this new source of information, and Andrew Jackson used this medium to engage voters, bypass the political elite, and communicate his message of rugged individualism and "the rise of the common man" to help him capture the White House in the 1828 election. The newspaper, which became a common person's medium, enabled Jackson to distribute his message widely to an audience that was willing and eager to read what he had to say. Jackson's use of the newspaper was critical to his success, just as Obama's use of social media was critical to his own success. Never again would presidential political campaigns be targeted exclusively at political elites, thanks to Jackson's use of the penny press to effectively appeal to the masses.

DEBATES OVER DIVERSITY
Changing Racial Categories in the U.S. Census

Since 1790, the U.S. government has implemented a nationwide census to count the population in the country every 10 years. This population information is used for a variety of reasons, including distribution of federal spending and planning for the growing population. The U.S. Census questionnaire has evolved considerably since 1790, often as a result of the changing understanding of diversity. The first census collected very rudimentary information on the racial makeup of the country—it was restricted to asking if the individual responding was white or owned slaves. The census racial categories have evolved; however, they are still limited to five basic categories, including White, Black or African American, American Indian or Alaska Native, Asian, and Native Hawaiian or Other Pacific Islander.

It was not until 1970 that the U.S. Census began to ask respondents about their ethnicity, which was restricted to asking a subsample of respondents whether they had a Hispanic family origin. After 2000, the Census began to allow respondents to choose more than one racial category. The most recent debate over census questions revolved around whether to include a question about citizenship. We are now challenged with understanding the true diversity of the U.S. population, which may require further Census revisions.

9. What is Person 1's race? *Mark* X *one or more boxes.*

☐ White
☐ Black, African Am., or Negro
☐ American Indian or Alaska Native — *Print name of enrolled or principal tribe.* ⤵

☐ Asian Indian   ☐ Japanese   ☐ Native Hawaiian
☐ Chinese   ☐ Korean   ☐ Guamanian or Chamorro
☐ Filipino   ☐ Vietnamese   ☐ Samoan
☐ Other Asian — *Print race, for example, Hmong, Laotian, Thai, Pakistani, Cambodian, and so on.* ⤵   ☐ Other Pacific Islander — *Print race, for example, Fijian, Tongan, and so on.* ⤵

☐ Some other race — *Print race.* ⤵

U.S. Census Bureau

The 2000 U.S. Census was the first to allow respondents to self-identify as a member of more than one race.

For Critical Thinking and Discussion

1. How would you answer the Census question on race and ethnicity?
2. Do you believe the current Census questions about race and ethnicity offer an accurate portrayal of the country's demographic makeup? Why or why not? How would you revise them?

This book explores the role of history as a guide to understanding contemporary American politics.

DEBATES OVER DIVERSITY IN AMERICAN POLITICS

As part of this book's exploration of our country's history, we also highlight the country's ongoing struggles with our growing diversity. It is critical to highlight and understand the unique role of diversity in our evolving democracy. We take a broad view of diversity to examine how differences in various identity characteristics (such as gender, race, ethnicity, and sexuality) can impact not only our place in society but also our opportunities to have a voice in American government. We hope to challenge you to think broadly on how your particular identity impacts your understanding of and participation in American politics.

Some people worry that growing diversity introduces an essential dilemma into American politics, as it requires society and government to evolve and change. During the 2016 presidential campaign, Donald Trump stirred up racial and religious tensions by speaking negatively about our nation's diversity, especially in terms of the supposed dangers brought by the Latino and Muslim populations in the country. Throughout this book we highlight not only how our diversity has always been viewed as a potential challenge but also how it has been seen as a source of our country's strength. In the first diversity dilemma the country faced, the U.S. government was challenged to define who was a citizen for purposes of the U.S. Census population count. Even though our definition of a citizen was rather limited at the time of our country's founding, we have thankfully evolved our understanding of the American people. We are now challenged to keep working on our country's evolution, which includes a discussion of how far we still need to go.

In this book we examine the major topics and concepts in American government and politics. We attempt to answer sweeping questions about how American government works: How does policy get made? Who are the major players and institutions that make the laws? How do these players achieve their position? How do disputes get resolved? What are the role and power of the people? Throughout these discussions, we pay special attention to millennials and Generation Z, the contributions and challenges of diversity, and how we might better understand American government today by observing the patterns of history.

1-2 FORMS AND FUNCTIONS OF GOVERNMENT

Government is the collection of public institutions in a nation that establish and enforce the rules by which the members of that nation must live. Even the most primitive of societies have found government to be necessary. Without government, society would be in a state of **anarchy**, a situation characterized by lawlessness and discord in the political system. Thomas Hobbes, a seventeenth-century British political philosopher, wrote that without government, life would be "solitary, poor, nasty, brutish and short."[1] Government is necessary to make the rules by which citizens must abide, promoting order, stability, and protection for the society. It exists in part to resolve conflicts that naturally arise when people live in communities. Elaborating on the role of government, Jean-Jacques Rousseau, an eighteenth-century French philosopher, posited that in fact a "social contract" exists.[2] A **social contract** is an agreement people make with one another to form a government and abide by its rules and laws. In return, the government promises to protect the people's rights and welfare and to promote their best interests.

A government's **authority** over its citizens refers to the ability of public institutions and the officials within them to make laws, independent of the power to execute them. People obey authority out of respect, whereas they obey power out of fear. Numerous different forms of government with governing authority can be found around the nations of the world. One such form—the form that will receive extended attention throughout this book—is **democracy**, defined as a government in which the people, either directly or through elected representatives, hold power and authority. The word *democracy* is derived from the Greek *demos kratos*, meaning "rule by the people."

By contrast, an **oligarchy** is a form of government in which a small exclusive class, which may or may not attempt to rule on behalf of the people as a whole, holds supreme power. In a **theocracy**, a particular religion or faith plays a dominant role in the government; Iran is just one example of a theocratic nation in the world today. A **monarchy** is a form of government in which one person, usually a member of a royal family or a royal designate, exercises supreme authority. The monarch may be a king or queen, such as Queen Elizabeth II of Great Britain. In the past, monarchies were quite common; today they are rarely practiced in the absolute sense. Although the United Kingdom continues to pay homage to its royalty, true political power rests in the Parliament, the members of which are elected by the people.

Many of the nations in the world today have an **authoritarian** form of government in which one political party, group, or person maintains such complete control over the nation that it may refuse to recognize, and may even choose to suppress, all other political parties and interests. The nation of Iraq, before the American military intervention in 2003, was considered by most to be an authoritarian government under the dictatorial rule of Saddam Hussein. North Korea under Kim Jong-un is an authoritarian government in existence today.

An important characteristic of any government, whether democratic or not, is its power to exercise authority over people. **Power** is the capacity to get individuals to do something that they may not otherwise do, such as pay taxes, stop for red lights, or submit to a search before boarding an airplane. Without power, a government would find it very difficult to enforce rules. The sustained power of any government largely rests on its legitimacy. **Legitimacy** is the extent to which the people (or the "governed") afford the government the authority and right to exercise power. The more that people subscribe to the goals of a government, and the greater the degree to which that government guarantees the people's welfare (e.g., by supporting a strong economy or providing protection from foreign enemies), the higher will

government The collection of public institutions in a nation that establish and enforce the rules by which the members of that nation must live.

anarchy A state of lawlessness and discord in the political system caused by lack of government.

social contract From the philosophy of Jean-Jacques Rousseau, an agreement people make with one another to form a government and abide by its rules and laws, and, in return, the government promises to protect the people's rights and welfare and promote their best interests.

authority The ability of public institutions and the officials within them to make laws, independent of the power to execute them.

democracy Form of government in which the people, either directly or through elected representatives, hold power and authority. The word *democracy* is derived from the Greek *demos kratos*, meaning "rule by the people."

oligarchy A form of government in which a small exclusive class, which may or may not attempt to rule on behalf of the people as a whole, holds supreme power.

theocracy A form of government in which a particular religion or faith plays a dominant role in the government.

monarchy A form of government in which one person, usually a member of a royal family or a royal designate, exercises supreme authority.

authoritarian A form of government in which one political party, group, or person maintains such complete control over the nation that it may refuse to recognize and may even suppress all other political parties and interests.

be the government's level of legitimacy. When the governed grant a high level of legitimacy to their government, the government wields its power to make and enforce rules more successfully.

1-3 AMERICAN GOVERNMENT AND POLITICS

Politics is defined as the way in which the institutions of government are organized to make laws, rules, and policies, and how those institutions are influenced. More than 80 years ago, political scientist Harold Lasswell proposed a brief but very useful definition of politics as "who gets what, when and how."[3] In American politics, the "who" includes actors within and outside the formal government, such as citizens, elected officials, interest groups, and state and local governments. The "what" are the decisions the government makes and take the form of what government funds, the way it raises revenue, and the policies it produces and enforces. The "when" relates to setting priorities about what government does. The concerns and issues that government addresses differ in importance, and issues of greater importance tend to be addressed more quickly. Finally, the "how" refers to the way in which the government goes about its work, based on the political institutions that exist and the formal and informal procedures and rules that define the governing process. In describing American politics, this book provides answers to Lasswell's "Who gets what, when and how?"

Government in the United States is especially complex. It is organized into multiple layers (national, state, and local) and contains many governing units, as shown in Table 1-1. It encompasses a number of political institutions that share power—the executive (the president), the legislature (Congress), and the judiciary (the courts)—and it provides countless methods for individuals and groups to influence the decisions made by those institutions. In this book, we examine this complex organization of American government, describe the political institutions that exercise power, and explore the varied ways that people and groups exert influence. As we sort through this complexity of American government, we explain how and why the American political system has been able to endure the conflicts, both internal and external, that it has faced and currently faces. We attempt to show how the American government is uniquely designed to stand up to its many challenges.

The strength and stability of the U.S. government are grounded in the high level of legitimacy it maintains with the American public. Americans may disagree vehemently with public officials, but rarely do they question their claim to authority. The framers of the U.S. Constitution were keenly aware of the importance of the legitimacy of the system.

power The ability to get individuals to do something that they may not otherwise do, such as pay taxes, stop for red lights, or submit to a search before boarding an airplane.

legitimacy The extent to which the people afford the government the authority and right to exercise power.

politics The way in which the institutions of government are organized to make laws, rules, and policies, and how those institutions are influenced.

TABLE 1-1

Governments in the United States

The government of the United States might be more correctly described as a system of governments. In addition to the federal government, there are 50 state governments and thousands of local governments. The 2012 U.S. Census Bureau's *Census of Governments* listed these totals for the number of governments operating throughout the nation.

Government	Number
Federal	1
State	50
County	3,013
Municipal	19,522
School district	13,051
Township/town	16,364
Special district	37,203
Total	**89,204**

U.S. Census Bureau.

They knew that if the government was to withstand the test of time, it must serve the people well. These ideas about legitimacy drew largely on the theories of seventeenth-century British political philosopher John Locke (1632–1704).[4] Locke proposed that people are born with certain *natural rights*, which derive from **natural law**, the rules of conduct inherent in the relationship among human beings and thus more fundamental than any law that a governing authority might make. Government cannot violate these natural rights, which include life, liberty, and property. Therefore, government, or human law, must be based on the "consent of the governed." That is, citizens are responsible for choosing their government and its leaders. This theory loomed large in the mind of Thomas Jefferson as he drafted the Declaration of Independence to justify the American colonies' split with the British government: "All men . . . are endowed by their creator with certain unalienable rights . . . [and] whenever any form of government becomes destructive of these ends, it is the right of the people to alter or abolish it." A government maintains legitimacy as long as the governed are served well and as long as government respects the natural rights of individuals.

Drawing on this philosophy, the framers drafted a Constitution that created a political system able to manage the inevitable conflicts that occur in any society. Mindful of Thomas Hobbes's notion that the essence of government is to manage naturally occurring conflicts, the framers designed a government that encourages conflict and competition rather than attempting to repress it. As we shall see in the chapters that follow, the U.S. Constitution includes a number of mechanisms that allow naturally occurring conflict to play out in as productive a manner as possible. Mechanisms are also in place to resolve conflicts and arrive at consensus on issues. Those who disagree and come up on the short side of political battles are guaranteed rights and liberties nonetheless. Further, the rules by which conflicts are settled are predicated on fairness and proper procedures.

The significance of what the framers of the Constitution accomplished cannot be overstated. They not only addressed the short-term problems challenging the new nation; they also drafted a blueprint for how government should go about dealing with problems and conflicts into the future. The U.S. Constitution has served as the cornerstone of an American political system that routinely attempts to tackle some of the thorniest problems imaginable. In Chapter 2 of this book, we examine the enduring principles and processes outlined in the Constitution.

The Constitution provides a way for the American government to navigate through the many problems and conflicts that have faced the nation, including severe economic depressions, two world wars, nuclear confrontations with the former Soviet Union, and persisting questions of equality. Through all these difficulties, the American government has endured. The foresight of the framers to create a Constitution that possesses the flexibility to adapt to changing times has served as a basis for the enduring democracy of the United States.

The preamble to the U.S. Constitution perhaps best summarizes the broad goals of American government:

> *We the People of the United States, in order to form a more perfect union, establish justice, insure domestic tranquility, provide for the common defence, promote the general welfare, and secure the blessings of liberty to ourselves and our posterity, do ordain and establish this Constitution for the United States of America.*

It is no accident that the first three words of the Constitution are "We the People." With this phrase, the framers acknowledged that the ultimate source of power rests with the people, a concept known as **popular sovereignty**. The U.S. Constitution provided for a form of **representative democracy**, under which regular elections are held to allow voters to choose those who govern on their behalf. In this sense, individual citizens do not directly make policies, rules, and other governing decisions (that system of government is known as a **direct democracy**). Rather, representative democracy, also referred to as *indirect democracy* or a *republican* form of government, rests on the notion that consent of the governed is achieved through free, open, and regular elections of those who are given the responsibility of governing.

An important source of the legitimacy of the U.S. government is the nation's commitment to representative democracy, which features the notion of majority rule. Majorities (more than 50 percent of the voters) and pluralities (the leading vote getters, whether or not they constitute absolute majorities) choose the winners of election contests, and so officeholders

natural law According to John Locke, the most fundamental type of law, which supersedes any law that is made by government. Citizens are born with certain natural rights (including life, liberty, and property) that derive from this law and that government cannot take away.

popular sovereignty The idea that the ultimate source of power in the nation is held by the people.

representative democracy A form of government designed by the U.S. Constitution: Free, open, and regular elections allow voters to choose those who govern on their behalf; it is also referred to as *indirect democracy* or a *republican* form of government.

direct democracy A system of government in which all citizens participate in making policy, rules, and governing decisions.

THEN & NOW
When the Popular Vote and the Electoral Vote Diverge

The Electoral College offers a unique, if sometimes controversial, system for selecting America's chief executive every four years. The Electoral College and the popular vote have produced different results in five presidential elections in American history, the most recent one being 2016.

Then

In 1888, the presidential race featured a contentious face-off between the Republican challenger, Benjamin Harrison, and the Democratic incumbent, President Grover Cleveland. On November 6 of that year, voters cast their ballots and the national vote tally provided nearly 100,000 more votes to Cleveland. However, the result in the Electoral College, which decides presidential elections, gave Harrison nearly 60 more electoral votes and thus a resounding victory. This electoral vote/popular vote divergence came only 12 years after the same event occurred in the course of Rutherford B. Hayes's victory over Samuel Tilden in 1876. That time, too, the Republican rode to victory, courtesy of the Electoral College.

Now

In 2016, at the end of the presidential contest, voters cast their ballots for Democrat Hillary Clinton, Republican Donald Trump, or one of two third-party candidates. After the election, the popular vote favored Clinton by about 2,800,000. Still, Donald Trump managed to muster 67 more electoral votes than Clinton to put him over the top in the Electoral College count. This electoral vote/popular vote divergence came only 16 years after the same anomaly resulted in George W. Bush's victory over Al Gore.

For Critical Thinking and Discussion

1. Do you think that the U.S. Constitution should be amended to eliminate the Electoral College and replace it with the national popular vote as the method of selecting a president? What are the advantages and disadvantages of such an amendment?
2. In two of the past five elections, the popular vote winner was not the electoral vote winner. In both instances (2000 and 2016) the GOP candidate lost the popular vote but won the electoral vote and thus the election. Why do you think the electoral vote benefits the GOP candidate?

take their positions on the basis of whom most voters prefer. If officeholders fall from public favor, they may be removed in subsequent elections.

Legitimacy is also enhanced by broad public support for the specific purposes of government stated in the preamble to the Constitution: to "insure domestic tranquility" (produce laws that maintain a peaceful and organized approach to living in the nation), to "provide for the common defence" (establish and maintain a military force to protect the nation from outside threats), to "promote the general welfare" (develop domestic policy programs to promote the welfare of the people), and to "secure the blessings of liberty" (guarantee basic freedoms, such as the rights of free expression and the ownership of property, even to those in the minority). Though people may have different opinions on how to achieve these broad goals, few in the United States would disagree with the ideals as stated in the abstract, or with the broad outlines of our republican form of government. Problems arise when public officials stray so far from these goals that their actions are deemed illegitimate by a near, if not absolute, majority. Yet the political system as a whole has been able to maintain its legitimacy, even under such trying circumstances, because it has been flexible enough to eventually rid itself of those ineffective actors, whether through elections, impeachment, or some other means. The relatively high degree of legitimacy that is maintained in the United States has helped the American government persist under the U.S. Constitution through good times and bad since 1789.

1-4 AMERICAN POLITICAL CULTURE

Political culture refers to the core values about the role of government and its operations and institutions that are widely held among citizens in a society. Political culture defines the

> **political culture** The values and beliefs about government, its purpose, and its operations and institutions that are widely held among citizens in a society; it defines the essence of how a society thinks politically and is transmitted from one generation to the next.

TABLE 1-2

Daniel Elazar's Typology of American Political Culture

Many observers of American politics have used different approaches and typologies to describe American political culture. The late political scientist Daniel Elazar described three competing political subcultures, which he believed differentiated American political culture from that found in any other country in the world.

According to Elazar, different subcultures can be found in different geographic areas and sometimes within a single area. For example, he described the political subculture in Texas as part traditionalistic (as manifested in the long history of one-party dominance in state politics) and part individualistic (as seen in the state government's commitment to support for private business and its opposition to big government).

Subculture	Description
Individualistic	Is skeptical of authority, keeps government's role limited, and celebrates the United States' general reliance on the marketplace
Moralistic	Has faith in the American government's capacity to advance the public interest and encourages citizens to participate in the noble cause of politics
Traditionalistic	Maintains a more ambivalent attitude toward both government and the marketplace, believing that politicians must come from society's elite, whereas ordinary citizens are free to stand on the sidelines

Adapted from Daniel J. Elazar, American Federalism: A View from the States (New York: Thomas Y. Cromwell, 1966)

essence of how a society thinks politically. It is transmitted from one generation to the next and thus has an enduring influence on the politics of a nation. Every nation has a political culture, and the United States is no exception.

Whereas common ancestry characterizes the core of the political culture of many other nations, the United States has no common ancestry. Most other nations around the world, such as France, Britain, China, and Japan, are bound by a common birth lineage that serves to define the cultural uniqueness of the nation. For example, the Russian people share common political values and beliefs as part of their ancestors' historical experiences with czars and then later with the communist regime. Britain, despite being a democracy, retains a monarchy as a symbolic gesture toward its historical antecedents. In many nations rich with such common ethnic traditions, these routines often serve to underscore the political culture of the nation.

The United States has no such common ancestry to help define its political culture. As seen in Table 1-2, Daniel Elazar presented a popular description of American political culture. Its land was first occupied by many different Native American tribes and then settled by people from many different parts of the world. Most of the immigrants who settled the colonies were seeking a better life from the political or religious persecution they experienced in their native countries, or they were seeking improved economic opportunities for themselves and their families. As America continued to grow through the centuries, it attracted immigrants from around the world, eager to find a better life. These circumstances had a profound influence on the core values that have become engrained in the American political culture. The ideas generated by democratic political philosophers such as Thomas Hobbes and John Locke also significantly contributed to American political culture. These ideas were used by the founders to justify the Declaration of Independence and the U.S. Constitution, and they continue to underlie American political culture today.

The circumstances surrounding America's first and current immigrants, as well as the great ideas generated by Enlightenment philosophers, form the core set of values that define the American political culture. One of these core values is **majority rule**. From its earliest times, the American nation has been committed to the notion that the "will of the people" ought to guide public policy, thus underscoring the importance of popular sovereignty in the thinking of the founders. Majority rule is the way in which popular sovereignty is actually exercised. Rarely will all of the people agree all of the time, and so it is what the majority of people prefer that generally guides decision-making. Early local governments, such as town governments in some of the New England colonies, relied on town meetings, where all citizens were invited to attend, discuss, and vote, to make governmental decisions. Elections for most local and state offices, and elections for the U.S. Congress, are all based on the idea

majority rule The notion that the will of the majority should guide decisions made by American government.

that those who make and enforce laws are duly elected by majorities. A more recent aspect of U.S. commitment to majority rule is its heavy reliance on public opinion polling as a gauge for assessing the performance of elected leaders and to ensure that leaders respect public preferences for certain policy positions.

Although the preferences of the majority rule the day, another core value in the American political culture is minority rights. Those in the minority enjoy certain rights and liberties that cannot be taken away by government. The idea of the natural law (e.g., that people are "endowed by their creator with certain unalienable rights" that government cannot deny) is an important corollary to majority rule. The rights to speak freely, to choose a religion, or to decide not to practice religion at all are among the many liberties that are protected by the U.S. Bill of Rights and are widely endorsed by the American public.

These rights are intended to inspire debate on issues, guarantee religious freedoms, and afford due process rights to those accused of crimes. The American political culture places a high value on individual liberty. The fact that many immigrants came to this country for the promise of greater freedom adds further credence to this proposition. Certainly there are some terrible black marks in American history that belie this claim. Among them are the perpetuation of slavery in the country up until the Civil War, the internment of Japanese Americans during World War II, and the treatment of early 1960s civil rights protesters in the South. Still, many Americans today view their nation as the world's "garden" of freedom and liberty, even if it has come to this status only slowly and sometimes with reluctance during its more than two centuries of existence.

Another core value in American political culture is the idea of **limited government**. Americans have generally supported the idea expressed by Thomas Jefferson that "the government that governs least governs best." From the days of the American Revolution, the colonists believed that the corruptive power of King George III and the British Parliament led to unfair treatment of the colonies. Suspicion of the government and those with power is firmly rooted in the psyche of American political culture. The "watchdog" function of the press, the separation of powers and the system of checks and balances among political institutions, and the rather negative connotation of the word *politics* all reflect an appreciation for limits and checks on those with authority. Corresponding to the value of limited government is the notion that communities and the private sector should take a role in helping fellow citizens. Problems that may be solved without government should be solved that way. The French journalist Alexis de Tocqueville observed this tradition when he visited the United States in the early 1800s and credited the success of the American political system in part to citizens' strong interest in community and helping one another apart from government.[5]

Because the United States has no common ancestral or cultural bloodline, American political culture recognizes the value and strength derived from the diversity of its population—another important core value. At the base of the Statue of Liberty in New York Harbor is inscribed a poem by Emma Lazarus that includes the phrase "Give me your tired, your poor, your huddled masses yearning to breathe free." Until the U.S. government adopted a restrictive immigration policy in the early 1920s, those huddled masses arrived in waves from different parts of the world, as the United States became the chosen destination for those seeking a better life. Joining freed African American slaves who were originally brought here against their will were legions of Italians, Irish, Germans, and other immigrants from Europe and elsewhere. This surge in immigration occurred from 1880 through 1920, as immigrants left the economic and political strife of Europe seeking jobs and opportunities in America.

One of the most profound population developments in the recent history of the United States has been the skyrocketing growth of the nation's Hispanic population. The Hispanic or

> **limited government** The value that promotes the idea that government power should be as restricted as possible.

Latina journalist and PBS senior correspondent Maria Hinojosa.

FIGURE 1-1

Asians Projected to Become the Largest Immigrant Group, Surpassing Hispanics

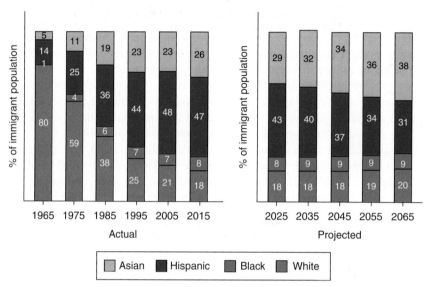

Projections of Asian Population in America

Actual — 1965, 1975, 1985, 1995, 2005, 2015

Projected — 2025, 2035, 2045, 2055, 2065

Asian · Hispanic · Black · White

Source: "Asians Projected to Become Largest Immigrant Group, Surpassing Hispanics," Pew Research Center, Washington, DC, September 23, 2015, https://www.pewhispanic.org/2015/09/28/modern-immigration-wave-brings-59-million-to-u-s-driving-population-growth-and-change-through-2065/ph_2015-09-28_immigration-through-2065-05/.

Note: Pew Research Center estimates for 1965–2015 based on adjusted census data; Pew Research Center projections for 2025–2065.

Note: Whites, blacks, and Asians include only single-race non-Hispanics. Asians include Pacific Islanders. Hispanics are of any race. Other races shown but not labeled.

Latino/a populations have expanded from what was once a small, regionally concentrated subgroup of fewer than 6 million in 1960 to a now widely dispersed population of more than 50 million (or 16 percent of the nation's population) today. The recent explosion of immigrants from Latin America is largely a product of the difficult economic and social conditions they face in their home countries, as well as the opportunity for a better life they believe is possible in the United States.

As shown in Figure 1-1, the Pew Research Center projects that this modern immigration wave will drive U.S. population growth and change at least through 2065. The projections also include a growing Asian American foreign-born population that will even surpass Hispanics as the country's largest immigrant group by 2055. Such a massive swelling in the ranks of Hispanics and Asian Americans has the potential to create major political change in America.

This population growth has transformed the United States to one of the most racially and ethnically diverse nations in the world. Integrating these many people into a united nation has not been easy; in fact, resistance to the notion of a "melting pot" has been common. The nation has been wracked at times with racial and ethnic strife to a degree that more homogeneous countries can more easily avoid. Government officials occasionally exacerbate these tensions by promoting policies that discriminate against various groups, including Native Americans, African Americans, Asian Americans, and Hispanics. No stranger to ethnic and racial tensions himself, German dictator Adolf Hitler calculated that the diversity of the United States would eventually hamper its resistance against Germany's totalitarian aggression; in fact, American soldiers of different backgrounds, ethnicities, and religions fought in

FIGURE 1-2

Individualism as a Value in the United States Compared to Other Democracies

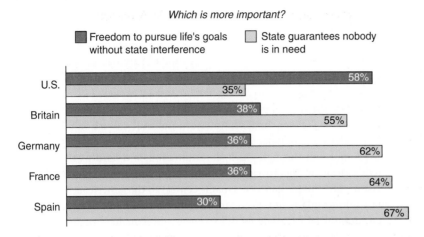

Which is more important?

■ Freedom to pursue life's goals without state interference　□ State guarantees nobody is in need

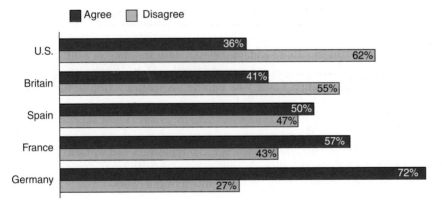

Would you agree that success in life is determined by forces outside our control?

■ Agree　□ Disagree

Source: "5 ways Americans and Europeans are different," Pew Research Center, Washington, DC, April 19, 2016, https://www.pewresearch.org/fact-tank/2016/04/19/5-ways-americans-and-europeans-are-different/.

A recent Pew Global Survey shows that Americans are more likely than their European counterparts to believe that "it is more important to pursue life's goals without government interference" and to disagree with the statement "success in life is determined by forces outside our control."

World War II. Much to Hitler's chagrin, U.S. diversity proved to be a source of strength rather than weakness. Indeed, many Americans today believe that the heterogeneity of our society enhances the quality of our culture and helps guarantee the fairness of the government.

Americans also generally subscribe to the notion that individuals are primarily responsible for their lot in life—a value referred to as **individualism**. The seeds of this value were sown hundreds of years ago with the Puritans and their commitment to a strong work ethic that stressed that "what one sows determines what one reaps." In other words, hard work and intelligence should be rewarded. Although the U.S. government has assumed some responsibility to provide a safety net for citizens who suffer economically, the American political culture, through its primary reliance on a capitalist economic system, free markets, and individual effort, is one that promotes individual initiative and responsibility. Figure 1-2 depicts the heightened importance of the value of individualism in the American political culture, compared to other European democracies.

individualism The value that individuals are primarily responsible for their own lot in life and that promotes and rewards individual initiative and responsibility. This value underlies America's reliance on a capitalist economy and free market system.

The value of individualism promotes another core value—equality of opportunity, or the idea that the role of government is to set the stage for individuals to achieve on their own and that everyone should be given the same opportunity to achieve success. Indeed, America has been an attractive place for highly motivated individuals from around the world to immigrate so that they might have a fair chance of achieving personal success. Many immigrants today, particularly from Asia and Latin America, are attracted to the United States for the opportunities to achieve individual success.

The United States has long set itself apart from those nations whose histories include traditions of a rigid class system of privileged aristocracies and oligarchies and peasants with few or no rights or freedoms. In the United States there is no formal recognition of a class system; nor is there a tradition of royalty, nobility, or monarchy. Indeed, Article I of the Constitution specifically prohibits both the federal government and the state governments from granting any title of nobility upon its citizens. Instead, American political culture values the so-called Horatio Alger myth. Alger was a popular writer in the late 1800s whose characters came from impoverished backgrounds but through pluck, determination, and hard work achieved huge success. Although this idealistic rags-to-riches notion often ignores the many harsh economic disparities that exist in the United States, it remains central to the American political culture. The stories of Benjamin Franklin and Abraham Lincoln exemplified this road to success, as do the more recent examples of Presidents Bill Clinton and Ronald Reagan, both of whom came from less-than-privileged circumstances to win the nation's highest political office and become leaders of the free world. Perhaps it is because of these success stories that so many Americans believe that they have boundless opportunities to better their lot on the basis of diligence and hard work.

These core values provide a window into American political culture. To be sure, there is plenty of room for disagreement as to how these values might be applied to specific situations, which we address in Chapter 10. In addition, these values are often in conflict. At the heart of the debate over affirmative action, for example, lies the value conflict pitting individualism against equality of opportunity. Those who oppose affirmative action in hiring claim that individuals should be evaluated exclusively based on who they are and what they can do rather than on their gender, race, or other demographic characteristic. Those supporting affirmative action claim that historical discrimination has led to a current job market that provides unequal opportunities for certain groups, such as racial minorities and women. Although these values do not always solve problems and policy debates, they do lay the groundwork for how American politics goes about settling problems and debating issues.

1-5 IS AMERICAN DEMOCRACY IN DECLINE?

The old saying that "those who ignore the problems of the past are destined to repeat them" holds as true in American politics as it does in any other context. Certainly new issues and problems may arise, requiring innovative new thinking to address them. But many other difficulties the United States faces can be effectively addressed by casting an eye on the distant or not-so-distant past. A historical view can help place modern dilemmas in proper perspective.

THE CASE FOR DECLINE

Some recent observers of American politics have suggested that the American political system is in decline. Are we currently witnessing a deterioration of democracy in the United States? Is the American political system in jeopardy? Are the problems that the American system of government faces today beyond repair? To try to answer these questions, let's first look at the factors some cite as contemporary indicators of the decline of American democracy.

1. **The decline of the United States as an economic superpower?** The growth of the national economy from the Industrial Revolution through the post–World War II era established the United States as the preeminent fiscal power in the world for much of the twentieth century. This fiscal strength enabled the United States to establish the dollar as the benchmark unit of currency for the world, defeat the Soviet Union in the Cold

TABLE 1-3

Projections of U.S. and Chinese Gross Domestic Product (GDP), in Billions

	China	United States
2015	22,210	20,169
2020	35,734	27,584
2025	57,145	35,963

Congressional Research Service.

War, build a military capability vastly superior to that of other nations, and provide the leadership that brought democracy to many other nations. However, the significant growth of the Chinese economy over the past decade, coupled with the exploding U.S. national debt (and the willingness of China to underwrite much of that debt), has raised serious questions about the future of U.S. dominance over the world's economy. Concerns over the economic rise of China and the decline of the United States are summarized in a recent study by the Congressional Research Service: "The emergence of China as a major economic superpower has raised concern among many U.S. policymakers . . . that China will overtake the United States as the world's largest trade economy in a few years and the world's largest economy within the next two decades. In this context, China's rise is viewed as America's relative decline."[6] This report offers evidence of a decline in economic power citing projections of U.S. and Chinese gross domestic product (GDP), depicted in Table 1-3.

2. **The death of capitalism?** The collapse of some of the largest financial institutions in the United States in 2008 and the subsequent "Great Recession" have raised questions about the viability of the free market system in contemporary society. In large part, the financial industry's drive in the 1990s and 2000s to capitalize on rising real estate markets drove financial institutions to rely on increasingly risky lending practices. Risky

A contentious 2019 meeting in the Oval Office addressed funding for a border wall. From left to right: House Speaker Pelosi, Vice President Pence, President Trump, and Senate minority leader Schumer.

loans were bundled and sold off to investors in the form of real estate securities. (These practices were depicted in the award-winning movie *The Big Short*.) Multibillion-dollar financial institutions, such as Citibank, Morgan Stanley, Lehman Brothers, Countrywide Mortgage, and AIG, among many others, found themselves in the red at the exact same time that the real estate market collapsed, thus freezing credit in the United States. The stock market tumbled, and the U.S. government needed to bail out many of the largest financial institutions just to keep the nation's financial system from collapse. The frantic drive for profits among the largest of these companies was identified as the source of economic ills not only in the United States but around the world. Greed, inspired by capitalism, seemed to be the culprit of the world's economic woes, thus leading to questions about the viability of the free market system in the modern age. The failure of markets during the Great Recession contributed to the popular presidential campaign of Democratic socialist Bernie Sanders in 2016, and the initial field of more than 20 Democratic contenders in 2020 featured several prospective candidates who advocated a much larger role for government in managing and regulating the nation's economic affairs.

3. **Policy paralysis caused by partisan gridlock?** Relations between the two major parties tend to ebb and flow with changing political moods and circumstances. Still, cross-party relations between Republicans and Democrats seemed to have reached such a low in the current era that policy-making all but ceases to function. In recent years, whichever party has carried the White House has been forced to brace for a Senate opposition that uses the filibuster freely and with few limitations to impose a supermajority requirement of 60 senators for all legislative enactments. Many other bills can never even get out of committee. Meanwhile, in the House of Representatives, the president's opposition has ruled with an iron hand, rendering matters that had in the past proven perfunctory (such as the routine raising of the nation's debt ceiling) into a knockdown, drag-out fight between the two parties in Congress. The prospect of a government shutdown has loomed over every budget fight, and in December 2018–January 2019 partisan tensions did in fact lead to the longest shutdown of many federal government functions in the nation's history. Party-line votes in Congress on most major legislative initiatives indicate a lack of any common ground whatsoever. Further, tensions between the Democrat-controlled House and President Trump inspired calls in the House of Representatives for the impeachment of the Chief Executive.

4. **Has money ruined American politics?** "Big money" now dominates American elections, in the form of contributions from those who seek to influence future officials, personal expenditures from candidates themselves, and general expenditures by political parties. The Supreme Court's landmark decision in *Citizens United v. Federal Election Commission* (2010) seemed to cement the role that big money plays in determining election outcomes, paving the way for independent-expenditure political action committees (often called "super-PACs") to accept unlimited contributions from individuals, unions, and corporations for the purpose of making so-called independent expenditures on behalf of candidates; it thus enabled wealthy individuals to dominate the process. In the year following *Citizens United*, just 22 donors provided the money for half of the $67 million funded by super-PACs! In some instances, anonymous outside groups poured millions of dollars into the process. Others were willing to stand up and be counted: consider that billionaire Sheldon Adelson singlehandedly kept Newt Gingrich's struggling presidential campaign afloat in 2012 with his donation of $10 million to a pro-Gingrich super PAC. With a handful of individuals responsible for a large percentage of the donations in these campaigns, the corruptive influence of money appears to have reached new, dangerous heights.

BUT DO THESE PROBLEMS REALLY SIGNIFY A DECLINE?

If we reexamine some of the criticisms of contemporary American politics with the benefit of historical perspective, we may reach far different conclusions about whether American democracy is now in a state of decline.

1. **The United States will remain an economic superpower.** Challenges to U.S. fiscal dominance, such as the current challenge of China, are nothing new. Forty years ago, for example, many policy-makers expressed similar concerns about the imminent decline of U.S. economic power. At that time the concern was focused not on China but on Japan. The Japanese economy flourished in the decades after World War II. A latecomer to modernization, Japan was able to avoid the pitfalls of industrialization experienced by the United States and other advanced democracies prior to World War II. Once converted to a free market system after the war, Japan's economy took off quickly. By the 1970s, Japan had the world's second largest economy and appeared to be closing in on the United States. Gross domestic product (GDP) in Japan grew from $8 billion in 1955, to $32 billion in 1965, to $148 billion in 1975, to $323 billion in 1985. By 1990 Japan's per capita GDP exceeded per capita GDP in the United States. The sharp upward trajectory alarmed many U.S. policy-makers, who felt that Japan's rise would ultimately derail the U.S. dominance of world fiscal policy. Yet today Japan offers no significant threat to the economic power of the United States. The rapid rise of Japan's economy left it unable to effectively deal with a recessionary period of any length. Consequently, the dire predictions of the U.S. economic fall to Japan were never realized. Furthermore, by 2016 China's economy had already showed signs of slower growth, leading economists to recognize the likely continued dominance of the United States well into the twenty-first century.[7]

2. **Capitalism is not dead.** The Great Recession of 2008 and the events that led up to it certainly do not mark the first time that speculation in free markets led to economic catastrophe. A panic in 1837 led to stymied economic growth for more than three years, a severe recession in 1873 retracted growth for six years, and an economic panic in 1893 set off a series of bank failures. A stock market crash in 1929 produced a decade-long "Great Depression." These and many other economic downturns in U.S. history, aggravated by speculation and overly exuberant investors, have led to extremely tough economic times. But the ills of the free market have never limited the ability of capitalism to provide the medicine for recovery, and then some. Panics, recessions, and depressions have always been corrected by bull markets, opportunities, and resurgences. Capitalism has been declared dead many times in U.S. history. The approach of each economic downturn was accompanied by claims that the U.S. experiment with a free market system had finally failed. In fact, the free markets operate in natural cycles of growth and retraction. Just as the free market system was declared dead at earlier times in American history, so, too, were many claiming that the Great Recession of 2008 was the last nail in the coffin of American capitalism. However, just as the cyclical nature of free market growth calmed the fears of the skeptics before, so, too, has the recent growth of the U.S. stock market and decline in unemployment quieted the naysayers once again.

3. **The polarization of the two major political parties has not paralyzed the lawmaking process.** The political parties' recent polarization is hardly unprecedented: at various times in history (e.g., during the Civil War, the New Deal) the parties have stood in stark contrast on nearly all the major issues of the time. Some democratic theorists argue that a marked differentiation between the two parties may actually contribute to democracy under a "responsive theory of democracy": the two parties disagree on the issues and then allow the public to express its opinion through elections. Despite all the talk of polarization, the 115th Congress passed and President Trump signed a number of new laws, including a vast tax cut bill in 2017. Nearly a decade earlier, in 2009–2010, the 111th Congress passed 43 major pieces of legislation, including the Obama administration's centerpiece, the 2010 health care reform law. Thus, while the two major parties continue to grow further apart, government continues to make decisions.

4. **The influence of money does not spell the end of American politics.** American elections have always been dominated by individuals with immense power and influence. For much of this nation's history, political machines all but controlled the nomination process and wielded heavy influence on politicians who benefitted from their respective

Courting the Youth Vote

Ann Hermes/The Christian Science Monitor via Getty Images

A student at the University of North Carolina, Charlotte, signs a voting pledge at a Rock the Vote campaign.

Candidates and political parties often try to increase turnout as a means of enhancing their prospects in an election. However, numerous nonpartisan organizations also engage in special efforts to encourage the so-called youth vote in particular. These organizations may target young voters primarily for two reasons: (1) young voters represent the future of American democracy, and (2) youth turnout has tended to be lower than turnout among older

Americans. In the 2016 presidential election barely half of eligible voters aged 18 to 29 voted, leaving that group well behind turnout rates of the electorate as a whole (60 percent).

Among the many organizations that run programs to encourage young voters to exercise their voting rights are the following:

1. Rock the Vote, which claims to have registered more than 5 million new voters in recent presidential elections (see rockthevote.org);
2. CIRCLE (Center for Information and Research on Civic Learning and Engagement), which studies the voting behavior of young people (see www.civicyouth .org); and
3. YouthVote.org, a website that provides a plethora of information to help young people learn how to register to vote and why it is important to do so.

For Critical Thinking and Discussion

1. Why do you think college-age students turn out in relatively lower numbers compared to older voters?
2. How effectively have the candidates in 2020 addressed issues that are important to college students?

---

handouts and other forms of largesse. Whether it was Boss Tweed and Tammany Hall in New York City, the Thomas Pendergast political machine in Missouri, or the Daley machine in Chicago, power has always been wielded by a relatively few, elite individuals. The recent dominance of money in politics has shifted the source of power from those machines to the extremely wealthy, but that may actually represent a positive development of sorts, as both parties have enjoyed their share of big donors and fundraising prowess in recent years. Moreover, well-financed campaigns like Governor Jeb Bush's unsuccessful bid for the White House in 2016 prove that money can only go so far without the right messenger and the right message. Those who think money corrupts politics might want to consider these caveats, as well as the far less attractive alternative that used to mark the elections process.

History does not literally repeat itself. The specific people, circumstances, and events certainly change. But history can help us identify patterns, recurring problems, and trends in how the American political system functions and resolves conflicts. The preceding discussion of some of the contemporary arguments for why American democracy may be in a state of decline helps us frame current conditions. In doing so, we may gain a greater understanding of the challenges facing the nation today. Certainly, many contemporary challenges are no less daunting than problems the nation has encountered over the past two centuries. Throughout this book, a historical perspective on contemporary problems offers a sense of how the past might help us understand politics today.

Summary

1-1 Presidential Campaigns, History, Diversity, and American Politics

- No event in American politics receives the level of attention that a presidential election elicits. The 2020 campaign is highly partisan, but many past campaigns were no stranger to divisive partisan battles.
- The patterns of history provide a powerful tool for understanding American politics today.

1-2 Forms and Functions of Government

- The development of the American political system is grounded in the philosophy of John Locke and Jean-Jacques Rousseau, who argued that government is necessary and that it exists for the purpose of protecting the people that it serves. The "social contract" theory states that natural law gives people certain unalienable rights that government cannot take away and that the people give government authority to rule, but the people can withdraw that authority if government does not serve the people's interests.
- Democracy may be distinguished from other forms of government in that it is a form of government in which the people, either directly or through elected representatives, hold power and authority.

1-3 American Government and Politics

- Democracy includes at its core the idea of popular sovereignty. The United States practices a form of democracy known as "representative democracy," where the people indirectly rule by electing leaders who are responsible for making and carrying out policies and laws.

1-4 American Political Culture

- The political culture in America is reflected in the Constitution and the way in which the political system deals with and decides political debates. Among the core values guiding the American political culture are majority rule, liberty, limited government, diversity, individualism, and equality of economic opportunity.

1-5 Is American Democracy in Decline?

- Although the current American government has been in place for more than 200 years, questions have been raised about whether this political system is in a state of decline. Lower voter turnout, confusing election outcomes, negativity, polarization in politics, and the influence of money in policy outcomes have been offered as evidence of a decline. However, a review of historical patterns in American politics suggests that these seemingly contemporary problems are chronic, and the American political system has effectively dealt with these and many other problems in the past.
- Viewing American government from a historical perspective may enrich our understanding of how the political system works. History can help us identify patterns, recurring problems, and trends in how the American political system functions and resolves conflicts. Many contemporary challenges are no more significant than problems the nation has encountered over the past two centuries.

Key Terms

anarchy (p. 6)
authoritarian (p. 6)
authority (p. 6)
democracy (p. 6)
direct democracy (p. 8)
government (p. 6)
individualism (p. 13)
legitimacy (p. 6)
limited government (p. 11)
majority rule (p. 10)
monarchy (p. 6)

natural law (p. 8)
oligarchy (p. 6)
political culture (p. 9)
politics (p. 7)
popular sovereignty (p. 8)
power (p. 6)
representative democracy (p. 8)
social contract (p. 6)
theocracy (p. 6)

2

THE FOUNDING AND THE CONSTITUTION

Zach Gibson / Getty Images

Tourists view an original copy of the U.S. Constitution at the National Archives in Washington, DC.

THE ENDURING CAPACITY of the U.S. Constitution to govern for better than two centuries represents something of a miracle: by one estimate, the average life-span of national constitutions over this same period was just 17 years. How has the American constitutional experiment succeeded where so many others have failed? The secret lies in its capacity to serve two functions at the same time: it provides stability (just 17 amendments passed during the past two centuries) while at the same time offering the flexibility to adapt to changes in America's political culture. Woodrow Wilson addressed this when he wrote, "The Constitution of the United States is not a mere lawyers' document: it is a vehicle of life, and its spirit is always the spirit of the age."

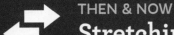

Stretching the Constitution to Serve Political Needs

Amendments to the Constitution provide the most visible form of change to our founding document, but they are exceedingly rare. There have been just 27 amendments in all, and just 17 have been ratified since the Bill of Rights first appeared in 1791. How can a republic adapt to changing times and realities when its written constitution is so impervious to formal change? In practice, less formal types of constitutional change (such as the decision by one of the three branches to offer its own newly formed interpretation of the document) can serve the needs of the nation as well. On the other hand, these forms of constitutional change can prove more controversial, as they can occur quickly and without the formal approval of a majority of the governed.

Then

As the United States sunk further into the Great Depression during the early 1930s, certain principles of intragovernment relations remained unchanged from the earliest days of the republic. That included the "nondelegation doctrine," which prohibited Congress from passing its constitutionally prescribed law-making powers on to other branches. Yet, beginning in 1933, a forceful new chief executive, Franklin Delano Roosevelt, was prepared to offer innovative new solutions to the nation's economic woes. Because the unwieldy size of Congress had left it largely powerless to hold previously unregulated businesses accountable, FDR's administration planned to stretch the Constitution's limits to allow for executive action in the matter. Thus, on June 16, 1933, FDR signed into law the National Industrial Recovery Act (NIRA), by which Congress authorized the chief executive to approve codes generated by trade associations regarding maximum hours of labor, minimum rates of pay, and working conditions in business. The administration approved more than 700 industry codes in all before the Supreme Court invalidated portions of the NIRA in 1935. Still, even that legal setback could not stop the growth of the welfare state under Roosevelt and his successors. Between 1935 and 1980 the federal government grew exponentially on the backs of executive agencies issuing rules and regulations that clearly amounted to law-making. The Constitution's capacity to stretch eventually afforded the federal government more flexibility to offer innovative solutions for an increasingly complex society.

Now

Upon assuming office as president in January 2017, Donald Trump quickly turned his attention to fulfilling campaign promises on immigration. The building of a newly fortified wall along the southern border would theoretically require funding from Congress, a slow-moving institution in even the best of circumstances. By contrast, the new president could take unilateral action to impose the so-called travel ban he had promised to voters. Thus, during his first week as president, Donald Trump issued Executive Order 13769, suspending the entry of Syrian refugees indefinitely and directing cabinet secretaries to suspend entry for at least 90 days of those from seven Muslim-majority countries that did not meet adjudication standards under U.S. immigration law. (The original list of countries included Iran, Iraq, Libya, Somalia, Sudan, Syria, and Yemen.) Critics complained that the order focused exclusively on countries that had a Muslim majority and thus constituted a "Muslim ban" in violation of the free exercise clause; they also claimed it exceeded the power of the executive to impose unilateral measures in the absence of an emergency. (The administration countered that the security of the country constituted just such an emergency.) As was the case with FDR's NIRA, the travel ban hit roadblocks in the courts, forcing the administration to rewrite the ban more than once. Yet the U.S. Supreme Court eventually upheld the reformulated ban in June 2018, endorsing unprecedented executive powers to secure the country's borders against travelers from several Muslim-majority countries. Once again the Constitution had been reshaped by bold new interpretations of the same text that had been in place for over two centuries.

For Critical Thinking and Discussion

1. Since 1803, the U.S. Supreme Court has assumed for itself the right to say what the Constitution means, including what it forbids. Does the president and/ or the Congress have the power to interpret the Constitution as well? If a political branch disagrees strongly with a Supreme Court decision, can it offer a contrary position?
2. Do you believe the Constitution should adapt and change according to the times, even when no amendment that spells out that change has been formally ratified? Why or why not?

2-1 THE BEGINNINGS OF A NEW NATION

Throughout the seventeenth and early eighteenth centuries, thousands of people migrated to North America. Many came in search of greater economic opportunities; others fled to escape religious persecution and sought freedom to worship as they pleased. Slowly, a culture dedicated to the protection of social and civil rights began to take shape in the colonies.

The political structures that governed the colonies up through the early 1760s roughly paralleled those of England during the same period: (1) Royal governors served as substitutes for the king in each individual colony; (2) a governor's council in each colony served as a mini House of Lords, with the most influential men in the colony serving effectively as a high court; and (3) the general assembly in each colony was elected directly by the qualified voters in each colony and served essentially as a House of Commons, passing ordinances and regulations that would govern the colony. Up until the middle of the eighteenth century, the colonies' diverse histories and economies had provided little incentive for them to join together to meet shared goals. In fact, those in Great Britain feared other European powers attempting to encroach on their American holdings far more than they feared any form of uprising on the part of the colonists.

The French and Indian War that was waged in the colonies from 1754 through 1763 was a significant turning point in British–colonial relations.[1] For nearly a decade, the French, from their base in Canada, fought the British in the colonies for control of the North American empire. Both nations were interested in rights to the territory that extended west of the colonial settlements along the Atlantic seaboard and over the Appalachian Mountains into the Ohio Valley. Britain defeated France, and under the terms of the Treaty of Paris (1763), which settled the war, all territory from the Arctic Ocean to the Gulf of Mexico between the Atlantic Ocean and the Mississippi River (except for New Orleans, which was ceded to Spain, an ally of Britain during the war) was awarded to Britain. But along with the acquisition of all this new territory came a staggering debt of approximately 130 million pounds. Administering its huge new North American empire would be a costly undertaking for Britain.

BRITISH ACTIONS

Following the war, Britain imposed upon its colonies a series of regulatory measures intended to make the colonists help pay the war debts and share the costs of governing the empire. To prevent colonists from ruining the prosperous British fur trade, the Proclamation of 1763 restricted them to the eastern side of the Appalachian chain, angering those interested in settling, cultivating, and trading in this new region. The Sugar Act of 1764 was the first law passed by Parliament for the specific purpose of raising money in the colonies for the Crown. (Other regulatory acts passed earlier had been enacted for the purpose of controlling trade.) The Sugar Act (1) increased the duties on sugar; (2) placed new import duties on textiles, coffee, indigo, wines, and other goods; and (3) doubled the duties on foreign goods shipped from England to the colonies. The Stamp Act (1765) required the payment of a tax on the purchase of all newspapers, pamphlets, almanacs, and commercial and legal documents in the colonies. Both acts drew outrage from colonists, who argued that Parliament could not tax those who were not formally represented in its chambers. Throughout late 1765 and early 1766, angry colonists protested the Stamp Act by attacking stamp agents who attempted to collect the tax, destroying the stamps, and boycotting British goods. When English merchants complained bitterly about the loss of revenue they were suffering as a result of these colonial protests, Parliament repealed the Stamp Act in March 1766.[2]

COLONIAL RESPONSES

As a result of the Stamp Act fiasco, positions on the state of British rule were articulated both in the colonies and in Parliament. Following the lead of the Virginia assembly, which sponsored the Virginia Resolves that had declared the principle of "no taxation without representation," an intercolonial Stamp Act Congress met in New York City in 1765. This first congressional body in America issued a Declaration of Rights and Grievances that acknowledged allegiance to the Crown but reiterated the right to not be taxed without consent. Meanwhile, the British Parliament—on the same day that it repealed the Stamp Act—passed into law the Declaratory Act, asserting that the king and Parliament had "full power and authority" to enact laws binding on the colonies "in all cases whatsoever."

Despite the colonists' protests, Parliament continued to pass legislation designed to raise revenue from the colonies. The Townshend Acts, passed in 1767, imposed duties on various items, including tea, imported into the colonies, and created a Board of Customs Commissioners to enforce the acts and collect the duties. When the colonists protested by boycotting British goods, in 1770 Parliament repealed all the duties except that on tea. The Tea Act, enacted in 1773, was passed to help the financially troubled British East India Company by relaxing export duties and allowing the company to sell its tea directly in the colonies. These advantages allowed the company to undersell colonial merchants. Angry colonists saw the act as a trick to lure them into buying the cheaper tea and thus ruining colonists' tea sellers. On December 16, 1773, colonists disguised as Mohawk Indians boarded ships in Boston Harbor and threw overboard their cargoes of tea. Outraged by this defiant Boston Tea Party, Parliament in 1774 passed the Intolerable Acts (known in the colonies as the Coercive Acts), designed to punish the rebellious colonists. The acts closed the port of Boston, revised the Massachusetts colonial government, and required the colonists to provide food and housing for British troops stationed in the colonies.

The colonists had had enough. In September 1774, 56 leaders from 12 colonies (there were no delegates from Georgia) met in Philadelphia to plan a united response to Parliament's actions. This First Continental Congress denounced British policy and organized a boycott of British goods. Although the Congress did not advocate outright independence from England, it did encourage the colonial militias to arm themselves and began to collect and store weapons in an arsenal in Concord, Massachusetts. The British governor general of Massachusetts ordered British troops to seize and destroy the weapons. On their way to Concord, the troops met a small force of colonial militiamen at Lexington. Shots were exchanged, but the militiamen were soon routed and the British troops marched on to Concord. There they encountered a much larger group of colonial militia. Shots again were fired, and this time the British retreated. The American Revolution had begun.

THE DECISION FOR INDEPENDENCE

Despite the events of the early 1770s, many leading colonists continued to hold out hope that some settlement could be reached between the colonies and Britain. The tide turned irrevocably in early 1776, when one of the most influential publications of this period, *Common Sense*, first appeared. In it, Thomas Paine attacked King George III as responsible for the provocations against the colonies and converted many wavering Americans to the cause of independence.[3]

On June 7, 1776, Richard Henry Lee, a delegate to the Second Continental Congress from Virginia, proposed a resolution stating that "these United Colonies are, and of right ought to be, free and independent States." Of course, the Congress needed a formal document both to state the colonies' list of grievances and to articulate their new intention to seek independence. The Congress thus appointed a committee to draft a document that would meet those objectives.

The committee, consisting of Thomas Jefferson, John Adams, Roger Sherman,

Patrick Henry, a leading revolutionary who coined the phrase "Give me liberty or give me death," speaking before the Virginia House of Burgesses in 1775.

Daniel Shays leads a rebellion of farmers to a Massachusetts courthouse in 1786 to protest the state legislature's inaction.

Robert Livingston, and Benjamin Franklin, appointed Jefferson, a popular delegate from a more populous state, to compose the document. The committee eventually submitted its draft to Congress on July 2, 1776; after making some changes, Congress formally adopted the document on July 4. The **Declaration of Independence** restated John Locke's theory of natural rights and the social contract between government and the governed.[4] Locke had argued that although citizens sacrifice certain rights when they consent to be governed as part of a social contract, they retain other inalienable rights. In the Declaration, Jefferson reiterated this argument with the riveting sentence: "We hold these truths to be self-evident, that all men are created equal, that they are endowed by their Creator with certain inalienable rights, that among these are life, liberty and the pursuit of happiness." Jefferson went on to state that whenever government fails in its duty to secure such rights, the people have the right to "alter" or "abolish" it and institute a new one. Through the centuries, America's political leaders have consistently invoked the Declaration of Independence as perhaps the truest written embodiment of the American Revolution. Before independence could become a reality, however, the colonists had to fight and win a war with Great Britain.

THE FIRST NATIONAL GOVERNMENT: THE ARTICLES OF CONFEDERATION

The colonies also needed some sort of plan of government to direct the war effort. The Second Continental Congress drew up the **Articles of Confederation**, a written statement of rules and principles to guide the first continent-wide government in the colonies during the war and beyond. Although the document was initially adopted by Congress in 1777, it was not formally ratified by all 13 states until 1781. The Articles of Confederation created a "league of friendship" among the states, but the states remained sovereign and independent, with the power and authority to rule the colonists' daily lives. The sole body of the new national government was the Congress, in which each state had one vote. As shown in Table 2-1, the Congress enjoyed only limited authority to govern the colonies: it could wage war and make peace, coin money, make treaties and alliances with other nations, operate a postal service, and manage relations with the Native Americans.[5] But Congress had no power to raise troops, regulate commerce, or levy taxes, which left it dependent on state legislatures to raise and support armies or provide other services. Congress's inability to raise funds significantly hampered the efforts of George Washington and the Continental Army during the war against Britain. Although Congress employed a "requisition system" in the 1780s, which essentially asked that states voluntarily meet contribution quotas to the federal government, the system proved ineffective. New Jersey, for example, consistently refused to pay such requisitions. Reflecting the colonists' distrust of a strong centralized government, the Articles made no provision for a chief executive who could enforce Congress's laws.

The limited powers of the central government posed many problems, but changing the Articles of Confederation to meet the needs of the new nation was no easy task. The Articles could be amended only by the assent of all 13 state legislatures, a provision that made change of any kind nearly impossible. Wealthy property owners and colonial merchants were frustrated with the Articles for various reasons. Because Congress lacked the power to regulate interstate and foreign commerce, it was exceedingly difficult to obtain commercial concessions from other nations. Quarrels among states disrupted interstate commerce and travel. Finally, a few state governments (most notably, that of Pennsylvania) had come to

Declaration of Independence Formal document listing colonists' grievances and articulating the colonists' intention to seek independence; formally adopted by the Second Continental Congress on July 4, 1776.

Articles of Confederation The document creating a "league of friendship" governing the 13 states during and immediately after the war for independence; hampered by the limited power the document vested in the legislature to collect revenue or regulate commerce, the Articles eventually proved unworkable for the new nation.

TABLE 2-1

The Articles of Confederation and the U.S. Constitution: Key Features

Articles of Confederation Provisions	Problems Generated	1787 Federal Constitution
Unicameral (one-house) Congress with each state having one vote, regardless of population	Gave smaller, less populated states disproportionate power in law-making	Bicameral (two-house) legislature with one house apportioned by population (House of Representatives) and second house (Senate) apportioned equally among states (two senators from each state)
Approval by 9 of 13 states required for most legislative matters	Restricted law-making by simple majorities, halting the legislative process in most cases	Approval of simple majority (one-half plus one) of both houses required for most legislation
No separate executive or judiciary	Legislative abuses went unchecked	Three separate branches of government: legislative, executive, and judicial
Congress did not have the power to regulate foreign or interstate commerce	States negotiated separately among themselves and with foreign powers on commercial matters, to the detriment of the overall economy	Congress given power to regulate interstate and foreign commerce
Congress did not have the power to levy or collect taxes	Suffering from the economic depression and saddled with their own war debts, states furnished only a small portion of the money sought by Congress	Congress given power to levy and collect taxes
Congress did not have the power to raise an army	Once the war with Britain had ended, states were reluctant to provide any support for an army	Congress given power to raise and support armies
Amendments to Articles required unanimous approval of state legislatures	Articles were practically immune from modification and thus inflexible to meet changing demands of a new nation	Amendments to Constitution require two-thirds vote of both houses of Congress, ratification by three-fourths of states

be dominated by radical movements that further threatened the property rights of many wealthy, land-owning colonists.

These difficulties did not disappear when the war ended with the Americans' victory in 1783. Instead, an economic depression, partially caused by the loss of trade with Great Britain and the West Indies, aggravated the problems facing the new nation. In January 1785, an alarmed Congress appointed a committee to consider amendments to the Articles. Although the committee called for expanded congressional powers to enter commercial treaties with other nations, no action was taken. Further proposals to revise the Articles by creating federal courts and strengthening the system of soliciting contributions from states were never even submitted to the states for approval; congressional leaders apparently despaired of ever winning the unanimous approval of the state legislatures needed to create such changes.

Then in September 1786, nine states accepted invitations to attend a convention in Annapolis, Maryland, to discuss interstate commerce. Yet, when the Annapolis Convention opened on September 11, delegates from only five states (New York, New Jersey, Delaware, Pennsylvania, and Virginia) attended. A committee led by Alexander Hamilton, a leading force at the Annapolis meeting, issued a report calling upon all 13 states to attend a convention in Philadelphia the following May to discuss all matters necessary "to render the constitution of the federal government adequate to the exigencies of the Union." At the time, few knew whether this proposal would attract more interest than had previous calls for a new government.

Events in Massachusetts in 1786–1787 proved a turning point in the creation of momentum for a new form of government. A Revolutionary War veteran, Daniel Shays was also one of many debt-ridden farmers in Massachusetts, where creditors controlled the state government. Shays and his men rebelled against the state courts' foreclosing on the farmers' mortgages for failure to pay debts and state taxes.[6] When the state legislature failed to resolve the farmers' grievances, Shays's rebels stormed two courthouses and a federal arsenal.[7] Eventually the state militia put down the insurrection, known as **Shays's Rebellion**, but the message was clear: a weak and unresponsive government carried with it the danger of disorder and violence. In February 1787, Congress endorsed the call for a convention to serve the purpose of drafting amendments to the Articles of Confederation, and by May 11, states had acted to name delegates to the convention to be held in Philadelphia.

2-2 THE CONSTITUTIONAL CONVENTION

The **Constitutional Convention** convened on May 25, 1787, with 29 delegates from nine states in attendance. Over the next four months, 55 delegates from 12 states would participate. Fiercely resistant to any centralized power, Rhode Island sent no delegates. Some heroes of the American Revolution, such as Patrick Henry, refused appointments because of their opposition to the feelings of nationalism that had spurred the convention to be held in the first place. Meanwhile, lending authority to the proceedings were such well-known American figures as George Washington, Alexander Hamilton, and Benjamin Franklin. (The 36-year-old James Madison of Virginia was only beginning to establish a reputation for himself when he arrived in Philadelphia; meanwhile, John Adams and Thomas Jefferson were both on diplomatic assignment in Europe.)

The delegates, who unanimously selected Washington to preside over the convention, were united by at least four common concerns: (1) The United States was being treated with contempt by other nations, and foreign trade had suffered as a consequence; (2) the economic radicalism of Shays's Rebellion might spread in the absence of a stronger central government; (3) Native Americans had responded to encroachment on their lands by threatening frontiersmen and land speculators, and the national government was ill-equipped to provide citizens with protection; and (4) the postwar economic depression had worsened, and the national government was powerless to take any action to address it.[8] Of course, on many other matters the delegates differed. Those from bigger, more heavily populated states such as Virginia and Pennsylvania wanted a central government that reflected their larger population bases, whereas those from smaller states like Georgia and Delaware hoped to maintain the one-state, one-vote principle of the Articles.

PLANS AND COMPROMISES

It quickly became evident that a convention originally called to discuss amendments to the Articles of Confederation would be undertaking a more drastic overhaul of the American system of government. Members of the Virginia delegation got the ball rolling when they introduced the **Virginia Plan**, also known as the "large states plan," which proposed a national government consisting of three branches—a legislature, an executive, and a judiciary. The legislature would consist of two houses, with membership in each house proportional to each state's population. The people would elect members of one house, and the members of that house would then choose members of the second house. The legislature would have the power to choose a chief executive and members of the judiciary, as well as the authority to legislate in "all cases to which the states are incompetent" or when the "harmony of the United States" demands it. Finally, the

Shays's Rebellion Armed uprising by debt-ridden Massachusetts farmers frustrated with the state government.

Constitutional Convention Meeting of delegates from 12 states in Philadelphia during the summer of 1787, at which was drafted an entirely new system to govern the United States.

Virginia Plan A proposal known also as the "large states plan" that empowered three separate branches of government, including a legislature with membership proportional to population.

Portrait of George Washington, circa 1775. Washington was elected president of the Constitutional Convention in Philadelphia.

legislature would have power to veto any state law. Under the plan, the only real check on the legislature would be a Council of Revision, consisting of the executive and several members of the judiciary, which could veto the legislature's acts.

To counter the Virginia Plan, delegates from less populous states proposed the **New Jersey Plan**, which called for a one-house legislature in which each state, regardless of size, would have equal representation. The New Jersey Plan also provided for a national judiciary and an executive committee chosen by the legislature, expanded the powers of Congress to include the power to levy taxes and regulate foreign and interstate commerce, and asserted that the new constitution and national laws would become the "supreme law of the United States." Both the Virginia and the New Jersey plans rejected a model of government in which the executive would be given extensive authority.

By July 2, 1787, disagreements over the design of the legislature and the issue of representation had brought the convention to a near dead end. The delegates then agreed to submit the matter to a smaller committee in the hope that it might craft some form of compromise.

The product of that committee's deliberations was a set of compromises, termed the **Great Compromise** by historians. (Formally proposed by delegate Roger Sherman of Connecticut, the agreement is also known as the "Connecticut Compromise.") As shown in Table 2-2, its critical features included (1) a bicameral (two-house) legislature with an upper house or "Senate," in which the states would have equal power with two representatives from each state, and a lower House of Representatives, in which membership would be apportioned on the basis of population; and (2) the guarantee that all revenue bills would originate in the lower house. The convention delegates settled as well on granting Congress the authority to regulate interstate and foreign commerce by a simple majority vote but required that treaties be approved by a two-thirds vote of the upper house. The Great Compromise was eventually approved by a narrow 5–4 margin of the state delegations.

Compromise also resolved disagreement over the nature of the executive. Although rejecting the New Jersey Plan's call for a plural executive—in which officials would have exercised executive power through a multiperson council—the delegates split on whether the executive should be elected by members of Congress or directly by the people. The

New Jersey Plan A proposal known also as the "small states plan" that would have retained the Articles of Confederation's principle of a legislature where states enjoyed equal representation.

Great Compromise A proposal also known as the "Connecticut Compromise" that provided for a bicameral legislature featuring an upper house based on equal representation among the states and a lower house whose membership was based on each state's population; approved by a 5–4 vote of the state delegations.

TABLE 2-2
The Virginia Plan, the New Jersey Plan, and the Great Compromise

The Virginia Plan	The New Jersey Plan	The Great Compromise
Introduced on May 29, 1787, by Edmund Randolph of Virginia; favored initially by delegates from Virginia, Pennsylvania, and Massachusetts	Introduced on June 15, 1787, by William Paterson of New Jersey; favored initially by delegates from New Jersey, New York, Connecticut, Maryland, and Delaware	Introduced by Roger Sherman of Connecticut; approved at the convention by a narrow 5–4 vote on July 16, 1787
Bicameral legislature with one house elected by the people and second house chosen by the first	Unicameral legislature elected by the people	Bicameral legislature with one house elected by the people and second house chosen by state legislatures
All representatives and senators apportioned by population	Equal representation among states	Members of one house (representatives) apportioned by population (five slaves counted as three free men); members of second house (senators) apportioned equally among states
Singular executive chosen by the legislature	Plural executive chosen by the legislature	Singular executive chosen by the "electoral college" (electors appointed by state legislatures choose president; if no one receives majority, House chooses president)
Congress can legislate wherever "states are incompetent" or to preserve the "harmony of the United States"	Congress has the power to tax and regulate commerce	Congress has power to tax only in proportion to representation in the lower House; all appropriation bills must originate in lower House

agreement reached called for the president (and vice president) to be elected by an electoral college. Because the number of electors equaled the number of representatives and senators from each state, this system gave disproportionately greater influence to smaller states. As chief executive, the president would have the power to veto acts of Congress, make treaties and appointments with the consent of the Senate, and serve as commander in chief of the nation's armed forces.

THE SLAVERY ISSUE

The issue of representation collided with another thorny issue looming over the convention proceedings: the issue of slavery. Four Southern states (Maryland, Virginia, North Carolina, and South Carolina) had slave populations of more than a hundred thousand each, two New England states (Maine and Massachusetts) had already banned slavery, and another four Northern states (Vermont, New Hampshire, Rhode Island, and Connecticut) maintained extremely low concentrations of slavery within their borders. The steady march of abolition in the North was matched by a Southern slave population that had been doubling every two decades. (As shown in Figure 2-1, slavery would continue to predominate in the Deep South up through the eve of the Civil War.) The convention delegates who advocated a new form of government were wary of the role slavery would play in this new nation, but they were even more wary of offending Southern sentiments to the point that consensus at the convention would be endangered.

FIGURE 2-1

The State of U.S. Slavery in 1850

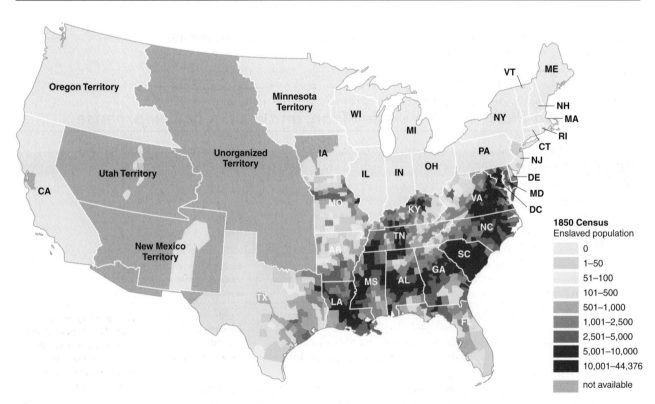

At the time of the founding, Northern states still featured limited slavery within their borders. Yet, over the following half-century, the concentration of slaves would shift to the point that by 1850, slavery had become an exclusively Southern institution. Thus the delicate compromise over slavery that the founding fathers struck at the Constitutional Convention would be put to the test during this later period.

Some delegates from the Northern states who had already voted in favor of banning slavery sought a similar emancipation of slaves in all of the colonies by constitutional edict. Southerners hoping to protect their plantation economy, which depended on slave labor, wanted to prevent future Congresses from interfering with the institution of slavery and the importation of slaves. Southern delegates also wanted slaves to be counted equally with free people in determining the apportionment of representatives; Northerners opposed such a scheme for representation because it would give the Southern states more power, but the North did want slaves counted equally for purposes of apportioning taxes among the states.

In an effort to forestall the convention's collapse, the delegates crafted a series of compromises that amounted to misdirection, and in some instances outright silence, on the issue of slavery.[9] By the agreement known as the **Three-Fifths Compromise**, five slaves would be counted as the equivalent of three "free persons" for purposes of taxes *and* representation. Delegates from Southern states also feared that a Congress dominated by representatives from more populous Northern states might take action against the slave trade. Most Northerners continued to favor gradual emancipation. Once again, neither side got exactly what it wanted. The new constitution said nothing about either preserving or outlawing slavery. Indeed, the only specific provision about slavery was a time limit on legislation banning slave importation: Congress was forbidden from doing so for at least 20 years. In 1807, however, with the slave population steadily outgrowing demand, many Southerners allied with opponents of the slave trade to ban the importation of slaves. Not until the Civil War decades later would the conflict over slavery finally be resolved.

On September 17, 1787, after four months of compromises and negotiations, the 12 state delegations present approved the final draft of the new constitution. By the terms of Article VII of the document, the new constitution was to become operative once ratified by 9 of the 13 states.

2-3 THE NEW CONSTITUTION

As a consequence of the many compromises in the draft constitution, few of the delegates were pleased with every aspect of the new document. Even James Madison, later heralded as the "Father of the Constitution" for his many contributions as a spokesman at the convention, had furiously opposed the Great Compromise; he hinted at one point that a majority of the states might be willing to form a union outside the convention if the compromise were ever approved, and he convinced the Virginia delegation to vote "no" when it came up for a formal vote.

Nonetheless, the central desire of most of the delegates to craft a new government framework led them to consensus on a set of guiding principles evident throughout the document. The following principles continue to guide politicians, lawyers, and scholars today as they study the many ambiguous provisions of the U.S. Constitution:

- Recognizing that calls for fairer representation of colonists' interests lay at the heart of the Declaration of Independence, popular sovereignty was a guiding principle behind the new constitution. The document's preamble beginning with "We the People" signified the coming together of people, not states, for the purposes of creating a new government. Under the proposed constitution, no law could be passed without the approval of the House of Representatives, a "people's house" composed of members apportioned by population and subject to direct election by the people every two years. Of even greater significance, the delegates agreed that all revenue measures must originate in the House, an explicit affirmation of the principle that there would be "no taxation without representation."
- The delegates recognized the need for a **separation of powers**. The founders drew upon the ideas of the French political philosopher Baron de Montesquieu, who had argued that when legislative, executive, and judicial power are not exercised by the same institution, power cannot be so easily abused. Mindful of the British model in which Parliament combined legislative and executive authority, the drafters of the new constitution assigned specific responsibilities and powers to each branch of the government—

Three-Fifths Compromise A compromise proposal in which five slaves would be counted as the equivalent of three free people for purposes of taxes and representation.

separation of powers The principle that each branch of government enjoys separate and independent powers and areas of responsibility.

checks and balances A system of limits imposed by the Constitution that gives each branch of government the limited right to change or cancel the acts of other branches.

Congress (the legislative power), the president (the executive power), and the Supreme Court (the judicial power). In the new government, individuals were generally prohibited from serving in more than one branch of government at the same time. The vice president's role as president of the Senate was a notable exception to this rule.

- While establishing separate institutions, the drafters of the new constitution also created a system of **checks and balances** to require that the branches of government would have to work together to formulate policies (see Figure 2-2). This system of "separate institutions sharing power" helped ensure that no one interest or faction

FIGURE 2-2

Checks and Balances in the U.S. Constitution

CHECKS BY JUDICIARY

Checks on Congress

✓ Federal judicial power extends to all cases arising under the laws of the United States (Art. III, § 2, Cl. 1) **(subsequently interpreted to include power to invalidate unconstitutional laws passed by Congress)**

Checks on Executive

✓ Federal judicial power extends to all cases or controversies to which the U.S. government is a party (Art. III, § 2, Cl. 1) **(subsequently interpreted to include power to invalidate unconstitutional acts by president)**

✓ Chief justice shall preside over Senate impeachment trials of the president (Art. I, § 3, Cl. 6)

CHECKS BY EXECUTIVE

Checks on Congress

✓ Presidential power to sign or veto bills (Art I, § 7, Cl. 2)

✓ In alternate role as president of Senate, vice president of United States can cast votes to break ties in a divided Senate (Art. I, § 3, Cl. 4)

✓ President can bypass Senate temporarily by filling vacancies during Senate recess that expire at end of next Senate session (Art. II, § 2, Cl. 3)

✓ President may "on extraordinary occasions" convene or adjourn either or both houses of Congress (Art. II, § 3)

✓ President must "take care" that congressional laws are faithfully executed (Art. II, § 3)

Checks on Judiciary

✓ President nominates and (with Senate advice and consent) appoints Supreme Court justices (Art. II, § 2, Cl. 2)

CHECKS BY CONGRESS

Checks on Executive

✓ Impeachment by House (Art. I, § 2, Cl. 5) and removal by Senate (Art. I, § 3, Cl. 6) of president, vice president, and all civil officers of the United States (Art. II, § 4)

✓ Congressional override of presidential vetoes by two-thirds of both houses (Art. I, § 7, Cl. 2)

✓ Senate must approve all treaties by two-thirds vote (Art. II, § 2, Cl. 2)

✓ House selection of president and Senate selection of vice president in event there is no Electoral College majority (Art. II, § 1, Cl. 3, Twelfth Amendment)

✓ Senate advice and consent required for appointment of "Officers of the United States" (Art. II, § 2, Cl. 2)

Checks on Judiciary

✓ Senate advice and consent required for appointment of Supreme Court justices (Art. II, § 2, Cl. 2)

✓ Impeachment by House (Art. I, § 2, Cl. 5) and removal by Senate (Art. I, § 3, Cl. 6) of Supreme Court justices

✓ Congress can make exceptions to appellate jurisdiction of the Supreme Court (Art. III, § 2, Cl. 2)

could easily dominate the government. Through the exercise of presidential vetoes, Senate advice and consent, and judicial interpretations and other tools, each institution would have an opportunity to contend for influence.

- Dividing sovereign powers between the states and the federal government—a system later termed *federalism* (discussed at greater length in Chapter 3)—is also a defining characteristic of the government framework established by the new constitution. Rather than entrusting all powers to a centralized government and essentially reducing the states to mere geographical subdivisions of the nation, the convention delegates divided powers between two levels of government: the states and the federal government. The distinction drawn between local concerns (controlled by state governments) and national concerns (controlled by the federal government) was nearly as confusing then as it is today. But the delegates determined that such a division was necessary to achieve a consensus.

- Although united by the belief that the national government needed to be strengthened, the framers of the new constitution were products of a revolutionary generation that had seen governmental power abused. Thus they were committed to a government of limited or **enumerated powers**. The new constitution spelled out the powers of the new federal government in detail, and it was assumed that the government's authority did not extend beyond those powers. By rejecting a government of unlimited discretionary power, James Madison argued, individual rights, including those "inalienable rights" cited in the Declaration of Independence, would be protected from the arbitrary exercise of authority.

- Finally, some delegates believed that the new constitution should be a "living" document; that is, it should have some measure of flexibility in order to meet the changing demands placed on it over time. Perhaps the most frustrating aspect of the Articles of Confederation was the near impossibility of any sort of modification. Because any change to the Articles required the unanimous consent of the states, even the most popular reform proposals stood little chance of being implemented. Thus, the framers decided that the new constitution would go into effect when it had been ratified by 9 of the 13 states. Furthermore, once ratified, the constitution could be amended by a two-thirds vote of each house of Congress (subject to subsequent ratification by three-fourths of the state legislatures).

2-4 THE RATIFICATION BATTLE

FEDERALISTS VERSUS ANTI-FEDERALISTS

Once Congress submitted the new constitution to the states for approval, battle lines were formed between the **Federalists**, who supported ratification of the new document, and the **Anti-Federalists**, who opposed it. From the outset, the Federalists enjoyed a number of structural and tactical advantages in this conflict.

- **Nonunanimous consent.** The rules of ratification for the new constitution, requiring approval of just 9 of the 13 states, were meant to ease the process of adopting the new document. The delegates understood that once the constitution had been approved, it would be difficult for even the most stubborn of state holdouts to exist as an independent nation surrounded by this formidable new national entity.
- **Special "ratifying conventions."** The delegates realized that whatever form the new constitution might take, state legislatures would have the most to lose from an abandonment of the Articles. Thus they decided that the constitution would be sent for ratification not to state legislatures but instead to special state ratifying conventions that would be more likely to approve it.
- **The rule of secrecy.** The Constitutional Convention's agreed-upon rule of secrecy, which forbade publication or discussion of the day-to-day proceedings of the convention, followed the precedent established in colonial assemblies and the First Continental Congress, where it was thought that members might speak more freely and openly if their remarks were not subject to daily scrutiny by the public at large.

enumerated powers Those powers granted to Congress that are listed in the Constitution, including exclusive federal powers as well as concurrent powers shared with the states.

Federalists Those who supported ratification of the proposed constitution of the United States between 1787 and 1789.

Anti-Federalists Those who opposed ratification of the proposed constitution of the United States between 1787 and 1789.

In the fall of 1787, the rule of secrecy also gave the Federalists on the inside a distinct advantage over outside opponents, who had little knowledge of the new document's provisions until publicized. As it turned out, five state ratifying conventions approved the new constitution within four months of the convention's formal conclusion, just as Anti-Federalist forces were marshalling their strength for the battle ahead.

- **Conventions held in the winter limited rural participation.** Winter was approaching in late 1787 just as the fight over the new constitution was being launched. This timing gave the Federalists another advantage, especially in the critical ratification battlegrounds of Massachusetts, New Hampshire, and New York. It would be difficult for rural dwellers—mostly poor farmers resistant to a strong central government and thus opposed to the new constitution—to attend the ratification conventions if they were held in the dead of winter. Supporters of the new constitution successfully pressed for the ratifying conventions to be held as soon as possible. Of the six states that held such conventions over the winter, all voted to ratify by substantial margins.

THE FEDERALIST PAPERS

Between the fall of 1787 and the summer of 1788, the Federalists launched an aggressive media campaign that was unusually well organized for its time. James Madison, Alexander Hamilton, and John Jay wrote 77 essays explaining and defending the new constitution and urging its ratification. Signed under the name "Publius," the essays were printed in New York newspapers and magazines. These essays—along with eight others by the same men—were then collected, printed, and published in book form under the title *The Federalist*.[10] The essays allayed fears and extolled the benefits of the new constitution by emphasizing the inadequacy of the Articles of Confederation and the need for a strong government. Today these essays are considered classic works of political philosophy. The following are among the most frequently cited **Federalist Papers**:

- **Federalist No. 10.** In Madison's first offering in the Federalist Papers, he analyzes the nature, causes, and effects of *factions*, by which he meant groups of people motivated by a common economic and/or political interest. Noting that such factions are both the product and price of liberty, Madison argued that by extending the sphere in which they can act, "you make it less probable that a majority of the whole will have a common motive to invade the rights of other citizens." Political theorists often cite Federalist No. 10 as justification for pluralist theory—the idea that competition among groups for power produces the best approximation of overall public good.
- **Federalist No. 15.** Hamilton launched his attack on the Articles of Confederation in this essay. Specifically, he pointed to the practical impossibility of engaging in concerted action when each of the 13 states retained virtual power to govern.
- **Federalist No. 46.** In this essay, Madison defended the system of federalism set up by the new constitution. He contended that the system allowed the states sufficient capacity to resist the "ambitious encroachments of the federal government."
- **Federalist No. 51.** In perhaps the most influential of the essays, Madison described how the new constitution would prevent the government from abusing its citizens. His argument is that the "multiplicity of interests" that influences so many different parts of the government would guarantee the security of individual rights. Because the federal system of government divides the government into so many parts (federal vs. state, legislative vs. executive vs. judicial branch, etc.), "the rights of the individual, or of the minority, will be in little danger from interested combinations of the majority."
- **Federalist No. 69.** Hamilton in this essay defined the "real character of the executive," which, unlike the king of Great Britain, is accountable to the other branches of government and to the people.
- **Federalist No. 70.** In this paper, Hamilton presented his views on executive power, which had tempered considerably since the convention, when he advocated an executive for life. Still, Hamilton argued for a unitary, one-person executive to play a critical role as a check on the legislative process (i.e., by exercising vetoes), as well as in the process of negotiating

Federalist Papers A series of articles authored by Alexander Hamilton, James Madison, and John Jay that argued in favor of ratifying the proposed constitution of the United States; the Federalist Papers outlined the philosophy and motivation of the document.

treaties and conducting war. According to Hamilton, "Energy in the executive is a leading character in the definition of good government"; by contrast, "the species of security" sought for by those who advocate a plural executive is "unattainable."

- **Federalist No. 78.** In this essay—cited in several landmark Supreme Court opinions—Hamilton argues that the judiciary would be the weakest of the three branches because it has "neither FORCE nor WILL, but merely judgment." Because the Court depends on the other branches to uphold that judgment, Hamilton called it "the least dangerous branch."

In late 1787 and early 1788, Anti-Federalists countered the Federalist Papers with a media campaign of their own.[11] In letters written under the pseudonyms "Brutus" and "The Federal Farmer" and published by newspapers throughout the colonies, the Anti-Federalists claimed that they were invoking a cause more consistent with that of the revolution—the cause of freedom from government tyranny. For them, the new national government's power to impose internal taxes on the states amounted to a revival of the British system of internal taxation. Perhaps the Anti-Federalists' most effective criticism was that the new constitution lacked a bill of rights that explicitly protected citizens' individual rights. They rejected Madison's contention in Federalist No. 51 that limitations on the central government provided those protections.

Ratification ultimately succeeded but by a somewhat narrow margin (see Table 2-3). Of the first five states to ratify, four (Delaware, New Jersey, Georgia, and Connecticut) did so with little or no opposition, whereas Pennsylvania did so only after a bitter conflict at its ratifying convention. Massachusetts became the sixth state to ratify when proponents of the new constitution swung the convention narrowly in their favor only by promising to push for a bill of rights after ratification. By June, three more states (Maryland, South Carolina, and New Hampshire) had voted to ratify, providing the critical threshold of nine states required under the new constitution. Still, the Federalists worried that without ratification by the major states of New York and Virginia, the new union would not succeed.

TABLE 2-3

Ratifying the Constitution

State	Vote	Date of Ratification
Delaware	30–0	December 7, 1787
Pennsylvania	43–23	December 12, 1787
New Jersey	38–0	December 18, 1787
Georgia	25–0	January 2, 1788
Connecticut	128–40	January 9, 1788
Massachusetts	187–168	February 16, 1788
Maryland	63–11	April 26, 1788
South Carolina	149–73	May 23, 1788
New Hampshire	57–46	June 21, 1788
Virginia	89–79	June 25, 1788
New York	30–27	June 26, 1788
North Carolina*	194–77	November 21, 1789
Rhode Island	34–32	May 29, 1790

* Despite strong Federalist sentiment at the convention, North Carolina withheld its vote in 1788 until a draft bill of rights was formally introduced. The submission by Congress of 12 proposed amendments to the states on September 25, 1789, led North Carolina to hold a second ratifying convention the following November.

Opposition in Virginia was formidable, with Patrick Henry leading the Anti-Federalist forces against James Madison and the Federalists.[12] Eventually Madison gained the upper hand with an assist from George Washington, whose eminent stature helped capture numerous votes for the Federalists. Madison also promised to support adding a bill of rights to the new constitution. Then, Alexander Hamilton and John Jay capitalized on the positive news from Virginia to secure victory at the New York ratifying convention. With more than the required nine states—including the crucial states of New York and Virginia—the Congress did not wait for the votes from North Carolina or Rhode Island; on July 2, 1788, it appointed a committee to prepare for the new government.

A BILL OF RIGHTS

Seven of the state constitutions created during the Revolutionary War featured a statement of individual rights in some form. The Virginia Declaration of Rights of 1776, for example, had borrowed (from John Locke) its grounding of individual rights in a conception of natural law and social contract: "All men are by nature equally free and independent, and have certain inherent rights, of which, when they enter into a state of society, they cannot, by any compact, deprive or divest their posterity." Later, during the battle over ratification, five state ratifying conventions had stressed the need for amendments to the proposed constitution in the form of a bill of rights, which would expressly protect fundamental rights against encroachment by the national government.[13]

Still, not all Federalists saw the need for a federal bill of rights. Madison, for one, believed a bill of rights was unnecessary because the central government held only those powers enumerated in the Constitution. He explained, "The rights in question are reserved by the manner in which the federal powers are granted . . . the limited powers of the federal government and the jealousy of the subordinate governments afford a security which has not existed in the case of the state governments, and exists in no other." Madison was also concerned about the dangers of trying to enumerate all important rights: "There is great reason to fear that a positive declaration of some of the most essential rights could not be obtained," leaving some essential rights omitted for the future. Hamilton underscored this sentiment in Federalist No. 84, arguing that such a list of rights might invite governmental attempts to exercise power over those rights not included in the list.

Among the most ardent supporters of adding a bill of rights to the Constitution was Thomas Jefferson, who warned about the dangers of abuses of power.[14] From his distant vantage point in France, where he continued to serve as an American minister, Jefferson was in the dark about the new constitution until November 1787. Then, in a December 20, 1787, letter to his friend and political protégé from Virginia, James Madison, Jefferson wrote, "A bill of rights is what the people are entitled to against every government on earth, general or particular, and what no just government should refuse, or rest on inference." Although recognizing Madison's fears of omissions as legitimate, Jefferson continued to argue the point. In a subsequent letter dated March 15, 1789, Jefferson argued that "half a loaf is better than no bread. If we cannot secure all our rights, let us secure what we can."

In the end, Jefferson's arguments prevailed, and Madison (by this time a congressman from Virginia) became a principal sponsor of a bill of rights in the first Congress. Introducing the bill in the House of Representatives, he declared, "They will be an impenetrable bulwark against every assumption of power in the legislative or executive." On September 9, 1789, the House of Representatives voted to submit a list of 12 **amendments** to the states; 10 of these were ratified by the required nine states by December 15, 1791, and compose today's **Bill of Rights**.

Among the rights protected by the Bill of Rights are the rights of free religious exercise, free speech, free press, and assembly (First Amendment); rights against search and seizure without a warrant stating "probable cause" (Fourth Amendment); and rights of due process and no self-incrimination (Fifth Amendment). The two amendments not ratified in 1791 did not relate to individual rights at all. They were (1) a prohibition on salary increases for legislators taking effect prior to the next congressional election (in 1992—more than two hundred years later—this became the Twenty-seventh Amendment) and (2) a provision defining the rules for determining the number of members of the House of Representatives.

amendments Modifications or additions to the U.S. Constitution passed in accordance with the amendment procedures laid out in Article V.

Bill of Rights The first 10 amendments to the U.S. Constitution, which protect various rights of the people against the new federal government.

2-5 CHANGING THE CONSTITUTION

THE FORMAL AMENDMENT PROCESS

Although political circumstances dictated that the Bill of Rights be passed quickly, future proposed amendments would not have it so easy. In crafting the rules for amending the new constitution, the framers sought to balance two competing interests: (1) the need to protect the Constitution from short-lived or temporary passions by making amendments exceedingly difficult to pass, and (2) sufficient flexibility to allow for amendments to be added when the needs of the nation demanded change. Their determination to strike such a balance was shaped by their experience in dealing with the Articles of Confederation, whose "unanimous consent of states" rule had left the document immune from even the most necessary of reforms.

As shown in Figure 2-3, Article V of the Constitution specifies two ways in which amendments can be proposed and two methods of ratification. Congress may propose an amendment by a two-thirds vote of both houses; alternatively, two-thirds of the state legislatures may apply to Congress to call a special national convention for proposing amendments. Amendments take effect when ratified either by a vote of three-fourths of the state legislatures or by special ratifying conventions held in three-fourths of the states. To date, all 27 amendments (including the Bill of Rights) have been proposed by Congress, and all but one (the Twenty-first Amendment) have been ratified by the state legislatures.

No national convention has ever been called for the purpose of proposing amendments. Indeed, the closest the states have ever come to applying to Congress for such an event occurred in 1967, when 33 states (just one short of the required number) petitioned Congress to call a convention that would propose an amendment reversing the 1964 Supreme Court ruling requiring that both houses of each state legislature be apportioned according to population. Given the ambiguity of Article V, numerous questions have been raised about the form such a convention would take.

How would delegates be chosen? When Congress proposed the Twenty-first Amendment, it left it to each state to determine the manner in which delegates to the ratifying conventions would be chosen. How would the convention be run? Could a convention go beyond the

FIGURE 2-3

How an Amendment Gets Proposed and Ratified

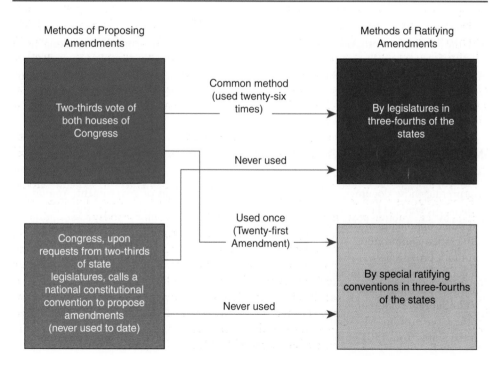

Methods of Proposing Amendments

Methods of Ratifying Amendments

Two-thirds vote of both houses of Congress

Common method (used twenty-six times)

By legislatures in three-fourths of the states

Never used

Congress, upon requests from two-thirds of state legislatures, calls a national constitutional convention to propose amendments (never used to date)

Used once (Twenty-first Amendment)

By special ratifying conventions in three-fourths of the states

Never used

limitations placed on it by Congress? What would happen if a convention went far afield and proposed an entirely new constitution, just as the convention in 1787 did? Congress has to date refused to pass laws dictating the terms of future conventions, in part because it has not wanted to encourage such an event.[15]

Critics of the amendment process charge that it is undemocratic, as today just 13 of the 50 states can block amendments desired by a large majority. Additionally, amendments, especially those ratified by special conventions, may be adopted even if they lack widespread popular support.

Although 27 amendments have been ratified since 1789, only 17 of those were ratified after 1791 (see Table 2-4). More than 11,000 amendments have been introduced in Congress since that time, but only 33 have been formally proposed by Congress. Today, different amendments sponsored by Congress garner varying levels of support. Among the proposed amendments that failed in the ratification process are the following:

- An amendment that would withdraw citizenship from any person who has accepted a title of nobility or who has received (without the consent of Congress) an office or salary from a foreign power (proposed in 1810)
- An amendment proposed on the eve of the Civil War in 1861 that would have prohibited further interference by the federal government with slavery in any state
- An amendment that would have prohibited labor by young children (proposed in 1924)

The Equal Rights Amendment (ERA) proposed by Congress in 1972 also came up short during the ratification process, after years of effort to secure its passage. Although the courts have consistently held that ratification of an amendment must take place within a "reasonable time," it has been left up to Congress to determine what constitutes a reasonable time. When drafting the proposed Eighteenth Amendment in 1917, Congress placed into the text of the amendment a seven-year limit on ratification and continued to do so with subsequent amendments it proposed up until 1960. That year, when Congress proposed the Twenty-third Amendment giving residents of the District of Columbia the right to vote in presidential elections, it began the practice of setting time limits in the resolution accompanying submission of the amendment to Congress, rather than in the formal part of the amendment. As a consequence, when it appeared that the ERA would not be ratified, proponents of the amendment managed to get the ratification period extended to June 30, 1982 (an additional three years and three months beyond the original deadline), by a majority vote of both houses. Despite the extension, however, the proposed amendment still failed to win the approval of more than 35 state legislatures.

The "reasonable time" requirement for ratification of an amendment reached an extreme with the Twenty-seventh Amendment (forbidding congressional pay raises from taking effect until an intervening election in the House of Representatives has occurred). Originally proposed in 1789 as part of the Bill of Rights, it was finally ratified in 1992, just over 202 years later. (See the "From Your Perspective" box in this chapter for more detailed discussion of what occurred.)

INFORMAL PROCESSES OF CHANGE

After the Constitution and Bill of Rights were ratified, there remained the difficult task of interpreting those documents for use by the different branches of government. Among the framers, Alexander Hamilton was perhaps most attuned to the danger that Anti-Federalists and other opponents of the Constitution might attempt to overturn the convention's carefully crafted compromises so many years later by judicial fiat. Certainly most of the Constitution's provisions were vague enough that they allowed discretion for maneuvering by the generation that interprets them, but how much discretion was justified in the process of constitutional interpretation?

The Supreme Court under Chief Justice John Marshall was the first to put its lasting imprint on the Constitution. Marshall, who hailed from Virginia, served as the chief justice of the United States from 1801 until his death in 1835.[16] Marshall believed in a **loose construction**

loose construction
Constitutional interpretation that gives constitutional provisions broad and open-ended meanings.

TABLE 2-4

Amendments, Date of Ratification, and Length of Ratification Process

Amendment Bill of Rights	Subject of Amendment	Date Proposed	Date Ratified	Length
First	Free speech, press, religion, assembly			
Second	Right to bear arms			
Third	No quartering of troops in homes			
Fourth	No unreasonable searches/seizures			
Fifth	Right to due process, grand jury, no double jeopardy, self-incrimination			
Sixth	Right to speedy and public trial, counsel	September 25, 1789	December 15, 1791	2+ years
Seventh	Right to trial by jury in civil cases			
Eighth	No excessive bail, fines, cruel/unusual punishment			
Ninth	Rights not enumerated retained by people			
Tenth	Powers not delegated to Congress or prohibited to states belong to states or people			
Eleventh	No federal cases between state, citizen of other state	March 5, 1794	January 8, 1798	3+ years
Twelfth	Modification of Electoral College rules	December 12, 1803	September 25, 1804	9+ months
Thirteenth	Ban on slavery	February 1, 1865	December 18, 1865	10+ months
Fourteenth	States can't deprive right to due process, equal protection, privileges and immunities	June 16, 1866	July 28, 1868	2+ years
Fifteenth	Right to vote can't be denied by race	February 27, 1869	March 30, 1870	1+ years
Sixteenth	Congress can levy individual income taxes	July 12, 1909	February 25, 1913	3+ years
Seventeenth	Direct election of senators	May 16, 1912	May 31, 1913	1+ years
Eighteenth	Prohibition of liquors	December 18, 1917	January 29, 1919	1+ years
Nineteenth	Women's right to vote	June 4, 1919	August 26, 1920	1+ years
Twentieth	Dates for inauguration, Congress's session	March 2, 1932	February 6, 1933	1+ months
Twenty-first	Repeal of prohibition	February 20, 1933	December 5, 1933	9+ months
Twenty-second	Presidential term limits	March 24, 1947	February 26, 1951	3+ years
Twenty-third	DC residents' vote for president	June 16, 1960	March 29, 1961	9+ months
Twenty-fourth	Ban on poll taxes	August 27, 1962	January 23, 1964	1+ years
Twenty-fifth	Appointment of new vice president, presidential incompetence	July 6, 1965	February 10, 1967	1+ years
Twenty-sixth	Eighteen-year-olds' right to vote	March 23, 1971	July 1, 1971	3+ months
Twenty-seventh	Congressional pay raises effective only after election	September 25, 1789	May 7, 1992	202+ years

Based on Paul Murphy, Background of the Bill of Rights (New York, NY: Taylor & Francis, 1990).

(or interpretation) of the Constitution, meaning that under his leadership, many of the Constitution's provisions enjoyed broad and quite open-ended meanings. Thus, for example, Article I, Section 8, Clause 18 empowered Congress "to make all laws which shall be necessary and proper for carrying into execution" any of the powers specifically listed in the

Constitution. Marshall's loose construction of that provision gave the federal government considerable implied powers (those not explicitly stated) to regulate the economy. Thus, in the 1819 case of *McCulloch v. Maryland*,[17] the Marshall court ruled that Congress had the power to create a national bank, even though the Constitution said nothing explicitly about such a power. The Court determined that a national bank was "necessary and proper" to assist in regulating commerce or raising armies. This philosophy of loose constitutional interpretation underlies the concept of a "living Constitution," one that is adaptable to changing times and conditions.

Thomas Jefferson, James Madison, and many others viewed the powers of the central government more narrowly. They favored a **strict construction**, arguing that the government possessed only those powers explicitly stated in the Constitution. Thus, although Article I, Section 8, Clause 3 gave Congress the power to regulate interstate commerce, it could not do so by creating a national bank or utilizing any other means not specifically mentioned in the Constitution. They supported a "fixed Constitution," one that could be changed only by the formal amendment process, not by congressional action or judicial ruling.

The tension between advocates of strict and loose constructions of the Constitution continues to this day. The late Supreme Court justice Antonin Scalia rejected the notion of constitutional standards evolving over time; in 2008 he told one reporter that while change in a society can be reflected in legislation, "society doesn't change through a Constitution."[18] In accordance with this philosophy, the more conservative Supreme Court of the late 1990s (which included Scalia) struck down federal statutes regulating guns in the schools and domestic violence, on the theory that such regulations were not grounded in any specifically enumerated power of Congress, such as the power to regulate interstate commerce.

This strict-construction approach contrasts markedly with the approach advocated by professors Lawrence Tribe[19] and John Hart Ely,[20] as well as the late Supreme Court justice William Brennan, who argued for a loose or more flexible interpretation of the Constitution.

strict construction
Constitutional interpretation that limits the government to only those powers explicitly stated in the Constitution.

FROM YOUR PERSPECTIVE

One Student's Term Paper Proves That the Constitution Is Indeed a "Living Document"

College students may be forgiven for assuming that classroom assignments that invite them to propose constitutional amendments are strictly theoretical exercises. Yet, in the case of one University of Texas student, such an assignment on constitutional change became much more than theoretical. Gregory Watson chose as his research topic a long-forgotten amendment to forbid congressional pay raises from taking effect until an intervening election in the House of Representatives had occurred. Originally proposed in 1789 as part of the Bill of Rights, the amendment was finally ratified 202 years later, thanks largely to Watson. In 1982, the sophomore college student had discovered the amendment while doing research for a paper on American government. Watson's final paper—in which he argued that the amendment was still viable for ratification—garnered a mere "C" from his professor. But Watson continued his quest to secure ratification of the amendment. Tapping into the

resentment of citizens over various instances in which members of Congress had quietly passed pay raises for themselves without calling attention to their actions, Watson joined forces with several state lawmakers to get the required number of states to ratify the provision. Their efforts succeeded, and the Twenty-seventh Amendment was eventually ratified in May 1992. Although Watson's grade from a decade earlier remained unchanged, he at least had the satisfaction of knowing that he had made history—literally.

For Critical Thinking and Discussion

1. What amendments to the Constitution would you like to see implemented?
2. Would you be willing to sacrifice your own time, energy, and resources to organize interest-group activities on an amendment's behalf?

Advocates of a loose construction view the document as evolving with the times. In the 1960s and 1970s, the Supreme Court (with Brennan presiding) utilized a loose-construction approach to interpret congressional power more broadly to include the power to create civil rights legislation and federal criminal laws.

With so few amendments proposed and ratified during the nation's history, students of American politics may wonder how a constitution written in 1787 has developed to meet the needs of a changing nation. In truth, an informal constitutional convention occurs on a frequent basis in the American political system. Congress, the president, and the courts engage in constitutional interpretation every day through their respective activities, both official and unofficial. Thus, the Constitution has not been a straitjacket at all—rather, its elegant vagueness has opened it up to a variety of interpretations.

Much of the rise in presidential power during the twentieth century occurred in the absence of any formal amendments conferring new powers on the chief executive. The

DEBATES OVER DIVERSITY
The Right to Sexual Autonomy, Sexual Expression, and Diverse Notions of Sexuality

The U.S. Constitution as amended does not explicitly spell out all individual rights; accordingly, it is left to politicians, judges, and society as a whole to address whatever gaps may exist. For example, throughout our country's history we have continually debated whether the Constitution implicitly protects rights to sexual autonomy and privacy. This debate has only intensified in recent times as society's notions of sexuality and sexual expression have quickly evolved. Today, individuals who favor the protection of these rights must often go to court to ensure that they are fully realized.

In the landmark Supreme Court case of *Obergefell v. Hodges* (2015),[21] the high court extended the fundamental right to marry to same-sex couples, even though no constitutional amendment was ratified on this subject. In his majority opinion, Supreme Court justice Anthony Kennedy wrote that the framers of the Constitution "did not presume to know the extent of freedom in all of its dimensions, and so they entrusted to future generations a charter protecting the right of all persons to enjoy liberty as we learn its meaning." Of course, future challenges to the definition of these rights remain: reformers continue to call for an amendment to the Constitution that would cement these gains into the law and force the actual language of the Constitution to reflect our nation's growing diversity on the nature of sexual autonomy, sexual expression, and sexuality more generally. Meanwhile, some critics of the *Obergefell* decision maintain the hope that a more conservative Supreme Court might one day reverse, or at a minimum undermine, those same protections.

Win McNamee / Getty Images

Vin Testa, a gay rights activist, waves a pride flag in front of the U.S. Supreme Court building in Washington, DC, in June 2013. The high court dismissed an appeal request on California's Proposition 8, which allowed for same-sex marriage to be reinstated in the state.

For Critical Thinking and Discussion

1. What rights of sexual autonomy, sexual expression, and sexuality more generally can be implied from the Constitution? Do these rights fall under the more general "right to privacy," or are they implied elsewhere?
2. What amendments to the Constitution are necessary to ensure our sexuality rights going forward? Would you prefer constitutional interpretation by judges that reflect evolving notions of sexuality over amendments as a method of reflecting these changes?

president of the United States reacted to circumstances facing the executive office by assuming greater authority over foreign and domestic policy-making, and the other branches of government deferred to the president in many such matters. With its ruling in *Marbury v. Madison* (1803),[22] the Supreme Court asserted its right of judicial review, that is, its authority to review acts of Congress for their constitutionality and void those that the Court determines are contrary to the Constitution. As part of its decision in *McCulloch v. Maryland*, the Court ruled that when state and federal powers collide, federal powers take precedence. With some notable exceptions, the other branches of the federal government and state courts have more or less acquiesced to such exercises of power.

When the states in 1791 ratified the Bill of Rights, citizens must have marveled at the flexibility of the new U.S. Constitution. After all, it had been amended 10 times in just two years! And yet the Constitution has proven remarkably resistant to change since then, incorporating only 17 additional amendments over the following two centuries. How has the federal Constitution survived so long and in nearly same form as the original document? The demands of modern government, which manages an advanced welfare state that serves the needs of hundreds of millions of Americans, press the Constitution into service even when traditional rules of constitutional interpretation would seem to offer an insurmountable obstacle. Advocates of the New Deal were undaunted by the strictures of the "nondelegation doctrine," and they stretched the Constitution's language to advance the modern welfare state; more than 80 years later, President Trump pressed ahead with his controversial travel ban, confident that his efforts would eventually be validated and his campaign promise duly fulfilled. The so-called higher law found in the Constitution must ultimately defer to the same public that vests it with that supreme authority in the first place.

Summary

2-1 The Beginnings of a New Nation

- The American Revolution arose a decade after Britain's victory in the French and Indian War; to pay off its significant war debts, Britain imposed numerous regulatory measures on the colonies, which generated outrage, protests, and eventually armed resistance from the colonists.
- The Articles of Confederation created a "league of friendship" among the 13 states by vesting them with equal authority in a weak government with only limited powers to raise revenue and regulate commerce. The weakness of the Articles hampered early American foreign policy and rendered Congress unable to stamp out political unrest throughout the states.

2-2 The Constitutional Convention

- In 1787 a Constitutional Convention of delegates from 12 states considered both the "Virginia Plan," which favored larger, more populous states, and a "New Jersey Plan" that gave equal representation to the states.
- The Convention ultimately accepted the "Great Compromise" and its bicameral legislature featuring a House of Representatives apportioned by

population and a Senate allotting equal power to each state.
- The delegates sidestepped the slavery issue by settling on the "Three-Fifths Compromise" (counting five slaves as three people for purposes of taxes and representation) and by deferring a ban on slave importation for at least 20 years.

2-3 The New Constitution

- The new constitution combined features of popular sovereignty, separation of powers, and checks and balances with a commitment to a system of "federalism" that divides sovereignty between state and federal governments.

2-4 The Ratification Battle

- The battle over ratification was waged between the Federalists, who supported the new constitution, and the Anti-Federalists, who opposed it. In advocating the merits of the document, Federalists benefitted from the convention's rule of secrecy and the rule requiring the approval of just 9 of 13 state ratifying conventions for ratifications.
- Additionally, Federalists employed a well-crafted media campaign in support of ratification; this

included the anonymous publication of the Federalist Papers in newspapers justifying various provisions of the new constitution. Several state ratifying conventions insisted that the new government add a bill of rights to the Constitution; James Madison, the "Father of the Constitution," was initially reluctant to propose such a bill for fear that it might omit important rights, but eventually he sponsored a new Bill of Rights in the first Congress.

2-5 Changing the Constitution

- Article V of the Constitution makes it exceedingly difficult to amend the document. Since the Bill of Rights was ratified in 1791, all but one of the 17 amendments that followed resulted from a two-step process: (1) two-thirds support of both houses of Congress, followed by (2) ratification by three-fourths of the state legislatures. (The Twenty-first Amendment was ratified by three-fourths of special state ratifying conventions). To date, a national constitutional convention (also authorized by Article V) has never been held.

- Informal constitutional change often occurs through U.S. Supreme Court interpretation of the document's text, as well as through bold actions from the president and Congress. The Supreme Court under Chief Justice Marshall favored a loose construction of several provisions, giving the federal government considerable implied powers; Thomas Jefferson and Jeffersonian Republicans favored a stricter construction of the Constitution's provisions.

Key Terms

amendments (p. 34)
Anti-Federalists (p. 31)
Articles of Confederation (p. 24)
Bill of Rights (p. 34)
checks and balances (p. 30)
Constitutional Convention (p. 26)
Declaration of Independence (p. 24)
enumerated powers (p. 31)
Federalist Papers (p. 32)

Federalists (p. 31)
Great Compromise (p. 27)
loose construction (p. 36)
New Jersey Plan (p. 27)
separation of powers (p. 29)
Shays's Rebellion (p. 26)
strict construction (p. 38)
Three-Fifths Compromise (p. 29)
Virginia Plan (p. 26)

3

FEDERALISM

Planetpix / Alamy Stock Photo

Members of the South Carolina State police lower the Confederate flag at the State House in Columbia on July 10, 2015.

THE TERM *FEDERAL* comes from the Latin *foedus*, which means a covenant, or an agreement linking different entities. A federal (or federated) system of government is one in which power is divided between a central authority and constituent political subunits. Both types of government are linked in order to provide for the pursuit of common ends; at the same time, each government maintains its own integrity. Federalism, the doctrine underlying such a system, generally requires the existence of a central government tier and at least one major subnational tier of governments (usually referred to as "states" or "provinces"). Each tier is then assigned its own significant government powers. What may sound simple in the abstract has proven quite difficult in practice. How exactly does a political system divide sovereignty between two thriving branches of government without creating animosities among the competing branches that may threaten to undermine the system?

Learning Objectives

3-1 What Is Federalism?

- Define *federalism* and explain how Articles I and IV of the U.S. Constitution differentiate between federal government powers, state government powers, and concurrent powers in accordance with the Supremacy Clause of Article VI.

3-2 The History of American Federalism

- Define the different eras of state–federal relations in American history, and assess the role played by the Supreme Court in articulating the various forms of federalism that prevailed in the modern era.

3-3 Why Federalism? Advantages and Disadvantages

- Identify the advantages and disadvantages of federalism in terms of fairness and accountability.

Compelling the States to Fall in Line

Citizens of the United States are also citizens of one of the 50 states. Policies in the states are by no means uniform. Notwithstanding some of the uniform testing requirements imposed by the Every Student Succeeds Act (ESSA) passed by Congress in 2015, educational policy differs widely from state to state. So, too, will an individual accused of a crime find one state's criminal justice system far more onerous and difficult than another's. And health care has traditionally fallen under the exclusive jurisdiction of state legislatures, leading to widely different types of coverage from state to state. The federal government (which includes federal courts) has occasionally stepped in to smooth out those differences, much to the chagrin of states that prefer to maintain their own unique identity on specific issues. Sometimes uniformity is favored as a matter of good policy; at other times it may be mandated by the Constitution itself. This delicate balancing act between state interests and the need to maintain states' unique political and cultural identities has never been easy to maintain.

Then

In 1963, uniformity in the treatment of criminal defendants was squarely at issue before the U.S. Supreme Court. By late 1962, close to half of the states were automatically providing indigent defendants a right to free counsel whenever jail time was a possibility. In fact, just prior to the landmark Supreme Court case *Gideon v. Wainwright* (1963),[1] 22 of those states urged the Court to adopt this right as a federal standard. By contrast, many states (including Florida) provided such counsel only on a case-by-case basis—if a poor defendant seemed competent enough to try his or her own case, judges usually insisted that he or she do so. Could such a patchwork of protections stand under the Sixth Amendment? "No," said the Supreme Court, which in *Gideon* effectively nationalized the requirement that counsel be provided to all needy defendants. Following the landmark decision, the second half of the 1960s witnessed the creation of public defender programs across the country.

Now

In 2012, the U.S. Supreme Court once again inserted itself into a partisan political debate. This time the issue was health care. For decades, presidents had tried to address the nation's health care crisis without blowing up the deficit in the process. In 2009 President Barack Obama introduced legislation that would allow children to stay on their parents' health care policies through the age of 26; it would also prohibit insurers from discriminating against individuals with "preexisting conditions" that might be expensive to treat. To pay for these increased costs, President Obama's plan further required that young and healthy individuals not otherwise insured would have to pay into the system along with everyone else. Did such a regulatory scheme exceed the limits of congressional power under the Constitution? The Supreme Court's answer came in *NFIB v. Sebelius* (2012)[2]: By a 5–4 vote, the Court held that Congress indeed had the authority to mandate that citizens purchase health care insurance pursuant to its "tax and spend" power under Article I. Though Congress would eventually repeal the controversial mandate in late 2017, it left the rest of Obamacare intact, ensuring that the federal government would continue to lead the way in regulating health care, a policy area that had once lay within the exclusive jurisdiction of states.

For Critical Thinking and Discussion

1. If the Constitution and the Bill of Rights were intended to provide rights to all citizens, shouldn't those rights be uniform from state to state?
2. Can you justify, for example, giving criminal defendants in one state less constitutional protection than defendants in another state? If so, on what basis?
3. If state legislatures fail to adequately address complex and difficult issues like health care, should the federal government be allowed to step in on that basis? Should the Supreme Court interpret congressional powers broadly or narrowly?

Stock Montage / Getty Images

Affordable Care Act (aka Obamacare) supporters wave signs outside the Supreme Court; that court narrowly upheld the controversial law on June 28, 2012.

New U.S. citizens take the oath at a citizenship ceremony in Idaho.

3-1 WHAT IS FEDERALISM?

Federalism is the doctrine underlying a political system in which power is divided between a central authority and constituent political subunits. For a system of federalism to maintain itself, it must sustain this division of powers by whatever means possible, including—but not limited to—a resort to the courts to define the proper bounds of authority. Perhaps the greatest challenge facing any federalist system is the task of determining sovereignty, defined as the supreme political power of a government to regulate its affairs without outside interference. In a system based on federalism, sovereignty resides not just in the central government but also within each of the subunits, which in the case of the United States are the individual 50 states. Yet how can there be two separate sovereign governments sharing power over the exact same territory? The distribution of national and local responsibilities to more than one sovereign power depends on how the terms *national* and *local* are defined. These definitions are important, for a government based on federalism must both achieve national unity for certain overarching purposes and also preserve local governments' autonomy to respond to diverse subsets of citizens.

Related to these issues are complex questions concerning the nature of national citizenship. American federalism rests on the principle that two separate sovereigns—the state government and the federal government—both exert authority over the individual. Thus U.S. citizens have official status as citizens both of the state where they reside and of the nation as a whole. Many take pride in *both* associations. What remains unclear are the obligations and duties that dual citizenship requires. Is national citizenship every citizen's primary form of identification? To which sovereign government is the citizen obligated when the nation and individual states are in conflict?

COMPARING FEDERALISM TO OTHER SYSTEMS OF GOVERNMENT

A federal system of government can be placed on a continuum of different forms of government. At one end of the continuum is a confederation (or "confederacy"), defined as a league of two or more independent states that unite to achieve certain specified common aims. Those aims may be quite limited, as is often the case with offensive or defensive military alliances. For example, the Articles of Confederation, which prescribed the rules of government for the newly independent colonies until 1788, featured 13 states entering into "a firm league of friendship with each other, for their common defense, the security of their liberties, and their mutual and general welfare." Recently the European Community, a collection of European nations united in a commercial alliance, has acquired its own status as a type of confederation.[3] Similarly, the United Nations is a league of countries from around the world that work together to enforce various provisions of international law. Although a confederation may be a useful arrangement to achieve some aims, it can result in political chaos, as when separate member countries bound only by limited rules strike out on their own at critical times, often to the detriment of the larger confederation.

At the other end of the continuum is a unitary system of government, which subordinates the independent aims of constituent states (if any even exist) to the goals of the central whole. Although individual states within such a government may enjoy some form of representation in the central legislature (such as through the election of state senators) and may even assert their own systems of municipal law, sovereignty rests in the central government alone, with states exerting authority over citizens only through the larger government entity. Of the Western industrialized nations, Great Britain and France perhaps come closest to this unitary government ideal, with their provinces and subunits having little power independent of the national government. Problems with a unitary system of government often arise from the tendency toward *hypercentralism*, that is, the more or less complete reliance on the central government and the extinguishing of individual state differences. Such a system often hampers local officials from responding to the particular needs of their varying constituencies.

As Figure 3-1 shows, a federal system of government sits in the middle of this continuum, granting its member states significant power but still subordinating them to the national

NFIB v. Sebelius (2012) The Supreme Court case that upheld as constitutional the bulk of the Patient Protection and Affordable Care Act (aka Obamacare), including the requirement that certain individuals pay a financial penalty for not obtaining health insurance.

Federalism The doctrine underlying a system of government in which power is divided between a central government and constituent political subunits.

sovereignty The supreme political power of a government to regulate its affairs without outside interference.

confederation A system of government (or "league") in which two or more independent states unite to achieve certain specified common aims.

unitary system of government A system of government in which the constituent states are strictly subordinated to the goals of the central government as a whole.

FIGURE 3-1

Comparing Systems of Government

Federal System

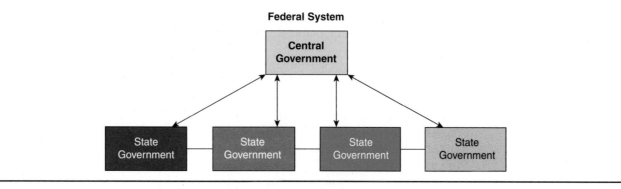

Unitary System of Government

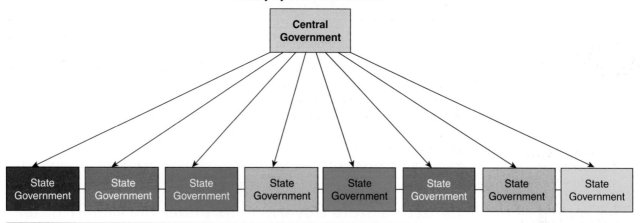

Confederate Government

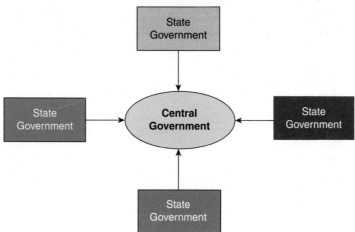

These three figures illustrate the most common configurations for (1) federal systems of government, (2) unitary systems of government, and (3) confederate systems of government. The directions of the arrows indicate the relationship that exists between the different forms of government. Note the two-way arrows found in the federal system.

government in critical instances. James Madison believed this federal system was the preferred "middle ground" of government types. At least 20 countries today, including Canada, Germany, Australia, and Switzerland, may be characterized as federal systems. It is the United States' brand of federalism, however—first established with the ratification of the Constitution in

1788—that represents the most significant breakthrough in the evolution of this government type among modern nation-states.

GOVERNMENT POWERS IN A FEDERAL SYSTEM

Under the U.S. Constitution, the national government of the United States was formed to serve a community of 13 states, and each state delegated to the new central government significant powers while retaining full powers within its own constitutionally designated sphere of authority. The framers of this new government relied on no overarching philosophy or political theory in designing this federalist form of government; "federalism" was simply a political compromise calculated to build consensus among them. The powers delegated to Congress under Article I of the Constitution are called enumerated powers. The powers retained by the states are reserved powers. And the powers shared by the federal and state governments are generally referred to as concurrent powers (see Table 3-1).

Article I, Section 8 enumerates the specific powers held by the national government. Among these are economic powers such as the authority to levy and collect taxes, borrow money, coin money, and regulate interstate commerce and bankruptcies; military powers such as the authority to provide for the common defense, declare war, raise and support armies and navies, and regulate the militia; and legislative powers such as the authority to establish regulations governing immigration and naturalization. Congress also enjoys the prerogative to make laws that are "necessary and proper" to carry out these foregoing powers.[4]

On its face, the Constitution appears to draw clear and explicit lines between the powers afforded the state and national governments: The national government assumes responsibility for great matters of national importance, including the protection of national economic interests, relations with other countries, and the military security of the United States. All

reserved powers Those powers expressly retained by the state governments under the Constitution.

concurrent powers Those powers shared by the federal and state governments under the Constitution.

TABLE 3-1

The Powers of the Federal and State Governments under the Constitution

Federal Government Powers (Enumerated Powers)	State Government Powers (Reserved Powers)	Concurrent Powers (Shared Powers)
Borrow money on U.S. credit	Regulate intrastate commerce	Spend money for general welfare
Regulate foreign commerce	Regulate state militias	Regulate interstate commerce
Regulate commerce with Indian nations	Conduct elections/qualify voters	Establish bankruptcy laws
Conduct foreign affairs	Regulate safety/health/morals	Lay and collect taxes
Coin money/punish counterfeiting	Ratify amendments	Charter/regulate banks
Establish courts inferior to Supreme Court		Establish courts
Establish post offices		Establish highways
Establish patent/copyright laws		Take private property for public purposes (with compensation)
Define/punish high-seas offenses		
Declare war		
Raise and support armies, navies		
Call forth militias		
Govern District of Columbia matters		
Admit new states to the Union		
Establish rules of naturalization		

local and/or internal matters—including the health, safety, and welfare of citizens—were to be to the province of state governments. Indeed, in a delayed victory for states' rights advocates who had opposed the proposed constitution before its ratification, the Tenth Amendment restates this fundamental division of powers: that any specific power not assigned to the federal government by the Constitution may be exercised by the states, unless the Constitution prohibits the states from exercising that power.

The framers of the Constitution believed that Congress should legislate only within its enumerated powers under Article I; in their view, the **necessary and proper clause** (later referred to as the elastic clause) was *not* to be used as an instrument to expand federal legislative authority unnecessarily. Yet, within a few years, competing views of the necessary and proper clause arose, giving the national government far more discretion in determining how to carry out its enumerated powers.

THE SUPREMACY CLAUSE

Overlaying this explicit system of enumerated powers for Congress and reserved powers for the states is the **supremacy clause** of Article VI, which provides that the Constitution and the laws passed by Congress shall be "the supreme law of the land," overriding any conflicting provisions in state constitutions or state laws. The supremacy clause gives special weight to the federal Constitution by ensuring that it cannot be interpreted differently from state to state. In the landmark case of *Martin v. Hunter's Lessee* (1816),[5] the U.S. Supreme Court rejected the Virginia Supreme Court's attempt to interpret the federal Constitution in a way that conflicted with the U.S. Supreme Court's own rulings. Accordingly, each state legislature and state judiciary must abide by not only the terms of the federal Constitution but also the interpretation of those terms laid out by the U.S. Supreme Court.

The language of the supremacy clause also gives rise to the doctrine of preemption. When Congress exercises power granted to it under Article I, the federal law it creates may supersede state laws, in effect "preempting" state authority. In practice, when a federal law clearly bars state action, the doctrine of **preemption** is relatively uncontroversial. For example, when the federal government acted to regulate the commercial advertising of tobacco products, it essentially "occupied the field," and all state rules governing tobacco advertising immediately gave way to the new federal standard. But when Congress enacts a law that does not clearly articulate its intentions with regard to state laws, a court may have to decide whether the doctrine of preemption applies, subject to later court review.

necessary and proper clause The clause in Article I, Section 8 of the Constitution that affords Congress the power to make laws that serve as a means to achieving its expressly delegated powers.

supremacy clause The provision in Article VI, Clause 2 of the Constitution that provides that the Constitution and federal laws override any conflicting provisions in state constitutions or state laws.

Martin v. Hunter's Lessee (1816) The Supreme Court case that established that state governments and state courts must abide by the U.S. Supreme Court's interpretation of the federal Constitution.

preemption The constitutional doctrine that holds that when Congress acts affirmatively in the exercise of its own granted power, federal laws supersede all state laws on the matter. (p. 58)

full faith and credit clause The provision in Article IV, Section 1 of the Constitution that forces states to abide by the official acts and proceedings of all other states.

RELATIONS BETWEEN THE STATES

A federalist system must not only manage relations between the state governments and the federal government but also arbitrate disagreements among member states. A feature of American federalism in this regard is the requirement that individual states must respect the civil laws of all other states, as guaranteed by the **full faith and credit clause** of Article IV, Section 1 of the Constitution. This clause provides that each state must abide by the decisions of other state and local governments, including their judicial proceedings. This clause acts to ensure stability in commercial and personal relations that extend beyond one state's borders. For example, contracts duly entered into in California under the laws of that state cannot simply be ignored or invalidated by the courts in Arizona or any other state. Similarly, when an unhappy married couple meet the legal requirements of divorce in one state and end the marriage, they are not required to meet new divorce requirements in other states, as the divorce decree of one state must be recognized as valid by every other state.

Gay marriage ceremony in Massachusetts.

The enforcement of immigration laws across the country has sparked a fierce debate on the nature of federalism in our modern constitutional system. Immigration is predominately a federal issue, as Article I vests in Congress the power to "establish a uniform rule of Naturalization," and with it, the power to determine how citizenship is conferred. However, many states and localities have taken up the issue of citizenship on their own to address increasing rates of immigration in the country, which (they argue) has not been adequately addressed by Congress.

In fact, many of the nation's border states have at one time or another tried to enact immigration-related laws and resolutions. This immigration-related legislation touches on a multitude of related issues affecting citizens, including the budget, education, employment, health, and public benefits. These policies vary drastically from state to state: some have passed severe restrictions on undocumented immigrants, denying them a host of government services. In recent years the most notable state immigration policies impose strict law enforcement over undocumented immigrants. For example, Arizona's controversial SB 1070 legislation required police to determine the immigration status of individuals held for "reasonable suspicion" by demanding that they "show me your papers." These state policies eventually came under the scrutiny of the Supreme Court, which ruled that the law requiring officials to verify the immigration status of all people stopped or detained for any reason was preempted by federal law and thus invalid.

For Critical Thinking and Discussion

1. Why do you think states have increased their efforts to enact immigration-related legislation? Do you expect that these efforts will increase over time? Why or why not?
2. How do statewide efforts to restrict immigration conflict with the federal government's constitutional authority over immigration?

Bill Clark / Getty Images

Immigration rights activists rally in Washington, DC.

Even though the full faith and credit clause has traditionally required states to respect the public proceedings of every other state, controversies over interstate recognition sometimes arise. Prior to the U.S. Supreme Court's decision in *Obergefell v. Hodges* (2015),[6] which established the right of same-sex marriage in all 50 states, many state legislatures attempted to prevent same-sex couples who married in one state from asserting their newfound status as married couples. At least 31 states at various times passed laws denying recognition to same-sex marriages before the Supreme Court stepped in to end the controversy, at least as a matter of constitutional law. The full faith and credit clause serves as a continued obstacle for states that refuse to recognize legal contracts or other actions duly taken in other states.

Another clause that provides for the equal treatment of out-of-state citizens is the privileges and immunities clause of Article IV. Through this clause, which guarantees that the citizens of each state are "entitled to all Privileges and Immunities of Citizens in the several States," the Constitution protects the rights of every citizen to travel through other states, to reside in any state, and to participate in trade, agriculture, and professional pursuits in any state.[7] Some states have tried to limit memberships to in-state residents or to impose hefty commuter taxes on out-of-staters who cross state lines each day for work. Such legislative efforts potentially conflict with the privileges and immunities clause. Article IV also provides that the criminal laws of individual states must be respected across state lines. When a criminal in one state escapes to another state, he or she is normally "extradited" (handed over) to the original state either to stand trial or to complete a previously imposed sentence.

Article III, Section 2 of the Constitution gives the U.S. Supreme Court the authority to decide disputes between states. Although such jurisdiction is rarely exercised, the Court has taken its responsibility to arbitrate state conflicts seriously on those occasions when it has been asked to do so. For example, when officials in New York and New Jersey were battling in the late 1990s over which of those two states could claim sovereign authority over Ellis Island, the Court ruled that Ellis Island was within the state boundaries of New Jersey—news no doubt to the millions of immigrants who thought they had disembarked in New York.[8] The framers of the Constitution believed it was critically important that the highest federal court retain the power to arbitrate disputes between state governments, a key component of American federalism.

3-2 THE HISTORY OF AMERICAN FEDERALISM

In the more than two centuries that have passed since the ratification of the Constitution, different conceptions of federalism have prevailed during different eras. Some of these shifting patterns in state–federal relations were inevitable given the changing state of the nation and the increasingly important role it would play in world politics. The dominance of a global economy in the late twentieth and early twenty-first centuries, changing patterns in population growth, and technological developments in communication and transportation all spurred wholesale reexamination of the nature of federal and state governmental functions. Various government figures—presidents, Supreme Court justices, and members of Congress—have also played a role in shaping the nature of federalism. The flexibility of the federalist system has allowed it to adapt to changing circumstances.

Although a clear delineation of periods may oversimplify history, scholars have identified at least five eras of American federalism:

1. state-centered federalism, 1789–1819;
2. national supremacy period, 1819–1837;
3. dual federalism, 1837–1937;
4. cooperative federalism, 1937–1990; and
5. the "new federalism," 1990–present.

Each of these periods is defined by some shift in the power relationship between the national and state governments.

STATE-CENTERED FEDERALISM, 1789–1819

The framers' vision of federalism was relatively clear at the time the Constitution was ratified: other than in those policy areas expressly identified in Article I as subject to the national government's control (the military, foreign affairs, creation of currency, etc.), state governments would have full sovereignty over all matters involving the health, safety, and welfare of individuals. Indeed, it is tough to imagine the Constitution being ratified by the requisite number of states had it called for any further subordination of traditional state authority. And with some notable exceptions, the national government's reach was exceedingly limited during the first 30 years of the Constitution's history.[9] At the urging of Treasury Secretary Alexander Hamilton, the Washington administration cautiously undertook some first steps in nationwide economic planning when it chartered the first National Bank of the United States and the federal government assumed all the debts of the state governments. Nevertheless, during this earliest period of federalism, states remained the principal authority for American citizens. For the most part, each state managed its own affairs, often with little interference from the federal government.

Chief Justice John Marshall, who led the U.S. Supreme Court from 1801 to 1835.

NATIONAL SUPREMACY PERIOD, 1819–1837

Just before leaving office in 1801, President John Adams installed as chief justice of the Supreme Court a fellow nationalist, John Marshall of Virginia. That appointment may have been the most significant act of Adams's presidency; although the Federalists would never again occupy the White House or control Congress, the national government–oriented party would influence American politics through Chief Justice Marshall for the next three decades.

Marshall's **national supremacy doctrine** of federalism is most evident in the Supreme Court decision in *McCulloch v. Maryland* (1819),[10] which concerned the National Bank of the United States. As secretary of the Treasury during the Washington administration, Alexander Hamilton successfully pushed for Congress to charter the first bank of the United States in 1792, arguing that such an institution would help provide for a sound national currency and a national system of credit. Thomas Jefferson, then secretary of state, and James Madison opposed the bank, believing that the Constitution gave Congress no authority to charter such a bank. Consequently, when the bank's 20-year charter expired, the Jeffersonian Republican–controlled Congress declined to recharter it. Recognizing that the lack of a national bank had hindered American efforts to obtain needed financial resources throughout the War of 1812, many in the Democratic-Republican Party, including Madison, who was now president, swallowed their pride and supported the chartering of a second national bank in 1816.

Marshall's court also refuted the power of state courts to interpret and apply the Constitution in ways that conflicted with the Supreme Court's own interpretations. Thus, the Constitution assumed its status as the uniform governing law of all the states. To Marshall, the U.S. Supreme Court's duty was not to preserve state sovereignty but rather "to protect national power against state encroachments." Consistent with this view, the Marshall court routinely interpreted Congress's legislative authority quite broadly. In *Gibbons v. Ogden* (1824),[11] for example, the Court invalidated a monopoly granted by the New York legislature covering the operation of steamboats in New York waters because the New York monopoly was in conflict with a federal license.

The national supremacy doctrine articulated by Marshall was not without its critics. State politicians accused the Court of ignoring the sovereign power of the states. As president, Andrew Jackson opposed the National Bank and all internal improvements (such as the building of roads or canals) ordered by Congress as unconstitutional. He even vetoed a rechartering of the bank in 1832. Yet, at the same time, he also applied Marshall's national supremacy doctrine in defending the Tariff of 1828. After Congress passed a highly protectionist tariff over the objections of Southern free-trade adherents, the South Carolina legislature adopted a series of resolutions negating the tariff on the theory that state sovereignty allowed each state to nullify any law passed by Congress that the state deemed unconstitutional. (New Englanders had used that same argument during the War of 1812 when a convention of the region's states met in Hartford, Connecticut, in early 1815 and endorsed the right of states to interpose themselves against "dangerous infractions" of the Constitution by the federal government.) In response to the action by South Carolina, President Jackson declared that such a nullification was an "impractical absurdity" and rejected the right of individual states to refuse to obey federal laws.[12]

DUAL FEDERALISM PERIOD, 1837–1937

Although the immorality of slavery as an institution would become a crucial component of the fight between the Union and the Confederacy, the Civil War began as a struggle about the relationship between the states and the federal government. The Union's victory undermined the premise that the nation was a mere "compact of states" by rejecting the authority of states

national supremacy doctrine Chief Justice John Marshall's interpretation of federalism as holding that states have extremely limited sovereign authority, whereas Congress is supreme within its own sphere of constitutional authority.

McCulloch v. Maryland (1819) The Supreme Court case that established that Congress enjoys broad and extensive authority to make all laws that are "necessary and proper" to carry out its constitutionally delegated powers.

Gibbons v. Ogden (1824) The Supreme Court case that held that under the Constitution, a federal license to operate steamboats overrides a state-granted monopoly of New York water rights.

FIGURE 3-2

Admission of States to the Union

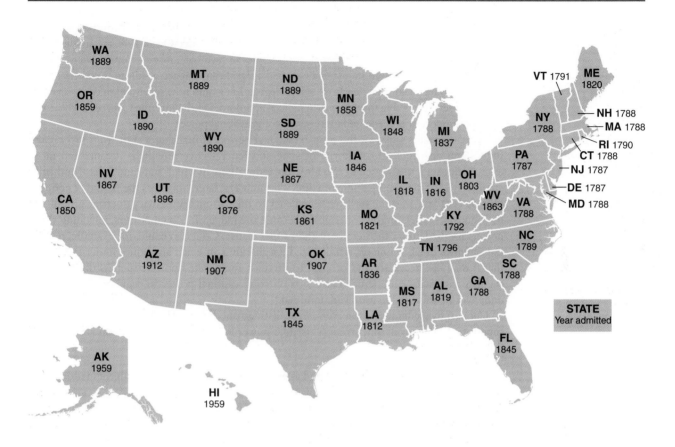

to leave the compact. Then, in a series of cases handed down after the Civil War, a newly constituted Supreme Court acknowledged national power and congressional authority to set the terms for readmitting former Confederate states into the Union. This power was considered an outgrowth of Congress's exclusive and unquestioned authority not only to regulate the territories of the United States but also to oversee the admission of new states to the Union. With 24 of the 50 states joining the Union between 1836 and 1912 (Figure 3-2), admission to statehood was an important function of the federal government during this period.

Under dual federalism, however, the states retained considerable authority to regulate economic affairs that were not directly within the "stream of commerce" between two or more states, including matters concerning the manufacturing of products and the health and safety of factory workers. Ignoring *McCulloch v. Maryland*, the Supreme Court refused to give Congress the discretionary authority it enjoyed during the era of the national supremacy doctrine. Regulatory legislation passed by Congress, such as child labor laws and many minimum wage laws, were set aside as unconstitutional. Later, in the 1930s, the Court also struck down a series of New Deal laws implementing pension and retirement systems for workers and regulating industrial relations.[13] In this way, dual federalism rendered Congress somewhat helpless in addressing the hardships brought on by the Industrial Revolution and the Great Depression.

COOPERATIVE FEDERALISM, 1937–1990

Faced with judicial opposition to New Deal policies regulating the workplace, retirement policies, and other subjects traditionally ceded to the states, President Franklin D. Roosevelt (FDR) and his supporters grew increasingly frustrated. To them, the economic hardships of the Great

> **dual federalism** The doctrine of federalism that holds that state authority acts as a significant limit on congressional power under the Constitution.

Depression demanded an activist federal government, and a conservative Supreme Court now stood in the way. FDR and his allies in Congress proposed slowly expanding the size of the Supreme Court from 9 to what would eventually become 15, which would allow Roosevelt to "pack" the Supreme Court with advocates of a broader vision of federal legislative power.[14] The proposed "court-packing plan" became unnecessary, however. As public frustration with the Court was mounting, one member of the Court in 1937, Justice Owen Roberts, suddenly did an about-face, abandoning dual federalist principles in favor of a more expansive view of congressional authority. A shift in just one vote had a significant impact; a shift in two votes on the Supreme Court meant that nearly all federal legislation would now survive high court scrutiny. Once Roosevelt was able to add his own judicial appointees to the mix, the Court as a whole was ready to support unprecedented exercises of congressional power.

Social scientists speak of the post–New Deal period as marking a shift from layer-cake federalism, in which the authority of state and federal governments is distinct and more easily delineated, to a system of marble-cake federalism, in which state and federal authority are intertwined in an inseparable mixture. This new era, later labeled as the period of cooperative federalism, in some ways harkened back to the national supremacy doctrine articulated by John Marshall. Congress once again became the judge of its own powers, including those powers implied under the necessary and proper clause. Congress could, for example, restrict the activities of labor unions, criminalize loan sharking, or enact any policy under the theory that it may be "necessary and proper" to exercise enumerated powers such as the power to regulate interstate commerce. The limits on congressional power to regulate the economy under cooperative federalism were minimal.[15]

Cooperative federalism, however, can be distinguished from Marshall's doctrine of national superiority. Whenever concurrent legislative power is exercised, Congress can act in one of three ways:

1. Preempt the states altogether and assert exclusive control over the subject matter.
2. Leave the states to act on their own.
3. Provide that the operation of its own law depends on or is qualified by existing state laws.

This last category provides an opening in state–federal relationships that even Marshall could not have anticipated: the possibility that the federal government might enlist state officials and other state actors to implement federal policies.

The positive aspects of cooperative federalism are obvious. The expansion of the central government beginning in the 1930s into the $4-trillion-per-year behemoth that it is today means that federal officials now have huge sums of money at their disposal, as shown in Figure 3-3. Individual states can benefit from this pool of funds whenever the federal government passes some of its revenues directly to the states to initiate and administer programs. Grants-in-aid from the federal government to the states have been used to fund state educational initiatives, build roads, and provide unemployment relief, among other programs that fulfill purposes expressly approved by Congress and/or its federal regulatory agencies. Federal grants also help balance the economic inequities that arise because states have vastly different tax bases. Occasionally the federal government has transformed grants-in-aid, which are allocated only for specific programs or policies, into block grants, which state or local governments may use at their discretion for more generalized programs.

The system of federalism dictates that the federal government, not the states, must provide national defense. By contrast, state expenditures focus on educational expenses, criminal justice, and social services in particular. Although different systems of categorization make budget comparisons among governments difficult, a glimpse of the budgets of the federal government and two state governments provides some interesting insights as to where your tax dollars are going . . . or not going.

The collaboration between state governments and the federal government in the era of cooperative federalism also carried some negative implications for state sovereignty. Federal government officials increasingly insisted that federal appropriations to the states be accompanied by various conditions. Often these consisted of "protective conditions," designed to ensure that the state would administer its program consistent with the objectives of Congress.

layer-cake federalism Description of federalism as maintaining that the authority of state and federal governments exists in distinct and separate spheres.

marble-cake federalism Description of federalism as intertwining state and federal authority in an inseparable mixture.

cooperative federalism The doctrine of federalism that affords Congress nearly unlimited authority to exercise its powers through means that often coerce states into administering and/or enforcing federal policies.

grants-in-aid Grants from the federal government to states that allow state governments to pursue specific federal policies, such as highway construction.

block grants Grants from the federal government to the states that may be used at the discretion of states to pursue more generalized aims.

FIGURE 3-3

Comparing Federal Expenditures to State Expenditures

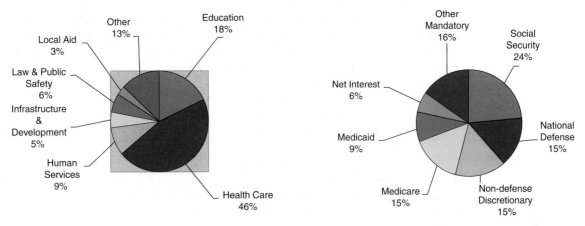

Massachusetts Government Expenditures - FY 2018

- Education 18%
- Other 13%
- Local Aid 3%
- Law & Public Safety 6%
- Infrastructure & Development 5%
- Human Services 9%
- Health Care 46%

Federal Government Expenditures - FY 2017

- Other Mandatory 16%
- Social Security 24%
- Net Interest 6%
- National Defense 15%
- Medicaid 9%
- Non-defense Discretionary 15%
- Medicare 15%

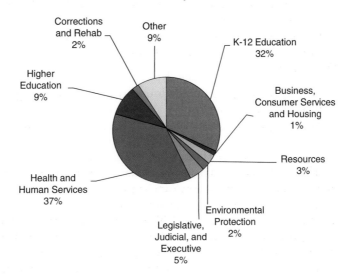

California Government Expenditures - 2018-19

- Corrections and Rehab 2%
- Other 9%
- K-12 Education 32%
- Higher Education 9%
- Business, Consumer Services and Housing 1%
- Resources 3%
- Health and Human Services 37%
- Environmental Protection 2%
- Legislative, Judicial, and Executive 5%

For example, Congress required that states receiving educational assistance meet federal requirements for educating handicapped children, including the creation of individualized education programs for students with special needs. On occasion, however, Congress has imposed coercive burdens on states that increasingly rely on such federal assistance. In 1984, for example, Congress passed the National Minimum Drinking Age Amendment, which withheld 5 percent of federal highway funds from any state "in which the purchase or public possession of any alcoholic beverage by a person who is less than 21 years of age" is lawful.[16] When Ronald Reagan was elected president in 1980, he openly trumpeted federal initiatives to return policy-making authority to the states. In the decade that followed, Congress curtailed a number of federal grant programs.

The voluntary transfer of power by the central government to state or local governments is known as "devolution."[17] As it turned out, strong resistance from the Democratic-controlled House led to the defeat of many of Reagan's devolution initiatives. Nonetheless, Reagan administration rhetoric emphasizing federal deregulation and increased state responsibilities set the stage for more sweeping reforms to be implemented in the years ahead.

THE "NEW FEDERALISM," 1990–PRESENT

Scholars assessing the state of federalism since 1990 have failed to reach a consensus on the proper label for characterizing what appears to be a counterthrust favoring states' rights. This new era of federal–state relations has been marked by a resuscitation of state authority, helped by a more conservative Supreme Court that, since the early 1990s, has been increasingly protective of state sovereignty on a number of fronts.

Since the mid-1990s, Congress's virtually unlimited authority to regulate interstate commerce has been scaled back to a degree. In *United States v. Lopez* (1995), the Supreme Court declared that Congress could not ban guns in school zones.[18] Whereas during the cooperative federalism era Congress regulated all manner of criminal and social activities, the present-day Supreme Court has more strenuously insisted that Congress must show a clear connection with commerce when exercising its power to regulate interstate commerce, for example. Then, in 1997, Congress ran into more obstacles when it enacted a law entitling sexual assault victims to sue their perpetrators in federal court. Once again, the Supreme Court stood firm for state sovereignty, ruling in *United States v. Morrison* (2000) that the law was unconstitutional, on the grounds that domestic abuse had only a slight connection to commerce.[19] Even when the Supreme Court upheld the controversial individual mandate provisions of the Patient Protection and Affordable Care Act in *NFIB v. Sebelius* (2012), it did so while offering a key concession to states' rights enthusiasts: that while the mandate to purchase insurance may have survived scrutiny as a valid exercise of Congress's power to tax, such a penalty on inactivity was *not* a proper use of Congress's commerce clause powers.[20] In that sense, the Court's decision in the case continued down the path set out by *Lopez* and *Morrison*.

Additionally, the high court has given new teeth to the Eleventh Amendment, which bars citizens of one state from bringing suit against another state in federal court. As a result of Court decisions, many plaintiffs are now restricted from bringing lawsuits in federal court against public employers; instead, plaintiffs must bring suit in state courts.[21]

Of course, Supreme Court decisions are not solely responsible for this recent resurrection of state sovereignty. The Reagan administration managed to push through deregulation initiatives in a number of partially preempted programs, and it relaxed federal oversight of state performance to a considerable degree. Then, six years after Reagan left office, Republicans took control of both the House and the Senate for the first time since the early 1950s. In 1994, Newt Gingrich (R-GA), then House minority whip, and 366 other Republican candidates for Congress rallied around the "Contract with America," a series of initiatives they promised to introduce in the first 100 days of the 104th Congress. The new Republican majority seemed poised to transfer large amounts of policy-making authority and administrative responsibility away from the national government and into the hands of state legislatures.

In the end, that Congress and the ones that followed passed few revolutionary new laws. Devolution of programs to the states has instead evolved far more gradually, through legislation such as the Personal Responsibility and Work Opportunity Reconciliation Act of 1996, which capped federal block grants to states for welfare aid. States have been encouraged by the law to create their own cost-efficient welfare benefits programs. But the states' rights movement stopped significantly short of the vaunted "devolution revolution" promised by Republican House leaders when they first took control in 1995.

In the wake of the terrorist attacks that occurred on September 11, 2001, Americans rallied around the flag, offering support for a bigger federal government presence. Yet, as Figure 3-4 shows, in the nearly two decades since then, Americans have grown increasingly skeptical about big government and the threat it poses. (The federal government is of course the biggest government by far.) For better or worse, public frustration with the immense size and power of the federal government is a modern reality, and politicians in Washington, DC, must account for this sentiment when they introduce new programs.

3-3 WHY FEDERALISM? ADVANTAGES AND DISADVANTAGES

Supporters of federalism point to several advantages offered by this form of government, and opponents of federalism counter with arguments of their own concerning the disadvantages of this form of government.

FIGURE 3-4

Has the Federal Government Gotten Too Big?

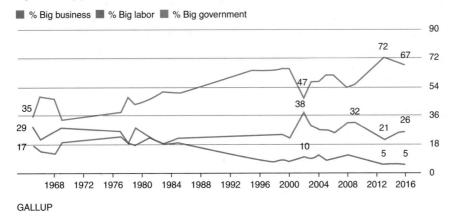

Americans' Perceptions of the Biggest Threat Facing the Country

In your opinion, which of the following will be the biggest threat to the country in the future -- big business, big labor or big government?

■ % Big business ■ % Big labor ■ % Big government

GALLUP

Source: Noam Fishman and Alyssa Davis, Gallup.com, January 5, 2017.

ADVANTAGES OF FEDERALISM

Supporters of federalism cite among the specific advantages of this form of government that it is more likely to accommodate the needs of a diverse citizenry, to strengthen liberty by dividing powers between levels of government, to encourage experimentation, and to respond to change.

ACCOMMODATION OF DIVERSITY. If a unitary system of government threatens to treat citizens of different states as interchangeable parts for purposes of quick and easy administration, federalism acts as an important counterbalance to this trend. A citizen of the United States can also take pride in being a citizen of Texas or some other state with a clearly defined culture or character. State and local politicians can perhaps respond to the specific demands or needs of their citizens better than a central government can. The culture of a state may be reflected in that state's handgun control laws, its rules on the distribution of alcohol, or many other of its laws.

STRENGTHENING OF LIBERTY THROUGH THE DIVISION OF POWERS. In Federalist No. 51, James Madison argued that "in the compound republic of America" the power surrendered by the people is divided between two distinct governments. This division provides security against a concentration of power in a single, unitary government. Madison also believed that in the unlikely event that one entire government turns corrupt, the other government would still be available to check that government's abuses. Thus, the existence of two distinct levels of government, combined with the separation of executive, legislative, and judicial powers within each of those governments, offers individuals "a double security" of protection.

LABORATORIES OF DEMOCRACY. In 1932, Supreme Court justice Louis Brandeis made famous a metaphor for creative federalism when he wrote that "a single courageous state may, if its citizens choose, serve as a laboratory, and try social and economic experiments without risk to the rest of the country."[22] This notion of states serving as "laboratories of democracy" is encouraged by a federalist system that gives the states authority to craft policies at the outset, while at the same time affording the central government authority to implement policies that prove successful throughout the nation. During the 1930s, FDR borrowed from the experience of various states in crafting many New Deal policies. In 2006, Massachusetts governor Mitt Romney signed into law a landmark health care bill that featured many elements (including the controversial individual mandate) that were later incorporated into the Affordable Health Care Act championed by the Obama administration. The flip side of such successes is also significant: state policies that proved to be failures discourage broad-based applications by the federal government.

DISADVANTAGES OF FEDERALISM

Opponents of federalism present arguments of their own concerning the disadvantages of this form of government. Their objections to a federalist system include (1) the unfairness to citizens caused by economic disparities among the states, (2) confusion over which government should be accountable for certain public programs, and (3) the excessive reliance on the courts to define the nature of federalism.

FISCAL DISPARITIES AMONG THE STATES. States differ markedly in the wealth of their citizens and thus in the taxable resources available to them for programs. According to the U.S. Census Bureau, Maryland's citizens in 2017 boasted a median household income of $80.776, almost twice as high as that enjoyed by Mississippi households ($43,529) that same year.[23] Because of these fiscal differences, the amount that states have available to spend on governmental programs varies widely. Furthermore, when the central government defers to state entities in the governing process, such as when it requires states to fund their own welfare programs, wide fiscal inequalities among states (and localities) may mean disparate—and inequitable—programs for citizens in different states. Advocates of social equity and justice routinely complain about this consequence of federalism.

LACK OF ACCOUNTABILITY. Numerous government programs fall under the exclusive authority of neither the state governments nor the federal government; both may act, either may act, or, in some cases, neither may act. At least in the abstract, federalism creates the prospect of multiple levels of government vying for the opportunity to address economic or social problems. In practice, however, the federal and state governments often play a game of "chicken," each hoping the other will act first and assume greater economic responsibility and perhaps accountability for failures. In an era when public frustration with rising taxes discourages government spending, this "blame game" may go on for years, with both sides accusing the other of shirking its responsibilities to the public. During the 1990s, for example, many state governments eliminated benefits for the needy and imposed stricter requirements on those seeking welfare. During this same period, Congress passed welfare legislation that transferred welfare responsibilities back to states. Critics charge that this arrangement of shared accountability quickly transforms into a lack of accountability, with neither government accepting responsibility for dealing with problems.

EXCESSIVE RELIANCE ON THE COURTS. When Congress and the states clash over which sovereign government has the primary power to regulate in a particular area, it is left to the courts to sort out the nature of power under the Constitution's scheme of federalism. This may pose significant challenges. Delegates at the constitutional convention invoked the concept of federalism as a political compromise between large and small states; accordingly, it offered little by way of clear legal principles. In some cases, the Supreme Court has been forced to reverse itself as it determined that its own judicial pronouncements about federalism proved unworkable. That occurred a few decades ago when the Supreme Court held in *Garcia v. SAMTA* (1985) that Congress had the power to extend federal minimum wage laws to state government workers. In doing so, the Supreme Court essentially reversed its position from just nine years earlier in *National League of Cities v. Usery* (1976). What changed in the interim? Nothing, other than the recognition by a handful of justices that federalism issues can prove so amorphous that they leave courts grappling for better answers.

The Real-Life Benefits of Attending College Close to Home

Kevork Djansezian / Getty Images

UCLA students walking to class on the school's Westwood campus. In recent years, state universities such as UCLA have increased the number of admissions offers extended to nonresidents as a means of generating more revenue.

Many high school seniors dream of attending colleges or universities in distant and exotic locations, far from the watchful eyes of parents or guardians who may be footing the bill. Did you ever dream of attending the University of Hawaii or perhaps the Florida Keys Community College?

While admission standards to such schools may or may not pose an obstacle, the bigger issue may be financial. State legislatures try to attract in-state students by offering lower-cost in-state tuition. They know that those students will often stay in the state after graduation and secure good jobs, contributing to the state's economy. For example, if you live in Wisconsin and you want to go to the University of Rhode Island, your college tuition in 2018 would have cost you $30,862. But if you were from Rhode Island, it would only cost you $14,138. UCLA offers perhaps the biggest home-state discount in the country: $42,217 in tuition per year for out-of-staters, as compared to just $13,225 for California residents.

For Critical Thinking and Discussion

1. Did you consider attending (or are you currently attending) a school far from your own home state? Were you aware of the significant disparities in tuition charged by some public universities to students from other states?
2. Should states be allowed to financially discriminate against out-of-state applicants? Why or why not?

Contentious issues in federalism often begin as debates over the substance of legislation: Should fugitive slaves who escape to freedom be returned to their masters? Should immigration enforcement extend to local police officers stopping individuals and demanding that they produce evidence of citizenship? Yet when significant questions about resources and enforcement inevitably arise, those issues quickly transform into even larger questions of jurisdiction and sovereignty: Can the federal government order states to accept Medicaid expansion funds? If it cannot, are states entitled to the money when they offer alternatives better suited to their own needs but that accomplish federal goals? States tend to respond to federal programs and the mandates that flow from those programs based on political factors as well: Do the citizens of the state want to be part of the federal program? Are they willing to pay more taxes to fund their own programs? Sweeping federal programs ensure a measure of uniformity from state to state; sometimes uniformity also helps to avoid confusion and prevent abuse; at other times, however, variations among the states allow for valuable policy experimentation as well as the protection of local concerns and interests. Dividing sovereignty is never easy. As long as federal and state governments keep the public interest in mind, the debate over applications of federalism should continue to serve as a mostly healthy (if a bit uncomfortable) form of political dialogue.

Summary

3-1 What Is Federalism?

- Federalism links the central government of the United States to all 50 state governments. Sovereignty resides concurrently in both the central government and state governments, as distinguished from confederations (simple alliances of powerful independent states) or unitary systems of government (in which the subunits are subordinate to the central government).
- The framers of the Constitution assigned to the federal government matters of great national importance (including foreign and military affairs) and assigned to the states all local and internal matters, including those relating to the health, safety, and welfare of citizens. Concurrent (or "shared") powers include taxation, banking and bankruptcy regulations, spending for highways, and other forms of general welfare.
- In addition to managing foreign and military affairs, Article I also vests Congress with the power to borrow money on U.S. credit, coin money, establish post offices, admit new states, and establish rules of naturalization, among other authorities.
- The supremacy clause of Article VI provides that the Constitution and all federal laws override (or "preempt") conflicting provisions in state constitutions or state laws. The full faith and credit clause of Article IV requires that states respect each other's acts and official proceedings.

3-2 The History of American Federalism

- Beginning in 1819, the Supreme Court under Chief Justice John Marshall substituted the framers' vision of state-centered federalism with a national supremacy doctrine that deferred to Congress as the supreme authority within the sphere of its own constitutional powers. Beginning in 1837 a system of "dual federalism," in which state authority served as a severe limit on congressional power, reigned for nearly a century. The Great Depression ushered in an era of "cooperative federalism" (1937–1990), which allowed Congress nearly free reign. During the current period of "new federalism" (1990–present), state sovereignty has once again been resuscitated to resist certain forms of congressional coercion.
- In the modern era, relatively clear divisions between state and federal authority (i.e., "layer-cake federalism") have given way to an intertwining of federal and state authority (i.e., "marble-cake federalism"). Through grants-in-aid and block grants, the national government has placed huge sums of federal money at the disposal of states, while still imposing conditions on states and state officials to help administer federal laws.

3-3 Why Federalism? Advantages and Disadvantages

- Supporters of federalism argue that it accommodates diversity, strengthens liberty, and encourages states to serve as "laboratories of democracy." Opponents of federalism object to the unfairness caused by economic disparities among the states. They also complain about the lack of government accountability for programs managed by competing sovereign powers, as well as the system's heavy reliance on the judiciary to define the nature of federalism and enforce its perimeters.

Key Terms

block grants (p. 52)
concurrent powers (p. 46)
confederation (p. 44)
cooperative federalism (p. 52)
dual federalism (p. 51)
federalism (p. 44)
full faith and credit clause (p. 47)
Gibbons v. Ogden (1824) (p. 50)
grants-in-aid (p. 52)
layer-cake federalism (p. 52)
marble-cake federalism (p. 52)

Martin v. Hunter's Lessee (1816) (p. 47)
McCulloch v. Maryland (1819) (p. 50)
national supremacy doctrine (p. 50)
necessary and proper clause (p. 47)
NFIB v. Sebelius (2012) (p. 43)
preemption (p. 47)
reserved powers (p. 46)
sovereignty (p. 44)
supremacy clause (p. 47)
unitary system of government (p. 44)

4
CIVIL LIBERTIES

"SAUL LOEB / Getty Images"

Abortion demonstrators rally outside the U.S. Supreme Court on January 18, 2019.

THE CONCEPT OF civil liberties—those specific individual rights that cannot be denied by government—dates all the way back to the original English legal charter, the Magna Carta of 1215. Yet civil liberties remain just as significant and hotly contested today. In the United States, most discussions of civil liberties begin with the Bill of Rights, which amended the Constitution in 1791. The Bill of Rights affords to individuals numerous protections, including the freedom of speech and the right of protection against self-incrimination. All these individual rights are subject to formal interpretation from the courts and to informal interpretation by those charged with their enforcement. Civil liberties may be distinguished from civil rights (sometimes called *equal rights*), which refer to rights that members of various groups (racial, ethnic, gender, etc.) have to equal treatment by government under the law as well as equal access to society's opportunities. This chapter deals with civil liberties, whereas Chapter 5 deals with civil rights.

Learning Objectives

4-1 The Bill of Rights: Origins and Evolution

- Compare civil rights to civil liberties; discuss the origins of the Bill of Rights and the process of incorporation.

4-2 Freedom of Religion and the Establishment Clause

- Describe the free exercise clause; identify the rules governing the separation of church and state, and explain the tests for upholding government accommodations of religion.

4-3 Free Expression Rights

- Assess the scope of free speech and free press rights, including the rules for exempting from protection lesser-value speech such as libel and obscenity.

4-4 The Right to Bear Arms and the Rights of the Criminally Accused

- Assess the scope of the Second, Fourth, and Fifth Amendment rights, as well as rights granted under the Sixth and Eighth Amendments.

4-5 The Modern Right to Privacy

- Define the modern privacy rights that apply to government restrictions on abortion, same-sex acts, and euthanasia.

4-1 THE BILL OF RIGHTS: ORIGINS AND EVOLUTION

What are rights? Strictly speaking, they are powers or privileges to which individuals are entitled. The central question is where do rights come from, and are they absolute? *Natural rights*, which are based on the natural laws of human society, exist even in the absence of a formal government. Because natural rights theoretically transcend government entities, no authority can legitimately take them away. As Thomas Jefferson so eloquently stated in the Declaration of Independence, human beings are endowed with certain rights that are "unalienable," which means they cannot be denied by government. *Positive rights*, by comparison, are granted by government authority and can usually be shaped and modified by that authority according to certain rules. A right to a lawyer paid by the state in felony cases for individuals who cannot afford counsel, for example, is a positive right.

The late Supreme Court justice Antonin Scalia once stated that individual rights are only "the fruits, rather than the roots, of the Constitutional tree."[1] The Constitution of the United States was intended to provide individuals with protection by guaranteeing a framework of limited government based on a theory of enumerated powers—the central government was allowed to exercise only those powers delegated to it by the Constitution. As James Madison wrote in Federalist No. 14, "the general government is not to be charged with the whole power of making and administering laws . . . its jurisdiction is limited to *certain enumerated objects*."[2] Thus, by Madison's logic, separate provisions for the protection of individual rights were unnecessary; protection for those rights was inherent in the nature of limited government with enumerated powers. Because the government possessed no explicit power to infringe on those rights in the first place, they should never be in danger.

Yet Madison's logic ran up against an early American tradition that called for the explicit delineation of individual rights. The Declaration of Independence not only formally recognized that certain "unalienable rights" exist, it also stated that when a government created by "the consent of the governed" fails to protect those rights, the people have the right to "alter or abolish such government." At the time of the founding, individual rights were considered an important element of America's political culture because they embodied the principles that justified the American Revolution. Many of the former colonists wanted those rights clearly spelled out, lest there be any doubt of their significance to the new nation.

When the U.S. Constitution was created in 1787, most state governments already maintained a bill of rights to protect citizens against government encroachment. As the final draft of the proposed constitution was being debated at ratification conventions in the states, it became evident to the new constitution's supporters that its approval was going to require the inclusion of a more formal bill of rights to protect citizens against the federal government. Thomas Jefferson in particular was an early proponent of a bill of rights. To Madison's fears that such a declaration of rights could never be comprehensive and thus might leave out something important, Jefferson replied: "Half a loaf is better than no bread."[3] Eventually it was Madison who framed the list of rights that the first Congress proposed in 1789—10 amendments to the Constitution were ratified by the required three-fourths of state legislatures. These are normally regarded as the "Bill of Rights." Whereas the first eight amendments guarantee specific rights, the Ninth and Tenth Amendments offer more general statements describing divisions of power between the federal and state governments under the Constitution.

The provisions listed in the Bill of Rights enjoyed little influence in late eighteenth- and early nineteenth-century America because they were understood to be restrictions only on the federal government, which was itself an exceedingly limited institution at the time. The Supreme Court confirmed as much in the case of *Barron v. Baltimore* (1833),[4] which pitted a wharf owner against the city of Baltimore. City officials had lowered the water level around the wharves, causing him a significant economic loss. The wharf owner thus sued the city under the Fifth Amendment's "taking clause," which stated that no private property could be taken from an individual for public use without just compensation. But the Supreme Court dismissed the suit because at that time only the federal government could be held up to the standards of the Bill of Rights. In light of the dominant role state governments played in regulating individuals' daily lives during most of this period, the *Barron v. Baltimore* decision essentially reduced the Bill of Rights to paper guarantees that only occasionally provided protection for ordinary citizens.

That all changed in the twentieth century, as the Supreme Court grew increasingly willing to protect individuals against intrusive state actions. Its instrument for doing so was the Fourteenth Amendment (ratified in 1868), which provided that no *state* could "deprive any person of life, liberty or property without due process of law." The Fourteenth Amendment had been passed immediately after the Civil War to protect freed slaves from discriminatory state laws. Yet, at the beginning of the twentieth century and increasingly throughout the century, the Supreme Court, by a process known as **incorporation** (or "nationalization"), demonstrated a new willingness to hold state governments accountable to the Bill of Rights by utilizing the Fourteenth Amendment's vague requirement that states respect "due process." Specifically, the Court carefully considered individual clauses from the Bill of Rights, and if the right was deemed fundamental enough, the Court held that no state could legitimately ignore the right without depriving an individual of the right to "life, liberty and property, without due process of law." By this incorporation process, states were required to live up to the dictates of the First Amendment free speech clause beginning in 1925, the Fourth Amendment right against unreasonable searches and seizures beginning in 1949, and the Sixth Amendment right to a speedy trial beginning in 1967. (See Table 4-1.) Slowly but surely the provisions of the Bill of Rights were incorporated by the Fourteenth Amendment to apply to state governments as well as to the federal government.

TABLE 4-1
Incorporating the Bill of Rights to Apply to the States

Provision (Amendment)	Year	Case
Protection from government taking property without just compensation (Fifth)	1897	*Chicago, Burlington & Quincy Railroad Co. v. City of Chicago*
Freedom of speech (First)	1925	*Gitlow v. New York*
Freedom of the press (First)	1931	*Near v. Minnesota*
Right to assistance of counsel in capital cases (Sixth)	1932	*Powell v. Alabama*
Freedom of assembly (First)	1937	*DeJonge v. Oregon*
Free exercise of religion (First)	1940	*Cantwell v. Connecticut*
Protection from establishment of religion (First)	1947	*Everson v. Board of Education*
Right to public trial (Sixth)	1948	*In re Oliver*
Right against unreasonable search and seizure (Fourth)	1949	*Wolf v. Colorado*
Exclusionary rule (Fourth and Fifth)	1961	*Mapp v. Ohio*
Protection against cruel and unusual punishment (Eighth)	1962	*Robinson v. California*
Right to paid counsel for indigents in felony cases (Sixth)	1963	*Gideon v. Wainwright*
Right against self-incrimination (Fifth)	1964	*Malloy v. Hogan*
Right to confront witnesses (Sixth)	1965	*Pointer v. Texas*
Right to an impartial jury (Sixth)	1966	*Parker v. Gladden*
Right to compulsory process to obtain witnesses (Sixth)	1967	*Washington v. Texas*
Right to speedy trial (Sixth)	1967	*Klopfer v. North Carolina*
Right to jury in nonpetty criminal cases (Sixth)	1968	*Duncan v. Louisiana*
Right against double jeopardy (Fifth)	1969	*Benton v. Maryland*
Right to keep and bear arms (Second)	2010	*McDonald v. Chicago*

incorporation The process by which the U.S. Supreme Court used the due process clause of the Fourteenth Amendment to make most of the individual rights guaranteed by the Bill of Rights also applicable to the states. Incorporation provided that state and local governments, as well as the federal government, could not deny these rights to citizens.

At present there remain just a handful of provisions of the Bill of Rights that theoretically provide protection against the federal government only:

- The Third Amendment safeguard against the involuntary quartering of troops
- The Fifth Amendment requirement that defendants be indicted by a grand jury
- The Seventh Amendment guarantee of a trial by jury in civil cases
- The Eighth Amendment prohibition against excessive bail and fines

Virtually all other provisions contained within the first eight amendments of the Constitution are considered applicable to all 50 state governments, the District of Columbia, and all local governments within the states in exactly the same manner as they are applicable to the federal government.

4-2 FREEDOM OF RELIGION AND THE ESTABLISHMENT CLAUSE

THE FIRST AMENDMENT: *Congress shall make no law respecting an establishment of religion, or prohibiting the free exercise thereof....*

Although the first words of the Bill of Rights speak to the freedom of religion, the actual rights guaranteeing religious freedom did not become widespread until the latter half of the twentieth century. In early America, Protestantism played a highly influential role in public life, and the First Amendment was intended to provide a limited barrier against its influence. In 1802, Thomas Jefferson described the First Amendment as erecting a "wall of separation" between church and state,[5] but that metaphor captured his hopes more than the reality of the time. Although there existed no official church of the United States, government aid to religion—in particular to certain Protestant sects—stood little chance of being overturned by a court on constitutional grounds. And for much of American history, minority religious groups such as Mormons, Jehovah's Witnesses, and the Amish were forced to change or abandon some of their religious practices whenever public policy conflicted with them. By the 1940s, however, American public life had grown increasingly secular, and application of the First Amendment's guarantees of freedom of religion was transformed. Even today the interest in accommodating religion continues to run up against the desire to create a "wall of separation" emphasizing government neutrality.

THE FREE EXERCISE OF RELIGION

The free exercise clause of the First Amendment bans government laws that prohibit the free exercise of religion. Debate over the clause has largely focused on whether government laws can force adherents of a certain religion to engage in activities that are prohibited by their religious beliefs or prevent them from performing acts that are compelled by their religious beliefs. During the heart of World War II, the Supreme Court in *West Virginia State Board of Education v. Barnette* (1943)[6] ordered school officials to reinstate the children of Jehovah's Witnesses who had been suspended for refusing to salute the American flag in their public school classrooms. Yet, although those children could claim legitimate religious objections to the law (the Jehovah's Witnesses' creed forbids them from saluting any "graven image"), they also could claim more generally the right of free expression—those who disagreed with the U.S. government were free to withhold displays of public support for the nation's symbol. It remained for the Court in subsequent years to sort out what rights of religious freedom might exist under the free exercise clause.

SEVENTH-DAY ADVENTISTS AND THE REFUSAL TO WORK. In the landmark case of *Sherbert v. Verner* (1963),[7] the Supreme Court ordered the state of South Carolina to pay unemployment benefits to a Seventh-day Adventist who refused to work on Saturdays. Even though the state's unemployment laws required that she make herself available for work on Saturday,

free exercise clause The religious freedom clause in the First Amendment that denies government the ability to prohibit the free exercise of religion. Debate over the clause has largely focused on whether government laws can force adherents of a certain religion to engage in activities that are prohibited by their religious beliefs or prevent them from performing acts that are compelled by their religious beliefs.

the Court refused to apply that law to this worker because Saturday is the Seventh-day Adventists' Sabbath. The Supreme Court declared that only a *compelling state interest* could justify denying her an exception to the Saturday work requirement on the basis of religion. What interest counts as "compelling"? Although no precise definition is available, the Court has held that administrative convenience is not compelling; rather, the Court must be convinced that the government program would be significantly undermined by religious exemptions.

THE AMISH AND MANDATORY SCHOOL ATTENDANCE. Continuing to accept exemptions for religious reasons, the Supreme Court in *Wisconsin v. Yoder* (1972)[8] held that members of the Amish religion were not required to send their children to school after the eighth grade. Even though

Amish children walking to school in Ohio. In 1972 the U.S. Supreme Court declared that members of the Amish religion could not be compelled to send their children to school after the eighth grade.

"*Stocktrek / Photodisc / Getty Images*"

Wisconsin law compelled high school attendance, the Court ruled that the enforcement of that law would undermine Amish religious principles, which include the value of "learning through doing" and support for "community welfare" over all other interests.

THE MORMONS AND POLYGAMY LAWS. Up until the late nineteenth century, a central tenet of the Church of Jesus Christ of Latter-day Saints (LDS), often referred to as the Mormon Church, required some of its adherents to practice polygamy—the act of having multiple spouses "when circumstances would permit." During the 1870s, many of these church members were prosecuted under a federal anti-bigamy statute. George Reynolds, secretary of one of the founders of the LDS Church in America as well as the founder of Brigham Young University, brought suit in 1878, challenging the law as destructive to the Church of Jesus Christ and thus a violation of the free exercise clause of the First Amendment. The Supreme Court, in a unanimous decision, rejected Reynolds's argument that the First Amendment protects plural marriage. According to the Court, these religious "practices" were to be distinguished from religious "beliefs," which the government had no power to regulate.[9] Thus polygamy today is banned in all 50 states and since 1890 the LDS Church has formally renounced the practice.

ILLEGAL DRUG USE AND THE SMITH CASE. In 1990, the Supreme Court adopted a new approach to the free exercise of religion, one that dramatically diminished the likelihood that future religious exemptions might be granted. Two Native Americans were dismissed from their jobs as drug rehabilitation counselors when it was discovered that they had ingested the illegal drug peyote as part of their tribe's religious rituals. Because their drug use violated the Oregon criminal code, the two men were subsequently denied unemployment compensation. The Supreme Court ruled in *Employment Division, Department of Human Resources of Oregon v. Smith* (1990)[10] that the state's legitimate interest in maintaining its unemployment insurance fund at a high level outweighed the Native Americans' religious rights and thus that it could deny the two men unemployment benefits. State governments may choose to accommodate otherwise illegal acts done in pursuit of religious beliefs, but they are not *required* to do so.[11]

Today *Smith* remains the rule for judicial interpretation of free exercise cases: instead of being forced to show a *compelling* government interest (which is extremely hard to do), a government interested in applying its neutral laws over religious objections may do so based on any *legitimate state interest* it might claim. What is a legitimate state interest? The bar here is quite low; only an arbitrary or irrational objective by government will fail the test of legitimacy.

THE ESTABLISHMENT CLAUSE

Even more controversial than the debate over religious exemptions from public policies has been the battle over what role religion may play in American public life under the **establishment clause**, which prohibits the government from enacting laws "respecting an establishment of religion." Most Americans take it for granted that during the holiday season they will see Christmas decorations prominently displayed in government buildings, in front of the town hall, and in public squares. But what about nativity scenes? Menorahs? The Ten Commandments? What types of religious activities and symbols are considered acceptable in public places, and which ones run afoul of the First Amendment, whose prohibition of government "respecting an establishment of religion" has been interpreted to mean creating a "wall of separation" between church and state?

Modern debates over the proper role religion may play under the establishment clause generally divide advocates into two camps. Those who advocate a strict dividing line between church and state support a principle of "separation," which holds that government should have no involvement whatsoever with religious practices, although religion remains free to flourish privately on its own, with its own resources.[12] Opponents of strict separation argue instead for the principle of "accommodation," which holds that government neutrality toward religion requires only that it treat all religions equally. Government should be free to aid and subsidize religious activities as long as it does so fairly across different religions and aids comparable nonreligious activities as well. In recent decades, the Supreme Court has moved from

> **establishment clause** The clause in the First Amendment that prohibits government from enacting any law "respecting an establishment of religion." Separationist interpretations of this clause affirm that government should not support any religious activity. Accommodationists say that support for a religion is legal provided that all religions are equally supported.

 ## DEBATES OVER DIVERSITY
Religious Divide in Teaching of Evolution

Those holding different religious beliefs often find themselves in conflict with each other or with the government. In the context of public education, adherents of different religions clash over the teaching of evolution to students. Central questions include "How was the universe created?" and "Which theory or scientific facts should be used for our public education science standards?" Some religious groups favor the teaching of intelligent design and creationism, as they believe the universe was either intelligently designed by some entity or by God. These beliefs may come into sharp conflict with those who favor the teaching of Charles Darwin's theory of evolution. Many states and school boards have sided with religious groups in challenging the teaching of evolution.

Are school boards required to balance religious or academic freedoms with the more secular focus of education standards? The Supreme Court has responded in various cases. Most notably in *Edwards v. Aguillard* (1987),[13] the high court outlawed the teaching of creationism in American public school science classes. Still, this battle remains far from settled, as statewide efforts challenging the teaching of evolution have continued in the decades since that landmark decision.

"Bettmann/Getty Images"

Attorney Clarence Darrow speaks at the infamous 1925 Scopes monkey trial in defense of his client, accused of teaching evolution in the public schools.

For Critical Thinking and Discussion

1. What side do you take in this religious divide over the teaching of evolution? Should school boards be allowed to dictate that teachers teach theories of intelligent design or creationism alongside the teaching of evolution theory?
2. Do you recall how your previous schools responded to the debate over evolution? Were you taught one theory or both?

a position of especially strict separation to one that shifts back and forth between principles of separation and accommodation.

HISTORICALLY ACCEPTED PRACTICES. Certain religious practices have been a part of political and public life for generations, and the Supreme Court has generally allowed such activities to continue. Congress, as well as some state and local legislatures, open each legislative session with a prayer from a clergy member. Chaplains serve in religious capacities with the U.S. armed forces, and U.S. currency proclaims "In God We Trust." Even the Supreme Court opens every court session to a marshal's bellowing pronouncement: "God save this honorable court!" All of these are considered acceptable practices, products of the American historical tradition. The high Court even held that one town's practice of opening its town board meetings with a sectarian prayer did not violate the establishment clause because it comported with the town's traditions and it did not coerce nonadherents. Still, not all religious displays on public property will be automatically deemed "historically accepted practices." On occasion, the Court has ordered the removal of nativity scenes and other religious displays during Christmastime.

In Kentucky, versions of the Ten Commandments were posted on the walls of several county courthouses. In Texas, a six-foot-high monolith inscribed with the Ten Commandments sits among numerous other monuments and historical markers outside the state capital building commemorating the "people, ideals, and events that compose Texan identity." Do these public displays of the Ten Commandments violate the establishment clause of the First Amendment? In a set of cases handed down in 2005, the Supreme Court ordered the Kentucky courthouses to remove their displays but allowed the Texas display to remain standing. In explaining its different approach to these cases, the Court ruled that even though the Ten Commandments are inherently religious, their placement in a monument outside the state capital is an essentially "passive" act, whereas their placement within the courthouse had been motivated by a desire on the part of legislators to advance religion.

RELIGIOUS PRAYERS IN PUBLIC SCHOOL CLASSROOMS. The public school classroom has always been viewed as a unique context in which to assess claims that the government has violated the establishment clause. Judges and politicians alike assume that students—particularly elementary school students—have not yet formed firm beliefs about religion and thus may be susceptible to even subtle forms of religious coercion. Public officials interested in promoting religion in society as a whole have focused on the school as a place to encourage religious practices; as a consequence, school policies touching on the subject of religion have undergone serious scrutiny in the courts.

In 1962, the Supreme Court in *Engel v. Vitale*[14] invalidated the New York public schools' policy of having each class recite a specified nondenominational religious prayer each day. That prayer, which proclaimed in nondenominational terms, "Almighty God, we acknowledge our dependence upon thee," was held to be a violation of the First Amendment's prohibition against the establishment of religion. In *Abington School District v. Schempp* (1963),[15] the Court refused to allow spiritual Bible readings in public school classrooms, and in *Wallace v. Jaffree* (1985)[16] it outlawed "moments of silence" authorized by government officials to encourage religious prayer during those moments. The Court held that in neither of those instances was the government acting with a "secular purpose"—one not grounded in a desire to "advance religion."

Despite these seemingly clear rulings against school prayer, enforcement issues remain as some teachers continue to lead students in prayer in public school classrooms across the country. Accordingly, at least one court in Alabama was forced to forbid prayer in schools throughout the state fully 35 years after the Supreme Court had formally invalidated the practice. Anecdotal evidence of violations continue to mount as well: in one highly publicized case, officials in DeKalb County, Georgia, helped lead a religious revival at a public high school in admitted disobedience of the Supreme Court. Defiance persists in part because of community sentiment, which tends to squelch potential litigation. Dissenting parents quickly realize that only continued and expensive litigation over many years will bring a defiant school into line.

A high school football team gathers in group prayer before a game in Mobile, Alabama.

FINANCIAL AID AND THE *LEMON* TEST. During the past several decades, government officials seeking to promote religion as part of the educational process have expanded the variety and scope of their efforts. Many initiatives have occurred in public schools—provisions for school prayer recitations, released-time programs (allowing students to visit religious schools for instruction during normal school hours), and the teaching of subjects with religious content, such as creationism. Efforts to provide religious private schools that teach students full-time with public funds have met with some recent success. In 2000, the Supreme Court approved of a program to provide government-funded computers and other teaching aids to certain parochial schools. Two years later, the Court in *Zelman v. Simmons-Harris* (2002)[17] upheld a system of private school vouchers, whereby parents are given coupons that can be used to pay tuition at private schools, including parochial schools. Such programs continue to be a source of heated policy debate between proponents of separation and accommodation.

Since 1971, issues involving the separation of church and state have often been governed by the *Lemon* test articulated by the Supreme Court in the landmark decision of *Lemon v. Kurtzman* (1971).[18] Under the test, government aid to public or private schools is considered unconstitutional if it fails to meet three separate criteria: "First, the statute must have a secular [that is, not religious] purpose; second, its principal or primary effect must be one that neither advances nor inhibits religion; finally, the statute must not foster 'an excessive government entanglement with religion.'" The test has been criticized by many, including a number of the Supreme Court justices, who assert that its requirements are so stringent that literally all deliberate government accommodation of religion is presumptively invalid. The Court has never renounced the test, and it continues to play a role in the consideration of various types of financial aid.

PRAYERS AT GRADUATION CEREMONIES AND FOOTBALL GAMES. In recent decades, some school officials have attempted to facilitate student prayers in school contexts outside of the classroom. Those efforts have met with little success. In *Lee v. Weisman* (1992),[19] the Supreme Court ordered a Providence, Rhode Island, middle school to stop its practice of permitting prayers to be read at the school's graduation ceremony, even though attendance was voluntary. Eight years later, in *Santa Fe Independent School District v. Doe* (2000),[20] the Court ruled that a student-led prayer before a football game at a Texas public high school violated the separation of church and state. The Court believed that both practices forced all of those present to participate in an act of religious worship. In addition, these practices could have been interpreted as state endorsements of prayer, which is unconstitutional.

The debate over the role religion should play in American public life remains a highly charged topic. Public schools especially will continue to be a focus of intense interest, as the proponents of a greater role for religion seek ever more creative ways to combine the educational process with efforts to encourage spirituality and religious participation.

4-3 FREE EXPRESSION RIGHTS

THE FIRST AMENDMENT: *Congress shall make no law ... abridging the freedom of speech, or of the press.*

Among the many civil liberties guaranteed by the Bill of Rights, the First Amendment rights of free speech and press enjoy especially revered status. That wasn't always the case. The Sedition

Lemon test The legal test that determines if a government statute aiding public or private schools is an unconstitutional violation of the establishment clause. The statute is unconstitutional if the statute has no secular purpose, if its principal or primary effect advances or inhibits religion, or if it fosters "an excessive government entanglement with religion."

Act of the late 1790s egregiously restricted speech that negatively reflected on the Federalists who were in power; during the Civil War, the Lincoln administration imprisoned editors and publishers who sought to undermine the Union's cause. Today, nearly all politicians openly celebrate rights of free expression, at least in the abstract. For many, these rights of free expression serve as a cornerstone for all other individual rights, facilitating the more effective realization of such freedoms as the right to vote and participate in the democratic process.

What accounts for the lofty status of free expression rights in the American political system? Several theories have been offered to justify this high level of respect:

- **"The marketplace of ideas,"** a phrase coined by Supreme Court justice Oliver Wendell Holmes in 1919, is a metaphor for the premise that the best test of truth is the free trade of ideas; only through such free exchange and presentation of all arguments, valid and invalid, can the truth prevail. To ensure a robust "marketplace of ideas," government restrictions on speech must be kept to a minimum.
- **Self-governance** is another frequently cited justification for protecting free expression. Speech is considered essential to representative government because it provides the mechanism by which citizens deliberate on important issues of public policy. Free speech also serves as a means for ordinary citizens to check the abuse of power by public officials.
- **Self-fulfillment.** Some philosophers have emphasized the importance of free speech and expression as a means of achieving individual self-fulfillment. The human capacity to create ideas and express oneself is thus considered central to human existence; government restrictions on free speech invariably threaten that human capacity. Such a justification of free speech rights would extend to the protection of music, pictures, and other forms of artistic expression.
- **A "safety valve."** Free speech also serves a critical role in encouraging adaptability and flexibility according to the changing circumstances in society. If the suppression of free speech forces citizens to adopt more extreme means of enacting change, such as violence, the promotion of free speech provides an essential mechanism for balancing the need for order with cries for reform.

Each of these justifications for free speech protection may be subject to legitimate criticisms as well. But for better or worse, the First Amendment's protection of free expression today enjoys a special status in our constitutional system, even though that was not always the case.

FREE SPEECH DURING THE EARLY TWENTIETH CENTURY: THE CLEAR AND PRESENT DANGER TEST

The modern status of free expression rights is a far cry from the low level of protection the First Amendment afforded to free speech a century ago. Many of the early twentieth-century cases pitting dissenting speakers against the government came before the Court when tensions were great—first during wartime, then at the height of the Cold War when fears of communist infiltration in American society gripped many ordinary Americans. In neither instance did free speech fare well.

The Supreme Court gave birth to the "clear and present danger" test in *Schenck v. United States* (1919).[21] In 1917, with the United States readying for active participation in World War I, Charles Schenck, a general secretary for the American Socialist Party, was tried and convicted for distributing leaflets arguing that the military draft was immoral. Although the pamphlet posed little actual

The KKK burn a cross in Madison, Indiana.

AP Photo

danger of interfering with the draft, the Supreme Court refused to release Schenck from jail. Writing the majority opinion for a unanimous court, Justice Oliver Wendell Holmes stated that there was in fact "a clear and present danger" that the pamphlet could bring about the damage being claimed by the government.

In practice, the clear and present danger test soon became a hammer on speakers' rights rather than a shield against government suppression. Under the doctrine, members of the Socialist and Communist parties were tried and punished for participating in organizational meetings or declaring allegiance to their party's principles. Justice Holmes was clearly alarmed by the legacy his *Schenck* decision had wrought; in subsequent decisions he modified his earlier view by insisting that the present danger must relate to an "immediate evil" and a specific action. But Holmes was now in the minority, and there was little he could do to stop the momentum.

THE WARREN COURT AND THE RISE OF THE "PREFERRED FREEDOMS" DOCTRINE

By the late 1950s, fears of subversion and communist infiltration in the United States were beginning to subside. However, it was the ascension of former California governor Earl Warren to the position of chief justice of the United States in 1953 that eventually changed the Court's free speech doctrine from one that offered little protection to dissenting speakers into one that protected even the most unpopular speakers against suppression by the majority. The Warren court brought about this change by embracing a doctrine first articulated by Justice Harlan Fiske Stone in 1938. In a footnote to the otherwise forgettable case of *United States v. Carolene Products* (1938),[22] Justice Stone declared that various civil liberties guaranteed in the Bill of Rights, including the right of free expression, enjoyed a "preferred position" in constitutional law. Stone's explicit support for this preferred freedoms doctrine did not take immediate hold. Yet in the 1960s, when new social tensions such as the battle over civil rights and resistance to the Vietnam War threatened to wreak havoc on civil liberties, the Warren court issued several key decisions that shattered any possibility that the government might be able to suppress the exercise of free speech rights under the Constitution, as it had in the earlier part of the century.

In 1969, the Supreme Court in *Brandenburg v. Ohio* (1969)[23] abandoned the clear and present danger test and replaced it with a test that was much more protective of free speech. A Ku Klux Klan rally in Cincinnati, Ohio, featured numerous figures in white hoods uttering phrases that demeaned African Americans and Jews. The principal speaker had argued that some form of vengeance be taken against both groups. The group's leader was convicted under a law criminalizing the advocacy of violence. The Supreme Court overturned his conviction. In the process, it declared a new "imminent danger" test for such speech: first, is the speech "directed to inciting or producing imminent lawless action," and second, is the advocacy *likely* to produce such action? Few of the speakers jailed in the previous half-century for seditious speech could have been convicted under this new standard.[24]

The preferred freedoms doctrine also offered protection to those exercising their rights of free expression in other contexts—to writers and publishers, filmmakers, and protesters, for example. Indeed, it provided a foundation for the protection of such modern activities as the dissemination of information on the Internet. Even speakers and publishers of certain categories of speech that have not traditionally enjoyed First Amendment protection—obscenity and libel, for example—soon discovered that the preferred freedoms doctrine provided protection for their activities.

THE FREEDOM OF THE PRESS, LIBEL LAWS, AND PRIOR RESTRAINTS

Freedom of the press enjoys a long and storied tradition in the United States. Well before the American Revolution or the drafting of the Constitution, the trial of newspaper publisher John Peter Zenger in 1734 on charges of libel laid the foundation for robust press freedoms. Libel is the crime of printing or disseminating false statements that harm someone. Zenger was accused of attacking the corrupt administration of New York's colonial governor in his weekly newspaper. When he was acquitted on the basis of his lawyer's argument that he had

libel Printing or disseminating false statements that harm someone.

FIGURE 4-1

Do You Know What Rights Are in the First Amendment?

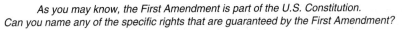

*As you may know, the First Amendment is part of the U.S. Constitution.
Can you name any of the specific rights that are guaranteed by the First Amendment?*

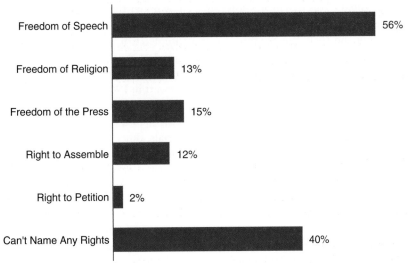

Freedom of Speech	56%
Freedom of Religion	13%
Freedom of the Press	15%
Right to Assemble	12%
Right to Petition	2%
Can't Name Any Rights	40%

A 2018 national survey conducted by the Freedom Forum found that few Americans are aware of all five rights in the First Amendment. And fully 40 percent couldn't even name one of those five rights.

printed true facts, Zenger's case helped to establish the legal principle that truth would serve as a defense to any libel action. In the late 1790s, after many Republican editors and publishers had been jailed under the highly controversial Sedition Act, public distaste for the act helped to catapult Thomas Jefferson and his Republican Party into power in the election of 1800.

Despite the general recognition of the importance of the press, newspapers traditionally enjoyed few special privileges under the law. Specifically, individuals whose reputations were harmed were free to bring libel suits against newspapers and other publications without any implications for the First Amendment. That changed in 1964 with the landmark decision of *New York Times v. Sullivan*.[25] A Montgomery, Alabama, police commissioner sued the *New York Times* in March 1960 for an advertisement the newspaper had published. The ad—charging the existence of "an unprecedented wave of terror" against blacks in Montgomery—had been signed by several black clergymen. In its description of events that had transpired, the ad also contained some minor inaccuracies. Although the police commissioner was unable to prove that he had suffered any actual economic harm, he still sought a $500,000 judgment against the *Times*. But the Supreme Court refused to allow the official to claim damages and in the process articulated a much more stringent test to be met by public officials suing for libel: they must prove that the newspapers had published false facts with malice (bad intentions) or reckless disregard for the truth (i.e., they ignored clear evidence of contrary facts).[26]

In subsequent years, the *New York Times v. Sullivan* decision has applied to public figures as well as public officials; today a libel lawsuit brought by any famous person—whether it's the president of the United States, LeBron James, or Julia Roberts—must prove that the newspaper or magazine in question not only printed false facts but did so either with "malicious intent" or in "reckless disregard" for the truth. Unlike such public figures, private figures seeking monetary damages need only show that the newspaper was "negligent."

Whereas libel laws punish publications after the fact, a **prior restraint** imposes a limit on publication *before* the material has actually been published. Securing a prior restraint is very difficult for the government to accomplish. In the *Pentagon Papers Case* (1971),[27] the Supreme Court refused the U.S. government's request to stop the *Washington Post* and the *New York Times* from publishing a classified study of U.S. decision-making about the Vietnam War. The

prior restraint The government's requirement that material be approved by government before it can be published.

courts have made it very difficult for government to implement a prior restraint of expression. In only the rarest of cases, such as the publication of information about troop movements during wartime, has government been able to block the publication of a story.

OBSCENITY AND PORNOGRAPHY

Despite the exalted status free expression rights enjoy under the Constitution, obscenity has long been recognized as an exception to the rule. Even through the so-called sexual revolution of the 1960s and 1970s, the Supreme Court continued to adhere to the premise that truly obscene speech—words or publications that tend to violate accepted standards of decency by their very lewdness—may, under certain circumstances, be regulated. When asked how he would define obscene pornography, Justice Potter Stewart in 1964 uttered his now celebrated phrase: "I can't define it, but I know it when I see it." Stewart's statement captures the often confusing state of obscenity law in the United States. The First Amendment does not allow governments simply to ban all sexually explicit materials. But what types of materials can be banned? Is all pornography to be considered "obscene"?

In *Miller v. California* (1973),[28] the Supreme Court created the modern legal test for determining what sexually explicit materials may be legitimately subject to regulation under the Constitution. According to the Court, a work is obscene if *all* of these three conditions are met:

1. The average person applying contemporary community standards would think that the work (taken as a whole) appeals to the "prurient" (that is, lustful) interest.
2. The work depicts sexual conduct in a patently offensive way.
3. The work taken as a whole lacks "serious literary, artistic, political or scientific value."

> **SLAPS test** A standard that courts established to determine if material is obscene based in part on whether the material has serious literary, artistic, political, or scientific value. If it does, then the material is not obscene.

This third condition has come to be known as the "**SLAPS test**" (derived from taking the first letter of each word in the quoted phrase). In theory, adherence to the SLAPS test allows a jury to apply its own conception of "contemporary community standards" and thus ban relatively innocent sexual materials. In practice, however, courts have found very few materials that would not receive protection under the SLAPS test (after all, who is to say what possesses "artistic value"?). None of the above rules apply to child pornography, which enjoys no First Amendment protection whatsoever.

The rise of the Internet over the past quarter century has caused even more confusion as to what types of obscenity and/or pornography can be regulated. In *Reno v. ACLU* (1997),[29] the Supreme Court invalidated a federal law passed to protect minors from "indecent" and "patently offensive" communications on the Internet. The Court feared that in denying minors access to potentially harmful speech, the law had suppressed a large amount of speech that adults have a constitutional right to receive. Still, the question of how to restrict sexually explicit speech on the Internet will remain an issue for years to come.

NOW YOU CAN SEE IT!

The most whispered about book in the world becomes the MOST TALKED ABOUT PICTURE OF THE YEAR!

THE FILM WITHOUT FALSE MODESTY!

D. H. LAWRENCE'S CONTROVERSIAL MASTERPIECE

"Lady Chatterley's Lover"

DANIELLE DARRIEUX
LEO GENN
and Introducing
ERNO CRISA

A Kingsley International Release

Everett Collection, Inc. / Alamy Stock Photo

Poster advertising Lady Chatterley's Lover. *The film was based on a book that was the target of a New York State ban during the 1950s.*

SYMBOLIC SPEECH AND THE FLAG-BURNING CONTROVERSY

When school officials in Des Moines, Iowa, suspended two students for wearing black armbands in protest of the Vietnam War in the 1960s, they claimed they were not restricting free speech rights at all—rather, the students were engaging in conduct at school that could be regulated.[30]

The Supreme Court in 1969 disagreed and the students were vindicated,[31] but the line between speech and conduct remains difficult to draw, whether it occurs at school or in the public square. Protesters may camp out in public parks overnight to bring attention to the plight of the homeless or burn their draft cards as a statement of opposition to a war. Are such forms of symbolic speech protected by the First Amendment?

In 1968, the Supreme Court in *United States v. O'Brien*[32] refused to allow a Vietnam War protester to burn his draft card in violation of federal law. That case introduced three criteria for determining whether the regulation of symbolic speech may be justified:

1. The government interest must be valid and important.
2. The interest must be unrelated to the suppression of free speech.
3. The restriction should be no greater than is essential to the furtherance of that interest.

In *United States v. O'Brien*, the key factor was motive: the Court believed the government actions were motivated by the need to operate a military registration system during wartime, rather than simply to suppress the ideas and message of this particular protester. Similarly, protesters do not have the right to violate federal park service rules and sleep in parks after closing—those rules were established for one reason: to prevent damage to public property. By contrast, students were granted the constitutional right to wear black armbands in school to protest the Vietnam War—their "conduct" was considered the equivalent of "pure speech" and school officials' arguments about the maintenance of order and discipline were given little credibility.

The constitutionality of flag-burning has been a source of considerable debate in recent years. To many, the American flag is a symbol of nationhood and national unity and thus must be preserved at all costs. For that very reason, protesters seeking to attract publicity for their ideas have burned or desecrated the flag in public places. The Supreme Court ended the legal debate over flag-burning with its decision in *Texas v. Johnson* (1989).[33] In 1984, Gregory Lee Johnson was arrested and convicted for "desecrating a venerated object" at a political demonstration in Dallas, the site of the Republican National Convention. Johnson had been leading a protest against the Reagan administration; he eventually set an American flag on fire, after which he and the other protesters chanted: "America, the red, white and blue, we spit on you." But the Supreme Court threw out Johnson's conviction because the "government may not prohibit the expression of an idea simply because society finds the idea itself offensive or disagreeable."[34]

Despite the Supreme Court's apparent resolution of the matter, heated feelings on both sides of the flag-burning issue have kept it alive. After an initial attempt by Congress to pass flag-burning legislation failed to withstand judicial scrutiny in 1990, some members of Congress proposed passage of an amendment to the Constitution that would make flag-burning unconstitutional. Although that proposed amendment has on several occasions achieved the necessary level of support in the House of Representatives, the U.S. Senate has so far failed to approve it, thus preventing it from being promulgated to state legislatures for ratification.

HATE SPEECH CODES

Since the 1970s, communities have sought to prevent speakers who preach hatred for certain groups—whether racial, religious, or some other classification—from exercising their rights of free speech in certain specified neighborhoods or other places where the perceived harms may be great. In one instance during the late 1970s, the courts refused to deny neo-Nazis the right to march in a parade in Skokie, Illinois, home to a large number of Holocaust victims.[35] By contrast, in *Virginia v. Black* (2003),[36] the U.S. Supreme Court ruled that the state of Virginia could prohibit cross-burning with the "intent to intimidate any person or group" because the law applied only to intimidation and it applied to all groups, not just racial or ethnic groups.

It is a considerable challenge for school officials to restrict hate speech by students at public colleges and universities, even when that speech proves disruptive to the school's mission of providing a constructive environment for learning.[37] In 1988, the University of Michigan passed a regulation subjecting individuals to discipline for "behavior, verbal or physical" that

symbolic speech
Nonspoken forms of speech that might be protected by the First Amendment, such as flag-burning, wearing armbands at school to protest a war, or camping out in public parks to protest the plight of the homeless.

New York University students and faculty rally in favor of the Black Lives Matter movement and against institutional racism.

stigmatized or victimized an individual on the basis of race, ethnicity, religion, sex, or a host of other criteria. Stanford University similarly attempted to prohibit "discriminatory harassment," which was defined to include speech intended to stigmatize or insult on the basis of sex, race, and so on. Lower courts invalidated both of these "hate speech codes" on grounds that they violated the First Amendment. More recently, student groups at colleges and universities have argued that there need to be "safe spaces" where students can relax without fear of being made to feel unwelcome on account of sex, race/ethnicity, sexual orientation, gender identity, or other traits they may possess. Depending on how they are applied, these efforts may or may not stand up against First Amendment free speech protections as well.

REGULATING THE INTERNET

Meanwhile, high school principals and superintendents face their own set of twenty-first-century challenges, thanks to the Internet and popular social networking sites like Facebook and Twitter. Public school students today may find themselves the target of "cyberbullying" from classmates who post nasty comments about them on social media sites. If the harassing posts originated from a school or library computer, the school would obviously have the authority to punish the cyberbullies. But what if a student posted the harassing comment from his or her own computer or a mobile device while at home? What if the student posted the offending comments on a discussion thread open only to his or her closest friends? Does school authority extend to students' behaviors in their own private spheres? Lower courts are still sorting out such issues as they await eventual judgment from the U.S. Supreme Court.

4-4 THE RIGHT TO BEAR ARMS AND THE RIGHTS OF THE CRIMINALLY ACCUSED

THE RIGHT TO BEAR ARMS

THE SECOND AMENDMENT: A well regulated militia, being necessary to the security of a free State, the right of the people to keep and bear Arms, shall not be infringed.

The Second Amendment "right to keep and bear arms" remains something of a puzzle for Americans. On one hand, the second part of the amendment appears to trumpet the "people's" right to own firearms at their discretion and has taken its place as a central tenet in the platforms of interest groups such as the National Rifle Association (NRA), which opposes nearly all government attempts to restrict gun ownership. On the other hand, the first part of the amendment speaks directly of a "well regulated militia," and implies that some relationship must exist between the private gun owner's rights and more formal state activities. The U.S. Supreme Court finally weighed in on the subject in 2008. In *District of Columbia v.*

Heller (2008),[38] the Supreme Court by a 5–4 vote held that the Second Amendment forbids the government from banning all forms of handgun possession in the home for purposes of immediate self-defense. In *McDonald v. Chicago* (2010),[39] the Supreme Court went a step further, ruling that the right to bear arms is incorporated by the due process clause of the Fourteenth Amendment and thus applies to all 50 states as well.

Second Amendment rights are not absolute: the Court in *Heller* noted that government can still regulate the commercial sale of handguns; it can also prohibit their possession by felons and the mentally ill, or in sensitive places such as school buildings. Still, Congress has been reluctant to regulate gun ownership—only rarely are the sponsors of gun control able to overcome fierce lobbying efforts by the NRA and others in opposition. The Brady Handgun Violence Prevention Act, signed by President Clinton in 1993, required a five-day waiting period and a background check on handgun purchases from licensed firearms dealers to ensure that felons, drug users, fugitives, and other specified categories of individuals are not permitted to purchase guns. Congress has also attempted to restrict the carrying of firearms near schools, even though some of these efforts have been invalidated by the Supreme Court. As a general matter, convicted fugitives and those involuntarily admitted to a mental facility are also prohibited from purchasing firearms, though their rights may be restored by law in some instances.

THE RIGHTS OF THE CRIMINALLY ACCUSED

A few rights for the accused may be found in the language of the original Constitution. Article I prohibits Congress from passing a **bill of attainder**, which is an act of a legislature declaring a person (or group) guilty of some crime and then carrying out punishment without a trial. It also prohibits **ex post facto laws**, which are new criminal laws retroactively applied to those who engaged in activities when they were not yet illegal. But the vast majority of constitutional rights for those accused of crimes are contained in the Fourth, Fifth, Sixth, and Eighth Amendments to the Constitution. Despite the seemingly explicit protections found in those four amendments, accused individuals enjoyed only limited substantive protection from arbitrary violations of criminal due process for the first century and a half of this nation's history, as they protected defendants only against intrusions by the federal government.

Much changed in the 1960s, as the Supreme Court applied many of the provisions of the Bill of Rights against state governments by incorporating protections given to accused persons in the federal judicial system. In addition, the Court gave increased substance to these rights, holding all government officials accountable for their actions at highway road stops, during the interrogation of witnesses at the police station, and elsewhere.[40] Even the right to counsel was broadened to extend to far more of those accused of committing crimes.

FOURTH AMENDMENT RIGHTS

> **THE FOURTH AMENDMENT:** *The right of the people to be secure in their persons, houses, papers and effects, against unreasonable searches and seizures, shall not be violated, and no Warrants shall issue, but upon probable cause. . . .*

The right of citizens to be free from unreasonable searches and seizures has a long history in America. Before the American Revolution, colonists loudly protested English abuses of the power to inspect merchants' goods through the use of an unlimited "general warrant." Although the Fourth Amendment had been in place for nearly two centuries, the Warren court modernized the rules governing police searches with its decision in *Katz v. United States* (1967).[41] The Court's ruling created the *Katz* test, which requires that the government attain a warrant demonstrating "probable cause" for any investigative activity that violates a person's reasonable expectation of privacy, whether or not the person is at home. A **warrant** is a document issued by a judge or magistrate that allows law enforcement to search or seize items at a home, business, or anywhere else that might be specified.

bill of attainder An act of a legislature declaring a person (or group) guilty of some crime, and then carrying out punishment without a trial. The Constitution denies Congress the ability to issue a bill of attainder.

ex post facto law A law that punishes someone for an act that took place in the past, at a time when the act was not illegal. The Constitution denies government the ability to write laws ex post facto.

***Katz* test** The legal standard that requires the government to attain a warrant demonstrating "probable cause" for any "search" that violates a person's actual and reasonable expectation of privacy.

warrant A document issued by a judge or magistrate that allows law enforcement to search or seize items at a home, business, or anywhere else that might be specified.

Balancing Police Surveillance Techniques with the Need for Individual Privacy

Americans have long accepted that even in a free society they must consent to some degree of police surveillance of their activities. When an individual takes a walk in a public park or drives a car along a public thoroughfare, he or she can expect those activities will be observed by complete strangers, including members of law enforcement. Under Fourth Amendment precedents, the government must have a warrant to search someone—even in a public place—if the person maintains a "reasonable expectation of privacy" in his or her actions. Of course, law enforcement officers' increasing use of technology for surveillance purposes complicates this area of the law, forcing the Court to weigh the interests of society against those of the individual in this context.

Then

In 1967, the Supreme Court for the first time ruled that nonphysical government intrusion may require a warrant. In *Katz v. United States*, the court considered the case of Charles Katz, who made illegal gambling wagers by using a public pay phone booth. The Federal Bureau of Investigation (FBI) had secretly attached an electronic bugging device (without a warrant or probable cause) to the outside of the booth to record all conversations. The government defended its actions by asserting that the phone booth was in the public, and the bugging device was on the outside of the booth, where others could legally go. The Supreme Court rejected this argument: by a 7–1 vote, it held that the recording of Katz's conversation violated the privacy "upon which he justifiably relied." Katz established that the Fourth Amendment protects not just "things" but the reasonable expectations of people as well.

In 1986, the Court ruled that this new Fourth Amendment doctrine was not unlimited. In *California v. Ciraolo*, Dante Ciraolo was charged with growing marijuana in his backyard. Ciraolo put up two large fences to keep the activity private; meanwhile, the Santa Clara police photographed the marijuana plants from a private airplane 400 feet above the ground. This time,

by a 5–4 vote, the Supreme Court held that so long as the plants were visible to the "naked eye" from above, the government did not require a search warrant, and Ciraolo's reasonable expectation of privacy was not violated.

Now

In 2018, the police learned that they could not overrely on the technology used by private cell phone companies to conduct surveillance. In *Carpenter v. United States*, the Supreme Court ruled that the government must obtain a warrant in order to access historical cell phone records, as they offer what are in effect "detailed, encyclopedic, and effortlessly compiled" data about a person's movements. Writing for a narrow 5-4 majority, Chief Justice John Roberts argued that technology thus "has afforded law enforcement a powerful new tool to carry out its important responsibilities … this tool risks Government encroachment of the sort the Framers, after consulting the lessons of history, drafted the Fourth Amendment to prevent." Unfortunately, the Court's opinion left some significant questions unanswered, such as Could the government require that cell phone companies provide them with cell tower data in the event of an emergency or if national security issues were implicated? As technology grows even more sophisticated, the police will continue to enjoy a significant advantage over targets, so long as privacy expectations do not raise more red flags with the Court.

For Critical Thinking and Discussion

1. How have advances in modern technology expanded or contracted citizens' conceptions of what privacy they actually enjoy? Is it still reasonable to assume that conversations on cell phones remain private? What about email messages and texts? Is anything that you do or write on a social networking site such as Facebook actually private?
2. What steps must an individual take to keep his or her activities private from government?

Perhaps the most controversial aspect of the Fourth Amendment is the mechanism by which it is enforced. Although no specific provision for enforcing civil liberties is provided in the amendment, since its 1961 decision in *Mapp v. Ohio*,[42] the Supreme Court has demanded that all 50 states adhere to the **exclusionary rule**, by which all evidence obtained by police in violation of the Bill of Rights must be "excluded" from admission in a court of law, even if it might have assisted in convicting those accused of committing crimes. Complaints about the exclusionary rule focus on its most likely beneficiaries: those who are factually guilty of committing some wrongdoing and thus have the most to gain from such exclusion. Detractors also complain about the "injustice" of the rule—whenever evidence is thrown out because of a warrantless search by police, "the criminal is to go free because the constable has blundered." Defenders of the rule counter that without a means of excluding such evidence, the government could violate the rights of guilty and innocent individuals alike by conducting the equivalent of fishing expeditions.

Since the 1960s, the Court has modified application of the exclusionary rule somewhat, although it has refused to back down from its central requirements. The most significant of these modifications is the **good faith exception** to the rule, which was first instituted in 1984: if a search warrant is invalid through no fault of the police (e.g., the judge puts the wrong date on the warrant), evidence obtained under that warrant may still be admitted into court. Police may also, under certain circumstances, conduct warrantless searches of a defendant's premises. The allowable circumstances for a warrantless search include any of the following: (1) the search is incidental to a lawful arrest, (2) the defendant has given consent to be searched, (3) the police are in "hot pursuit" of the defendant, and (4) the evidence is in "plain view" of police standing in a place where they have the legal right to be. Police may also briefly stop individuals driving in their cars or conduct a "pat down" of suspicious individuals for weapons—in neither case is a warrant required.

Advances in technology used by the police have invited new types of Fourth Amendment civil liberties claims and a potential reinterpretation of those rights by the U.S. Supreme Court. The testing of defendants for drug or alcohol use through breathalyzer tests and the taking of blood samples may require the police to jump through a series of procedural hoops imposed on them by the state, but no warrant is generally required in either instance when the defendant is in the legitimate custody of the police. Similarly, the DNA testing of defendants has provided a significant breakthrough in the prosecution of difficult cases that lack eyewitnesses or other "hard" evidence of the crime.

On the other hand, the use of thermal imaging scans, which operate somewhat like a video camera showing heat images, was banned by the Supreme Court in *Kyllo v. United States* (2001).[43] The Court held that "where the Government uses a device that is not in general public use, to explore details of the home that would previously have been unknowable without physical intrusion, the surveillance is a 'search' and is presumptively unreasonable without a warrant." And as noted in the **Then & Now** feature, the justices also held in 2018 that government authorities generally must obtain a warrant to gain access to cell tower records that can provide a virtual timeline and map of a person's whereabouts from their cell phone usage.

Recently, some communities have posted cameras at stoplights that produce photographic evidence of traffic violations. Other communities have installed cameras on street corners in busy areas. When used in conjunction

exclusionary rule The legal rule requiring that all evidence illegally obtained by police in violation of the Bill of Rights must be "excluded" from admission in a court of law, where it might have assisted in convicting those accused of committing crimes.

good faith exception An exception to the exclusionary rule stating that if a search warrant is invalid through no fault of the police, evidence obtained under that warrant may still be admitted into court.

Peter Steiner / Alamy Stock Photo

The Syracuse Common Council spent $150,000 on police surveillance cameras such as these. Critics complain that this type of comprehensive surveillance by police violates citizens' privacy rights.

with facial recognition software and computer databanks of convicted criminals, these cameras can provide surveillance capable of instantly detecting the presence of such figures on the street. Officials in Tampa, Florida, have turned to closed-circuit television systems to assist police departments in performing such surveillance of wanted individuals and alert authorities quickly and efficiently of their presence.

Civil libertarians complain that the use of surveillance cameras in general violates many citizens' privacy rights, which they believe extend beyond the privacy of their own homes. As the use of these techniques is broadened—perhaps to facilitate racial profiling or other controversial forms of police investigation—it is certain that even more legal challenges will be waged.

FIFTH AMENDMENT RIGHTS

THE FIFTH AMENDMENT: No person shall be held to answer for a capital, or otherwise infamous crime, unless on a presentment or indictment of a grand jury . . . nor shall any person be subject for the same offense to be twice put in jeopardy of life or limb; nor shall be compelled in any criminal case to be a witness against himself.

Under the Fifth Amendment, the accused enjoy an assortment of rights that may prove crucial to their defense. The requirement that a grand jury, a jury that meets to decide whether the evidence is sufficient to justify a prosecutor's request that a case go to trial, be convened for serious crimes is theoretically significant; it forces prosecutors to convince an initial jury that a defendant should rightfully be forced to go to trial. (Grand juries do not decide on a defendant's guilt or innocence.) In practice, however, the grand jury requirement is rarely much of an obstacle to a skilled prosecutor, who can selectively present evidence to the jury members outside the view of the defendant or the defendant's lawyer. Moreover, because the grand jury requirement was never incorporated through the Fourteenth Amendment, it applies only to federal prosecutors in federal court.[44] The **double jeopardy clause** is a source of much greater protection for defendants: it provides that no defendant may be tried twice for the same crime. Prosecutors must weigh carefully their probability of success at trial and bring forth all the relevant resources at their disposal. If the jury acquits the defendant, the prosecutor cannot try the defendant again. Still, the double jeopardy clause does not stop an altogether different government from retrying the defendant for violating that government's own laws. This occurred in the high-profile case of several white Los Angeles police officers who were accused in 1991 of beating Rodney King, an African American motorist whom they had stopped for a traffic violation. The acquittal of the police set off a series of race riots in Los Angeles. Later, federal charges were brought against the police for violating King's civil rights. At the federal trial, the officers were convicted.

Another provision of the Fifth Amendment is the self-incrimination clause, which prevents individuals from being compelled to testify against themselves. Although originally interpreted to provide protection for defendants only in the courtroom, the self-incrimination clause today offers substantial protection to defendants being questioned by police at the station house or elsewhere. Certainly the clause protects defendants from being coerced or tortured into confessing to crimes. But the Warren court truly changed this area of the law in the now famous case of *Miranda v. Arizona* (1966).[45] In that ruling, the Supreme Court announced the requirement that *Miranda* warnings be read to all defendants in custody before they are questioned by police.

Ernesto Miranda was convicted of the March 1963 kidnapping and rape of an 18-year-old girl in Phoenix, Arizona. Soon after the crime, the police picked up Miranda, who fit the description of the girl's attacker. Officers immediately took him into an interrogation room and told him (falsely) that he had been positively identified by his victim. After two hours of questioning, Miranda confessed. At trial, the defense counsel prodded one of the detectives into admitting that Miranda had never been given the opportunity to seek advice from an attorney prior to his interrogation. Miranda was nevertheless convicted and sentenced to 40 to 60 years in prison. On appeal, the U.S. Supreme Court in 1966 set aside Miranda's conviction. Chief

double jeopardy clause The constitutional protection that those accused of a crime cannot be tried twice for the same crime.

***Miranda* warning** The U.S. Supreme Court's requirement that an individual who is arrested must be read a statement that explains the person's right to remain silent and the right to an attorney.

Justice Warren wrote, "Prior to any questioning, the person must be warned that he has a right to remain silent, that any statement he does make may be used as evidence against him, and that he has a right to the presence of an attorney, either retained or appointed."

Thanks to police drama shows and movies, the *Miranda* warnings are better known to citizens today than almost any other constitutional protections: police must routinely tell suspects being questioned that they have the right to remain silent and the right to a court-appointed attorney, and police must confirm that the suspects understand these rights. Perhaps that's why a more conservative Supreme Court conceded in the case of *Dickerson v. United States* (2000)[46] that *Miranda* has become so "embedded in routine police practice" that the warnings have become "part of our national culture." Thus a failure to read the list of *Miranda* rights to witnesses may still result in any subsequent confession to the police being thrown out of court by virtue of the exclusionary rule.[47]

SIXTH AMENDMENT RIGHTS

THE SIXTH AMENDMENT: *In all criminal prosecutions, the accused shall … have the Assistance of Counsel for his defense.*

Images of beleaguered and confused defendants trying desperately to defend themselves against experienced and well-seasoned prosecutors are now mostly a thing of the past. In 1963, the Supreme Court in *Gideon v. Wainwright*[48] ordered a new trial for an indigent defendant (i.e., one who could not afford legal counsel) who had been ordered by the state of Florida to defend himself in a criminal trial, even though he possessed no legal training. Under prevailing Sixth Amendment standards today, no indigent criminal defendant can be sentenced to jail unless the defendant has been provided with a lawyer at no cost. This constitutional right to the assistance of counsel even extends beyond the trial: a court-appointed lawyer must assist the defendant in preparing the case and in all other hearings and meetings before trial. Some critics of the criminal justice system cite the disparity that often exists between the quality of court-appointed counsel and of paid counsel for well-off defendants. Nevertheless, public defenders' offices have been established all over the country in response to the requirement that indigent defendants be provided with lawyers.

EIGHTH AMENDMENT RIGHTS

THE EIGHTH AMENDMENT: *Excessive bail shall not be required, nor excessive fines imposed, nor cruel and unusual punishments inflicted.*

The Eighth Amendment deals in a limited way with defendants being held for trial. According to the language of the Eighth Amendment, bail, which is an amount of money paid to the court as security against a defendant's illegal flight before trial, may not be excessive. In practice, that provision applies only when bail is proper in the first place; many high-risk defendants are held either to prevent flight or to ensure that they do not cause more harm while on release. In those instances, bail may be denied altogether without any violation of the Constitution.

Far more significant are the concluding words of the Eighth Amendment with respect to "cruel and unusual punishment." No government may impose a cruel and unusual punishment on an individual, but there remains heated debate over what is "cruel and unusual." Traditionally, the clause prohibited only those punishments that even the drafters of the Bill of Rights would have disapproved of—drawing and quartering, beheading, and other forms of extreme torture. In recent times, the Court has added to the mix the requirement of "proportionality," in which serious punishments may not be imposed for relatively minor offenses. Thus, for instance, the Court in *Robinson v. California* (1962) struck down imprisonment for the controversial offense of "being addicted to the use of narcotics" on the ground that the state was punishing someone for an illness.

The Supreme Court currently rejects the premise that all applications of the death penalty are inherently "cruel and unusual." Most modern lawsuits by prisoners on "death row" focus on the manner by which the death sentence has been imposed. Any judge or jury that imposes capital punishment must have the opportunity to consider mitigating circumstances that might generate some sympathy for the accused. Nor can a jury impose a death sentence

bail An amount of money determined by a judge that the accused must pay to a court as security against his or her freedom before trial.

at the same time that it finds the defendant guilty; the defendant's lawyers must be given a chance to argue against imposition of the death penalty without also having to prove the defendant is innocent. Finally, certain defendants may not receive the death penalty. In 2002, the Court in *Atkins v. Virginia* ruled executions impermissible in the case of defendants with an intellectual disability.[49] Then in 2005, the Court also ruled executions impermissible for defendants who committed their crimes while under the age of 18.

Critics of the system claim that so many death penalty cases are held up on appeal that bad luck and randomness are inevitable in the process.[50] Furthermore, advances in DNA testing technology have revealed that some prisoners on death row were innocent of the crime for which they had been sentenced to death. Even in the face of unrelenting popular support for the death penalty, governors in Illinois and Maryland recently announced a "moratorium" on executions in their respective states, to be continued as long as the process by which death sentences are determined remains so riddled with errors.

4-5 THE MODERN RIGHT TO PRIVACY

Perhaps no single constitutional right garnered more controversial attention during the second half of the twentieth century than the right to have an abortion. Unlike all the other rights mentioned so far in this chapter, however, neither the specific right to abortion nor the more general right to privacy is explicitly referred to in the Constitution or in the amendments to the Constitution. The right to privacy is thus often referred to as an unwritten or "unenumerated" right. The Ninth Amendment counsels against dismissing such rights offhand. It reads: "The enumeration in the Constitution of certain rights, shall not be construed to deny or disparage others retained by the people." In other words, the fact that other rights such as freedom of speech are written down in the Bill of Rights does not mean that the Constitution doesn't also recognize certain unwritten rights.

The recognition of unstated rights in the Constitution raises difficult questions, such as how to justify recognizing certain unenumerated rights but not others. In 1965, the Supreme Court stepped into this controversy with its decision in *Griswold v. Connecticut*,[51] when it invalidated an 1879 Connecticut law prohibiting the dissemination of information about and the sale of contraceptives. Seven of the nine justices ruled that although the right to birth control is not explicitly mentioned in the Constitution, several provisions of the Bill of Rights (the First, Third, Fourth, and Fifth) and the Fourteenth Amendment, taken together, suggest that these provisions create a "zone of privacy" that includes within it the right to decide whether or not to bear a child. Although the Supreme Court's methods were considered highly speculative, widespread acceptance of birth control devices allowed the Supreme Court to avoid controversy in the years following the decision.[52]

No such sidestepping of heated controversy was possible in 1973, when the Supreme Court formally recognized the constitutional right to abortion in *Roe v. Wade*.[53] By the early 1970s, nearly 15 states had passed liberal abortion laws, but lawyers for Norma McCorvey (she used the pseudonym of "Jane Roe" for purposes of her lawsuit) argued that the decision to end a pregnancy was a constitutional right that *all 50 states* must adhere to. McCorvey herself had been unable to secure a legal abortion in Texas and so eventually gave birth and put her baby up for adoption. The Supreme Court agreed to take her case and rule on the general constitutionality of abortion restrictions.

In ruling in McCorvey's favor, the Supreme Court affirmed that the Constitution recognizes a right to privacy in general—and thus a right to abortion more specifically—even though neither of those rights is ever spelled out explicitly. Such a right is not absolute throughout the term of the pregnancy, however. The author of the opinion, Justice Harry Blackmun, divided the pregnancy into three stages as part of a highly controversial *trimester framework*. During the first trimester, a woman's right to end her pregnancy is absolute. During the second trimester, the right is nearly absolute, although the government has the right to restrict abortions that might pose threats to a woman's health. Finally, in the third trimester (when the fetus is potentially viable), the state government is allowed to impose any abortion restrictions on the mother, so long as they do not limit efforts to protect the life or health of the mother.[54]

The number of legal abortions that occurred in the United States rose dramatically in the years immediately following *Roe v. Wade*. The decision also unleashed a fury of controversy from anti-abortion interest groups and conservative lawmakers. The election of Ronald Reagan to the presidency in 1980 and his reelection in 1984 set the stage for *Roe v. Wade's* weakening; as a candidate for high office, Reagan had specifically targeted *Roe v. Wade* as a case of illegitimate judicial activism and had promised to nominate Supreme Court justices who would overturn the controversial decision. Reagan's more conservative Supreme Court appointments began to make their presence known during the late 1980s, when increasingly severe restrictions on abortion were upheld by the Court.

In 1992, the Supreme Court overhauled *Roe v. Wade's* controversial trimester framework in *Planned Parenthood v. Casey*.[55] Although the Court did not specifically overturn *Roe*, the justices replaced the trimester framework with a less stringent *undue burden test*: does the restriction at issue—regardless of what trimester it affects—*unduly burden* a woman's right to privacy under the Constitution? One example of this new constitutional test at work can be found in the Court's approach to state-mandated 24-hour waiting periods for abortions. Under *Roe v. Wade*, the requirement that a woman wait for an abortion in either of the first two trimesters would have been unconstitutional. Yet in *Casey*, the Court held that such a waiting period does not unduly burden the woman's right to privacy. Other regulations that have been upheld under the *Casey* framework include the requirement that minors seek permission from a parent or a court before having an abortion and the requirement that women seeking abortions be provided information about the specific medical effects an abortion will have on the fetus.

Not all abortion restrictions are allowed under this new framework. In *Casey*, the Supreme Court invalidated a requirement that women notify their spouses of their intention to have abortions. Yet many more provisions restricting abortion have been upheld since 1992 under the less restrictive *Casey* doctrine. In *Gonzales v. Carhart* (2007),[56] the Supreme Court upheld the Partial Birth Abortion Act of 2003, which effectively banned the use of the "intact dilation and extraction" abortion procedure, most often performed during the second trimester of pregnancy. By contrast, the Court more recently held that laws which place substantial obstacles in the path of women seeking abortions may be unconstitutional if those obstacles cannot be defended on clear medical or other legitimate grounds.

Once the unwritten right to privacy became a reality in constitutional law, it was inevitable that citizens might try to claim other unwritten rights implicating privacy in the same fashion. Although most efforts to expand the right to privacy beyond abortion and birth control have met with limited success, the Court has not always shut the door on these claims. In 1986, the Court held that a Georgia law that criminalized same-sex acts was constitutional. Seventeen years later in the case of *Lawrence v. Texas*,[57] the Court reversed itself, holding that a Texas law making it a crime for two people of the same sex to engage in certain types of intimate sexual conduct did in fact violate the individual's right to due process. (The Court treated the right to same-sex marriage as an issue of equal protection; that subject is discussed at greater length in Chapter 5.)

In the 1990s, the highly visible prosecutions of Dr. Jack Kevorkian for helping terminally ill patients end their lives brought added attention to the issue of physician-assisted suicide. On April 13, 1999, Kevorkian, a retired pathologist, was sentenced to jail in Michigan for helping a terminally ill man die by direct injection, a form of voluntary euthanasia. Kevorkian, labeled by many of his opponents as "Dr. Death," had already acknowledged publicly that he had helped at least 90 other people to die by assisted suicide in Michigan between 1990 and 1997. Do terminally ill patients have the right to end their lives and, if so, can a licensed physician assist them in doing so? Although the Court has been willing to recognize a right of terminally ill patients to end their medical treatment, it has steadfastly refused to extend that privilege to the active termination of one's life. In 1997, the Supreme Court held that no such constitutional right exists.

Arming Teachers behind the Schoolhouse Door

In response to incidents of gun violence on college campuses, the Texas state legislature in 2015 passed a law allowing licensed gun owners to carry concealed handguns in classrooms, libraries, and other campus buildings. President Trump has offered White House support for teachers to carry licensed weapons in high schools, middle schools, and even some elementary schools. Does the constitutionally guaranteed right to possess a firearm extend to teachers seeking to protect themselves and their students in the classroom? In more than half of the 50 states, adults who legally own guns are not prohibited from carrying them in public schools, and in seven of those states, teachers and staff are explicitly empowered to do so. In most cases, they do not have to inform principals, other teachers, or parents that they have done so. School administrations, of course, can decide to gather the information from their employees, but they may decide not to disclose the information to anyone else. Consider that since the Utah legislature in 2004 specifically authorized teachers to carry guns in classrooms, no fatal K–12 school shootings have occurred in that state. Still, some parent groups argue that guns in classrooms present more risk than the potential for reward.

A sign in English and Spanish on the grounds of Lyndon Baines Johnson High School in Austin, Texas, warns of a prohibition against weapons on school grounds.

Robert Daemmrich Photography Inc / Getty Images

For Critical Thinking and Discussion

1. Do you think the Second Amendment right to bear arms extends to teachers who teach in K–12 public schools? Why or why not?

2. If arming teachers reduces the number of violent incidents that take place in schools, does the reward justify the potential risks?

3. Does the government have a compelling reason to prohibit teachers from bringing lawfully owned firearms into schools? What reason could they offer?

Yet the Supreme Court also indicated that states are free to legalize physician-assisted suicide for terminally ill patients who are suffering significantly. Since then, "physician-assisted death" has been effectively legalized in eight jurisdictions: California, Colorado, District of Columbia, Hawaii, Montana, Oregon, Vermont, and Washington. Most of these states specifically distinguish the legal act of "medical aid in dying" from the act of suicide, which may lead to penalties for those who attempt it. Physician-assisted suicide now enjoys widespread support. According to a 2017 poll from Gallup, 73 percent of Americans support laws allowing patients to seek the assistance of a physician in ending their life.[58] Even so, it remains illegal in a clear majority of states.

Summary

4-1 The Bill of Rights: Origins and Evolution

- Civil liberties are rights that government cannot deny to citizens, whereas civil rights are owed to members of certain groups that afford them equal treatment under the law. The framers guaranteed ratification of the proposed constitution by promising that Congress would propose a "bill of rights" protected from intrusion by the federal government; not until the mid-twentieth century did the U.S. Supreme Court, through a process known as incorporation, use the Fourteenth Amendment's due process clause to require that state governments uphold most of these protections as well.

4-2 Freedom of Religion and the Establishment Clause

- The free exercise clause arguably bans the government from forcing adherents of a certain religion to engage in activities that would otherwise violate their religious beliefs, except through neutral, generally applicable laws. The establishment clause prohibits the government from enacting any law "respecting an establishment of religion"; in recent decades this has led to a strict separation between church and state on some issues, while allowing significant accommodations to religion in other cases.

4-3 Free Expression Rights

- The First Amendment rights of free speech and press are "preferred freedoms" that enjoy heightened protection under the Constitution because free expression promotes the marketplace of ideas, acts as a watchdog on government, and advances the capacity for individuals to create ideas and improve society.
- Speech includes such activities as flag-burning (referred to as symbolic speech) and other forms of expressive conduct, all of which enjoy a high level of protection from the courts. By contrast, the Supreme Court has exempted obscenity, libel, fighting words, and other lesser-value speech from this heightened level of protection. Meanwhile, the press is afforded significant protection from libel suits (which are exceedingly difficult to prosecute) and from prior restraints, granted only under extremely rare conditions.

4-4 The Right to Bear Arms and the Rights of the Criminally Accused

- The Constitution protects the right of individuals to possess a firearm, although government retains the power to enact a broad range of firearms laws, including reasonable restrictions on possession by felons, or in sensitive places such as schools or government buildings.
- The Fourth Amendment protects the right of citizens to be free from unreasonable searches and seizures; with some exceptions, a warrant (issued only based on probable cause) is necessary for a valid search. Additional rights of the accused are articulated in the Fifth Amendment, including the double jeopardy clause, the grand jury requirement, and the self-incrimination clause. The Supreme Court has ruled that police must read the *Miranda* warnings to anyone who is arrested, which indicates not only the right to remain silent but also the right to an attorney. (A failure to read *Miranda* rights to a suspect in custody may lead to a confession being excluded as evidence at trial.)
- A more comprehensive right to counsel is protected by the Sixth Amendment, and the Eighth Amendment protects against the government imposing excessive bail requirements or cruel and unusual punishment.

4-5 The Modern Right to Privacy

- The Supreme Court has recognized a general right to privacy under the due process clause, which includes a qualified right to abortion and a limited right to die. *Roe v. Wade* was the 1973 case that first established abortion rights under the Constitution; however, a more conservative Supreme Court in recent years has allowed the states to place more restrictions on abortion rights, so long as those restrictions are justified on some medical or other ground beyond simply the desire to reduce the number of abortions. And although the Court has recognized the right of terminally ill patients to end their medical treatment, it has refused to extend that privilege to the active termination of one's life. By contrast, the Court has recognized greater rights of sexual privacy in recent years.

Key Terms

bail (p. 77)

bill of attainder (p. 73)

civil liberties (p. 59)

double jeopardy clause (p. 76)

establishment clause (p. 64)

ex post facto law (p. 73)

exclusionary rule (p. 75)

free exercise clause (p. 62)

good faith exception (p. 75)

incorporation (p. 61)

Katz test (p. 73)

Lemon test (p. 66)

libel (p. 68)

Miranda warning (p. 76)

prior restraint (p. 69)

SLAPS test (p. 70)

symbolic speech (p. 71)

warrant (p. 73)

5

CIVIL RIGHTS, EQUALITY, AND SOCIAL MOVEMENTS

Protesters walk during the Women's March on Washington, January 21, 2017.

IN THE ABSTRACT, the word *equality* sits alongside lofty terms such as *liberty, freedom,* and *justice* as values that underlie American political culture. Unfortunately, when it comes to settling on a formal definition of equality, no consensus exists. "All men are created equal" was the phrase Thomas Jefferson penned in the Declaration of Independence of 1776. But Jefferson never intended that document to extend to African American slaves, at least not in the short run. When Abraham Lincoln warned in 1859 that "those who deny freedom to others, deserve it not for themselves," the future president of the United States did not consider the lot of women in American society, who at that time were not yet guaranteed the freedom to vote or own property, among other rights. As with any other abstract ideal, we must fully define *equality* and appreciate its implications in order to understand all that it encompasses.

5-1 TYPES OF EQUALITY

References to different types of equality tend to appear again and again in discussions of American politics; political equality, social equality, and economic equality are among the most common.

Political equality generally refers to a condition in which members of different groups possess substantially the same rights to participate actively in the political system. These rights include voting, running for office, and formally petitioning the government for redress of grievances. In a democracy, the rights to free speech, to free press, and to a quality education may also be considered necessary elements of political equality, as those who are denied such rights often are less able to exercise influence over the political process in any meaningful way. In the years immediately following the Civil War, some moderates in Congress argued that if freed slaves were simply given formal political equality, other benefits and privileges would inevitably follow. Reality quickly proved otherwise, as even African Americans in the North who were able to exercise their right to vote were generally unable to influence the political process.

Social equality extends beyond the granting of political rights; it refers additionally to equality and fair treatment within the various institutions in society, both public and private, that serve the public at large. Social equality calls for a sameness of treatment in stores, theaters, restaurants, hotels, and public transportation facilities, among many other operations open to the public. Jim Crow laws passed in the South during the late nineteenth century segregated many of these institutions, thus denying social equality to racial and ethnic minorities.

Economic equality remains the most controversial form of equality. To some, society's responsibility to promote economic equality requires only that it provide equality of economic "opportunity," by which different groups enjoy substantially the same rights to enter contracts, marry, purchase and sell property, and otherwise compete for resources in society. To others, economic equality extends beyond equality of economic opportunity to something approaching an "equality of results." Whichever meaning one gives to the term, economic equality has been exceedingly difficult to achieve. Although the government has introduced a graduated income tax and other resource-leveling measures during the past century to improve economic opportunities for the poor, large variances in the quality of education afforded to different groups continue to render economic equality an elusive ideal.

The term civil rights refers to those positive rights, whether political, social, or economic, conferred by the government on individuals or groups that had previously been denied them. What type of equality does the guarantee of civil rights promote? Immediately after the Civil War, civil rights legislation that provided for greater social equality (equal accommodations in hotels, restaurants, trains, and other public facilities) was struck down as unconstitutional by the U.S. Supreme Court. As a result, the package of civil rights granted to freed slaves included only limited political rights, including the right to vote. In the late 1950s and 1960s, renewed efforts to guarantee equality in all areas of American life led to the civil rights movement.

Many civil rights battles in American history have been waged by members of racial and ethnic minority groups, women, people with disabilities, seniors, and the LGBTQ community who have also sought the equality denied them. The Constitution of the United States and the amendments to it have provided a framework for these groups to use to win equality. As a result, the meaning of civil rights has been significantly expanded both in the scope of its protection and in the variety of groups who seek its guarantees.

5-2 THE STRUGGLE FOR EQUALITY: APPROACHES AND TACTICS

The methods and tactics various groups use to achieve equality have evolved since the end of the Civil War. Initially, the battle over what constituted the most effective means of fostering change—at least in the context of challenging racial discrimination—pitted two competing philosophies against each other. Booker T. Washington, who founded Tuskegee Normal and Industrial Institute (today Tuskegee University) in Alabama in 1881, advocated a philosophy of *accommodation*, which promoted vocational education for African Americans and opposed confrontation with the mostly white power structure in place in post–Civil War America. Washington urged his fellow African Americans to accept existing conditions, even to the point

political equality
A condition in which members of different groups possess substantially the same rights to participate actively in the political system. In the United States, these rights include voting, running for office, petitioning the government for redress of grievances, free speech, free press, and the access to an education.

social equality
Equality and fair treatment of all groups within the various institutions in society, both public and private, that serve the public at large, including in stores, theaters, restaurants, hotels, and public transportation facilities, among many other operations open to the public.

economic equality
May be defined as providing all groups the equality of opportunity for economic success, or as the equality of results. In the United States, the latter has been the more common understanding of economic equality.

civil rights Those positive rights, whether political, social, or economic, conferred by the government on individuals or groups.

of tolerating racial segregation and all but surrendering the newly won right to vote. According to his philosophy, engaging in law-abiding practices and standing by former white oppressors would best prepare African Americans for the exercise of the franchise. Washington's philosophy of accommodation fit comfortably within the dominant conservative political and economic structure of his time. Although some critics charged him with accepting second-class citizenship for his race, Washington was perhaps the most powerful and influential figure in African American affairs until his death in 1915.[1]

Washington's passive approach contrasted with the philosophy of *agitation*, which challenged racial discrimination and injustice through various forms of political activity. Among Washington's contemporaries, the most widely recognized proponent of this

Representative Karen Bass (D-CA) speaks at the Smithsonian Museum, November 2018 in Washington, DC.

alternative approach was W. E. B. Du Bois. At the beginning of the twentieth century, Du Bois and his associates proposed a specific platform of legal, political, and social reforms to achieve equality for African Americans.[2] Their demands included the right to vote and an immediate end to all segregation. Agitation eventually replaced accommodation as the dominant mode by which African Americans and other groups sought equality in twentieth-century America. New debates emerged, however, over what would be the most effective means and methods for achieving these reforms.

The following are the tactics that various groups have used to seek their civil rights:

Working within the Political System. Some groups have used the political process to implement reforms to end discrimination. In recent decades, for example, African Americans have used their substantial power as a voting bloc to influence the outcome of some elections. Various groups have expanded their influence more directly over public policies and programs by lobbying and petitioning government officials; in some cases, members of these groups have been elected to high public office, giving them a place at the table of political power.

Litigation. When the political arena fails to provide adequate remedies to discrimination, a lawsuit brought before a court may afford a better opportunity for success. Founded in 1909 for the purpose of ensuring the political, educational, social, and economic equality of rights of all Americans, the National Association for the Advancement of Colored People (NAACP) focused its efforts on legal challenges to discrimination and segregation because the political arena had offered inadequate remedies. Civil rights legislation in particular had proven ineffective, with southern state legislatures either ignoring or circumventing the laws. The NAACP and the Mexican American Legal Defense and Education Fund, among other groups, won numerous legal battles that gradually broke down racial and ethnic barriers in education and elsewhere. These efforts culminated with high court decisions such as *Brown v. Board of Education* (1954),[3] which ordered desegregation of public schools. In subsequent years, women's groups, people with disabilities, and other victims of discrimination have similarly turned to the courts for remedies to discriminatory practices.

Legal Boycott. The organized refusal to buy, sell, or use certain goods or to perform certain services has long been a tool in economic battles waged between employers and unions. Adopting this tactic for use in the war on racial discrimination, African American citizens of Montgomery, Alabama, refused to ride the city's buses for more than a year in the mid-1950s; their efforts drained the city's public transportation budget and ultimately forced city officials to desegregate the bus system. In 2003,

Brown v. Board of Education (1954)
The 1954 U.S. Supreme Court decision that declared school segregation to be unconstitutional.

women's rights organizations discouraged some companies from sponsoring the Masters Golf Tournament held at the all-male Augusta National Golf Club in Augusta, Georgia.

Civil Disobedience. Sometimes citizens resort to passive resistance to what they see as an unjust government policy or law by openly refusing to obey it. Such a tactic may result in arrests, fines, or even jail time for those who practice it. Still, civil disobedience may also call attention to a group's plight in an especially effective way. The Reverend Martin Luther King Jr., who had studied the methods used by Mohandas Gandhi of India and other nonviolent protestors, applied these methods to the civil rights movement in the American South.

5-3 THE STRUGGLE FOR EQUALITY: RACE, ETHNICITY, AND CIVIL RIGHTS

The metaphor of the "melting pot" evokes an image of cultural assimilation in America achieved by the fusion of different nationalities, ethnicities, and cultures into a greater whole. In recent decades, some have rejected the melting pot image in favor of *multiculturalism*, a theory that views ethnic and racial groups as maintaining their own cultural distinctions and integrity within American society. The reality of the immigrant experience in America probably resides somewhere in between these two competing theories. Regardless, prejudice, stereotyping, and other discriminatory practices targeting racial and ethnic minorities have been a persistent theme throughout American history, and any rendering of how American society has evolved must take careful account of that reality.

Colonists who supported the American Revolution trumpeted the notion of equality as a means of justifying their war with England. Yet, when the U.S. Constitution was drafted in 1787, the document said nothing about such a call to equality, nor did the Bill of Rights (ratified in 1791) guarantee to all citizens "equal protection of the law." The period following the Revolution offered equality primarily to property-owning white men. Throughout the North, African Americans were denied the right to vote and numerous other economic and social privileges enjoyed by whites. In the South, the institution of slavery thrived for more than a half-century after the Constitution was ratified.

Meanwhile, immigrants from a multitude of Spanish-speaking nations, Asia, and elsewhere were treated as second-class citizens as well, suffering especially intense forms of discrimination both economically as well as in society as a whole.

RACIAL DISCRIMINATION: FROM SLAVERY TO RECONSTRUCTION

The organized antislavery movement in the United States began in the late eighteenth century as an effort to eradicate slavery through progressive elimination. Advocates of gradual emancipation believed that by preventing the extension of slavery to new areas and relocating emancipated slaves to areas outside the United States, slavery would eventually die out. Opposed to gradual emancipation were the abolitionists, who sought the immediate emancipation of all slaves. A leader of the abolitionist movement was William Lloyd Garrison, who founded the antislavery periodical *The Liberator* in 1831. It is noteworthy, however, that even extreme abolitionists such as Garrison believed that the "fatal characteristic" of slavery was that it denied African Americans the basic legal rights to own property, enter into contracts, and testify in court. Many abolitionists at the time did *not* believe that emancipation automatically entitled freed slaves to the right to vote or serve on juries. Even among some of the most ardent advocates of equality before the Civil War, a sharp distinction was often drawn between economic rights—which they felt African Americans were entitled to—and basic political rights including suffrage, which were somehow not viewed as natural entitlements.

Neither conception of civil rights for slaves gained much favor in the South, where the economy of the plantation system depended on slave labor. The Southerners' approach to racial equality was perhaps best summed up by Chief Justice Roger Taney of Maryland, who in the landmark Supreme Court case of *Dred Scott v. Sandford* (1857)[4] wrote that blacks were "so far inferior that they had no rights which the white man was bound to respect." The initial rhetoric surrounding the outbreak of the Civil War in 1861 focused on issues such as states' rights and territorial expansion in addition to slavery. The Emancipation Proclamation issued by President Lincoln in 1863 declared the freedom of all slaves in states fighting the Union and allowed blacks to enlist in the Union Army. By the end of the struggle in 1865, the war was essentially transformed into a battle over the end of the institution of slavery.

With the Union victory in the Civil War, the complete emancipation of African Americans after the war was a foregone conclusion. Former slaves were able to legally marry, worship as they wished, and migrate to different parts of the country. But the years following the Civil War—normally referred to as the Reconstruction era (1865–1877) in American history—proved a mixed blessing for the newly freed slaves.[5] The Civil War Amendments to the Constitution granted African Americans the rights of citizenship. The Republican-controlled Congress hoped that these three amendments would institutionalize freedom for the former slaves and protect their rights from being undermined by future generations.

- **Thirteenth Amendment** (ratified 1865) banished slavery from all U.S. states/territories.
- **Fourteenth Amendment** (ratified 1868) granted full U.S. and state citizenship to all people born or naturalized in the United States and guaranteed to each person "the equal protection of the laws."
- **Fifteenth Amendment** (1870) forbade the denial or abridgement of the right to vote by any government on account of race.

During the Reconstruction era, many freed slaves were successful in getting on ballots in the former Confederate states—in all, 22 African Americans were elected to the House and 1 (Hiram Revels of Mississippi) was elected to the Senate during the latter part of the nineteenth century. African American participation in Congress trailed off at the beginning of the twentieth century, however, because restrictions on the franchise curtailed the political viability of most black candidates. No African American served in either house of Congress for most of the first three decades of the twentieth century, and just four served in the House up to 1954.

Although African Americans achieved some gains during Reconstruction, the Reconstruction-era generation posed the greatest threat to those civil rights victories. The Fourteenth Amendment had been proposed in part to negate the infamous Black Codes passed by the Southern states, which denied African Americans numerous economic and social rights. However, in the *Slaughterhouse Cases* (1873),[6] a conservative U.S. Supreme Court narrowly defined the scope of rights protected by the Fourteenth Amendment, holding that the great body of civil rights still lay under the protection of state governments, not the U.S. Constitution. The Civil Rights Act of 1875 attempted to ensure the social and political rights of freed slaves by, among other provisions, prohibiting discrimination in public accommodations. The Supreme Court invalidated the act in the *Civil Rights Cases* (1883),[7] ruling that whereas the Constitution prohibits the states from discriminating by race against certain civil rights, it does not protect the invasion of such civil rights by private individuals unaided by state authority. Therefore, privately owned restaurants and hotels could freely discriminate on the basis of race without violating the Constitution.

This judicial gutting of federal civil rights guarantees opened the way for numerous abuses of freed slaves once the federal government's military occupation of the South ended in 1877. Although the Fifteenth Amendment had given African American men the right to vote, the Southern states imposed new barriers to disenfranchise the former slaves and other people of color, which included:

- **poll taxes**: a fee a voter had to pay before being allowed to vote.
- **literacy tests**: prospective voters had to pass a test of literacy in order to vote.
- **property requirements**: demanded some form of property-owning and residency documentation to be eligible to vote.
- **grandfather clause requirement**: stated that to be eligible to vote, one's grandfather had to have voted.
- **white-only primaries**: restricted African Americans and other people of color from participating in crucial party primaries.

Thirteenth Amendment (ratified in 1865) Banished slavery from all states and U.S. territories.

Fourteenth Amendment The 1868 amendment that granted full U.S. and state citizenship to all people born or naturalized in the United States and guaranteed to each person "the equal protection of the laws."

Fifteenth Amendment The 1870 amendment to the Constitution that guaranteed the franchise regardless of race, color, or previous condition of servitude.

poll tax Fee a voter had to pay before being allowed to vote.

literacy test The requirement that individuals prove that they can read and write before being allowed to vote.

property requirements Need for some form of property-owning and residency documentation to be eligible to vote.

grandfather clause requirement Need for proof that one's grandfather had previously voted in order to be eligible to vote.

white-only primaries Restricted political party primaries that did not allow African Americans and other people of color to participate in choosing nominees for the general election.

Discrimination against racial and ethnic minorities in all areas of public life soon became the norm. The Ku Klux Klan intimidated or threatened African Americans to keep them under control, sometimes backing up their threats with beatings, arson, or murder. White vigilante groups resorted to lynching in an effort to restore white supremacy and deny blacks their rights. Thus, while post–Civil War no longer allowed for slavery, many could hardly be considered equal citizens under the laws in place during the latter parts of the nineteenth century.

OTHER FORMS OF DISCRIMINATION IN NINETEENTH- AND EARLY TWENTIETH-CENTURY AMERICA

Other groups also struggled during this post-bellum period, suffering terrible hardships at the hands of the government and private groups. Hispanics—many of whom were descended from Mexicans living in the Southwest along the Mexican border when it became part of the United States in the 1840s—were among the earliest victims of governmental discrimination. Even after immigration laws were tightened in the 1890s, hundreds of thousands of Mexicans continued to enter the United States both legally and illegally, drawn by opportunities in farming, mining, and other industries. Unfortunately, beginning in 1885, California and other states formally segregated Hispanic students from white students in schools; this pattern continued up through the 1950s.

While white Americans migrated west during this period, millions of Native Americans were herded onto reservations according to a removal policy backed by the federal government. By a federal law passed in 1871, the government no longer agreed to recognize Native American tribes or nations as independent powers capable of entering treaties with the United States—all future tribal affairs were to be managed by the federal government without tribal consent. With passage of the Dawes Severalty Act in 1887, the U.S. government divided tribal lands still in existence among individual Indians who renounced their tribal holdings, further undermining tribal cultures and structures.

Although certain Native American tribes received piecemeal U.S. citizenship beginning in the 1850s and the Dawes Act granted citizenship to those who ceded their tribal holdings, the class of Native Americans as a whole was not admitted to full citizenship until 1924, nearly 60 years after freed slaves had been afforded that same privilege. The federal government's attempt to undo the tribal structure did not produce widespread assimilation of Indians into American society as proponents of the Dawes Act intended; many chose to remain on reservations in an attempt to protect their culture from outside influences.

Asian Americans were also victims of prejudice. While immigrants from Japan and China in particular supplied much of the labor for building U.S. railroads in the nineteenth century, most were excluded from labor unions and denied other civil rights in the process. In the years that followed, the government enacted several immigration acts specifically designed to limit or prevent Asian immigration. For example, the Chinese Exclusion Act, passed in 1882, prohibited Chinese laborers from immigrating and denied U.S. citizenship to Chinese living in the United States. Later, the 1907 Gentleman's Agreement with Japan prohibited the immigration of Japanese laborers; the National Origins Act of 1924 then banned *all* Asians from further immigration to the United States. In many West Coast cities, Asian children were segregated into separate public schools in San Francisco, and the state of California restricted Japanese immigrants' rights to own farmland.

RACIAL AND ETHNIC SEGREGATION AND GOVERNMENTAL BARRIERS TO EQUALITY

Following the Civil War, some groups were able to use public accommodations as long as they could afford to pay for them. By the turn of the twentieth century, however, growing racial tensions, exacerbated by urbanization and industrialization, led to racial segregation throughout America. The southern states enacted Jim Crow laws, which required segregation of whites and nonwhites in public schools, railroads, buses, restaurants, hotels, theaters, and other public facilities. The laws excluded nonwhites from militias and denied them certain education and welfare services. When Homer Plessy (described in court filings as being

Jim Crow laws
Laws used by some southern states that required segregation of nonwhites and whites in public schools, railroads, buses, restaurants, hotels, theaters, and other public facilities. The laws excluded nonwhites from militias and denied them certain education and welfare services.

"seven-eighths Caucasian and one-eighth African blood") was arrested on a Louisiana train for refusing to leave a seat in a coach section designated for whites, he challenged the Louisiana law requiring segregated railroad cars, arguing that the law violated the equal protection clause of the Fourteenth Amendment. In *Plessy v. Ferguson* (1896),[8] the Supreme Court upheld the Louisiana law on the theory that as long as the accommodations between the racially segregated cars were equal, the equal protection clause was not violated. The Court's ruling established the constitutionality of racial segregation according to the "separate but equal" doctrine. To the argument that such an enforced separation of the two races stamps the colored race with a "badge of inferiority," the Supreme Court replied matter-of-factly, "If this be so, it is not by reason of anything found in the act, but solely because the colored race *chooses* to put that construction upon it."

Civil rights leaders responded to the spread of racial segregation throughout the United States in markedly different ways. Initially, Booker T. Washington's accommodationist philosophy prevailed. W. E. B. Du Bois, by contrast, advocated direct and militant challenges to segregation. Perhaps the greatest breakthrough against segregation occurred through the legal arm of the organization that Du Bois helped found: the NAACP. Beginning in the late 1930s, NAACP lawyers Charles Houston and Thurgood Marshall began attacking the legal basis for segregation in the courts.[9] As detailed in Table 5-1, they won their first battles against state-mandated segregation in institutions of higher education, as the Supreme Court eventually recognized that separate accommodations in law schools and colleges had failed to meet the essential requirements of equality mandated by the Fourteenth Amendment.

Plessy v. Ferguson (1896) The Supreme Court case that upheld a Louisiana segregation law on the theory that as long as the accommodations between the racially segregated facilities were equal, the equal protection clause was not violated. The Court's ruling effectively established the constitutionality of racial segregation and the notion of "separate but equal."

TABLE 5-1

Tracking the Legal Assault on Racially Segregated Education

U.S. Supreme Court Case	Description
Missouri ex rel. Gaines v. Canada (1938)	Invalidated the exclusion of black students from the University of Missouri's School of Law absent some other provision for their legal training.
Mendez et al v. Westminster School District of Orange County (1947)	Ruled the school segregation of Mexican students into separate schools was unconstitutional.
Sipuel v. Board of Regents of University of Oklahoma (1948)	Rejected Oklahoma's attempt to create a separate law school for blacks by roping off a section of the state capitol for black law students and assigning three law teachers to them; such a form of separation failed to comply with the constitutional requirement of "equality."
Sweatt v. Painter (1950)	Invalidated Texas's attempt to create an alternative to the University of Texas law school for blacks because any such alternative would be inherently different in the reputation of its faculty, the experience of its administration, the position and influence of its alumni, its standing in the community, and so on.
McLaurin v. Oklahoma State Regents (1950)	Rejected as "unequal," Oklahoma's attempt to provide graduate education to a black student by making him sit in a classroom surrounded by a railing marked "reserved for colored," assigning him a segregated desk in the library, and requiring him to sit separately from whites in the cafeteria.
Brown v. Board of Education (1954)	Rejected the "separate but equal" doctrine altogether, declaring that in the field of public education, "separate educational facilities are inherently unequal."
Hernandez v. Texas (1954)	Held that Mexican Americans and all other racial or national groups in the United States enjoyed the right to equal protection under the Fourteenth Amendment of the U.S. Constitution.
Cooper v. Aaron (1958)	Condemned the attempts of the Little Rock, Arkansas, school board to postpone desegregation efforts, ruling that no scheme of racial discrimination against black schoolchildren can stand if "there is state participation through any arrangement, management, funds, or property."

World War II eventually proved to be a rallying point for many in the ongoing battle against racial and ethnic discrimination. Perhaps the most notorious incident of state-sponsored discrimination occurred in 1942, when the U.S. government—in response to the Japanese bombing of Pearl Harbor—forcibly relocated 110,000 Japanese Americans to inland internment camps and seized their property. The Supreme Court upheld the internment policy in 1944, perpetuating an especially egregious brand of racial discrimination committed against legal residents of the country, including more than 60,000 legal U.S. citizens. National security concerns used to justify the policy at that time were later exposed as essentially baseless. Other racial and ethnic minorities returned from the fighting in Europe to find their home country of the United States far less enlightened on race issues. Nor did they fail to see the irony that Adolf Hitler's defeated Third Reich had been built on a theory of racist superiority that still held sway in large portions of America.

Some federal courts led the way in ending ethnic segregation within the public schools soon after the war had concluded. In *Mendez v. Westminster* (1947),[10] the U.S. Court of Appeals for the Ninth Circuit upheld a lower court order striking down the policy of Orange County, California, to segregate Hispanic children into separate schools in what was the first ruling by a U.S. court in favor of desegregation. Though the lower court found the policy to be an unconstitutional denial of equal protection, the Court of Appeals did not go that far—rather, it held that the segregationist policy was invalid because it had not been specifically authorized by state law. Still, the case offered hope that courts might be willing to take on legislatures and school boards that proved equally determined to protect the "separate but equal" doctrine for as long as possible.

Following in those footsteps, the NAACP utilized its own incremental approach to eliminate racial segregation in education. Its efforts eventually reached their climax in 1954 with the Supreme Court's landmark decision in *Brown v. Board of Education*. Chief Justice Earl Warren, writing for a unanimous Supreme Court, held that racial segregation in any facet of public education constituted a denial of equal protection by the laws. Recognizing the psychological harms of segregation on racial and ethnic minority children, the Court declared that segregated schools were "inherently unequal."

The *Brown* decision also confirmed that in all future cases related to racial and ethnic discrimination, the Court would apply a standard of strict scrutiny, a level of judicial review that requires the government to prove that the racial classification of the law or practice in question is "narrowly tailored" to meet a "compelling state interest." What precisely does this mean? At a minimum, there should be no less-restrictive alternative means available for achieving the government's objectives, and those objectives should stand among the most necessary that may be pursued by any government. Many legal scholars and judges say the strict scrutiny standard tends to invalidate nearly all government laws and programs. In the years following *Brown*, the courts would apply the standard of strict scrutiny in decisions on segregated public swimming pools, police forces, and laws banning interracial marriages.

A year after handing down the *Brown* decision, the Supreme Court declared that its implementation should proceed "with all deliberate speed." Despite that decree, many local school boards resisted desegregation. The school board of Little Rock, Arkansas, adopted a plan for "phased integration" over a 10-year period, spurring more lawsuits to speed up the process. Undeterred, Arkansas governor Orval Faubus declared that no "*Brown* decisions" enjoyed "the force of law" in his state. In one famous instance, he placed soldiers of the Arkansas National Guard at Little Rock's Central High School to stop African American students from entering the school. Mississippi governor Ross Barnett refused to comply with court desegregation orders on so many occasions that a federal court held him in contempt. Alabama governor George Wallace blocked a University of Alabama doorway, refusing to allow black students to pass through, in 1963. One hundred members of Congress signed a "Southern Manifesto" declaring their intention to use "all lawful means" to reverse the *Brown* decision. On several occasions, the Supreme Court was forced to reassert its authority over state governments. In *Cooper v. Aaron* (1958),[11] for example, the Court held that the rights of African American students could "neither be nullified openly and directly by state legislatures or state executive officials . . . by evasive schemes for segregation."

Mendez v. Westminster (1947) The federal court decision that ended the segregation of Mexican Americans in California primary schools.

strict scrutiny A legal standard set in *Brown v. Board of Education* for cases related to racial discrimination that tends to invalidate almost all state laws that segregate racial groups.

Other racial and ethnic groups also made significant civil rights gains beginning in the 1950s. The ban on Asian immigration was officially lifted in 1952, and provisions of federal law encouraging the immigration of professionals helped attract to the United States large numbers of educated and highly skilled Asian professionals.

Despite the Supreme Court's increasingly clear edicts against segregation, many school districts in the South and North continued to drag their feet.[12] Significant and widespread change would not occur until after passage of civil rights legislation in the mid-1960s, which gave the executive branch of the government increased power to enforce school desegregation in local districts. Additionally, a sudden influx of federal money into local schools gave extra bite to court desegregation decrees. Many school districts in the Deep South where less than half of all blacks were being educated alongside whites as late as 1967 were almost fully integrated by 1971.

In urban areas where whites and racial/ethnic minorities lived largely apart, strict adherence to a neighborhood school system meant indefinitely perpetuating a racially unmixed setting; thus, massive court-ordered "busing" in the late 1960s and 1970s became a controversial feature of efforts to integrate these schools. Many such court orders were issued in both northern and southern cities, as the Supreme Court required communities to cease both *de jure discrimination* (segregation sanctioned by the law), which was found mostly in the South, and *de facto discrimination* (segregation in reality, such as that which occurs when different racial groups voluntarily choose to live in different neighborhoods or attend different schools), which was found in both the North and the South. Yet busing was a remedy that was limited in scope, and comprehensive efforts to integrate schools were further hindered by white flight to suburbia, which left inner-city school districts in many large northern cities predominantly black and Hispanic. Today, a majority of "U.S. public school students attend schools where at least half of students are of their race or ethnicity."[13] Thus, more than 50 years after the *Brown* decision, de facto discrimination in public education remains a reality in many parts of America.

THE BEGINNINGS OF THE CIVIL RIGHTS MOVEMENT

Although *Mendez* and *Brown* signaled the end of state-sponsored segregation, the Supreme Court took pains to note that its holding applied only to discriminatory acts by the government. The extension of civil rights protections to all public accommodations did not occur until the civil rights movement began to gather momentum in the late 1950s and early 1960s. In December 1955, Rosa Parks, an African American seamstress in Montgomery, Alabama, was arrested for refusing to give up her seat at the front of a city bus. Her arrest sparked a racial boycott of the city's bus system. Leading the boycott was Martin Luther King Jr., pastor of the Dexter Avenue Baptist Church. King's eloquent speeches and his methods of nonviolent civil disobedience brought national attention to the boycott. King had been introduced to these tactics of nonviolent protest when he was a student at Crozer Theological Seminary in Chester, Pennsylvania, and studied the pacifist philosophy of Mohandas Gandhi of India, whose unshakable belief in nonviolent protest and religious tolerance helped secure independence for his country from Great Britain.

In 1957, King and other African American ministers in the South formed the Southern Christian Leadership Conference (SCLC), which encouraged Gandhian practices of nonviolent civil disobedience as a way to gain equal rights for blacks and spur white politicians into action. African American and white college students in numerous cities across the South eventually became the engine for pressing such change. One early tactic the students used was the sit-in. On February 1, 1960, four freshmen from the black North Carolina A&T College in Greensboro sat down at a whites-only lunch counter and refused to move after being denied service. The next day, more students—black and white—joined them. Angry mobs harassed the students verbally and physically. Committed to nonviolence, the students endured the abuse. The episode brought considerable publicity to the civil rights movement. In 1961, interracial groups of students sponsored "Freedom Rides," traveling

"Michael Evans/Hulton Archive / Getty Images"

A 19-year-old student named Martin Luther King Jr. was first introduced to the pacifist philosophy of Mohandas Gandhi. By seeking a nonviolent confrontation with the segregation laws, King's followers practiced Gandhi's philosophy in a way that sent shock waves throughout the South and eventually the entire nation. King would continue to preach Gandhi's call for nonviolent protest up until his assassination in 1968.

In 1963, firefighters in Birmingham, Alabama, sprayed civil rights demonstrators with fire hoses.

together from Washington, DC, to the South to test court decisions prohibiting segregation on interstate buses and in bus terminals; many within the groups of interstate travelers of mixed races were beaten when their buses arrived in Alabama. Eventually President John F. Kennedy was forced to nationalize the Alabama police to help ensure safe passage for the freedom riders.

Hispanics also charged ahead in the battle for civil rights. Although its origins dated back to the mid-nineteenth century, the "Chicano movement" (one example of Latino civil rights movements) reached its peak as a symbol of self-determination and ethnic pride in the 1960s. Spurred on by the Supreme Court's holding in *Hernandez v. Texas* (1954)[14] that Latinos and other subordinated groups were entitled to equal protection under the Fourteenth Amendment, the movement addressed private and public discrimination in the courts and elsewhere. Cesar Chavez, Dolores Huerta, and the National Farm Workers Association fought to make the struggle of migrant workers in particular and Latino empowerment more generally a moral cause through the use of hunger strikes and other nonviolent tactics. Meanwhile, the American GI Forum and the Mexican American Legal Defense and Education Fund continued its battle in the courts.

BIRMINGHAM 1963: THE TURNING POINT OF THE CIVIL RIGHTS MOVEMENT

The civil rights movement's strategy of nonviolent civil disobedience reached a climax between 1963 and 1965.[15] The year 1963 will long be remembered as the "Year of Birmingham." Tension was growing between King's SCLC and new civil rights groups that favored more radical and militant action, including the use of violence. Looking for a site where nonviolent demonstrations might succeed and draw national attention to the civil rights movement, King and his followers settled on Birmingham, Alabama. Birmingham was an obvious target, for several reasons. First, as an industrial city (unlike most southern cities), it had a sizable concentration of workers. Also, during the 1930s and 1940s, the labor movement had introduced to the city a tradition of organized protest unusual throughout most of the South. And finally, the city was a stronghold of segregation; city leaders included the notoriously racist Public Safety Commissioner Eugene "Bull" Connor, who ruthlessly enforced segregation laws throughout the city.

In Birmingham, King led other demonstrators in a nonviolent march downtown, where he was arrested and placed in solitary confinement. While confined, he wrote his famous "Letter from Birmingham City Jail," addressed to the white Alabama clergymen who had criticized King's campaign. In the letter, King explained his philosophy and defended his strategy of nonviolent protest. Despite King's arrest, the demonstration in Birmingham continued. The marchers, including more than a thousand black schoolchildren, were met by attack dogs, cattle prods, and fire hoses. Pictures of children being attacked flashed across the nation's television sets, and the violence was covered by newspapers and magazines across the world. The nation would be forever provoked by these events; the civil rights movement had finally been transformed into a truly national cause.

Birmingham businessmen, fearing damage to their downtown stores, hastened negotiations with King and his fellow civil rights leaders. An accord was eventually reached on May 10, 1963, with merchants agreeing to desegregate lunch counters and hire more black workers for clerical and sales positions. Yet the agreement did not bring peace to Birmingham. On the night of May 11, a Ku Klux Klan rally outside the city was followed by the explosion of bombs at the motel where King was staying. Riots erupted and some stores were set ablaze. This time, however, the federal government got involved; President Kennedy dispatched soldiers to Fort McClellan, 30 miles outside of Birmingham. Nevertheless, in September a bombing at the city's Sixteenth Street Baptist Church killed four African American schoolgirls.

The events in Birmingham were not the last of the civil rights demonstrations, nor did they mark the end of violence in response to those activities. In August 1963, more than 250,000 people participated in the March on Washington, where King delivered his memorable "I Have a Dream" speech from the steps of the Lincoln Memorial. In 1964, the murder of three civil rights workers and a local NAACP leader in Mississippi revealed the depth of continuing opposition to racial equality. In 1965, King and other civil rights leaders organized a march from Selma, Alabama, to the state capital in Montgomery to bring attention to harsh political realities in the South, where African Americans had been denied the right to vote by illegitimate tests and, in some instances, outright intimidation.

President Lyndon Johnson and the U.S. Congress were eventually prodded into action. Johnson signed into law the **Civil Rights Act of 1964**, which banned racial discrimination in all public accommodations, including those that were privately owned; it also prohibited discrimination by employers and created the Equal Employment Opportunity Commission to investigate complaints of discrimination; and it denied public funds to schools that continued to discriminate on the basis of race.[16]

The **Voting Rights Act of 1965**, enacted the following year, invalidated literacy tests and property requirements. Section 5 of the law then required that certain states and cities with a history of voting discrimination obtain preclearance from the U.S. Department of Justice for all future changes to their voting laws. As shown in Table 5-2, the act proved largely successful, as millions of African Americans were effectively re-enfranchised in the South in subsequent decades. The 1965 Voting Rights Act (VRA) was further updated to extend the protections to other racial/ethnic groups, starting in 1970.

Notable extensions of the VRA included the following:

- 1970: Congress extended the threshold for coverage.
- 1975: Congress extended VRA protection to all language minorities.
- 1982: Congress eliminated at-large districts and replaced them with single-member districts that increased opportunities for minority groups' representation.
- 1992: Congress extended bilingual voting assistance.
- 2006: Congress extended Section 5 for an additional 25 years.

The Voting Rights Act was dramatically weakened by the Supreme Court's ruling in *Shelby County v. Holder* (2013), which held that the act's coverage formula, which determines which jurisdictions are subjected to preclearance, is based on outdated data and thus impermissibly burdens the sovereignty of states under the Constitution.

The **Civil Rights Act of 1968** banned race discrimination in housing and made interference with a citizen's civil rights a federal crime. Even the state legislatures played a role in this civil rights transformation by ratifying the **Twenty-fourth Amendment** in 1964, which banned poll taxes in federal elections.

The focus of the civil rights movement began to shift in the mid to late 1960s with the rise of "black and brown nationalism," which was grounded in the belief that African Americans and Latinos/Chicanos could not effectively work within the confines of a racist political system to produce effective change. Malcolm X, a leading advocate of Black Nationalism, sought to turn the characteristic of being black-skinned into a source of strength, and he urged African Americans to shun white culture and the values promoted by white society. He and other black nationalists criticized the civil rights leaders who advocated integration into white society rather than building separate black institutions. The influence of Black Nationalism in the civil rights movement reached its peak during the late 1960s and early 1970s following the assassination of Martin Luther King Jr. in 1968. Epitomizing a revolutionary vision of society that replaced the strategy of nonviolence with confrontational tactics, the Black Panther Party became a controversial militant presence in some cities.

Civil Rights Act of 1964 The federal law that banned racial discrimination in all public accommodations, including those that were privately owned; prohibited discrimination by employers and created the Equal Employment Opportunity Commission to investigate complaints of discrimination; and denied public funds to schools that continued to discriminate on the basis of race.

Voting Rights Act of 1965 The federal law that invalidated literacy tests and property requirements and required select states and cities to apply for permission to the Justice Department to change their voting laws. As a consequence, millions of African Americans were effectively re-enfranchised in the South.

Civil Rights Act of 1968 The federal law that banned race discrimination in housing and made interference with a citizen's civil rights a federal crime.

Twenty-fourth Amendment A 1964 constitutional amendment that banned poll taxes in federal elections.

TABLE 5-2

The Effect of the Voting Rights Act on Registration Rates in the South

The following table compares black voter registration rates with white voter registration rates in seven southern states in 1965 and 1988. All numbers are percentage rates.

State	March 1965			November 1988		
	Black	White	Gap	Black	White	Gap
Alabama	19.3	69.2	49.9	68.4	75.0	6.6
Georgia	27.4	62.6	35.2	56.8	63.9	7.1
Louisiana	31.6	80.5	48.9	77.1	75.1	–2.0
Mississippi	6.7	69.9	63.2	74.2	80.5	6.3
North Carolina	46.8	96.8	50.0	58.2	65.6	7.4
South Carolina	37.3	75.7	38.4	56.7	61.8	5.1
Virginia	38.3	61.1	22.8	63.8	68.5	4.7

Sources: U.S. Commission on Civil Rights; Chandler Davidson and Bernard Grofman, Quiet Revolution in the South *(Princeton, NJ: Princeton University Press, 1994).*

DEBATES OVER DIVERSITY
Contemporary Challenge to Voting Rights

Today we take for granted that all citizens may effectively exercise the right to vote. Unfortunately, some political actors continue to place obstacles in the way of voters, and their efforts could well influence elections in some cases. The recent controversy over strict voter identification laws exemplifies this problem. As of 2018, a total of 34 states had already passed laws requiring voters to show some form of identification at the polls. This included strict photo ID requirements instituted by Georgia, Indiana, Kansas, Mississippi, Tennessee, Virginia, and Wisconsin.[17] Supporters of such voter restrictions argue that they are necessary to curb voter fraud. However, the laws' opponents argue that they place undue discriminatory restrictions on an individual's ability to vote, especially among certain groups (including racial/ethnic minorities, women, low-income persons, seniors, and college-age citizens). These groups are disproportionately less likely to own the required government-issued photo identification, and they normally have fewer opportunities to obtain the needed documents. So far, this battle remains unsettled, as civil rights groups continue to challenge many of the stricter state voter ID laws in the courts, enjoying only mixed success to date.

Voter ID laws in Texas and elsewhere that require driver's licenses (or similar forms of validation) to vote have been challenged in court by civil rights groups.

For Critical Thinking and Discussion

1. Do you think photo identification should be required to vote? If so, why? Should it be more difficult to vote than it is to purchase gas for one's car?
2. What are the ramifications of government efforts to place obstacles in the way of greater voter turnout? Do you think strict voter ID restrictions significantly influence voter turnout in elections?

Although the Black Panther Party had all but faded as a significant entity by 1972, black separatist organizations continue to maintain a strong presence. For example, the Nation of Islam (Black Muslims), led by Louis Farrakhan, preaches class consciousness and the concept of black self-rule. In 1995, Farrakhan's Nation of Islam led the Million Man March in Washington, DC, which far outdrew the 1963 March on Washington. Four years later, African American women held their own million women march (the Women's March on the Pentagon).

Beginning in the latter part of the twentieth century, some Native Americans also embraced activism to protest their mistreatment by government authorities. From November 1969 until June 1971, 78 members of one tribe occupied Alcatraz Island in San Francisco Bay, demanding that it be made available as a cultural center to the tribes. Members of the American Indian Movement (AIM), an organization founded in 1968 to promote civil rights for Native Americans, occupied the Washington, DC, offices of the Bureau of Indian Affairs in 1972, demanding that they receive the rights and privileges that had been promised them under the original treaties entered into by the federal government. This activism drew public attention to Native American causes and spurred action by Congress, which formally terminated its policy of assimilation and began to recognize the autonomy of Native American tribes to administer federal programs on their own lands. In the past quarter century, the U.S. government has settled millions of dollars in legal claims pressed by Native American tribes and has returned nearly half a million acres of land to the Navajo and Hopi tribes alone.

The end of the Vietnam War in 1975 also brought a great influx of immigrants from Vietnam, Laos, and Cambodia to the United States. With increasing numbers of immigrants from South Korea and the Philippines, the Asian American population today stands at approximately 4 percent of the American population as a whole.

Barack Obama's historic election as the first African American president may have fundamentally changed how African Americans as well as other racial and ethnic minorities perceive their national government. Still, members of those groups continue to face immense challenges in making their voices heard in other institutions on the national political scene. Consider that Obama left a Senate chamber in November 2008 in which he had been the only African American then serving, and where he was just the third popularly elected African American senator to serve since Reconstruction. Since Obama departed the Senate, just three African Americans have been elected as U.S. senators: Sen. Tim Scott (R-SC), Sen. Corey Booker (D-NJ), and Sen. Kamala Harris (R-CA). African Americans have enjoyed more success in the other house of Congress, as a record 54 African American members (12.4 percent of the total membership) held seats at the start of the 116th Congress.

Meanwhile, Hispanics form the nation's largest language minority today, as more than 35 million people of Hispanic descent currently live in the United States. In recent years, Mexico in particular has been the source of 29 percent of the overall growth in foreign-born persons living in the United States. As you can see in Table 5-3, Latin America as a whole has accounted for 58 percent of the growth in the immigrant population since 2000. Thus, Mexicans, Cubans, Puerto Ricans, and numerous immigrants and refugees from other Central American countries all contribute to the ranks of this rapidly growing minority group.

Some of the Cubans who left their native land hailed from privileged socioeconomic conditions. Their goal was to flee Fidel Castro's communistic agenda, but they also immigrated to the United States as part of an effort to preserve their standard of living. Barack Obama's historic visit to Havana during the spring of 2016 received only a mix of support from this politically active community. By contrast, most immigrants from Latin American countries such as Mexico and Cuba sought to escape some severely adverse economic circumstances in those nations.

Of course, discrimination against Hispanics also contributes to the overall disproportionate levels of poverty and unemployment in this group. In New Mexico and California they have been a large and influential minority for several decades. And yet despite the large number of Hispanics, the group's political power has yet to receive its due influence on public policy in those southwestern states, perhaps because many Hispanics are not yet citizens and thus do not have the right to vote. Certainly, the appointment of Judge Sonia Sotomayor as the first Latina (and more specifically, Puerto Rican) to the U.S. Supreme Court in 2009 was a source of pride among the Hispanic community, and officials in both major parties made appeals to the Hispanic community a top priority going into the 2016 presidential election. Given that hopeful

TABLE 5-3

Countries Sending the Most Immigrants to the United States, 1990, 2000, and 2010

Country	2010	2000	1990
1 Mexico	11,711,103	9,177,487	4,298,014
2 China, Hong Kong, and Taiwan	2,166,526	1,518,652	921,070
3 India	1,780,322	1,022,552	450,406
4 Philippines	1,777,588	1,369,070	912,674
5 Vietnam	1,240,542	988,174	543,262
6 El Salvador	1,214,049	817,336	465,433
7 Cuba	1,104,679	872,716	736,971
8 Korea	1,100,422	864,125	568,397
9 Dominican Republic	879,187	687,677	347,858
10 Guatemala	830,824	480,665	225,739
All of Latin America	**21,224,087**	**16,086,974**	**8,407,837**

Sources: Steven A. Camarota, "A Record-Setting Decade of Immigration: 2000 to 2010," Center for Immigration Studies, October 2011, https://cis.org/sites/cis.org/files/articles/2011/record-setting-decade.pdf.

backdrop, leaders of the Hispanic community were particularly dismayed by comments in 2016 from then Republican presidential nominee Donald Trump that compared Mexican immigrants (and all Latinos) to rapists and drug dealers. President Trump continued his controversial and dramatic actions once in office with continued fights with Congress to seek funding for a border wall and his "zero-tolerance" policy of family separation and detention at the border. The quest to implement comprehensive immigration reform and reward this exploding Latino population with political clout reflective of its numbers is certain to remain a continuing challenge.

5-4 THE WOMEN'S MOVEMENT AND GENDER EQUALITY

The process by which women achieved their own degree of equality during the course of the twentieth century took a circuitous route. In the early part of the twentieth century, women's rights leaders linked their calls for equality to other social movements of the same period, including those calling for child labor laws and increased literacy for immigrants. Initially, the women's rights movement pressed for protective laws, arguing that such legislation was necessary because of women's otherwise inferior legal status. For example, in *Muller v. Oregon* (1908),[18] the Supreme Court upheld an Oregon law that prohibited women laundry workers from being required to work more than 10 hours a day; similar laws applied to male workers had been invalidated as beyond the government's authority. Yet the reason for the holding could hardly have cheered advocates of women's equality: according to the Court, "A woman's physical structure and the performance of maternal functions place her at a disadvantage in the struggle for subsistence."

JUDICIAL SCRUTINY OF GENDER DISCRIMINATION AND THE EQUAL RIGHTS AMENDMENT

After ratification of the Nineteenth Amendment in 1920 guaranteed women the right to vote, women's rights groups began to alter their strategy for pursuing gender equality through the courts. In attempting to expand women's legal rights, these groups now argued

social movements
A large informal grouping of individuals and/or organizations focused on specific political or social issues.

Nineteenth Amendment
The constitutional amendment that guarantees women equal voting rights.

that men and women should be treated equally. Their efforts met with only limited success at first. Although the NAACP achieved a string of successful challenges to racial discrimination in the 1940s and 1950s, the Supreme Court refused to view gender discrimination as similarly deserving of suspect scrutiny. In *Goesaert v. Cleary* (1948),[19] the Court upheld a Michigan law that banned women from tending bar unless they were the daughter or wife of the bar owner. Thirteen years later, the Court accepted as legitimate a Florida law that gave only women the right to excuse themselves from jury duty. In both cases, the Court continued to accept sex-role stereotypes of women as weak and as dedicated above all else to taking care of the children at home. As the Court pointed out in *Hoyt v. Florida* (1961), "Despite the enlightened emancipation of women from the restrictions and protections of bygone years . . . woman is still regarded as the center of home and family life."[20]

The women's rights movement did not achieve any significant breakthroughs in this regard until the early 1970s. Although the National Women's Party had first proposed an equal rights amendment to the Constitution in 1923 and in nearly every session of Congress since then, the amendment never got very far. In 1966, the newly formed National Organization for Women (NOW) became a new and forceful advocate for the Equal Rights Amendment (ERA) and other equal rights in education, employment, and political opportunities for women. NOW and other women's groups vigorously pressed for passage of the ERA, which stated simply that "equality of rights under the law shall not be denied or abridged by the United States or any state on account of sex." In 1972, Congress passed the amendment and sent it to the state legislatures for ratification. Even after the deadline for ratification was extended to June 1982, the amendment failed to achieve the approval of the three-fourths of state legislatures necessary for passage, falling just three states shy. Members of Congress reintroduce the ERA in nearly every session of Congress and the amendment is currently just one state shy of approval from the required 38 state legislatures. Still, if a 38th state ever does ratify the ERA, it would be up to Congress and the courts to determine whether or not the ratification deadline renders the issue moot.

Although the ERA has not passed, women have recently achieved some noteworthy victories in politics. For example, women made political history in 2003 when Democrat Nancy Pelosi of California was elected minority leader in the House, the first woman ever to hold that high of a position in either branch of Congress. When Democrats won control of Congress after the 2006 and 2018 midterm elections, Pelosi was elected Speaker of the House. (Between 2011 and 2018, she served as minority leader in the Republican-controlled House of Representatives.) Pelosi's ascension to such high congressional leadership positions contrasts with the way women in Congress were often relegated to lesser committees and noninfluential positions in the past. Beginning in 2019, the 116th Congress included over 100 women serving in the U.S. House of Representatives and 24 in the U.S. Senate.

When Hillary Clinton became the first female to serve as a major party's presidential nominee, her campaign hoped the women's vote would provide her with the electoral edge she needed to win the White House. Yet, as it turned out, while women voters overall preferred Clinton by 13 percentage points (54 to 41 percent) to Donald Trump, white women preferred Trump by 10 points (53 to 43 percent) and white women without a college degree preferred Trump by an overwhelming 28 percentage points (62 to 34 percent). In that sense, Hillary Clinton performed about the same among women voters as Barack Obama did in 2012. Clearly, the first woman president may have to wait for a time when she can inspire women across the board to support her in realizing that history-making moment.

LEGAL CHALLENGES TO GENDER DISCRIMINATION

Ironically, some attributed the failure of the Equal Rights Amendment to other legal developments that may have rendered it unnecessary. The American Civil Liberties Union (ACLU), an organization traditionally dedicated to protecting the First Amendment rights of political dissidents and labor unions, turned its attention to women's rights in the late 1960s. Led in court by board member Ruth Bader Ginsburg (who was later appointed by President Clinton to the U.S. Supreme Court), the ACLU brought suit on behalf of women who charged that they had been victims of gender discrimination. Although the Court refused to accord gender discrimination the strict scrutiny normally reserved for racial discrimination, the ACLU achieved several victories in cases brought before the Supreme Court. In *Reed v. Reed* (1971),[21] the Court invalidated an Idaho law that gave males preference over females as administrators of estates. In *Frontiero v. Richardson* (1973),[22] the Court struck down a federal law requiring only female members of the armed forces to show proof that they contributed more than 50 percent to the income of their household in order to receive certain fringe benefits. And in the landmark case of *Craig v. Boren* (1976),[23] the Court invalidated an Oklahoma law that prohibited the sale of 3.2 percent beer to males under the age of 21 and to women under the age of 18.

Since *Craig*, the Supreme Court has applied *intermediate scrutiny* in all gender discrimination cases, a standard requiring the government to show that the gender classification is "substantially related to an important state interest." This level of scrutiny is less than that of strict scrutiny, which tends to invalidate all racial classifications. But under intermediate scrutiny, *nearly* all laws that discriminate against women will be invalidated. That fact alone distinguishes intermediate scrutiny from *rational basis* (or *minimum*) *scrutiny*, which asks only whether the law is "rationally related to a legitimate state interest"—a question to which courts can readily answer "yes" in nearly every instance.

In fact, in the modern era the Court has upheld only a handful of gender classifications as constitutional. For example, in 1981 the Court upheld a challenge to federal laws that required selective military service registration for males but not for females. That same year the Court upheld a statutory rape law in California that punished men for having sex with underage females, although not vice versa. In each of those two instances, perceptions of real and relevant differences between men and women persuaded the Court to allow the discrimination to stand.

The highest-profile lawsuits charging gender discrimination targeted two all-male southern military academies, the Citadel in Charleston, South Carolina, and the Virginia Military Institute (VMI) in Lexington, Virginia. Both were classified as state institutions because they accepted significant funds from their respective states' budgets; thus, each was hard-pressed to continue excluding women in violation of the Fourteenth Amendment's equal protection clause. Shannon Faulkner's frustrating experience as the first female cadet at the Citadel paved the way for future women to apply and be accepted to the institution in subsequent years. In an attempt to fend off gender integration of its own student body, VMI contracted with nearby Mary Baldwin College to create a parallel military program for women called the Virginia Women's Institute for Leadership (VWIL). But in 1996, the Supreme Court ruled that VWIL did not approximate VMI in terms of student body, faculty, course offerings, facilities, or opportunities for its alumni and ordered VMI to accept women. The issue of "separate but equal" that was resolved by the Supreme Court for racial classifications in 1954 was still being litigated for gender classifications well into the 1990s.

As with race discrimination, discrimination against women has been mostly eliminated in the formal sense. Title IX of the Federal Educational Amendments of 1972 prohibited the exclusion of women from an educational program or activity receiving financial assistance from the federal government. Courts have interpreted those provisions to force colleges and universities to provide as many athletic teams for women as they do for men. Title VII of the Civil Rights Act of 1964 extended to women protection against discrimination in private and public businesses alike. Armed with equal rights to education and to entry in the workforce, women made considerable occupational gains during the twentieth century.

Women have also benefited from affirmative action programs, especially in the workplace and in admission to professional and trade schools. Affirmative action programs are generally laws or practices designed to remedy past discriminatory hiring practices, government contracting, and school admissions. To rectify long traditions of excluding women from certain occupations, scores of businesses and firms have aggressively recruited women. The period of most striking change occurred over the two decades between 1970 and 1990, when the proportion of women physicians doubled from 7.6 percent to 16.9 percent, and the percentage of women lawyers and judges nearly quadrupled from 5.8 percent to 22.7 percent. Still, complaints remain that in some occupations women continue to be clustered in low-paying positions. Some observers contend that a "glass ceiling" exists in many businesses,

Title IX
The section of the Federal Educational Amendments Law of 1972 that prohibits the exclusion of women from an educational program or activity receiving financial assistance from the federal government. Courts have interpreted those provisions to force colleges and universities to provide as many athletic teams for women as they do for men.

affirmative action
Programs, laws, or practices designed to remedy past discriminatory hiring practices, government contracting, and school admissions.

whereby women are prevented from receiving raises and promotions due them because of the subjective biases of their male bosses.

The securing of formal equality under the law and the proliferation of affirmative action programs have not always translated into actual equal opportunities to succeed. Women today continue to earn less than men in comparable positions. Calls for "equal pay for equal work" have not always generated substantive changes in the pay structures of private companies or even the government. When women's salaries are compared with those of equally qualified men, the differences remain dramatic. Although Congress passed the Equal Pay Act in 1963 to ensure that women would be paid the same as men for work that is "substantially equal" (i.e., almost identical unless the pay difference is based on seniority, experience, or other legitimate factors), in the year 2018 a woman on average still earned less than 78 cents for every dollar a man received.[24] During the 2008 presidential campaign, Barack Obama highlighted the issue of equal pay and he followed through by signing the Lilly Ledbetter Fair Pay Act of 2009 as his first official act after he became president. This act provided some important revisions to the Civil Rights Act of 1964 by instituting more flexibility in the statute of limitations for filing an equal-pay lawsuit.

In April 2014 President Barack Obama also issued two executive orders meant to pressure federal contractors on pay equity, a move that drew praise from advocates and criticism from conservatives who accused the administration of pandering to female voters. Even the president's own Office of Personnel Management conceded that factors other than discrimination could contribute to the differences in pay between men and women, including differences in prior work experience, care-giving responsibilities, motivation, and work performance. Given the growing political power of women in the electorate, officials from both political parties can expect to answer even more questions about pay equity in the years to come.

Sexual harassment, normally in the form of unwelcome sexual advances by superiors, continues to pose a threat to working women in America. Since the mid-1980s the Supreme Court has considered such harassment—which includes any and all actions that create a hostile working environment, such as putting up provocative posters, making lewd comments, and so forth—to be a form of sexual discrimination actionable under Title VII of the 1964 Civil Rights Act. Still, many such sexual advances in the workplace continue despite the law, either because women remain unclear about the bounds of permissible conduct or because they fear reprisals for reporting the legal violations of superiors. Indeed, more than 4 in 10 women employed in federal agencies say they have experienced some form of harassment.[25] Recent events, including several high-profile sexual assault and harassment cases in the entertainment industry, have increasingly focused the public's attention on gender discrimination and assault. In 2017, #MeToo became a national movement of victims against sexual assault and harassment. The subsequent founding of the Time's Up movement in January 2018 energized national and international forces against sexual assault, harassment, and inequality in the workplace.

5-5 OTHER GROUP STRUGGLES FOR EQUALITY

American history is replete with accounts of discrimination against other underrepresented groups as well. In recent years these other groups have begun to see their own claims to fairness and equal treatment recognized and vindicated within the American political system.

OLDER AMERICANS

Today approximately 13 percent of Americans are over the age of 65, compared with just 4 percent of Americans who were at that age at the beginning of the twentieth century. With their increased numbers has come increased political power; older Americans are among the most politically active of all citizens, and groups such as AARP (formerly the American Association of Retired Persons), with more than 40 million members on its rolls, have become especially influential players on the political scene. This increased influence has been used to counteract incidents of age discrimination in the workplace and elsewhere. The Age Discrimination in Employment Act, passed in 1967 and broadened in 1986, makes it

Members of Rise and Resist hold a protest outside the MTA NYC Headquarters in 2017 to advocate for the importance of accessible subway stations.

unlawful to hire or fire a person on the basis of age. Older Americans have also been at the forefront of lobbying efforts to protect Social Security trust funds and to ensure the continuation of cost-of-living adjustments to their payments. Ironically, older Americans' success at wielding influence within the political system has given credence to the suggestion that age classifications do not require suspect scrutiny by courts; at least in this instance, the political system appears to protect the civil rights of this particular subset of Americans.

INDIVIDUALS WITH DISABILITIES

As with age classifications, discrimination against Americans with physical and mental disabilities has never received heightened scrutiny from the courts. Misperceptions about the nature of certain disabilities have on occasion led to discriminatory treatment of individuals with disabilities. In the 1920s, some states passed laws authorizing the sterilization of institutionalized "mental defectives"—Justice Oliver Wendell Holmes callously dismissed all legal challenges to such laws with the statement that "three generations of imbeciles are enough."

Today, thanks to significant technological and medical advances, a more enlightened social understanding, and a more sophisticated approach to educating citizens about the nature of these limitations, millions of Americans with disabilities have been mainstreamed into society, attending school, going to work, and living otherwise normal lives. The Americans with Disabilities Act of 1990 established a national commitment to such mainstreaming efforts and extended to those with disabilities protection from discrimination in employment and public accommodations comparable to that afforded women and racial minorities under the 1964 Civil Rights Act.

LGBTQ PERSONS

Of the many groups that have legitimate claims as victims of discrimination in the United States, LGBTQ (lesbian, gay, bisexual, transgender, and queer) persons once stood among the least successful in seeing those claims vindicated. Up through the end of the twentieth century, LGBTQ members suffered significant discrimination in society, whether from those whose religions frowned on homosexuality in general or from those who were simply uncomfortable with them. In the period immediately following World War II, a movement for gay rights emerged with generally integrationist goals, encouraging gays and lesbians to conform to most existing social standards. LGBTQ individuals then assumed a more activist quest for equality beginning in the late 1960s, marching for "gay power," urging reluctant gays to "out" themselves by openly admitting their sexual orientation, and interrupting government meetings to draw attention to their cause of equal treatment and nondiscrimination.

Although LGBTQ activists made some limited advances, no significant antidiscrimination legislation followed. Some communities reacted by passing laws that prohibited the granting of "any special rights or privileges" to LGBTQ persons. The Supreme Court in *Romer v. Evans* (1996)[26] struck down such a provision of the Colorado Constitution in 1996. Yet perhaps the biggest court victory of all for gays and lesbians occurred in 2003, when the Supreme Court in *Lawrence v. Texas* (2003)[27] struck down a Texas law that forbade same-sex partners from engaging in certain types of intimate relations. Despite these victories, the Supreme Court has still never recognized the LGBTQ population as a protected class on a par with women or African Americans. Battles over the right to same-sex marriage were

The Shifting Battle Lines of Equality

Then

Beginning in the 1860s and continuing through World War I, demands for women's suffrage stood front and center in the battle lines of equality. Activists at the outset were mostly older women of English or German descent. Frustrated that Congress had placed the African American male's right to vote as a higher priority, several women's groups, including the New England Woman Suffrage Association and the American Woman Suffrage Association, began working to achieve the right to vote. By the 1890s, these voices had merged into a movement, led at first by Susan B. Anthony. Opposition was widespread: upper-class women worried that their behind-the-scenes influence would be diluted once all women could vote, southern white males feared that African American women would vote, and liquor interests worried that women voters would favor prohibition. Pro-suffrage groups managed some limited victories, particularly in the newly settled western states of Utah, Colorado, Idaho, and Wyoming, which all granted women suffrage before the turn of the century. Still, they experienced continued setbacks at the federal level during the first decade of the new century. The tide may have finally turned with President Woodrow Wilson's call for American entry into World War I. When Wilson termed the battle ahead as a "war for democracy," his point rang hollow among disenfranchised women. Reluctantly, Wilson shifted his position in favor of women's suffrage. Finally, in 1919, the Nineteenth Amendment passed, guaranteeing women the right to vote nationwide.

Now

By the 1970s, gay and lesbian advocacy groups had begun organizing to achieve equality on a number of fronts. The going was tough at first. In 1973, just three years after Jack Baker and Michael McConnell applied unsuccessfully for a marriage license in Minnesota, Maryland became the first state to statutorily ban same-sex marriage. During the remainder of the twentieth century, 44 more states followed Maryland's lead, undermining gay advocacy groups' efforts to secure equal access to marriage at every turn. Even the Democratic Party, which strategically embraced gay rights as a general matter, refused support for same-sex

Same-sex marriage supporters rejoice after the U.S Supreme Court hands down a ruling regarding same-sex marriage on June 26, 2015.

Alex Wong / Staff / Getty Images

marriage in its party platform. Then in 1996 President Bill Clinton signed into law the Defense of Marriage Act (DOMA), which banned federal recognition of same-sex unions. During the first decade of the twenty-first century, however, the tide began to turn in the opposite direction. First, gay and lesbian groups achieved some limited success in Vermont, which established a law providing for same-sex civil unions. The movement for same-sex marriage then earned its first major breakthrough in 2004 when Massachusetts became the first state to formally authorize marriages for gay and lesbian couples. In the decade that followed, at least 17 states and the District of Columbia followed suit. By 2014, a Gallup poll registered 54 percent of Americans supporting gay marriage, and the Supreme Court eventually validated this progress, holding that same-sex marriage was a constitutional right in *Obergefell v. Hodges* (2015).[28]

For Critical Thinking and Discussion

1. How was the modern battle over same-sex marriage similar to the century-old battle over a woman's right to vote? How were they different?
2. The suffragettes did not rest until the right to vote had been established as a permanent part of the Constitution in the form of the Nineteenth Amendment. Should gay rights activists pursue a same-sex marriage amendment as well? Would pursuing such a goal require a shift in strategy or tactics?

initially waged state by state during the first decade of the twenty-first century. All those legislative gains were rendered irrelevant, however, when the Court in *Obergefell v. Hodges* (2015) held that a fundamental right to marry was guaranteed to same-sex couples by the Fourteenth Amendment to the U.S Constitution.

Of course, anti-LGBTQ discrimination remains. The issue of LGBTQs in the military first drew intense national attention when U.S. Army Colonel Margarethe Cammermeyer was discharged from the armed forces in June 1992; during a routine security clearance interview, she acknowledged that she was a lesbian. Cammermeyer hinged her hopes for reinstatement on a promise made to her by candidate Bill Clinton during his successful presidential campaign that fall. Yet, soon after taking office, President Clinton began to backtrack on his promise and indicated he might go along with a supposed compromise that would segregate gays within the military. The ultimate compromise reached was a "don't ask, don't tell" policy that would allow gays still in the closet to stay in the military, so long as they never publicized their status. Later, after a federal court ruled in July 2011 that a ban on openly gay troops was unconstitutional, President Obama and the chairman of the Joint Chiefs of Staff certified to Congress that ending the "don't ask, don't tell" policy would not harm the nation's "military readiness." With the support of Congress, the federal government then formally ended the controversial policy on September 20, 2011. Renewed fights over who can join the military arose once again when Department of Defense regulations banning transgender persons from U.S. military service were repealed by the Obama administration on June 30, 2016. President Trump attempted to reverse these efforts in 2017, when he called for a ban of transgender people serving in the military; these plans were later challenged and blocked by a federal court in 2018. However, transgender people continue to face obstacles in joining the military, as their applications face long delays.

Despite suffering countless setbacks, members of the LGBTQ community continue to enjoy a significant presence in the political system, forging alliances with more liberal administrations and even electing some openly gay or trans politicians. Clearly, the LGBTQ community represents a political force in America today that can no longer be ignored by officials of both major political parties.

5-6 CONTINUING STRUGGLES OVER EQUALITY IN THE MODERN ERA

There are several contemporary and hotly debated topics related to equality, including those related to the war on terrorism, affirmative action initiatives, and racial profiling.

THE WAR ON TERRORISM AND ITS IMPACT ON MUSLIM AMERICANS

The events of September 11, 2001, had a profound impact on America's foreign policy priorities and its approach to international terrorism. Those events have also taken a toll on citizens' perceptions of Muslim Americans, a group already set apart by its members' distinct religious practices and forms of dress. When plans for an Islamic community center and mosque to be built near the site of "Ground Zero" in New York City were revealed in early 2010, anger directed at Muslim Americans suddenly found a new cause. Polls showed a clear majority of Americans opposed the project, even though most of those surveyed also recognized that the Muslim group had a legal right to build there. Politicians of all stripes were quick to oppose the proposal, knowing that such opposition would offer them immediate political benefits.

The stereotype that associates the Islamic religion with terrorism is hardly applicable to the vast majority who practice the faith, but post–September 11 initiatives sanctioned by Congress under the USA PATRIOT Act targeted many Muslim Americans for questioning and, in some cases, temporary detention. Of course, African Americans, Hispanics, and other racial and ethnic minorities have long suffered from racial profiling in criminal law enforcement; still, the level and degree to which Muslim Americans have been singled out has been a special source of worry for civil rights groups. Their fears only escalated when in 2017, President Trump began issuing temporary bans on all Muslims entering the United States. The Supreme Court upheld Trump's third iteration of the Muslim travel ban in *Trump v. Hawaii* in June 2018. Clearly Muslim Americans have a long way to go in their quest to debunk negative stereotypes, especially those that unfairly label all members of the religious group as perpetrators of terrorism.

AFFIRMATIVE ACTION

Some observers have called the civil rights movement a "Second Reconstruction" because it eliminated most of the vestiges of racial discrimination and segregation from the books. But would this successful legal revolution translate into real change? Various civil rights leaders in the 1970s and 1980s shifted their focus to affirmative action

Students at the University of Michigan rally in support of affirmative action. In 2003 the U.S. Supreme Court upheld the use of affirmative action by the University of Michigan's Law School but struck down the affirmative action program utilized by that university's undergraduate admissions.

as a means of promoting racial, ethnic, and gender gains in education and the workplace. Although "quotas" (specifically defined numerical goals for hiring or admitting members of certain groups) have been used in the past, more often such programs involve giving some form of preferential treatment, whether by adding points to a mathematical score due to a person's status as a member of a particular racial group, or by creating economic or other incentives for administrative bodies to increase the diversity of their incoming workforce and/or educational institutions.

Proponents of affirmative action argue that past discriminatory practices have deprived certain racial groups and women of opportunities to get the skills or experiences they need to compete for jobs or college admissions on an equal footing with those who have not experienced such discrimination. The issue of affirmative action reached the U.S. Supreme Court in the case of *Regents of the University of California v. Bakke* (1978).[29] In 1973, Alan Bakke, one of 2,664 applicants for 100 seats at the University of California–Davis Medical School, interviewed with one of the school's officials, Dr. Theodore West. At that time, West told Bakke that he was a "very desirable applicant to the medical school." Thus Bakke was quite surprised when he was denied admission twice: in 1973 and again in 1974. In both instances, 16 applicants with lower grade point averages and MCAT (Medical College Admission Test) scores than Bakke's were admitted to the school under a special minority admissions program. Bakke challenged the program as a violation of the Fourteenth Amendment's equal protection clause.

In deciding the case, the Supreme Court ruled that a university could take into account race and ethnicity when making decisions about the admission of students, as long as it did not utilize specifically assigned numerical goals. To the Court, no constitutional infirmity exists where "race or ethnic background is simply one element—to be weighed fairly against other elements—in the selection process." In his majority opinion, Justice Lewis Powell also heralded the benefits of a diverse student body, noting that students with particular racial backgrounds may bring to a school "experiences, outlooks and ideas that enrich the training of its student body."[30]

Five years after he was first denied admission, Bakke got what he wanted: on June 28, 1978, the U.S. Supreme Court directed that he be admitted to the university's medical school. Opponents of affirmative action thought they had received the victory they were looking for; after all, the Court held that the university could not use fixed racial quotas in this instance. But schools and universities took refuge in the Court's statements favoring the consideration of racial criteria more generally, and in the quarter century that followed, countless schools of higher education utilized race-conscious admissions programs.

Opponents of affirmative action complain that such programs punish white applicants who played no role at all in the original discriminatory practices. They also claim that a racial divide that currently exists in this country may be exacerbated by affirmative action because members of racial groups who benefit from such programs may be stigmatized by the perception that they are not fully deserving. Finally, affirmative action programs are explicit racial classifications and thus may be thought to violate the principle of a "color-blind Constitution" that was celebrated by the Supreme Court's decision in *Brown v. Board of Education*.

A string of Supreme Court decisions in the late 1980s and 1990s effectively ended explicit affirmative action programs in public employment and contracting. The final nail in the coffin for affirmative action in contracting may have been the Court's decision in *Adarand v. Peña* (1995),[31] which held that any racial classification may be considered unconstitutional unless it meets the test of strict scrutiny: it must be "narrowly tailored" to further a "compelling governmental interest," a standard that has proved nearly impossible for the government to meet. In fact, no affirmative action employment plan has been upheld as constitutional by the Supreme Court since the early 1990s.

By contrast, affirmative action in education remains steeped in controversy; the confusion over what is legal in this context was only partially resolved by two University of Michigan cases in 2003 that essentially reaffirmed *Bakke*'s finding that diversity constitutes

FROM YOUR PERSPECTIVE
Protesting Injustice on College Campuses

"Chip Somodevilla / Staff / Getty Images"

Protestors in Washington, DC, on December 13, 2014, march against police brutality and the killing of unarmed black men by police.

In 2012, George M. Zimmerman, a neighborhood watch coordinator for a gated community in Sanford, Florida, shot and killed 17-year-old African American high school student Trayvon Martin. At the time, Martin was temporarily staying in the community where the shooting took place. After Zimmerman was acquitted in 2013, the international activist movement titled Black Lives Matter (BLM) began to campaign on social media and

elsewhere against violence committed by law enforcement officials against African Americans, as well as against police brutality and racial equality more generally. The movement received national acclaim after it successfully organized street demonstrations around the country; later it began to lobby for politicians to state their positions on BLM issues. In 2015 the BLM movement and related groups such as the Black Justice League took their battle to college campuses following the failure of several college administrations to adequately respond to racist incidents on campus. At least two university presidents and numerous deans and administrators resigned over allegations of racial insensitivity. In addition, some colleges have considered the removal of statues and the renaming of buildings that celebrate racist founders or donors. In pressing for such actions, the BLM movement on campuses makes it clear that colleges and universities matter in the continuing quest for social equality.

For Critical Thinking and Discussion

1. Have you ever participated in protests for equal treatment on your college campus or elsewhere?
2. Do you think campus buildings should be renamed due to the racist political stances and policies associated with the names on those buildings?

a "compelling state interest" under certain circumstances. In *Grutter v. Bollinger* (2003),[32] the Court upheld the university's law school admission program because it only considered race as a positive factor in a review process where all individual applications were carefully reviewed and analyzed on their own merits. Yet that same day in *Gratz v. Bollinger* (2003),[33] the Supreme Court struck down the same university's undergraduate admissions program because instead of providing such careful, individualized review, it automatically awarded 20 points to all students from underrepresented groups, greatly enhancing their chances of being admitted. The Court declared that such a blanket award of benefits was not "narrowly tailored" enough to promote diversity.

In an attempt to balance the interests of having a diverse student body with frequently heard criticisms of affirmative action, state governments in Texas, Florida, and California have enacted alternative programs that would guarantee a place at the state's top universities for every student who finishes in the upper tier (normally the top 5 or 10 percent) of his or her high school class. Critics of the plans charge that they capitalize on patterns of segregation in housing and geography. Regardless, the Supreme Court upheld this type of program in *Fisher v. Texas* (2016). By a 4–3 vote, the Court affirmed a University of Texas admission policy that featured both a "top 10 percent plan" as well as a secondary plan by which race was considered, along with other factors, as part of an individualized review.

RACIAL PROFILING

Statistics pertaining to the criminal justice system also testify to continuing racial inequality and racial tensions. For instance, although African American youth at the end of the twentieth century represented just 15 percent of the nation's total youth population, they made up 26 percent of the youth arrested, 31 percent of the youth referred to juvenile court, and 44 percent of the youth detained by the police.[34] African American and Hispanic males in particular compose a disproportionate number of those imprisoned. Critics of the system charge that it is racially biased, especially in how it metes out capital punishment. A study conducted by social scientist David Baldus in the early 1990s concluded that the victim's race was a significant factor in predicting which convicted murderers receive the death penalty. Specifically, killers of whites were 4.3 times more likely to be sentenced to death than killers of African Americans.

Racial discrimination may also characterize the initial phases of gathering information about a crime. For example, some law enforcement officials admit to using **racial profiling**—the practice of taking race into account when investigating crimes. Racial/ethnic minorities may be stopped, questioned, and even held in custody not because there is specific evidence that links them to a particular crime but because they fit a "profile" of the perpetrator that includes the characteristic of race.

Even in the wake of the civil rights revolution of the 1960s, little objection was raised against the practice, provided that it was done for purposes of "bona fide law enforcement" and not racial harassment, and so long as race was one of several factors that police officers considered when investigating crimes. But racial profiling became a source of considerable controversy in the 1990s. During the spring of 1999, victims of the New Jersey State Police force's allegedly overaggressive racial profiling testified at hearings held by the Black and Latino Caucus of the state's legislature. President Bill Clinton publicly condemned racial profiling as a "morally indefensible, deeply corrosive practice." Finally, in March 2003, New Jersey became the first state in the nation to enact an anti-profiling law, which made any profiling by police punishable by five years in prison and a $15,000 fine. Yet, by the end of that decade, a majority of states still had not banned racial profiling as a law enforcement practice. In June 2003, President George W. Bush issued a directive that banned racial profiling by federal law enforcement agencies, although critics complained about both the law's exception for the use of racial profiling in "national security" investigations and the lack of enforcement mechanisms provided. Accordingly, claims of profiling in the past decade have focused on Naturalization, Customs, and Border Patrol agents accused of improperly restricting Muslims' entry or reentry into the United States.

racial profiling The law enforcement practice of taking race into account when identifying possible suspects of crimes.

More recently, Arizona law enforcement officials were accused of racial profiling under the auspices of the Arizona Law Enforcement and Safe Neighborhoods Act, better known as SB 1070. Passed in 2010, the act authorized the police to arrest individuals if there was a mere "suspicion" that the persons were undocumented immigrants. Critics were quick to complain that the law was directed at those who merely "looked" like they were from foreign countries, a clear form of racial profiling. In 2012, the Supreme Court struck down most provisions of the Arizona law, including the power of police to arrest a person on the mere suspicion that he or she is an undocumented immigrant.

Are criticisms of racial profiling exaggerated? Statistics overwhelmingly confirm that African American young men commit a disproportionate share of street crime in the United States. Thus, not all racial profiling may be driven by prejudice against African Americans. At the same time, defenders of racial profiling (as one of many factors in the investigative process) tend to minimize the extent to which the practice adds to the sense of resentment of law enforcement felt by rich and poor minorities alike. No court has ever banned the practice outright. Moreover, even if a court did take such a bold action, it would be difficult to disprove an officer's claim that nonracial factors were in fact the primary consideration in his or her decision-making process.

The controversy over racial profiling entered the national conversation once again in 2012 with the fatal shooting of an unarmed 17-year-old African American, Trayvon Martin, by a multiracial neighborhood watch coordinator in a Sanford, Florida, gated community. Although there was no indication that Martin was involved in any criminal activity, the coordinator, George Zimmerman, initially reported Martin to the police and then shot him in an altercation that took place before the police arrived. The local police chose not to charge Zimmerman; nearly six weeks passed before Zimmerman was charged by a specially appointed prosecutor with second-degree murder. In the meantime, allegations of racist motivations by both the shooter and the police dominated media coverage of the incident. Critics also charged that laws like Florida's "Stand Your Ground Law"—which allows the use of force in self-defense without a duty to retreat—encourages racial profiling by citizens. Thus, few were surprised when Zimmerman was acquitted on charges of second-degree murder and manslaughter in June 2013. The riots in Ferguson, Missouri, over the killing of Michael Brown by a white police officer added even more fuel to the fire of resentment that this issue continues.

Controversies surrounding the war on terrorism, affirmative action, and racial profiling highlight a vexing challenge in modern society. Even if all vestiges of formal racial classifications under the law are eliminated, calculations of racial differences inevitably enter into the subjective judgments of those in positions of authority. Thus, for all successful challenges launched against the racist legal and political structures that prevailed in American society during the twentieth century, the greater challenge remains of winning over the "hearts and minds" of individuals.

Summary

5-1 Types of Equality

- Civil rights are those political rights (focusing on the right to participate in the political system), social rights (focusing on equality within institutions that serve the public), or economic rights (focusing on competition over resources) conferred by the government on members of groups that had previously been denied those rights.

5-2 The Struggle for Equality: Approaches and Tactics

- The tactics used by groups seeking to achieve civil rights include working within the existing rules and political process, litigation, boycotts, and civil disobedience.

5-3 The Struggle for Equality: Race, Ethnicity, and Civil Rights

- The hard-fought struggle by racial/ethnic minorities for equality dates back to the Constitutional Convention, which controversially left the institution of slavery intact in the South. The Civil War Amendments ended slavery, granted citizenship to former slaves, guaranteed all Americans "equal protection under the laws," and denied states the ability to prevent voting rights on the basis of race.
- The states used many means to prevent racial/ethnic minorities from obtaining equality, including Black Codes, literacy tests, poll taxes, and Jim Crow laws, and by distinguishing state action from private discrimination and upholding the controversial "separate but equal" doctrine in public accommodations.
- The movement toward civil rights for racial and ethnic minorities in all public accommodations began in the late 1950s and emerged as a major force under the leadership of Martin Luther King Jr., Cesar Chavez, and others. A number of court decisions, including *Mendez v. Westminster* (1947) and *Brown v. Board of Education* (1954), eventually eliminated the "separate but equal" doctrine. The Civil Rights Act of 1964 and the Voting Rights Act of 1965 brought America closer to the goal of equality for racial/ethnic minorities.

5-4 The Women's Movement and Gender Equality

- The seeds were sown for the movement toward gender equality in the early twentieth century with the ratification of the Nineteenth Amendment, guaranteeing women the right to vote. However, not until the formation of the National Organization for Women (NOW) and its emergence as a significant political force did women's equality start to capture national attention. Beginning in the 1970s, the Supreme Court gave intermediate scrutiny to gender classifications as well, invalidating all but a handful of laws that discriminated on the basis of gender.
- Congress passed Title IX in 1972, prohibiting the exclusion of women from any educational programs receiving financial assistance from the federal government. Courts have interpreted Title IX as requiring colleges to provide as many opportunities for female athletes as male athletes.

5-5 Other Group Struggles for Equality

- More recent debates over racial and ethnic equality have focused on discrimination against older Americans, disabled Americans, and LGBTQ persons.
- Courts have vindicated some of the rights of LGBTQ persons, upholding the constitutional right of same-sex marriage. Additionally, Congress has passed laws protecting the rights of older Americans and disabled Americans from discrimination, especially in the workplace.

5-6 Continuing Struggles over Equality in the Modern Era

- Racial and ethnic differences are not the only type of discrimination practiced by governments. Recent battles have focused on discrimination against Muslim Americans (and how to protect their civil rights in the post-9/11 era).
- Two contemporary issues relating to civil rights are affirmative action and racial profiling. The courts have struck down affirmative action programs that feature quotas and other fixed advantages for racial minorities. Racial profiling remains a controversial practice, especially as practiced by state officials against immigrant populations and others.

Key Terms

affirmative action (p. 98)
Brown v. Board of Education (1954) (p. 85)
civil rights (p. 84)
Civil Rights Act of 1964 (p. 93)
Civil Rights Act of 1968 (p. 93)
economic equality (p. 84)
Fifteenth Amendment (p. 87)
Fourteenth Amendment (p. 87)
grandfather clause requirement (p. 87)
Jim Crow laws (p. 88)
literacy tests (p. 87)
Mendez v. Westminster (1947) (p. 90)
Nineteenth Amendment (p. 96)

Plessy v. Ferguson (1896) (p. 89)
political equality (p. 84)
poll taxes (p. 87)
property requirements (p. 87)
racial profiling (p. 105)
social equality (p. 84)
social movements (p. 96)
strict scrutiny (p. 90)
Thirteenth Amendment (p. 87)
Title IX (p. 98)
Twenty-fourth Amendment (p. 93)
Voting Rights Act of 1965 (p. 93)
white-only primaries (p. 87)

Part II
INSTITUTIONS

6

CONGRESS

Cynthia Johnson/The LIFE Images Collection/Getty Images

The U.S. Capitol Building

CONGRESS IS A large and complex institution. It is the branch of government that is primarily responsible for creating new laws. Although the Constitution makes no mention of the role that political parties might play in making laws, partisanship is the primary factor that organizes Congress and its daily operations. The 2018 congressional elections resulted in the Democrats taking the House majority and Republicans holding their majority in the Senate, further reflecting the nation's partisan divisions. Nonetheless, there are ample opportunities for either party, or even a small set of members, to thwart new laws from passage, contributing to the gridlock in Washington, DC. In this chapter, we explore the organization of the Congress and its leadership structure. We trace the steps of the complex law-making process, the checks that Congress has on the other branches of government, and the important role that members play in their home districts.

Partisan Divisiveness in the Halls of Congress

Partisan divisiveness often prevails in the U.S. Congress; still, during certain periods of our nation's history, the level of partisan nastiness and incivility has been especially high, all but paralyzing the legislative branch.

Then

In the 1850s, just before the Civil War, Congress was frequently stymied by especially hostile relations between the two major parties. On one occasion, actual physical violence erupted on the floor of the U.S. Senate. House member Preston Brooks of South Carolina walked over to the Senate and clubbed Senator Charles Sumner of Massachusetts nearly to death because of their disagreements over slavery. The term *filibuster*—from a Dutch word meaning "pirate"—first became popular during the 1850s, when it was applied to efforts by the Senate minority to hold the Senate floor in order to prevent a vote on a bill. The heightened divisiveness of the 1850s led to extreme dysfunction, driven by congressional party-based factions that could not work together to solve America's problems.

Now

During the past decade, congressional approval ratings have fallen to all-time lows, averaging 10 percent or lower. Such dismal ratings are a product of the vitriol and partisanship that began in 2009 when the Senate witnessed a record number of filibusters, as not one simple majority vote on a substantive bill prevailed throughout this period. The legislative battle over the Affordable Care Act ("Obamacare") in 2010 epitomized this bitter partisan reality, as Senate Republicans voted over and over along party lines to reject any and all bills proposed by the Democrats. The election of President Donald Trump in 2016 took partisan divisiveness in Congress to a new level over issues such as immigration bans from predominantly Muslim countries, tax cuts for corporations, and the building of a U.S.–Mexican border wall, to name just a few.

For Critical Thinking and Discussion

1. Why has partisan divisiveness and gridlock in Congress become so prevalent over the past decade? What issues and events contribute to the intense partisan bickering we have witnessed in the modern era?
2. Do you think that the results of the 2020 congressional elections are likely to improve the cooperation of the parties in Congress, or do you believe they will contribute to even more partisan divisiveness?

North Wind Picture Archives / Alamy Stock Photo

Senator Preston Brooks shown clubbing Senator Charles Sumner on the floor of the U.S. Senate during an antislavery debate in 1856.

6-1 ARTICLE I AND THE CREATION OF CONGRESS

Article I of the U.S. Constitution created Congress, and the fact that it came first was no accident. James Madison, the father of the Constitution, referred to Congress as the "first branch of government," and as a graduate student, Woodrow Wilson (later the 28th president of the United States) wrote in his book *Congressional Government* (1885) that "anyone who is unfamiliar with what Congress actually does and how it does it . . . is very far from a knowledge of the constitutional system under which we live."[1] As the legislative branch of the federal government, Congress has ultimate authority for enacting new laws. Because this authority is central to any system of government, the founders engaged in considerable debate and took great care in building this first branch.

There was little question that a congress of some type would be the central institution in the new political system—a congress had been a central feature in all attempts to organize the states up through and including the Constitutional Convention of 1787. The Albany Congress of 1754 was the first attempt to unite the colonies—at the time for common defense against the French in the pending French and Indian War. The Albany Plan of Union called for the colonies to organize through the vehicle of a "congress." In addition, colonial efforts to deal with emerging conflicts with the British led to the formation of two congresses: the First Continental Congress in 1774 and then the Second Continental Congress in 1775. After the Revolutionary War was won, the first official government of the United States, created under the Articles of Confederation, again used a congress as its organizing principle. It is not surprising, then, that Article I, Section 1 of the U.S. Constitution states: "All legislative Powers herein granted shall be vested in a Congress of the United States."

The founders engaged in plenty of debate, negotiation, and compromise in defining the powers, functions, and structure of the U.S. Congress. The complexity of this institution continues today. Congress is filled with paradoxes. On one hand, it is a highly democratic institution in which senators and representatives are selected in free and open elections; on the other hand, Congress often is responsive to an exceedingly narrow set of specialized interests. Citizens and journalists frequently criticize the institution as being too slow to act responsively; yet voters return more than 9 in 10 of their elected members to office. At times, such as in the weeks following the terrorist attacks of September 11, 2001, Congress can show enthusiasm for tackling large issues expeditiously: within days of the attacks, it passed the USA PATRIOT Act, which featured numerous antiterrorism measures. At other times, it seems to avoid taking positions on important issues, such as immigration policies and abortion rights. Many of these factors have led to very low confidence ratings in Congress from the American public. Figure 6-1 shows the results of the Gallup Poll's survey on confidence levels in a variety of institutions. As the chart shows, confidence in Congress has declined significantly since the mid-1970s.

Most significantly, Congress is the branch of the U.S. government that ensures representation of the people through the direct election of members of the House and, in more recent times, of members of the Senate as well. Through its 535 members, Congress provides

FIGURE 6-1

Confidence in Congress (1976–2016)

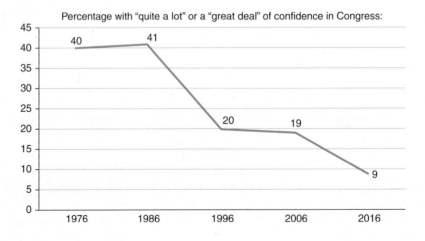

Percentage with "quite a lot" or a "great deal" of confidence in Congress:

Source: Based on data from National Survey of American Adults conducted by the Gallup Organization.

representation of many groups throughout the country, such as women, African Americans, Native Americans, LGBTQ persons, and Latinos.

6-2 THE STRUCTURE AND ORGANIZATION OF CONGRESS

Congress is organized into two separate chambers, the Senate and the House of Representatives, and is thus termed a **bicameral legislature**. Creating a bicameral legislature enabled the founders to reach a compromise between two factions at the Constitutional Convention—those who represented large states and wanted congressional representation according to population and those from small states who favored the model of the Articles of Confederation (i.e., that each state, regardless of population, would be equally represented in Congress). The "Great Compromise" reached by the convention delegates allowed for equal state representation in the Senate and representation based on population in the House. These two chambers have shared law-making responsibilities since 1789.[2]

This nearly equal sharing of legislative power between the two chambers is significant. Many other nations in the world have bicameral legislatures, but the two legislative houses are rarely equal in power and usually do not share power. In the British Parliament, for example, the House of Lords has little power and serves a mostly symbolic function in that nation's politics, whereas the House of Commons wields the most authoritative power. Legislatures in other nations, such as Canada, France, Germany, Israel, and Japan, are also heavily dominated

> **bicameral legislature**
> A legislature composed of two separate chambers.

DEBATES OVER DIVERSITY
Does Congress Look Diverse?

Does the racial, ethnic, and gender diversity of Congress reflect the reality of the America that it purports to represent? One way to evaluate congressional representation is to examine descriptive representation, or the descriptive characteristics of members of Congress as compared to the corresponding makeup of the U.S. population. Such an exercise depicts a congressional delegation far from reflective of the American population.

The Reflective Democracy Campaign project calls attention to this lack of diversity in the national legislature. The project created a National Representation Index, which measures political representation by race and gender, then weighted to account for geographic population differences across the country.[3] Their stark figures show that white men are 31 percent of the population but hold 65 percent of elected positions. In other words, they have four times more political representation than other gender/racial groups. Women represent 51 percent of the U.S. population but hold only 23 percent of congressional seats. Racial/ethnic minorities represent 38 percent of the U.S. population but occupy only 11 percent of the seats in Congress (7 percent minority males and 4 percent minority females).

For Critical Thinking and Discussion

1. Are you surprised or concerned about the lack of racial, ethnic, and gender diversity in Congress?
2. What are the important implications of this lack of congressional diversity?

Win McNamee / Staff / Getty Images

Members of the Congressional Black Caucus holding a press conference in Washington, DC.

by one house. By contrast, in the U.S. Congress, the Senate and House are coequal chambers, with each enjoying about as much power as the other. Similar to the United States, the national legislatures in Italy and Mexico include two houses with nearly equal power. Many nations have *unicameral* legislatures that consist of only one body, such as the 275-member legislature elected to govern in Iraq in 2005.

Bicameralism has important implications for the legislative process in American politics. Passing new laws is difficult because the two chambers, constructed so differently, must come to agreement before a new law is enacted. The slowness that often characterizes law-making in Congress is, in part, a product of this reality. The sharing of power and the "checks" that each chamber has on the other are no mistake. Indeed, the founders intentionally built a Congress that would move slowly and carefully in the adoption of new laws, a process that, although often characterized as gridlock, ensures that change is well contemplated before it is adopted.

THE HOUSE OF REPRESENTATIVES: THE "PEOPLE'S HOUSE"

The founders intended the House of Representatives to be the "people's house," or the institution through which ordinary people would be represented in government. At the time the Constitution was adopted, the only federal officials directly elected by the people were members of the House of Representatives. Senators were chosen by state legislatures; the president and vice president were selected by electors in the Electoral College; and judges, ambassadors, and high-ranking officials in the executive branch were nominated by the president and approved by the Senate. In Federalist No. 51, James Madison admonished, "As it is essential to liberty that the government in general should have a common interest with the people, so it is particularly essential that the branch of it under consideration [the House] should have an immediate dependence on, and an intimate sympathy with, the people."[4] The House of Representatives thus directly connects voter sentiment with popular representation.

So that members of the House would be held accountable, Article I, Section 2 sets the term of a House member at two years, keeping members constantly attentive to public opinion. Indeed, because of their relatively brief term of office, members of the House are typically consumed with concerns about winning reelection. This preoccupation has been well documented by scholars such as Thomas Mann, who argues that incumbent House members are in campaign mode most of the time, feeling "unsafe at any margin" of victory.[5]

Article I also ensures that the House of Representatives reflects the popular will by requiring that the number of representatives from each state be proportional to each state's population. States are not equally represented in the House of Representatives; rather, the population of each state is proportionately represented, at least to a large degree. This means that a more populous state has greater representation than a less populous one. The state of California, for example, now has 53 seats in the House of Representatives, compared to Wyoming, which has only 1 seat.

The first Congress in 1789 included 65 members, consistent with the Article I requirement that the number of House members should not exceed 1 for every 30,000 people in a state. As the nation grew in both the number of states and number of people, the number of members of the House of Representatives also grew. If the ratio of 30,000 people to 1 representative applied today, there would be about 10,000 members of the House of Representatives! By the mid-1800s, Congress began enlarging the population size of a congressional district to keep the membership of the House from getting too large. Public Law 62-5, passed in 1911 to take effect in 1913, capped the total number of House seats at 435.[6]

Today there are still 435 congressional districts, each represented by one House member. The number of people who are represented in a congressional district is tied to a number that changes after every census. Since fixing the number of seats at 435, Congress has struggled to find an equitable way to allocate House seats to the states. This process is known as reapportionment.

Several U.S. Supreme Court decisions in the early 1960s[7] established the basic principle that guides the process of reapportionment after every census—the "one person, one vote" principle. According to this principle, the population size of congressional districts

congressional district A geographic region (either a state itself or a region located entirely within one state) whose residents select one member to represent it in the House of Representatives.

reapportionment The allocation of a fixed number of House seats to the states.

must be as equal as possible. Currently, that amounts to roughly 710,000 people per district. The requirement that each state maintain at least one House district causes some variance among the population sizes of each district. The single congressional district for Wyoming, for example, has a population of about 580,000 because that is the number of people who live in that state. Consequently, Wyoming's population is proportionately "overrepresented," compared to most other congressional districts. Because congressional districts cannot cross state boundaries, the population size of congressional districts across states also varies. Yet, once congressional districts are officially allocated to states based on the U.S. Census, the size of each district within a state must be as close to equal as possible.

The Constitution requires that a new census of the population be taken every 10 years, which is used to reapportion seats in the House of Representatives to each state. The states are then responsible for redistricting congressional boundary lines to achieve equal representation in each of the congressional districts, that is, redrawing congressional district lines to achieve the "one person, one vote" principle within the borders of the state.

In addition to equalizing the size of congressional districts, parties in each state try to optimize the partisan characteristics of each district to their advantage. This drawing of district boundaries to favor one party over the other is referred to as gerrymandering, a term named for Elbridge Gerry, who was a signer of the Declaration of Independence, a Massachusetts delegate to the Constitutional Convention, a U.S. congressman, governor of Massachusetts, and vice president under James Madison. While governor, he endorsed legislation that redrew districts in Massachusetts, resulting in huge advantages for his political party, the Democratic-Republicans. The map of one of the new districts took on an odd shape, that of a salamander. Gerry's political opponents, the Federalists, dubbed the plan the "gerrymander plan." The political fallout for Gerry was significant—he lost his next bid for governor. But the legacy of gerrymandering continues. Every decade or so, parties in states with more than one House member must ultimately negotiate a redistricting plan based on gerrymandered district boundaries that each party hopes will optimize its electoral successes.

Amendments to the Voting Rights Act in 1982 have previously required that some states apply the gerrymandering concept to create majority-minority districts. That is, the boundaries of some congressional districts are drawn to ensure that the majority of voters are members of minority groups, thus enhancing the chances that a minority group member will win the congressional seat. Such "racial gerrymandering" is intended to prevent the dilution of minority representation in Congress. The creation of majority-minority districts substantially increased racial/ethnic minority representation in the House. However, weakening of the Voting Rights Act and several Supreme Court decisions have lessened the possibility for creating majority-minority districts in the future.

Article I requires that all members of the House of Representatives be at least 25 years of age, have been a U.S. citizen for a minimum of seven years, and live in the state (though not necessarily the congressional district) from which they are elected. These requirements are somewhat less restrictive than those for the Senate—another indication of the founders' intention to give the people a greater role in deciding on who members of the House should be.

THE SENATE: A STABILIZING FACTOR

Whereas the founders wanted to make the House of Representatives highly responsive to the people, their idea for the Senate was quite different. The Senate was to represent the states—with each state having two senators, or equal representation. As adopted, the Constitution specified that senators were to be elected not by the people of the state but by the state legislatures, another way to recognize states' importance. Not until passage of the Seventeenth Amendment to the Constitution in 1913 were senators elected directly by the people of the state they represented.

The founders were also concerned that the "people's house" might be too prone to radical changes in membership resulting from swift changes in popular opinion. James Madison in particular regarded the U.S. Senate as "a necessary fence against this danger,"[8] able to resist fast changes in federal legislation because it was less accessible to the people. In fact, during the first five years of our constitutional government, the U.S. Senate met in closed session. By sharing legislative power with the House of Representatives, the Senate, a slower, more

redistricting The act of redrawing congressional boundaries to achieve equal representation in each of the congressional districts.

gerrymandering The drawing of House district boundaries to the benefit of one political party over another. The term is named for Elbridge Gerry, a Massachusetts delegate to the Constitutional Convention, who (as governor) redrew districts in this fashion to favor the Democratic-Republicans.

majority-minority district A congressional district drawn with geographic boundaries that promote the chances of electing a minority member to represent that district.

deliberative body, would be the mechanism for protecting against the potential tyranny of the masses. Thus, the creation of new laws would be forced to proceed at a more thoughtful pace.

The Constitution sets the term of a U.S. senator at six years, three times the length of that for a House member. The founders staggered the terms of senators. Every two years, only one-third of the seats in the Senate are up for reelection, as compared to all of the seats in the House. So, although in theory all of the seats in the House can change every other year, the Senate may change only by a maximum of 34 seats every two years and is thus less prone to drastic changes in membership.

The qualifications for becoming a U.S. senator are also tighter. The minimum age is 30, five years older than in the House. The founders based this provision on the theory that older people would be less likely to endorse radical change. Also, a U.S. senator must have been a citizen for at least nine years (rather than seven for the House) and be a resident of the state that he or she represents.

Article I requires that there be two senators from each state. The total number of senators grew from 26 in 1789 to 100 in 1959, the year Alaska and Hawaii became the 49th and 50th states, respectively. Although the size of the Senate has grown, it still remains small, at least relative to the size of the House of Representatives. The smaller size of the Senate is often cited as the primary reason why debate in the Senate tends to be more civil and camaraderie between individuals more important.

LEADERSHIP IN CONGRESS

Unlike the executive branch, which is headed by the president, no one person or office leads Congress as a whole. Leadership is distinct in the Senate and the House of Representatives. Though both chambers must work together to pass new laws, each chamber maintains its own leadership structure to work on bills, pass laws, and conduct its other business. Cooperation between the House and Senate is necessary to accomplish legislation.

The principal factor driving leadership in each chamber is the political party system, which, interestingly, is not mentioned in the U.S. Constitution.[9] The two-party system in America generates a majority of members from one of the two major parties, in both the Senate and the House of Representatives. Since 1851, the majority party in each house has been either the Democratic Party or the Republican Party. Members of the party that has the majority of seats constitute the **majority caucus**, whereas those who are members of the party with a minority of seats constitute the **minority caucus**. The majority caucus in the House and the majority caucus in the Senate use their respective majorities to elect leaders and maintain control of their chamber. The larger the party's majority is, and the more discipline and unity among party members, the stronger the power of the majority party's leadership ability will be.

From 1954 through 1980, the Democrats held the majority caucus in the Senate. Since then, partisan control of the Senate has shifted seven times, with the Democrats having a majority for 18 years and the GOP for 20 years. The outcome of the 2018 elections ensured that Republicans would maintain their majority in the Senate.

In the House of Representatives, the Democrats enjoyed its status as majority caucus from 1954 up through 1994. Finally, after 40 years, the 1994 elections transformed a Democratic majority to a Republican majority. The Republicans continued to dominate the House until the 2006 midterm

majority caucus The members of the party that has the majority of seats in a particular chamber.

minority caucus The members of the party that has a minority of seats in a particular chamber.

SAUL LOEB / AFP / Getty Images

Rep. Nancy Pelosi (D-CA) takes the oath as Speaker of the House on January 3, 2019. She is the only woman to ever hold that post.

elections, at which point the Democrats regained leadership of the people's chamber. Democratic control of the House, however, proved short-lived. In 2010, the GOP won back 63 House seats from the Democrats and reestablished a Republican majority, only to be reversed with Democrats taking over the majority after the 2018 midterm elections.

LEADERSHIP IN THE HOUSE OF REPRESENTATIVES

The only guidance the Constitution offers regarding House leadership is contained in Article I, Section 2: "The House of Representatives shall choose their Speaker and other Officers." The **Speaker of the House** is the title given to the leader of this chamber. Every two years, when a new Congress takes office, the full House of Representatives votes to determine who the Speaker will be from among its 435 members. In practice, the selection of Speaker is made by the majority caucus, which meets prior to the vote for Speaker and agrees on their leader, who receives virtually all the votes from the majority party members, thus guaranteeing that the majority party will occupy the Speaker of the House post.

As presiding officer, the Speaker of the House is the most powerful member of the House of Representatives, although the position was not always so powerful. Through the 1800s, the Speaker acted mostly as procedural leader, or presiding officer, of the House. However, with the accession of Joe Cannon to Speaker in 1903, this post became much more powerful. Cannon, a Republican from Illinois, served in the House for more than 50 years and was Speaker from 1903 to 1911. As Speaker, Cannon used the House Rules Committee to amass a tremendous amount of power.[10] Known as "Uncle Joe," he arbitrarily recognized who could speak in the House chamber and required that any measure passing the Rules Committee would have to be personally approved by him. Cannon also made a practice of filling important committee posts with those who were loyal to him. A coalition of Democrats and insurgent Republicans eventually unseated Cannon, but Uncle Joe permanently changed the visibility and power of the Speaker position.

The Speaker remains powerful today for a variety of reasons, as shown in Table 6-1.

Partisan control of the House is the key factor regarding how that body is organized to do its work. Because the party that holds a majority of seats selects the Speaker, the majority party controls the legislative agenda through members serving in other leadership posts, including chairs of committees.

> **Speaker of the House** The leader of the House of Representatives, responsible for assigning new bills to committees, recognizing members to speak in the House chamber, and assigning chairs of committees.

TABLE 6-1

Why the Speaker of the House Is a Powerful Position

1. As the person responsible for assigning new bills to committees, the Speaker can delay the assignment of a bill or assign it to a committee that is either friendly or hostile to its contents, a power that gives the Speaker control over much of the House agenda.

2. The Speaker has the ability to recognize members to speak in the House chamber. Because an important part of the legislative process involves members debating bills on the House floor, the Speaker's authority over this process is significant.

3. The Speaker is the ultimate arbiter and interpreter of House rules. The ability to cast final judgment on a rule of order can make or break a piece of legislation.

4. The Speaker appoints members to serve on special committees, including conference committees, which iron out differences between similar bills passed in the House and Senate. The Speaker's influence is thus felt in the final changes made to a bill before Congress completes work on it.

5. The Speaker plays an influential role in assigning members to particular permanent committees. Some committees, as we will see later in this chapter, are more important than others. Being on the Speaker's "good side" can help in getting a good committee assignment. In addition, the Speaker hand-picks the nine members of the all-important Rules Committee.

6. The Speaker has ultimate authority to schedule votes in the full House on a bill, an authority that allows the Speaker to speed the process or delay it, using timing to either improve or subvert a bill's chances of being passed.

To promote partisan leadership, the majority caucus in the House votes for a House **majority leader**, and the minority caucus for a House **minority leader**. These leaders oversee the development of their party platforms and are responsible for achieving party coherence in voting. Other important party leadership positions in the House are the House minority and majority **whips**. Whips report to their respective party leaders in the House and are primarily responsible for counting up the partisan votes on bills—that is, they contact members of their party caucus and try to convince them to vote the way their party leadership wants them to vote. The whips spend much of their time on the floor of the House, on the phone, or in the offices of their party colleagues, counting votes and urging their members to vote the party line on bills.

LEADERSHIP IN THE SENATE

The Constitution prescribes that the presiding officer of the Senate is the vice president of the United States. In this capacity, the vice president also holds the title of president of the Senate. Unlike the Speaker of the House, who is necessarily a member of the House of Representatives, the president of the Senate is not a member of the Senate. The president of the Senate cannot engage in debate on the floor of the Senate and has no legislative duties in the Senate, with one notable exception: to cast a vote in the Senate in the event of a tie. John Adams, the first vice president of the United States, was the most frequent tiebreaker in U.S. history, casting a vote 21 times in the Senate. Some vice presidents (such as Joe Biden, who held the office from 2009 through 2016) are never called to cast a tie-breaking vote. The current vice president, Mike Pence, however, cast nine tie-breaking votes during the Trump administration's first two years in office.

In practice, the vice president rarely shows up on the Senate floor to preside over its session. The presiding officer, in the absence of the vice president, is the **president pro tempore** (*pro tempore* is Latin, meaning "for the time being"). By custom, the official president pro tempore is the senator in the majority caucus who has served the longest number of consecutive years in the Senate. Again, however, in practice the president pro tempore rarely exercises the authority to preside over the Senate. With fewer rules and a greater culture of respect to fellow members than in the House, the presiding officer of the Senate serves what is largely a ceremonial role.

Leadership in the Senate is principally a function of partisanship, with the majority and minority caucuses organizing through leadership posts similar to those of the House of Representatives. Once again, the majority party exercises tremendous power by controlling the agenda and mobilizing majority votes on important issues for the party. The majority caucus elects a Senate majority leader, and the minority caucus a Senate minority leader. These leaders are the main party spokespersons in the Senate, lead their party caucuses in proposing new laws, and are the chief architects of their party's platform. As leader of the majority, the Senate majority leader enjoys special power in making assignments to leadership of committees.

As in the House, the Senate majority and minority leaders are supported by whips, majority and minority. The whips in the Senate serve the same function as those in the House—they keep track of how caucus members are planning to vote on upcoming bills, and they communicate the positions of party leaders on upcoming legislative votes.

Leaders in the Senate generally have far less power than their counterparts in the House. The smaller number of senators requires less discipline in membership, and the culture of the Senate includes a greater amount of deference from one senator to another. Because there are fewer rules and formal procedures in the Senate, leaders and rule-making members have less power to control debate in that body.

majority leader In the Senate, the controlling party's main spokesperson who leads his or her party in proposing new laws and crafting the party's platform. The Senate majority leader also enjoys the power to make committee assignments. In the House, the majority leader is the controlling party's second in command, who helps the Speaker to oversee the development of the party platform.

minority leader The leader of the minority party in each chamber.

whips (majority and minority) Member of Congress elected by his or her party to count potential votes and promote party unity in voting.

president pro tempore In the absence of the vice president, the senator who presides over the Senate session. By tradition, this is usually the senator from the majority caucus who has served the longest number of consecutive years in the Senate.

Senate GOP majority leader Mitch McConnell (left) confers with Democratic minority leader Chuck Schumer (right) during a congressional awards ceremony.

6-3 THE COMMITTEE SYSTEM

The work of a member of Congress can be classified into four categories: (1) running for reelection, (2) serving constituents, (3) working on legislation, and (4) providing oversight of federal agencies. Working on legislation involves two activities: working on bills in committees and voting on proposed bills.[11] The bulk of work on legislation consists of what members do in committees, which includes generating ideas for new laws, debating the merits of those ideas, holding hearings, conducting investigations, listening to the testimony of experts, offering modifications and additions to proposed bills, and giving important advice to all House and Senate members regarding how they should vote on a new bill. Committee work also is the means through which members fulfill their role of oversight of federal agencies. Voting, on the other hand, is a rather simple and straightforward process. Members show up on the House or Senate floor and cast a vote of either "aye," "nay," or "present," indicating their support for, opposition to, or abstention from voting on a proposed piece of legislation.

Every year about 10,000 bills are introduced in Congress. A bill is a formally proposed piece of legislation, and many bills are long, complex documents with much legal and technical information. It is not practical to assume that each senator and House member reads and digests every bill that is introduced. As a way to manage the workload, both chambers of Congress rely heavily on a committee system. In both the House and Senate, each member is assigned to a few committees and becomes an expert in the subject area of the committee. Most of the members' legislative work revolves around the committees to which they are assigned.

Congressional committees also include subcommittees, providing for even more specialization and division of labor. Currently there are more than 100 subcommittees in the House alone. Each of the subcommittees is also assigned a chair, so many members in the majority party of the House are chairs of either a committee or subcommittee. In the Senate, with fewer members, all members of the majority are usually the chair of at least one committee or subcommittee. A House member sits on an average of five different committees, whereas a senator sits on an average of seven committees.

What makes the committee system so powerful a force in legislation? It is the deference that most members give to the work of their colleagues in committees. Recognizing specialized knowledge, respecting the need for division of labor, and protecting one's own authority in the committees in which one serves all lead senators and House members to vote on the basis of a committee's recommendation on a bill.

TYPES OF COMMITTEES IN CONGRESS

There are four general types of congressional committees: standing committees, select committees, conference committees, and joint committees.

Standing committees are permanent committees that exist in both the House and the Senate. Most standing committees focus on a particular substantive area of public policy, such as transportation, labor, foreign affairs, or the federal budget. A few focus on procedural matters of the House and Senate, such as the House Rules Committee and the Senate Rules and Administration Committee. The most significant power of the standing committee is that of **reporting legislation**, which means that the full House or Senate cannot vote on a bill unless the committee votes to approve it first. No other type of congressional committee has the power to report legislation. Table 6-2 lists the standing committees of the House and Senate.

Standing committees have been the heart and soul of congressional legislative work since the early 1800s. Just like today, standing committees at that time were divided into substantive policy areas and had plenty of authority to determine the future of a bill within their jurisdiction. For example, in 1802 the House of Representatives established the Ways and Means Committee to set policies for America's federal tax system. Any bill dealing with changes in the tax system had to pass through this committee, as it still does today. The House Ways and Means Committee remains the primary author of tax bills.

Though most standing committees focus on a substantive area of public policy, such areas of focus are often broad and complex. To further divide labor and provide for even greater

bill A proposed law presented for consideration to a legislative body.

standing committee A permanent committee that exists in both the House and Senate; most standing committees focus on a particular substantive area of public policy, such as transportation, labor, foreign affairs, and the federal budget.

reporting legislation The exclusive power of standing committees to forward legislation to the full House or Senate. Neither chamber can vote on a bill unless the committee votes to approve it first.

TABLE 6-2

The Standing Committees in Congress

Committees in the House	Committees in the Senate
Agriculture	Agriculture, Nutrition, and Forestry
Appropriations	Appropriations
Armed Services	Armed Services
Budgets	Banking, Housing, and Urban Affairs
Education and Labor	Budget
Energy and Commerce	Commerce, Science, and Transportation
Financial Services	Energy and Natural Resources
Homeland Security	Environment and Public Works
House Administration	Finance
Intelligence*	Foreign Relations
Judiciary	Health, Education, Labor, and Pensions
Natural Resources	Homeland Security and Governmental Affairs
Oversight and Government Reform	Judiciary
Rules	Rules and Administration
Science and Technology	Small Business and Entrepreneurship
Small Business	Veterans Affairs
Standards of Official Conduct	
Transportation and Infrastructure	
Veterans Affairs	
Ways and Means	

* Technically a "permanent select committee."

levels of specialization, most standing committees include subcommittees. For example, the House Transportation and Infrastructure Committee includes the following subcommittees: Aviation; Coast Guard and Marine Transportation; Economic Development, Public Buildings, Hazardous Materials, and Pipeline Transportation; Ground Transportation; Oversight, Investigations, and Emergency Management; and Water Resources and Environment.

Before the House of Representatives or the Senate can vote on any bill, it must first be approved by a majority of members on the committee. A number of factors can affect a committee's consideration of a bill, which can seriously slow down the process of a bill becoming law and create a sense of "legislative gridlock." When a committee gets a new bill, the chair usually directs the bill to a subcommittee. The subcommittee discusses the bill, holds hearings, and makes changes, additions, or deletions to the bill. Usually, after a successful subcommittee vote, the bill moves back to the full committee, where additional debate and hearings might occur. Only after a successful committee vote is the bill ready to be considered by the full House and/or Senate. This process occurs in both the House and the Senate. There are, therefore, many opportunities for standing committees to slow the policy-making process or bring it to a grinding halt.

A second general type of committee in Congress is the **select committee**, a special committee established to examine a particular issue of concern. Select committees do not have the power to report legislation, and they are not permanent. Once their work on a particular issue

select committee
A committee established by a resolution in either the House or the Senate for a specific purpose and, usually, for a limited time.

of the day is complete, the select committee is dissolved. Select committees are often formed to deal with a particularly serious national problem—a problem for which legislation may not be considered but rather a recommendation might be made. In 2009, for example, the Democratic leadership in both houses established the Select Committee on Energy Independence and Global Warming. When the GOP won back the House, its new leaders indicated they no longer wanted this committee to continue its work, and so it was disbanded.

A third type of committee found in Congress is the conference committee. As described earlier in this chapter, the House and Senate are equal players in the legislative process. This means that both chambers debate, hold hearings on, comment on, and vote on individual pieces of legislation. A bill, then, is considered, modified, and voted on by both the House and the Senate. Assuming that a bill survives both chambers and passes, it is likely that the changes made to the bill during the standing committee process will differ between the House and Senate. Conference committees consist of both House members and senators, who work together to iron out differences in the House and Senate versions of a bill.

A fourth type of committee is the joint committee, which consists of members from both chambers. Joint committees do not propose legislation and have no reporting power but rather are investigative in nature, focusing on issues of general concern, such as oversight of programs that are administered by the executive branch of the federal government. Unlike select committees, which are temporary and focus on a narrower topic, joint committees are typically permanent and focus on broader policy areas. An example is Congress's Joint Economic Committee. This committee keeps tabs on the performance of the nation's economy and provides oversight to the Federal Reserve Board, the unit that, among other things, has authority to adjust the federal prime interest rate.

conference committee
A joint committee of Congress appointed by the House of Representatives and the Senate to resolve differences on a particular bill.

joint committee
A committee composed of members of both the House and the Senate that is investigative in nature.

LEADERSHIP OF CONGRESSIONAL COMMITTEES

Although there are a handful of broad leadership positions such as presiding officers and "party leaders" in the House and Senate, the vast majority of leaders are the chairs of the many committees and subcommittees in the two chambers. The power of the majority caucus is fully felt in the committee and subcommittee chairs, as all chairs are members of the majority caucus. Committees are where Congress gets most of its work done, and the chairs of committees have a great deal of power in determining what gets done and when it gets done.[12]

For example, the chairs decide how much time, if any, to spend on a new bill; they choose the people who will testify before the committee; and they allot the time to be spent on testimony and committee discussion. House and Senate leaders choose committee chairs from members of the majority caucus, selections generally based on seniority and party allegiance. For each committee, the majority party's ranking, or senior, member is typically the person who becomes the committee chair, although the Speaker of the House ultimately determines the chairs for House committees and the Senate majority leader does the same for Senate committees.[13] Though still important, congressional reforms in 1974 and 1994 have somewhat reduced the power of seniority in the determination of committee chairs. More recently, the selection of chairs and the chairs' adherence to party leadership have provided a strong basis for party influence in congressional leadership.

PARTISAN NATURE OF THE COMMITTEE SYSTEM

The large number of standing committees and subcommittees, along with the significant power of the committee given its expertise in the policy area, disperses legislative power. It is in the interest of the majority party, however, to control what bills are given priority, how bills are written, and what bills get passed. Thus, the primary organizational characteristic of most committees in Congress is partisanship. To control the committee agenda and the committee votes, the majority caucus ensures that all committees have a majority of members of their party.[14] Furthermore, the chair of each committee is from the majority caucus. In addition, the majority caucus typically reserves a "supermajority" of seats on the most powerful committees, such as the Rules and Appropriations Committees.

CONGRESSIONAL STAFFING

The 435 House members and 100 senators are supported by a large professional staff, many of whom are young, recent college graduates. Staffers perform a variety of support functions related to the roles of members of Congress. They conduct background research on bills, help generate new ideas for bills, provide services to constituents, and aid in the oversight of executive agencies. There are three categories of congressional staff.

First is the member's congressional personal staff. Members of Congress are given a budget to support a group of staffers to assist them. They typically have a staff in their Washington, DC, office and one in their home district office. The personal staffers serve a number

FROM YOUR PERSPECTIVE
An Internship as a Stepping Stone

Shannon Finney / WireImage / Getty Images

The Congressional Hispanic Caucus Institute honors the 2018 Capitol Hill interns at its annual awards gala in Washington, DC.

Many college students interested in politics and public policy seek internships with Congress during the summer. Such an experience allows them to see firsthand how Congress works, gain valuable experience, and prepare for a possible job with the federal government. Students often earn course credit for their internship experience; they may also acquire valuable skills and unique perspectives that enable them to more fully engage in the civic process.

Recently, the job-search website Monster.com estimated that job opportunities in the federal government would grow from 2.1 million to 2.5 million. Building one's résumé with an internship in Congress can help to jump-start a successful career in public service. The dozens of committees in Congress all have spots for college interns, as do large congressional agencies such as the Government Accountability Office, the Congressional Budget Office, and the Library of Congress. In addition, all 535 members of Congress maintain offices in Washington, DC, as well

as in their home state or district. Interns are commonly found helping with casework in many of these offices. Moreover, the partisan leadership offices, such as the majority and minority leaders and whips, frequently hire college interns to help them do their work, as do the Democratic and GOP House and Senate campaign committees. Many senators and representatives were first introduced to Congress through internships they had. At a minimum, an internship with Congress provides a great résumé item when applying for a full-time job in some part of the federal government.

If you are interested in a congressional internship, there are a number of ways to get one. You can contact the office of a member of the House or Senate directly and inquire about future openings. You can visit the internship coordinator at your college or in your university's political science department and ask what might be available and how to apply. Or you can visit the following websites for information about ongoing internship opportunities:

dc.about.com/od/jobs/a/Internships.htm
www.twc.edu
www.cbo.gov/about/careers/internships

For Critical Thinking and Discussion

1. An internship in Congress provides a wonderful experience for interested students to learn firsthand how our government works. However, there are only a handful of these internships, and so getting them is not easy. Should students who are interested in spending a semester in Washington, DC, have more opportunities to do so?
2. Where would you like to complete an internship? (You may want to discuss the options available to you with your college advisor.)

of legislative support functions, including tracking bills that the member has introduced and conducting research on ideas for new bills. They also work with the local media in the member's home district, answering journalists' questions and providing information on the member's legislative activities. Perhaps the personal staffers' most important responsibility is responding to constituents in the district. House and Senate members receive many kinds of communications from constituents, ranging from requests for information about bills and explanations of why they voted a particular way, to letters expressing opinions on various issues and requests for speaking engagements. The personal staffers are responsible for dealing with these myriad constituent inquiries.

A second type of staffing resource at Congress's disposal is the congressional committee staff. Each standing committee of Congress employs a professional staff, many of whom are policy or legal experts in the policy area of the committee.

The third form of support for members of Congress is congressional agencies. The volume of legislative work has grown substantially over the years, as has the complexity of the federal budget and the policy issues with which Congress deals. One way that Congress has dealt with problems of growth and complexity has been to delegate authority to executive agencies. Consequently, Congress began to lose control of the ability to keep tabs on what those agencies were doing. The explosion of budget deficits in the 1970s and suspicions about the administration that were inspired by the Watergate scandal also left Congress feeling that it lacked necessary information for effective executive oversight. Through the 1970s, Congress relied on budget data from the Office of Management and Budget (OMB), which reports to the president. Congress suspected that the budget figures produced by the OMB were compiled with an eye toward supporting the president's point of view. In response, in 1974 Congress created a new congressional agency, the Congressional Budget Office (CBO), to monitor the nation's economic situation and provide objective projections of the national budget. It reports directly to Congress. With the CBO, Congress no longer relies exclusively on the executive branch to gather economic data and produce information to help Congress oversee the budget process.

At the same time, Congress also substantially expanded the size and funding of the Government Accountability Office (GAO; formerly called the General Accounting Office) and the Congressional Research Service (CRS). Congress uses the GAO to monitor executive agency expenditures. Essentially, the GAO audits the spending of federal organizations to find and remove any abuses. The CRS is Congress's information and statistical data archive. It provides members with information they might need in preparation for writing a bill, conducting a hearing or investigation, or making a speech. Other important agencies of Congress include the Library of Congress, which acts as the de facto national library of the United States as well as a research arm for congressional members, and the Government Printing Office, which prints and provides access to documents produced by and for all three branches of the federal government.

congressional committee staff A group of workers assigned to congressional committees to support each committee's legislative work.

congressional agencies Government bodies formed by and relied on by Congress to support members of Congress in performing their functions.

6-4 HOW A BILL BECOMES A LAW

It is not easy for a bill to become a law. Though most work on bills occurs in committees, there are numerous other points at which a bill might be "killed." The Speaker of the House, the Senate majority leader, and the president all have means at their disposal to kill a bill. There are other points, as well, when bills might be stopped dead in their tracks. Not surprisingly, of the 10,000 or so bills introduced annually in Congress, only about 500 to 1,000 end up becoming law. Rarely does a bill, as originally introduced, become law without significant revision on its way to becoming law. An important book on the process of a bill becoming law is *The Dance of Legislation*, by Eric Redman.[15] As the title suggests, the law-making process involves many people and much politicking; the process is difficult and often follows no regular or consistent path. The steps to a bill becoming law (highlighted in Figure 6-2) are also highly influenced by partisan politics, lobbyists and special interest groups, public opinion, and powerful voices in and out of government. Even though the actual dance of legislation typically follows no neat pattern or order, we describe here the general steps in which a bill becomes a law.

FIGURE 6-2

How a Bill Becomes Law

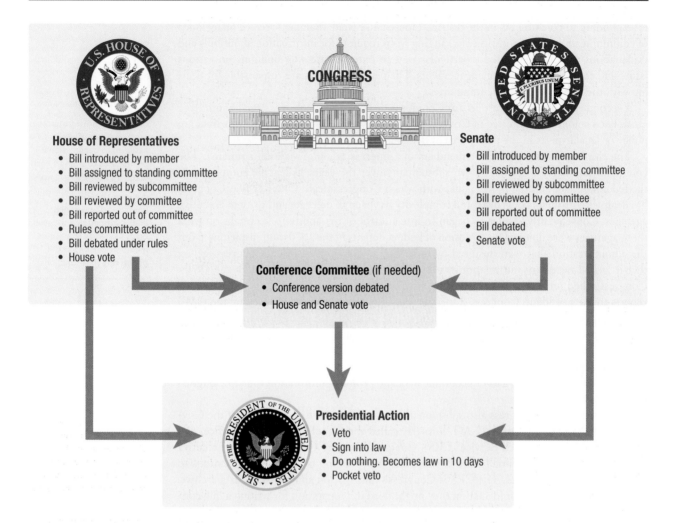

House of Representatives
- Bill introduced by member
- Bill assigned to standing committee
- Bill reviewed by subcommittee
- Bill reviewed by committee
- Bill reported out of committee
- Rules committee action
- Bill debated under rules
- House vote

Senate
- Bill introduced by member
- Bill assigned to standing committee
- Bill reviewed by subcommittee
- Bill reviewed by committee
- Bill reported out of committee
- Bill debated
- Senate vote

Conference Committee (if needed)
- Conference version debated
- House and Senate vote

Presidential Action
- Veto
- Sign into law
- Do nothing. Becomes law in 10 days
- Pocket veto

STEP 1: A BILL IS INTRODUCED

With the exception of tax or revenue proposals, which must originate in the House of Representatives, a bill can be first introduced into either the Senate or the House. The revenue exception, as stipulated in the Constitution, is a product of the American colonial experience with England, and the famous cry "no taxation without representation." Because the House provides popular representation, and representation is the philosophical basis undergirding taxation, the founders gave the House sole authority to originate tax and revenue bills.

Whereas the Constitution requires that only a House member or a senator can introduce a bill, the ideas for new bills come from a variety of sources. Many come from the president of the United States or someone in the president's office or executive branch of government. Others come from lobbyists. Because House members and senators depend on lobbyists for information, and lobbyists represent groups who support candidates for congressional office, those with access to members are an important source of ideas for new legislation. Business leaders, educators, journalists, and regular constituents may also generate ideas for new bills. The next step for those with a suggestion for a new law is to find a sponsor in the House or Senate to introduce the idea in the form of a bill.

Whether the idea for a law comes directly from a member of Congress or from some other source, the first official step in the process is for the sponsoring member to submit the bill to the House or Senate clerk, who issues a unique number to the bill. The clerk in the House sends the bill to the Speaker of the House; the Senate clerk forwards the bill to the Senate majority leader.

STEP 2: THE BILL IS SENT TO A STANDING COMMITTEE FOR ACTION

Next, the bill is assigned to the standing committee that has policy jurisdiction over the topic the bill addresses. Sometimes a bill never makes it to this step. For example, the GOP majority in the House introduced dozens of bills from 2011 through 2013 aimed at contracting or eliminating Obamacare. None of these bills was even sent to a Senate committee by Democratic majority leader Harry Reid.

More times than not, however, the Speaker and majority leader do assign a bill for committee work. A bill introduced in the Senate to raise the minimum wage, for example, would likely be sent to the Senate Labor and Human Resources Committee; a bill proposing increased criminal penalties for mail fraud introduced into the House might be assigned to the House Judiciary Committee.

Most bills die during their initial consideration by the committee. In some cases, the committee chair simply ignores it. In other cases, the full committee, without deliberation, votes to kill the bill. If the committee decides to give the bill serious consideration, the committee chair usually assigns it to a subcommittee. The subcommittee may hold hearings, conduct investigations, and deliberate on the merits of the bill. Often the subcommittee will make amendments to the bill before sending it back to the full committee.

When a bill is back in full committee, the recommendations of the subcommittee may be accepted, rejected, or further revised. The full committee may conduct additional hearings, call more witnesses and experts to testify, and debate the bill. At the end of this process, a "markup," or final version of the bill, is prepared. The markup is the proposed legislation on which the full committee will vote. If a majority of committee members vote against the bill, the bill goes no further, so here is another point in the process where a bill might be stopped. If a majority of committee members vote in favor of the bill, it moves forward in the process.

STEP 3: THE BILL GOES TO THE FULL HOUSE AND SENATE FOR CONSIDERATION

At this next stage, the full House or Senate debates the bill and proposes amendments. The start of this process differs in the House and Senate. In the House, a bill that makes it through the committee is immediately assigned to the House **Rules Committee**. The Rules Committee decides when the bill will be debated, the amount of time that will be allotted for debate, and the extent to which amendments may be added from the floor of the House. The ability to control the timing and amount of time for debate is significant, thus making this committee one of the most important ones in the House. The ability to control the amendment process is even more powerful. If the Rules Committee issues a **closed rule**, House members are severely limited in their ability to amend the bill. An **open rule** order, on the other hand, permits amendments to the bill.

In the Senate, there are no rules set up ahead of time for debate. The Senate majority leader decides when to bring a bill to the floor. But, in theory, there are no limits on the amount of time the bill will be debated, and all senators are given the courtesy of speaking on any bill, if they so wish. The fact that the Senate includes far fewer members than the House allows for less structured debate. With no rules about how long a senator might speak, there is a possibility that a minority of senators—or even one senator—might try to block a bill from passage by refusing to end discussion, a process known as a **filibuster**.[16]

In 1917, a group of senators successfully filibustered to thwart a bill that would have armed American ships in anticipation of the nation's entry into World War I. In response to this event, the Senate adopted a **cloture** rule, which permitted the Senate to end debate and force a vote on a bill by approval of a two-thirds vote. The Senate left a loophole in place, however: if any senator, once properly recognized, refuses to concede the floor, he or she can exercise the equivalent of a one-person filibuster for as long as his or her voice will hold out. Accordingly, in 1957 South Carolina Senator Strom Thurmond spoke for more than 24 hours in an attempt to block the Senate from passing civil rights legislation. For many years, Senate filibusters successfully blocked legislation supported by a majority of senators. Then in 1975, the Senate modified the cloture requirement, so that currently a less stringent three-fifths vote of the Senate (60 out of 100 senators) is required to end debate.

Rules Committee A committee in the House of Representatives that determines the rules by which bills will come to the floor, be debated, and so on.

closed rule A rule of procedure adopted by the House Rules Committee that severely limits the ability of members of Congress to amend a bill.

open rule A rule of procedure adopted by the House Rules Committee that permits amendments to a bill.

filibuster The action by a single senator or a minority of senators to block a bill from passage by refusing to end discussion. Under modern Senate rules, not all legislation or presidential appointments are subject to the filibuster.

cloture A Senate debate procedure that permits that body to end debate and force a vote on a bill by a vote of 60 senators.

Senator Ted Cruz (R-TX) speaking to reporters at the Capitol following his 21-hour filibuster opposing Obamacare.

Between 2009 and 2015, Senate Republicans who were in the minority increasingly resorted to the use of filibusters, averaging 126 filibusters per two-year congressional term during that period, in their attempts to block the Democratic majority from passing legislation endorsed by the Obama administration. Similarly, the Democrat minority during the 115th Congress (2017–2018) resorted to the filibuster more than 160 times.

Frustrated by GOP filibusters to many of President Obama's judicial and senior executive nominees, the Democratic Senate majority in 2013 modified its rules by eliminating the use of the filibuster for such nominees. At the time, the new rule did not apply to Supreme Court nominees. Yet, with the GOP in charge of both the legislative and executive branches beginning in January 2017, the Republican Senate majority moved quickly to pass that reform as well, eliminating the filibuster in the case of high court appointments so that body could confirm President Trump's first two Supreme Court nominees (Neil Gorsuch and Brett Kavanaugh) on the strength of quite narrow Senate majorities. Despite these changes in the appointment process, the tool of minority power remains a thorn in the side of the Senate majority in trying to enact legislation outside of these presidential appointments.

At the end of the debate and amendment process, the House and Senate take a vote on the proposed bill. Passage of a bill must achieve a majority of votes (half of all present for voting, plus one) from members on the floor. A majority of votes must be achieved in both the Senate and the House for the bill to survive to the next step in the legislative process.

How any one member of the House or Senate makes the decision to vote "aye" or "nay" on a given proposed bill differs from one bill to another, and from one member to another. The six common explanations are shown in Table 6-3.

Many Americans have expressed frustration over how Congress makes decisions on important bills before it. During the highly charged debate over the health care reform legislation in 2009 and 2010, for example, most Americans felt that Congress paid too little

> **logrolling** The trading of influence or votes among legislators to achieve passage of projects that are of interest to one another.

TABLE 6-3

Why Legislators Vote the Way They Do

1. **Personal opinion and judgment.** Many members of Congress have strong personal opinions and convictions on issues and cast their votes on bills on the basis of those opinions. When members use their own personal judgment, they are said to be exercising their role as a "trustee."

2. **Constituent opinion.** Members of Congress want to be liked by their constituents, and most want to be reelected. In voting on particular bills, members often use results from polls, commentary in local media, and constituent letters to help them make up their minds. When members use constituent opinion as a cue, they are said to be exercising their role as a "delegate" of the people they represent.

3. **Interest groups and lobbying.** Members use both information provided by interest group lobbyists to aid in their voting and the campaign support from interest groups to prompt how they will vote.

4. **Political parties.** The party of a member often conveys quite a bit about his or her political positions and ideology, with Democrats tending to be more liberal on social and economic issues and Republicans tending to be more conservative on these issues. In addition, the leadership of each party is organized to influence party members to vote the "party line" on bills. Members voting with their party tend to be rewarded with better committee assignments and greater campaign funding.

5. **The president.** Presidents are quite influential in directing congressional members of their own party how to vote, but they often exert influence on members of the opposition party as well. Particularly in times of international crisis, presidents can effectively make appeals to put partisanship aside and convince members to vote in the interests of the country.

6. **Logrolling.** Members often enter into an agreement with other members to vote a certain way on one bill in exchange for a favorable vote on another bill. This process is known as logrolling. Giving up a vote on less important bills in exchange for favorable votes on more important bills is a common practice that often guides congressional voting behavior.

attention to the public and people who would be affected by the changes to health care and too much attention to the media and interest groups, as shown in Figure 6-3.

STEP 4: CONFERENCE COMMITTEE ACTION

Often, the version of a bill that passes the Senate differs from that passed by the House. To iron out any differences between Senate and House bills, Congress has two options. The first and most common route is to work out the differences informally. Of course, the ability to do this depends on the extent of differences in the two versions of the bill and the closeness of the votes in committee and in the full chambers. When the versions are not far apart in content and when the margins of approval are large, informal discussions between House and Senate leaders and committee chairs are usually sufficient to strike a deal. When the prospects for informal agreement are less likely, then House and Senate leaders select a conference committee to work out the kinks. The conference committee consists of House and Senate members—usually drawn from the standing committees that worked on the bills.

STEP 5: PRESIDENTIAL ACTION

The president plays both an informal and a formal role in the passage of new laws. The president's informal role is to develop new ideas for laws and urge members of Congress to introduce them. The president also lobbies Congress, attempting to persuade members to support or oppose certain bills. The president's strong presence in the American political system, along with attention from the national media, offers the president a unique platform from which to lobby on behalf of or against certain legislation.

The formal constitutional role that the president plays in legislation is the fifth step in the process by which a bill becomes law. Once both chambers of Congress have agreed to a bill,

FIGURE 6-3

Whom Does Congress Listen to?

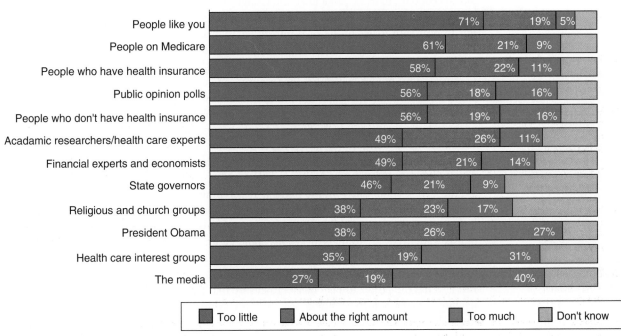

Do you think members of Congress are paying too much, too little, or about the right amount of attention to what the following groups are saying about changes to the health care system?

Source: Based on data from NPR/Kaiser Foundation Survey of Americans, conducted August–September 2009.

In the Oval Office, President Trump signs the marquee GOP legislation of his first term, the Tax Cuts and Jobs Act of 2017.

the bill is sent to the president for action. The president has three options for dealing with the congressionally approved bill. First, the president can sign the bill, which officially makes it new law. Second, the president can **veto** (or refuse assent to) the bill, which stops the bill from becoming law. If the bill is vetoed, Congress has one more opportunity to pass the bill, by **overriding** the presidential veto. This requires a two-thirds vote in favor of passage in both the Senate and the House, a margin substantially more difficult to achieve than the simple majority vote required prior to a presidential veto. Third, the president can decide not to act on a bill (i.e., neither sign nor veto it), in which case the bill automatically becomes law after it has sat on the president's desk for 10 days. If Congress passes a bill and sends it to the president within 10 days of the end of a congressional session and the president does not act on the bill, then the bill does not become law; this is a process known as a **pocket veto**.

6-5 OVERSIGHT AND PERSONNEL FUNCTIONS OF CONGRESS

In addition to creating new laws, Congress performs a number of oversight functions, including oversight of federal agencies, confirmation of top federal executives and judges, approval of treaties, and impeachment of top federal executives and judges.

CONGRESSIONAL OVERSIGHT

Congress's principal responsibility is to enact new laws to deal with national problems and concerns. However, many of these issues are complex (e.g., disposing of nuclear and toxic wastes, creating new sources of energy, promoting the role of high technology, and enhancing the performance of a multitrillion-dollar economy that has become highly integrated in the global economy, to name just a few), and Congress often lacks the scientific and technological expertise needed to enact laws. In addition, for political reasons, sometimes Congress prefers not to deal with issues on its own but rather to "pass the buck" to a bureaucratic agency. Defining the limits of genetic cloning is one such political hot potato. Whether the reason is technical capability or politics, Congress often delegates more specific legislative authority to the executive branch, which has the resources and expertise to make more highly technical policy decisions. The delegation of congressional power to the executive branch has become more frequent as our society has become more complex.

This delegation of authority, however, is not carried out blindly or without accountability. When Congress delegates its authority, it generally monitors the activities of agencies and administrators who are given this power through congressional oversight. One agency to which Congress has delegated considerable authority is the Federal Reserve Board (known as "the Fed"). Established by the Federal Reserve Act of 1913, the Fed has authority over credit rates and lending activities of the nation's banks. Congress created the agency because it recognized that specialized monitoring of the economy and the technical expertise of economists were necessary to make decisions about credit rates and lending activities in order to maintain a viable economy. The act gave the Fed the authority to adjust the supply of money to banks and to shift money from where there is too much to where there is too little. The Fed also has the power to take means to ensure that banks do not overextend themselves in lending so that a sudden economic scare will not cause a sudden run on banks for money. For over 100 years, Congress has given this agency the power to set important monetary policy for the nation. But Congress retains its authority to exercise oversight of the Fed. The Joint Economic Committee in Congress carefully monitors the Fed's performance and regularly

veto The constitutional procedure by which the president refuses to approve a bill or joint resolution and thus prevents its enactment into law.

overriding (a veto) The power of the Congress to enact legislation despite a president's veto of that legislation; requires a two-thirds vote of both houses of Congress.

pocket veto The indirect veto of a bill received by the president within 10 days of the adjournment of Congress, effected by the president's retaining the bill unsigned until Congress adjourns.

holds hearings to inquire about its policies and decisions. In addition, newly appointed members of the Federal Reserve Board must be approved by Congress.

In his book on Congress titled *Congress: Keystone of the Washington Establishment*,[17] political scientist Morris Fiorina notes other important reasons for congressional delegation of power to executive agencies, including garnering political rewards while shifting blame to the executive branch, enabling Congress to blame federal agencies for failing to fulfill legislative intent, and taking credit for problem-solving by holding oversight and investigative hearings.

CONFIRMATION OF PRESIDENTIAL NOMINATIONS AND APPROVAL OF TREATIES

The U.S. Senate plays a pivotal role in the selection of cabinet officers, other agency and executive branch heads, federal judges, and foreign ambassadors. The president nominates individuals for these posts, but the Senate must consent to the nomination with a majority vote in favor of the candidate. This function is one performed solely by the U.S. Senate, and not the House of Representatives.

At the beginning of a new presidential administration, the U.S. Senate is typically quite busy reviewing the president's nominations for high executive office positions.[18] Although the Senate usually endorses most nominees, there have been a number of high-profile instances when the Senate has been unwilling to confirm the nominee, typically occurring during eras of divided government when the political party of the president is different from the majority party in the Senate. The threat of a denial has become somewhat less likely since the Senate modified its rules in 2013 to eliminate the possibility of a filibuster for presidential appointments to the judicial and executive branches.

When there is a vacancy on the U.S. Supreme Court, a situation that often draws considerable interest from both the press and the public, the president nominates a new justice, whom the Senate also must confirm with a majority vote. Conflict between the Senate and the president over Supreme Court nominees goes all the way back to the first U.S. president, George Washington, and his choice of John Rutledge for chief justice of the United States. Although Rutledge appeared eminently qualified for the post (he was associate justice on the Supreme Court from 1789 to 1791 and chief justice of the South Carolina Court of Common Pleas from 1791 to 1795), he had openly criticized the highly controversial Jay Treaty with Britain (backed by Washington and the Federalists), which reneged on the terms of America's 1778 treaty with France. Although Washington stood behind his nominee and gave him a temporary recess appointment as chief justice, Federalist senators argued that confirmation of Rutledge would be an extreme embarrassment to their party and denounced him publicly. On December 15, 1795, the Senate rejected Rutledge's nomination by a 14–10 vote.

A more recent example of Senate opposition to a Supreme Court nominee occurred in the case of Brett Kavanaugh, nominated to the high court by President Trump in 2018. The Democrats opposed Kavanaugh, who held conservative views on numerous issues. Kavanaugh's problems mounted further when a female professor from California, Dr. Christine Blasey Ford, accused him of sexually attacking her decades earlier when the two were in high school. Kavanaugh ultimately won confirmation by a close 50–48 vote and currently sits on the Supreme Court.

Win McNamee / Getty Images

Judge Brett Kavanaugh is sworn in prior to testifying before the Senate Judiciary Committee's confirmation hearings on his nomination to the Supreme Court in September 2018.

Under certain circumstances, Congress may also become involved in the selection of president and vice president of the United States. When no candidate receives a majority of electoral votes, the House of Representatives chooses the president and the Senate chooses the vice president. This has happened three times in the history of the nation: in 1801 when the House chose Thomas Jefferson as president, in 1825 when the House chose John Quincy Adams, and in 1877 when the House appointed a commission to resolve the controversial 1876 election (it chose Rutherford B. Hayes).

In the event of a vacancy in the vice presidency, the Twenty-fifth Amendment to the Constitution stipulates that the president's nomination of an individual to fill that position is subject to the approval of both the House and Senate by majority vote. This has happened twice since adoption of that amendment: in 1973 when Vice President Spiro Agnew resigned and Nixon's nomination of Gerald Ford was quickly approved and in 1974 when Ford became president due to Nixon's resignation and Congress approved Ford's nomination of Nelson Rockefeller as vice president.

Finally, the Senate has the power to approve treaties that the president negotiates with foreign countries. The Constitution stipulates that approval of a treaty requires the consent of two-thirds of the Senate. Even though the standard for treaty approval is much higher than a simple majority, most treaties do obtain the necessary two-thirds approval. The relatively low number of rejected treaties may be due to presidents' reluctance to negotiate treaties that they are not reasonably certain will pass. Perhaps the most important rejection concerned the Treaty of Versailles following World War I. President Woodrow Wilson's failure to consult with the Senate and consider its objections to the Treaty of Versailles led to the treaty's twice being rejected by the Senate, once in 1919 and again in 1920. More recently, the House has also played an important role in approving treaties because most of them involve financial issues that require the approval of that chamber.

IMPEACHMENT AND REMOVAL OF FEDERAL JUDGES AND HIGH EXECUTIVES

Congress also has the authority to impeach and remove federal judges, cabinet officers, the president, the vice president, and other civil officers. The removal process requires an impeachment action from the House and a trial in the Senate. Only two presidents (Andrew Johnson in 1867 and Bill Clinton in 1998) have been impeached, and neither was actually removed from office. (A third president, Richard Nixon, resigned from office before the full House had actually voted for impeachment).

Impeachment is the formal process by which the House brings charges against federal officials. A judge, president, or executive official who is "impeached" by the House is not removed; he or she is charged with an offense. In this sense, the House acts as an initial forum that makes the decision about whether a trial is warranted. An impeachment occurs by a majority vote in the House of Representatives. An official may be impeached by the House on more than one charge, each of which is referred to as an article of impeachment.

Assuming the House passes at least one article of impeachment, the official must then stand trial in the Senate. The prosecutors in the trial are members of the House of Representatives and are referred to as House "managers." Selected by the House leadership, the House managers present the case for removal to the full Senate. If the defendant is the president, the chief justice of the U.S. Supreme Court presides over the trial; otherwise, the vice president of the United States (who is president of the Senate) or

Rep. Maxine Waters (D-CA), chair of the House Financial Services Committee, talks to reporters at the outset of the 116th Congress in January 2019. Waters is a harsh critic of President Trump and was one of the first House members to call for his impeachment.

the president pro tempore of the Senate presides. Other than in the impeachment of a president or vice president, the Senate in recent times has usually designated a committee to receive evidence and question the witnesses. The impeached official provides lawyers in his or her own defense. A two-thirds vote of the full Senate is required for removal of an official.

6-6 CONSTITUENT SERVICE: HELPING PEOPLE BACK HOME

Much of what has been discussed thus far in this chapter pertains to what members of Congress do in Washington. As the people's representatives, members are sent to Washington to develop new laws and deliberate on important issues. They are expected to safeguard the nation's security, act as watchdogs against fraud, and ensure that judges and high-ranking executive officers are qualified for office. An integral part of the way members serve their constituents is by reflecting the opinions and input of those whom they represent while carrying out these legislative functions.

However, the service of members of Congress does not stop with the work they do in Washington. Often constituents will call upon a House member or senator to provide information about federal programs, to render assistance in getting benefits from federal programs, or to prepare a talk or visit with a community group to educate its members about the political system or on a specific legislative or policy topic. Members are often asked by officials in state or local government to facilitate federal help for a local or state issue. The direct assistance that a member provides to a constituent, community group, or local or state official is referred to as casework. A now classic book by Richard F. Fenno Jr., titled *Home Style: House Members in Their Districts*, provides a rich description of this role played by members of Congress.[19]

Casework is important for a number of reasons. First is its electoral importance to members of Congress. Casework raises the visibility of members in their home state or district, which reflects positively on how well those members are regarded and gives them an advantage over their opponents in elections. More than 90 percent of House and Senate members who run for reelection are returned to office, and effectively managing casework is an important reason for this high return rate.

It has also become an implicit responsibility of members to help their constituents navigate the complex federal bureaucracy. Federal programs are varied and complex, and constituents are often overwhelmed in their efforts to obtain the benefits for which they are eligible. For example, under the Workforce Development Act, the federal government has programs that provide assistance to "displaced workers," defined as those who have lost their jobs due to technological or broad trends in the workplace. Many workers in the manufacturing industry in the United States have lost their jobs over the past two decades as the national economy has shifted away from manufacturing and toward technology and information services. Various programs are available for these displaced workers to help them obtain training in new skills necessary to adapt to the new workforce. Finding these programs is often difficult, and members provide information to connect constituents with available programs.

Third, casework provides a direct connection between members and their constituents. Casework requires members to keep in touch with those whom they represent. Giving a speech to a local Rotary club or League of Women Voters meeting, showing up to cut the ribbon at an opening of a new local school building or park, and coming to speak to a group of students or employees all provide face time between the members and their constituents. The experiences that members have and the type of work they do in Washington can shelter them from the real-life concerns of their constituents back home. Casework provides a constant reminder of the needs and interests of those whom members represent.

Another aspect of constituent service involves what is known as "pork-barrel" politics. The federal budget includes a great deal of money for local projects, such as parks, dams, and road improvements. Members secure federal funds to support these projects in their states and districts through what is often referred to as pork-barrel legislation.

casework The direct assistance that a member of Congress provides to a constituent, community group, or local or state official.

pork-barrel legislation A government project or appropriation that yields jobs or other benefits to a specific locale and patronage opportunities to its political representative.

The pork-barrel reference is based on the idea that members are "bringing home the bacon." Members use their influence on congressional committees and leadership positions to add amendments to bills that authorize pork-barrel spending on projects back home. Though many observers of the political system decry the unfairness of pork-barrel legislation, it has been an important aspect of constituent service since the beginning of our political system and promises to remain so in the future.

When Congress is dealing with major problems or issues of the day, the process of creating new laws, approving new treaties, and approving presidential appointments can be very slow indeed—many observers use the word gridlock to describe congressional inaction. Congress's actions are slow and deliberate; there are many points at which the process may be halted and many actors with the capacity to hinder progress. Further, the compromises necessary to achieve success in Congress rarely prove entirely satisfactory to everyone involved. The slow and grinding legislative process can even lead to bad behavior on the part of members of Congress, such as with Senator Preston Brooks's clubbing of Senator Charles Sumner in a debate on slavery in 1856 and Representative Joe Wilson's "You lie!" shout at President Obama in 2009 during Obama's health care address. The power and significance of individual actors in the legislative process are also significant to understanding how Congress works. Strong individuals such as former Senate majority leader Harry Reid and former House Speaker John Boehner dominated the debate in recent years. Congress is not simply two houses of 535 individuals who vote, with a majority obtaining victory. Those in leadership positions can exert a disproportionate influence on the process. Those with special communication skills enjoy more power, as do those who are highly informed on a particular issue.

Summary

6-1 Article I and the Creation of Congress

- Congress, the legislative branch of the government, was the central institution in America's new political system at the beginning of the republic. It is the branch of government that represents the people, and its primary function is to create laws.

6-2 The Structure and Organization of Congress

- Congress consists of two houses: a "people's house" apportioned by population (the House of Representatives) and a Senate in which the states, regardless of population, have equal representation. States are equally represented in the Senate whereas the House represents the population.
- Although not mentioned in the Constitution, leadership in Congress is primarily determined based on political parties. The majority party controls the legislative process.
- The Constitution designates that the leader of the House carry the title Speaker of the House. The Speaker is responsible for assigning new bills to committees and recognizing members to speak in the House chamber. The Constitution

also prescribes that the vice president is to be the presiding officer of the Senate. Unlike the Speaker, the president of the Senate can vote only to break ties. When the vice president is absent from the Senate chamber, as is quite often the case, the presiding officer is the president pro tempore ("for the time being").

- To ensure the principle of "one person, one vote" in the House, the size of congressional districts must be "reapportioned" so that they are as even as possible, based on the results of the decennial census. Political parties try to maximize their advantage in the redistricting process that occurs after each census by "gerrymandering," which means that the party in control in each state draws district boundaries to favor the dominant party in elections.

6-3 The Committee System

- There are four types of congressional committees: standing committees (permanent), select committees (established to look at a particular issue for a limited time), conference committees (reconcile differences between House and Senate versions of a bill), and joint committees (includes members from both houses, investigative in nature). Most members defer to committee recommendations on a bill.

6-4 How a Bill Becomes a Law

- The law-making process is often slow, and bills that survive frequently receive significant revisions along the way. After a bill is introduced by a member of Congress, it is usually sent to a committee for consideration (often in the form of hearings) and possible action. If the bill is endorsed by a majority of the committee, it then goes to the full House and Senate for consideration. Finally, if it is endorsed by a majority of each chamber, a conference committee reconciles differences in versions between the chambers, and then after a vote on the bill's final version, it goes to the president for signature. If the president vetoes the final bill, Congress can override the presidential veto by a two-thirds vote of both houses of Congress.

6-5 Oversight and Personnel Functions of Congress

- Congress delegates considerable legislative authority to the executive branch, whether because it lacks the expertise of bureaucrats or because it

wishes to shift blame for policies to the executive branch. Still, Congress may exercise oversight to ensure that the implementation of laws and regulations is consistent with national problems and concerns.

- The U.S. Senate plays an important role in consenting to the president's selection of cabinet officers, other executive branch officials, and judges. Senate confirmation of Supreme Court nominees in particular has been the subject of considerable controversy. If a majority in the House of Representative impeaches a president, federal judge, or other executive official, the official must stand trial in the Senate. A two-thirds vote of the full Senate is required for the removal of an official from office.

6-6 Constituent Service: Helping People Back Home

- Members of Congress play an important role doing casework for local constituents, whether by assisting them in getting federal benefits, educating them on policy issues, or performing some other service on their behalf. Casework provides a direct connection between members and their constituents.

Key Terms

bicameral legislature (p. 113)
bill (p. 119)
casework (p. 131)
closed rule (p. 125)
cloture (p. 125)
conference committee (p. 121)
congressional agencies (p. 123)
congressional committee staff (p. 123)
congressional district (p. 114)
congressional personal staff (p. 122)
filibuster (p. 125)
gerrymandering (p. 115)
joint committee (p. 121)
logrolling (p. 126)
majority caucus (p. 116)
majority leader (p. 118)
majority-minority district (p. 115)

minority caucus (p. 116)
minority leader (p. 118)
open rule (p. 125)
overriding (a veto) (p. 128)
pocket veto (p. 128)
pork-barrel legislation (p. 131)
president pro tempore (p. 118)
reapportionment (p. 114)
redistricting (p. 115)
reporting legislation (p. 119)
Rules Committee (p. 125)
select committee (p. 120)
Speaker of the House (p. 117)
standing committee (p. 119)
veto (p. 128)
whips (majority and minority) (p. 118)

7
THE PRESIDENCY

The Washington Post / Getty Images

President Trump delivers his State of the Union Address in February 2019.

THE WORLD'S OLDEST CONTINUOUS republican chief executive office remains the U.S. presidency. Whereas most other countries divide political and symbolic functions among different officials, the Constitution combines both sets of functions into just one office: the president of the United States is both head of state and chief executive of the federal government. Unfortunately, the Constitution is deliberately vague on the meaning of the chief executive's primary responsibility under Article II: To "take Care that the Laws be faithfully executed." For more than a century it was the U.S. Congress—disciplined by the two major political parties—that served as the dominant institution of government. It was not until the twentieth century that the presidency became the central institution of American political life, with its executive powers expanded to include vast legislative, judicial, economic, administrative, and foreign policy responsibilities. Of course, with that immense power comes an unprecedented level of accountability as well, especially in the modern era when the public watches the president's every move in real time thanks to wall-to-wall television coverage and the power of the internet. Is presidential government in the early twenty-first century compatible with the Constitution and traditional notions of representative government? This much we know: the individual who occupies the White House will stand at the apex of international attention and power for as long as he or she remains president.

Learning Objectives

7-1 Where Do Presidents Come From? Presidential Comings and Goings

- Identify the most common traits of presidents, the constitutional requirements for the position, and the process by which presidents may be removed from office.

7-2 The Evolution of the American Presidency

- Trace the evolution of the presidency from "chief clerk" in the late eighteenth and nineteenth centuries to near dominance over the political system.

7-3 Express Powers and Responsibilities of the President

- Define the formal powers vested in the president under Article II of the Constitution, including the veto, appointments, the pardon, and commander in chief of the armed forces.

7-4 Implied Powers and Responsibilities of the President

- Discuss those implied powers of the presidency not spelled out in the Constitution, including the issuing of executive orders and agreements.

7-5 Presidential Resources

- Describe the other individuals and offices in the executive branch that contribute to the modern presidency.

7-6 Important Presidential Relationships

- Assess how the power of the presidency is enhanced by communications with the public, the Congress, and the media.

7-1 WHERE DO PRESIDENTS COME FROM? PRESIDENTIAL COMINGS AND GOINGS

What career experiences have provided the most effective launching pads for the 44 separate individuals who have attained the presidency? Many vice presidents have gone on to immediate election as president, including most recently George H. W. Bush, vice president under Ronald Reagan, who in 1988 won the White House in his own right. Yet that form of promotion is actually quite rare. Although 5 of the last 14 vice presidents (up through Joseph Biden) eventually became president, among them only Bush won election as a sitting vice president. In fact, in the 132-year period between Vice President Martin Van Buren's presidential victory in 1836 and former vice president Richard Nixon's election in 1968, every vice president who rose to the presidency did so (at least initially) as a direct consequence of the president's untimely death in office.

Although the U.S. Senate has been aptly described as a body of 100 individuals who all think they should be president, only 16 senators have eventually gone on to the White House. (And only three of those individuals—Warren Harding, John F. Kennedy, and Barack Obama—moved *directly* from the Senate to the presidency.) By comparison, 19 governors and 19 members of the House of Representatives eventually served as president. Three presidents—William Henry Harrison, John Tyler, and Andrew Johnson—served in all three of those jobs. Another nine presidents formerly served in another president's cabinet. The military has also been something of a breeding ground for presidents: 29 had some military experience, and 12 served as generals. Fully 27 of the 45 chief executives have been lawyers, but the cohort of presidents also includes among its ranks a mining engineer (Herbert Hoover), a peanut farmer (Jimmy Carter), a baseball team executive (George W. Bush), and even a hat salesman (Harry Truman). The current president, Donald Trump, was previously a businessman and real estate magnate who built office towers, hotels, casinos, and golf courses, among other properties. And unlike these other businessmen, he held no public office before assuming the presidency.

As a formal matter, the adage that "anyone can grow up to be president" is not literally true. Article II of the Constitution imposes three prerequisites on those who aspire to the Oval Office. Every president must be (1) a "natural-born" citizen, (2) 35 years of age or older, and (3) a resident within the United States for at least 14 years. Although the Constitution poses no other formal obstacles to the presidency, as a practical matter the first 44 individual holders of the office have tended to fall into several clearly identifiable categories. All but one of these chief executives have been white males (Barack Obama is the lone African American president) between the ages of 42 and 77. All were born Christians, and nearly all identified themselves as Protestants at one point or another in their lifetimes. (John Kennedy was Catholic; Lyndon Johnson was mostly nonobservant in his adulthood.) Twenty-four were firstborn children in their families, and all but nine attended college (since 1897, every president except Harry Truman received some type of higher education degree). Some states have served as birthplaces for a disproportionate share of presidents, including Virginia (eight), Ohio (seven), New York (five), and Massachusetts (four). Birthright has also played a role in helping an individual reach the Oval Office. Twenty-six presidents have been related to other presidents by blood; these relationships encompass two father–son combinations (John and John Quincy Adams; George H. W. and George W. Bush), a grandfather–grandson combination (William Henry Harrison and Benjamin Harrison), and cousins (James Madison and Zachary Taylor were second cousins; Theodore Roosevelt and Franklin Roosevelt were fifth cousins).

When George Washington, after serving two terms as the nation's first president, declined to run again, he established an unwritten two-term precedent. No president challenged that tradition until Franklin Delano Roosevelt (FDR) sought a third term in 1940. FDR's successful election to four consecutive terms (he won in 1932, 1936, 1940, and 1944) led to passage of the **Twenty-second Amendment** in 1951, which restricts any one person from being elected to the presidency "more than twice," or from acting as president for longer than two and a half terms. Four chief executives were assassinated while in office, and four others died of natural causes while still serving as president, including FDR, who died in 1945, only a few months into his unprecedented fourth term.

Twenty-second Amendment Passed in 1951, this constitutional amendment restricts any one person from being elected to the presidency "more than twice," or from acting as president for longer than two and a half terms.

Public Support for Diverse Presidential Candidates

The 2016 presidential campaign was unique in various ways, including its historically diverse pool of candidates in both the Republican and the Democratic primary battles, spanning both genders and a variety of racial, ethnic, and other categories. Doubts still arise as to whether or not a majority of Americans are ready to support such a diverse set of political candidates. The

Gallup Poll Results

Percentage of voters that would consider a presidential candidate who was:

Catholic (93%)
A woman (92%)
Black (92%)
Hispanic (91%)
Jewish (91%)
Mormon (81%)
Gay or lesbian (74%)
An evangelical Christian (73%)
Muslim (60%)
An atheist (58%)
A socialist (47%)

Source: Justin McCarthy, "In U.S., Socialist Presidential Candidates Least Appealing," Gallup.com, June 22, 2015, https://news.gallup.com/poll/183713/socialist-presidential-candidates-least-appealing.aspx.

Gallup poll, among other well-known survey research companies, continues to ask questions that seek to gauge the public's receptivity to such candidates.[1]

The public's willingness to support diverse candidates for president has gradually risen since Gallup began asking about these issues in 1937. Gallup started polling the public about its willingness to support a black presidential candidate in 1958; at that time, only 37 percent expressed support for such a candidate. Of course, this type of questioning became much more than just a hypothetical exercise with the election of President Obama in 2008 and the subsequent campaigns of frontrunner Hillary Clinton in both 2008 and 2016. In June 2015, this same Gallup question invited a markedly different response: a clear majority of the American public expressed a willingness to support a variety of diverse presidential candidates, including the categories listed in the table to the left.

For Critical Thinking and Discussion

1. In the wake of Barack Obama's presidency and Hillary Clinton's candidacy, which won a plurality of voters in 2016, are Americans now ready to vote for presidential candidates in an array of different demographic categories? In short, do you believe the polling results referenced above will translate into real political results now that President Obama and Clinton have paved the way?

2. What did you learn from the 2016 presidential election on this score? Did the election results serve to confirm or deny these earlier poll results?

impeachment The first step in a two-step process outlined in Article II, Section 4, of the U.S. Constitution to remove a president or other high official from office. The House of Representatives, by majority vote, may impeach if the official has committed "Treason, Bribery, or other high Crimes and Misdemeanors." The second step requires a conviction in the Senate by a two-thirds vote.

The constitutional means of removing a president from office is by **impeachment** and subsequent conviction. Article II, Section 4, of the U.S. Constitution provides that the president may be removed from office upon impeachment by a majority vote of the House and conviction by two-thirds of the Senate of "Treason, Bribery, or other high Crimes and Misdemeanors." Just what type of offense qualifies as a "high crime and misdemeanor"? It is difficult to say. Just two presidents, Andrew Johnson and Bill Clinton, have ever been impeached under these provisions, and both were impeached for primarily political reasons: Johnson was charged with illegally firing a cabinet member, pardoning traitors, and impeding ratification of the Fourteenth Amendment; Clinton was accused of lying to a grand jury about his sexual relationship with an intern and of obstructing justice. Both men were acquitted on all charges by the U.S. Senate and served out their respective terms. The only president to resign was Richard Nixon, who was accused of obstructing justice in the now infamous Watergate scandal. Nixon left office less than halfway through his second term in 1974 under the looming threat of impeachment. In practice, unpopular presidents are usually turned out of office not by removal but by a failed reelection.

When President John Adams was defeated for reelection in 1800 and turned over the White House to archrival Thomas Jefferson, he helped establish a precedent of peaceful transition between chief executives that has held firm to this day, despite the hostile feelings that sometimes exist between successive presidents. In the case of the president's removal by death, resignation, or inability to serve, the Constitution requires that the powers and duties of the president "devolve" on the vice president. When William Henry Harrison died barely a month after becoming president in 1841, Vice President John Tyler took over all the powers, duties, and responsibilities of the presidency, rejecting any notion that he was simply there to serve as a more limited "acting president" until the next election. Since Tyler, seven vice presidents have become chief executive in this manner, including most recently Lyndon Johnson, who assumed office after John F. Kennedy was assassinated in November 1963. Of the last six vice presidents thrust unexpectedly into office, four—Theodore Roosevelt, Calvin Coolidge, Harry Truman, and Lyndon Johnson—eventually secured election as presidents in their own right.

7-2 THE EVOLUTION OF THE AMERICAN PRESIDENCY

The U.S. Constitution places as many limitations on the office of the presidency as it grants the president specific powers and duties. Wary of the excessive authority wielded by the king of England, most of the founders rejected Alexander Hamilton's radical suggestion that the president should be elected for life; instead, they designed a chief executive who would be powerful enough to respond quickly when necessary but who would be limited by lack of law-making power and the need to gain congressional approval for most long-term commitments, whether foreign or domestic.

The presidency has evolved over the past two centuries not so much because of any constitutional amendments that affected the chief executive's powers but rather through practice, tradition, and the personal energy of some presidents. The changing dynamics of policy-making in the United States from a mostly local focus to a national phenomenon has given presidents the opportunity to exert unprecedented influence over the process, and many have done exactly that. In many ways, the growth of the power of the presidency has paralleled the growth of the United States.

THE PRESIDENT AS "CHIEF CLERK" OF THE UNITED STATES, 1789–1836

The earliest presidents established the office as a forceful power in the national government. Still, even the most popular presidents of the period were careful to avoid interfering with the clear legislative prerogatives of Congress. Several played a major role in helping steer America away from or toward war, despite the inclinations of Congress. But the truly dominant chief executive would not emerge until many years later.

When George Washington, the immensely popular former general of the Continental Army, agreed to be nominated as the nation's first president, widespread public confidence in his abilities helped secure immediate respect for this new office. Serving as the first chief executive from 1789 to 1797, Washington established various precedents that helped preserve a republican form of government in the nation's infancy. Washington rejected entrapments of royalty such as being referred to as "Your Majesty," preferring instead to be called "Mr. President." As a practical matter, Washington consulted constantly with the other branches—at one point he even asked the Supreme Court for an advisory opinion about his own interpretations of a foreign treaty. (The Court declined his invitation for comment.) Washington also established the executive's influential role in crafting public policy, siding with Secretary of Treasury Alexander Hamilton's plans for industrialization and the creation of a national bank, and striving to maintain an

William Henry Harrison, a military war hero, won election to the presidency in 1840. Yet, for all of his strengths as a war hero, he was ultimately a victim of his own stubbornness. Inauguration Day, March 4, 1841, was one of the coldest and most blustery days of the year in Washington, DC. Harrison refused to wear a hat and coat, and his nearly two-hour inaugural address was one of the longest in history. One month later Harrison died of pneumonia, probably contracted during his inaugural speech. He was the first president to die in office, but perhaps the last not to bundle up warmly for his Inauguration Day celebration.

isolationist foreign policy. Washington thus rejected the less interventionist, farmer-friendly policies favored by his secretary of state, Thomas Jefferson.[2] For better or worse, most subsequent presidents would be forced to work within the framework of a divided party system that originated as an intramural fight within the Washington administration.

During the four decades after Washington's retirement, most presidents served more as chief "clerks" than as chief "executives," doing Congress's bidding and performing mostly administrative duties on behalf of the federal government. Upon winning the presidency in 1800, Thomas Jefferson (1801–1809)[3] put into practice his own theory "that government is best which governs least." Accordingly, the Jefferson administration abolished many judgeships, trimmed government's economic planning efforts, and scaled back the armed forces. The one crucial exception to such downsizing occurred in the area of land acquisition: Jefferson arranged for the purchase of the vast Louisiana territory from France, more than doubling the physical size of the country.

A presidency characterized by limited executive powers soon confronted unexpected challenges. When tensions between Great Britain and the United States erupted into the War of 1812, President James Madison (1809–1817) found himself hampered both by the small size of the federal army and by the lack of a powerful national bank capable of funding the government's prosecution of the war. This war with Britain revealed the limited powers of the president to influence national matters without strong institutional resources at his disposal. Madison's successor, James Monroe (1817–1825), exercised most of his influence in foreign affairs. Monroe's secretary of state, John Quincy Adams, who himself was president from 1825 to 1829, helped craft the "Monroe Doctrine," which declared that the United States would thereafter regard as an "unfriendly act" any attempt by a European nation to increase its possession or otherwise intervene on the American continent. Meanwhile, Congress led the way in domestic matters, crafting key compromises over slavery and paying off much of the public debt incurred during the War of 1812.

Andrew Jackson, who served as president from 1829 to 1837, remade the presidency into an office of tremendous political power. The military hero of the Battle of New Orleans in 1815, Jackson came to the White House as a political outsider but with overwhelming popular support. Capitalizing on this resource, Jackson wielded presidential power in a way that few of his predecessors had, dismissing hundreds of office-holders, forcing out cabinet members who angered him, using his constitutionally authorized power to veto Congress's bill to recharter the Second National Bank of the United States, and introducing the so-called spoils system of doling out federal offices to individuals as rewards for political service.[4]

THE WEAKENED PRESIDENCY IN THE WILDERNESS YEARS, 1837–1900

Andrew Jackson raised the profile and authority of the presidency to unprecedented heights, but its ascendancy was largely a product of his own popularity and energetic personality. The pre–Civil War presidents who followed Jackson also proved to be much weaker. The model of president as chief clerk seemed once again alive and well. Typical of this period were such weak presidents as Franklin Pierce and James Buchanan; the failures of both to address growing sectional tensions over slavery in the 1850s left proslavery and abolitionist interests alike bitterly frustrated.

The presidency of Abraham Lincoln (1861–1865) thrived due to a rare combination of factors. Frequently underestimated as a great political mind, Lincoln was confronted with the single greatest threat in the history of the republic—the secession of 11 Southern states and the great battle between North and South to restore the Union. Although Lincoln proceeded carefully in his prosecution of the war against the South for fear of alienating crucial border states, those acts he did undertake were bold and unprecedented. At the outset of the war in April 1861, with Congress not even in session, Lincoln proclaimed a blockade of Southern ports and called on the Northern states to provide 75,000 soldiers for battle. He (at least in one court's opinion[5]) unconstitutionally suspended the writ of habeas corpus, by which anyone arrested was to be brought before a judge or court to determine if there is sufficient reason to hold the person for trial. Suspending the writ allowed Lincoln to hold some criminal defendants indefinitely. The president also spent freely from the U.S. Treasury without congressional approval. Although Congress ultimately ratified all his actions after the fact, Lincoln's bold exercise of authority essentially reinterpreted Article II into a source of executive authority during emergencies.

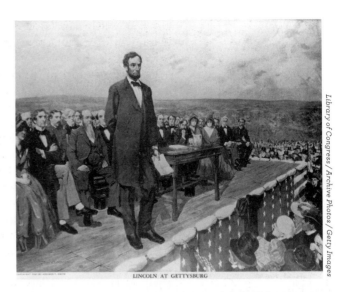

LINCOLN AT GETTYSBURG

President Abraham Lincoln delivering the Gettysburg Address in 1863.

Following Lincoln's assassination in April 1865, Congress, dominated at that time by radical Republicans determined to punish the former Confederate states, quickly reasserted its control over the nation's agenda. For the remainder of the century, Congress would determine domestic policy. Indeed, after the former Civil War hero Ulysses Grant left office in 1877, no sitting president won election to a second term until William McKinley accomplished the feat in 1900.

THE BIRTH OF THE MODERN PRESIDENCY AND ITS RISE TO DOMINANCE, 1901–1945

The beginning of the twentieth century marked the onset of a new era for the American presidency. In an increasingly global and interconnected world, the power of the presidency grew disproportionately. By the time two world wars had concluded, the presidency had emerged as the premier institution in American politics.

In the fall of 1901, William McKinley was assassinated during the first year of his second term, thrusting his young and ebullient vice president, 42-year-old Theodore Roosevelt, into office. Roosevelt's presidency (1901–1909) ushered in a new era of presidential authority. He injected a forceful energy and enthusiasm into the White House, using his position as "a bully pulpit" (Roosevelt's own words). As one observer noted, "He wanted to be the bride at every wedding; the corpse at every funeral." Unlike many of his predecessors, Roosevelt was willing to gamble political capital on bold assertions of presidential power. Most notably, the Supreme Court narrowly upheld his efforts to break up corporate monopolies. Through the creative use of executive orders, he also increased the acreage of national parks fivefold. When Roosevelt became president, foreign affairs were assuming an ever more significant place in the nation's list of priorities. As the first president to travel to foreign lands, Roosevelt expanded the Monroe Doctrine by advancing the "Roosevelt Corollary," which declared that the United States would serve as a police power to maintain stability in the Western Hemisphere by opposing any European interference in the affairs of Latin American nations. In foreign affairs, where force of personality is so important, Congress proved little match for this charismatic young president.

As president from 1913 to 1921, Woodrow Wilson achieved some significant successes and suffered some great failures: his aggressive industrial reform agenda marked a successful first term in office; during his second term he eventually led the United States into World War I and received accolades at the Paris Peace Conference following the war. But Wilson's hopes for a stable international order based on a system of collective security ultimately confronted political reality, as Senate leaders whom Wilson had excluded from the peace talks rejected U.S. membership in the League of Nations. Still, Wilson's presidency illustrated just how much more powerful the presidency had become since the mid-nineteenth century. In the early part of the twentieth century, the president came to dominate the political landscape.

The onset of the Great Depression during Herbert Hoover's presidency (1929–1933) and the looming threat of a second world war in the late 1930s demanded a new and innovative approach to the office. Franklin Delano Roosevelt placed his own indelible stamp on the nation by transforming the presidency into an institution marked by permanent bureaucracies and well-established repositories of power. FDR tackled the Great Depression with **New Deal** policies that tied the economic fate of millions of Americans to the fate of the American government: a Social Security program of old-age insurance and unemployment insurance would provide income for the elderly and the jobless; the government would guarantee deposit accounts in commercial banks through the Federal Deposit Insurance Corporation (FDIC); and the government would provide federal jobs to the unemployed to perform various public works. Roosevelt communicated extensively with the American people through the media—millions listened to his "fireside chats" on the radio. By restoring public confidence with his energetic support for New Deal programs, FDR redefined the presidency as a source of national leadership. As indicated in Table 7-1, FDR would go down in history as one of the greatest U.S. presidents, largely because of these domestic accomplishments.

More than half a century ago, historian Arthur M. Schlesinger Jr. began the process of polling historians to rank the presidents of the United States. Recent surveys continue to borrow heavily from Schlesinger's original methodology. In 2017, C-SPAN surveyed presidential historians, asking them to rate the president on various qualities of leadership. The categories were given equal weight in arriving at a president's total score. The Siena College Research Institute conducted a similar survey of presidential scholars in 2018. Interestingly, the results vary. Whereas Washington, Lincoln, and Franklin D. Roosevelt usually top most lists, presidential scholars often disagree on how to complete the list of greatest presidents.

Still, like Theodore Roosevelt and Woodrow Wilson, FDR felt especially at home in foreign affairs. Although adhering to popular sentiment that the United States should maintain strict neutrality in foreign wars, in the early days of World War II, Roosevelt met with British royalty and the British prime minister as a show of support, initiated a "lend-lease" policy by which Britain could purchase war supplies from the United States as long as it paid cash and

TABLE 7-1

Ranking the 10 Greatest Presidents of All Time

C-SPAN Survey—2017 Top 10	Siena College Research Institute—2018 Top 10
1. Lincoln	1. Washington
2. Washington	2. F. Roosevelt
3. Roosevelt, F.	3. Lincoln
4. Roosevelt, T.	4. T. Roosevelt
5. Eisenhower	5. Jefferson
6. Truman	6. Eisenhower
7. Jefferson	7. Madison
8. Kennedy	8. Monroe
9. Wilson	9. Truman
10. Obama	10. Kennedy

Source: "Presidential Historians Survey 2017," C-SPAN.org, https://www.c-span.org/presidentsurvey2017/; "Siena's 6th Presidential Expert Poll 1982–2018," https://scri.siena.edu/2019/02/13/sienas-6th-presidential-expert-poll-1982-2018/.

New Deal A set of aggressive federal domestic policies proposed by President Franklin Delano Roosevelt in the 1930s and passed by Congress as a response to the Great Depression; it ultimately transformed the presidency into an institution marked by permanent bureaucracies and well-established repositories of power.

transported the supplies in its own ships, and traded Britain 50 destroyers in exchange for rights to build military bases on British possessions in the Western Hemisphere—all without the consent of Congress. With the president playing a dominant role in both national and world affairs, the imperial presidency that took root at the beginning of the twentieth century came to fruition by the mid-1940s.

THE IMPERIAL PRESIDENCY COMES UNDER ATTACK, 1945–1980

By the end of World War II, the presidency had emerged as a very powerful office. Those who followed in the footsteps of FDR confronted a new and unprecedented threat to American national security: the presence of a second world military superpower—the Soviet Union. With presidential authority greatest in the area of national security, waging the Cold War that began in the late 1940s consumed much of these presidents' energies. Harry Truman, FDR's immediate successor, proclaimed the "Truman Doctrine" in foreign policy, by which the United States pledged military and economic aid to any nation threatened by communism or the Soviet Union. Like Truman, Presidents Eisenhower and Kennedy also focused their administrations' energies on containing the Soviet communist threat. As long as the Soviet Union challenged American interests, the presidency would remain the focus of attention in the American political system.

Not until the presidency of Lyndon Johnson (1963–1969) was a president able to enact a sweeping domestic agenda similar to FDR's New Deal. Johnson's Great Society program featured more than 60 reform measures, including increases in federal aid to education, the enactment of Medicare and Medicaid, and a voting rights act for racial/ethnic minorities. But Johnson's domestic policy success was offset by his failures in foreign policy. Exercising his authority as commander in chief, Johnson sent more than half a million troops to Vietnam to fight an increasingly unpopular war. The failure to stop the communists from taking over South Vietnam was laid squarely at the feet of Johnson, just as earlier foreign policy successes had been credited to his predecessors.

The presidents who followed Johnson came under increasing attack in the 1970s. Richard Nixon achieved foreign policy success by improving America's relationship with the Soviet Union and China, but in 1974 he became the first president in history to resign from office before the end of his term when the Watergate scandal enveloped his presidency. Jimmy Carter's presidency (1977–1981) was beset with hardships, as the nation's economy faltered in the 1970s. Carter's failure to resolve an Iranian revolution that included the taking of 50 American hostages further cemented his image as an inept commander in chief. Carter thus became the first elected president since 1932 to lose a reelection bid. By the end of the 1970s, the modern presidency created by Theodore Roosevelt and brought to new heights by Franklin Delano Roosevelt found itself increasingly under attack from an emboldened Congress and a frustrated public.

REDEFINING THE PRESIDENCY IN AN ERA OF DIVISIVENESS, 1981–PRESENT

The election of Ronald Reagan to the White House in 1980 marked the return of the chief executive as an unmatched force in American politics. No president in the twentieth century (save perhaps FDR) could match Reagan's prowess as a "great communicator"; by speaking directly to the American people in terms they could understand, Reagan bypassed Congress and enjoyed early victories with passage of an economic program marked by tax cuts, decreased social spending, and a marked increase in defense spending. Reagan's legislative success was all the more remarkable given that he was working with a divided-party government. In foreign policy, Reagan's aggressive program of military buildup combined with his own hardline position against the Soviet Union is credited with helping bring about the fall of communist regimes in Eastern Europe, the breakup of the USSR, and thus victory in the Cold War. In addition, Reagan's immense popularity allowed him to weather numerous crises and scandals in a way that few of his predecessors had.

Reagan's successors also faced the reality of divided-party government at different points in their respective presidencies. George H. W. Bush took the lead in foreign policy, overseeing

Great Society A set of aggressive federal domestic policies proposed by President Lyndon Johnson and passed by Congress in the 1960s that further enhanced the role of the presidency.

the dismantling of the Soviet Union and forging international alliances prior to mounting a successful war against Iraqi aggression in Kuwait. However, by compromising with the opposition Democrats on tax legislation, he frustrated some of his more conservative constituencies and undermined his efforts at reelection. Bill Clinton became the first Democratic president in a half-century to serve two full terms. Clinton appealed to moderates largely by borrowing central elements of the opposition party's domestic program: his three main legislative successes (free trade agreements, budget cutting, and welfare reform) were all programs that had been more closely associated with Republicans than Democrats at the time Clinton took office in the early 1990s.

In the aftermath of the terrorist attacks of September 11, 2001, President George W. Bush moved quickly to position his administration as the eminent world leader in an emerging "war on terrorism." His aggressive military intervention against the Taliban-controlled government in Afghanistan in late 2001 proved extremely popular and helped cement his administration's image of toughness and resolve. Yet, when the Bush administration expanded the war on terrorism to include military intervention in Iraq, justified on the basis of inaccurate reports that Iraq possessed weapons of mass destruction, these same policies became much more divisive.

Barack Obama's presidency began—as most presidential terms do—buoyed by feelings of goodwill and optimism. At the outset, President Obama benefitted from strong Democratic majorities in Congress; he muscled through his legislative agenda almost entirely on the strength of those majorities, and with little support from Republicans. Most partisan of all was the landmark health care reform bill of 2010. The final legislation, the Patient Protection and Affordable Care Act (aka Obamacare), garnered not a single Republican vote from either branch of Congress. Facing an emboldened Republican majority following the 2010 midterm elections, Obama soon found himself at loggerheads with the GOP House leadership—this led to a series of threatened government shutdowns prior to the 2012 election and a near paralysis of government following President Obama's successful reelection bid in 2012. Eventually, a frustrated Obama resorted to more limited executive orders addressing gun violence and immigration. This much was clear: Obama's rhetoric celebrating bipartisanship rarely translated into legislation passed with bipartisan votes.

Like his predecessor, President Donald J. Trump began his first term with partisan majorities in his party in the House and Senate. United GOP government led to a major tax relief law, an increase in defense spending, and the appointment of two Supreme Court justices and many lower federal court judges. Also, like his predecessor, President Trump's party lost control of the House in the 2018 midterm elections, after which he became even more combative. Trump catered to his loyal Republican base, pressing for more restrictive immigration policies (including the building of a southern border wall) and an all-out assault on Obamacare. What Trump could not achieve through legislation, he took on through bold executive orders. For example, in February 2019 he declared a national emergency in order to divert funds to the construction of the border wall. President Trump's refusal to compromise on his budget requests regarding the border wall led to the longest government shutdown in American history. Far from limiting presidential power, this hyperpartisan era in Washington, DC, has emboldened modern presidents to seek less traditional and ever more audacious means of achieving their partisan and political goals.

7-3 EXPRESS POWERS AND RESPONSIBILITIES OF THE PRESIDENT

Article II of the Constitution provides that the president of the United States holds executive power, but it is not very detailed about what constitutes executive power. In fact, the Constitution lists only four specific powers of the president: (1) commander in chief of the armed forces, (2) power to grant reprieves or pardons, (3) power to make treaties (subject to Senate approval), and (4) power to make certain appointments, including those of ambassadors and justices of the Supreme Court (again subject to Senate approval). Despite this limited number of constitutionally expressed powers, presidents today serve many important functions in the American political system. Noting these varied roles, political scientist Clinton Rossiter referred to the many different hats that the president must wear during the course of a week, or even during just one day.[6] Some of these are specified in the Constitution and laws of the United States, which conceive of a limited executive but one who possesses the authority to react quickly and energetically to unexpected crises.

HEAD OF STATE

The office of the presidency combines the political and symbolic functions that are often divided in other countries. As the nation's head of state, the president fulfills numerous formal duties and obligations on behalf of the country. Most visiting foreign heads of state meet directly with the president; sometimes those visits include an official state dinner at the White House hosted by the president and attended by

AP Photo / Evan Vucci

President Trump meets in the Oval Office with Democratic congressional leaders Nancy Pelosi (far left) and Chuck Schumer (far right), as well as Vice President Mike Pence, in December 2018.

key political leaders from throughout Washington. Article II of the Constitution also carves out a more formal role for the president in foreign affairs; the president's role in receiving ambassadors and other public ministers has often been interpreted as granting the president the discretion to give or deny official recognition to foreign governments. Although such a power may seem mostly honorary, it can have a real political impact in some circumstances. President Woodrow Wilson's refusal to recognize the new government of Mexico in 1913 caused considerable consternation among American supporters of the Mexican revolution and led to growing tensions between the two neighbors. More recently, American presidents during the 1970s and 1980s refused to recognize the Palestine Liberation Organization as the legitimate representative of the Palestinian people, buttressing Israel's own hardline stance against that organization.

CHIEF EXECUTIVE AND HEAD OF GOVERNMENT

In his *Second Treatise of Government*, political theorist John Locke argued that executive power was so fundamental that it predated civil society.[7] According to Locke, legislatures were ill-equipped to enforce their own laws, as they might be tempted to "suit the law to their own particular advantage," regardless of the law's language. Another political theorist, Baron de Montesquieu, also advocated the separation of legislative and executive powers— specifically, he decried the tendency of legislatures to exert too much influence over the executive, increasing the opportunity for abuse.[8]

Influenced in part by these arguments, the framers of the Constitution vested all executive power in the president alone. However, they failed to define that power with any specificity. At a minimum, the Constitution grants presidents alone the responsibility to execute the laws of the United States, which encompasses the implementation and enforcement of measures passed by Congress—in other words, to see that Americans actually abide by those laws in practice. A president's failure to "take Care that the Laws be faithfully executed"—whether intentionally or due to negligent administration of his subordinates—can have obvious implications for the effectiveness of such laws. Actual levels of execution sometimes lie squarely within the discretion of the chief executive. Presidents Obama and Trump, for example, defined civil rights laws in markedly different ways simply by offering contrasting approaches to the execution of those laws. For example, while the Obama administration conducted high-profile investigations of police departments across the country for potential civil-rights abuses, Trump's Justice Department was more deferential to state and local police departments in that context.

President Richard Nixon and Vice President Gerald Ford conferring on August 9, 1974, the day Nixon resigned from office.

The president's power to see that laws are faithfully executed also implies some power to hire and fire those charged with administrative authority to help execute federal laws. The **power of appointment** thus stands among the president's most important executive powers.[9] The Constitution specifically authorizes the president to appoint ambassadors and other public ministers, judges of the Supreme Court, and all other federal officers under his charge. Additionally, the president appoints all federal judges. Most of these appointments require the consent of the Senate. In recent years, senators have subjected the president's nominees to intense scrutiny, occasionally even rejecting the president's choices. President George W. Bush withdrew his second choice for the Supreme Court, White House counsel Harriet Miers, amid mounting opposition from his own party. And President Obama faced stubborn opposition from Senate Republicans when he nominated Judge Merrick Garland to a vacant Supreme Court seat in 2016. Led by majority leader Mitch McConnell, the Senate refused to even hold hearings for Garland before Election Day, asserting that body's power to withhold consent for the president's nominee during a presidential election year.

Although Supreme Court nominees often receive the most intense investigation, the Senate may occasionally question other presidential appointments as well. In 1989, the U.S. Senate rejected President George H. W. Bush's choice for defense secretary, John Tower, due to allegations that Tower had a drinking problem. Barack Obama's first choice as secretary of health and human services, former Senate majority leader Tom Daschle, withdrew his name from consideration in February 2009 amid a growing controversy over his failure to accurately report and pay income taxes.

The president's removal power has been a source of controversy as well. The Supreme Court's decision in *Myers v. United States* (1926)[10] established that chief executives have the power to remove "purely executive officers" without congressional consent. Although independent agency heads can be removed only by congressional action, cabinet heads and military officials can be terminated by the president alone. In one famous instance during the Korean War, President Truman decided in 1951 to fire the extremely popular General Douglas MacArthur, commander of the United Nations forces in Korea.

Not only is the president responsible for the enforcement of all federal laws, he or she is also authorized by the Constitution to grant reprieves and pardons to individuals who violate those laws. The founders vested this power in the chief executive because they believed that the prerogative of mercy, on which the pardon power is based, is most efficiently and equitably exercised by a single individual as opposed to a body of legislators or judges. A **reprieve** reduces the severity of a punishment without removing the guilt; a full **pardon** relieves an individual of both the punishment and the guilt. A president's decision to exercise the pardon power can invite considerable negative comment and political backlash. Not surprisingly, then, most presidents wait until the end of their presidential terms to grant pardons. Less than two months after being denied his bid for reelection in 1992, President George H. W. Bush pardoned six officials for their involvement in the Iran-Contra scandal from 1987, including former defense secretary Casper Weinberger. President Clinton issued 140 pardons on his last day in office in 2001, including one to Marc Rich, who had previously fled the country for tax evasion and whose wife was a major contributor to Clinton's political campaigns. No president received more criticism for granting a pardon than Gerald Ford, who

power of appointment The president's constitutional power to hire and fire those charged with administrative authority to help execute federal laws, such as ambassadors; federal judges, including those on the Supreme Court; and all other federal officers under the president's charge. Most of these appointments require the consent of the Senate.

reprieve The president's constitutional authority to reduce the severity of a punishment without removing the guilt for those who have violated the law.

pardon The president's constitutional authority to relieve an individual of both the punishment and the guilt of violating the law.

Making History on the Road to the White House . . . Yet Again

When President Obama was inaugurated on January 20, 2009, nearly 2 million people crowded onto the Washington, DC, mall to be part of history, as the first African American president took the formal oath of office. Eight years later, the Republican nominee Donald J. Trump became the first U.S. president to arrive in office without any government experience (military or civilian) whatsoever. As Democrats were preparing for their own set of primary battles to take on President Trump in 2020, a brand-new set of candidates with history-making potential rose to prominence in the Democratic field. Included among the contenders were Kamala Harris (who would, if elected, become the first African American female president), Bernie Sanders (who would, if elected, become the first Jewish president), and Pete Buttigieg (vying to become the first openly gay president of the United States). In a nation where Caucasian, male heterosexual Protestants have dominated the presidential scene, 2020 offers yet another opportunity to buck this trend in some fashion. Consider some other presidential election firsts as well.

John F. Kennedy, Inauguration Day, January 20, 1961.

Bettmann / Getty Images

Then

In 1836, Martin Van Buren became the first man elected president who was born in the United States of America (he was born a U.S. citizen in Kinderhook, New York, in 1782—the previous seven presidents were born as British subjects). Van Buren would also become the first president born after the Declaration of Independence.

In 1960, America elected the first Catholic president in Senator John F. Kennedy (D-MA). At 43, Kennedy was also the youngest man ever elected president, the first president born in the twentieth century, and the first president to have previously served in the U.S. Navy.

In 1980, Ronald Reagan became the first divorced individual and the first professional actor to be elected president. The 69-year-old former governor of California was also the oldest man to be elected president for the first time; he was also the first president to be born and raised in Illinois.

In 2008, Barack Obama became the first African American (and the first multiracial American) to be elected president. Born in Hawaii, he was also the first president to be born outside of the contiguous 48 states.

President Trump delivers his inaugural address after being sworn in as the 45th president on January 20, 2017.

AP Photo / Patrick Semansky

Now

In 2016, America elected its first true "outsider"—someone with absolutely no military or government experience—as president. After earning his bachelor's degree from the Wharton School of Business, Donald Trump rose to prominence by building a real estate and

(Continued)

construction firm that was eventually valued in the billions. Trump effectively used television to become a national celebrity—first, by appearing at Miss USA pageants (which he owned from 1996 to 2015) and then later as the host and co-producer of *The Apprentice*, a successful reality television show that ran from 2004 to 2015. Trump toyed with politics often during his career: He had first sought the Reform Party presidential nomination in 2000 but withdrew before voting began. He was also considered as a possible vice presidential running mate by George H. W. Bush in 1988. Still, when Trump declared that he was running for president in June 2015, few pundits or long-time political observers gave his campaign any real chance of success. And yet 17 months later Trump had overcome exceedingly long odds to win

the White House. In doing so, he rewrote the rulebook for what qualifications are necessary to hold the highest office in the government.

For Critical Thinking and Discussion

1. Why do you think Americans take so much pride (at least initially) in historical breakthroughs when electing a new president?
2. Rather than serving as a source of pride, should the election of an individual with an unusual racial or ethnic background (as compared to past chief executives) serve instead as a sober reminder to the public that the White House has not been a source of access for many such groups in the past?

---

as vice president succeeded to the presidency when Richard Nixon resigned in 1974. Ford's pardon of his former boss for involvement in the Watergate scandal helped undermine his prospects for election to the White House in his own right two years later.

CHIEF DIPLOMAT

As chief diplomat of the United States, the president has the power to negotiate treaties and appoint diplomatic representatives to other countries, including ambassadors, ministers, and consuls. The president's power over treaties is limited to negotiation and execution—enactment of any treaties requires approval by two-thirds of the Senate. Still, the power to negotiate and execute the terms of treaties affords the president immense authority in the field of foreign affairs. John F. Kennedy used this power to negotiate an end to the Cuban missile crisis in 1962;[11] Jimmy Carter personally presided over the negotiation of the Panama Canal Treaty of 1977–1978, which relinquished U.S. control over the canal by the year 2000. Bill Clinton surprised many in his own party in 1993 when he completed negotiations on the North American Free Trade Agreement, an economic treaty with Canada and Mexico that was favored primarily by Republican presidents who came before him. Twenty-five years later, the Trump administration renegotiated NAFTA and entered new trade pacts with Canada and Mexico.

CHIEF LEGISLATOR

Although Congress is the branch of government authorized to make laws, modern presidents are involved in nearly every stage of federal law-making.[12] The Constitution's express provision that the president recommend for the consideration of Congress "such Measures as he shall judge necessary and expedient" barely hints at the president's real role in this context: major legislation is often the product of a give-and-take process between the president and congressional leaders. Indeed, the president plays a critically important role in helping to set the law-making agenda for Congress, especially when the president's party is also in control of the legislative branch of government. While campaigning for the White House, the future president will lay out a policy agenda; once elected, he will claim a legislative mandate to follow through on those campaign proposals. In the State of the Union address, an annual speech made to Congress laying out the status of the nation, the president typically

State of the Union address An annual speech that the president delivers to Congress laying out the status of the nation and offering suggestions for new legislation.

proposes suggestions for legislation. The legislative programs of FDR's New Deal and Lyndon Johnson's Great Society were both influenced heavily by the executive branch. Similarly, Congress's reorganization of various executive branch agencies into a unified Department of Homeland Security in 2002 was based on a plan drafted by officials within the George W. Bush administration. According to social scientist Paul Light, recent presidents have tended to offer fewer legislative proposals than did presidents of the mid-twentieth century, consistent with the modern administrations' increased emphasis on reducing the size of the federal government.[13] Still, when a national crisis demands legislative solutions, Congress often looks to the president for leadership. House and Senate leaders made few significant modifications to their respective health care bills in 2009 without first huddling with President Obama and his top White House aides, and it was the president's willingness to meet frequently with moderate Democratic members of Congress that kept many in the fold for the final passage of health care reform in 2010.

The White House Office of Legislative Affairs serves as a liaison between the president and Congress and helps develop the strategy used to promote passage of the president's legislative agenda. Administration officials often testify before congressional subcommittees on behalf of legislation, and presidents meet with congressional leaders frequently throughout the law-making process to negotiate details and discuss strategy. Many bills have the

> **White House Office of Legislative Affairs**
> A presidential office that serves as a liaison between the president and Congress. This office helps the president develop the strategy used to promote passage of the president's legislative agenda.

TABLE 7-2
Vetoes Issued by Modern Presidents (through August 27, 2019)

President	Congresses	White	Pocket Vetoes	Total Vetoes	Vetoes Overridden
Theodore Roosevelt	57th–60th	42	40	82	1
William Taft	61st–62nd	30	9	39	1
Woodrow Wilson	63rd–66th	33	11	44	6
Warren Harding	67th	5	1	6	0
Calvin Coolidge	68th–70th	20	30	50	4
Herbert Hoover	71st–72nd	21	16	37	3
Franklin D. Roosevelt	73rd–79th	372	263	635	9
Harry Truman	79th–82nd	180	70	250	12
Dwight Eisenhower	83rd–86th	73	108	181	2
John F. Kennedy	87th–88th	12	9	21	0
Lyndon B. Johnson	88th–90th	16	14	30	0
Richard M. Nixon	91st–93rd	26	17	43	7
Gerald Ford	93rd–94th	48	18	66	12
Jimmy Carter	95th–96th	13	18	31	2
Ronald Reagan	97th–100th	39	39	78	9
George H. W. Bush	101st–102nd	29	15	44	1
William Clinton	103rd–106th	37	1	38	2
George W. Bush	107th–110th	11	1	12	4
Barack Obama	111th–114th	12	0	12	1
Donald Trump	115th–116th	5	0	5	0

Source: U.S. Senate, "Summary of Bills Vetoed, 1789–Present," www.senate.gov/reference/Legislation/Vetoes/vetoCounts.htm.

president's imprint squarely upon them, even though the power of law-making rests formally with Congress. The president's legislative authority also includes the constitutional power to veto, or reject, legislation that he opposes. Although Congress can technically override a veto by a two-thirds vote of both houses, barely 4 percent of presidential vetoes have been overridden in history.

During the twentieth century, vetoes became a routine form of political exercise for presidents, especially those confronting Congresses controlled by the opposite political party (see Table 7-2). That power includes so-called pocket vetoes, by which presidents may refuse to sign a bill within 10 days of the adjournment of Congress, thus rendering it void. For Richard Nixon, Gerald Ford, and George H. W. Bush, the only three presidents during this span who were never the beneficiaries of unified party rule, the veto became something of an art form. Nixon and Bush vetoed 43 and 44 bills, respectively. (Only eight of those vetoes were overridden.) Gerald Ford vetoed 66 bills in just two and a half years, but more than 1 in 5 were overridden, a clear sign of the limited power Ford held during his brief term as president. With Republicans controlling the House during George W. Bush's first six years in office, he did not need to veto any bill until July 19, 2006, when he vetoed the Stem Cell Research Enhancement Bill, legislation that would have eased restrictions on federal funding for embryonic stem cell research. However, after the Democrats' takeover of Congress in 2007, Bush vetoed 11 more bills sent to him by the Democratic Congress. President Obama vetoed just 12 bills during the course of his presidency, including the controversial Keystone Pipeline Approval Act and several other environmental bills. Meanwhile, President Trump waited until March 2019 to veto his first bill: he rejected a joint resolution of Congress seeking to overturn his declaration of a national emergency at the Mexico–U.S. border.

In recent times, presidents have resorted to other means to undermine laws that stop short of an actual veto. For example, the president's distaste for a law may be so strong that even while signing the bill into law (perhaps for political reasons), the president will still express his intent to thereafter ignore the law in the form of a "signing statement." The past three decades have seen a notable surge in such signing statements (see Figure 7-1). President George W. Bush

FIGURE 7-1

Signing Statements Past and Present

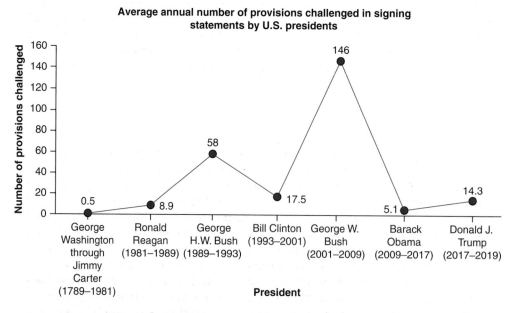

Average annual number of provisions challenged in signing statements by U.S. presidents

Source: The Center for Media and Democracy's "PR Watch," www.prwatch.org/node/5156; The American Presidency Project, https://www.presidency.ucsb.edu/documents/presidential-documents-archive-guidebook/presidential-signing-statements-hoover-1929-obama

in particular heavily relied on such signing statements (over 800 times during his eight years in office); thus, for example, in signing the Detainee Treatment Act of 2005, which prohibited cruel, inhumane, and degrading treatment of detainees in U.S. custody, Bush warned that the executive branch would construe the act in a manner consistent with his own views on a president's constitutional authority. Though signing statements have appeared less frequently during the Obama and Trump administrations, neither of those two chief executives have shied away from using the device as necessary to insert their own views on legislation into the public record.

COMMANDER IN CHIEF

One of the defining features of the American political system is its commitment to civil control of the military, embodied in the president's status as head of the nation's armed forces. As commander in chief, the president is the nation's principal military leader, responsible for formulating and directing all military strategy and policy. Although the Constitution awards to Congress the formal power to "declare war," the balance of war-making power has shifted overwhelmingly from Congress to the president during the past century, as modern executives have assumed the nearly unlimited power to send troops into combat.[14] Calling it a "police action," President Harry Truman sent troops to Korea in June 1950 without even asking Congress for a formal declaration of war. In 1973, over President Nixon's veto, Congress passed the War Powers Resolution, which theoretically limits the power of the president to unilaterally commit troops to battle. Ignoring its provisions, Presidents Reagan, George H. W. Bush, and Clinton deployed U.S. troops to invade Grenada (1983), Panama (1989), and Haiti (1994), respectively. In February 2009 President Obama announced his plans to bolster the U.S. military presence in Afghanistan by committing over 17,000 new troops to the region. Of course, no president is entirely immune from public pressures in this context. After initially threatening to use military action in response to Syria's use of chemical weapons against some of its own citizens in 2013, President Obama eventually backtracked from that position in the face of a conflict-weary American public.

7-4 IMPLIED POWERS AND RESPONSIBILITIES OF THE PRESIDENT

Article II of the Constitution does not spell out all the powers that a president may exercise; during the past two centuries, presidents have assumed the right to exercise some "implied" or "inherent" powers not listed in the Constitution, and the Supreme Court for the most part has acceded in their right do so. These implied powers allow the president to act quickly in crisis situations, to serve as leader of his political party, and to issue executive orders and make executive agreements that do not require congressional approval.

CRISIS MANAGER

More than any other official in government, the president is in a unique position to respond quickly and effectively to unexpected crises. Consequently, Americans look immediately to the president under such circumstances to provide assurances, comfort, and, where appropriate, a plan to address the difficulties. When a natural disaster strikes, the president will often visit the scene, meet with family members, and in many cases provide aid from the Federal Emergency Management Agency (FEMA). In the days following the September 11 attacks, George W. Bush redefined his presidency as a fight against terrorism—his visits to "Ground Zero," the site of the attacks on the World Trade Center, and his address to a joint session of Congress created indelible images in the media and won him widespread public support. When Hurricane Sandy demolished parts of New Jersey in 2012, President Obama signed an emergency declaration and personally visited the site of the damage to reassure residents that federal assistance would be provided. President Trump was urged to take similar actions when Hurricane Maria devastated Puerto Rico several years later. Although the U.S. military performed well in that crisis, humanitarian groups such as Refugees International severely criticized the slow response of federal authorities.

PARTY LEADER

Once elected, the president of the United States assumes the position of de facto leader of his or her own political party. Not surprisingly, presidents are normally well attuned to how their political decisions will reflect on the party as a whole. A popular president is often expected to campaign for the party's congressional candidates and, if possible, help secure control of Congress for the party. Any assistance the president provides to congressional candidates seeking election may have an important side effect: the president may now have the leverage to demand support from those members of Congress for his own legislative programs. Similarly, the "coattail effect," by which congressional candidates and state and local officials benefit at the polls from the votes of the president's supporters, may strengthen the president's position with party members during the upcoming term.

EXECUTIVE ORDERS AND AGREEMENTS

On their own, presidents can issue executive orders, which are rules or regulations issued by the chief executive that have the force of law. Once thought to be an unconstitutional exercise of Congress's law-making power, executive orders have now become a routine feature of American government.[15] Since the beginning of the twentieth century, presidents have issued more than 13,000 executive orders regulating all manner of topics, including affirmative action, civil service, federal holidays, the classification of government documents, public land designations, and federal disaster relief. President George W. Bush issued more than 150 executive orders during his first term in office alone. On his first full day in office, Obama issued an executive order mandating that the interrogation of terrorism suspects not include torture. He issued 275 more executive orders, establishing federal rules on such controversial subjects as immigration, gun control, and gender discrimination by federal contractors. Donald Trump has similarly deployed executive power in this fashion: during his first two years as president, he issued 92 separate orders.

Though executive orders carry the force of federal law, they are subject to judicial review and can be partially or even fully revoked by an act of Congress. FDR strategically issued executive orders to create agencies that Congress refused to establish; eventually, however, he was frustrated by the legislature's refusal to fund those agencies near the end of his presidency. Similarly, Richard Nixon's efforts to dismantle by executive order certain agencies created by his Democratic predecessors, such as the Office of Economic Opportunity, were often stymied because the courts refused to allow the elimination of an agency established with the approval of Congress. Though Presidents Obama and Trump held contrasting positions on most immigration issues, both chief executives resorted to executive orders affecting immigration policies in the wake of partisan gridlock that stymied efforts to achieve more comprehensive legislative solutions on that subject.

An executive agreement is a pact, written or oral, reached between the president and a foreign government. As with executive orders, these agreements do not require the consent of Congress, although Congress does have the power to revoke them. Executive agreements have become important tools by which presidents conduct foreign affairs. FDR agreed to trade U.S. destroyers for British military bases in 1940, more than a year before the United States formally declared war on Germany, thus implicitly supporting the British military cause against Germany. In recent years, the U.S. government's military alliances with Great Britain and other countries in response to Iraqi aggression have not been spelled out in any treaties that required the advice and consent of the Senate; rather, those alliances came in the form of executive agreements between President George W. Bush and the British government.

7-5 PRESIDENTIAL RESOURCES

More than a half-century ago, Richard Neustadt, in his landmark book *Presidential Power and the Modern Presidents: The Politics of Leadership* (1960), defined the central problem that all presidents face from the moment they are sworn into office: How do presidents mobilize the powers of the office to work for them? The federal bureaucracy has grown so vast that

executive orders Rules or regulations issued by the chief executive that have the force of law and do not require the consent of Congress.

executive agreement A pact reached between the president and a foreign government that does not require the consent of Congress.

presents cannot simply "command" the bureaucracy to do their will. So what exactly can presidents do to make their will felt within the executive branch and to carry out their choices through that "maze of personalities and institutions called the government of the United States"?

Neustadt argued that the president's most fundamental power is the "power to persuade."[16] Presidents use this power most effectively by keeping themselves informed, employing a system of information that allows them to be at the center of the decision-making apparatus, and carefully cultivating the image of a powerful president. Modern presidents have tended to emphasize certain individuals and offices under their control that play critical roles in the success of their administrations.

THE VICE PRESIDENT

Vice President Mike Pence (left) shakes hands with former vice president Joe Biden at the Capitol in January 2018.

After Vice President Martin Van Buren's successful election to the White House in 1836, few vice presidents rose to the presidency by running and winning on their own accord. In fact, after Van Buren, no sitting vice president even emerged as a serious contender for the presidency until the Republicans nominated Richard Nixon, who lost to John F. Kennedy in 1960. And the next sitting vice president after Van Buren to be elected president was George H. W. Bush in 1988.

Next in line for succession and thus "only a heartbeat away" from the presidency, vice presidents have often been relegated to the very fringes of presidential power.[17] FDR barely communicated with John Nance Garner, who was vice president during FDR's first two terms in office. Of course, Garner did not have a very high opinion of the vice presidency either, referring to the position (in a sanitized version of his remarks) as not worth "a bucket of warm spit." When asked toward the end of his presidency what ideas Vice President Richard Nixon had offered within his own administration, President Dwight D. Eisenhower quipped: "If you give me a week, I might think of one." In fact, up through the 1950s, vice presidents maintained their principal offices on Capitol Hill near the Senate Chamber, where they occasionally performed their one clearly defined constitutional responsibility: to preside over the Senate and to cast a vote in the event of a tie.

The vice presidency, however, has undergone a transformation in recent decades. Modern-day vice presidents have assumed roles as key advisers and executive branch officials working on behalf of the president. Walter Mondale developed U.S. policy on South Africa and was one of President Jimmy Carter's most trusted advisers. Al Gore headed the National Performance Review for the Clinton administration, leading to reforms to increase the federal government's efficiency and reduce its costs. Perhaps no federal official was more influential with President George W. Bush than Vice President Dick Cheney, the driving force behind Bush's controversial decision to invade Iraq in March 2003.[18] Barack Obama's vice president, Joe Biden, was famous for his salty language and verbal gaffes; notably, Biden's public declaration that he was comfortable with legalizing marriage for gay and lesbian couples may have forced President Obama to declare similar support for same-sex marriage just a few days later. Both Biden and his successor as vice president, Mike Pence, sought to press their respective administrations' legislative agendas by personally lobbying members of Congress.

Constitutionally, the vice president is first in line to succeed the president in the event of death or incapacitation. By statute, if the vice president is not available to serve, succession falls in turn to the Speaker of the House, the president pro tempore of the Senate, and then to cabinet-level officials.

THE CABINET

The Constitution specifically affords presidents the power to solicit the advice of the principal officers in each of the executive departments. Thus, in addition to running their own executive departments within the large federal bureaucracy, principal officers also serve as key advisers. Together, they form the president's **cabinet**. Today's cabinet consists of 15 heads of departments and 6 other important officials considered of "cabinet rank." In reality, such a large body of individuals with different areas of expertise can serve only limited functions for a president, and recent chief executives have convened their full cabinets to serve more as a sounding board and a communications device than as a significant instrument of policy-making. Nevertheless, in individual meetings cabinet-level officials may still provide critical input to the president on issues related to their own departments.

THE EXECUTIVE OFFICE OF THE PRESIDENT AND THE WHITE HOUSE STAFF

Created in 1939 to bring executive branch activities under tighter control, the Executive Office of the President (EOP) and its 2,000 federal employees consists of numerous agencies that assist with the management and administration of executive branch departments. Some of these agencies, such as the Office of Management and Budget, the President's Council of Economic Advisors, the National Security Council, and the Office of the U.S. Trade Representative, have near-permanent status. Other EOP agencies come and go, depending on the policy priorities of the current administration. Thus, during the height of the Cold War, the EOP included agencies that focused on preparedness and civil defense in the event of a nuclear attack.

The EOP also includes an expanded White House staff. Until 1939, this staff consisted mostly of assistant secretaries and clerks who helped the president with correspondence; the White House staff today consists of nearly 600 employees and runs on an annual budget of almost $730 million. In charge of this bureaucracy is the **White House chief of staff**, who manages and organizes the staff to serve the president. Some modern presidents, including Ronald Reagan and George H. W. Bush, have adopted management styles that rely heavily on the chief of staff to control access to the president. Others, such as President Clinton, have utilized a "spokes-of-a-wheel" arrangement in which five or six different advisers have direct access to the president.[19] Regardless of the arrangement chosen, the White House chief of staff has a significant hand in the success of the modern presidency. The principal duties of the White House staff include, but are not limited to, speechwriting, advance work for presidential appearances, scheduling, congressional relations, public relations, and communications.

cabinet The collection of the principal officers in each of the executive departments of the federal government who serve as key advisers to the president.

White House chief of staff The manager of the White House staff, which serves the president's organizational needs, including speechwriting, advance work for presidential appearances, scheduling, congressional relations, public relations, and communications.

Slovenian-born, Melania Trump is the first First Lady born outside the United States since Louisa Adams, the British-born wife of the sixth president, John Quincy Adams (1825–1829).

THE FIRST LADY

All but one president (James Buchanan) have been married at some point in their lifetimes, and the spouses of sitting presidents, now referred to as first ladies, have come to assume an important role in the affairs of the nation. Until recently, presidents mainly relied on their spouses to help them perform social obligations, such as hosting state dinners. Woodrow Wilson's two wives broke somewhat with this mold: his first wife, Ellen, took public positions on bills being considered for Congress and his second wife, Edith, served as an intermediary between the president and other government leaders while Wilson was recovering from a massive stroke in the fall of 1919. Eleanor Roosevelt, wife to Franklin Delano Roosevelt, charted a course for first ladies as aggressive public advocates. Mrs. Roosevelt launched one of the earliest civil rights organizations, the Southern Conference on Human Welfare; she actively supported the building of model communities; and she lobbied for refugees fleeing Nazi persecution. Occasionally, Mrs. Roosevelt even disagreed publicly with some of FDR's policies in foreign affairs.

Although no first lady after Eleanor Roosevelt was willing to so boldly challenge her husband's policies in the media, many staked out policy areas where they could contribute, and some became active members of their husbands' administrations.[20] They have been assisted in this regard by a formal Office of the First Lady, now staffed by more than 20 aides. Rosalynn Carter lobbied Congress for mental health initiatives, Nancy Reagan became the public voice of the "Just Say No" to drugs campaign, and Barbara Bush (wife of George H. W. Bush) campaigned widely against the problem of illiteracy. A distinguished lawyer, Hillary Rodham Clinton led a task force in 1994 charged with reforming the nation's health care system; Mrs. Clinton's complex plan ultimately proved too ambitious, and it was rebuffed by Congress. In another series of unprecedented moves, Hillary Clinton ran for and won a seat in the U.S. Senate in 2000 and was reelected to the Senate in 2006; she was the front-running Democratic candidate for president in 2008, and became secretary of state in 2009. Finally, in 2016 she rose to even greater political heights, carrying her party's mantle as the Democratic nominee for president. Unfortunately for Clinton, her quest to become the first female president in U.S. history came up just short, when she was defeated by Donald Trump on Election Day.

Regardless of what roles first ladies may assume, modern presidents have increasingly come to rely on their spouses as advisers on a range of issues.

7-6 IMPORTANT PRESIDENTIAL RELATIONSHIPS

The power of the president is influenced by the relationships that a president develops and cultivates with three important constituencies: the public, Congress, and the news media.

THE PRESIDENT AND THE PUBLIC

Catering to the needs and demands of the public mattered little to presidents prior to 1824, when presidential nominees were chosen by congressional leaders in secret caucuses. By contrast, the presidency today is a truly public institution that depends heavily on its public popularity for political effectiveness. Modern presidential nominations and elections are won on an arduous campaign trail in which aspiring chief executives must reach out to, communicate with, and ultimately gain acceptance from large segments of the public. Once in office, presidents must remain constantly attentive to the sentiments of the public at large. FDR was the first president to rely on public opinion polls, and his administration utilized them to monitor support for his New Deal policies. Through his fireside chats, he reached into the living rooms of millions of Americans, winning their support for and confidence in his domestic and foreign policies.

Most modern presidents continuously engage the public to support administration policies, whether through the annual State of the Union address to Congress and other special televised messages, staged events, or interviews and press conferences with the media where they attempt to promote the benefits of their programs. Presidents Richard Nixon and Ronald Reagan preferred the "set piece" speech presented from the Oval Office during prime time; Presidents Jimmy Carter and Bill Clinton occasionally held "town meetings" to discuss issues in open forums with concerned citizens. In bypassing legislators and appealing directly to their constituents, modern presidents have perfected the art of what social scientist Samuel Kernell calls "going public."[21] Presidents Obama and Trump utilized Twitter to communicate directly to constituents in an especially timely fashion.

Some recent presidents have come under criticism for being too dependent on public opinion polls. President Clinton's critics charged that he too quickly withdrew support for some of his more controversial appointments when public opinion swung against them. Notably, President Obama's decision in May 2012 to declare his own personal support for same-sex marriage coincided with recent polls showing a bare majority's support for that right for the first time in American history. On the other hand, presidents may find themselves in even greater political trouble when they refuse to heed public opinion. President Johnson's escalation of troops in Vietnam during the late 1960s ignored growing public opposition against that war and undermined his hopes for reelection. Just as the Watergate scandal began to engulf Richard Nixon's presidency, his decision to hold press conferences less frequently only fed the impression that he was hiding from the public and fueled even more calls for his resignation. Whereas high levels of public support increase a president's chances to get legislation passed, precipitous drops in public support may stop a president's program in its tracks.

THE PRESIDENT AND CONGRESS

The history of the American political system is marked by the ebb and flow of power between the president and Congress. For much of the nineteenth century, a form of "congressional government" prevailed, with most presidents acting as dutiful administrators of the laws passed by Congress. Buoyed by advances in communications technology that placed modern presidents at the center of American politics, presidents today play far more influential roles in the legislative process, at times even prodding Congress forward to meet their administrations' goals. Since the 1970s, the frequency of divided-party government, with the executive and the legislature controlled by opposing political parties, has placed the two branches in a near continuous battle over the nation's domestic policy agenda. Because credit for a program's success is rarely spread evenly among the two branches, tensions are inevitable and compromises often difficult to come by. President Reagan managed to get the Democrat-controlled House of Representatives to pass his program of tax decreases and spending cuts in 1981; when the economy rebounded a few years later, Reagan and the Republican Party benefited politically far more than did the Democrats. President Clinton's willingness to sign a welfare reform bill in 1996 aided him in that year's election, when he claimed to have lived up to his earlier promise to "end welfare as we know it." The Republican Congress that actually drafted and passed the welfare bill received far less credit for its accomplishments. In foreign policy, presidents continue to act nearly independent of Congress.

Presidents have many tools at their disposal to influence Congress. As party leader, the president can campaign for congressional candidates and then leverage that assistance into support. Personal contacts by the president with members of Congress can be effective as well. The White House Office of Congressional Relations serves as a liaison to Congress, rounding up support and monitoring events on Capitol Hill. Still, the most effective lobbying for a president's policies comes from members of Congress friendly to the administration, who persuade other members of Congress to vote in favor of the policies. The rewards for such service often come in the form of future appointments, pork-barrel projects for home districts or states, or financial support from the political party for future election bids. FDR rewarded Hugo Black, a key Senate supporter of the president's controversial 1937 plan to increase the size of the Supreme Court, with an appointment to the Court; Bill Clinton was prepared to reward Senate majority leader George Mitchell with the same prize in 1994 but held back because he needed Mitchell's support in Congress for a pending health care bill. (Despite Mitchell's efforts, Clinton's health care bill was defeated.)[22]

White House press secretary The person on the White House staff who plays an especially important role in briefing the press, organizing news conferences, and even briefing the president on questions that may be asked.

THE PRESIDENT AND THE MEDIA

The relationship between presidents and the media that cover their administrations is important. The media provide perhaps the most effective channel through which presidents can communicate information about their policies to the public. At the same time, the media's desire for interesting headlines to attract greater numbers of readers, listeners, viewers, and online observers leaves them to rely heavily on the executive branch for information. Effective media management has been a hallmark of the most successful modern presidents. Much of the responsibility rests with the White House press secretary, who plays an especially important role in briefing the press, organizing news conferences, and briefing the president on questions he may be forced to address. Thus, during President Trump's first term, White House press secretary Sarah Huckabee Sanders was one of the most visible faces of the administration.

Of course, the administration that ignores media management does so at its own peril. Social scientists Kathleen Hall Jamieson and Paul Waldman revealed how the mainstream media today do not so much report the news about presidents as create it, transforming "the raw stuff of experience into presumed fact" and "arranging facts into coherent stories" that can prove crucial to presidential success.[23] President Obama enjoyed considerable positive media coverage during his

Bloomberg / Getty Images

Former White House press secretary Sarah Huckabee Sanders served in the position for nearly two years before resigning on July 1, 2019.

initial months in office. By contrast, after Islamic militants attacked the American diplomatic mission in Benghazi, Libya, in September 2012, CBS and other media outlets noted possible contradictions in the Obama administration's description of the attack (i.e., was it terrorism or a spontaneous protest?), driving negative media coverage in the months that followed.

Today the president relies heavily on the White House director of communications to articulate a consistent and effective message to the public.[24] But even before that office came into being, chief executives felt the need to craft a message and hone their public images. Although known best for his fireside chats and effective public speeches, Franklin Delano Roosevelt worked hard to cultivate good relations with the media, allowing his administration to set the news agenda and influence the content of the news. Many of his press conferences included off-the-record commentary that fed the media's appetite for information yet allowed the president to change his position as circumstances changed. John F. Kennedy perfected the modern press conference in the East Room of the White House; his colorful banter with reporters played well as sound bites on the evening television news. Ronald Reagan's reputation as the "great communicator" was enhanced by positive media coverage. His administration perfected the use of "staged" or "pseudo" events, which presented the president in a positive light—perhaps visiting flag factories or reading Shakespeare to children at elementary schools—all packaged in time for the evening newscasts. Even when scandals rocked Reagan's second term in office, his mostly friendly relations with the press paid off when they painted him as the unwitting victim of his own administration's follies.

Borrowing from Reagan's playbook, recent presidents have avoided live press conferences wherever possible, preferring controlled situations that could be molded to fit their respective styles and messages. The George W. Bush administration attempted to cultivate the image of a president working hard for the American people—even while vacationing at his ranch in Crawford, Texas, the president was often pictured clearing brush and performing various chores, rather than simply relaxing. President Obama in particular relished hitting the road to drum up support for his policies at large pep rallies. President Trump has employed two devices to communicate with the masses: (1) speeches given around the country at large rallies attended by his most loyal followers and (2) presidential tweets (in 140 characters—280 since Twitter's November 2017 update—or fewer) reacting off the cuff to events as they take place. Although President Obama was the first president to use social media sites such as Twitter to promote legislation and support for his policies, President Trump has taken this to a whole new level, tweeting to followers more than 6,000 times during his first two years as president. (See the "From Your Perspective" box later in this chapter.)

Another Tweet from the Commander in Chief: The Interactive Presidency of Donald J. Trump

AP Photo / Alex Brandon

President Trump, with one of his tweets shown in the inset.

Twitter, an online social networking service, allows every registered user to follow friends, experts, celebrities, and breaking news in posts of up to 280 characters, known as "tweets." Enter the president of the United States into this modern world of communication by tweeting. President Obama was the first president to make extensive use of the social networking service at its peak, Obama's "tweets" were followed by more than 70 million people around the world. Yet President Trump has made far more extensive use of Twitter than his predecessor, using his own personal account rather than the official government account. During the first two years of his presidency, Trump tweeted more than 6,200 times, offering reactions to everything from news coverage of his presidency to critics of his administration. His favorite Twitter targets early in his presidency included certain federal judges who ruled against him, Hillary Clinton (he called her "Crooked Hillary"), Attorney General Jeff Sessions, and Special Counsel Robert Mueller (Trump said his investigation was a "witch hunt").

For Critical Thinking and Discussion

1. What advantages does a modern president have in his or her ability to communicate with a younger and more social media–savvy generation of citizens through Twitter?
2. Do you think Twitter users tend to only follow presidents they already support? Or does Twitter allow presidents to effectively communicate to supporters and opponents alike?

Summary

The Constitution does not spell out all of the roles and responsibilities that have become central to the modern presidency. The office has evolved over the course of the nation's history, and much of that evolution has occurred in response to crisis situations, economic or otherwise. Unlike the Congress, the president is just one person and so can act quickly and decisively. Additionally, the president and the vice president are the only two officials elected by the entire nation—thus, the president alone can claim a mandate to act on behalf of the American people as a whole, rather than on behalf of a state, a district, or one political party. In times of crisis, citizens look to presidents for strength because they alone are in a position to provide it. For that reason, more than any other, presidents only rarely have to demonstrate their continued relevance in the modern political system.

7-1 Where Do Presidents Come From? Presidential Comings and Goings

- Although theoretically any American who is at least 35 years old, is a "natural-born" citizen, and has lived in the United States for 14 years is eligible to be president, the vast majority of individuals who have held the office have been older, well-educated,

Caucasian Protestant men who have had prior experience in government.

- Although the House of Representatives can impeach the president for committing "High Crimes and Misdemeanors," the Senate alone has the power to actually remove the impeached president by a two-thirds vote. Only two presidents in history have ever been impeached by the House, and none were removed by the Senate.

7-2 The Evolution of the American Presidency

- The office of the president has evolved from what was principally a "chief clerk" in a federal government dominated by Congress, to a modern presidency in which a "chief executive" has come to dominate the political system. This more modern presidency began with the ascension of Theodore Roosevelt, whose strong positions in foreign and domestic policy promoted power in the executive office; it then gained unprecedented strength when FDR's New Deal policies cemented a large role for the president in the American constitutional system.

- Despite an increasingly polarized political system, the emergence of the United States as a superpower after World War II helped to cement the role of the U.S. president as a dominant player in world and national politics. Thus, even weak contemporary presidents find themselves as the focal points of policy-making, setting the political and legislative agenda and leading American foreign and domestic policy.

7-3 Express Powers and Responsibilities of the President

- The powers of the president, as expressly stated in the Constitution, are (1) to be commander in chief of the armed forces, (2) to grant reprieves or pardons, (3) to "make" treaties (subject to Senate approval), and (4) to make certain appointments, including those of ambassadors and justices of the Supreme Court (again subject to Senate approval).

7-4 Implied Powers and Responsibilities of the President

- Beyond the express powers granted to the president in the Constitution, presidents today also play a key role in setting the legislative agenda, managing national and international crises, and serving as leader of their political party. The singularity of leadership in the executive branch gives presidents the power to command the attention of the nation's people, Congress, and the media, thus enhancing their ability to persuade others concerning what to do.

7-5 Presidential Resources

- The cabinet, the Executive Office of the President, and the White House staff provide large organizational support for the president to administer federal programs and agencies and lead the national government.

7-6 Important Presidential Relationships

- The president enhances his power by continually communicating with the public, maintaining a strong working relationship with congressional leaders from both parties, and cultivating a good relationship with the media through strategic management of the White House's activities.

Key Terms

cabinet (p. 152)
executive agreement (p. 150)
executive orders (p. 150)
Great Society (p. 141)
impeachment (p. 136)
New Deal (p. 140)
pardon (p. 144)

power of appointment (p. 144)
reprieve (p. 144)
State of the Union address (p. 146)
Twenty-second Amendment (p. 135)
White House chief of staff (p. 152)
White House Office of Legislative Affairs (p. 147)
White House press secretary (p. 154)

8

THE FEDERAL BUREAUCRACY

iStock.com/Gromit702

The EPA plaque at the agency's building in Washington, DC.

BUREAUCRACY IS A TERM that usually conjures up negative images. It often refers to overgrown government, excessive rules and paperwork, or a burdensome process for getting something done. Political candidates often extol the vices of "the unresponsive, fat bureaucracy" to strike a sympathetic chord with voters.[1] Despite the negative connotations of the term, bureaucracy is necessary for any government to function. Laws must be enforced, programs must be administered, and regulations must be implemented. Without a federal bureaucracy, the government could not function. To be sure, there are many problems with bureaucracy. It is often hard to get things done in an efficient manner, or to fire workers who do not perform well, or to reward deserving workers. The buck often passes from one desk to another, and silly or irrelevant rules sometimes dictate the actions of the bureaucrats. Despite its problems and the "bad rep" that the term often conjures up, bureaucracy is absolutely essential for any government to implement and carry out its laws and public policies.[2] New presidents quickly learn that to accomplish their policy goals, they must rely on the federal bureaucracy. They frequently are elected to office and claim a mandate to get things done. Getting things done not only requires the passage of laws but also needs a bureaucracy to carry out those new laws.

8-1 WHAT IS BUREAUCRACY?

A bureaucracy is an organization set up in a logical and rational manner for the purpose of accomplishing specific functions. Sociologist Max Weber (pronounced VAY-ber), an early student of bureaucratic organizations, identified six characteristics of effective bureaucracies:[3]

1. **Bureaucracies are organized on the basis of specialization, expertise, and division of labor.** The organization is divided into subunits based on function, and subunits are staffed by employees who are qualified to administer those tasks.
2. **Bureaucracies are organized in a hierarchical manner with an identifiable "chain of command" from top to bottom.**
3. **A common set of rules for carrying out functions characterizes the operation.** These rules are often referred to as standard operating procedures (SOPs). Employees are trained to know and use these SOPs so that functions are performed smoothly and consistently.
4. **Bureaucracies maintain good records, or a "paper trail," of actions taken and decisions made.** Good record maintenance enables periodic review, efficiency of operation, and proof of action.
5. **Bureaucracies are characterized by an air of professionalism on the part of employees.**
6. **The hiring and promotion process within effective bureaucracies is characterized by merit-based criteria and is insulated from "politics."**

Bureaucracies are created within many types of organizations. Organizations typically exist to carry out a function, or set of functions. Bureaucracies are what actually carry out these functions. Large private companies typically have bureaucracies that divide labor functions into categories or departments such as sales, accounting, human resources (HR), management information systems (MISs), and other divisions. Colleges and universities have bureaucracies that usually include an admissions department, a registrar's office, an academic counseling center, an athletics department, and others. Even small organizations such as physicians' offices feature a bureaucracy that includes medical support staff (e.g., nurses), a front-office staff (receptionist and secretary), and business offices (accountant and medical insurance specialist).

Governments maintain bureaucracies to carry out specific functions, and the federal government is no exception. As with political parties, there is no reference to the bureaucracy in the U.S. Constitution. But like parties, the federal bureaucracy is arguably one of the most important features of the American political system because Americans have come to depend on it for many important things, such as the defense of U.S. interests around the world, protection against terrorist attacks, cleaning up of the destruction caused by natural disasters, a financial safety net for those who are unemployed or retired, the maintenance and expansion of the nation's roads and airways, and research for cures to such health problems as heart disease, cancer, and AIDS. In American government, the federal bureaucracy has traditionally come under the authority and jurisdiction of the president and the executive branch. As we will see, however, the modern federal bureaucracy is a complex set of agencies and organizations, parts of which are accountable to the legislative and judicial branches as well.

Citizens are more likely to come into direct contact with the bureaucracy than any other part of government, and so for many Americans the bureaucracy comes to symbolize what government is. A visit to an unemployment office to register for unemployment benefits, a check in the mail from the Social Security Administration, a trip to the Department of Motor Vehicles to renew a driver's license, or a visit to the website of the Consumer Protection Agency to inquire about the safety of a child's car seat—these are just a few of the many ways citizens interact with the bureaucracy.

The federal bureaucracy, in fact, is a huge set of organizations that is expected to serve many different functions. It includes numerous departments, offices, agencies, bureaus, councils, foundations, commissions, boards, services, and authorities. Each of these units, as Weber's analysis of bureaucracies suggests, specializes in an area of public policy, is hierarchically organized to carry out its particular duties, conducts its operation on the basis of a set of standard operating procedures, maintains records of its actions and decisions, is trained to

bureaucracy An organization set up in a logical and rational manner for the purpose of accomplishing specific functions.

carry out functions in a professional manner, and engages in hiring practices that are based on merit. The vast size and level of responsibility that these units have make the federal bureaucracy a complex and often confusing system to study.

8-2 WHAT DOES THE FEDERAL BUREAUCRACY DO?

Most of the federal bureaucracy is contained within the executive branch of government, and ultimately reports to the president of the United States.[4] Article II of the Constitution states that "the executive Power shall be vested in a President of the United States of America." The executive power, or the power to carry out, administer, and enforce specific laws, then, falls mainly under the purview of presidential responsibility. The president uses the federal bureaucracy to exercise executive authority.

POLICY IMPLEMENTATION

The full range of activities in which the federal bureaucracy engages is known as **policy implementation**. Policy implementation is the process of carrying out a law. Laws that are passed by Congress often include the development of new or modification of existing federal programs or services. In order to carry out the specific programs or services outlined in a law, the federal bureaucracy is assigned the task of implementation. For example, in 1935 Congress passed the Social Security Act to provide older Americans with a stable source of income during their retirement years and to offer support for the children of deceased workers. The act created the Social Security Administration as the agency in the federal government that had the authority to carry out the provisions of the act. Today, the Social Security Administration remains the unit in the federal bureaucracy responsible for maintaining records and authorizing benefits to those eligible for Social Security payments.

Implementation of a law requires translating the congressional legislation into action. Bureaucratic units begin the process of implementation by developing **regulations**, or sets of rules that guide employees of the agency in carrying out its programs or services. These rules are supported by the force of law. The Social Security Administration, for example, has written a detailed set of regulations defining who is and who is not eligible for Social Security retirement benefits. The rules include a schedule for the amount of monthly payment benefit based on a person's age, the number of years he or she contributed to the Social Security system while working, and other criteria. Regulations are useful not only because they translate laws into actions, but, because they are written down and are usually very specific, they also provide a basis for employees in the bureaucracy to consistently apply them from one case to the next.

Once an agency drafts a set of regulations to implement a program, the regulations are published in the *Federal Register*. This federal government publication is widely accessible to elected leaders, interest groups, corporations, the media, and regular citizens. The agencies authoring the regulations have an open period when they accept comments on the proposed rules and decide whether to redraft based on the commentary they receive. If the agency refuses to redraft based on an objection, the objector can ask Congress to require the agency to modify the regulations, or the objector might take the matter to court on the basis that the agency was acting outside of Congress's intentions in the law.

BUREAUCRATIC LEGISLATION

The types of laws passed by Congress are many and varied, and thus policy implementation encompasses many different bureaucratic activities. Some laws are very vague and offer agencies very little guidance about implementation. Other laws can be very specific in directing the agency on how to implement them. When laws are vague, agencies are said to have **administrative discretion**, which gives them considerable freedom in deciding how to implement the laws. Vague laws require an agency to spend more time and effort in developing regulations.

policy implementation The process of carrying out laws, and the specific programs or services outlined in those laws

regulations Rules or other directives issued by government agencies.

Federal Register The journal that publishes regulations that implement federal programs.

administrative discretion The freedom of agencies to decide how to implement a vague or ambiguous law passed by Congress.

Creating New Agencies to Tackle Chronic Problems

Joseph P. Kennedy, the first chairman of the Securities and Exchange Commission.

Although public skepticism of big government is an ongoing reality, officials charged with tackling big problems invariably turn to new bureaucracies for answers.

Then

Consider the economic crisis that emerged at the end of the "roaring 1920s." American industry flourished in the six years prior to the 1929 stock market crash. The Dow Jones Industrial index grew by a factor of five over that period, luring Americans to the stock market with unprecedented returns on their investments. And invest they did. Few considered what they were actually risking in buying shares in companies that could just as easily fail as succeed. All of this blind risk-taking came to a halt on October 24, 1929, when the six-year-old stock bubble burst. On that day alone, the Dow Jones Industrial index suffered an 11 percent decline; through July 1932 the market suffered an 89 percent slide, gutting the savings of hundreds of thousands of Americans. Many investors were left to wonder what happened to their money. In response, Congress established the Securities and Exchange Commission (SEC). Movie mogul and steel industry executive Joseph P. Kennedy was one of few Americans who escaped the stock market crash unscathed thanks to insider information and friends in high places. Who better than him to prevent other "insiders" like himself from manipulating the

Richard Cordray, the first director of the Consumer Financial Protection Bureau.

future market? Under the leadership of Kennedy, also the father of the 35th U.S. president, the SEC promulgated new rules governing the disclosure of information affecting the sale and trade of stocks. Thereafter, issuers of securities would be forced to fully disclose all the information that a potential shareholder might need to help make up his or her mind about the investment, thus protecting consumers from deceptive corporate practices.

Now

As the dark cloud of recession cast a shadow over the American economy in 2007 and 2008, millions of homeowners found themselves unable to afford their mortgage payments. The housing market had experienced high growth in the decade leading up to this recession as low interest rates, high levels of employment, and federal policies supporting the issuance of subprime loans lured Americans eager to take part in the American dream of homeownership. With the high demand for housing, property values skyrocketed and homeowners took pride in their suddenly lucrative investments. Financial institutions also cashed in on the booming real estate market by closing on new loans and selling those loans off in the form of market-based securities. Unfortunately, the race for profits led some financial institutions to engage in lending practices that caused unwitting consumers to sign up for risky loans they could not afford over the long run.

(Continued)

These so-called predatory lending practices included forgoing proper background checks on loan applicants and "qualifying" homebuyers at artificially low initial interest rates, which over time ballooned to much higher rates. When the economy slowed, millions of new homeowners found themselves out of work and holding mortgage payments far higher than what they initially paid. By 2010, a record 2.87 million homes in the United States were in foreclosure. In response, Congress created the Bureau of Consumer Financial Protection (BCFP). The BCFP was charged with establishing new rules for loan-making practices and enforcing those rules to ensure that consumers didn't fall prey to predatory lending practices. Eighty years after the stock market crash kicked off the Great Depression, a new administration had once again retooled the federal bureaucracy to safeguard consumers.

For Critical Thinking and Discussion

1. Do you think that the BCFP and the SEC "solved" the problems of the Great Recession and Great Depression, or were they an overreach of government's authority?
2. The BCFP remains a controversial agency today. Should Congress reconsider its existence, or should it reaffirm its authority?

Two policy areas where congressional legislation tends to be vague and where agencies have much latitude in making rules and regulations are environmental quality and workplace safety. Important pieces of legislation, such as the Clean Air Act and the Occupational Safety and Health Act, have given agencies such as the Environmental Protection Agency (EPA) and Occupational Safety and Health Administration (OSHA) much discretion in setting specific standards for car emissions, pollution, and workplace safety standards. This discretion usually is the product of at least one of two conditions. First, Congress often does not have the technical expertise to define how to achieve clean air or workplace safety, so it gives agencies that have such technical capabilities the discretion to set standards. Second, Congress sometimes chooses not to deal with politically difficult issues such as how to clean up toxic-waste dumps, and so it shifts the responsibility to the bureaucracy, forcing an agency to resolve the problem. When an agency makes an unpopular decision as a result of Congress's "passing the buck," the agency's action contributes further to the negative image of bureaucracies.

When Congress writes vague legislation and thus transfers legislative authority to an agency, it gives that agency the effective power to make laws, a constitutional power that is supposed to rest with the Congress alone. When Congress does this, it is said to have delegated congressional power. Laws that relate to the authority of administrative agencies and the rules promulgated by those agencies are referred to as administrative law. Congress has delegated considerable legislative authority to the EPA and OSHA to craft both environmental and workplace safety laws. Similarly, Congress has delegated a substantial amount of authority to the Federal Reserve to manage the nation's economy. The "Fed" has the power to adjust the prime interest rate in response to economic conditions to encourage investments and ward off inflation.

Delegation of power from Congress to bureaucratic agencies is not, however, typically open-ended. Congress may cede law-making authority to the bureaucracy, but it does not relinquish all power. Congressional oversight is the term used to describe Congress's regular monitoring of bureaucratic agency performance for the purpose of achieving accountability. Although the vast bulk of bureaucratic agencies ultimately report to the president as chief executive, Congress, through its oversight function, commands a significant amount of accountability from executive agencies.[5]

If Congress is not satisfied with an agency's performance, it has a variety of means to coerce change: it can reduce or eliminate an agency's budget, it can refuse to confirm presidential appointments to that agency, it can eliminate the agency, it can conduct investigations into the activities and performance of the agency, or it can establish a new agency and shift resources and powers to it. This strong system of checks often renders the federal bureaucracy just as (if not more) responsive to Congress as to the president.

delegated congressional power Congress's transferring of its law-making authority to the executive branch of government.

administrative law A law that relates to the authority of administrative agencies and the rules promulgated by those agencies.

congressional oversight Congress's exercise of its authority to monitor the activities of agencies and administrators.

Specific congressional oversight functions may be carried out in a number of ways. Particular committees (or subcommittees) in Congress hold hearings, on either a regularly scheduled or an ad hoc basis, to review agency performance. For example, the House Armed Services Committee meets with the secretary of defense and Joint Chiefs of Staff to review Pentagon programs. The Senate Environment and Public Works Committee holds regular meetings with the administrator of the EPA to review that agency's activities. The House Science and Technology Committee reviews the activities of the National Aeronautics and Space Administration (NASA). In addition, the House Appropriations Committee is divided into a number of subcommittees, each of which regularly reviews pending authorizations for funding individual agencies. These subcommittees often scrutinize agency spending.

Two bureaucratic agencies under the direct control of Congress (rather than the president) that support the oversight function of congressional committees are the Congressional Budget Office (CBO) and the Government Accountability Office (GAO). These offices compile data on federal programs and are staffed with program review and accounting professionals who comply with members' and committees' requests for information on agency performance and cost. Congress uses the GAO to investigate the actions or inactions of an agency, and it uses the CBO to conduct research, such as program effectiveness studies.

BUREAUCRATIC ADJUDICATION

Just as policy implementation sometimes includes the writing of legislation, it also may involve bureaucratic adjudicating, or determining the rights and duties of particular parties within the scope of an agency's rules or regulations. Such adjudication might include ruling on whether an individual is eligible to receive Social Security payments or whether a company has violated an air pollution rule. Most adjudication takes place in the court system. However Congress, which has the authority to create federal adjudicating agencies, has placed judicial power in some bureaucratic agencies as well. For example, the Equal Employment Opportunity Commission (EEOC) has the authority to adjudicate cases where an individual or group of individuals charges that a company has violated federal laws preventing discrimination in hiring or promotion practices in the workplace. The EEOC can try a case against a company, and if the finding is that the company violated federal law, the EEOC is authorized to prescribe a punishment or corrective action.

The EEOC and other agencies such as the EPA, the National Labor Relations Board, and the Federal Communications Commission (FCC) employ the personnel, procedures, and case law more typically seen in the judicial branch. Bureaucratic judicial personnel and powers include administrative judges, appellate courts within the agency, and administrative hearings that resemble a trial. Ultimately, any administrative court decision may be appealed to the federal court system because the power of adjudication ultimately rests in the hands of the judicial branch. In reality, however, federal courts routinely uphold cases appealed from administrative courts.

8-3 THE DEVELOPMENT OF THE FEDERAL BUREAUCRACY

The executive branch of government during the first four years of George Washington's presidency was very limited. Congress created just three departments to aid the first president in executing the law: the Department of State to oversee foreign affairs, the Department of Treasury to oversee fiscal affairs, and the Department of War to oversee military affairs. Washington selected and the Senate confirmed Thomas Jefferson, Alexander Hamilton, and Henry Knox to lead these departments, respectively. Shortly after these departments were created, the president was authorized to hire an attorney general and a postmaster general. During the first year of the Washington administration, the federal bureaucracy employed only about 50 individuals.

bureaucratic adjudicating Determining the rights and duties of particular parties within the scope of an agency's rules or regulations.

Many of the federal bureaucracy's "alphabet soup" agencies were created as New Deal programs during the administration of President Franklin Delano Roosevelt. Pictured are workers at one such agency, the Tennessee Valley Authority, assembling a new power generator at the Cherokee Dam on the Holston River in east Tennessee.

As the role of government expanded, and as the United States added new territories, there was a need to expand the size of the federal bureaucracy. Military operations, such as those conducted during the War of 1812, required increased support services and agencies to support military operations. Westward expansion brought with it the need for federal services to settle the new areas. A centralized national bank required federal agencies to centralize the economic and monetary system. By the mid-1800s, Congress saw the need to create a new cabinet department, the Department of the Interior, to manage federally owned lands and to aid in the westward expansion of the nation. The important role of farming in the nation's growth and development led to the establishment of the Department of Agriculture in 1862 to support and promote farming and farm-product commercialization. The Department of Justice was established in 1870 to aid the attorney general in the post–Civil War era in prosecuting violators of federal law and representing the federal government in the courts.

In 1884, a Bureau of Labor was created to address the concerns of the labor force that arose with the growth of the industrial economy. Large-scale industrialization and economic development led to the development of a Commerce Agency in 1888 to help regulate interstate and foreign trade. These agencies were elevated to cabinet status in the early 1900s to reflect the growing role they played in the federal government. The Great Depression set the stage for the election of Franklin Delano Roosevelt (FDR) in 1932. The FDR administration advocated an activist role for the federal government in responding to the economic crisis. Consequently, FDR's New Deal created a myriad of new federal agencies to deal with the nation's fiscal woes, including the Social Security Administration, the Securities and Exchange Commission, the Civilian Conservation Corps, and a host of public works programs to provide jobs for the large number of unemployed. In 1936, Roosevelt established the Brownlow Committee (named for its chair Louis Brownlow) to investigate how to make the growing bureaucracy more efficient and more responsive to the president.[6] The committee unanimously agreed that the president's power should be enhanced to give the president greater authority as manager of the bureaucracy. The Brownlow Committee's recommendations led to the consolidation of presidential authority over the bureaucracy.

By 1940, the federal government accounted for 10 percent of the nation's gross domestic product (GDP), with $9.5 billion spent on federal programs, including the employment of about 700,000 Americans in the federal bureaucracy. The increased role of government led to greater demands for federal services, which in turn necessitated growth in the federal bureaucracy. Between 1940 and 1975, the federal bureaucracy experienced an unprecedented growth spurt. During this period, the number of federal employees more than tripled to 2.2 million, the federal budget increased to $332 billion, and the federal budget as a percentage of GDP reached 22 percent.[7]

Two factors accounted for this massive growth in the bureaucracy. First was President Lyndon B. Johnson's Great Society program of the 1960s. The Great Society encompassed numerous new laws aimed at social and economic improvements to American society through a highly activist role of the federal government. The post–World War II prosperity of the American economy allowed Johnson to convince a Democratic Congress that programs promoting social justice, a safety net for the impoverished, improvements to urban life, health care for the elderly, and greater access to educational opportunities should be guaranteed to all Americans and funded by the great wealth of the American economy. These programs had a large influence on growth of the bureaucracy through the 1970s.

A second factor contributing to the massive growth in the bureaucracy was the Cold War. World War II resulted in two superpowers, the United States and the Soviet Union, vying against each other for global influence. From 1945 to 1991, these superpowers developed expensive nuclear and other war technologies in search of military superiority. The federal budget for defense programs grew dramatically, as did the programs to support intelligence operations and aid to foreign nations for diplomatic purposes.

8-4 GETTING CONTROL OF THE GROWING BUREAUCRACY

During the mid- to late 1970s, the American economy began to slump. Whereas the prosperity of the 1960s facilitated the creation of a larger-size government to accomplish a number of policy goals, the sluggish economy of the late 1970s was unable to support the very large federal bureaucracy. Federal budget deficits began to accumulate, and the United States could no longer afford the huge federal bureaucracy that it had created. During this period critics of the massive federal bureaucracy pointed to many programs that, at least on the surface, appeared to represent wasteful spending (see Table 8-1).

TABLE 8-1
The "Golden Fleece" Awards

Stories of waste in bureaucratic spending always become fodder for calls to cut federal spending and eliminate unnecessary federal programs. Much of this "wasteful" spending is rooted in congressional pork-barrel spending, that is, spending on projects that benefit individual members' home districts. Perhaps no one took better aim at wasteful pork-barrel spending in the federal bureaucracy than U.S. Senator William Proxmire (D-WI). In 1975, Proxmire began what he called the "Golden Fleece Awards" to target bureaucratic agencies that spent money on wasteful programs. Proxmire announced 150 awards in all. Asked to identify the top 10 most egregious spending wastes, Proxmire provided the following list:

- **Tequila fish.** The National Institute on Alcohol Abuse and Alcoholism for spending millions of dollars to find out if drunken fish are more aggressive than sober fish, if young rats are more likely than old rats to consume alcohol in order to reduce anxiety, and if rats can be turned into alcoholics.

- **The Great Wall of Bedford.** The U.S. Department of Commerce for spending $20,000 to build an 800-foot limestone replica of the Great Wall of China in Bedford, Indiana.

- **Buying Worcestershire sauce.** The Department of the Army for spending $6,000 to prepare a 17-page document that told the federal government how to buy a bottle of Worcestershire sauce.

- **The New Jersey Sewer Museum.** The Environmental Protection Agency for spending $1 million to preserve a Trenton, New Jersey, sewer as a historical monument.

- **Lessons in watching TV.** The Office of Education for spending $220,000 to develop a curriculum to teach college students how to watch television.

- **Tennis cheating.** The National Endowment for the Humanities for a $25,000 grant to study why people cheat and act rudely on tennis courts in Virginia.

- **Tailhook.** The Department of the Navy for using 64 planes to fly 1,334 officers to the Hilton Hotel in Las Vegas for a reunion of the Tailhook Association (a nonprofit organization that supports sea-based aviation).

- **Patrol car.** The Law Enforcement Assistance Administration for spending $2 million on a prototype police car that was never completed.

- **Basketball therapy.** The Health Care Financing Administration for Medicaid payments to psychiatrists for unscheduled meetings with patients who were attending basketball games, which cost the federal government between $40 million and $80 million.

- **Surfing subsidy.** The Department of Commerce for giving the Honolulu city government $28,000 to study how to spend $250,000 for a good surfing beach.

Based on data from Taxpayers for Common Sense, found at www.taxpayer.net.

Ronald Reagan was elected president in 1980 with an agenda to scale back the federal bureaucracy. The Reagan administration targeted domestic programs to achieve the reduction in government. Since the 1980s, various administrations have attempted to reduce the size of the federal bureaucracy. The methods they have used include privatization, deregulation, devolution, and "reinventing government."

PRIVATIZATION

Privatization means replacing government-provided services with services provided by the private sector. The theory of privatization is that if private companies compete to provide services, the cost of those services will be less than if government provides those services directly. Additionally, some contend that private corporations can more flexibly adapt to changing circumstances because they are not weighed down by civil service restrictions and government red tape. Accordingly, a number of federal programs were privatized during the 1980s. For example, the U.S. Department of Labor frequently provided job-training services to the unemployed during the 1960s and 1970s. Federal laws passed in the 1980s eliminated much of the federal management of job training and contracted out these services to private companies. More recently, the federal government has used a number of private contractors, including Halliburton (the company once run by former vice president Dick Cheney) to help rebuild Iraq after the second Persian Gulf War, under the idea that the costs would be even greater if the federal government played a more direct role.

DEREGULATION

The development of rules and regulations to achieve a policy goal requires units in the bureaucracy to ensure that such rules and regulations are followed. Deregulation, that is, eliminating government oversight and regulation of certain activities, results in less government to do the regulating. Prior to the mid-1970s, the trucking and railroad industries, long-distance telephone service, prices for air flights, and the activities of savings and loan institutions were regulated by the federal government. Deregulation of these and other activities resulted in the abolition of a number of federal agencies, including the Civil Aeronautics Board and eventually the Interstate Commerce Commission.

DEVOLUTION

A central question in our federal system of government is which level of government—national or state—should have the authority to provide programs and services to citizens. The New Deal and Great Society programs gave the national government increased responsibility and authority for such services. In response to extensive growth of the national government, the 1980s witnessed a devolution of power and responsibility back to the states, mainly to shrink the size of the national government. For example, welfare reform in the mid-1990s shifted much responsibility for welfare from the federal to the state governments.

privatization The process of replacing government-provided services with services provided by the private sector.

deregulation The elimination of government oversight and government regulation of certain activities.

devolution The transfer of power and responsibilities for certain regulatory programs from the federal government back to the states.

"REINVENTING GOVERNMENT"

When Bill Clinton was elected president in 1992, he promised to "reinvent government." This promise translated into an eight-year effort to promote bureaucratic accountability. The Clinton administration instituted mechanisms such as customer satisfaction research with those who received federal services and freedom-of-information policies that gave the public and the news media access to government documents to help promote accountability. In addition, the Government Performance and Results Act, passed in 1997, required that agencies establish goals and set out a plan for achieving those goals. In the book *Reinventing Government*, David Osborne and Ted Gaebler describe how bureaucracy and other aspects of the public sector in the United States have undergone a transformation.[8] They contend that the "entrepreneurial spirit" brought to bear on government performance, which includes market-driven and business-oriented planning, has improved the effectiveness and efficiency of bureaucracy at all levels of government.

In addition to implementing these strategies for reducing the size of the federal bureaucracy, the Cold War, which concluded in 1991 with the collapse of the Soviet Union, put an end to escalating defense budgets to support the arms race with the Soviets.

The end of the Cold War and the implementation of strategies that contain, if not reduce, the size of the federal bureaucracy do appear to have reversed the decades-long trend toward increasing the size of government. Between 1990 and 2000, the number of civilian employees in the federal government declined by about 500,000,[9] and the percentage of the GDP accounted for by federal spending dropped from 21.9 percent to 18.2 percent. Despite these efforts, however, federal spending on the bureaucracy continues to increase annually at a pace that exceeds inflation. In particular, defense spending to fight the war on terrorism and the war in Iraq in recent years has increased federal spending. Also, the Department of Homeland Security, created in response to the terrorist attacks of September 11, 2001, required increased federal dollars to protect the nation within its own borders.

The administration of President Barack Obama ushered in a new growth spurt for the federal bureaucracy. A $787 billion federal spending plan to provide an economic stimulus along with a health care reform package and increased regulations on the financial services industry all significantly increased the scope and size of the bureaucracy. The national debt during the Obama years more than doubled. In addition, early in the Trump administration, Congress supported the president's calls for increased spending on national defense. Despite the rhetoric of both Democrats and Republicans to address the problem of the growing national debt, the recent trend toward larger government continues.

8-5 THE ORGANIZATION OF THE FEDERAL BUREAUCRACY

As shown in Figure 8-1, the federal bureaucracy is made up of a variety of different types of agencies that are empowered to carry out laws and federal programs. Some of these organizations have broad authority over a public policy area, whereas others have a narrow focus; some are empowered to implement laws and programs established by Congress, whereas others have the added responsibility of creating rules and policies, and adjudicating. Some report directly to the president, whereas others answer to both the president and Congress. Also, although most organizations in the federal bureaucracy are part of the executive branch, some are part of the legislative and judicial branches. Units of the federal bureaucracy include cabinet departments, independent agencies, regulatory agencies, government corporations, and the Executive Office of the President.

CABINET DEPARTMENTS

Amid the complex web of bureaucratic units is a select set of 15 organizations called **cabinet departments**, which are the major administrative organizations of the executive branch. These departments vary in terms of both size and importance. The Department of Defense, for example, employs nearly 1 million civilian workers and another 1.5 million military personnel. By contrast, the Department of Education has only about 5,000 employees.

At the head of each cabinet department is a secretary (with the exception of the Justice Department, which is headed by the attorney general) who reports directly to the president. Along with a few other high-level presidential advisers and the vice president, these secretaries compose the president's cabinet, a set of high-level administrators who report directly to the president. Cabinet heads and their deputies are nominated by the president and must be confirmed by the Senate. Typically, a secretary shares the same views as the president on policy matters and often is a loyal political supporter (if not close friend) of the chief executive. The *inner cabinet* is a term used to describe the secretaries of the most important departments in the cabinet—State, Defense, Treasury, and Justice. Whereas the cabinet once served as the president's primary advisory panel, the growth in the Executive Office of the President, discussed later in this chapter, has shifted primary advisory responsibilities to that office.

cabinet departments Those federal agencies that qualify as the major administrative organizations of the executive branch.

FIGURE 8-1

The Organization of the Federal Bureaucracy

Branches

1. LEGISLATIVE BRANCH	2. EXECUTIVE BRANCH	3. JUDICIAL BRANCH
Architect of the Capitol Congressional Budget Office (CBO) Congressional Research Service General Accounting Office (GAO) Government Printing Office (GPO) Library of Congress Stennis Center for Public Service	**Executive Office of the President** The First Lady The President The Vice President The White House Home Page Offices within the Executive Office of the President	Administrative Office of the United States Courts Federal Judicial Center U.S. Sentencing Commission

Cabinet Departments

Department of Agriculture (USDA)
Department of Commerce (DOC)
Department of Defense (DOD)
Department of Education (ED)
Department of Energy (DOE)
Department of Health and Human Services (HHS)

Department of Homeland Security (DHS)
Department of Housing and Urban Development (HUD)
Department of the Interior (DOI)
Department of Justice (DOJ)
Department of Labor (DOL)

Department of the State (DOS)
Department of Transportation (DOT)
Department of the Treasury
Department of Veterans Affairs (VA)

Independent Agencies, Regulatory Agencies, and Government Corporations

Advisory Council on Historic Preservation
African Development Foundation
Bureau of Consumer Financial Protection
Central Intelligence Agency (CIA)
Commission on Civil Rights
Commodity Futures Trading Commission
Consumer Financial Protection Bureau (CFPB)
Consumer Product Safety Commission (CPSC)
Corporation for National and Community Service
Defense Nuclear Facilities Safety Board
Election Assistance Commission
Environmental Protection Agency (EPA)
Equal Employment Opportunity Commission (EEOC)
Export-Import Bank of the United States
Farm Credit Administration
Federal Communications Commission (FCC)
Federal Deposit Insurance Corporation (FDIC)
Federal Election Commission (FEC)
Federal Housing Finance Board
Federal Labor Relations Authority
Federal Maritime Commission
Federal Mediation and Conciliation Service
Federal Mine Safety and Health Review Commission
Federal Reserve System
Federal Retirement Thrift Investment Board
Federal Trade Commission (FTC)
General Services Administration (GSA)
Institute of Museum and Library Services
Inter-American Foundation
International Broadcasting Bureau (IBB)
Merit Systems Protection Board
National Aeronautics and Space Administration (NASA)
National Archives and Records Administration (NARA)

National Capitol Planning Commission
National Council on Disability
National Credit Union Administration (NCUA)
National Endowment for the Arts
National Endowment for the Humanities
National Labor Relations Board (NLRB)
National Mediation Board
National Railroad Passenger Corporation (AMTRAK)
National Science Foundation (NSF)
National Transportation Safety Board
Nuclear Regulatory Commission (NRC)
Occupational Safety and Health Review Commission
Office of Compliance
Office of Government Ethics
Office of National Counterintelligence Executive
Office of Personnel Management
Office of Special Counsel
Overseas Private Investment Corporation
Panama Canal Commission
Peace Corps
Pension Benefit Guaranty Corporation
Postal Rate Commission
Railroad Retirement Board
Securities and Exchange Commission (SEC)
Selective Service System
Small Business Administration (SBA)
Social Security Administration (SSA)
Tennessee Valley Authority
Trade and Development Agency
United States Agency for International Development
United States International Trade Commission
United States Postal Service (USPS)

Source: www.firstgov.gov.

Cabinet departments (sometimes referred to as executive departments) generally have a broad scope of authority over a particular policy area, such as the nation's military (the Department of Defense), federal law enforcement (the Department of Justice), the federal road and highway system (the Department of Transportation), and protection of the nation from terrorism and response to emergency situations (Department of Homeland Security). The scope of activities in any one department tends to be so broad that most departments are best viewed as a collection of many different agencies and subagencies, each with a narrower policy focus.

The U.S. Department of Labor, for example, is charged with promoting the American labor force and the interests of labor. It is organized into a large array of agencies and offices, each of which focuses on a particular aspect of labor issues. The Occupational Safety and Health Administration (OSHA) develops standards to promote safe workplace environments and implements regulations to ensure that employers live up to these standards. The Bureau of Labor Statistics is responsible for compiling data on the labor force on a regular basis. The Office of Labor-Management Standards sets policies for the conduct of negotiations between employers and employees.

Likewise, the U.S. Department of Defense manages the armed forces and is organized into a number of subunits, including the U.S. Army, Navy, Air Force, and National Guard. The hierarchical organization of departments facilitates the bureaucratic goals of area specialization, division of labor, and chain of command.

Although the head of a cabinet department advises and reports directly to the president, only Congress has the authority to create a new department or eliminate an existing one. The power to define the scope, authority, and, indeed, the very existence of a specific major department in the federal bureaucracy is an important "check" that Congress exercises over the president.

Special situations, and particularly crises, have led the U.S. government to create cabinet-level departments to deal with large-scale national problems. The creation of the Department of Defense in 1947, for example, was in response to large and costly inefficiencies in military operations during World War II. The Department of Energy was established in 1977 in response to the severe energy crisis and gasoline shortage that plagued the country during the 1970s. President Reagan successfully pressed for the creation of a Veterans Affairs Department in 1988 in order to promote his administration's appreciation of those who served in the U.S. military. The newest cabinet department is the Department of Homeland Security (DHS), established in 2002.

In addition to maintaining the authority to carry out many of the nation's laws, the cabinet also plays a symbolic role in the political system. Many interest groups provide input to the president through leaders in the cabinet, and the voices of community and business leaders are often heard first by cabinet-department officials. As the highest-level units in the bureaucracy, cabinet departments theoretically represent the most important policy areas. Increasingly, presidents have used their cabinet secretary appointments to demonstrate diversity in government. For nearly two centuries, cabinet secretaries were almost exclusively white men, but over the past 25 years presidents have used race and gender as factors influencing their appointments. President Clinton made history by naming women to the inner cabinet for the first time: Janet Reno as attorney general in 1993 and Madeleine Albright as secretary of state in 1997. President George W. Bush then made history by appointing the first African American to the inner cabinet—Colin Powell as secretary of state in 2001, and then an African American woman, Condoleezza Rice, as Powell's replacement in 2005; he also appointed the first Hispanic to the inner cabinet when he named Alberto Gonzales as the nation's attorney general during his second term in office.

President Obama's cabinet was also diverse: it featured prominent positions for nine women, several Latinos, and two African Americans. Although less diverse than the cabinet of his predecessor, the 22-member cabinet of President Trump includes five women, one African American, one Latino, and one Asian American.

President Trump meeting with his Cabinet at the White House Cabinet Room in April 2019.

Diversity in the President's Cabinet

Every president has the opportunity to increase or decrease the diversity of executive branch personnel, including the most prominent appointments in the presidential cabinet. Decades ago, the vast majority of cabinet members were white males. The demographic diversity of these high-level appointees has changed over time, particularly over the past 25 years. During his two terms in office, President Obama made the most headway of all on this issue. Specifically, Obama's cabinet featured increased representation from women (35.3 percent), African Americans (14.4 percent), Latinos (8.5 percent), and Asian Americans (4.6 percent).[10] The *New York Times* did an analysis of the first cabinet appointments of presidents since Bill Clinton in 1993. Clinton's initial cabinet in 1993 included 10 white men; George W. Bush's first cabinet in 2001 featured 11 white males; President Obama's first cabinet in 2009 was composed of 8 white men. This trend toward greater diversity in the cabinet, however, was reversed with Donald Trump's initial appointment of 18 white males in 2017.[11]

For Critical Thinking and Discussion

1. How important is it that the top managers in the federal government are represented by diverse gender and racial groups?
2. Can you identify members of President Trump's cabinet who are women or belong to a racial minority group?

INDEPENDENT AGENCIES

independent agencies Departments that focus on a narrower set of issues than do higher-status cabinet departments.

regulatory agencies Government bodies responsible for the control and supervision of specified activities or areas of public interest.

A number of units in the federal bureaucracy do not have the high status of a cabinet department but do report directly to the president. Whereas cabinet departments tend to concentrate on broad areas, such as labor, energy, defense, or education, these independent agencies, which are not part of any executive cabinet department, tend to focus on a narrower scope of issues. NASA, for example, focuses on the U.S. space program, while the Small Business Administration concentrates on low-cost loans and support to encourage the development of small businesses. Independent agencies tend to be smaller than cabinet departments. The heads of these agencies are appointed by and report to the president.

REGULATORY AGENCIES

Regulatory agencies are responsible for implementing rules and regulations with respect to individual or corporate conduct related to some aspect of the economy. Such agencies are supposed to be staffed by nonpartisan individuals who are entrusted to make sound decisions that promote fairness and weed out corrupt practices on fiscal matters. To accomplish this, regulatory agencies (unlike cabinet departments and independent agencies) are not under the direct control of the president. They are created by Congress and are run by independent boards or commissions that are not supposed to exert partisan influence.

The first regulatory agency was the Interstate Commerce Commission (ICC), created by Congress in 1887.[12] As with the creation of most regulatory agencies, the ICC was the federal government's response to widespread corruption. In the case of the ICC, the target was corruption in the railroad industry, which led to the high cost of railroad transportation. The ICC's scope of responsibility extended to regulation of commerce via not only

AP Photo / Kevin Wolf

The chair of the Federal Reserve regularly testifies before the Senate Banking Committee, as Congress oversees the activities of the Fed. Here Fed chair Jerome Powell appears at one such testimony in April 2019.

railroad but also pipeline, barge, automobile, and aircraft. The ICC established a complex set of rates for both passenger and freight transportation via the various modes of transport. ICC rules were intended to guarantee that transportation companies pay a fair fee on the value of property they used in carrying out their services. Congress abolished the ICC in 1995 because it determined that the agency was overregulating and thus stymieing growth in certain business sectors.

Today's federal bureaucracy includes a number of important regulatory agencies:

- **The Federal Trade Commission (FTC).** The FTC was established in 1914 and has the authority to develop and implement rules and regulations to encourage competition in industry. Over the years, the FTC has played an instrumental role in preventing price-fixing policies of corporations.
- **The Federal Communications Commission (FCC).** The FCC was established in 1934 with the authority to regulate radio, television, and interstate telephone companies. Unlike newspapers, which are not regulated, radio and TV stations use public airwaves, making them subject to regulations developed and administered by the FCC.
- **The Securities and Exchange Commission (SEC).** The SEC is responsible for rule-making with respect to the stock market and corporate bookkeeping practices. It was created in 1934 in response to the stock market crash of 1929.
- **The Equal Employment Opportunity Commission (EEOC).** Created by Congress to help administer the Civil Rights Acts of 1964, the EEOC is charged with investigating violations of the act.
- **The Environmental Protection Agency (EPA).** The EPA was created in response to the environmental protection movement of the 1960s and 1970s. Concerns about air and water quality, as well as hazardous-waste materials, led Congress to pass a number of important laws that addressed antipollution measures and empowered the EPA (in 1970) to implement environmental regulations. The EPA is the largest of the regulatory agencies.
- **The Consumer Product Safety Commission (CPSC).** Consumer advocacy was another movement that gained steam in the 1960s and 1970s. Efforts to make manufacturers produce products that were safer for consumers were an important feature of that movement. The CPSC was created in 1972 to protect the public against risks associated with consumer products.

GOVERNMENT CORPORATIONS

A small number of units in the federal bureaucracy are set up to run like private companies even though they serve an important public purpose. These are called government corporations. The idea behind a government corporation is that there is a market of customers who are willing to pay individually for the services provided by the corporation. The revenue on which the government corporation relies comes primarily from citizens paying for the service provided by the corporation. Unlike private corporations, government has a special interest in the solvency of government corporations because they serve an important public purpose. Consequently, when the revenue of a government corporation falls short of meeting expenses, government often will intervene to keep the unit in business.

The most widely known and used government corporation is the U.S. Postal Service (USPS), which employs nearly 1 million workers. The primary source of funds for the USPS comes from the sale of U.S. postage stamps. Similar to a private business, the USPS has a product to offer (mail delivery) and charges a fee (the cost of postage) for use of that service.

Another government corporation is the Tennessee Valley Authority (TVA), which serves the power needs of seven states in the Tennessee Valley and operates the system for navigation and flood control of the Tennessee River. Users of TVA's generated power pay for service, as do those who navigate on the Tennessee River. Another well-known government corporation is Amtrak, a railroad service operated by the National Railroad Passenger Corporation. Amtrak maintains more than 20,000 miles of track and operates 500 stations across the nation. Its revenue is largely derived from the sale of passenger tickets; however, in recent years low ridership has forced Congress to subsidize Amtrak from the general revenue fund.

government corporations Units in the federal bureaucracy set up to run like private companies that depend on revenue from citizens to provide their services.

THE EXECUTIVE OFFICE OF THE PRESIDENT

The president of the United States has an office staff that reports directly to the president, provides advice and counsel, and helps the president manage the rest of the federal bureaucracy. The Executive Office of the President is managed by the White House chief of staff and includes a Communications Office, a press secretary, a Council of Economic Advisors (to provide advice and management of the bureaucratic agencies responsible to the economy), a National Security Council (to provide advice on foreign and military affairs), an Office of Management and Budget (to coordinate and provide data on the national budget), a White House counsel (to provide legal advice to the president), an Office of Science and Technology, an Office of the U.S. Trade Representative, and an Office of National Drug Control Policy, among others.

8-6 THE FEDERAL WORKFORCE

The federal bureaucracy encompasses an immense workforce. Currently it employs nearly 2 million civilian personnel, plus an additional 850,000 postal workers.[13] In addition, there are about 1.5 million active-duty U.S. military personnel. Although the federal government remains the single largest employer in the United States, the total number of federal employees has remained steady over the past half-decade, despite the fact that the total population has nearly doubled (from 179 million to 329 million).

POLITICAL APPOINTEES AND CAREER PROFESSIONALS

About 8,000 members of the federal workforce are presidential appointees, some of whom must be confirmed by the Senate. Those requiring Senate confirmation include cabinet secretaries and the attorney general, heads of independent agencies, ambassadors, U.S. attorneys, and other high-level officers who have administrative responsibility. When a president's term of office expires, the new president generally fills these positions with new appointees. Presidential appointees are frequently referred to as "political" appointees because the job often represents a political reward for past service to the president or the president's political party.

Another 7,500 civilian federal employees are part of what is called the Senior Executive Service (SES). These are senior officers in the federal bureaucracy who are career professionals. Those in the SES do not leave their positions when a new president takes office but work closely with presidential appointees and provide continuity in the operations of the federal bureaucracy from one presidential administration to the next. Congress established the SES in the late 1970s as a means of providing this continuity in leadership. Congress also spelled out a nonpartisan process for hiring SES officers based on educational background, work experience, and other qualifications.

Presidential appointees are largely selected to reflect the political orientation of the president, and senior executives are selected primarily to find highly qualified career professionals who will maintain stability in the operations of the bureaucracy. Together, these groups of employees provide leadership and senior management of the units in the federal bureaucracy.

THE CIVIL SERVICE

The vast majority of the federal bureaucracy workforce is known as the civil service. Today's civil service includes approximately 3 million federal workers. This workforce is highly diverse, with 43 percent women and 28 percent racial/ethnic minority employees. Although many of these workers are located in Washington, DC, the vast majority (90 percent) work outside of the federal Capitol.[14] Similar to the SES, civil service workers in the federal bureaucracy are theoretically hired for their position based on their qualifications and remain employees beyond the term of a particular president. Thus, they are supposed to be immune from partisan political maneuvering. Civil service jobs were not always insulated from partisan politics, as they are today. To understand the rules and processes for employment in the federal bureaucracy, it is useful to examine how employment in the federal workforce has changed over the years.

During the early years of the American republic, continuous recruitment of well-educated, upper-middle-class men characterized the development of the federal bureaucracy. Presidents

Executive Office of the President The staffers who help the president of the United States manage the rest of the federal bureaucracy.

Senior Executive Service (SES) Since the late 1970s, a defined group of approximately 7,500 career professionals in the federal bureaucracy who provide continuity in the operations of the bureaucracy from one presidential administration to the next.

civil service The system whereby workers in the federal bureaucracy are supposed to be immune from partisan political maneuvering.

Washington, Adams, and Jefferson hired political, business, and social elites to carry out the activities of the federal bureaucracy. With the exception of top posts in government such as cabinet secretaries, those in federal jobs usually remained from one presidential administration to the next. This tradition ensured an able and effective federal workforce, albeit a nondiverse one.

President Andrew Jackson, elected to office in 1828, undertook a massive restructuring of the federal workforce. Jackson ran for the presidency as a populist advocating for the interests of the "common man." Upon taking office, he chose to remove individuals in the bureaucracy who were not at all "common" and who found themselves politically at odds with the new president. Resistance among many in the bureaucracy to follow Jackson's orders, along with the president's own desire to see that the bureaucracy more closely reflected the demographics of American society, led Jackson to undertake a major overhaul of the bureaucratic workforce.

Jackson replaced the long-term, upper-middle-class bureaucrats with political supporters and friends who came from many walks of life. This spoils system of hiring federal workers quickly became a steadfast American tradition. To the victors of presidential elections went the spoils of jobs in the federal government. Under this system of patronage, campaigning, political party activities, and governing became intertwined. Political parties enticed people to work on political campaigns by promising the payoff of a good federal job with an electoral victory. Often, those who were given a job were expected to return a percentage of their salary to the political party—a very clever fund-raising strategy. Strength of partisan support became the key criterion for landing and maintaining a good job.

Needless to say, this system of hiring workers produced a number of problems. Because qualifications to do the job were not important in the hiring decision, the bureaucracy became inefficient. Bureaucrats were more concerned about campaigning and supporting the political party than they were about doing their job. Further, the bureaucracy lacked any sort of continuity—for example, when the partisan control of the presidency changed hands, federal workers were fired en masse and replaced by a new set of underqualified political appointees.

By the time of the Civil War, the spoils system was entrenched and the bureaucracy was thoroughly corrupt. A civil service reform movement arose in the post–Civil War era, advocating an end to the spoils system and the development of a "professionalized" bureaucracy. Strong resistance from the political party bosses stalled the reform movement's agenda. But the 1881 assassination of President James Garfield by a disgruntled party worker who did not receive the federal job he thought he deserved gave strength to the movement. In 1883, Congress passed the Pendleton Civil Service Reform Act, which did the following:[15]

- It created a merit system for hiring many federal workers based on qualifications for the job, including educational background, related job experience, and performance on civil service tests.
- It prevented employees from losing their federal jobs when the presidency changed hands.
- It set up a Civil Service Commission to oversee federal hiring and firing practices.

Initially, the Pendleton Act applied only to a limited portion of the federal workforce, but it provided the basis for Progressive Era reformers of the early 1900s to develop a more professional bureaucracy through additional reform legislation. Today job qualifications in federal hiring and federal worker immunity from patronage are firmly rooted in the federal bureaucracy's employment practices. These principles now apply to more than 90 percent of federal workers.

The Hatch Act of 1939 further insulated the civil service from partisan politics by (1) prohibiting the dismissal of an employee for partisan reasons (with the exception of certain high-level political appointments) and (2) prohibiting federal workers from running for office or actively campaigning for a political candidate. In the early 1990s, revisions to the Hatch Act relaxed some of the more stringent requirements of the law and allowed federal workers more flexibility in engaging in political activities. Those in the civil service can now participate in campaigns outside of their work hours, contribute money to a candidate or party, express partisan opinions, and wear campaign buttons, among other activities. However, under the current law, federal workers still cannot be candidates in a partisan election or use their official position to raise money or influence votes.

The Civil Service Reform Act of 1978 replaced the Civil Service Commission with the Office of Personnel Management (OPM) and the Merit Systems Protection Board (MSPB). The OPM and MSPB, bureaucratic agencies themselves, manage the civil service system today.

spoils system The postelection practice of rewarding loyal supporters of the winning candidates and party with appointive public offices.

patronage The act of appointing people to government positions in return for their partisan and/or political support.

Pendleton Civil Service Reform Act The 1883 law that created a merit system for hiring many federal workers, protected them from being fired for partisan reasons, and set up a Civil Service Commission to oversee the hiring and firing process.

merit system A system of appointing and promoting civil service personnel based on merit rather than political affiliation or loyalty.

Civil Service Reform Act of 1978 The federal act that replaced the Civil Service Commission (the agency that oversaw federal hiring and firing practices) with the Office of Personnel Management (OPM) and the Merit Systems Protection Board (MSPB).

Their functions include administering the system of federal hiring, protecting the rights of federal employees, conducting hearings and deciding cases where there are charges of wrongdoing in hiring and firing of employees, evaluating the effectiveness of federal hiring and retention practices, and regulating the ways in which federal workers can participate in politics.

The federal bureaucracy has grown dramatically, particularly since the New Deal era of the 1930s. As new presidents seek to advance new policy goals, federal departments and agencies have been created and expanded. These agencies have aided presidents in accomplishing new feats and bringing the United States to world "superpower" status. These include Lincoln's efforts to withstand the secession of the Southern states and preserve the Union, Theodore Roosevelt's drive to tame the corporate monopolies, Franklin Delano Roosevelt's priming of the federal workforce to tackle the Great Depression, and Barack Obama's attempt to jumpstart the economy through a major stimulus spending plan. Over the centuries, presidents, with the support of the American people, have used the bureaucracy to accomplish important policy goals. The bureaucracy has also served as the "whipping boy" in rhetorical campaigns for political office. In many instances, the bureaucracy has earned its reputation as wasteful, inefficient, and bloated. But without the federal bureaucracy, the most important national initiatives could not have been realized. Even those presidents who campaigned on a platform to cut the bureaucracy ended up using it to advance important initiatives. The federal bureaucracy is an easy target of criticism, yet there is no denying the fact that it has contributed as much to the development of the American political system as any other part.

FROM YOUR PERSPECTIVE
The Dreaded FAFSA Form

You have probably seen it. Your parents or legal guardians have seen it. Most of your college friends have seen it, too. It is the dreaded FAFSA (Free Application for Student Aid) form. The joy and satisfaction of getting accepted into college are often met with the red tape and complexity of applying for student financial aid. The FAFSA form must be filled out by all students applying for federal support to offset the increasingly high costs of college tuition. Most states and colleges also require the FAFSA to help make their own decisions about a student's financial need and thus the aid that may be required. The U.S. Department of Education begins accepting FAFSA applications on January 1 for eligibility during the school year that begins the following fall. FAFSA requires documentation for a myriad of financial information about college students and their legal guardians. If you have never seen the form, take a look at it at on the web at www.fafsa.ed.gov.

Financial planners and other consultants have built an industry out of aiding college students and their families in their efforts to navigate the cumbersome FAFSA form. The detailed financial information that FAFSA requires is not always handy—gathering that information can be an especially time-consuming and aggravating task. However, the goal of FAFSA remains a laudable one: to fairly and equitably distribute aid to college students based on documented financial need. Still, the challenge of filling out FAFSA and meeting all its requirements can offer a rude awakening to prospective and returning students

The 2019 FAFSA application form.

who have never before been confronted by the federal bureaucracy in all its glory.

For Critical Thinking and Discussion

1. What do you think about the FAFSA form? Is it too cumbersome or tedious?
2. Is the federal government transforming a simple process into one that is too complex to be effective? Or do you believe this form of red tape is necessary to ensure that colleges and universities can make fair decisions about financial aid for the nation's college students?

Summary

8-1 What Is Bureaucracy?

- Although the term *bureaucracy* often conjures up negative images, the government could not function effectively without bureaucratic organizations.
- Most units in the vast federal bureaucracy are located within the executive branch of government, and most engage primarily in policy implementation. Such implementation begins with the development of regulations that guide employees of the agency in carrying out particular programs or services.

8-2 What Does the Federal Bureaucracy Do?

- Because Congress lacks technical expertise, it often gives agencies wide administrative discretion to decide how to implement laws. Sometimes Congress also delegates important programs to agencies because it wants to avoid thorny political issues.
- Congressional oversight of executive agencies may occur through legislative hearings or through the use of congressional agencies such as the CBO and GAO. Congress may threaten poorly performing agencies with reduced funding, a refusal to confirm appointments to the agency, or (in some extreme cases) the elimination of the agency altogether.
- Congress has placed judicial power in some bureaucratic agencies to help determine the rights and duties of parties within the scope of an agency's authority.

8-3 The Development of the Federal Bureaucracy

- The size of the federal bureaucracy exploded as the federal government played an increasingly active role in regulating the U.S. economy, overseeing new territories, and conducting overseas military operations. After FDR's New Deal was enacted during the 1930s, the federal government accounted for a sizeable portion of the nation's economy as a whole. The bureaucracy continued to expand in the 1960s and beyond to meet the needs of President Lyndon Johnson's Great Society program and to compete with the Soviet Union in the Cold War.

8-4 Getting Control of the Growing Bureaucracy

- Beginning in the 1980s, some administrations attempted to reduce the size of the federal bureaucracy through (1) the privatization of certain government-provided services, (2) the deregulation of some federal activities, (3) the devolution of various powers and responsibilities back to the states, and (4) efforts to promote greater bureaucratic accountability through initiatives such as the Government Performance and Results Act.

8-5 The Organization of the Federal Bureaucracy

- The federal bureaucracy is organized into 15 cabinet departments, including the recently created Department of Homeland Security, numerous independent agencies that focus on a narrower scope of issues, regulatory agencies that implement rules and regulations of private conduct, government corporations, and the Executive Office of the President.

8-6 The Federal Workforce

- The federal workforce includes 8,000 presidential employees who received their positions through political patronage, a Senior Executive Service consisting of approximately 7,500 senior career professionals, and a vast number of civil service workers whose jobs are immune from partisan politics. Today, most lower-level federal workers are hired through a merit system, rather than through the spoils systems that prevailed throughout much of the nineteenth and early twentieth centuries.

Key Terms

administrative discretion (p. 160)
administrative law (p. 162)
bureaucracy (p. 159)
bureaucratic adjudicating (p. 163)
cabinet departments (p. 167)
civil service (p. 172)
Civil Service Reform Act of 1978 (p. 173)
congressional oversight (p. 162)
delegated congressional power (p. 162)
deregulation (p. 166)
devolution (p. 166)
Executive Office of the President (p. 172)

Federal Register (p. 160)
government corporations (p. 171)
independent agencies (p. 170)
merit system (p. 173)
patronage (p. 173)
Pendleton Civil Service Reform Act (p. 173)
policy implementation (p. 160)
privatization (p. 166)
regulations (p. 160)
regulatory agencies (p. 170)
Senior Executive Service (SES) (p. 172)
spoils system (p. 173)

9

THE JUDICIARY

The sculptor James Earle Fraser's "Guardian or Authority of Law" sits in front of the facade of the U.S. Supreme Court building in Washington, DC.

ARTICLE III OF THE U.S. Constitution vests in the Supreme Court the power to decide legal cases or controversies that come before it. As one of the three primary branches of the federal government, the judiciary enjoys a special status in our constitutional system. Many scholars have suggested that courts enjoy heightened prestige over other actors in government as a result of their own conscious efforts to foster the perception that they somehow stand above the political fray. The solemn formalities that pervade so many judicial proceedings conducted by "high priests of the law"—the black robes, the prohibition of cameras in the U.S. Supreme Court, and the general reluctance of judges to seek out publicity—contribute to a mythology about courts in general and to a "cult of the robe" that carries credence with many Americans.[1] This chapter explores the nature of the federal judiciary and the specific role it plays in the U.S. political system by examining types of law and the manner in which the legal system in the United States is organized. It also explores the role state courts play in the political system and then focuses on the U.S. Supreme Court more closely, with an eye toward understanding how that court is confronting some of the great issues of the day.

9-1 TYPES OF LAW

The concept of law defies simple understanding. Although law is normally defined simply as "authoritative rules made by government," the philosopher John Locke argued that certain laws precede society and government. These natural laws are God-given, exist within human beings from the time they are born, and are intrinsic to the nature of individuals. Civil law (also called "statutory law") refers to legislative codes, laws, or sets of rules that are enacted by authorized law-making bodies such as Congress, state and local legislatures, or any executive authority entrusted with the power to make laws.[2] Common law refers to judge-made laws handed down through judicial opinions, which establish slowly evolving precedents over time. Many European legal systems, such as those in France, Germany, and Italy, are characterized as primarily "civil law systems" due to their extensive reliance on detailed legislative codes. The legal system in Britain, by contrast, is recognized as mainly a common law system.

The modern U.S. legal system features a combination of these two approaches: although the common law held sway for most of the nation's history, legislatures in all 50 states and Congress during the past century have replaced many traditional common law rules with detailed legislative codes on a number of important topics, including commercial law, probate law, and various aspects of criminal law. Other categories of law include the following:

- *Criminal law* is the body of rules and regulations that declare what types of conduct constitute an "offense against society" and prescribe the punishment to be imposed for those offenses. Criminal laws against murder, rape, and burglary can be found in almost any legal system. The body of noncriminal law—which includes the law of property, contracts, and other issues dealing with the private rights of citizens—is sometimes referred to as "civil law." (Be careful not to confuse references to "civil law" in this context with the "civil law" referenced earlier, which primarily concerns the enactment of statutes and codes.) Serious criminal offenses may lead to jail time; by contrast, those who violate noncriminal laws can be fined but not imprisoned. Of course, criminal law and civil law may touch on the same events—for example, a person alleged to have killed someone may be criminally prosecuted for murder and also separately sued in a "wrongful death action" for the same incident.
- *Constitutional law* is the body of rules and judicial interpretations of rules found in the fundamental law of the nation or state, such as the Constitution of the United States. Normally constitutional law is considered "supreme" and overrides any statutes or executive decisions with which it comes into conflict.
- *Administrative law* is the body of rules, regulations, orders, and decisions issued by administrative agencies of a government, such as the Federal Trade Commission, the Environmental Protection Agency, or a state department of health.
- *Public law*, a term used more by academics than practitioners, refers to the laws and rules that govern disputes and issues involving the government directly acting in its official capacity. Constitutional, administrative, and criminal laws are all subcategories of the general rubric of public law.
- *Private law* refers to all parts of the law concerned with the definition, regulation, and enforcement of rights in cases where either (1) all the parties directly implicated are private individuals (such as a divorce settlement) or (2) the government is acting like any other private citizen when it sues or is being sued. For example, when a private person crashes his car into a government mail truck, the government's lawsuit against that person is usually a matter of private law rather than public law.

Significant overlap exists among all these categories of law. Knowing something about the different types of law is useful in helping to understand courts and the functions they serve in the American political system.

civil law This term has two meanings: (1) legislative codes, laws, or sets of rules enacted by duly authorized law-making bodies such as Congress, state and local legislatures, or any executive authority entrusted with the power to make laws; (2) the body of noncriminal laws of a nation or state that deal with the rights of private citizens.

common law Judge-made law handed down through judicial opinions, which over time establish precedents.

9-2 THE STRUCTURE OF THE U.S. LEGAL SYSTEM

Every court occupies a unique position within the larger hierarchy of state and federal courts. As a result, each court performs a variety of specific roles dictated by where it happens to be situated within the larger court structure.

STATE LEGAL SYSTEMS AND STATE COURTS

Most criminal and civil law matters in the United States first find their way into one of the 50 states' legal systems. Together, the state governments process nearly 35 million cases per year, more than 95 percent of the nation's litigation. About a third of the cases in state legal systems involve criminal matters. Each state system features its own unique characteristics and different nuances, an outgrowth of the states' different historical origins and significant population differences. Still, as shown in Figure 9-1, some common elements exist across the vast majority of, if not all, states.

Every state maintains trial courts, which do the bulk of the work processing cases at the lower levels of the state legal system. These trial courts (often called *district courts* or *circuit courts* depending on the state or locality) may hear appeals from subordinate courts such as traffic courts; they also serve as sites for trials of more significant crimes. Thirty-nine of the 50 states have intermediate appellate courts, to which all appeals from trial courts must first be directed. All 50 states maintain at least one supreme court. (Texas and Oklahoma have separate supreme courts for criminal and civil cases.) State supreme courts (or their equivalent of a different name) generally provide the final source of appeal for each state legal system.[3] To appeal beyond the state supreme court directly to the U.S. Supreme Court, a losing party must first exhaust all the remedies available at the state level, including losing his or her case at the state system's court of final appeal. He or she must also demonstrate there is a federal question at issue, whether based on the interpretation of a federal statute or of the U.S. Constitution.

In theory, state courts must comply with pronouncements from the U.S. Supreme Court over the meaning of the federal Constitution. The reality is much more complicated. During various periods of American history, rebellious state courts tried to evade certain Supreme Court pronouncements by distinguishing or limiting the Supreme Court ruling, and on occasion even by denying the Supreme Court's jurisdiction over the matter. The Virginia Supreme Court resisted various pronouncements of the U.S. Supreme Court in the early part of the nineteenth century; more than a century later, state courts sometimes ignored U.S. Supreme Court decisions protecting the accused. Although the Supreme Court can usually exert its will over defiant state courts, it must be willing to expend key institutional resources and prestige to do so.

FIGURE 9-1

Common Features of a State Court System

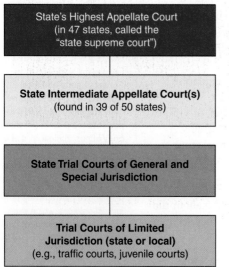

State's Highest Appellate Court
(in 47 states, called the "state supreme court")

State Intermediate Appellate Court(s)
(found in 39 of 50 states)

State Trial Courts of General and Special Jurisdiction

Trial Courts of Limited Jurisdiction (state or local)
(e.g., traffic courts, juvenile courts)

DEVELOPMENT OF THE FEDERAL COURT SYSTEM

Article III of the Constitution establishes a Supreme Court and any "inferior courts" that Congress may wish to create. Accordingly, at the nation's outset, Congress provided for the creation of district and circuit courts, the latter of which bear little resemblance to modern circuit courts. Specifically, these early federal circuit courts were staffed by Supreme Court justices and district court judges, and they performed both trial and appellate functions. Thus, in addition to their formal duties on the high court, Supreme Court justices in the early days of the Republic were also required to "ride circuit," traveling to their assigned circuits on a regular basis. (This practice formally ended when Congress reestablished the U.S. courts of appeals in 1891.)

During the nation's early history, the Supreme Court was seen as a weak third branch of government, with limited enforcement powers. With his ruling in *Marbury v. Madison* (1803),[4] Chief Justice John Marshall established the Court's power to review all acts of Congress for their constitutionality; even so, during Marshall's 34-year reign as chief justice, the Court struck down just one act of Congress as unconstitutional.

The Constitution makes no reference to the specific size of the Supreme Court. Thus, Congress during the eighteenth and nineteenth centuries altered the size of the Court to consist of one chief justice and anywhere from five to nine associate justices serving on the Court at one time. Occasionally the issue of Court size comes up as a matter of strategic politics: in 1937 President Franklin Delano Roosevelt's ill-fated plan to expand the size of the Court (to up to 15 members depending on the age of the sitting justices) was driven by the president's desire to appoint new justices who would support his New Deal program. Since 1869 the Court's composition of nine members (one chief justice and eight associate justices) has remained essentially unchanged. Meanwhile, Congress has been active in creating, disbanding, and modifying the number of other judges who serve throughout the federal court system.

Cases today begin in the federal court system, rather than the state court system, only when they fit into one of three categories: (1) the lawsuit requires interpretation of the U.S. Constitution, a federal law, or a treaty of the United States; (2) the federal government is suing or prosecuting someone, or is itself being sued; or (3) the lawsuit is between two citizens of different states suing for an amount of more than $75,000. Many of the highest-profile legal cases in recent years became federal cases because they featured defendants accused of committing federal crimes. Included on this list are the trial of boxer Muhammad Ali, who refused to comply with the Vietnam War draft, and the prosecution of some of the terrorists involved (directly or indirectly) in the attacks of September 11, 2001. In recent decades

THEN & NOW

Challenging the Norm of a Nine-Member Supreme Court

To many, the Supreme Court is a symbol of justice that rises above the partisanship that characterizes the other branches. Accordingly, the Court has held onto certain traditions throughout the years: the wearing of black robes, the confidentiality of discussions in conference, and the refusal of members to think of themselves as beholden to one or the other political party. Although the number of justices has shifted occasionally during the early and mid-eighteenth century, the norm of a nine-justice court has become another sacred tradition . . . at least since 1868. That year, Congress settled on nine justices following the turbulent Civil War. Would later Congresses consider altering that fundamental convention to provide more vacancies to a like-minded executive?

Then

The first real test of that new nine-justice norm occurred in 1937. Frustrated by a Supreme Court intent on striking down his administration's landmark New Deal initiatives, President Franklin Roosevelt settled on a plan to

Keystone Features / Hulton Archive / Getty Images

President Franklin Delano Roosevelt, whose administration proposed an expansion of the size of the Supreme Court in early 1937.

dramatically alter the court: he urged that for every justice who reached the age of 70 and did not retire within six months, the president would be able to appoint a younger

(Continued)

(Continued)

Supreme Court justice Owen Roberts's notable shift in voting to uphold the New Deal may have staved off passage of FDR's court packing plan.

justice to help out. (The Court could increase in size to a maximum of 15 justices under FDR's plan.) Ultimately the plan failed to pass, but FDR enjoyed the last laugh, as the contemporary composition of the Court shifted its votes just enough to validate key parts of the New Deal going forward. The Supreme Court had thus weathered a major storm and came out on the other size with its nine-member court still intact.

Now

In 2016, the Republican-controlled U.S. Senate refused to hold hearings for President Obama's Supreme Court nominee, Judge Merrick Garland. A vacancy on the U.S. Supreme Court thus remained open through that year's presidential election; the following year, President Trump successfully appointed Neil Gorsuch to that still-vacant seat, handsomely rewarding the Senate leadership for its election-year gambit. Yet, to frustrated Senate Democrats, Justice Gorsuch had occupied a "stolen seat," one that should rightfully have been filled by Obama. As they witnessed Justice Gorsuch cast his vote on an increasingly conservative Supreme Court, liberal interest groups in 2019 began to hatch plans for a daring response that could be implemented only once the Democrats took

back the White House and Congress in due course. For the first time in eight decades, leaders from one of the two major parties began speaking openly of devising a "court-packing" plan: with a Democratic president in place, they would increase the size of the Court by at least two more justices in hopes of transforming the high court and the constitutional landscape in a more liberal direction. As a sign of the plan's seriousness, candidates for the Democratic presidential nomination were forced to take a position on these court-packing proposals. Though such a bold reform would surely be an uphill climb, anything is possible in an era when even the most cherished norms of government find themselves under attack.

Merrick Garland, the president's nominee to replace the late Supreme Court justice Antonin Scalia, delivers remarks in the Rose Garden of the White House, March 16, 2016.

For Critical Thinking and Discussion

1. Do you think the prestige of the Supreme Court would suffer if Congress altered its size in response to partisan political pressures? How should the Court respond, if at all, to allegations that the hyper-partisan appointment process has threatened its legitimacy?
2. If you were a senator, would you vote to increase the size of the Supreme Court in response to unfair tactics by the opposition in waging past Supreme Court appointment battles? If not, what action would you take?

Congress has become increasingly active in passing legislation to declare new federal crimes. Thus, carjacking, the sale or possession of many types of illegal drugs, and money laundering are now considered federal crimes, and defendants who commit such offenses may face prosecution in federal courts.

The federal judicial system today also features a number of specialized courts, including tax courts, bankruptcy courts, and military courts. Most parties to a federal case start out in one of the 94 federal district courts located throughout the country. Federal district court judges have original jurisdiction (the power to rule in the first instance) over criminal and civil trials, and, along with federal magistrates, they provide the initial sources of potential legal relief available in the federal judicial system.

Figure 9-2 depicts the flow of cases in the federal system. After the federal district court has rendered its judgment, appeal is available to one of the 13 federal appeals courts (also referred to as *circuit courts of appeals*) across the country. With some exceptions, federal appeals are normally decided by a panel of three judges selected at random from the pool of 10 or more judges authorized to serve on that court. In some cases, litigants can appeal from the three-judge panel to the full circuit court—this type of hearing is called *en banc*. Because the San Francisco–based Ninth Circuit maintains a roster of 47 judges (spread out from Hawaii and California in the west, to Arizona, Nevada, Montana,

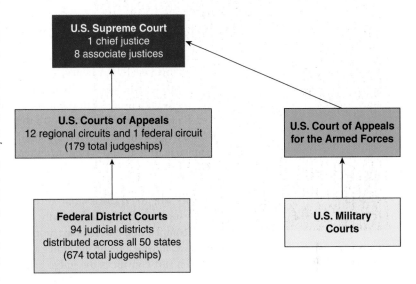

FIGURE 9-2
*The Federal Court System**

*Chart does not include specialized courts, including courts of international trade, tax courts, claims courts, and others.

and Idaho in the east), the phrase *en banc* on that court refers to 11-judge panels that perform essentially the same function as en banc panels in other circuits.[5]

Litigants who receive an adverse judgment in the federal appeals court and wish to be heard in the U.S. Supreme Court may petition for a *writ of certiorari* (discussed later in this chapter), in which a losing party asks the Supreme Court to review the decision of a lower court. Currently the Supreme Court enjoys near absolute discretion over its docket, and so it remains a long shot (less than 3 percent) that it will even grant the writ of certiorari in the first place.

Petitioning the U.S. Supreme Court for review is the final option available to state court litigants who suffer adverse decisions in the highest state court and to federal court litigants who suffer adverse decisions after exhausting all forms of appeal in the federal court system. In a normal year, approximately half of the cases heard by the Supreme Court come from federal appellate courts and the other half from the 50 state court systems.

9-3 THE ADVERSARIAL SYSTEM OF JUSTICE

Some European legal systems are based on an inquisitorial system of justice, in which judges, working on behalf of the government, are responsible for gathering information relevant to the disposition of a particular case. For example, in France (which adheres to the inquisitorial model), judges may initiate a criminal investigation against an individual, commission experts to investigate and report on special aspects of the crime, and even call witnesses and question them intensely. By contrast, the American legal system is primarily an adversarial system of justice, in which opposing parties contend against each other for a result favorable to themselves. In jury trials, judges act merely as independent referees overseeing the contest; in so-called bench trials where no jury is present, judges must still remain objective arbiters as they prepare to make final decisions on the merits.[6] In an adversarial system, the judge is entrusted only with ensuring that the litigants achieve procedural fairness and plays no active role in evidence-gathering or in the advocacy of one side over the other. Supporters of this system contend that adversarial proceedings pitting zealous representatives of parties against one another offer the best prospect of allowing the judge or jury to determine the truth. Critics counter that inquisitorial systems tend to be free of the

inquisitorial system
a system of justice in which the court (in the form of one or more judges) is actively involved in investigating the facts of the case.

adversarial system
A system of justice in which opposing groups contend against each other; the judge is not actively involved in investigating the facts of the case.

many strategic "maneuvers" parties so frequently practice in U.S. courtrooms, such as the withholding of crucial evidence or the presentation of evidence that bears only a minimal relationship to the actual facts at issue.

ELEMENTS OF CIVIL LITIGATION

Countless disputes among individuals or entities are resolved quietly, long before the threat to litigate is even invoked. Still, whenever one private party contests another over the definition or enforcement of certain legal rights or the legal relationship that may exist between them, the disagreement may wind up in the form of a lawsuit brought before a judge in a court of law. Any such judicial contest, including all the events that lead up to a possible court event, is referred to as litigation. Although the procedural rules governing such private disputes vary widely from state to state and system to system, some elements of civil litigation are common among all systems. Normally the complaining party who chooses to initiate formal legal proceedings (usually called the plaintiff) does so by filing a complaint, which is a written document justifying why the court is empowered to hear the case and explaining why the plaintiff is entitled to some form of relief (usually an amount of money) under the current law. The target of the complaint, the defendant, normally must respond to the complaint with a formal written defense, in which he or she either admits to or denies what the plaintiff has said.

If the defendant convinces the judge either that the court has no power to hear the case (perhaps it was filed in the wrong court) or that there is no law that provides a remedy to the plaintiff, the case may be dismissed. If the defendant's argument is unsuccessful, the case then moves forward to the stage of pretrial litigation normally referred to as discovery. During discovery, each side has the right to find out what information the other side has about the case by requesting documents or materials, access to property, and/or examinations, or by offering answers to questions about the litigation either in written form or verbally at a deposition. Of course, the vast majority of civil disputes never make it to trial. In some cases, one party may succeed in convincing the judge that no trial is necessary and that the judge should rule in that party's favor immediately. Far more often, the sides agree to a legally binding "settlement" of claims made against each other, in which one side pays money to the other side or agrees to cease and desist a certain practice in order to avoid the costs and uncertainties of trial.

In some instances, the parties are not able to reach an out-of-court settlement, and a formal trial becomes necessary. In a *bench trial*, the parties present evidence to a judge rather than a jury of citizens. A jury trial usually takes far longer than a bench trial because of the many procedures required to prevent undue prejudice of the jury. Even if a jury trial is necessary, the judge still plays a role in the courtroom by ensuring that the jury is properly selected and that fair procedures are adhered to during the trial, including limitations on the admissibility of evidence that may be used to reach a decision. Only relevant evidence, which logically tends to prove or disprove a disputed fact, may be admitted into the trial proceedings. In civil cases, the complaining party is obligated to prove its allegations by a "preponderance of the evidence," which is generally thought to be anything greater than 50 percent. Although there is widespread disagreement on what this standard exactly means, it is clearly well below the high standard imposed on prosecutors in criminal cases to prove guilt "beyond a reasonable doubt."

Once the judge or jury has reached a final decision on the case, normally called the *verdict* in the case of a jury trial or the *judgment* in a bench trial, and the judge or jury has settled on a monetary amount to be awarded, the trial stage of the process comes to an end. Some posttrial motions may be available, and a dissatisfied party is also free to appeal the decision to a higher court.

THE CRIMINAL JUSTICE SYSTEM AT WORK

Although the rules of criminal procedure also vary widely, most criminal prosecutions begin with the arrest of a suspect by some law enforcement official at the federal, state, or local level. Once the suspect is formally accused, he or she is referred to as the *defendant*. Because some criminal charges may be later revealed as groundless or unsubstantiated, the government must quickly demonstrate in one of two ways that the charges against the defendant

litigation Any judicial contest, including all the events that lead up to a possible court event.

plaintiff The party that chooses to initiate formal legal proceedings in a civil case.

complaint A document written by the plaintiff arguing why the court is empowered to hear the case and explaining why the plaintiff is entitled to some form of relief under the current law.

defendant The target of a plaintiff's complaint.

discovery A stage of pretrial litigation in which the plaintiff and defendant have the right to learn what information the other side has about the case by requesting documents or materials, access to property, and/or examinations, or by offering answers to questions about the litigation either in written form or verbally at a deposition.

are valid. Some prosecutors elect to present initial evidence at a preliminary hearing held before a magistrate or trial judge, where they must demonstrate that there is probable cause to proceed to trial against the suspect. Far more often, the prosecutor convenes a **grand jury**, whose duty it is to receive complaints, hear the evidence offered by the prosecutor, and determine whether a trial is justified. Grand juries comprise a greater number of jurors than an ordinary trial jury. Unlike regular juries, which hear only one case, grand juries may be asked to hear evidence on numerous cases over a period of several weeks or even months. Because the grand jury process is supervised entirely by the prosecutor, he or she maintains a distinct advantage—as former New York state chief judge Sol Wachtler once joked, prosecutors have so much influence over grand juries that they could probably "indict a ham sandwich." In the overwhelming majority of cases, the grand jury does indeed return a bill of **indictment** authorizing the government to proceed to trial against the defendant.

High-profile defendant George Zimmerman, consulting with his lawyer at trial. Zimmerman fatally shot Trayvon Martin, an unarmed African American teen, in Sanford, Florida, in 2012. The events surrounding the murder, Zimmerman's arrest, and his subsequent trial invited charges of racism from Martin's family and others. In 2013, Zimmerman was acquitted.

Whereas discovery is far-ranging and extensive in civil litigation, it is far more limited in criminal trials. Defense attorneys are usually under little or no obligation to provide any evidence at all to prosecutors; as a general matter, prosecutors are under an obligation to provide defense attorneys only with evidence that tends to "clear" the accused from alleged fault or guilt, although some states and localities provide additional discovery rights to the accused.

Most criminal prosecutions in the United States are resolved through a negotiated **plea bargain** between the defendant and the prosecutor.[7] Indeed, over 90 percent of convictions are the direct product of negotiated plea bargains. Many defendants seek to reduce their jail sentences by entering plea agreements that lead to lesser punishments. Much of the negotiation that occurs between prosecutors and defense attorneys is over the appropriate charges that will be formally filed, as most courts have adopted the equivalent of "going rates" for particular crimes.[8] Prosecutors willingly trade down penalties for crimes either because they are seeking that defendant's cooperation at another trial or because they wish to avoid the uncertainty and huge expenditure of resources that come with a trial.

In criminal cases that do go to trial, the burden rests squarely on the prosecutor to prove that the defendant committed the crime "beyond a reasonable doubt." Defendants, by contrast, do not have to prove their innocence. Unless a defendant waives the right to a jury trial, she or he must be tried by a jury of peers. Numerous constitutional safeguards are available to the defendant, including the right to a public and speedy trial and the right to directly confront witnesses. If the jury renders a "not guilty" verdict, the double jeopardy clause of the Fifth Amendment generally forbids the government from trying the defendant again for the same crime. A defendant who is convicted has a constitutional right to appeal the conviction or the resulting sentence to a higher court.

The Sixth Amendment has been interpreted to guarantee each indigent (poor) defendant the right to a government-provided lawyer in any instance where he or she faces the possibility of jail time. Unfortunately, many public defenders' offices are overworked and underfunded, placing defendants at a relative disadvantage. By comparison, wealthy or well-connected defendants who enjoy access to top legal talent and other resources at trial often fare much better. For example, in 2005 the late recording star Michael Jackson was acquitted on charges of child abduction, molestation, and attempted molestation of

grand jury A jury whose duty it is to hear the evidence offered by a prosecutor and determine whether a trial is justified.

indictment A decision by a grand jury authorizing the government to proceed to trial against the defendant.

plea bargain A pretrial negotiated resolution in a criminal case in which the defendants seek to reduce their jail sentences by pleading guilty and in return prosecutors are willing to trade down the severity of the punishment.

several minor boys at his Neverland Ranch in Southern California. That result—contradicted by the accounts that some of his victims provided many years later—was due in no small part to the efforts of some of the nation's best-known lawyers, including celebrity advocates Susan Yu, Mark Geragos, and Benjamin Brafman. Clearly, the American legal system does not always offer the same types of outcomes to those who are not similarly situated or well connected. For the vast majority of defendants, "justice" in the courtroom is meted out at lightning speed, with judges and prosecutors running through multiple criminal trials in a matter of hours. Thus, the picture of drama-filled trials seen so often on television or in the movies hardly depicts the reality of what goes on in this nation's criminal courtrooms.

9-4 JUDICIAL REVIEW AND ITS IMPLICATIONS

Courts in general, and judges in particular, serve in a variety of capacities: supervising the disposition of legal controversies between private parties, overseeing preliminary hearings or trials of criminal defendants, and ruling on important issues concerning the procedures to be followed or the evidence to be introduced at trial. Indeed, the role many judges play as "independent magistrates" is fundamental to the effective functioning of the American legal system. But courts and judges also play a significant and far-reaching role in overseeing the operations of the other branches of government, both by supervising conflicts between those branches and by protecting citizens against government action that may violate the Constitution.

This judicial authority has been magnified by the general recognition that American courts enjoy the added power of judicial review, by which they may declare acts of the other branches of the federal or state governments unconstitutional and thus invalid. This dimension of judicial authority is not mentioned anywhere in the U.S. Constitution. Although Article VI of the Constitution declares the Constitution of the United States to be the "supreme Law of the Land," nowhere does the document explicitly vest any specific court (including the U.S. Supreme Court) with the authority to determine whether state laws are unconstitutional. Nor does the Constitution authorize the Supreme Court to serve as the authoritative interpreter of the document over the president, Congress, and other federal officials, all of whom are equally sworn to uphold the Constitution. In fact, scholars of the early constitutional period believe the drafters of the Constitution were unable to reach any consensus at all on this issue. How, then, did the power of judicial review arise?

The power of the Supreme Court to exercise judicial review was first established by the fourth chief justice of the United States, John Marshall, in the highly controversial case of *Marbury v. Madison* (1803).[9] With Thomas Jefferson's victory in the presidential election of 1800 and the Jeffersonian Republicans' rise to power that year, nearly all of the nation's most powerful Federalists, including John Adams, were soon to be relegated to outsider status in the federal government. In his final hours as president, however, Adams appointed 16 circuit court judges and 42 new justices of the peace for the District of Columbia (all loyal Federalists); each of the individuals chosen for the posts was confirmed by the lame-duck Federalist Congress that remained loyal to Adams. President Adams also named John Marshall as chief justice of the United States. Immediately after Thomas Jefferson and his secretary of state James Madison formally took office in March 1801, they learned that several of the commissions for the new justices of the peace appointed by Adams had never been delivered—including one for William Marbury. When Jefferson ordered Madison to withhold the commissions for partisan reasons, Marbury asked the Supreme Court to issue a *writ of mandamus*, a judicial order commanding an official (in this case, Madison) to perform a ministerial duty over which his or her discretion is limited (namely, the formal delivery of a duly signed and sealed commission). As authority for the Supreme Court's power to issue such a writ, Marbury cited the Judiciary Act of 1789, which appeared to give the U.S. Supreme Court exactly that authority.

Marbury was seeking to have the Supreme Court decide the case immediately, without first having to suffer a loss in a lower court. Because Chief Justice Marshall was an ardent Federalist, Marbury further assumed the Court would be sympathetic to his plight. In truth, it was Marshall who was really at fault in the case—as Adams's secretary of state, he had failed to properly mail the commission. Indeed, given his intimate knowledge of the facts,

judicial review The power of a court to declare acts of the other branches of government or of a subordinate government to be unconstitutional and thus invalid.

Marshall should have recused himself from the case, refusing to participate as a judge in the first place. Yet Marshall's Supreme Court rejected Marbury's request. Recognizing the tense political situation that surrounded the case—and all too aware that Jefferson might not abide by court order—Marshall lambasted the Jefferson administration for its refusal to perform its statutorily mandated duty but denied that the Supreme Court possessed the power to issue the writ as requested.

Why the refusal to help his fellow Federalist? Marshall acknowledged that the 1789 law did in fact authorize the Court to issue such a writ in "original jurisdiction." But, Marshall ruled, that law was in explicit violation of Article III, Section 2, Clause 2, which did not specifically list "writs of mandamus" among the types of cases over which the Supreme Court had original jurisdiction. Nor could Congress extend the Court's original jurisdiction by mere statute. Thus, Marshall decided, the 1789 law was repugnant to the Constitution and was therefore null and void. With this decision, Marshall seized for the Court a power of judicial review over congressional laws that is unmentioned in the Constitution. The Supreme Court exercised this power only once more before the Civil War, although it has struck down well over 150 acts of Congress since then.

Two rulings more than a decade later further established the Supreme Court's authority in interpreting the Constitution. In *McCulloch v. Maryland* (1819),[10] the Court upheld the constitutionality of the Bank of the United States, thereby establishing the precedent that congressional power extends beyond those powers specifically listed in Article I of the Constitution. In *Martin v. Hunter's Lessee* (1816),[11] the Supreme Court ruled that the power of federal courts to review government actions for their constitutionality was not just applicable to other federal institutions; the supremacy clause ("The Constitution . . . shall be the Supreme Law of the Land") meant that the Supreme Court could also invalidate any actions of state governments that it believed to be in conflict with the U.S. Constitution. During his 34 years as chief justice, Marshall wrote 519 opinions, many of which remain influential commentary on constitutional power and authority. Under Marshall's leadership, the Court consistently rejected claims of state sovereignty that conflicted with federal interests. It was the special duty of the Supreme Court, Marshall believed, to make difficult judgments on the Constitution that either limited or affirmed the exercise of federal authority. In doing so, Marshall's court defined a strong role for the federal government, which was more clearly realized beginning in the twentieth century.

In the two centuries since Marshall served as chief justice, the Supreme Court has invalidated more than 1,200 state laws. In 1958, it once again reaffirmed the principle of judicial supremacy in *Cooper v. Aaron*[12] in response to official defiance of a lower court's desegregation rulings: governors and state legislatures were bound to uphold decisions of the Supreme Court just as they were bound by oath to uphold the Constitution. At times, the exercise of judicial review has been extremely controversial. For example, the Supreme Court in *Dred Scott v. Sandford* (1857)[13] ruled that slaves were forever the property of their owners, even when they were brought temporarily into free states. The decision overturned a congressional law regulating the extension of slavery in the territories and may have helped to precipitate the Civil War four years later. During the Great Depression, the Supreme Court's rulings that many of FDR's New Deal proposals were unconstitutional instigated another constitutional crisis. More recently, President Obama suggested that if the Court invalidated his administration's signature health care reform legislation, it would be engaging in improper "judicial activism." As it turned out, the Supreme Court modified just one aspect of the legislation (the Medicare funding provision), leaving the rest of the Patient Protection and Affordable Care Act of 2010 intact. Despite the uncertain beginnings that led to this practice and the tense moments in the nation's history that it has given rise to, judicial review of federal and state laws has become an unchallenged dimension of judicial power within the U.S. political system.

9-5 LIMITATIONS ON COURTS

In Federalist No. 78, Alexander Hamilton deemed the judiciary "the least dangerous" branch because it had "no influence over either the sword or the purse . . . and can take no active resolution whatsoever." Despite Hamilton's opinion, courts have played a critically influential role in the American political system. When the Supreme Court aggressively interposes itself between aggrieved citizens and the government, as it did when it ordered desegregation of public schools in *Brown v. Board of Education* (1954),[14] or when it helps resolve some great political crisis, as it did when it ordered President Richard Nixon to hand over controversial tapes of White House conversations in *United States v. Nixon* (1974),[15] the judiciary appears more like an all-powerful branch than one that is weak and inconsequential.

The power of American courts is great, but the method by which courts participate in the political system is far more circumscribed than that of the other two branches. The limitations that courts must adhere to include the following:

1. **Courts cannot initiate or maintain lawsuits.** Unlike legislatures, which can propose and pass bills on their own initiative, judges in the United States cannot decide issues that are not currently before them in a legitimately filed lawsuit. If none of the actors in a controversy elects to involve the courts directly, the court has no role whatsoever in resolution of the conflict.

2. **Courts can hear only those lawsuits that constitute true "cases" or "controversies."** Article III imposes on the Supreme Court and all federal courts the same type of limitation that applies to nearly all other courts: judges may hear and resolve only those lawsuits that amount to legitimate "cases" or "controversies" and must ignore mere "hypothetical" or "theoretical" conflicts. In practice, courts tend to refuse to decide lawsuits that are moot (i.e., it is too late to provide any effective remedy), including lawsuits involving affirmative action programs and policies brought against educational institutions by applicants who have since enrolled in (and, in many cases, graduated from) another institution. Courts are equally reluctant to decide cases that are not yet ripe (i.e., the actual conflict is still sometime in the future). Accordingly, courts normally refuse to provide executives with what amounts to "legal advice" about hypothetical future controversies. Courts similarly refuse to hear cases that were contrived by the parties in the form of collusion or cases in which jurisdiction has not been properly invoked.

The courts have also maintained a long-standing tradition of refusing to decide cases where the Constitution has explicitly entrusted the issue to be decided by one of the other branches of government; such issues are generally referred to as *political questions*. Courts also limit lawsuits to parties that have proper standing, meaning those who are "uniquely" and "singularly affected" by the controversy. For example, courts usually reject lawsuits brought by individuals who are frustrated with the allotment of their tax dollars because those individuals are not "singularly affected." In the mid-twentieth century, Congress and many state legislatures loosened these standing requirements by authorizing lawsuits brought by large numbers of people with clearly defined common interests. These class action lawsuits can proceed through the legal system even without every member of the affected class. High-visibility class action lawsuits in recent years include those brought by tobacco users across the country and those by people who have suffered from the effects of asbestos.

3. **Courts must rely on other branches for enforcement.** Unlike the other branches of government, courts rely on other political institutions to put their opinions or orders into direct effect—police officers, marshals, and executive branch officers, among others, must carry out the courts' mandates. Whereas Congress can cut off funding to executive agencies that ignore its dictates, no similar tool is available to the judiciary. In the vast majority of instances, disobedience of the court is not in question. Yet, when a court makes a controversial pronouncement, officials may be reluctant to adhere to the court's decision. In rare cases, a court's decisions may even be met with outright disobedience. Sometimes courts even may react negatively to another court's rulings. In 1832, President Andrew Jackson declined to enforce the Supreme Court's decision in *Worcester v. Georgia*,[16] which ordered that a white Christian missionary be freed from a Georgia prison. Responding to Chief Justice Marshall's ruling that Georgia could not imprison the missionary for residing on Cherokee Indian property, President Jackson declared—perhaps apocryphally—that "John Marshall has made his decision . . . now let him enforce it." Over a century later, the high court in *Brown v. Board of Education*[17] held that segregated public schools violated the equal protection clause and then

standing The requirement that a party must be uniquely or singularly affected by a controversy in order to be eligible to file a lawsuit.

class action lawsuits Lawsuits filed by a large group of people with clearly defined common interests.

commanded that public schools be desegregated "with all deliberate speed. " That decision met with violent reaction in the South, forcing President Dwight Eisenhower to send U.S. marshals to enforce the desegregation decrees. Meanwhile, the Supreme Court's 1962 decision invalidating school-sponsored religious prayer in public schools (*Engel v. Vitale*[18]) is ignored in many parts of this country even today.

In addition to these limitations, courts must also adhere to limitations that arise from constitutional or statutory law. For example, Congress can, by statute, alter the Supreme Court's appellate jurisdiction, which is the power to review prior decisions handed down by state and lower federal courts. Thus Congress could in theory declare that federal courts as a whole are not empowered to hear abortion cases. (In fact, foes of the Supreme Court's abortion decisions proposed such a bill in the 1980s, but it was never passed.) However, Congress cannot alter the Court's original jurisdiction, which is the power to hear a lawsuit at the outset. Article III authorizes the Court's original jurisdiction in cases involving ambassadors and cases in which states are the only parties.

One final limitation on courts is harder to see but is no less significant. Because judges and justices are normally appointed by politically accountable entities such as executives and legislatures, or in some states elected by the public itself, courts in general rarely stray too far from the reigning political majority. Social scientist Robert Dahl affirmed this hypothesis in his landmark 1957 article, "Decision-Making in a Democracy."[19] Dahl's study of Supreme Court opinions revealed that although the Supreme Court often defies public opinion in the short run, its opinions usually fall in line with the dominant national majority coalition in the long run. The Court's eventual adaptability to shifts in the national mood, although much more subtle and slow-moving than the more political branches of government, has helped sustain it as a vital force in the American political system.

9-6 ELECTING AND APPOINTING JUDGES

The state and federal court systems differ dramatically in the way judges are selected. State court judges tend to be selected in one of five ways. Partisan elections are utilized in some states, with prospective and sitting justices required to campaign for their party's nomination and then to run in a general election. Nonpartisan elections, held in many other states, eliminate party designations from the election process. The "Missouri Plan," or merit plan, features a three-step selection process by which a judicial nominating commission initially screens candidates and then submits a list of three potential nominees to the governor, who then selects the judge from the list. Shortly thereafter, the new judge must then secure voter approval in a nonpartisan retention election.[20] Several other states authorize gubernatorial appointment of judges, in which the governor appoints judges, subject to approval of the state senate. Finally, a handful of states require that the state legislature appoint judges.

The selection of federal judges follows a more universal formula: all federal district court judges, federal appeals court judges, and Supreme Court justices are appointed by the president, subject to confirmation by a majority vote in the U.S. Senate. Whereas the Constitution dictates this formula for appointment of Supreme Court justices, Congress in its discretion authorized the appointment of lower federal court judges to require the Senate's advice and consent as well. Because all federal judges and Supreme Court justices hold their offices during "good behavior"—the functional equivalent of life tenure—they are thought of as more independent than those state judges who must run for reelection. In fact, the retention rate for state judges is often so high (due to low voter turnout and other factors) that even elected state judges tend to enjoy a large degree of independence in rendering decisions.

THE NOMINATION PROCESS

During a single term in office, a president can expect to make hundreds of federal judicial appointments. The Constitution does not impose any requirements or limits on those who aspire to membership on a federal court or even on the U.S. Supreme Court; it left the question of qualifications—whether education, experience, or anything else—to the political

appellate jurisdiction The authority of a court to review decisions handed down by another court.

original jurisdiction The authority of a court to be the initial court in which a legal decision is rendered.

actors who control the process. In practice, a tradition of deference to home-state senators (often called *senatorial courtesy*) provides legislators in the upper chamber—especially those hailing from the president's party—with considerable influence over the selection of district court judges in their own states. (Senatorial courtesy also has a more limited impact on the selection of appeals court judges, as circuits cross individual state boundaries.) In recent decades, presidents have not only relied on senators' recommendations to generate nominees for judgeships; they also consider ideological factors and the personal characteristics of potential nominees.

Some modern presidents have sought to place their own ideological stamp on the lower courts (whether liberal or conservative) by utilizing a committee of White House and Justice Department attorneys to screen and suggest candidates.[21] The Reagan and George W. Bush administrations were especially active in seeking to use the appointment of lower-court judges as a means of moving the constitutional landscape in a conservative ideological direction. When the presidency and the Senate are held by different parties, battles over judicial nominees may become especially fierce. In 2002 and 2007–2008, the Democrat-controlled Senate Judiciary Committee gave heightened scrutiny to President George W. Bush's more conservative nominees. Although in the minority, Senate Republicans sought to return the favor to President Obama, delaying many of his court nominees in 2009 and 2010.

Given its place atop the U.S. legal system, vacancies on the U.S. Supreme Court tend to draw far more political attention than do other judicial vacancies. Because the president, the U.S. Senate, and the media follow personnel changes on the Supreme Court more closely, the process by which justices are nominated and confirmed is a major news event. A president may have the opportunity to appoint several Supreme Court justices—Presidents George H. W. Bush, Bill Clinton, and Barack Obama appointed two justices each, whereas President Ronald Reagan appointed three associate justices and promoted one associate to chief justice (the justice responsible for administering the Court's affairs and heading the federal justice system as a whole) during his eight years in office. President Trump appointed two new justices during his first two years as president. George W. Bush appointed no justices during his first term but filled two vacancies (including the chief justiceship) during the latter half of 2005. Bush's reelection as president helped him escape the fate suffered by President Carter, whose lone term in office witnessed no Supreme Court vacancies at all.

If a vacancy occurs in the position of chief justice, the president may choose to promote one of the eight associate Supreme Court justices to this prestigious position, as President Reagan did when he promoted William Rehnquist to the Court's center seat in 1986. More often, presidents reach outside the confines of the current Supreme Court for someone to take the position of chief justice. Chief Justice Earl Warren, for example, served as governor of California immediately prior to becoming chief justice in 1953. President George W. Bush named a lower-court judge, John Roberts of the U.S. Court of Appeals for the District of Columbia Circuit, to succeed Rehnquist.

The court's membership as of August 1, 2019, is listed in Table 9-1. In choosing nominees to the high court, presidents in recent decades have considered several factors.

The nominee's ideological and policy preferences. This factor has enjoyed a place of special importance in presidential calculations. A nominee's views on abortion, school prayer, and other hot-button issues may well tip the balance of the Court in favor of the president's stated views. Certainly there exists little evidence that presidents employ "litmus tests" on nominees, by which they might refuse to appoint individuals unless they explicitly state their views on such issues to the president in advance. President Dwight Eisenhower allegedly referred to his appointments of Chief Justice Earl Warren and Justice William Brennan as the "two biggest mistakes" of his presidency because both men decided cases in a far more liberal direction than Eisenhower would have preferred. More recently, the elder George Bush may have been frustrated by the moderate-to-liberal opinions of Justice David Souter, his first appointment to the Supreme Court. Still, most modern presidents have mobilized White House and Justice Department resources to conduct extensive research on each candidate's past writings and opinions in hopes of eliminating any surprises.

TABLE 9-1

Membership of the U.S. Supreme Court as of 2019

Member	Gender	Position	Date Born	Year Appointed (President)	Law School	Party	Religion
John Roberts	M	Chief Justice	1/27/55	2005 (G. W. Bush)	Harvard	Republican	Roman Catholic
Clarence Thomas	M	Associate Justice	6/23/48	1991 (G. H. W. Bush)	Yale	Republican	Roman Catholic†
Ruth Bader Ginsburg	F	Associate Justice	3/15/33	1993 (Clinton)	Harvard/Columbia	Democrat	Jewish
Stephen Breyer	M	Associate Justice	8/15/38	1994 (Clinton)	Harvard	Democrat	Jewish
Samuel Alito	M	Associate Justice	4/1/50	2006 (G. W. Bush)	Yale	Republican	Roman Catholic
Sonia Sotomayor	F	Associate Justice	6/25/54	2009 (Obama)	Yale	Democrat	Roman Catholic
Elena Kagan	F	Associate Justice	4/28/60	2010 (Obama)	Harvard	Democrat	Jewish
Neil Gorsuch	M	Associate Justice	8/29/67	2017 (Trump)	Harvard	Republican	Roman Catholic/Protestant*
Brett Kavanaugh	M	Associate Justice	2/12/65	2018 (Trump)	Yale	Republican	Roman Catholic

† At the time of his 1991 appointment, Clarence Thomas regularly attended an Episcopal church, but he later returned to Roman Catholicism, the faith in which he had been raised.

* Neil Gorsuch was raised in a Catholic church but later attended an Episcopal church. It remains unclear whether he considers himself a Catholic who is also a member of a Protestant church, or simply a Protestant.

Judicial competence. Most presidents have an interest in appointing especially qualified candidates for the high court, if only because it assists in speeding along the confirmation process. The American Bar Association (ABA), an interest group of lawyers, rates candidates for every federal judicial vacancy on a scale from "highly qualified" to "not qualified" on the basis of their legal background and accomplishments.

Political loyalty. Although loyalty has diminished somewhat as a priority in recent years, presidents still occasionally practice old-fashioned politics in the selection of Supreme Court nominees, choosing a justice based on a background of service to the president's party or to the president. Since 1900, well over 90 percent of all Supreme Court nominees have been members of the president's political party. Of these, many emerged from the president's cabinet, from the members of Congress loyal to the president's legislative program, or from other positions close to the chief executive or his subordinates at the time the appointment was made. Every one of the four justices appointed by Presidents John Kennedy and Lyndon Johnson served in their respective administrations. More recently, President Obama tapped his own solicitor general, Elena Kagan, to be his second Supreme Court nominee in 2010.

Demographic factors. A president may choose a candidate for the diversity the nominee adds to the demographics of the current Supreme Court.[22] Lyndon Johnson appointed Thurgood Marshall as the first African American to the Court in 1967, Ronald Reagan appointed Sandra Day O'Connor as the first female justice in 1981, and President Obama appointed Sonia Sotomayor as the first Latina justice in 2009. When Obama appointed Elena Kagan to the Court the following year, he brought the number of women on the Court up to three for the time being. The selection of nominees who can diversify the Court may pay political

SAUL LOEB / AFP / Getty Images

President Donald Trump shakes hands with Judge Brett Kavanaugh, his second nominee to the U.S. Supreme Court.

dividends for the White House as well: the president may be counting on such nominations to build support among certain groups.

The current political environment. Supreme Court vacancies do not occur in a vacuum; presidents are well aware of the political conditions that surround a particular court vacancy, and more often than not they respond to it through their nomination choices. Such factors as low presidential approval ratings, a Senate controlled by the political opposition, or the need to achieve other legislative proposals may convince the president to select a more moderate or less controversial nominee. President Obama hoped that his 2016 nomination of Merrick Garland, a more moderate judge who several Republican senators had openly praised, might garner bipartisan support during a presidential election year. (Senate Republicans dashed those hopes, leaving the vacancy for President Trump to fill in 2017.) On the other hand, a president who enjoys a strong political position may decide to name a more controversial Supreme Court nominee, regardless of the political circumstances.

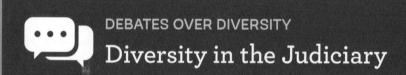

DEBATES OVER DIVERSITY
Diversity in the Judiciary

The increasingly diverse U.S. population is now reflected in the demographic composition of law school classes at leading law schools and within the membership of state bar associations across the country. Unfortunately, this diversity is not yet fully reflected in many of our nation's courts. The American Bar Association (ABA) has articulated that part of its mission is to "promote full and equal participation in the association, our profession, and the justice system by all persons" and to "eliminate bias in the legal profession and the justice system."[23] This clearly expressed goal has led this prestigious organization to carefully monitor diversity on the nation's courts, as well as to promote efforts that might increase their diversity. In 2010, the state judiciaries featured 24 percent African American jurists, 4 percent Asian/Pacific Islanders, 11 percent Hispanics, and 2 percent who were classified as Native American/Other. A report by the American Constitution Society for Law and Policy shows stalled progress as of 2014, as white men comprised 58 percent of all judges, as compared to 22 percent white women, 12 percent men of color, and 8 percent women of color. A closer examination shows that some state supreme courts are still majority white and most states are making agonizingly slow progress at diversifying. Scholars at the Brennan Center for Justice at NYU Law School believe the method of selecting judges (whether it is through judicial elections or judicial nominations) does not significantly affect the level of diversity. Instead, they recommend that state judicial nominating commissions implement systematic recruitment efforts, which can in turn expand the pool of diverse applicants and bring about real progress in diversifying state courts.[24]

For Critical Thinking and Discussion

1. What are the ramifications of a lack of diversity in the lower federal courts or in the state judiciaries? Are the ramifications different, depending on what level of the court system is under consideration?
2. What reforms would you favor to promote a more diverse judiciary? Do you agree with the Brennan Center's recommendations?

Source: http://gavelgap.org/.

THE CONFIRMATION PROCESS

Until the late 1960s, confirmation hearings for judicial nominees tended to be little-noticed events, drawing scarce public attention or press coverage. Around that time, however, with the growth of federal regulatory schemes placing more and more cases in the federal courts, presidents began to utilize judicial appointments as a means of shaping public policy. Consequently, the confirmation process for Supreme Court nominees was simultaneously opened up to unprecedented high levels of public scrutiny. All hearings for Supreme Court nominees have been televised live on C-SPAN since 1981. Interest groups have become increasingly active in confirmation proceedings, lobbying senators directly and testifying in favor of or against particular nominees. With the ideological stakes raised, presidents and their aides have become increasingly active in lobbying for their nominees.[25]

The Senate confirms the vast majority of Supreme Court nominees; between 1900 and 2018, 61 of the 65 Supreme Court candidates who came up for a formal Senate vote on their respective nominations were confirmed. Nevertheless, as shown in Table 9-2, controversial nominees in recent decades have experienced their share of public scrutiny—and, in some cases, outright rejection by the Senate—when subjected to the glare of the confirmation process. One of Richard Nixon's nominees to the Supreme Court in 1970, court of appeals judge G. Harrold Carswell of Florida, was rejected by a six-vote margin in the Senate in part because of his alleged links to white supremacist groups. Carswell was also dogged by charges that he was not competent to serve on the bench; to that came the deadly retort of one Senate supporter that even the mediocre judges "are entitled to a little" representation on the Supreme Court too.[26]

Less than two decades later, the Senate rejected Ronald Reagan's nomination of Judge Robert Bork amid some interest-group cries that Bork would reverse liberal precedents on free speech and abortion.[27] Bork, a former Yale law professor, wrote in opposition to many Supreme Court doctrines supported by political liberals, including the doctrine of constitutionally protected abortion rights that the Court first articulated in *Roe v. Wade* (1973).[28] Accordingly, liberal interest groups that were determined to defeat Bork employed "a wide variety of tactics, including advertising, grassroots events, focus groups and polling" to increase public awareness of Bork's controversial positions. The Senate eventually defeated Bork's nomination by a 58–42 vote. The ill-fated Bork nomination gave rise to a new verb in Washington's political lexicon—"to Bork," which is defined as the act of challenging a president's nominee through well-financed and well-organized interest-group opposition.

At first, the Bork confirmation fiasco encouraged subsequent presidents to favor nominees who either possessed no paper trail at all or would be far more circumspect than Bork in their

TABLE 9-2

Failed Supreme Court Nominees Since 1900

Nominee	Year Nominated	Nominating President	Result
John J. Parker	1930	Hoover	Rejected, 39–41
Abe Fortas	1968	L. B. Johnson	Withdrawn*
Homer Thornberry	1968	L. B. Johnson	Nullified**
Clement Haynsworth	1969	Nixon	Rejected, 55–45
G. Harrold Carswell	1970	Nixon	Rejected, 51–45
Robert H. Bork	1987	Reagan	Rejected, 58–42
Douglas H. Ginsburg	1987	Reagan	Withdrawn***
Harriet Miers	2005	G. W. Bush	Withdrawn
Merrick Garland	2018	Obama	No action taken

* Nomination for chief justice withdrawn.

** Nomination for associate justice voided by withdrawal of Fortas nomination.

*** Ginsburg withdrew his nomination before it was formally submitted to the U.S. Senate.

The U.S. Supreme Court justices, as pictured at the start of the Court's fall 2018 term. Sitting, from left to right: Justice Stephen G. Breyer, Justice Clarence Thomas, Chief Justice John G. Roberts Jr., Justice Ruth Bader Ginsburg, and Justice Samuel A. Alito. Standing, from left to right: Justice Neil M. Gorsuch, Justice Sonia Sotomayor, Justice Elena Kagan, and Justice Brett M. Kavanaugh.

willingness to engage the Senate on constitutional issues. In 1990, the first Supreme Court vacancy of George H. W. Bush's presidency went to David Souter, a little-known judge from New Hampshire whose position on issues such as abortion were never really tested (he was confirmed easily by a 90–9 Senate vote). However, in the current era of hyper-partisanship, party-line votes on Supreme Court nominees have become the norm; accordingly, when the White House and the Senate are held by the same political party, confirmation of Supreme Court nominees becomes a near certainty. In 2017, the Senate smoothed the path for controversial nominees further by passing a rule change that eliminated the possibility of filibusters in this context. Thus, when Brett Kavanaugh's 2018 Supreme Court nomination was threatened by allegations that he had sexually assaulted a young woman decades earlier (when both were in high school), nearly every Republican Senator lined up to support President Trump's embattled nominee. Kavanaugh was confirmed on a mostly party-line vote of 50–48.

The modern-day confirmation process for lower-court nominees has been politicized as well, with battles being waged with extra ferocity over appointments to the U.S. courts of appeals. During the Clinton and Obama administrations, Senate Republicans in control of that chamber often delayed or outright refused to take votes on nominees they felt were too liberal; Senate Democrats did the same to President George W. Bush's nominees in 2001. In the early part of the twenty-first century, obstruction became the norm. Utilizing the threat of a filibuster in almost every case, Senate opposition to judicial nominees effectively required a commitment of at least 60 Senate votes to allow nominations to reach the Senate floor for a full confirmation vote. Finally, in 2013, Senate Democrats, increasingly frustrated with Republican resistance to President Obama's lower-court nominees, eliminated the filibuster for all lower-court nominees going forward. Thus, as is the case with Supreme Court nominees, united party government can overcome most obstacles to confirming a president's selections for the federal bench.

9-7 HOW A CASE PROCEEDS WITHIN THE U.S. SUPREME COURT

The vast majority of cases that come before the U.S. Supreme Court arrive by a **writ of certiorari**, the formal term for an order by which the Court acts in its discretion to hear a case on appeal. Losing parties in the highest state court, a federal circuit court, or (in extremely rare cases) a federal district court can properly file a "cert petition" with the Supreme Court, asking the Court to hear its case. Decisions to grant a writ of certiorari generally follow the "*rule of four*": if four of the nine justices vote to hear the case, it is placed on the Court's official docket of cases that it will hear during the coming year. Of the many thousands of cert petitions that arrive at the Court during a given year, barely more than 1 percent (fewer than 90 overall) are normally granted.

In theory, the justices decide to hear only those cases that are considered so important that they justify intervention at such a high level. Two other factors may also increase the likelihood that the Supreme Court will grant a writ of certiorari: (1) when the federal government intervenes in the case or (2) when there is a split among two or more of the U.S. circuit courts of appeals on a similar issue. Additionally, some justices as a matter of strategy may vote to deny the petition for cert, even when they think the lower-court case was wrongly

writ of certiorari
The formal term for an order by which the Supreme Court acts in its discretion to review a case from a lower court.

decided, because they do not want their colleagues to transform the lower-court precedent into a Supreme Court edict applicable throughout the land. Regardless of the justices' many motives, denial of a cert petition theoretically casts no aspersions whatsoever on whether a case has been wrongly or rightly decided, although it does allow the lower-court decision to stand as the controlling legal decision for the parties in that case. For example, the Supreme Court's 1997 denial of a cert petition in a case concerning affirmative action at the University of Texas did not necessarily imply high court dissatisfaction with affirmative action; rather, it simply left intact a U.S. Court of Appeals decision that applied only to the three states in that circuit: Texas, Mississippi, and Louisiana. The U.S. Supreme Court waited until six years later to articulate new rules for affirmative action that would become applicable in all 50 states.

As shown in Figure 9-3, if the Court elects to issue a writ of certiorari and hear a case, both the losing and winning parties in the lower court file written documents called **briefs** arguing why constitutional or federal statutory law weighs in favor of their respective positions. Outside parties with an interest in the litigation may also elect to file briefs, known formally as **amicus curiae briefs** (*amicus curiae* is Latin for "friend of the court"), expressing their own views on how the Court should decide a particular case. Interest groups frequently file amicus briefs in Supreme Court cases that affect their members; in doing so, they offer a version of

> **briefs** Written documents filed by parties in an appealed case arguing why constitutional or statutory law weighs in favor of their respective positions.
>
> **amicus curiae briefs** Written documents filed by outside parties in the case with an interest in the outcome of the litigation expressing their own views on how the Court should decide a particular case.

FIGURE 9-3

From Cert Petition to Final Judgment in the U.S. Supreme Court

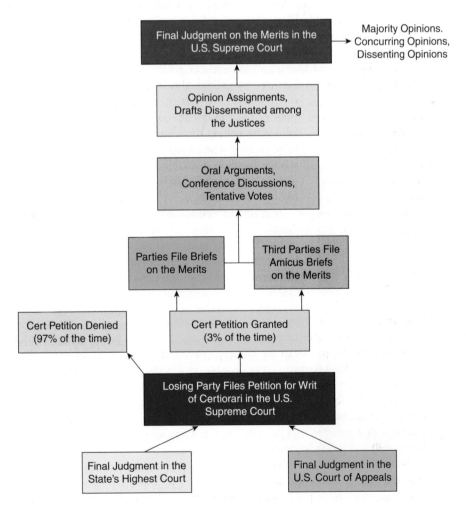

In some exceptionally rare cases, a final judgment from a federal district court may receive expedited review from the U.S. Supreme Court and thus bypass the U.S. Court of Appeals.

"expert testimony" on the law, albeit with their own strategic bent on the issue in question. The American Medical Association, for example, routinely files amicus briefs in abortion cases; the American Trial Lawyers Association may express its opinion in cases interpreting rules of trial procedure through amicus briefs as well. In some high-profile cases, literally hundreds of such briefs may be filed, offering the Court an admittedly informal tally of the state of public opinion on the issue.

The solicitor general argues on behalf of the U.S. government in most cases where the federal government is a party. That office also stands among the most influential "friends of the court," filing amicus briefs on behalf of the federal government in approximately a quarter of all cases heard by the Supreme Court each year. Acting through the solicitor general, the U.S. government has enjoyed a disproportionate share of success in affecting Supreme Court case discretionary grants of review and case outcomes.[29]

After all party and amicus briefs have been filed, the Supreme Court justices normally hear oral arguments from opposing counsel in the Supreme Court's chamber. Attorneys licensed to practice before the Supreme Court present their clients' view of the law and facts within an allotted period of time (normally 30 minutes); most of that time is spent answering questions and inquiries from the justices. If a justice is truly undecided, he or she may be affected in the margins by the positions of advocates at oral arguments; the give-and-take with the lawyers may also suggest ways to more effectively draft the final opinion. Still, there remains little evidence that the oral arguments shift the votes of most justices. Regardless, the hearings in the Supreme Court chamber can still offer moments of high drama, such as when Richard Nixon's attorneys argued for an especially broad interpretation of executive privilege in the 1974 Watergate tapes case. Their argument was ultimately rejected, and Nixon resigned just days after the Court's decision was handed down.

Shortly after the oral arguments are completed and the case has been formally submitted, the justices meet in conference to discuss the case, offer initial votes, and assign opinions. The chief justice presides over all conferences, which culminate in the assignment of opinions to be researched and written by individual justices in accordance with the conference discussions. Each justice employs four clerks—selected from a pool of the top law school graduates from across the country—who work behind the scenes researching the law and creating initial drafts of written opinions according to the justice's specific wishes. In some cases, clerks enjoy even more influence over the justices they work for, assisting them as they sort through competing legal arguments.

A majority opinion requires agreement of at least five of the Court's nine members; only a majority opinion carries the force of law. The chief justice has just one vote like his colleagues, but if he is in the majority, the chief justice also has the crucial power to choose who will write the Court's main opinion. (If the chief justice is not in the majority, the senior-most associate justice in the majority retains that power of assignment.) Individual justices may choose to write other opinions either on their own or on behalf of a minority of justices. A concurring opinion agrees with the end result reached by the majority but disagrees with the reasons offered for the decision. A dissenting opinion, on the other hand, disagrees with the result reached by the majority. Justices write concurring and dissenting opinions both to register their differences with the majority and to lay the groundwork for the future, when those alternate grounds may one day secure the support of a Court majority.

The dissents written by Oliver Wendell Holmes Jr., who served on the U.S. Supreme Court from 1902 to 1932, established him as one of the most important legal thinkers in American history. With speech restrictions on the rise in America during and immediately after World War I, Holmes eventually promoted a broad

solicitor general The lawyer representing the U.S. government before the U.S. Supreme Court.

majority opinion The opinion of a majority of members of the U.S. Supreme Court, which carries the force of law.

concurring opinion The opinion of one or more justices that agrees with the end result reached by the majority but disagrees with the reasons offered for the decision.

dissenting opinion The opinion of one or more justices who disagree with the result reached by the majority.

MPI / Archive Photos / Getty Images

The "great dissenter," Justice Oliver Wendell Holmes Jr., was appointed to the Supreme Court by President Theodore Roosevelt in 1902. Holmes's dissenting opinions on behalf of the freedom of expression would garner the support of Supreme Court majorities several decades later.

conception of free speech under the Constitution. Along with fellow justice Louis Brandeis, Holmes dissented from the majority's opinions allowing the government to punish minority views. (Holmes also made famous the metaphor of a "marketplace of ideas" and cautioned that even liberal protections of free speech would not protect a man from "falsely shouting 'fire!' in a crowded theater.")

Once drafts of the justices' opinions in a case have been circulated and finalized, the decision can be announced. Occasionally the justices can shift their votes near the end of the process. For example, in 1986 Justice Lewis Powell seemingly resolved his own inner struggles over the scope of privacy rights when he chose to join Justice Byron White's four-person opinion in *Bowers v. Hardwick*.[30] Powell's vote gave White the slim majority and determined that the right to homosexual sodomy would not receive constitutional protection. That decision was finally reversed in 2003, when the Court overturned *Bowers* in *Lawrence v. Texas*.[31] Powell later publicly recanted his support of *Bowers*, proving that his inner struggle had actually continued. Normally the justices issue written opinions only, but on special occasions, the justices may even decide to read from key passages of the opinions they authored.

9-8 JUDICIAL DECISION-MAKING AND DEBATES OVER THE EXERCISE OF JUDICIAL POWER

Although it is difficult to determine what causes Supreme Court justices to vote as they do on certain issues, social scientists and legal scholars have identified a number of factors that may play a role in a judge's decision-making:

- **Legal rules and precedents.** The law itself—including constitutional law, statutes, rules and regulations, and past court decisions interpreting those sources—may be unambiguous enough to counsel one particular application to the case at hand. Previous court decisions are especially hard to avoid—when judges follow the decisions of past judges' rulings in similar cases, they are adhering to the long-standing doctrine of *stare decisis*, which is Latin for "stand by the decision" that has already been settled. For example, although Justice Byron White dissented from the original decision in *Miranda v. Arizona* (1966)[32] providing unprecedented rights to the accused, in later decisions he actively applied the *Miranda* holding to other cases, deferring to a high court precedent that he personally opposed. Although the language of Supreme Court opinions suggests that *stare decisis* is always at work, often more than one reasonable interpretation of a law or legal opinion exists. In recent years, some judges have turned to international law and judicial opinions handed down in foreign courts as well. Most notably, Justice Anthony Kennedy in *Lawrence v. Texas* (2003) cited the European Court of Human Rights in support of the Court's protection of gay privacy rights. Defenders of this practice claim that because Americans share some values with the wider civilization, judges should be able to cite any and all sources of law in rendering their decisions; critics respond that there is no basis for U.S. judges to impose foreign "moods or fads" on Americans.
- **Changes in circumstances.** Sometimes changes in real-life conditions and circumstances may influence how laws are interpreted. In the school desegregation cases of the 1950s, the Supreme Court openly considered the newly discovered harmful effects of segregation on African American children. Similarly, in 1973, the Supreme Court took into account changes in modern medicine when it formulated the definition of constitutionally protected abortion rights in *Roe v. Wade*. Some jurists and scholars believe such changes in circumstances are irrelevant; rather, they view the Constitution as fixed in time and thus limited in scope to what the framers envisioned. The search for the framers' original intent about the Constitution is often referred to as "originalism." By contrast, other judges and scholars advocate the more flexible view of the Constitution as a "living, breathing document," which must adapt to changing circumstances and conditions.
- **Ideological "attitudes."** Many political scientists argue that Supreme Court justices' personal attitudes (liberal or conservative on law enforcement issues, free speech, etc.)

stare decisis A Latin term meaning "stand by the decision" that has already been settled by the court.

AP Photo / PABLO MARTINEZ MONSIVAIS

John Roberts, nominee for chief justice of the United States, testifying before the Senate Judiciary Committee in September 2005.

influence their judicial decision-making. This model of understanding how justices decide cases has been labeled "the attitudinal model." Defenders of the model cite numerous statistics that support their understanding of the way judges decide cases. For example, William O. Douglas was a New Deal liberal who voted in the liberal direction in criminal procedure cases nearly 90 percent of the time and in civil rights cases 93 percent of the time.[33]

- **Personal traits and characteristics.** Males and females may approach political events differently; accordingly, the gender of a Supreme Court justice affects his or her reaction to legal issues and cases to some degree. Before arriving on the Supreme Court, Justice Sonia Sotomayor famously expressed the hope that "a wise Latina woman with the richness of her experiences would more often than not reach a better conclusion than a white male who hasn't lived that life." Certainly a justice's personal experiences will play some role in how he or she judges. Biographers of Justice Oliver Wendell Holmes, for example, contend that Holmes's near-death experiences as a soldier in the Civil War colored his approach to judging.[34]

- **Intracourt politics.** A justice's interest in maintaining good relations with fellow justices may push him or her to vote in a certain way; behind-the-scenes bargaining and negotiating have also been features of Supreme Court politics throughout its history. In the late 1950s and early 1960s, Chief Justice Earl Warren and Justice William Brennan were famed for their ability to sway undecided justices in their favor; by contrast, Justice Felix Frankfurter's condescending attitude toward his fellow justices persuaded few and alienated many.

- **External political pressures.** Although Supreme Court justices enjoy life tenure and are thus theoretically immune to outside political pressures, the reality is much more complicated. Aware that the Court's prestige often rests on its ability to persuade the other branches, as well as the public, to comply with the Court's decisions, justices often react to the political environment that surrounds the Court when issuing legal opinions. *Roe v. Wade* survived its widely predicted demise in 1992 because at least two conservative justices feared its reversal would deal a blow to the Supreme Court's prestige. Chief Justice Roberts's concern with threats to the Court's prestige may have led him to defer to the political branches in the health care case of *NFIB v. Sebelius* (2012).[35] Public opinion may thus play a role in determining the language of opinions and even the outcome of some cases.

Regardless of how individual justices arrive at their decisions, the U.S. Supreme Court (and American courts in general) frequently find themselves the subject of controversy. Many of the recurring debates over the proper role of courts include the following:

- **Judicial restraint versus judicial activism.** The Supreme Court struck down several New Deal statutes in the 1930s; a few decades later, it invalidated state laws banning the use of contraceptive devices (in 1965) and state laws restricting the right to abortion (in 1973). Critics of those decisions protested the exercise of judicial activism by the high court. Specifically, they charged that rather than deferring to the elected branches of government as a general matter, the justices responsible for those controversial decisions had effectively turned the Court into a "super legislature" that makes social policy. More recent cases such as *Citizens United v. Federal Election Commission* (2010),[36] in which the Court struck down a federal law banning corporations from most forms of participation in election campaigns, have revived those charges once again. Critics of judicial activism argue in favor of a philosophy of judicial restraint by which judges act more slowly and incrementally, affording the democratically elected branches considerable discretion to enact whatever laws they choose, so long as there is no clear and unambiguous prohibition against those laws in the Constitution itself.

The late Supreme Court justice Antonin Scalia, being interviewed by Chris Wallace on Fox News Sunday in 2013. Justice Scalia was consistently opposed to televising the Supreme Court's oral arguments during his nearly 30 years of service on the high court.

- **Electing judges versus appointing judges**. Federal judges are appointed by the president with the advice and consent of the Senate and then serve for life. Many state judges are appointed as well, for either fixed or indefinite terms; others must run for election and then must seek reelection to stay on the bench. These varying methods of judicial selection may have significant implications on judicial decision-making. Appointed judges no longer accountable to the public or to any political processes enjoy increased independence in their decision-making. On the other hand, what elected judges may lack in independence, they make up for in accountability; unlike judges appointed for life, elected judges should be more responsive to the public as a whole. The debate over judicial selection mechanisms often boils down to a question of how to strike the proper balance between the competing interests of judicial independence and accountability to the public.

- **Law versus politics.** Do judges sit on a court of law, or is their institution simply another political body exercising its political will? Certainly the judicial process is fashioned to trumpet the court's role as a legal body that transcends ordinary politics. The judicial robes, magisterial courtrooms, and reliance on formality give rise to this "cult of the robe" as the "apolitical" branch. Canons of judicial ethics require that judges avoid even the appearance of impropriety by not participating in political debates and lobbying other branches on various matters. At the same time, the U.S. Supreme Court in particular often finds itself at the storm center of American politics. In some instances the other branches actually come to the Court in search of legal answers to what are essentially political problems. The Court's 5–4 decision in *Bush v. Gore* (2000),[37] which ended the manual recounts for the 2000 presidential election in Florida and made George W. Bush the president-elect, illustrates just one way that law and politics can become intertwined. Over a decade later, the Supreme Court's decision to uphold President Obama's health care reform legislation offered political fodder for both sides of the political spectrum in the months leading up to the 2012 presidential election. In extremely rare cases, the elected branches essentially abdicate their responsibility to act altogether, forcing the courts to step in by enforcing judicial decrees. For example, federal courts have on rare occasions supervised the construction of prisons and the implementation of busing programs. The highly political manner in which judges are chosen and the ambiguous nature of so many legal provisions mean that the tension between law and politics is perhaps inevitable in the U.S. political system.

- **Cameras in the courtroom.** The Constitution guarantees to every criminal defendant a public trial; courts can satisfy that requirement by allowing the media and some members of the public access to the trial. Many states go a step further, allowing television cameras in state courtrooms, but the federal judicial system has so far resisted any such development. Even the justices of the U.S. Supreme Court have resisted calls for televising their proceedings, though that court typically releases audio recordings of the oral arguments within a matter of days. Do lawyers play up to the television cameras, undermining the interests of justice? It's hard to say. Chief Justice John Roberts continues to defer to the majority of justices who remain adamantly opposed to television coverage. The late justice Antonin Scalia noted his objection in especially stark terms during a 2005 interview when he was still serving on the high court: "I think there's something sick about making entertainment out of other people's legal problems . . . I don't like it in the lower courts, and I don't particularly like it in the Supreme Court."[38] Until the makeup of the current Court changes significantly, Supreme Court observers unable to observe oral arguments in person will have to settle for audiotapes of the oral arguments made available a short time later.

Since the outset of the republic, U.S. presidents have appointed justices to the Court who have gone on to make decisions that transform the constitutional landscape for decades after those same presidents have passed from the scene. That explains much of the controversy surrounding the 2018 confirmation of Brett Kavanaugh, President Trump's nominee to replace the retiring justice Anthony Kennedy. During his 30-plus years on the high court, Kennedy was often the "swing justice" on the most controversial issues of the day, providing a critical fifth vote in abortion, same-sex marriage, and religious freedom cases. Both political sides realized that if he were confirmed, Kavanaugh might well hold the balance of power in many future Supreme Court decisions. At the judge's confirmation hearings, opponents seized on sexual assault allegations leveled against the candidate in hopes of derailing his nomination; meanwhile, supporters of Donald Trump and the Republicans circled the wagons in support of their nominee.

FROM YOUR PERSPECTIVE

Is Law School the Right Choice for You and, If So, When Should You Apply?

Currently there are almost two hundred law schools in the United States accredited by the American Bar Association (ABA) that award juris doctor degrees to students upon completion of three years or more of legal education. You are no doubt familiar with the names of many of these schools: Harvard, Yale, Columbia, the University of Chicago, and several others that enjoy sterling reputations and are well known around the world. Many graduates of these schools work in prestigious short-term clerkships for judges and then go on to enjoy their pick of legal jobs at extremely high starting salaries. Other law school graduates are not so fortunate, however. According to lawjobs.com, graduates of law schools ranked below the top 25 have a less-than-one-in-five chance of beginning their careers at a large law firm with relatively high starting salaries, and nearly 15 percent of all students at ABA-accredited schools either flunk out or are unemployed for at least nine months after graduation. Considering the high price of law school today (many students graduate with debts of $100,000 or more), these are daunting figures indeed.

Of course, for many college graduates who attend the right law school at the right moment in their young careers, legal education offers significant benefits, including the prospect of an exciting and lucrative career. Because the average age of entering law students across the nation is 25 years old (the average age is higher at some top-ranked schools), most college graduates will consider other post-graduation opportunities before law school, both to prepare them for the rigors of law school and to enhance their chances of admission at top schools.

For Critical Thinking and Discussion

1. Can you think of any benefits that accrue to law students who take time off after college?
2. Many college graduates apply to law school not so much because they dream of a legal career but because they are unaware of any other promising options. What other types of graduate schools might be of interest to students who enjoy debating public policy?

Of course, life appointments to the Court allow justices to rule without regard for their own political futures, and sometimes the justices' decisions do not fit into a well-understood political or legal framework. Consider Justice Kennedy, an appointment of Republican president Ronald Reagan, who dashed conservative hopes with many of his votes. Recent presidents have made it a top priority to choose predictable nominees with sound ideological credentials on one end or the other of the political spectrum. Unfortunately for them, the political circumstances and the legal issues that face the Court may change as well, rendering those predictions useless for future times. That won't stop interest groups and other political forces from investing considerable resources in the nomination fights of today. The least dangerous branch has never been more powerful, and ambitious presidents will not stop in their capacity to tame the highest court in the land.

Summary

9-1 Types of Law

- *Civil law* refers to statutes enacted most often by legislative bodies; *common law* consists of the rulings handed down by judges that establish precedents. Other types of law include criminal, constitutional, and administrative law.

9-2 The Structure of the U.S. Legal System

- Article III of the U.S. Constitution established the judicial branch, including the U.S. Supreme Court. Federal district courts are the trial courts, whose decisions may be appealed to the U.S. courts of appeals and then in turn to the U.S. Supreme Court. The decisions of the 50 state supreme courts that raise federal issues may also be brought directly to the U.S. Supreme Court.

9-3 The Adversarial System of Justice

- The U.S. legal system is an adversarial system of justice in which opposing parties contend against each other for a result favorable to themselves; disputes between parties may be settled through civil litigation, whereas those accused of crimes are prosecuted through a criminal justice system that primarily produces plea bargains between defendants and the government.

9-4 Judicial Review and Its Implications

- Chief Justice John Marshall's opinion in *Marbury v. Madison* (1803) established the Supreme Court's authority to review the constitutionality of any act passed by Congress as well as any order of the U.S. president.

9-5 Limitations on Courts

- Courts in the United States cannot initiate lawsuits. They can only hear true controversies, their decisions affect only those parties that are part of a case, and they have no ability to enforce their decisions.

9-6 Electing and Appointing Judges

- State judges are selected in various ways: some are appointed by governors or legislatures; others must run in an election; still others are chosen by a merit plan system. By comparison, all federal court judges are nominated by the president and must be confirmed by the U.S. Senate.

9-7 How a Case Proceeds within the U.S. Supreme Court

- In order to grant a writ of certiorari to review a case, four of the nine justices must approve. After briefs are filed and oral arguments are heard, the justices vote on the merits and issue their majority opinion accordingly; concurring and dissenting opinions may also be issued.

9-8 Judicial Decision-Making and Debates over the Exercise of Judicial Power

- Various factors influence a judge's decision-making, including legal precedents, new circumstances, ideological attitudes, personal traits, intracourt politics, and external pressures. Justices who frequently overturn state and federal laws, or who must run for reelection, may be accused of practicing politics on the bench. And a majority of justices continue to oppose allowing television cameras to cover oral arguments.

Key Terms

adversarial system (p. 181)

amicus curiae briefs (p. 193)

appellate jurisdiction (p. 187)

briefs (p. 193)

civil law (p. 177)

class action lawsuits (p. 186)

common law (p. 177)

complaint (p. 182)

concurring opinion (p. 194)

defendant (p. 182)

discovery (p. 182)

dissenting opinion (p. 194)

grand jury (p. 183)

indictment (p. 183)

inquisitorial system (p. 181)

judicial review (p. 184)

litigation (p. 182)

majority opinion (p. 194)

original jurisdiction (p. 187)

plaintiff (p. 182)

plea bargain (p. 183)

solicitor general (p. 194)

standing (p. 186)

stare decisis (p. 195)

writ of certiorari (p. 192)

Part III
POLITICAL BEHAVIOR

10

PUBLIC OPINION

A poll worker helping voters in Miami, FL.

FOR POLITICAL LEADERS and citizens alike, the appetite for information on what the public thinks has always been hearty. Today, this appetite is fed through the large number of opinion polls whose results are disseminated through newspapers, magazines, television, radio, and the internet. Increasingly this information is shared through social media outlets, which allows for more rapid exposure and a more diverse audience. The methods of gauging public opinion have advanced quite dramatically over the nation's history, and this advancement has been driven in no small part by the obsession to know what Americans think. The nation's democratic roots, featuring a commitment to majoritarian rule and the "consent of the governed," raise public opinion to a lofty status in the workings of American politics. Indeed, the willingness of officials to heed the people's voice has become firmly entrenched in American political culture. Scientific measurement of public opinion is a relatively recent phenomenon in American politics, but the significant role that public opinion plays in the formulation of policy is as old as American democracy itself. Understanding what public opinion is, how it is expressed, how it forms, and how it is measured in contemporary politics is critical to understanding how American government works.

10-1 PUBLIC OPINION IN AMERICAN POLITICS

Public opinion is a vague, although important, concept. It is regularly used by presidents to justify their policies, by political candidates to mount campaigns, by interest groups to promote their causes, by journalists to describe public preferences, and by scholars to understand the American government. The concept of public opinion is central to the American system of government. But the way in which public opinion is gauged and its relevance and uses in American politics have changed over the nation's history.

OVERVIEW OF PUBLIC OPINION

The U.S. Constitution begins with the words "We the People," highlighting the important role of the *public* in the creation of the government. Nonetheless, there is no mention of the term *public opinion* in the Constitution. The word *democracy* literally translated (from its Greek roots *demos* and *kratos*) means "rule by the people," and thus the opinions of the public take on a particularly important role in governing. The American system of government was founded on a set of democratic principles, first articulated by Plato and Aristotle and later popularized by political philosophers of the eighteenth-century Enlightenment, such as Montesquieu.[1] These principles herald the role of the public in governing and in consenting to what government does.

From the time of the founders up through the present day, the virtues of public opinion and its role in American democracy have been continually extolled. James Madison argued that the "public voice" and its formal role in voting provided primary justification for adopting the proposed Constitution. Borrowing from the political theories of John Locke, Madison acknowledged that government must serve the "will of the people." Andrew Jackson's presidency encouraged and empowered the rise of the "common man" to express his opinion for the purpose of influencing government.

Political leaders recognize that public opinion plays not only a theoretically important role in our democratic form of government but an important tactical role as well. Political scientist E. E. Schattschneider, in an influential book titled *The Semisovereign People*, argued that "public opinion can emerge as a key factor in any political context" and that public opinion often is responsible for determining the outcome of important political battles. Long before Schattschneider, President Abraham Lincoln expressed this idea based on his own experiences, saying: "Public sentiment is everything. With public sentiment, nothing can fail; without it, nothing can succeed."[2]

Although most scholars, elected leaders, and everyday citizens would agree that public opinion is and should be very important in our system of government, the concept remains hard to define and measure. Many scholars regard public opinion as simply the summation of individual opinions on any particular issue or topic. Political scientist V. O. Key Jr., however, defined public opinion more specifically as "those opinions held by private persons which government finds it prudent to heed."[3]

Today opinion polls—for better or worse—have become the yardstick through which public opinion is understood and evaluated. The barrage of polls released daily by major media organizations provides a plethora of data describing the American psyche. There are, however, numerous practices in addition to polling through which public opinion in America may be expressed.

HOW IS PUBLIC OPINION EXPRESSED?

The formal constitutional mechanism by which public opinion influences the federal government is the free, open, and regular election of House members. Since ratification of the Seventeenth Amendment in 1913, the direct election of U.S. senators has served as yet another constitutional means for the expression of public opinion. Chapter 14 covers this form of expressing public opinion in detail. Voting is one important expression of public opinion and provides guarantees that officials are responsive to voters. In many state and local elections, voters are asked to respond to referendum questions, which empower the public to directly resolve policy issues. But there are a number of additional ways beyond voting in which

public opinion The summation of individual opinions on any particular issue or topic.

public opinion has an influence on government. The First Amendment's guarantees that the people have the right to free speech, to peaceably assemble, and to petition their government pave the way for political rallies and protest rallies, which are important manifestations of public opinion.

Supporting a candidate and engaging in attempts to elect an individual or political party to office through a monetary contribution or a contribution of time and effort is another way that public opinion is expressed. Likewise, contributing time or money to an interest group or political action committee enables individuals to express their opinion indirectly and may have a significant impact on what government does.

Public opinion is also expressed through the news media. Journalists often provide commentary on politics and public issues through talk radio shows, websites, editorial pages, and television news talk shows that provide perspectives on public opinion. Individual citizens may also use the media to express their opinion. In addition, members of the public often choose to express their opinion directly to elected officials by contacting them, via either a letter or email, a phone call, or the internet, for their views on a particular issue. Although many politically aware Americans still express their opinions on politics in these *traditional* ways, millions of others now take advantage of their laptops, smartphones, and tablets to post comments on blogs or social media outlets. One of the first political blogs was Andrew Sullivan's "The Daily Dish," founded in 2000. Since then, the number of blogs has exploded. Today, blogs vary widely in form, but most feature some type of personal commentary, references to data, and links to other sources on the internet related to a topic of political discussion. Most bloggers don't aspire to the goal of providing *objective* commentary. Rather, they aim to provide up-to-date, personal, and often partisan perspectives on current political topics. Many liberals tend to flock to more left-leaning blogs such as *The Daily Kos* and *Talking Points Memo*, whereas conservatives frequent conservative blog sites, such as *Powerline* or the blog of conservative author Michelle Malkin. Social networks, such as Facebook, Twitter, and Tumblr, also provide a means for people to express opinions to their "friends" or others in their network.

In addition, a highly visible and widely used expression of public opinion in contemporary politics is the public opinion poll. Most major and many smaller media organizations today regularly conduct polls on politics and policy issues and publish the results of those polls in the form of news stories. The *USA Today*/Gallup Poll, the CBS/*New York Times* poll, the Fox News/Opinion Dynamics poll, and the NBC/*Wall Street Journal* poll are only a few examples of media-based polls that, on a regular basis, provide data on American public opinion.

10-2 THE LEVELS OF PUBLIC OPINION

Public opinion exists at three basic levels: the broad level of values and beliefs, an intermediate level of political orientations, and the specific level of preferences about particular topics.

VALUES AND BELIEFS

At the highest, most abstract level are the values and beliefs of the American people. Values are the broad principles underlying the American political culture that most citizens support and adhere to; they represent that which people find most important in life. Beliefs are the facts derived from values that people take for granted about the world. Although there are many values that Americans hold dear, political scientist Samuel Huntington[4] has identified four politically relevant values that are widely accepted in the American political culture and serve as the basis for defining political beliefs on which there is great consensus in America: liberty, equality, individualism, and the rule of law.

The vast majority of Americans support the idea of basic freedoms and liberties, such as freedom of religion and freedom of speech. These liberties are embedded in our political culture and serve as the basis for many government policies. Because Americans value liberty, for example, they believe that people should have the right to choose a religion or not to choose a religion, the right to publicly disagree with the president or the party in power, and the right to publish articles or news stories without government retribution.

values and beliefs The broad principles underlying the American political culture that citizens support and adhere to.

Likewise, a majority of Americans firmly value the concept stated in the Declaration of Independence that "all men are created equal." Regardless of economic status, race, or gender, the American public on the whole subscribes to the belief that all people should be treated equally under the law and that all people should have equal opportunities for economic success.

Americans also show a strong propensity to support the value of individualism. Over the years, Americans have consistently shown a preference for rewarding individual hard work and for limiting the role of government.[5] Jefferson's maxim "that government is best which governs the least" presumes that society will advance by encouraging individuals to succeed and leads to a belief in capitalism and free enterprise as the optimal economic system. Also, the Puritan work ethic that served as an important value in early American society continues to be reflected in Americans' affinity for the value of individualism.

Finally, the value of the "rule of law" encourages a strong belief in the legitimacy of the U.S. Constitution, in the importance of elections as a way to configure government, and in the beliefs that the opinion of the majority should prevail, that those in the minority should have the right to challenge the majority, and that those accused of a crime should be entitled to fair procedures.

Unlike other levels of public opinion, values and beliefs are unique in that they generally receive a high level of support and consensus. Whether individuals are Democrats or Republicans, from the far right or the far left, elites or more representative of the masses, the vast majority generally subscribes to these broad values. Accordingly, values are the level of public opinion that define our political culture; widespread agreement and support for them is thus critical to the maintenance of the American political system.

POLITICAL ORIENTATIONS

Values and beliefs are very broad and abstract notions held by Americans that provide general guidance to people in thinking about politics. Political orientations are the translation of these values and beliefs into a systematic way of assessing the political environment. Although there may be broad consensus about values and beliefs among Americans, the translation of these values into an organized way of thinking about politics and issues is considerably more varied.

The two primary ways in which Americans orient themselves toward political topics and issues are partisanship (see Figure 10-1) and political ideology. Partisanship, which is discussed in a later chapter, features a psychological attachment to one of the main political parties, generally either the Democrats or the Republicans.[6] A partisan identification provides an orientational mechanism for understanding how to apply one's values and beliefs to the political world. Consider, for example, the political debate over affirmative action policies. A Democratic orientation largely applies the value of equality and the belief that people of all races and creeds should enjoy equal opportunities, therefore suggesting support for affirmative action programs, which attempt to level the playing field and make corrections for policies that have historically benefited white males. A Republican orientation, on the other hand, generally places a higher priority on the value of individualism and the belief that government should not interfere with individual initiatives to succeed, thus suggesting opposition to affirmative action programs. Partisan orientation often helps people translate values into specific opinions.

Likewise, political ideology provides an orientation for translating values into specific opinions. Political ideology is a philosophical guide that people use to help translate their values and beliefs into specific political preferences. The dominant ideologies in America are liberalism and conservatism. The contemporary liberal ideology, which is more closely associated with the modern Democratic Party, prefers that government take a more assertive role in the redistribution of economic resources but that government advocate positions that emphasize individual freedom on a range of social issues. Today's conservative ideology, which is more closely identified with the Republican Party, favors government activism in defense of more traditional values on social issues but prefers government restraint in economic redistribution.

political orientations
The translation of values and beliefs into a systematic way of assessing the political environment.

political ideology
A philosophical guide that people use to help translate their values and beliefs into political preferences.

liberal ideology A political orientation that favors a more assertive role in the redistribution of economic resources but emphasizes individual freedom on a range of social issues.

conservative ideology
A political orientation that generally favors government activism in defense of more traditional values on social issues but favors government restraint in economic redistribution.

FIGURE 10-1

Partisanship in America

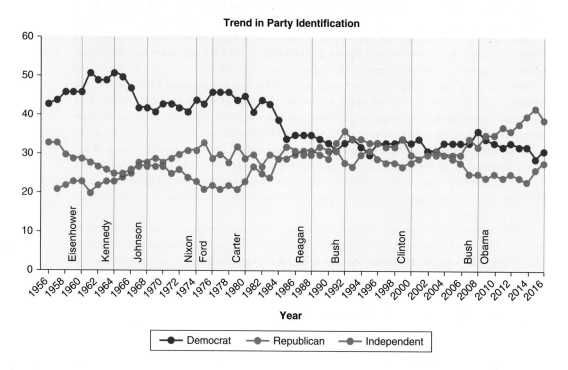

Trend in Party Identification

Source: https://news.gallup.com/poll/201638/independent-political-lowest-six-years.aspx.

The liberal and conservative camps largely agree on the basic values and beliefs of the American political culture—in the rule of law and majority rule and minority rights and in the idea that the free enterprise system will generally guarantee the most robust economy. But liberals and conservatives often differ when seeking to translate these values and beliefs into actual policies.

Partisanship and political ideology are two very important topics in the study of American public opinion. They provide a framework for individuals to translate broad values and beliefs into preferences for issue positions and political candidates. These orientations help people to efficiently form opinions and express those opinions. Partisanship and political ideology also enable both political leaders and scholars to better understand why Americans think what they think about particular issues and vote the way they vote in elections.

The political orientations of Americans tend to be quite stable and lasting[7]—more so than the specific preferences that people have toward policies and political actors. The stability in American political orientations provides an order and consistency to American public opinion, which ultimately promotes stability in the political system as a whole.

POLITICAL PREFERENCES

> **political preferences** The attitudes people maintain regarding the performance of political leaders and institutions, their candidate preferences in elections, and specific policy issues.

The most discussed level of public opinion is the particular **political preferences** that Americans have on policy issues, their attitudes regarding the performance of political leaders and institutions, and their candidate preferences in elections. Support for the minimum wage, gun control proposals, the use of U.S. troops in fighting terrorism, abortion policy, campaign finance reform proposals, tax increases, and tax cuts are all specific policy issues on which the American public expresses opinions. In addition to policies, Americans also hold specific opinions about the performance of their elected leaders such as the president, as well as their confidence in institutions such as Congress, the U.S. Supreme Court, and the military.

What Americans think about the minimum wage, the performance of the president, or the candidates in a political campaign is highly influenced by their political orientations. For example, an individual who identifies as a Democrat and considers herself ideologically liberal is much less likely to say she approves of President Trump's performance than would a Republican who considers himself to be conservative.

Figure 10-2 depicts public opinion on two preference questions that have experienced considerable change in the recent past: attitudes about gay marriage (for which public support has increased) and the percentage saying that the most important problem in America relates to economic conditions (which spiked in 2008 at the outset of the economic recession and then dropped significantly as the economy rebounded).

FIGURE 10-2

Preferences of Americans

Two in Three Americans Support Gay Marriage in 2018

Do you think marriages between same-sex couples should or should not be recognized by the law as valid. with the same rights as traditional marriages?

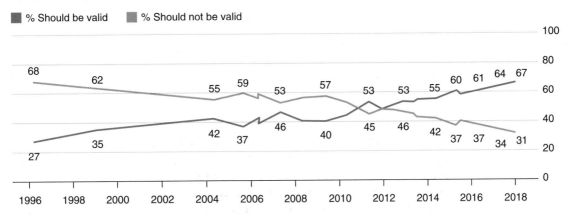

Percentage of Americans Mentioning Economic Issues as the Nation's Most Important Problem

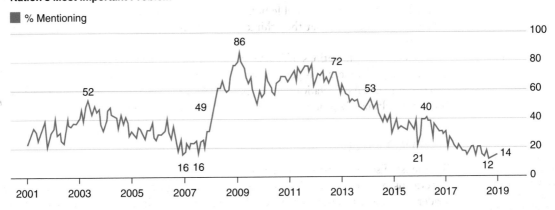

Source: https://news.gallup.com/poll/234866/two-three-americans-support-sex-marriage.aspx and https://news.gallup. com/poll/242189/record-low-cite-economic-issues-top-problem.aspx.

10-3 HOW INFORMED IS PUBLIC OPINION?

As discussed earlier in this chapter, American democracy relies on public opinion to choose leaders and inform public policy. This reliance is based on an important assumption about democracy—that citizens have the necessary information and skills to be able to understand political issues and provide informed input. Since the time of Plato and Aristotle, political philosophers have dealt with questions about this important assumption: is the public capable of democracy?

In the Federalist Papers, Alexander Hamilton and James Madison expressed concerns about the fickleness of public opinion and the potential "tyranny of the masses," which could lead to instability in governance.[8] Hamilton's solution for this problem was a republican form of government, in which the public chooses leaders who run the government, rather than a direct democracy, in which the public rules directly.

Suspicions about the capacity of the public for meaningful contributions to governance were also articulated quite well by Walter Lippmann in the early twentieth century.[9] Lippmann, a well-known public opinion scholar, delivered withering attacks on ordinary citizens' lack of knowledge regarding politics. He argued that citizens invest very little energy and effort in acquiring information about politics, and, as a consequence, the public lacks the necessary knowledge for their opinions to provide value. Subsequent research in the 1960s and 1970s, most notably by Angus Campbell and his colleagues in *The American Voter*, used scientific surveys to support the argument that ordinary citizens tend to be ill-informed about political issues, ill-equipped to understand politics, and quite fickle in how they stand on issues.[10]

More contemporary studies indicate that the American public today is uninformed about politics. For example, a 2017 poll from the University of Pennsylvania's Annenberg Public Policy Center found that many Americans lack knowledge on some important aspects of the American political system, including 37 percent of Americans who "could not name a single right protected by the First Amendment" or 33 percent who can't name any branch of the federal government.[11]

Some political scientists have come to the defense of the American public in this regard. V. O. Key Jr., in his work *The Responsible Electorate*,[12] stated that although "many voters act in odd ways indeed," if one studies the electorate more carefully, one would find that "voters are not fools." Key observed that "in the large, the electorate behaves about as rationally and responsibly as we should expect, given the clarity of the alternatives presented to it and the character of the information available to it." If political leaders don't rationally discuss issues and provide a framework for voters to use to understand politics, it is not the voters who should be blamed but rather the leaders. Considering this caveat, Key extolled the capacity of the public to form stable, responsible opinions and to contribute to the governing process.

Benjamin Page and Robert Shapiro extended Key's ideas in their book *The Rational Public*.[13] They used decades of public opinion poll data to show that over the long haul, public opinion on many issues remains fairly stable, and when it changes, it moves in logical directions. The aggregate responses of the public in polls, Page and Shapiro found, make sense and demonstrate rationality. They also found that the public makes distinctions between important policy areas and that public opinion tends to form meaningful patterns, consistent with a set of underlying beliefs and values.

The link between public opinion on an issue and public policy is a difficult one to establish. Page and Shapiro report that over the long haul, a relationship develops between public attitudes on policy issues and the public policies that emerge from government. These researchers also argue that when public opinion shifts, a corresponding shift in public policy is likely to follow.

Political scientist Samuel Kernell has noted a more indirect link between public opinion and public policy: political actors (most notably the president) who have high levels of public support are generally better able to get legislation passed.[14] President Bush, for example, in 2003 was able to get Congress to pass a new tax cut package in part because of the high job performance ratings Americans gave him at that time. High levels of public support may be translated into an office-holder's greater political power to influence the legislative process.

10-4 HOW DOES PUBLIC OPINION FORM?

Through voting, opinion polls, protest rallies, communications with leaders, and editorials published online or in print, public opinion is expressed and provides an important input for public policy-making. But how do individuals develop their particular political orientations, and how do they come to hold their specific political preferences? How do the more deep-seated values and beliefs form? What influences the values that people hold, their partisan and ideological orientations, and their opinions on specific issues?

Political socialization is the process by which an individual acquires values, beliefs, and opinions about politics. Political socialization is a lifelong process, beginning in early child-hood and continuing throughout an individual's life. The learning process that leads to the acquisition of values and opinions applies not only to politics but also to other orientations of people, including their beliefs about religion and culture.

Just as there are many factors and influences that lead individuals to consider themselves Democrats or Republicans or supporters of gun control or gun rights, there are also numer-ous factors and influences that lead people to choose a particular religion or to choose no religion at all. Socialization is important not only in the development of political learning for individuals but also in the transmission of the fundamental beliefs and values of the American political culture from one generation to the next.

Although political socialization is a lifelong process, there are certain times in life when political learning is greater. For example, the political socialization that occurs early in life has a more profound impact on political orientations than does learning that occurs in adulthood. The impressions and information that are acquired while an individual is younger tend to be most influential and the longest lasting. Psychologists refer to this as the primacy tendency.

Early political learning tends to be most profound, but socialization to politics remains at work through a number of influences over the course of a person's life. Numerous factors and institutions, known as agents of political socialization,[15] have been identified as having a particularly relevant impact on one's socialization to politics.

Certainly demographic factors such as race, ethnicity, gender, age, and economic status go a long way toward defining individuals' identities and can influence their political values. But a list of the most important agents of political socialization also includes such influences as family, friends and peer groups, schools, the media, and religion. Collectively, these agents promote the acquisition of the political values, beliefs, and opinions that an individual comes to hold.

FAMILY

Because much of the early years in a person's life is dominated by experiences with the family, the primacy tendency leads many to develop values and beliefs consistent with par-ents' values and beliefs. Parents begin to teach their children about the political world early in the child's life. They transfer feelings about such concepts as authority, freedom, democracy, and racial prejudice to their children in both formal and informal ways. By standing at attention during the playing of the national anthem or attending a Memorial Day service, parents are informally communicating important values about politics. Telling children that skin color should not affect how to think about a particular person or explaining why it is import-ant to vote in an election are formal ways political information is communicated.

These early formal and informal cues from parents have a long-term and lasting impact on a child's political socialization. Over the years, researchers have found that children whose parents are more involved in politics tend to be more involved in politics themselves. The transference of party identification from parent to child is also significant. Children who grow up in homes where parents regard politics as important also tend to regard politics as

political socialization The process by which an individual acquires values, beliefs, and opinions about politics.

primacy tendency The theory that impressions acquired while an individual is younger are likely to be more influential and longer lasting.

agents of political socialization Factors that have a significant impact on an individual's socialization to politics.

A father teaches his son to appreciate the values associated with Independence Day.

iStock.com/EpicStockMedia

Competitors in the National High School Mock Trial Championship.

Grade school children reciting the national anthem in class.

important throughout their lives. Because children generally want to be like their parents, the many cues, both formal and informal, that they receive from their parents are a strong influence on the formation of political orientation.

FRIENDS AND PEER GROUPS

As children grow older, they begin to interact with people outside of their immediate family. They seek friendships with others and show a desire to get along in social groups. Children acquire a great deal of new political learning through their friends and associates, as well as from the social groups that they join. Often, the values, beliefs, and opinions of social peers are the same as or similar to those of the family, so friends and peers reinforce what is learned from parents. For example, wealthy people tend to live together in particular neighborhoods, and so as children from wealthy families find friends and peers, they are likely to find people who have been socialized by their parents in ways similar to themselves.

By the fifth or sixth grade, children become cognitively equipped to better understand the world of politics. Whereas previous learning tends to be based on unquestioned acceptance of what is being communicated, young adults have the ability to critically analyze new information. This cognitive skill development comes at a time in life (young adolescence) when friends and peer groups are particularly influential. Thus the desire to get along and to form social relationships has an important influence on political learning at this point in life.

THE SCHOOLS

Part of the curriculum in many school systems across the United States focuses on the development of political values, such as respect for authority, the legitimacy of our political institutions, patriotism, and capitalism. Classes in civic education and American government, the daily morning pledge of allegiance to the flag, and pictures of American presidents are just some of the mechanisms by which schools act as an agent of socialization.

Schools serve as an important mechanism for the positive development of attitudes about basic American democratic values, thus promoting general positive attitudes about the legitimacy of the democratic system. Research conducted by David Easton and his colleagues in the 1950s and 1960s demonstrated that schools promoted a positive affective attachment to the concept of "democracy" by the third grade.[16] During the early grades, children acquire beliefs regarding a citizen's role in politics—obeying laws, voting, and paying attention to political events.

Political socialization from the school is not limited to elementary and high school. The college experience also has an important socializing effect on citizens' political development. College graduates tend to be more likely to vote and participate in politics, are more likely to follow news and political campaigns, and are better able to understand the political world in which they live. The effects of formal education, even beyond the specific civics education curriculum of the earlier grades, make an important positive contribution to an individual's political socialization.

THE MEDIA

Americans spend a great deal of time accessing news information and being entertained by the mass media. It is not surprising, then, that the media act as an important agent of political socialization as well. Information that citizens glean from media news coverage about political events and political campaigns has an impact on their values, beliefs, and opinions. Research has shown that heavy users of the news media are more politically informed than lighter users;[17] they are also more supportive of basic American values, such as individualism, equality, and free speech rights.

The media's impact as a socialization agent extends beyond the provision of news information. Entertainment television, the movies, talk radio, and other media forms also inspire various types of political learning. Studies have shown, for example, that entertainment television tends to promote negative stereotypes of women and minorities, which may reinforce negative attitudes about race or affirmative action. Use of internet websites and blogs may also help shape a person's political outlook.

Social networking sites are newer and constitute a medium that may socialize people in a way like no other medium. Social network users can select whether to allow or shut out those who want to communicate with them. The audience for each user is a familiar one. A user's network of friends is likely to be more trusted, more connected, and more likely to be open and receptive to others' views. Some research shows strong and positive relationships between social media use and youth political engagement.[18] As a result, social networking has the potential to play an important role in the political socialization of younger generations. This is significant considering that a recent Pew Center survey found that more than one-third of social network users around the world use this medium to express political views.[19]

RELIGION

Throughout American history, religious organizations have played an important role in the political socialization process. The values of individualism and hard work, based on the Protestant work ethic, were important influences in establishing a capitalist economy and continue to underpin economic policy in the United States. These values continue to influence the socialization process. More recently, the Christian-based fundamentalist movement has utilized religious teaching to influence opinions about political issues. Also, the Catholic Church's opposition to abortion affects many Catholics' position on that issue.

10-5 HOW IS PUBLIC OPINION MEASURED?

When Americans think about the term *public opinion* in contemporary politics, they often focus on the results of public opinion polls. A public opinion poll is a method of measuring the opinions of a large group of people by selecting a subset of the larger group, asking them a set of questions, and generalizing the findings to the larger group.

Public opinion polls are not the only way that public opinion in America is either expressed or understood, but polls have become the most obvious and important instrument for gauging public opinion. Polls provide information that elected leaders use in making public policy, thus providing an important way for public sentiment to influence public policy. Polls have also become a centerpiece of elections, used both by the candidates to shape a winning strategy and by journalists to provide news coverage of campaigns.

public opinion poll A method of measuring the opinions of a large group of people by asking questions of a subset of the larger group and then generalizing the findings to the larger group.

Polling has become a huge industry in the United States. To the public, the most visible polls are those that are regularly conducted by media organizations, asking Americans what they think about a variety of topics, such as whom they plan to vote for in an upcoming election, how they rate the job the president is doing, how they feel about the condition of the economy, and many other topics. Media polls are conducted with the purpose of broadcasting results as news stories. However, the polling industry extends far beyond media polls. Candidates at all levels conduct polls to identify strategies for waging a successful election campaign. Federal, state, and local government agencies conduct polls to evaluate the successes and failures of public programs. Interest groups conduct polls to promote their agendas.

Even though polls have come to play an important and visible role in American politics, the manner in which they are conducted is often misunderstood, and questions about their accuracy are often raised. What makes a poll "scientific"? How is it possible to interview 1,000 Americans and conclude how more than 200 million Americans think? How can two polls be conducted on the same topic and produce different findings? An understanding of polling techniques can help answer these questions.

THE HISTORY OF POLITICAL POLLING

The immediate predecessor to modern scientific polling in the United States dates back to the 1824 presidential campaign. Newspapers such as the *Boston Globe*, *New York Herald*, and *Harrisburg Pennsylvanian* attempted to gauge voter attitudes about the presidential candidates and predict the election outcome that year by conducting what has come to be known as the straw poll. A straw poll gathers the opinions of people who are conveniently available in a particular gathering place. (Today, many refer to these polls as "convenience" polls.) Back in 1824, the newspapers sent "counters" to public places (such as taverns and public meetings) to ask patrons and attendees whom they planned to vote for in the upcoming election. Newspaper publishers quickly found a hearty appetite among readers for stories that attempted to predict the outcome of political races—an appetite modern media executives continue to find quite strong today.

Early straw polls assumed that the accuracy of polls was based on the total number of respondents included in each poll. The larger the number of respondents, the more accurate the results, so it was thought. Straw polls remained the basic methodology for conducting polls for more than a century.[20]

By the early 1930s, the most famous national straw poll was the *Literary Digest* poll. In addition to conducting straw polls on policy issues, this poll correctly predicted the winners of the 1920, 1924, 1928, and 1932 presidential elections. The *Literary Digest* conducted its polls by mailing ballots to millions of people. Mailing addresses were obtained from the *Digest's* own readership lists as well as telephone directories and automobile registration lists. The *Digest* assumed its accuracy in predicting election outcomes was based on the large number of ballots that it counted from voters across the country.

In the 1936 election between Franklin Roosevelt and Alfred Landon, the *Literary Digest* collected ballots from more than 2 million people and confidently predicted that Landon would receive 55 percent of the vote, Roosevelt would get 41 percent, and the remaining 4 percent would go to Union Party candidate William Lemke. The actual election results stunned the *Literary Digest* and its many readers. Roosevelt won the election with a whopping 61 percent of the popular vote. Landon garnered 36.5 percent, whereas Lemke won less than 2 percent. The missed projection put the *Literary Digest* out of business.

This widely publicized missed call by the *Literary Digest* is explained by the faulty assumption of the straw-poll methodology, that is, the assumption that the greater the number of respondents, the more accurate the poll. The number of interviews in a poll is only one of a number of factors that affect poll accuracy. In 1936, the United States was still fighting the effects of the Great Depression, when many Americans had difficulty making ends meet. Those Americans with telephones, automobiles, and subscriptions to the *Literary Digest* (the sources of the mailing addresses for the ballots) tended to be wealthier, less affected by the Depression, and disproportionately less likely to support the liberal economic policies of FDR's New Deal.

straw poll An unscientific poll that gathers the opinions of people who are conveniently available in a gathering place, such as a shopping center.

At the time, the *Literary Digest* debacle was aptly explained by several researchers who had already begun to conduct polls with more accurate methodologies. Chief among these was Dr. George Gallup, who was applying probability sampling methods to the polls he conducted. During the 1936 campaign, Gallup argued that the *Literary Digest* methodology was producing faulty results. His cries fell on many deaf ears until after the election, when his advice sowed the seeds for a healthy polling industry based on more scientific methods. However, his scientific methods of polling would quickly become adopted as standards of the polling industry in the decades to come.

SCIENTIFIC SAMPLING

The polling procedures popularized by Gallup in the aftermath of the 1936 election relied on the principles of probability theory and focused on the sampling of the population under study.[21] A *sample* is a subgroup of people from a population who are studied for the purpose of learning something about the whole population. Based on the laws of probability, it is possible to draw a sample from a population, administer a set of questions to those in the sample, and understand something about the entire population, within a known level of error.

A scientific sample is one that uses probability theory as a guide to selecting people from the population who will compose the sample. Random selection of respondents in the sample is key to achieving a scientific, or representative, sample. *Random sampling* is achieved by giving each possible respondent in the population a known chance of being selected in the sample. There are a number of ways of achieving a random sample.

The polls projected Thomas Dewey would defeat President Harry Truman in 1948. The polls were wrong, but they led many newspapers across the country to prematurely project Truman's defeat as they went to press.

W. Eugene Smith / The LIFE Picture Collection / Getty Images

UNSCIENTIFIC POLLS

In a scientific poll, the results of the poll are generalizable to a population that is represented by the sample of people who are interviewed. Unscientific polls differ from scientific ones in that the sample of people who are interviewed is not representative of any group beyond those who register their opinion. There are many examples of unscientific polls in politics. What makes a poll unscientific is the way respondents are selected for the sample. If the vast majority of people in a population are given a chance of being sampled, then the poll is scientific. If not, then the sample represents nothing beyond itself. In an unscientific sample, some individuals in the population have no chance of being included. Many unscientific polls are conducted even today. A good example is the use of Twitter polls, which allow people to weigh in on a variety of questions posed by other people on Twitter. These polls are unscientific because only those people who are viewing the tweets have an opportunity to respond. Email surveys conducted by CNN.com and ESPN.com are similarly unscientific surveys. The sample of people who respond is not representative of any group beyond the respondents themselves. Other examples of unscientific polls include the following:

- **Log-in polls.** A poll question pops up as you enter your computer's web browser with the question: Do you think Elizabeth Warren would make a good president? Click here for "yes" or click here for "no." Many services, such as Yahoo! and MSN, include questions such as these on their home page and then present a tally of the results. This type of poll is an unscientific one because only those people who click on the browser and decide to take the time to answer the question have their opinion registered. Those who don't have a computer (e.g., poorer and older people), those who don't have

scientific sample A randomly selected subgroup drawn from a population using probability theory.

unscientific poll A poll in which the sample of people interviewed is not representative of any group beyond those who register their opinion.

The Presidential Honeymoon

When President Donald Trump took the oath of office to become the nation's 45th chief executive, he enjoyed a level of support (near 45 percent) that, although hardly overwhelming, was likely to stand as among the highest recorded during his first term in office. The "presidential honeymoon period" refers to the early portion of a new president's term in office when public opinion tends to rally in support of the new chief executive. Despite partisan differences, Americans offer large-scale support with the hope that the new president might successfully move the nation in a positive direction. The honeymoon period generally reflects higher-than-normal approval ratings from Americans as he is given the benefit of the doubt as his term commences. Generally, this translates into initial policy successes.

The Gallup Organization has been measuring presidential approval from the start through the end of each president's term since Harry Truman became president in 1945. From Truman through Obama, that's 13 presidents in all. Figure 10-3 shows the "honeymoon" approval rating (i.e., the approval rating as the new president took office) as well as the "overall average" approval rating through the presidents' full term in office.

FIGURE 10-3

Presidential Approval Rating

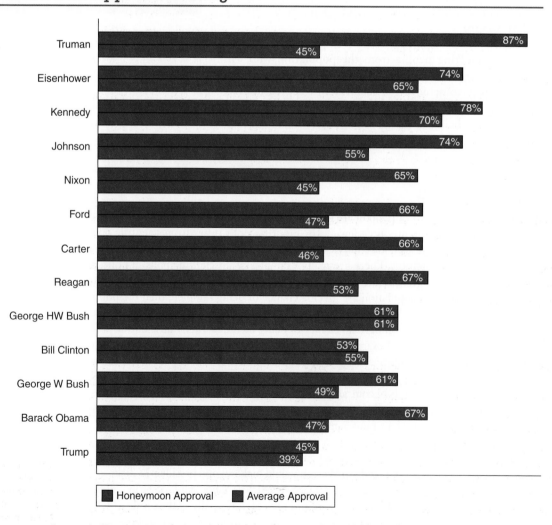

Source: www.gallup.com/poll/124922/presidential-job-approval-center.aspx.

internet access, and those who are less interested in politics have no chance or far fewer chances of being selected for such a poll. The results of those polls represent nothing more than the people who answer the poll question.

- **SLOPs, or self-selected listener opinion polls.** Television and radio news/talk shows sometimes conduct polls during the course of a broadcast by offering an 800 or 900 phone number for registered listeners to call and express their opinion on some topic. SLOPs are also known as "call-in" polls. These polls are unscientific because only those people who happen to be tuned in to the broadcast have any opportunity to be included in the sample.

- **CRAPs, or computerized response audience polling.** This kind of poll is often used by local news organizations. Telecommunications equipment places a call, and automated voice systems ask the poll questions. Respondents are asked to use the keypad of their telephone to register their answers to the questions. The extremely high rate of refusal (e.g., most people hang up when they hear the automated voice) renders them highly unscientific.

- **Intercept polls.** Have you ever been in a shopping mall when someone with a clipboard comes up to you and asks if you would answer some questions? If so, you've been solicited to participate in an intercept poll (i.e., an interviewer "intercepted" you). Respondents in such polls are conveniently selected into the sample because they are spotted by the interviewer. Because people who are at shopping malls or other public places are not representative of all people, this is regarded as an unscientific type of poll.

The *Literary Digest* mishap highlights the problem with unscientific samples—those people who have no chance of being included in the sample may be very different from those who are included. Voters who had no car or published telephone number had no chance of being selected in the *Literary Digest* sample described earlier. Even though the total number of people in the sample was quite high (more than 2 million), it was not representative of the population of voters because poorer people had little to no chance of being included in the sample.

PSEUDO-POLLS

Recently, some unscrupulous political campaigns and political action committees (PACs) have been disguising themselves as pollsters for the purpose of planting messages with voters rather than measuring public opinion. Some of these campaigners or PAC members present themselves as pollsters for the purpose of fund-raising as well. These phone calls have come to be known as pseudo-polls. As the term implies, there is no polling going on with a pseudo-poll. Pretending to be pollsters, callers often contact tens of thousands of voters and ask hypothetical (i.e., untrue) questions about their political opponents, such as "Did you happen to know that John Smith is reported to have beaten his wife in the past? Does this make you any less likely to support him in his race for senator?" Respondents to the call believe they are being interviewed by a legitimate polling firm and take away from the conversation a contrived and false message about a political candidate. This type of pseudo-poll is called a "push poll" because the intention of the call is to "push," or influence, people to vote a particular way.

pseudo-poll Phone calls from members of political campaigns or PACs who present themselves as pollsters for the purpose of planting messages with voters rather than measuring public opinion.

Another type of pseudo-poll is referred to as "FRUGing," or fund-raising under the guise of polling. This is an unethical practice that tricks people into thinking they are being polled by a legitimate organization, when they are really being set up for a fund-raising attempt. "SUGing," or selling under the guise of polling, is a pseudo-poll that engages in telemarketing. The individual—who will ultimately receive a sales pitch at the end of the call—believes that she or he is answering a legitimate poll.

SAMPLE SIZE

A fundamental characteristic of a scientific public opinion poll is the nature of the procedures used to draw a sample from the population. The size of the sample is also a factor in poll quality. Sampling error is the term used to indicate the amount of error in the poll that results from interviewing a sample of people rather than the whole population under study. Sampling error is largely a function of sample size: the larger the sample size, the less sampling error with the poll. However, there is a law of diminishing returns associated with increasing the size of the sample.

For example, a national scientifically drawn sample of 200 Americans has a sampling error of about +/–7 percent at the 95 percent level of confidence. This means that with a sample of 200, chances are 95 in 100 that the sample will produce results within 7 points above or below the survey result. By increasing the sample size by 400 respondents, from 200 to 600, the sampling error is reduced to +/–4 percent. An additional 600 respondents in the sample, bringing the sample size to 1,200, reduces the sampling error to +/–3 percent.

Media organizations that report poll findings often attempt to convey information about the poll to help the reader/audience understand the sampling error associated with the results. Typically, a news report on a poll will include a statement like this: "The survey was conducted by telephone with a random sample of 1,200 American adults. Sampling error for the survey is +/–3 percent at the 95 percent level of confidence."

What does this statement mean? Suppose the poll found that 45 percent of the respondents approved of the job that Donald Trump was doing as president. The statement indicates that there was a "random sample" of American adults. This means that the poll was a scientific poll and the results can be generalized to the full American adult public.

With any scientific poll, there is sampling error, and probability theory allows us to calculate what the sampling error might be. This calculation is thus expressed as a "confidence interval," or range, which is reported to be +/–3 percent of the poll result (or a 6-point range). The level of confidence typically reported is at the "95 percent level of confidence" (meaning that 95 out of 100 similarly conducted polls would produce results in this range). Thus, what the statement says, then, is that we can be 95 percent confident that the approval rating for President Trump is somewhere between 48 and 42 percent.

In addition to random selection and sample size, the quality of the sample is affected by "nonresponse" error. Once a sample is selected, it is necessary to contact and conduct interviews with those in the sample. Rarely is it possible to obtain an interview with 100 percent of those sampled. Some people refuse to be interviewed, some are not home when contacts are made, and others screen their phone calls. Nonresponse is problematic when those who do not respond tend to answer the questions differently than those who do respond. The goal is to achieve as high a response to the poll as possible in order to limit possible nonresponse error.

Modern-day scientific polls of Americans and voters typically use a probability technique known as random-digit dialing (RDD) to obtain scientific telephone samples. RDD uses known information about telephone area codes and exchanges and randomly assigns the last four digits to these. RDD sampling, however, only covers landline telephones. Pollsters using RDD now generally supplement their RDD samples with randomly selected cell phone numbers so that the sampling adequately reflects the growing number of Americans who use cell phones exclusively.

sampling error The amount of error in a poll that results from interviewing a sample of people rather than the whole population under study; the larger the sample, the less the sampling error.

random-digit dialing (RDD) A probability technique for scientific telephone polling that randomly assigns the last four digits to known information about telephone area codes and exchanges.

ASKING QUESTIONS ON POLLS

Accurate and reliable polls require not only scientific sampling procedures but also significant attention to the way in which polling questions are asked. The way in which a question is worded can have a large impact on the type of answers that are given by survey respondents. Consider the following example of a question asked on a national survey conducted by the Roper Organization in 1993: "Does it seem possible or does it seem impossible to you that the Nazi extermination of the Jews never happened?" More than one in five respondents to the poll indicated that he or she thought it was possible that the Holocaust never happened. The results from this question led to a series of news stories expressing concern that nearly one-quarter of the American public questioned the reality of the Holocaust. However, researchers noted an important problem with the wording of the question; namely, it included a double negative. It is difficult for respondents, particularly in a telephone interview (where they are not looking at the words of the question), to interpret what it means to "seem impossible" that something "never happened." The confusing question led to the exaggerated survey result. To test the notion that the question was confusing, the Gallup organization instead asked this question in a 1994 survey: "In your opinion, did the Holocaust definitely happen, probably happen, probably not happen, or definitely not happen?" In this form of the question, only 2 percent said that the Holocaust probably did not happen, and 0 percent said that it definitely did not happen.

Another example of how wording can influence the responses to a question involves two questions, on separate surveys, intended to measure attitudes about the legality of flag-burning. A CBS/*New York Times* poll asked, "Should burning or destroying the American flag as a form of political protest be legal or should it be against the law?" Fourteen percent said it should be legal and 83 percent said it should be against the law. A Gallup Poll asked the question this way: "The Supreme Court ruled that burning the American flag, though highly offensive, is protected under the free speech guarantee of the First Amendment to the Constitution. Do you agree or disagree?" Thirty-eight percent agreed that flag-burning should be legal based on this question—fully 24 percentage points higher than what was found with the CBS/*New York Times* question. In this case, the context in which Gallup framed the question—that the Supreme Court said flag-burning was legal based on the First Amendment—produced the different result.

Many polls conducted in the United States are intended to provide information for public consumption. These polls are referred to as "public polls." The *USA Today*/CNN/Gallup Poll and the *New York Times*/CBS Poll are just a few of the organizations that regularly conduct polling intended for public consumption.

Because there are so many polling organizations, people often have a hard time ascertaining the quality of a poll. The National Council on Public Polls (NCPP) is an association of organizations that regularly conduct public polls. Members of NCPP have articulated the following list of items that should be disclosed about any poll that is released publicly, as a way to help the poll consumer evaluate the quality of the poll:

- The name of the organization that sponsored or paid for the poll
- The dates of interviewing
- The method for obtaining the interviews (e.g., telephone, email, in-person)
- A definition of the population that was sampled
- The size of the sample (i.e., the number of interviews conducted)
- The size and description of subsamples, if the poll relies primarily on less than the total sample
- The complete wording of questions on which the poll results are based
- The percentages from the poll on which conclusions are based

Are Minority Voters Counted in Exit Polls?

Political pollsters aim to follow rules for scientific polls, which include specifications on sampling so that results can be generalizable to the general public. Unfortunately, traditional polling sometimes provides results that may be more generalizable to the national white population than to the wider population, which includes significant numbers of racial and ethnic minorities. Professor Gary Segura of the University of California, Los Angeles, has cautioned the news media and the public to be especially wary of the National Exit Poll in particular, as it may not accurately capture the minority vote.[22] Dr. Segura urges that reporters raise three different questions when presented with exit polls of Latinos and other minority populations:

1. *How do the pollsters select the precincts for surveys?* Segura warns that traditional exit polls have selected precincts that do not have sizeable racial/ethnic minority populations.
2. *What share of these surveys are done in the respondents' native language?* Immigrant-based groups, such as Latinos and Asians, include some foreign-born individuals who prefer to be interviewed in their dominant language. Yet the traditional pollsters generally rely on English.

3. *How reflective is the exit poll of the true population?* Segura warns that traditional exit polls generally overrepresent minority populations that are more middle-class and highly educated.

For Critical Thinking and Discussion

1. Have you ever questioned the results of national exit polls that were disseminated to the general public?
2. What are the ramifications of national exit polls that provide results that misrepresent the racial and ethnic minority vote?

iStock.com / shank_ali

A pollster going door-to-door asking questions.

10-6 INTERPRETING PUBLIC OPINION DATA

Understanding public opinion requires attention not only to the scientific aspects of sampling and the wording of questions but also to the analysis and interpretation of the results of a poll. In assessing results, analysts are concerned with three important characteristics of public opinion data: direction, intensity, and continuity.[23]

To understand the direction of public opinion, the analyst seeks to find which position or preference a majority of people hold as their opinion. On most topics, there are two possible directions in which public opinion might lean—a positive direction or a negative direction. For example, with respect to presidential approval, respondents might either approve or disapprove of the job the president is doing. Similarly, the public might either trust or distrust their political leaders, or they might support or oppose a proposal for a policy that makes it more difficult to buy a handgun. On any given opinion question, direction is a basic characteristic that the analyst seeks to gauge.

Intensity is also an important characteristic of public opinion. Often, the analyst seeks not only to find the direction of opinion but also to determine how strongly or how committed the public feels about the opinion that it holds. For example, the public can be asked how strongly or mildly they agree or disagree with a statement.

direction (of public opinion) A tendency toward a particular preference, usually (though not always) characterized as either positive or negative.

intensity (of public opinion) The degree of strength or commitment the public feels about the opinion it holds.

Continuity is a third important characteristic of public opinion. Political preferences may remain very stable over time, they may gradually change, or they may fluctuate wildly over short periods of time. Continuity (or "changeability," its opposite) is often an important dimension of public opinion. The presidential approval rating is often analyzed from the context of the continuity/change dimension. When major political events occur, we often see change. Figure 10-4 shows the changing views of Americans on their worry about global warming. In 2017, 42 percent of Americans polled by Gallup believed that yes, global warming will pose a serious threat to themselves or their way of life in their lifetime, which is up from 25 percent in 1997.

Public opinion plays an important role in any system of government. Even authoritarian regimes such as the French government under King Louis XVI in the late eighteenth century, the Soviet Union in the late twentieth century, and the Egyptian dictatorship of Hosni Mubarak in 2011 were susceptible to being overthrown by the forces of the popular will. But in a democratic society, public opinion is freely expressed and willingly heeded by those running the government. In contemporary American politics, there are a variety of ways in which public opinion may be expressed. Presidents have learned that public opinion can change drastically over the course of their term in office, keeping chief executives and other public officials continuously accountable to the popular will. In 2018 President Trump's deteriorating approval rating significantly curbed his ability to achieve legislative goals. Modern technology and the advancement of social science research have enabled political scientists, journalists, political candidates, and elected leaders to measure accurately and understand better not only what public opinion is but also how and why it changes. Modern presidents have the resources of scientific public opinion polls at their disposal and use them quite extensively. But although the scientific opinion poll is a modern phenomenon, the importance of public opinion has always been central to the life of American politics.

continuity (in public opinion) A tendency for political preferences to remain generally stable over time.

FIGURE 10-4

Concern over Global Warming Posing a Serious Threat in One's Lifetime

Do you think that global warming will pose a serious threat to you or your way of life in your lifetime?

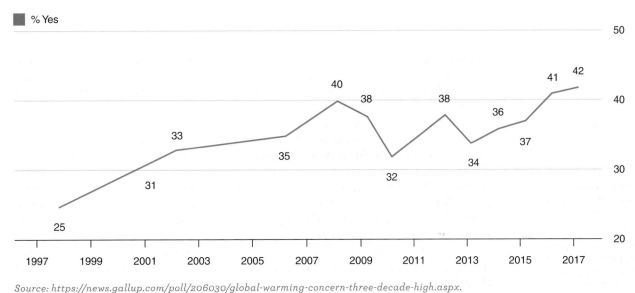

Source: https://news.gallup.com/poll/206030/global-warming-concern-three-decade-high.aspx.

Using Social Networking to Express Your Political Opinions

The use of social networking has spread around the world like wildfire, and young adults with a college education are one of the largest demographics to adopt it. Many social networkers are making use of this medium to express their political views. Certainly, social networks like Facebook and Twitter provide a unique forum for the expression of public opinion: a familiar audience, a selective audience, an audience more likely to take expressed views seriously, and an audience that can opt to engage in the conversation or express its approval or disapproval of the opinion. As social networking grows in popularity, it is certain that this format for political expression will become even more important.

However, many people feel that social media is an especially negative venue for political discussions. A 2016 Pew Research Center Survey found there is a range of opinion about whether social media political interactions can be viewed as stressful/frustrating or interesting/informative. In fact, at least 37 percent of social media users say they are "worn out" by the amount of political content they see in their feeds. As people increasingly use social networking to express their political opinions, we will have to navigate all the potential benefits with the potential negative repercussions to our political discourse.

For Critical Thinking and Discussion

1. Have you ever expressed your opinion about politics on Facebook, Twitter, or another social networking site? If so, did you get feedback from your friends? Was the feedback positive or negative?
2. Do your friends often express their political opinions? How much do you think your own opinions are influenced by what your friends say on social networking sites?

FIGURE 10-5

Political Content and Social Media Use

More than one-third of social media users are worn out by the amount of political content they encounter

% of social media users who say they... about politics on social media

Like seeing lots of political posts and discussions — 20%

Are worn out by how many political posts and discussions they see — 37%

Don't feel strongly one way or another — 41%

When discussing politics on social media with people they disagree with, % of social media users who say these things

They find it to be...

Interesting and informative — 35%

Stressful and frustrating — 59%

They have... than they thought

More in common politically — 29%

Less in common politically — 64%

Source: Pew Research Center, "More than One-Third of Social Media Users Are Worn Out by the Amount of Political Content They Encounter," Washington, DC, October 24, 2016, http://www.pewinternet.org/2016/10/25/the-political-environment-on-social-media/pi_2016-10-25_politics-and-social-media_0-01/.

Summary

10-1 Public Opinion in American Politics

- Public opinion plays an important role in ensuring that citizens' beliefs are embraced in a democracy; public opinion also plays a tactical role for political officials, influencing the outcome of many important political battles.
- Public opinion may be expressed through a variety of means, including public opinion polls, voting, free speech and assembly, political blogging, the support of particular candidates for political office, and the contribution of time and effort to interest groups. The news media also serve as an outlet for public opinion, whether by publishing articles about important individuals' opinions or by sponsoring their own public opinion polls on politics and policy issues. Still, many members of the public prefer to express their opinions directly to elected officials through letters, phone calls, or emails. Blogs have become an increasingly popular way for individuals to express their views on issues.

10-2 The Levels of Public Opinion

- Public opinion exists at its most abstract level in the form of values and beliefs; it exists in a more specific form through political orientations, which translate values and beliefs into a systematic way of assessing political realities, and in an even more specific way in the form of particular political preferences.

10-3 How Informed Is Public Opinion?

- Many noted scholars in the early and mid-twentieth century argued that the public lacks the necessary knowledge for their opinions to provide value. Contemporary surveys continue to confirm that the public maintains a low interest in politics generally, and that most Americans are uninformed about basic political facts. By contrast, numerous other scholars, beginning with V. O. Key Jr. in the 1960s, have argued that regardless of its specific knowledge of politics, the public as a whole behaves quite rationally over the long haul, expressing stable opinions that move (if at all) in logical and meaningful directions based on people's values and beliefs.

10-4 How Does Public Opinion Form?

- Individuals' opinions are shaped in part by political socialization; impressions formed during youth often last well into adulthood. Opinions are also shaped by demographics (race, ethnicity, gender, age, etc.), family members, friends and peer groups, schools, the media, and religious organizations.

10-5 How Is Public Opinion Measured?

- Public opinion polls measure the opinions of a large group of people by selecting a subset of the larger group and then generalizing the findings from the small group back to the large group. To ensure that the poll is scientific, the sample must be chosen randomly using probability theory through techniques such as random-digit dialing. Unscientific polls can produce misleading results.
- The way in which questions on a poll are worded is also an important factor in assessing the quality of a poll. Misleading questions, whether intentional or unintentional, may produce faulty results.

10-6 Interpreting Public Opinion Data

- The proper interpretation of public opinion data requires attention to the direction, intensity, and continuity of the public's expressions. With regard to the third characteristic, political preferences may fluctuate wildly over short periods of time.

Key Terms

agents of political socialization (p. 209)
conservative ideology (p. 205)
continuity (in public opinion) (p. 219)
direction (of public opinion) (p. 218)
intensity (of public opinion) (p. 218)
liberal ideology (p. 205)
political ideology (p. 205)
political orientations (p. 205)
political preferences (p. 206)
political socialization (p. 209)

primacy tendency (p. 209)
pseudo-poll (p. 215)
public opinion (p. 203)
public opinion poll (p. 211)
random-digit dialing (RDD) (p. 216)
sampling error (p. 216)
scientific sample (p. 213)
straw poll (p. 212)
unscientific polls (p. 213)
values and beliefs (p. 204)

11

INTEREST GROUPS

Members of the AARP (American Association of Retired People) participate in a rally to encourage Congress and the president to expand Medicare benefits.

THE U.S. POLITICAL SYSTEM provides numerous opportunities for people to influence public policy. Voting in elections to choose leaders offers one such opportunity. The guarantees of freedom of speech to speak one's mind about political issues and freedom of the press to critically assess issues and leaders' performance are others. Public opinion polls are yet another mechanism that solicits input from the masses. But perhaps the most natural—and arguably the most influential—form of public input arrives by way of the activities of interest groups. Interest groups today play a central role in making laws, regulating industries, and even influencing court decisions. The vast influence of interest groups makes them a target of criticism, particularly when scandals emerge. Thus, a persistent issue regarding interest-group activities is just how far we should allow such groups to press their interests. At what point do interest groups become a negative force in democracy? This chapter assesses the workings and performance of American politics from the perspective of interest-group activity. What are interest groups? How do they work? Who belongs to them? Which ones are more and less powerful? How do they exert influence on what government does?

The Political Power of the NRA

The National Rifle Association (NRA) has demonstrated time and time again how a powerful interest group can impact public policy, even against the currents of public opinion. Its political work in the1960s and again over the past decade are examples of how a well-organized interest group created very real policy consequences.

Then

After the gun assassinations of President John F. Kennedy in 1963, civil rights leader Martin Luther King Jr. in April of 1968, and presidential candidate Robert Kennedy in June of 1968, many congressional leaders felt the time was right for new gun control legislation. A Gallup poll conducted at the time found that as many as half of all Americans explicitly favored the banning of all handguns, whereas just 44 percent opposed such a law. Maryland Senator Joseph Tydings, a personal friend and colleague of Senator Robert Kennedy, took Kennedy's place on NBC's *Meet the Press* a few days after the assassination to announce that he would be introducing a new bill into Congress, the Firearms Registration and Licensing Act. If passed, the bill would have mandated the registration of all guns and created licensing requirements to keep guns out of the hands of criminals. The reaction to Tydings's bill was initially favorable, winning public praise from the Kennedy family as well as many commentators. The bill made it out of committee and onto the Senate floor. Then, as Tydings later lamented, "the NRA (National Rifle Association) got to work." The NRA, under the direction of its president at the time, Franklin Orth, used its vast resources to lobby Congress and engage in a public campaign that eventually not only defeated the bill in the Senate, but also defeated Tydings in his 1970 bid for reelection. At least for the time being, the powerful NRA had thwarted any measure to control the registration and licensing of guns.

Franklin Orth, president of the National Rifle Association, in 1969.

Dave Buresh / Denver Post / Getty Images

Now

In the wake of the December 2012 shootings of 20 children and staff at the Sandy Hook Elementary School in Newtown, Connecticut, public opinion polls showed that Americans were ready for new gun control laws. The Newtown event followed the 2011 gunning down of five people at an Arizona shopping center; included among the victims was Congressperson Gabby Giffords, who suffered a chronic brain injury in the incident. After the Newtown shooting, a Gallup poll found that 58 percent of Americans favored stricter gun control laws and nearly 9 in 10 favored stricter recordkeeping requirements for gun purchasers. California Senator Diane Feinstein took to the airwaves on *Meet the Press* a few days after the Newtown incident to try to convince Americans that new control measures were needed to curb the senseless gun violence. Several weeks later she introduced into Congress the Assault Weapons Ban of 2013, which would have stopped the sale, manufacturing, and transfer of military-style assault weapons such as the ones used in the Newtown murders. The bill won praise from the President, the families of many of the Newtown victims, and Rep. Giffords herself. The tide of public opinion and support from political elites, however, proved no match for the powerful NRA. Just a few months after the bill was introduced into Congress, it died in the Senate. A well-orchestrated public

Bloomberg / Getty Images

Wayne LaPierre, the current CEO of the National Rifle Association, speaks at the 2019 annual meeting of his organization.

(Continued)

information campaign by the NRA under the direction of Wayne LaPierre, along with strong lobbying efforts stopped the gun ban legislation in its tracks. Even in the wake of more recent shootings such as in 2018 at Parkland Elementary School in Florida, Congress has passed no new anti-gun laws.

For Critical Thinking and Discussion

1. Why do you think the NRA has been so successful in pressing for its agenda?
2. If a large segment of the public favors gun regulations, why do they find it so hard to match the NRA's organization and lobbying efforts?

11-1 PLURALISM AND THE INTEREST-GROUP SYSTEM

An influential form of public input into policy-making arrives by way of the activities of interest groups. James Madison, in Federalist No. 10, admonished that "the latent causes of faction are thus sown in the nature of man."[1] By faction, Madison was referring to what we now term *interest group*. Madison was concerned about the potential influence of factions on the government. But at the same time, he understood that people were drawn by nature toward the organization of collective interests and the use of that organization to influence government. Madison expected that if enough interest groups vied to influence policy, they would act as checks on each other.

WHAT IS AN INTEREST GROUP?

An **interest group** (also referred to as a *pressure group* or *organized interest*) is an organization of people with shared goals that tries to influence public policy through a variety of activities. Every individual has interests, and interest groups are a mechanism for people with shared goals to protect or advance their own interests. People can try to influence government on their own—such as by calling or writing their elected representatives to voice their opinion or by voting in an election. Another way that people can influence government is by joining a group that is organized to accomplish an objective.

Senior citizens, for example, have a shared interest in securing cost-of-living adjustments (COLAs) in the Social Security system that disburses checks to them each month. Each year, the president and Congress determine the percentage rate increase in the COLA. The larger the increase, the higher will be an individual's monthly Social Security check. Each individual senior citizen might call his or her representatives in Congress to try to influence the vote for a larger COLA increase. Another way senior citizens may try to influence government is by joining and supporting the AARP (formerly the American Association of Retired Persons), an interest group that, among other activities, tries to influence government to approve large increases in the annual COLA for Social Security. AARP is large, with many resources and lobbyists to influence legislators. Although an individual citizen's call to a representative may carry some weight, it is no match for the vast resources and activities of the AARP.

Interest groups link people with government policies. The linkage created by interest groups is constitutionally protected by the First Amendment, which guarantees the people's right "to peaceably assemble, and to petition the Government for redress of grievances." People assembling in groups that carry out activities to foster group members' goals is a common activity in Washington, in the 50 state capitals, and in thousands of local governments.

Alexis de Tocqueville, a Frenchman who toured the United States in the early 1830s and observed the early workings of the U.S. political system, was struck by the extent to which group association and activity dominated the American system. In his now-classic 1835 book titled *Democracy in America*,[2] de Tocqueville praised the extent to which group activity underpins American democracy:

> The [citizen] of the United States learns from birth that he must rely on himself to combat the ills and trials of life. . . . If some obstacle blocks the public road halting . . . traffic, neighbors at

interest group An organization of people with shared goals that tries to influence public policy through a variety of activities.

once form a deliberative body; this improvised assembly produces an authority which remedies the trouble before anyone has thought of the possibility beyond that of those concerned . . . associations are formed to combat moral troubles. Public security, trade and industry, and morals and religion all provide the aims for associations in the United States. There is no end to which the human will despair of attaining by the free action of the collective power of individuals.

When a political association is allowed to form centers of action at certain important places in the country, its activity becomes greater and its influence more widespread.

More than his fellow French citizens and other Europeans that he observed, de Tocqueville found that Americans were particularly prone to organize in groups and use their associations to influence the political process.

Pluralism refers to the theory that public policy largely results from a variety of interest groups competing with one another to promote laws that benefit members of their respective groups. By contrast, majoritarianism refers to the theory that public policy is a product of what majorities of citizens prefer. Whereas the majoritarian perspective focuses on public opinion, voting results, and mass representation to describe how democracy in America actually works, the pluralist perspective suggests that in fact the majority rarely rules.

Political scientist Robert Dahl, an architect of pluralist ideas, suggested in *A Preface to Democratic Theory*[3] that the American people are represented in government primarily through interest-group activity. The products of public policy are largely a function of support for and membership in interest groups that compete for influence through activities such as lobbying, which is discussed later in this chapter. The U.S. political system, according to Dahl, offers a number of "access points" for any given group to provide input. These access points include Congress, executive branch offices, the courts, elections, and the news media. David B. Truman, another political scientist, has advanced the notion that group activity and mobilization are natural consequences of shared concerns.[4] The free and open competition among groups advances the democratic system, just as a free and open marketplace of ideas promotes the adoption of the best ideas in society.

THE PROS AND CONS OF INTEREST GROUPS

The political power of group organization for the purpose of influencing government outputs can be quite strong. "Are interest groups good or bad for American democracy?" is a question akin to the old cliché "Is the glass half full or half empty?" The answer, of course, depends on one's perspective. Madison recognized that interest groups were powerful and that they could be dangerous. But he also acknowledged that factions could not be eliminated. Channeling them into productive devices for promoting public input was a primary challenge his generation faced in framing the government.

Interest groups in America invite criticism from some circles and praise from others. Listed next are the primary arguments for the advantages and disadvantages of interest-group activity.

The Pros. Many observers today sing the praises of an interest-group system that advances the interests of the people. Their arguments in support of interest groups include the following:

- Interest groups provide all groups in society with an opportunity to win support for their ideas and positions. The vast number of interest groups represents a wide array of political opinions, economic perspectives, and social class differences.
- By their very nature, humans seek out others who have ideas similar to their own. Joining groups and working for the interests of the group are natural inclinations of citizens and should be encouraged as a method of representation in our democracy.
- The right of association is a basic right protected implicitly by the First Amendment to the U.S. Constitution, which affords individuals the right "peaceably to assemble."
- A wide array of diverse groups in society—rich and poor, urban and nonurban, male and female, northern and southern, liberal and conservative—potentially may organize and attempt to influence government. The system is fair in that it gives all groups an opportunity to compete.

pluralism The theory that public policy largely results from a variety of interest groups competing with one another to promote laws that benefit members of their respective groups.

majoritarianism The theory that public policy is a product of what majorities of citizens prefer.

Former lobbyist Jack Abramoff is a recent example of a corrupt lobbyist whose actions contribute to negative feelings about lobbying. Abramoff illegally spent millions of dollars to influence elected officials by offering them extravagant meals, vacations, and professional sporting events tickets, among other things. He was prosecuted by the federal government and eventually pled guilty to an array of charges.

The Cons. Many other observers of the U.S. political system are quite critical of the power exerted by interest groups. In *The Power Elite*, C. Wright Mills[5] characterizes interest groups as a tool of the political elite rather than a system that enables broad participation in influencing public policy. Along this line, many criticize the ability of wealthy corporations and individuals to exert disproportionate influence on government through well-financed interest-group activities. John Heinz and his colleagues argue further that the influence of interest groups is contingent on a number of factors and that their influence may be quite limited.[6] Other criticisms of interest groups include the following:

- Use of interest groups to make public policy is unfair because groups supported by the wealthy have far greater resources to promote their interests in the political system.
- Large corporations exist to maximize profits. They dominate the interest-group system and tend to be ruthless in achieving their policy goals. The interest-group system thus promotes the advancement of interests that do not always strive for the common good.

FROM YOUR PERSPECTIVE

"Before the Lecture Begins, Students from PIRG Have an Announcement . . ."

A college student solicits signatures for a PIRG petition.

If you have spent significant time on a college campus, you have probably heard about PIRG (Public Interest Research Group). PIRG is a federation of state-based public-interest groups that, in the words of its website, "stand up to powerful special interests on behalf of the American public."[7]

The PIRG model of a national campus network was proposed by public-interest advocate Ralph Nader in 1970 and now has expanded to include 30 state-based organizations.

State PIRGs are particularly active in recruiting students on college campuses. At the start of the semester, student members of PIRG ask professors for a few minutes of class time to pitch PIRG-related activities to the class. For many students, this is their first exposure to an interest group. Those who join will quickly get involved in PIRG's public-interest causes and sometimes even become interns and get course credit for the experience.

For Critical Thinking and Discussion

1. Does PIRG operate on your campus? If so, how effective has it been in influencing state legislative decisions?
2. Take a look at your campus PIRG's website or that of another campus if PIRG is not active at your institution. What positions does it advance on which issues? Do you support its lobbying efforts, or do you oppose its lobbying efforts?

- The amount of interest-group activity is so great that it has made it difficult to get things done in government. Too many groups are operating, slowing down the policy-making process to a state of gridlock in many arenas.
- Interest-group leaders are not elected, distinguishing them from many of the policy-making institutions that have been constitutionally ordained—such as Congress and the executive branch. Thus, interest-group dominance of the political system is an affront to democracy.
- Interest groups work to concentrate benefits for the few while distributing costs to the many.

11-2 INTEREST GROUPS IN ACTION

Interest groups have always played an important role in American politics. Even in the colonial period, groups such as the Sons of Liberty gathered members, collected donations, and organized protests to achieve the goal of American freedom from British taxation. The Sons of Liberty were successful in their aims because they tied their actions to the economic interests of their members. As Madison acknowledged, economic interests tend to be the type of concerns that are most salient to people and thus move them to collective action.

In 1886, the American Federation of Labor (AFL) was formed as the first broad-based national labor union. The AFL was originally established to advocate the rights of craft unions and ensure the terms of union contracts. Organized and led by Samuel Gompers for 40 years, it attracted many members and raised funds to promote laws benefiting organized labor. The AFL was the principal advocate for establishing a cabinet department, the U.S. Department of Labor, to administer labor programs. This department continues to serve as one of the largest executive departments in the nation. In the 1950s, the AFL merged with the Congress of Industrial Organizations (CIO) to create the AFL-CIO, an interest group still very active in promoting the labor agenda.

The National Association of Manufacturers (NAM) was organized in 1885 for the purpose of advancing the interests of the manufacturing businesses. Although setting protective tariffs was its core objective, the NAM also became a primary opponent of the AFL and other labor interest groups. The goals of organized labor (such as higher wages for workers, better working conditions, increased benefits, and job security) and the goals of business owners (maximizing profits) often came into conflict.

Tensions between labor and business interests intensified with the tremendous growth of the American economy beginning in the late 1800s and continued to mount as the economy expanded. Large companies, focusing on maximizing profits (which in turn appealed to shareholders), opposed laborers' demands for increased wages, better working conditions, and worker benefits. Today, labor and business interest groups continue to be among the largest and most powerful interest groups in the nation.

THE GROWTH OF INTEREST GROUPS

Perhaps the most significant factor leading to an increase in the number of interest groups has been the overall growth in government. Interest groups attempt to advance their agenda by influencing various aspects of government. As the number of government programs and agencies has expanded, along with their reach, opportunities for influencing what government does through interest-group activities have expanded as well.

The New Deal programs of the 1930s and the Great Society programs of the 1960s led to tremendous growth in the federal government and huge increases in the federal budget. Government began to assume a more active role not only in promoting its economic policies but in promoting social policies as well. In response, a vast number of interest groups formed. Both proponents and opponents of a more active government organized interest groups to advocate their views. As the number of interest groups advocating economic issues expanded, so, too, did the number of groups promoting ideological perspectives, positions on single issues, and political reforms.

Contemporary Movements for Civil Rights

We are now witnessing a new force in American politics: the proliferation of identity-based social movements that have organized to advocate for civil rights and to provide brand new avenues for increased political participation. Groups such as Black Lives Matter (BLM) and the DREAMers exemplify this phenomenon, which you can see from their two websites: blacklivesmatter.com and unitedwedream.org.

The DREAMers movement began in the early 2000s as an immigrant youth network that worked on behalf of immigrant rights. The network developed out of stalled congressional efforts to pass the Development, Relief, and Education for Alien Minors Act (the "Dream Act"), which would have provided a path to citizenship for undocumented youth brought to the United States as young children. The network eventually grew to encompass the largest youth-led organization in the country, which "runs programs to advocate for access to higher education; stops deportations of undocumented youth and their parents; and strengthens alliances and support for DREAMers at the intersection of queer and immigrant rights."[9]

BLM is a chapter-based national organization that works for black civil rights. The organization was created in 2012 following George Zimmerman's acquittal for

A Black Lives Matter rally in 2019, in Washington, DC.

the death of Trayvon Martin. The organization aims to broaden the "conversation around state violence to include all of the ways in which Black people are intentionally left powerless at the hands of the state."[10] Both movements aim to advocate for human rights and unite people in social action.

For Critical Thinking and Discussion

1. How do BLM and DREAMers differ from more traditional groups or movements?
2. Do you think these new identity-based groups can be successful advocating for political and social change? What advantages, if any, do they offer?

Although interest groups have been part of the American system since its beginning, the number of groups has increased dramatically over the past half-century. Between 1960 and 2000, the number of official associations increased by 400 percent (from 5,843 to 23,298); the total amount of lobbying spending in Washington, DC, increased from $1.45 billion in 1998 to $3.37 billion in 2017; and from 1998 through 2017 the total number of registered lobbyists in Washington, DC, increased from 10,405 to 11,551.[8] Major political developments, such as the antiwar movement, the civil rights movement, and the Watergate scandal of the Nixon administration, mobilized a better-educated mass public to become increasingly concerned about political issues. This heightened concern about social and political issues fostered a significant amount of new interest-group activity. The sophisticated use of mass-media technologies such as television, the computer, and the internet has facilitated the ability of groups to emerge and flourish.

Another factor contributing to the increase in interest-group activity has been the escalating cost of financing political campaigns. As costs have increased, interest groups have come to play a greater role in supporting political parties and the election of candidates. The Federal Election Campaign Act of 1971 placed limits on individual and corporate contributions to political campaigns. As a means of financing campaigns through alternative methods, interest groups have formed **political action committees (PACs)**, which raise money from individuals and provide a source of funding for candidates and political parties. PACs also engage in "soft money" spending on advertising and other political work independent of candidates and parties. The Supreme Court ruled in *Citizens United v. Federal Election Commission* (2010)[11] that corporations, like individuals, may make contributions to PACs. In 2012 this controversial opinion facilitated the rise of the so-called super-PACs. As we will see in Chapter 14, PACs are a source of much controversy.

IRON TRIANGLES, ISSUE NETWORKS, AND THE INFLUENCE OF GROUPS

The influence of interest groups is buoyed by the process in which public policy is created and modified. As shown in Figure 11-1, in any policy area, three key sets of actors interact to produce public policy: (1) congressional committees and subcommittees assigned to a specific policy area, (2) executive agencies of government that have the authority to administer policies in a particular area, and (3) private interest groups that have an interest in influencing that policy area. Members of congressional committees, managers of agencies, and leaders of interest groups all have vested interests in any specific policy area. As political scientist Theodore Lowi has noted, although these parties may not always agree on particular positions, they all seek to promote policies favorable to their interests, and they come to depend on one another for support and influence. Together, this network of actors dominates the development of public policies. This durable and seemingly impenetrable three-sided network has come to be known as the **iron triangle** of policy-making.[12]

The development of U.S. defense policy illustrates how iron triangles work. The armed services and defense committees and subcommittees in Congress are responsible for appropriating funds for defense contracts (e.g., for the building of new military aircraft). Members of Congress on these committees are committed to maintaining a strong national defense,

FIGURE 11-1

The Iron Triangle of Policy-Making

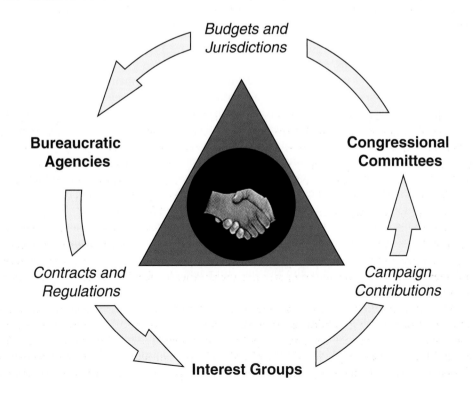

political action committee (PAC) The political arm of an interest group that promotes candidates in election campaigns primarily through financial contributions.

iron triangle A three-sided network of policy-making that includes congressional committees (and subcommittees) in a specific policy area, executive agencies with authority over that area, and private interest groups focused on influencing that area.

and they control the purse strings for developing new defense systems. Leaders in the U.S. Department of Defense are responsible for implementing defense systems under the orders of the president and rely on congressional committees to fund strong systems. Private contractors such as Pratt & Whitney (an airplane engine manufacturer) employ the engineers and researchers to design superior systems and provide valuable information to the congressional committees and the defense department.

The committees and the Department of Defense depend on Pratt & Whitney for advanced engine technologies, advice on aircraft design, and the capacity to produce cutting-edge aircraft engines. Pratt & Whitney benefits from winning federal contracts to produce defense systems. The congressional committees, Department of Defense managers, and corporate leaders and lobbyists from Pratt & Whitney are familiar with one another, depend on one another, and use one another in the development of defense systems. The iron-triangle approach to public policy-making has institutionalized the role of interest groups in the exercise of American democracy.

Although an iron triangle refers to the interdependent relationship between legislators, bureaucrats, and lobbyists in a particular policy area, it is also possible to identify a broader set of actors who all have a vested interest in an area of public policy and try to collectively influence their policy area. Political scientists have used the term issue networks to describe this broader array of actors beyond legislators, bureaucrats, and lobbyists who try to influence a particular policy area. These networks include congressional staff people, journalists or other members of the media who often report on the policy area, and researchers who have done work on and are experts in the policy area.[13]

MEMBERSHIP IN GROUPS

Many Americans belong to interest groups, and many businesses, nonprofit organizations, and public entities belong to interest groups as well. It is estimated that about four in five citizens belong to at least one interest group. Many of the more common groups Americans belong to include labor unions (e.g., the AFL-CIO, which boasts a total of about 12.7 million members), professional associations (e.g., the 240,000 physicians and medical students who belong to the American Medical Association), and organizations such as the AARP, to which many of the nation's senior citizens belong. As many as 3 million businesses across the United States belong to the U.S. Chamber of Commerce.[14]

Although the number of Americans who belong to interest groups is high, certain types of people are more likely than others to engage in interest-group activity. Americans with higher incomes and greater resources, and those who are better educated and employed in professional occupations, are much more likely to belong to groups. Those with more financial resources tend to better appreciate the utility of group membership and interest groups' impact on the political process; wealthier individuals are also more likely to have the resources to support interest-group activities. Thus, many critics of interest-group politics charge that the pluralist model of democracy favors the upper middle class and upper class of society. Because those with more resources can and do support interest groups, they are more likely to influence public policy to their financial advantage.

Various reasons have been proposed to explain why people or organizations might join and support certain interest groups. One is that they receive specific, tangible benefits from membership. These are referred to as material benefits of group membership.[15] For instance, local units of the National Education Association (NEA) work for its teacher members to win salary increases, and so the benefits of membership often produce a favorable material benefit to teachers in the form of higher wages. Many interest groups provide their members with other material benefits such as health and auto insurance discounts, magazine subscriptions, and free products.

Another reason why interest groups are appealing is the purposive benefits (or expressive benefits) of membership.[16] Purposive rewards are those that do not directly benefit the individual member but benefit society more generally. Some interest groups, for example, are committed to the goal of improving the environment and promoting policies that better protect the natural environment. The Sierra Club is one such organization that endorses

issue network The broad array of actors (beyond just the iron triangle) that try to collectively influence a policy area in which they maintain a vested interest.

material benefits (of group membership) The specific, tangible benefits individuals receive from interest-group membership, such as economic concessions, discounts on products, and so forth.

purposive benefits (of group membership) Rewards that do not directly benefit the individual member, but benefit society as a whole.

FIGURE 11-2

Donations to Interest Groups Are No Secret

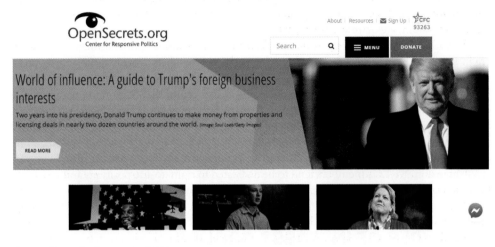

Source: Center for Responsive Politics, www.opensecrets.org.

these goals, and members of the Sierra Club receive purposive benefits from membership and support of the group's activities.

A third type of incentive for interest-group membership is the solidary benefits[17] of membership, or the satisfaction that individuals receive from interacting with like-minded individuals for a cause. Solidary rewards derive less from the interest group's goals and more from the process of interacting with others to achieve a goal. For example, a union worker who attends a labor rally to support increases in a new contract may receive satisfaction from simply being with colleagues in support of a cause.

WHAT MAKES SOME GROUPS MORE POWERFUL THAN OTHERS?

Although there are thousands of interest groups operating in the United States, some groups are more successful than others in promoting their cause and affecting public policy. There are three general characteristics of an interest group that may have significant bearing on how powerful that group's influence will be in Washington:

1. **The size of the membership.** There is, undoubtedly, power in numbers. The more members an interest group has, the more powerful that group will be. Large membership alone makes elected leaders responsive to a group's concerns. An interest group with a large number of members can increase its power and influence by convincing its members to vote for a candidate or candidates. The Christian Coalition of America (CCA) is a Christian political advocacy group that includes fundamentalists, evangelicals, Pentecostals, and many members of mainline Protestant churches. Officials of the CCA often communicate with the organization's huge membership regarding the endorsement of political candidates. Not surprisingly, the CCA attracts the attention of candidates as well as office-holders who plan on running for another term. Groups with large numbers of members also have an advantage in raising funds to support their activities. With many members, the potential for fund-raising is great. And funding goes a long way in advancing the effectiveness of interest-group activities. A good example of a group that exhibits strength through numbers is the American Farm Bureau Federation (AFBF), which boasts 4.7 million members and has proven especially effective at promoting policies that provide large subsidies and other benefits to American farmers. A bilateral trade agreement between the United States and Russia in late 2006 was a testament to AFBF influence, as it substantially expanded the export market for U.S. farmers.

> **solidary benefits (of group membership)** Satisfaction that individuals receive from interacting with like-minded individuals for a cause.

2. **The wealth of the members.** The number of members is an important indicator of the potential amount of money that interest groups might be able to raise, but just as important is the wealth of the membership. Certain interest groups enjoy a huge advantage when it comes to the average wealth of members. For example, the American Trial Lawyers Association (ATLA) is made up of trial lawyers, who, by virtue of their occupation, are quite wealthy when compared to average Americans. Thus, whereas the number of members of the ATLA is only about 60,000, the wealth of its membership and the consequent level of financial contributions from members provide sufficient resources to make it an especially powerful interest group in Washington, DC.

3. **The dedication of members to the goals of the group.** In addition to the number of members and wealth of members, groups that have a loyal following based on member commitment to the cause of the group can be a powerful resource.[18] The National Right to Life Committee (NRLC) is a good example. The NRLC organized and began to solicit members and contributions in 1973, after the *Roe v. Wade*[19] decision legalized abortion. NRLC's members tend to be dedicated to right-to-life positions and willing to contribute much time, effort, and resources to advance its pro-life agenda.

11-3 TYPES OF INTEREST GROUPS

Although interest groups represent a wide array of interests in American society, there are two basic types of interest groups: economic groups and noneconomic groups. Many groups engage in both economic and noneconomic pursuits, but most can be classified as either primarily economic or noneconomic in nature.

ECONOMIC GROUPS

Although the specific goals of different interest groups vary greatly, the vast majority of groups in America have goals that are economic in nature. Two out of every three interest groups in America are economic interest groups, or groups that exist to promote favorable economic conditions and economic opportunities for their members. Economic groups also tend to be the largest and most powerful groups because members of such groups maintain a vested personal financial stake in having the group achieve its goals.

As well as being the most numerous, economic groups also tend to be the best organized and most influential interest groups. Because economic interests are those that generally inspire more concern from businesses and citizens alike, they tend to feature greater individual involvement, commitment, resources, and organization.

There are thousands of interest groups that focus primarily on advancing the economic goals of members. These groups include private businesses, labor unions, business and industry associations, and professional associations.

Business Groups. The largest companies in the nation and the world typically maintain internal units that function as an interest group for the company. Very large companies, such as General Motors (GM) and IBM, for example, have their own interest groups. Such companies typically have wide and varied interests. GM, for example, is affected by environmental laws (tougher air pollution laws often require GM to spend more on technologies to reduce emissions from its cars), labor laws (increases in the minimum wage require higher pay for some workers), and product safety laws (increased safety standards might increase the cost of assembling a car). GM needs a well-staffed interest group to try to influence these and many other types of legislation.

Most businesses belong to associations, and often these associations engage in interest-group activities to advocate for the interests of their members. Some associations are very broad in scope, such as the U.S. Chamber of Commerce, with its 3 million members. These businesses range from small neighborhood auto mechanics to large billion-dollar financial institutions. The U.S. Chamber of Commerce seeks to broadly advance the interests of business owners.

Another type of business association is a trade association. A trade association typically focuses on one particular industry, and members of the association are drawn exclusively from

economic interest group An organized group that exists to promote favorable economic conditions and economic opportunities for its members.

trade association A business association that focuses on one particular industry, with membership drawn exclusively from that industry.

that industry. Businesses in a particular trade often face similar types of concerns, and the trade association looks out for the specific interests of a classification of businesses. For example, the American Society of Travel Agents (ASTA) is a trade association whose 24,000 member institutions include travel agencies, hotels, airlines, car rental agencies, and the like. ASTA promotes legislation and regulations favoring the travel industry.

Businesses, business associations, and trade associations have an advantage over associations and other organizations whose members are individual citizens or consumers. Businesses quickly see the advantage of joining an association, which collectively advocates for the interests of like businesses. Individuals, however, are less likely to join and contribute to an association that advocates for such things as

A California teacher participates in a strike rally in Los Angeles in January 2019. Tens of thousands of teachers in L.A. went on strike, demanding pay raises, smaller classes, and greater staffing support in the public schools.

consumer protection. Because there are so many consumers, an individual consumer is less likely to see a benefit in his or her own contribution. But because there are fewer businesses that belong to any given trade association, businesses are more likely to perceive a benefit from participating in the organization. As Mancur Olson, a well-known scholar on interest groups, put it, smaller groups are more likely to organize and associate because members can more readily see the benefits and "logic of collective action."[20] That is, people with common interests working together in groups are more effective than the same number of people working independently.

Certainly members of smaller groups are more likely to perceive direct benefits from their membership; smaller groups are also less likely to suffer from the free-rider problem. Free riders are those individuals who do not join or contribute to an interest group that is representing their interests. Thus, they enjoy the benefits of membership without paying for the costs. The free-rider problem is more common in larger groups, which may have trouble convincing individuals to contribute because of the perception that others will work to achieve the group's goal.

Labor Unions. Whereas business groups promote the interests of companies and corporations, labor unions promote the interests of American workers. Initially, labor unions emerged from the expansion of the U.S. economy in the late 1800s and early 1900s. The new technologies that resulted from the Industrial Revolution led to the rapid growth of large-scale farming and manufacturing and created many new jobs. Many business owners exploited their laborers, providing low pay, few benefits, and often poor and unsafe working conditions. Workers then organized into unions, using the threat of a strike to improve their conditions.

In the early 1940s, as many as 35 percent of workers in America were union members. Over the years, however, the percentage of union workers has declined. Today only about 13 percent of workers belong to a union. An important reason for this decline relates to changes in the type of jobs that Americans hold. Skilled and unskilled laborers are most likely to be unionized, but these types of jobs represent an increasingly smaller proportion of the workforce. Professional and service jobs, which are less likely to be unionized, now dominate the American workforce, and so union membership has declined. Rather than unionizing, professionals tend to organize and join professional associations. Some professionals, however, have unionized. The largest union in the United States today is a teachers' union, the National Education Association.

Unions differ from professional associations in that the laws provide certain bargaining rights to unions. Union membership may be required for all employees as well. State laws

free rider An individual who does not join or contribute to an interest group that is representing his or her interests.

vary on this issue. Some states are open shop, which means that employees in that state maintain the option of whether or not to join a certified union. Of course, in open-shop states, workers who do not join the union may benefit from union activities without "paying the price"—another form of the free-rider problem. Since 1947, the federal Taft-Hartley Act has technically banned the closed shop, which requires union membership as a condition of employment in a unionized workplace. Still, unions have successfully convinced some state legislatures that because all workers enjoy the benefits of union advocacy (e.g., promoting pay increases), all workers should at least be required to pay dues to the union. Thus, many states allow so-called union shops, which require that employees in unionized workplaces either join the union or pay the equivalent of union dues to it after a set period of time.

Professional Associations. Higher levels of education and advances in technology have transformed the American workforce over the past half-century. One of the major changes has been an increase in professional, technical, and service jobs and a decrease in the number of skilled and unskilled labor jobs. Professionals have organized to promote and protect their economic interests through membership in professional organizations, which lobby on their behalf.

Two large and growing classes of professionals are lawyers and medical doctors, both of which have high-profile and powerful interest groups—the American Bar Association (ABA) for lawyers and the American Medical Association (AMA) for doctors. The medical and legal professions are regulated by state governments, and the ABA and AMA have been quite successful in influencing the regulatory process—for example, by establishing licensing requirements for doctors and lawyers.

Another large and influential professional association is the National Association of Realtors (NAR), with a total membership of over 700,000, an annual budget of over $60 million, and an organizational staff of more than 400 people. The size, budget, and organization of the NAR provide it with ample resources to advocate the interests of the nation's real estate agents.

NONECONOMIC GROUPS

Economic groups exist primarily to advance the commercial and financial interests of their members. Whereas economic interests (as demonstrated in Table 11-1) dominate pluralist activities, many other interest groups advocate for primarily noneconomic concerns. Three general categories of noneconomic interest groups are public-interest groups, issue or ideological groups, and government groups.

Public-Interest Groups. Public-interest groups promote the broad, collective good of citizens and consumers. Many public-interest groups seek to promote political reforms that enhance the role of the public in the political process. The League of Women Voters is one such group. Initially formed as an interest group that promoted women's suffrage, the League has become a leading advocate for improving turnout among all citizens in elections. The League of Women Voters has also taken the lead in promoting candidate engagement on issues of importance to the voters by sponsoring campaign debates.

Another highly active public-interest group is Common Cause. This group's literature describes itself in the following way: "Common Cause is a nonprofit, nonpartisan citizen's lobbying organization promoting open, honest and accountable government. Supported by the dues and contributions of over 200,000 members in every state across the nation, Common Cause represents the unified voice of the people against corruption in government and big money special interests."[21]

Common Cause promotes reforming the political system in ways that enhance the role of the average citizen. Thus, it supports laws limiting elected officials from taking gifts from special interests, banning large speaking honoraria for members of Congress, and reforming the presidential campaign finance system. Ironically, Common Cause is an interest group that tries to limit the role of interest groups.

Ralph Nader and the various citizens' advocacy groups he helped to start (including Public Citizen and the Center for Auto Safety) are among the nation's leading public-interest groups. Nader's best-selling book *Unsafe at Any Speed: The Designed-in Dangers of the American Automobile*[22] forced the president of General Motors to publicly admit to the U.S. Senate that

open shop The law that allows employees the option of joining or not joining the certified union at a unionized workplace.

closed shop The law that requires employees to become members of the union as a condition of employment in unionized workplaces.

union shop The law that requires that employees in unionized workplaces either join the union or pay the equivalent of union dues to it after a set period of time.

noneconomic interest group An organized group that advocates for reasons other than its membership's commercial and financial interests.

public-interest group An organized group that promotes the broad, collective good of citizens and consumers.

TABLE 11-1

Who Spends the Most on Lobbying?

Each year interest groups spend more than $3 billion on lobbying activities in Washington, DC. This table shows the 10 biggest spenders on lobbying in 2018.

U.S. Chamber of Commerce	$82,260,000
National Association of Realtors	$54,530,861
Business Roundtable	$27,380,000
Pharmaceutical Research & Manufacturers of America	$25,847,500
Blue Cross/Blue Shield	$24,330,306
American Hospitals Associations	$22,094,214
American Medical Association	$21,535,000
AT&T	$19,717,000
Alphabet, Inc.	$18,370,000
Boeing Co.	$16,740,000

Source: Center for Responsive Politics, www.opensecrets.org.

the company ignored automobile safety problems. Nader's Raiders, the name later given to the hundreds of young activists who arrived in Washington, DC, to help Nader investigate government corruption, were highly influential in pushing automobile safety legislation in the late 1960s, which dramatically raised safety standards for cars and trucks. Their efforts effectively launched a widespread consumer movement, which remains strong. Today these groups advocate campaign finance reform, monitor the health care industry, and promote consumer safety and consumer rights, among other public-interest activities.

Issue and Ideological Groups. Interest groups that focus on specific issues and ideological perspectives are known as issue and ideological groups. Abortion, women's rights, and the environment are just a few of the policy issues that have produced interest groups such as the National Right to Life Committee (pro-life), Americans for Free Choice (pro-choice), the National Organization for Women (NOW; women's rights), and the Sierra Club and the Nature Conservancy (both environmental groups). Each of these groups maintains effective lobbies on behalf of its positions.

Some groups have a broader focus than a particular issue or set of policy issues. These are known as ideological groups, and they promote a more general ideological approach on how government should deal with a host of issues. Both liberal and conservative ideological groups operate in the American pluralist system. Americans for Democratic Action (ADA), for example, is an interest group that promotes government policies with a liberal orientation. Since 1947, the voting records of members of Congress on certain issues have served as the standard measure of political liberalism. The ADA supports candidates for office whose votes on key issues score a high liberal quotient.

The American Civil Liberties Union (ACLU) is an interest group that advocates for the civil rights and liberties of American citizens. Specifically, the ACLU adamantly supports the rights of the accused, free speech rights, free press rights, religious liberty rights, and many other liberties guaranteed by the Bill of Rights. The ACLU has also become a strong advocate for students' rights, the rights of workers, lesbian/gay rights, and immigrants' rights.

The Christian Coalition of America (CCA) is another ideological group that has become a lobbying powerhouse in recent decades; it offers a vehicle to become involved in influencing public policy. The CCA's agenda advocates pro-life positions, promotes the role of religion as a part of what government does, favors reducing tax burdens on families, and supports victims' rights.

issue and ideological group An organized group that focuses on specific issues and ideological perspectives.

Government Interest Groups. Most interest-group activity organizes private concerns (of either individuals or businesses) for the purpose of influencing public policy. But private interests are not the only ones represented in the pluralist system. Groups representing the interests of governments also operate in this complex system.

Cities and states across the nation have organized to exert influence on the federal government. Most states and large cities employ their own lobbyists in Washington, DC. But states, cities, and other governments also organize collectively through a variety of interest groups, which are generally referred to as intergovernmental lobbies. The National League of Cities, for example, is an interest group that advocates for the broad interests of local governments. Another intergovernmental lobby advancing the cause of the nation's cities is the U.S. Conference of Mayors. The Council of State Governments and the National Governors Association lobby on behalf of the states' interests.

Not only do state and local governments lobby in Washington, DC, but foreign governments also organize and lobby. Many nations have embassies in the Washington, DC, area, and many of these embassies engage in interest-group activities of their own.

11-4 HOW INTEREST GROUPS ACHIEVE THEIR GOALS

Interest groups engage in a number of activities to advance the goals of the group and influence public policy. These activities usually involve lobbying, supporting candidates and parties in election campaigns, litigating, and mounting persuasion campaigns.

LOBBYING

Interest groups attempt to influence elected and other public leaders to make decisions that are favorable toward the group's goals. Lobbying is the term used to describe how interest groups go about influencing government officials. Lobbyists are the professionals who do the lobbying.

Lobbyists provide information to public officials, with the hope that the information will convince the official to vote or act in a manner favorable to the group's interest. Lobbyists perform a valuable function to public officials by providing not only information and perspectives on issues, but expertise as well. In the iron-triangle system, lobbyists seek access to members of Congress and to managers in executive agencies in a particular policy area. Public officials come to depend on the lobbyists for information and knowledge. For example, managers in the Department of Defense and members of Congress on the Armed Services Committee rely on lobbyists from Pratt & Whitney for information on emerging jet engine technologies, engine performance data, and other information, which allows the military to plan and improve the nation's defenses.

Similarly, the congressional committees responsible for workplace safety standards and the Occupational Safety and Health Administration (OSHA), the executive agency responsible for administering those standards, depend on the lobbyists representing labor unions and product safety groups for data and information on workplace hazards and for recommendations for remediation. Of course, these same public officials are likely to be lobbied by business interests concerned about the increased costs associated with remediation of hazards.

Lobbyists communicate with public officials in many different ways, including formal presentations, written memos and policy papers, informal emails or notes, face-to-face meetings, and informal discussions over a meal or a drink. The most effective lobbyists are those who provide valuable, truthful information on policy issues and who make persuasive arguments. Having a good working relationship with public officials and a quality reputation provides the lobbyist with access to officials, which is crucial to the lobbyist's success.

A common depiction of lobbying is that of an individual offering money, gifts, trips, or other goods in return for a favorable action, such as a congressperson's vote on a particular bill. Though such activities do take place, in modern times they have become the exception rather than the rule. The activities of lobbyists today are strictly regulated by federal and state governments. Lobbyist gift-giving and bribery of public officials are illegal in most states and

intergovernmental lobby Any interest group that represents the collective interests of states, cities, and other governments.

lobbying The means by which interest groups attempt to influence government officials to make decisions favorable to their goals.

can be prosecuted. States require lobbyists to provide financial statements, report expenses, and maintain official registration for interest groups and individuals who provide lobbying services.

Lobbyists are regularly seen in the halls of the Capitol building and the House and Senate office buildings. They are also common fixtures in the halls and offices of the state capitol buildings. Many lobbyists own their own lobbying firms and contract with interest groups to provide services, similar to the way that an organization might hire a law firm to conduct legal work. More commonly, however, lobbyists are employed by businesses, associations, or other organizations to lobby for that employer alone. Large organizations and businesses have the resources to hire full-time lobbyists; contract lobbyists often work for smaller organizations that do not have the resources to hire their own full-time lobbying staff.

A form of lobbying that has been used more frequently in recent years is known as grassroots lobbying. The idea behind grassroots lobbying is that interest groups communicate with government officials by mobilizing public opinion to exert influence on government action. Because elected leaders are often quite sensitive to the opinions of voters, if a group can demonstrate that public opinion supports a particular position or that the public is willing to contact officials to express their view, office-holders will respond favorably because they want to enhance their chances of being reelected to office. Interest groups with a large number of members are particularly effective at grassroots lobbying, mainly because they can produce large numbers of potential votes in a given election. The AARP, with more than 40 million members, has successfully used grassroots methods of lobbying to put pressure on Congress to protect the Social Security and Medicare systems—two primary goals of the AARP.

SUPPORTING CANDIDATES AND PARTIES IN ELECTIONS

Interest groups are also quite active in electoral politics, providing resources for candidates and parties that support the interest groups' goals. Table 11-2 lists the groups that have contributed the most money to political campaigns over the past quarter century. PACs,

TABLE 11-2
Big Givers to Campaigns

These 11 organizations were the biggest contributors to American political campaigns between 1989 and 2012. AT&T, the National Association of Realtors, and Goldman Sachs gave about equally to Democrats and Republicans, whereas the remaining top 8 givers heavily tilted toward giving to Democratic Party candidates. None of the top 11 tilted toward the GOP.

Organization	Contributions
ActBlue	$58,511,226
AT&T, Inc.	48,196,209
American Federation of State, County and Municipal Employees	47,347,798
National Association of Realtors	41,687,376
Service Employees International Union	38,083,375
National Education Association	37,937,019
Goldman Sachs	37,343,517
American Association for Justice	35,673,179
International Brotherhood of Electrical Workers	34,821,537
American Federation of Teachers	32,833,966
Laborers Union	32,409,200

grassroots lobbying
Communications by interest groups with government officials through the mobilization of public opinion to exert influence on government action.

Source: Center for Responsive Politics, www.opensecrets.org.

described earlier in this chapter, are an important instrument through which interest groups provide financial support to candidates and political parties.

In addition to providing financing to support candidates, there are other ways in which groups play an important role in campaigns. For example, a labor union might endorse a candidate and communicate that endorsement to its members, urging members to vote for the candidate. A group might also use its resources to hire a phone bank to make "get out the vote" phone calls on behalf of a candidate or slate of candidates. Groups have also provided support by drafting speeches for candidates on policy matters or hosting rallies for office seekers.

Business groups tend to support Republican candidates, largely because Republicans are more likely to agree with their goals. Similarly, labor unions tend to support Democratic candidates because Democrats are likely to support labor's positions on many issues, such as increases in the minimum wage and family leave laws. On social issues, Republican candidates tend to receive the support of conservative groups, such as pro-life groups and groups advocating stiffer crime-control measures. Groups that advocate a more liberal social agenda (such as the ACLU and Sierra Club) tend to support Democratic candidates, whose issue agenda is more consistent with the groups' goals.

LITIGATION

Interest groups have become adept at using the court system as a means of achieving their goals. Groups regularly initiate lawsuits, request injunctions, defend members, and file briefs. Consumer product safety groups, for example, regularly file for injunctions in courts seeking to order companies to cease the sale of products that are unsafe.

Some interest groups focus primarily on the courts to achieve their goals. For example, the ACLU regularly initiates lawsuits in circumstances in which it believes the government is compromising individual civil liberties. The ACLU is very active in litigating gender discrimination cases. One of the advantages of interest-group litigation is its capitalization of interest groups' financial resources; average citizens do not have sufficient resources to initiate so many lawsuits. Also, because interest groups often specialize in particular kinds of lawsuits, they are able to litigate more skillfully.

Another way interest groups use the court system to exert influence is by the filing of amicus curiae ("friend of the court") briefs, which are companion briefs supporting an argument or set of arguments in an existing Supreme Court case.[23] Although the interest group is not a direct litigant in a matter, it can use an amicus brief to further or better articulate a position and thus aid litigants in their respective case.

Interest groups have also influenced the court system by engaging in lobbying activities to influence the appointment of judges. Pro-life and pro-choice groups are very active in supporting or opposing particular judicial nominees, based on the nominees' position and past decisions on abortion cases. The American Bar Association uses a rating system to rank individuals nominated for federal judgeships that has become extremely influential in the appointment process.

PERSUASION CAMPAIGNS

Many interest groups run media campaigns to persuade the public to support their position on issues. Some of this persuasion occurs during election campaigns when groups create and place ads intended to help a political candidate or political party achieve victory. But increasingly, groups have run such campaigns outside of election campaigns to persuade or educate others to the group's way of thinking.

Groups have developed sophisticated public relations operations to communicate their positions. They use tactics such as targeted mass mailings, in which they mail a pamphlet or other document to a large list of individuals that the group is attempting to influence. For example, the Americans for Democratic Action (ADA) group maintains a list of voters who are not registered with any particular political party. The ADA often sends mailings to those on the list to try to persuade them to support the ADA's position on a particular issue. In addition to mass mailings, groups regularly use television, radio, newspapers, magazines, or even billboards to communicate positions and try to persuade. They also use the internet to send messages to the wider public.

Interest groups have become firmly entrenched within the American political landscape. Their influence is both certain and controversial. More than two centuries ago, James Madison expressed concerns about the influence of "factions." Today, many observers of American politics continue to express concerns about the influence of groups and the value of pluralism as a mode of governance. Nevertheless, interest groups offer an important and unique linkage between American citizens' varied interests and public policy. This does not diminish the importance of other linkages, such as free and open elections. But the linkage offered by interest groups is unique in that it allows citizens to exert influence by interacting with one another and collectively attempting to influence what government does. Few would argue with the premise that interest groups have been responsible for leading the charge in promoting political and social policies that have significantly improved the lot of millions of Americans.

Summary

11-1 Pluralism and the Interest-Group System

- Interest groups are a popular mechanism by which groups of people attempt to influence government to advance their shared goals.
- Pluralism is the theory that public policy largely results from a variety of interest groups competing with one another to promote laws that benefit members of their respective groups.
- Many praise the interest-group system in the United States because it provides all groups in society with access and a fair opportunity to compete for influence over public policy. By contrast, critics of the interest-group system say that it allows wealthy corporations and individuals a disproportionate influence on public policy, encourages many groups to promote their own causes even if they run counter to the public interest, and significantly slows down the policy-making process.

11-2 Interest Groups in Action

- The growth of interest groups in the United States during the twentieth century was a product of the tremendous growth of government in general over that same period and the increased concerns about political issues that are expressed by a better-educated mass public.
- Interest-group influence over public policy is theoretically informal; in reality, interest-group participation has become ingrained in the process through structures such as iron triangles and issue networks.

- Individuals tend to join or support interest groups in order to receive material benefits, purposive benefits (those that benefit society more generally), and solidary benefits based on individuals' satisfaction from interacting with like-minded people in pursuit of a goal.
- The most successful interest groups tend to maintain a large membership of individuals, at least some of whom are wealthy, as well as a loyal following based on members' commitment to the cause.

11-3 Types of Interest Groups

- Economic interest groups that pursue favorable monetary benefits for their members include business groups such as industry trade associations, labor unions, and professional associations. Noneconomic interest groups that pursue goals other than the commercial interests of their members include public-interest groups, issue or ideological groups, and government interest groups.
- Large interest groups must always concern themselves with the problem of "free riders," that is, those who benefit from the groups' activities without ever joining or contributing to the groups.

11-4 How Interest Groups Achieve Their Goals

- Interest groups achieve their goals through lobbying activities, supporting candidates in election contests, litigating, and mounting persuasion campaigns.

Key Terms

closed shop (p. 234)

economic interest group (p. 232)

free rider (p. 233)

grassroots lobbying (p. 237)

interest group (p. 224)

intergovernmental lobby (p. 236)

iron triangle (p. 229)

issue and ideological group (p. 235)

issue network (p. 230)

lobbying (p. 236)

majoritarianism (p. 225)

material benefits (of group membership) (p. 230)

noneconomic interest group (p. 234)

open shop (p. 234)

pluralism (p. 225)

political action committee (PAC) (p. 229)

public-interest group (p. 234)

purposive benefits (of group membership) (p. 230)

solidary benefits (of group membership) (p. 231)

trade association (p. 232)

union shop (p. 234)

12

THE MEDIA AND AMERICAN POLITICS

2020 Democratic presidential candidate Bernie Sanders appears as a guest on The Late Show with Stephen Colbert in August 2018.

THE NEWS MEDIA serve a number of important political functions in the United States, operating through a large and growing number of outlets. Voters' primary source of information about political candidates and political issues is the news media, and political leaders constantly monitor and attempt to influence the content of news stories to their political advantage. The technologies of television and the internet both allow citizens to observe events on the battlefield, look into the eyes of presidential candidates, and watch tragedies unfold. Further, social media have facilitated the ability of anyone—so-called citizen journalists—to publish the news in real time as it is happening in front of them. Events, and government's reaction to those events, now unfold live before a worldwide audience at the flip of a switch or click of a mouse. Not only do the media serve as an important information source, but they also help set the political agenda, provide perspective and commentary on issues and political candidates, and help keep the government accountable to the people.

Learning Objectives

12-1 The Media in American Politics

- Compare and contrast the various functions that the media serve in the American political system.

12-2 Historical Development of the Media

- Assess the evolution from a partisan press to a media focused on objectivity and how changes in technology have transformed the nature of the media.

12-3 The Mass Media Today

- Identify the large variety of traditional and "new" media that provide news and opinion about government and politics, and how media ownership is concentrated in large corporations.

12-4 Effects of the Media

- Compare and contrast the different theories that have been developed to explain the effect that exposure to news has on viewers/readers.

12-5 Criticisms of the News Media

- Critique media coverage of politics, including bias, sensationalism, and the concentration of corporate ownership.

241

12-1 THE MEDIA IN AMERICAN POLITICS

Consider the following facts about media use in the United States: more than two-thirds of all Americans use Facebook (nearly 2 billion worldwide), and each user has an average of over 300 "friends"; the average American spends more time (about three hours per day) watching television than working or going to school; all forms of media considered, the average person is engaged in media consumption for 3,500 hours each year—that's almost 40 percent of the 8,760 hours that exist in a year. There are even more TV sets per household than there are toilets. The media clearly have a pervasive presence in the everyday life of most Americans. From watching the political comedy of *The Late Show with Stephen Colbert*, to listening to the political commentary of Rush Limbaugh, to catching up on the latest news from around the world on cable TV's CNN or Politico on the internet, Americans make ample use of media sources available to them for getting political information.

Most news media organizations in the United States are owned by private companies, which, like most other private companies, seek to make a profit. Unlike other industries, however, the media enjoy a special constitutionally granted protection. The First Amendment to the U.S. Constitution specifically provides that "Congress shall make no law . . . abridging the freedom . . . of the press." When the First Amendment was adopted in 1791, the press was mostly a small collection of newspapers and magazines. Over the years, the press, now more commonly referred to as the media, has expanded to include radio, television, book publishers, music producers, the internet, and motion pictures.

One early event that helped shape America's perspective on freedom of the press was the trial in 1735 of newspaper printer Peter Zenger, who in the *New York Weekly Journal* published a series of articles highly critical of the British-appointed governor of New York. Zenger was arrested on charges of criminal libel. He was defended by Philadelphia lawyer Andrew Hamilton, who won the case with his argument that Zenger had printed the truth and the truth cannot be considered libelous. Hamilton's argument thus established the principle of truth as a defense against libel.

The argument for a free press in the United States today largely rests upon the concept of the "free marketplace of ideas," a phrase coined by Supreme Court justice Oliver Wendell Holmes in his dissenting opinion in *Abrams v. United States* (1919),[1] which suggests that allowing people to freely communicate their ideas will provide a larger variety of ideas to consider. Encouraging the publication and dissemination of a wide variety of political ideas offers citizens a diversity of opinions and perspectives and facilitates the free flow of information about local, national, and global events. Of course, for ideas to flow freely, government must be prevented from using its power to stifle perspectives with which it disagrees.

GOVERNMENT REGULATION OF THE MEDIA

Congress created the Federal Communications Commission (FCC) in 1934 to regulate the electronic media (primarily radio and eventually television) through licensing broadcasters and creating rules for broadcasters to follow. The FCC does not have authority to regulate the print media, such as newspapers. In fact, regulation of print media is rare, and courts have consistently treated the right of print media to publish free of government regulation. Some electronic media require broadcast frequencies that are scarce and thus need to be regulated to ensure the orderly transmission of programs.

Among the tools that the FCC may employ to regulate the activities of broadcasters is the threat of revoking a license or fining a station for violating its rules. The FCC has used these tools to limit the language and type of sexual material that broadcasters might use. For example, the FCC imposed fines on the owners of radio stations that broadcast "shock jock" Howard Stern. Stern's program often included graphic descriptions of sexual acts and sex games, as well as language that the FCC deems unacceptable. Some of those stations fined then dropped the Stern show from their program schedule. To avoid further legal battles with the FCC, in 2005 Stern moved his show to a satellite radio station, which is not subject to FCC regulations because satellite radio is purchased by users and does not rely on the publicly controlled airwaves.

Have you noticed the lack of diversity on your nightly news program or on the cable news networks? We occasionally hear about the lack of diversity at key events, such as the annual announcement of Oscar nominees. However, a lack of diversity is also evident in various types of media sources. The Women's Media Center (WMC) publishes an annual report to highlight the status of women in U.S. media. Their findings are pretty bleak: in 2019, there was a sizeable news gender gap, with men generating 63 percent and women generating 37 percent of the news.[3] In addition, U.S. print news stories are far

Roy Rochlin / Getty Images

Ainsley Earhardt is an anchor on the Fox News Network.

more likely to be reported by men (59 percent) than by women (41 percent). Overall, the WMC report warns that gender inequality among journalists can be found across all media outlets and across most issues. The media gender gap is further exacerbated by the disproportional number of white men holding key leadership and management posts across media organizations, which in turn plays a key role in agenda-setting. In particular, the 2016 WMC report highlights the lack of diversity in staffing of newspaper newsrooms, where minority journalists comprised just 17 percent and women journalists a mere 38.1 percent of staffs at daily newspapers.

For Critical Thinking and Discussion

1. What are the ramifications of such wide gender and racial gaps across our news media outlets?
2. Do we need more diversity in the news media to ensure the availability of different perspectives? Why or why not?

One of the most visible instances of the FCC clamping down on material in broadcast transmission involved comedian George Carlin's "Seven Dirty Words" skit, which satirized attitudes toward vulgar language. In the skit, Carlin continually repeated the seven words that you can't say on TV or radio. The piece was played on a radio station licensed to the Pacifica Foundation. Prior to playing the piece, the announcer warned the audience about its content. Nevertheless, a listener complained to the FCC, and the FCC in turn warned the radio station not to replay the piece. The station challenged the FCC's authority to regulate programming content, and the case made its way to the U.S. Supreme Court in *FCC v. Pacifica Foundation* (1978).[2] In that case, the Supreme Court upheld the FCC's power to regulate the broadcast media on the criteria of indecent material.

The FCC's **equal time rule** mandates that radio and TV broadcast stations must offer equal amounts of airtime to all political candidates who want to broadcast advertisements. This rule also now includes a provision requiring that if a station broadcasts the president's State of the Union message, then that station must also provide free airtime for the opposing political party to broadcast a response.

From 1950 through the late 1980s, the FCC also enforced the so-called fairness doctrine, requiring broadcasters to set aside time for public affairs programming. The proliferation of news sources and technologies for transmitting electronic messages during the 1980s effectively ended the FCC's fairness doctrine requirements. These changes in technologies also resulted in the passage of the 1996 Telecommunications Act, which shifted the emphasis of government policy from regulating to facilitating competition. This law deregulated cable television providers, eliminated monopolies held by local phone companies, and allowed local phone companies to provide long-distance phone services. The Telecommunications Act transformed the FCC from a regulator of the telecommunications industry into an aggressive supporter of competition within that industry.

equal time rule The FCC mandate that radio and TV broadcast stations offer equal amounts of airtime to all political candidates who want to broadcast advertisements.

FUNCTIONS OF THE MEDIA IN AMERICAN POLITICS

Throughout the history of the United States, the media have come to serve a number of functions in the political system, all of which promote the free flow of information to the public. Principal functions of the media include (1) providing objective coverage of events, (2) facilitating public debate, and (3) serving as government watchdog.

Providing Objective Coverage of Events. The media's most basic role involves monitoring events around the nation and the world and communicating those events to the public. Through modern communications technologies, the media have become proficient at reporting major events as they happen. Live coverage of presidential addresses, campaign debates, war operations, prominent trials, natural disasters, and other important world events have made their way almost instantaneously onto front-page headlines and into television's round-the-clock news coverage.

Providing information about news and events is perhaps the most basic and most important function of the media. Factual news information is an essential component of evaluating events and forming political opinions. Operating free of government control, the U.S. media can provide objective coverage of events to the American public. Objectivity refers to the media reporting events factually, accurately, fairly, and equitably—an important goal for many journalists. In addition to providing factual information about events, objective journalism requires signaling when important events occur and providing perspectives on all sides of an issue or policy debate. The goal of objectivity, however, is itself the subject of some debate. Objectivity is hard to define and measure, and journalists sometimes take a shortcut by trying to give equal weight to all sides without making any judgments of their own. This approach permitted Senator Joseph McCarthy to falsely but very publicly accuse people of being communists in the 1950s, it let cigarette companies get away with denying that smoking causes cancer, and it is prolonging the current national debate on global warming. Journalism professor Philip Meyer has advocated for a science-based definition of objectivity by getting journalists to seek more independent verification of facts.[4]

Numerous media formats strive to provide objective coverage of news information. Most of the content of newspapers (with the notable exception of the editorial pages) is aimed at objectively covering news events and politics at the global, national, and local levels.

The 24-hour cable news channels, such as CNN, Fox News, and MSNBC, provide news of events on a continuous basis. Many other formats are aimed at providing an objective look at news information to readers and viewers.

Moreover, the proliferation of cable television has broadened the role of the media as provider of information. Channels like the Biography Channel, the History Channel, local government access channels, and C-SPAN offer programming that gives historical context to local, national, and international events.

Facilitating Public Debate. In addition to monitoring and reporting events, the media also facilitate public dialogue and debate on important political issues. By helping frame issues, offering perspectives on how a problem might be solved, and providing context and commentary on political campaigns, the media serve a vital role in a democratic system that depends heavily on voters to make informed choices in elections.

The media facilitate public debate through a variety of forms, both print and electronic. Newspaper editorials provide perspectives on policy debates and political candidates. Websites, such as the left-leaning *HuffPost* and the right-leaning *Townhall.com*, offer their respective partisan audiences a source of online political information. Syndicated columnists publish columns in newspapers around the nation on a regular basis, presenting their own perspectives on issues. Most newspapers dedicate space on their editorial pages for citizens to write opinion pieces ("op-eds") and letters to the editor offering their points of view. Many news magazines adhere to a liberal or conservative approach to discussing issues or evaluating candidates for office. *The Nation*, for example, has a liberal perspective, whereas *The National Review* presents a conservative perspective. Even magazines devoted to one perspective or another, however, usually offer a forum for readers to assess issues. Radio talk shows that offer perspectives on politics, such as those of conservative radio talk show host Rush Limbaugh,

objectivity The journalistic standard that news reporting of events must be factual, accurate, fair, and equitable.

also facilitate public debate, as do television programs like MSNBC's *Hard Ball with Chris Matthews* and Fox News' *Hannity*, which often feature debates between the anchors and their ideological opponents.

These media formats go beyond objectively reporting news to analyzing events and presenting arguments from varying ideological perspectives that readers and viewers can evaluate and use in forming their own opinions about public policies and political candidates.

Government Watchdog. Since the founding of the nation, American political culture has been characterized by a healthy skepticism about government. To govern is to have power, and power (in the minds of many) corrupts. The federal system that divides power between the federal government and state and local governments; the system of shared power among the legislative, executive, and judicial branches of government; and the system of checks and balances among these three branches are mechanisms that help guard against the potential abuse of government power. The news media also help prevent the abuse of government power through their role as government watchdog. In this role, the media are sometimes referred to as the fourth branch of government, or the "fourth estate," checking the power of the other branches. Rooting out corruption and abuses of power through investigative journalism is a core function of the American media, no less important today than it was two centuries ago.

More than a century ago, a group of journalists, who came to be known as "muckrakers"[5] (they were given this name by one of their top admirers, President Theodore Roosevelt), investigated and exposed corporate and political corruption in American life, including the corrupting effect of corporate contributions on presidential candidates who won office. In the late 1800s, corporate wealth was concentrated in a handful of companies in the railroad and banking industries, and those companies bought favors and influence with various presidential administrations. The muckrakers exposed the rash of influence peddling and by doing so helped spawn new laws curbing corporate contributions to federal campaigns.

MSNBC's Hardball with Chris Matthews *is a left-leaning TV show on political topics.*

Fox News Channel's Sean Hannity hosts a right-leaning TV show on political topics.

Perhaps the most well-known case of the media uncovering and exposing government corruption was the investigative reporting of *Washington Post* reporters Bob Woodward and Carl Bernstein in the early 1970s concerning the Watergate corruption scandal of President Richard M. Nixon's administration. Their work led in part to the resignation of President Nixon in 1974 for his role in covering up the details of the Republican-led break-in of the Democratic National Headquarters in the Watergate Hotel during the 1972 presidential campaign.[6] Woodward and Bernstein largely depended on an anonymous administration source, who came to be known as "Deep Throat," for information that ultimately exposed the White House cover-up of a number of criminal activities in Nixon's 1972 campaign for reelection.

The media also exercise their watchdog function through television programs such as *60 Minutes, Dateline,* and *Meet the Press* and through internet websites set up by groups like Common Cause, which provides data on the negative influence of corporate donations on political campaigns. The media also carry out their watchdog function through books. For example, a 2014 book (*Duty: Memoirs of a Secretary at War*) by Robert Gates, former secretary of defense to Presidents George W. Bush and Barack Obama, criticized the Obama administration's foreign policy decision-making.

12-2 HISTORICAL DEVELOPMENT OF THE MEDIA

Before the American Revolution, the news media consisted of a handful of newspapers that were published by printers.[7] The main job of the printer was not to publish a newspaper, but rather to prepare official documents (such as marriage licenses, deeds to land, and government documents), political pamphlets, and religious books. Newspapers of the time mostly featured notices of public events and advertisements for local merchants. These early newspapers carried little information about politics or news events.

The political events that led up to the American Revolution and the events of the Revolution itself changed the nature and functions of the colonial newspapers. Many colonists were intensely interested in the disputes with Great Britain and eager for news about the battles of the Revolution. Newspapers responded to these interests with news stories about the events. Stories about the economic turmoil of the post-Revolution period, particularly the bitter partisan fight between the Federalists and Anti-Federalists over ratification of the Constitution, also appeared in the nation's early newspapers.

THE ERA OF THE PARTISAN PRESS

The Federalist/Anti-Federalist battle ushered in the partisan press era, a period characterized by newspapers supporting a particular political party. This period lasted from the late 1700s through the mid-1850s. Newspapers advocating the Federalist position that favored a stronger central government included John Fenno's *Gazette of the United States* and Noah Webster's *American Minerva*. The Anti-Federalists and later the Jeffersonian-Republicans, who supported states' rights, had their own partisan newspapers, such as the *National Gazette* and the *National Intelligencer*.

Partisan newspapers appealed mostly to readers who already agreed with the political positions advocated by those publications. Partisan-oriented news eventually became big business, and government printing contracts to partisan publications became a regular part of the spoils system.

During the early nineteenth century, a number of technological developments had a significant impact on the newspaper business. The invention of the rotary press in 1815 enabled the mass production of newspapers. The invention of the telegraph and the development of the telegraph system across the United States in the 1840s provided for the widespread electronic dissemination of news information. The expansion of the railroad system across the nation facilitated the mass distribution of newspapers across the continent. These developments allowed newspapers to print news events more quickly and distribute their publications to a larger number of people in a shorter period of time. These technologies also helped reduce production costs, making newspapers affordable for most Americans. The term *penny press* aptly described the low cost of newspapers during the early to mid-nineteenth century.

By the 1850s, newspapers found that they could increase their circulation by distancing themselves from particular partisan positions. Eyeing ever-larger markets, newspapers began to appeal to all Americans. Journalists began to tout the goals of objective reporting of the facts, rather than providing a biased or partisan perspective on events. By the end of the nineteenth century, the technological innovations and the desire of newspaper publishers to reach larger numbers of readers and maximize profits through the selling of advertisements had transformed the newspaper industry from a mostly partisan press to one focused on objective reporting of the news.

THE EMERGENCE OF ELECTRONIC MEDIA

The development of the radio in the early twentieth century provided a new means for Americans to get information about politics. Most notably, communication from the media source to the audience was instantaneous. In addition, the technology allowed political leaders to directly communicate with the American people. The first radio station was KDKA in Pittsburgh, established in 1923. The first network of radio stations, which was established in 1926

partisan press era The period from the late 1700s to the mid-1800s when newspapers typically supported a particular political party.

as the National Broadcasting Company (NBC), provided common programming and newscasts that were made available to the first truly mass audiences.

Franklin Delano Roosevelt, elected president in 1932, used the radio to deliver comforting and inspiring messages to the nation, then suffering in the midst of the Great Depression. FDR's weekly radio addresses, which the president called "fireside chats," represented the first significant use of this medium by a political leader to communicate to the nation's people. In addition to FDR's fireside chats, radio commentators such as Father Charles Coughlin (Detroit's anti-Semitic "fighting priest") and Louisiana senator Huey Long popularized radio as a medium that could provide a great deal of political commentary and debate. During World War II, Americans eager for news about the progress of the war turned to the radio for information. Edward R. Murrow's live radio reports from London during the Nazi bombings of that city and from other battle sites captivated the nation. More recently, President Donald Trump used his Twitter account to communicate directly with voters throughout the 2016 presidential campaign, and as president he has tweeted on a daily basis, offering his perspective on politics and a wide variety of topics.

Numerous technological advancements have had a large impact on the scope and importance of the news media through American history, but none has had a more profound influence than the invention of television. In the post–World War II boom of the American economy, the nation quickly adopted TV as its primary medium for getting news about politics and the world. NBC and CBS developed the standard TV news show format in the early 1950s with a 15-minute daily news program. The program featured a news anchor reading the news, supported by film footage and reporters. This format—now modified into a half-hour program produced each evening—continues to be widely used today by all the major networks. In the 1950s, TV networks broadcast the Army–McCarthy hearings of the U.S. Senate that exposed Senator Joseph McCarthy as a crude bully and resulted in his censure for ethical misconduct. Live television coverage of the Republican and Democratic national conventions set the standard for live broadcasts of major political events. The networks also sold advertising time to the major party candidates in the presidential election of 1952, revolutionizing the way in which candidates would wage their bids for elective office.

President Franklin Delano Roosevelt, delivering one of his famous "fireside chats" in 1933.

Donald J. Trump ✔
@realDonaldTrump

Tariffs will make our Country MUCH STRONGER, not weaker. Just sit back and watch! In the meantime, China should not renegotiate deals with the U.S. at the last minute. This is not the Obama Administration, or the Administration of Sleepy Joe, who let China get away with "murder!"

7:48 AM · May 10, 2019 · Twitter for iPhone

15.6K Retweets **61.3K** Likes

A tweet from President Donald Trump sent to his Twitter followers in May 2019.

PRESIDENTIAL DEBATES AND THE POWER OF TELEVISION. A defining moment in revealing the political power of electronic media was the live television broadcast of the debates between Republican Richard Nixon and Democrat John Kennedy, candidates in the presidential election of 1960. For the first time, all Americans were able to watch a live debate between the candidates. Many observers credit Kennedy's favorable TV performance as an important factor contributing to his razor-thin victory over Nixon in the November election. During the first of three televised debates, Kennedy won over the audience with his relaxed and self-assured manner before the camera; by contrast, Nixon seemed nervous and uncomfortable.

Nixon prepared for the debate by studying briefing documents but spent little time practicing debate style. Kennedy, on the other hand, spent a great deal of time practicing answers to questions out loud. For the two days prior to the first debate, Kennedy and his inner circle of advisers didn't leave the practice session in their hotel room. On the night of the debate, a tanned Kennedy looked strong and healthy. He wore a navy blue suit that contrasted sharply

Using New Media to Change Public Policy

Throughout American history, presidents have taken advantage of new and emerging technologies to advance their respective policy agendas.

Then

In 1964, President Lyndon Johnson used the relatively new medium of television to push through civil rights reforms that had eluded his predecessors. Past presidents had tried and failed to pass civil rights laws: Johnson's ambitious civil rights agenda might have met a similar fate had the plight of African Americans in the South not been seen by the rest of the nation through extensive television coverage. Footage from television cameras in late 1963 and early 1964 allowed viewers at home to witness police officials directing full-pressure water hoses on African American school children, police dogs set loose on civil rights demonstrators, and numerous brutal beatings. Donations to the civil rights movement increased dramatically after the general public became an eyewitness to these dramatic events, and legislative leaders from both parties soon felt public pressure to overcome the objections of opponents. After waiting out a 54-day filibuster, the Senate eventually joined the House in approving major civil rights legislation. Thus, on July 2, 1964, President Lyndon Johnson signed the Civil Rights Act into law. Clearly, the "small screen" had played a large role in the process.

Black Star/Alamy Stock Photo

A still shot from a television report showing a Birmingham fireman hosing down protesters in 1963.

Now

Civil rights reform was not the only legislation that benefitted from a president's use of a new communications medium. Early in his presidency, President Barack Obama had been determined to achieve legislative success on a subject that had proved elusive to so many of his predecessors: comprehensive health care reform. In those earlier battles, the American Medical Association and other opponents used media campaigns to prey upon public fears that the legislation might separate individuals from their own doctors. The Obama administration's efforts to pass health care reform would overcome similar opposition campaigns by embarking on a successful media effort of its own, using the internet. Obama's forces effectively used the newest communications medium to bring the full debate over health care out into the open, exposing backroom deals and revealing opponents' exaggerations about negative consequences of the reform proposals. Through a continuous bombardment of information released over the internet, Obama successfully justified the plan to many of the millions of Americans who were busy lapping up online news and information. The legislation eventually overcame all obstacles in its path, including a Republican party-line filibuster. Had the public not been privy to the immense amounts of information pouring forth from the internet, the arguments against the administration's plan might once again have proved too difficult to overcome.

For Critical Thinking and Discussion

1. How much does the media type influence the message received by citizens?
2. In your opinion, would civil rights reforms have progressed so quickly in the 1960s if the civil rights movement had been covered exclusively by radio? If President Obama had been restricted to more traditional media sources like print, would the Affordable Care Act (aka Obamacare) have even passed? Why or why not?

with the light walls of the TV studio. Nixon, on the other hand, looked ill and underweight. Just before the debate he had been hospitalized with an infection, exhausted from a hard week of campaigning. He wore makeup to cover up his five o'clock shadow and dressed in a light gray suit that blended into the background.

The candidates debated the important issues, and both did well in articulating their positions. But TV analysts reported that Kennedy won the debate. His stage presence, practice addressing the camera, tanned complexion, hand gestures, and commanding appearance compared favorably to the somber, pale Nixon. It was a lesson that no future presidential candidate would forget.

Interestingly, research on this debate[8] reveals that those who listened to the debate on the radio thought Nixon won, whereas those who watched the debate on TV tended to think that Kennedy won, proving that the medium through which events are communicated can indeed influence the way in which people evaluate those events. That the medium itself may have an important effect on the way in which people receive and perceive news was suggested by communications researcher Marshall McLuhan, who summarized this idea with his memorable phrase "the medium is the message."[9]

Drew Angerer/Getty Images

At a Democratic debate in June 2019: Andrew Yang, Pete Buttigieg, Joe Biden, Bernie Sanders, Kamala Harris, and Kirsten Gillibrand.

Live televised debates between the candidates for president did not occur again until 1976, when Republican president Gerald Ford and Democratic challenger Jimmy Carter met. This time both candidates were well prepared to convey the image they wanted to the American viewing audience. Dressed to coordinate with the set background, prepped with numerous practice sessions, and made up to ensure a favorable skin color tone, both Carter and Ford sought to communicate a positive image. Live broadcasts of presidential campaign debates have been a part of every presidential election contest since 1976.[10]

Today, presidential debates are routinely featured not only in general election campaigns, but in presidential primary contests as well. In the 2016 primaries, the GOP candidates debated 12 times and the Democrats debated 9 times. In the general election campaign of 2016, there were three debates. In March 2019 the Democratic National Committee announced that there would be 12 debates among the large number of candidates contending for their party's nomination, with the first one to be held as early as June 2019.

PRESIDENTIAL PRESS CONFERENCES. The power of televised images has also altered the governing process. Whereas President Woodrow Wilson was the first to hold regular and formal presidential news conferences, President Dwight D. Eisenhower was the first to hold regular news conferences as we know them today, as a means of explaining his administration's policies and appealing directly to the public for support. Before Eisenhower, the news media's access to the president was primarily through appointments that the chief executive would give to favored reporters. Eisenhower opened up the press conference to reporters from all types of news organizations. The questions were not prescreened, and Eisenhower addressed whatever topics were on reporters' agendas. This format for addressing the nation, coupled with the capability of television to show Americans the event, opened up the Presidency to the public.

Eisenhower's successor, President John F. Kennedy, quickly mastered the art of the presidential press conference. He made events seem even more dramatic and intriguing by allowing TV to broadcast them live. Kennedy's preparedness on issues, strong intellect, charismatic personality, and sense of humor made his press conferences interesting and successful events. President Lyndon B. Johnson continued the press conference tradition set by his predecessors, but such events became more difficult for Johnson as America's involvement in the Vietnam War escalated, with press questions increasingly focused on war casualties and military ineffectiveness.

Chip Somodevilla / Getty Images

President Trump frequently uses meetings in the Oval Office, such as this one in August 2018, to answer questions from the media.

Eisenhower, Kennedy, and Johnson averaged about two press conferences every month, but Presidents Nixon, Ford, Carter, and Reagan held fewer—less than one per month. Nixon, Ford, and Carter each dealt with crisis situations (Vietnam, Watergate, a severe energy crisis, and the Iranian hostage crisis), which led to uncomfortable open questioning from journalists, and so each president cut back on the number of conferences. Reagan, despite his acting background and ease in front of a camera, had a difficult time dealing with reporters' questions in a press conference setting, and so he began a weekly radio address as a regular means of communicating with the American public. All presidents from Reagan to Obama have used this form of weekly address to speak to the nation. President Trump discontinued the weekly address in 2017. He also differs from most modern presidents in the use of the formal press conference. Specifically, President Trump prefers to more informally take questions from the press after events, such as the signing of a new bill into law or as he is entering or exiting the White House.

12-3 THE MASS MEDIA TODAY

Today's mass media include a variety of channels of communication through which news content is disseminated to audiences. Channels of communication may be either print or electronic. Print media largely include newspapers, magazines, and books. Electronic media include television, radio, the internet, and movies. In addition, forms of content on any medium may be classified as either news or entertainment.

Even media sources that are intended primarily to provide entertainment programming sometimes include content that may fall within the realm of politics. One very popular show that combines news with comedy is *The Daily Show*, hosted by political comedian Trevor Noah. During recent presidential elections, the cable television station MTV broadcast programming that attempted to increase voter turnout among young people.

Paul Morigi / WireImage / Getty Images

Darryl "DMC" McDaniels performs at Rock-the-Vote's 25th anniversary concert in Washington, DC.

THE PRINT MEDIA

The modern print media mostly include newspapers, magazines, and books. Use of these print media has declined in recent decades, as consumers of news increasingly turn to the internet and television as sources of information. These and other news magazines often rely on photojournalism to support their longer stories to engage readers.

Books also enjoy an important place in American journalism. For example, *Plan of Attack*, a 2004 book by Bob Woodward, documented the role of the Bush administration in preparing for the second Iraq War. Woodward, through interviews with top White House sources, including the president and the secretary of state, concluded that the Bush administration had actively begun preparations for war long before the U.S. invasion and well before notifying Congress of its intentions. Woodward's work became an important topic during the 2004 presidential campaign. Thirty years earlier, in a book called *All the President's Men*, cowritten with Carl Bernstein, Woodward documented the Nixon administration's role in the Watergate affair.

A century ago there were about 2,200 newspapers published daily; today there are only about 1,300 daily newspapers—a 30 percent decline—purchased by about 76 million readers. Once the prime source of news for Americans, newspapers now

Bettmann / Getty Images

Pulitzer Prize–winning investigative reporters Carl Bernstein and Bob Woodward in 1973. Woodward and Bernstein investigated the Watergate scandal of the Nixon administration from 1972 through 1974 for the Washington Post.

FIGURE 12-1
The Generational Divide in the Use of Social Media

Studies show that within every age group social media usage has increased. The data also show the large differences between age groups.

Social Platform Usage by Age Group

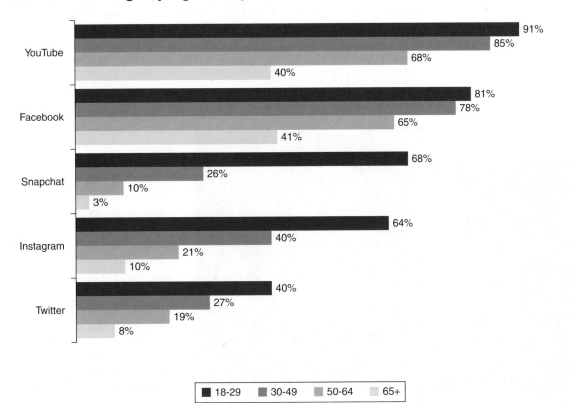

YouTube
- 91%
- 85%
- 68%
- 40%

Facebook
- 81%
- 78%
- 65%
- 41%

Snapchat
- 68%
- 26%
- 10%
- 3%

Instagram
- 64%
- 40%
- 21%
- 10%

Twitter
- 40%
- 27%
- 19%
- 8%

Legend: ■ 18-29   ■ 30-49   ■ 50-64   ■ 65+

Source: Pew Research Center, 2018.

take a back seat to television as the nation's main news source. Just as the number of newspaper readers has declined steadily since the 1950s, today the internet is becoming a more popular source of news and, as a result, the number of newspaper readers is falling at an even greater rate than before. The youngest generation of news consumers—those in high school—are most likely to be using digital media to get their news and information, as demonstrated in Figure 12-1. As the American population ages, it is likely that the trend toward greater use of the internet and lesser use of traditional media such as newspapers will continue.

The vast majority of newspapers are regional metropolitan and suburban publications. They range from those that cover large metropolitan areas, such as the *Chicago Tribune*, the *Miami Herald*, the *Dallas Morning News*, and the *San Francisco Chronicle*, to those covering much smaller towns. A handful of newspapers such as the *New York Times, the Wall Street Journal*, and *USA Today* are considered national dailies and are designed to appeal to a national readership. The *New York Times* trumpets its supposed status as the "paper of record" of events from around the world; *the Wall Street Journal* has the niche of being the nation's leading newspaper on financial markets and commerce; *USA Today*'s format of brief stories along with colorful graphics and pictures has helped it attract a nationwide following.

Wire services provide a clearinghouse for news as it is occurring. The largest wire service by far is the Associated Press (AP). The AP employs a large number of reporters throughout the nation and around the world to write stories on news events. Newspapers and television and radio stations that are members of the AP share the news services it produces. Using the AP as their news source allows smaller regional newspapers and local TV and radio stations to cover events from around the world in an efficient, informative, and cost-effective manner.

> **new media** Media outlets that rely on relatively newer technologies for communicating, such as the internet, DVDs, fax machines, cell phones, satellites, cable TV, and broadband.

THE ELECTRONIC MEDIA

The major electronic media are television, radio, and the internet. Television and radio have played an important role in American politics for many decades, and the internet has been responsible for more recent changes in the news and the way in which Americans use the news. The internet along with other relatively new media technologies, such as smartphones, satellites, and cable TV, have come to be known as the *digital media*, which have revolutionized the news business at every level.

Democratic presidential candidate Senator Kamala Harris (D-CA) shares some laughs with Stephen Colbert on The Late Show *in January 2019, shortly after announcing her candidacy.*

TELEVISION. With its mass adoption by households in the early 1950s, television became and has remained the primary source of news for most Americans. More than 98 percent of households in the United States report having at least one television set. News programming on TV is provided mostly by broadcast television networks and their local affiliates. The broadcast networks include ABC, CBS, and NBC. Cable television stations, such as CNN, Fox News, and MSNBC, provide 24-hour news programming as well. Other cable stations, such as C-SPAN and local public access stations, provide specialized coverage—for example, the live broadcast of congressional debates and committee meetings.

The defining characteristic of television is its visual nature.[11] The implied "reality" of seeing video of events, or live broadcasts of events, can be quite powerful, as civil rights demonstrators learned in the mid-1960s. Many argue that film footage of reporters covering the Vietnam War contributed to the erosion of public support for America's involvement there. The daily barrage of video showing dead soldiers brought new meaning to Americans' understanding of war and helped influence President Lyndon Johnson's decision not to seek reelection in 1968. In 2012, video of terrorist attacks at the U.S embassy in Benghazi, Libya, killing four American diplomats, captured a great deal of attention and reduced support for the Obama administration's foreign policy. Likewise, vivid pictures of American mistreatment of Iraqi detainees at Abu Ghraib prison did not help the George W. Bush administration's effort to defeat the Iraqi insurgents.

New satellite technologies further facilitate the live and instantaneous coverage of events not only around every corner of the globe, but also from the moon, Mars, and Jupiter. The new high-tech satellites provide an opportunity for people to view events as they occur even from the outer reaches of the universe, such as the live pictures sent back from satellites on the 2004 U.S. spaceship mission to Mars.

RADIO. Contemporary radio largely programs commercial music, with several minutes of each hour allotted for news, sports, traffic reports, and weather forecasts. These short news reports are an important source of information (particularly for commuters who use their cars to get to and from work or school) about news events and politics. Many radio stations carry a specialized form of programming referred to as **talk radio**, in which one or more hosts provide commentary and often invite listeners to call in to the show and offer their opinions. Talk radio steadily gained popularity in the late 1980s and early 1990s, marked by a growing interest in political talk shows, as increasing numbers of commuters with cell phones began to take time while sitting in traffic to listen to these shows and call in to offer their views.

Some of the more popular call-in shows focus on politics. The hosts often provide an ideological perspective on policies, issues, and political candidates and campaigns. Listeners of a particular ideological persuasion enjoy hearing what the host and others have to say, and small numbers call in to offer their own views. Many local radio stations provide political talk radio programs, ranging from very modestly ideological debates to extremely partisan ones. Several nationally syndicated shows have also attracted an especially large listening audience, such as conservative commentator Rush Limbaugh's show.

A trend in ownership of radio is the purchase of smaller, local radio stations by large media organizations. Critics of this trend contend that the large corporate owners typically impose standardized programming through satellite feeds, thus depriving these stations of their local character.

THE INTERNET. In 1993, a group of students at the University of Illinois developed MOSAIC, the first graphical internet browser. MOSAIC allowed users to view pictures and color images on the World Wide Web. MOSAIC soon went commercial and became Netscape, and by the mid-1990s it was attracting tens of millions of users. Coupled with huge worldwide increases in sales of personal computers through the 1990s, the ease and user-friendliness of accessing the internet made the medium an attractive source of news and information for people around the world.

The internet's rise as a mass medium has many implications for news, information, and the American political system. One such effect is the way in which people use the internet compared to other news sources. From the viewers' perspective, TV watching is a passive activity. Once they've tuned into a particular channel, viewers have no other choice but to get whatever news is being presented. They cannot ask questions or seek specific answers to questions they might have. Likewise, listening to a radio broadcast is a fairly passive activity for listeners unless, of course, they choose to call in to the show. While reading a newspaper, people can pick and choose the articles they prefer to read. However, newspapers are also limited in the amount of content they can provide, and readers cannot query a newspaper to get answers on specific questions they might have.

The internet, however, allows users to pursue exactly the kind of news and information they are interested in. Search engines such as Google and Yahoo allow users to find whatever they are looking for. Furthermore, most news websites include a "search" feature that allows users to search the website and/or newspaper database for information relevant to a particular query.

talk radio A specialized form of radio programming in which one or more hosts provide commentary and often invite listeners to call in to the show and offer their own opinions.

Unlike other media, the internet also enables individual users to be their own mass publisher, largely through social media such as Facebook and Twitter. Most word-processing packages include the option to "Save As Web Page," enabling users to place information, data, and graphics on their own web page. Web-design software enables users to put a web page on a server and thus make that page available to millions of other users. In this way, internet users can publish material that is accessible to a mass audience.

Most newspapers and television stations maintain websites that include the organization's news content and links to other sources, such as the Associated Press. Many of these sites also include a searchable database of archived news stories. Some of the most-used news websites are CNN (www.cnn.com) and *the New York Times* (www.nytimes.com). With searchable indices to past stories, links to other sites, online forums, and audio and video files, these sites offer a broad array of content that users can easily access.

The internet has transformed the flow of news and information about politics in other ways as well. It has become a common source of information about political campaigns, because candidates for office often create web pages and post them on servers for voters to access. Widely varying "chat rooms" and online forums serve as venues for users to post their opinions, ask questions, and engage in dialogue on political issues. Blogs (derived from the term *weblogs*) are also popular among many internet users. In 2008 and 2012, for example, the significant amount of fund-raising and voter communication by Obama supporters substantially buoyed that campaign's success. Since then, most presidential candidates make ample use of blogs for fund-raising. Blogs provide a combination editorial page, personal web page, and online diary offering personal observations in real time about news events and issues. Some of the more popular blogs are published by journalists and political commentators.

Smartphones and social media have also created a new type of news reporter—the so-called citizen journalist. These technologies allow anyone to play a role in gathering, analyzing, and reporting news and information. Prior to the emergence of these new technologies, only journalists employed at news organizations had the capability to gather and report the news to mass audiences through television, radio, and newspapers. But today, any citizen with a camera-equipped smartphone and a Facebook or Twitter account can gather news by taking videos and pictures and simply "tweeting" (or even retweeting) what they have viewed or experienced.

Some of the more salient national news stories that have been reported recently include reporting from citizen journalists, such as video of questionable police use of force in Brooklyn and South Carolina. Far more common on social media and local news media are pictures and video of events that citizens record as they see it happen.

Social media in particular may be having a particularly transformative effect on media and politics. Increasingly, Americans say that they get more and more of their news and information about politics from places like Facebook, Twitter, and YouTube. Although these media are still very new and research into their impact is largely not yet available, some preliminary work suggests that the social media may potentially be significant. One early study found that use of social media increases understanding and support for constitutional values.[12] Another study conducted on Election Day 2010 found that use of Facebook increased voter turnout.[13] As use of social media for political news and information continues to grow, their potential impact on American politics will grow as well.

Another issue of concern to some is that those who use the internet are more likely to be younger, middle- and upper-class, better educated, and nonminority—a disparity that has been referred to as the digital divide. Greater access to the internet facilitates access to news and information, and those who have access clearly enjoy an advantage. However, as computers and internet access costs decline, and as younger generations with computer skills replace older generations, the digital divide is likely to become less and less pronounced. Public libraries have provided another remedy to the digital divide. In 1996, 28 percent of all libraries had public access to the internet. Today, 99 percent of libraries offer internet access to patrons.[14] Because they are eager to gain access, the number of visitors to public libraries has increased by nearly 20 percent over the past six years.

blogs Internet sites that include a combination of editorial page, personal web page, and online diary of personal observations in real time about news events and issues.

citizen journalist A member of the general public who collects, disseminates, and analyzes news and information, especially by means of the internet.

digital divide The large differences in usage of the internet between older and younger people, lower- and middle-/upper-class people, lesser and better educated people, and minority groups and nonminority groups.

OWNERSHIP OF THE MEDIA

The Framers of the Constitution were clearly committed to the freedom of the press. Government ownership of the press was then and is today regarded as a threat to the basic freedoms that Americans enjoy. If government controls the news and the flow of information to citizens, it holds too much power. Private ownership of the media allows for the free and open exchange of ideas. Ironically, some today argue that the concentration of ownership of the news media by large nonmedia corporations, such as Comcast Corporation and the Disney Corporation, has stifled diversity in news content and blurred the line between what is news and what is entertainment. One large corporation that owns multiple media outlets has become the norm, whereas in the past most media outlets were

FIGURE 12-2

Corporate Ownership of the Major Television News Outlets

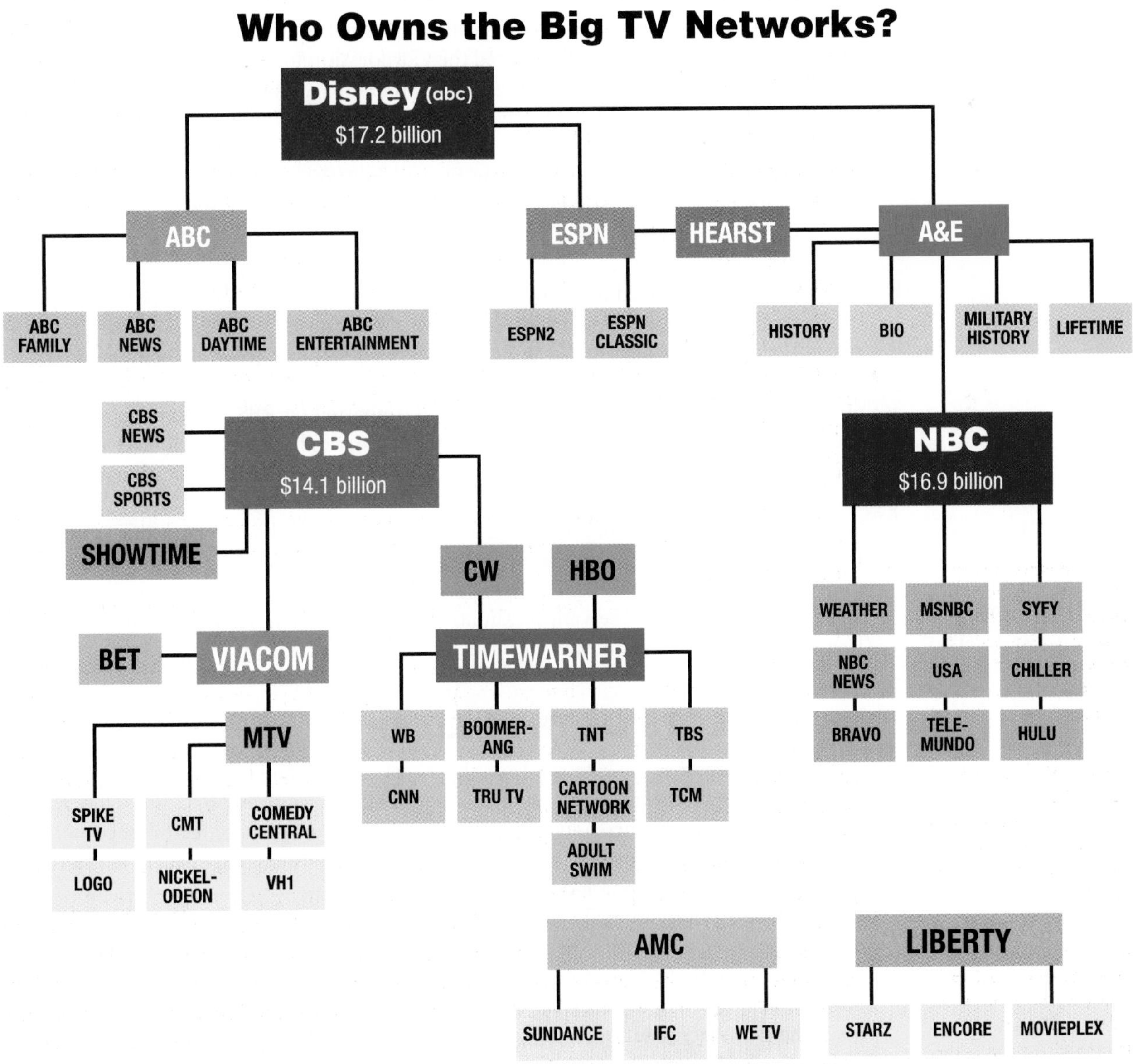

Who Owns the Big TV Networks?

Source: www.theglobalmovement.info/wp/wp-content/uploads/2013/06/media-ownership.jpg.

independently owned. It is also argued that ownership of media organizations by a conglomerate such as Comcast Corporation might compromise the objectivity of the news. When NBC, which is owned by Comcast, reports on a story about Comcast, might that story be biased?

The big-three television networks—ABC, CBS, and NBC—have dominated television viewership since the early 1950s. By 1956, more than 9 in 10 stations were affiliated with one of these networks. Over the past several decades, the growing popularity of cable and satellite TV has challenged the predominant position of the three networks. With hundreds of channels now available, the three networks' share of the viewing market continues to shrink. This competition led the networks to focus on greater efficiencies in the day-to-day operation of their businesses. By the mid-1980s, all three networks had experienced a change in corporate ownership, and all three now are part of "vertically integrated" corporations that are involved in video production as well as national and local distribution. In the late 1980s, competition between the networks further increased with the addition of the Fox Network. Figure 12-2 suggests the extent to which these three corporate owners control other media.

Not all television and radio stations in the United States are privately owned. The Public Broadcasting Act of 1967 created the Corporation for Public Broadcasting (CPB), which is responsible for distributing federal funds to support public, noncommercial radio and television stations. These stations have had a difficult time surviving economically in a marketplace dominated by commercial interests. CPB funds the Public Broadcasting Service (PBS), which was formed in 1969 to distribute programming to the nation's public television stations. CPB-funded radio programs are distributed by National Public Radio (NPR), American Public Media, and Public Radio International to member stations.

The 1967 law provided much-needed support for noncommercial TV and radio and has established a rather impressive network of stations that provide some very popular programming. *Morning Edition* and *All Things Considered* are highly regarded radio news shows with a very loyal following; the same goes for the PBS-supported *NewsHour. Frontline* is a popular, award-winning investigative reporting program supported by PBS. Documentary series on the Civil War, produced by Ken Burns, and on other topics have been well received by large audiences. PBS has also supported a significant amount of children's educational programming, including *Sesame Street*.

An important assumption underlying federal support for public broadcasting is that government is obligated to ensure that offerings are diverse and that ample numbers of educational programs are developed. Federal support for public TV and radio, however, is often a political hot potato. Conservatives claim that public television has a liberal bias, and many have attempted, unsuccessfully, to curb federal funding for CPB.

12-4 EFFECTS OF THE MEDIA

There is no doubt that Americans rely on the media for news and information about politics. What is less clear is the influence that media exposure has on citizens' opinions (Does watching a news story on the increase in crime rates make the viewer more fearful of crime?) and behavior (Does reading an article about Donald Trump's business experiences lead a reader to vote for or against him on Election Day?).

Researchers can quite easily gauge the exposure and use of the media. It is much more difficult, however, to identify the impact of media exposure on opinions and behavior. Citizens are constantly bombarded by news stories from a variety of different media. Isolating how one news story, or even several stories in one medium, influences opinions or behaviors is very hard to determine.

Despite the difficulty of proving media effects, political leaders and candidates for election certainly act as though the effects are powerful. Leaders constantly try to influence campaign stories and news stories to favor their own positions. Presidents use press conferences to send messages and attempt to win public support. Candidates buy advertising time to try to influence voters. Political parties orchestrate events at party conventions to send favorable partisan messages to voters.

Early research studies of media effects examined how citizen exposure to media content during a campaign influenced how they voted. In classic books on the subject (such as *The Voter Decides* and *The American Voter*), the media were credited with having little or no effect on voters' decisions. These studies, which led to a theory known as minimal effects theory, found that deep-seated, long-term political attitudes had a much greater influence on the vote decision.[15] Such enduring and preexisting attitudes lead to selective perception and retention of news content. People evaluate news material from their own partisan perspectives (selective perception) and tend to process and remember the material more consistent with their preexisting attitudes (selective retention).[16]

Moreover, preexisting attitudes often influence what kinds of news people choose to pay attention to in the first place (selective exposure). Psychologists suggest that people's desire to achieve cognitive consistency and avoid cognitive dissonance explains why they process new information in such a way as to assimilate with existing attitudes. These early studies that found "minimal effects" were largely focused on partisan elections and attempted to evaluate the effects of media exposure on the vote decision.

Subsequent research, although not refuting the findings of the media's minimal effects on partisan behavior, examined other areas where media exposure might have an impact. Social learning theory, for example, argued that viewers imitate what they view on television through observational learning.[17] Television's focus on sex and violence has led to a large number of studies that try to assess whether exposure to such material leads viewers to become more violent, with reduced moral standards. Some of this research suggests that viewers do learn negative, antisocial behavior from TV.

Some communications researchers have advanced the notion of *priming*,[18] which suggests that the activation of one thought also activates other thoughts, and exposure to media provides cues to people on this thought-activation process. For example, watching the Road Runner beat up on Wile E. Coyote in the old Warner Brothers cartoon may make one child act violently against another child after watching the cartoon. The rash of injuries related to the show *Jackass* is another example of the priming theory in action.

Critics of media often use social learning and priming theories to advocate for government controls of the media. The Telecommunications Act of 1996, for example, required television set manufacturers to include a V-chip in new units to allow parents to block programs they did not wish their children or families to view. Another law, passed in 1997, required the television industry to develop a rating system for television shows based on the show's level of sex, violence, and profanity. Studies that demonstrated a connection between TV exposure and negative behavior were important pieces of evidence used to promote support for the V-chip requirement and the TV ratings system.

The cultivation theory of media effects suggests that heavy television exposure helps develop an individual's overall view of the world.[19] According to this theory, the emphasis on violence and crime in both news and entertainment programming would lead the heavy viewer to overestimate and be disproportionately concerned about the extent of crime and violence.

A final theory of media effects is best known as agenda-setting theory. This theory suggests that although the effects of exposure may be minimal or difficult to gauge, the media are quite influential in telling the public what to think about. For example, Monica Lewinsky's affair with President Bill Clinton was a lead story in the news throughout 1998, and the prominent placement of that story in numerous media outlets helped to keep it a popular topic of conversation. Daily news coverage of the number of soldiers and civilians killed in Iraq focuses public attention on the U.S. military engagement there.

The media set the public agenda for the issues and activities that many Americans choose to think about and talk about. Prominently placed and frequently repeated headlines in newspapers, lead stories on television news shows and on talk radio, and highlighted stories on well-trafficked websites set the stage for public discourse. Citizens pick up a newspaper, flip on an all-news TV station, or go to their favorite social media site to become informed about what is happening in their community, the nation, and the world. In this sense, the news

minimal effects theory The theory that deep-seated, long-term political attitudes have much greater influence on an individual's vote decisions than does news media coverage.

social learning theory The theory that viewers imitate what they view on television through observational learning.

cultivation theory The theory of media effects that suggests that heavy television exposure helps develop an individual's overall view of the world.

agenda-setting theory The theory holding that although the effects of television exposure may be minimal or difficult to gauge, the media are quite influential in telling the public what to think about.

media have a powerful impact on public debate.[20] As news media scholar Doris Graber has noted, "When media make events seem important, average people as well as politicians discuss them and form opinions. This enhances the perceived importance of these events and ensures even more public attention and, possibly, political action."[21]

12-5 CRITICISMS OF THE NEWS MEDIA

Although Americans rely on the media for information about what is going on in the nation and around the world, the news media are also the subject of a number of criticisms. For example, despite the vast array of news sources available, most news programming follows a standard format that makes it appear the same to the public. Many newspapers are owned by a handful of publishers (such as Tribune Publishing Company and Gannett) and follow a standard format for news. Similarly, just a few companies own many of the nation's radio and TV stations and employ a similar format in their programming. Critics charge that this concentration in ownership could result in a handful of companies promoting their own political objectives.

Polls have also demonstrated that there has been a decline in the percentage of Americans who say that news reporting is fair and accurate. Figure 12-3 demonstrates this erosion in public sentiment in the context of social media.

Another criticism of the private ownership of the media stems from the premise that the media, like most other privately-owned companies, are in business primarily to make money. For the media, increasing profits requires attracting larger audiences and more readers, and as many media companies have found, providing higher-quality news programming on politically important topics does not always guarantee increased audience ratings or numbers of readers. Rather, news that provides more entertainment tends to get larger audience shares.

Often, the result is news that is characterized by sensationalized content. Stories that highlight or exploit crime, violence, disasters, personal conflicts, competition, and scandals tend to increase the sale of newspapers and improve the ratings of TV news programs. Thus, the profit motive of private ownership drives companies in the news business to disproportionately cover events that include sensationalized content. Stories about the untimely deaths of Michael Jackson and Prince, the extramarital affairs of Donald Trump, and the prostitution scandal involving New England Patriots owner Robert Kraft all received a tremendous amount of coverage recently at the expense of other, more important and politically relevant stories.

FIGURE 12-3

Perceptions of Accuracy in Social Media

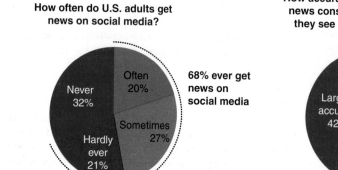

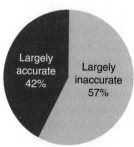

Source: Based on data from "News Use across Social Media Platforms 2018," Pew Research Center, Washington, DC (September 10, 2018), https://www.journalism.org/2018/09/10/news-use-across-social-media-platforms-2018/.

Sensationalism extends to coverage of elections as well. Studies of election coverage have found that most news dwells more on stories about the candidates' personal background than on their positions on the issues. Political scientists note that this emphasis on covering "character" issues rather than policy positions characterizes modern presidential election campaign news. For example, in 2016, significant coverage targeted Hillary Clinton's use of a private server to send official email and the scandal that ensued. Likewise, in 2016, a nine-year-old video of Donald Trump making insulting comments about women garnered a great deal of coverage. Critics of election coverage also charge that there is too much focus on preelection polls and the competitiveness of the "horse race," which crowds out the more substantive coverage of the issues and the candidates' positions on them.

Another common criticism of the news media is that they are politically biased. Some critics, for example, charge that corporate owners of media organizations are more likely to hold a conservative ideology, which is reflected in their news products. Others cite studies indicating that journalists and reporters tend to hold a more liberal philosophy, and that this orientation seeps into their stories. Certainly there is evidence to support the assertions that owners and managers are more conservative than the citizenry as a whole and that journalists are more liberal. But the issue of whether personal ideology or partisanship is reflected in news stories is less clear. In some elections, research has demonstrated that newspapers and TV news programs have shown a pro-Republican bias, whereas in others it has found a pro-Democratic bias.[22]

The media serve a number of important functions in the American political system. In addition to providing information, signaling events, and "watchdogging" what

Do You Use Social Media to Participate in National Political Discussions?

Social media have significantly changed the way that people across the country participate in American politics. They offer anyone with a computer and access to the internet the opportunity to publish their political opinions in the mass media, to share ideas and perspectives with others, to recommend the views of others, and to debate and challenge the positions of those with whom they disagree. Social media sites such as Facebook, Twitter, and Instagram are used by 200 million Americans, and billions of people worldwide, to express their opinions and perspectives on politics and to try to convince their "friends" to vote for or support a particular policy position.

Americans between the ages of 18 and 35 have been especially active in contributing their ideas to this particular media marketplace. Some of their efforts have had a significant impact on political events. For example, during a 2006 Virginia Senate campaign, a supporter of Democratic candidate Jim Webb was following Webb's opponent, incumbent senator George Allen, with a video camera. Annoyed at being followed, Allen referred to the Webb supporter as a "Macaca," a term that refers to a species of

monkey and is considered an ethnic slur. The videotaper, S. R. Sidarth, was also a blogger and immediately posted the video of Allen's slur on YouTube. Many other blogs and national news organizations began to cover the clip of Allen's slur. The posting is credited with clinching Webb's narrow victory in the race.

Another way people have used social media to influence politics is through the "moneybomb," a blog-driven grassroots fund-raising campaign that is usually generated over a short period of time: supporters use the blogs to create a frenzied atmosphere to quickly raise money.

For Critical Thinking and Discussion

1. Search for a blog or Facebook page that aligns with your own political interests or attitudes and read at least a week's worth of postings and comments. What do you notice? Do opinions tend to get debated or echoed within that blog?
2. What are the advantages and disadvantages of engaging in this form of political participation?

government does, the media also provide an infrastructure that leaders use to communicate with citizens. In the examples used at the outset of this chapter, we saw how Presidents Johnson and Obama took advantage of relatively new media (television and the internet, respectively) to successfully win long-term political struggles to pass civil rights and health care reform legislation. Technological innovations have served to change the forms and nature of the media throughout the course of American history. These changes have opened up new opportunities for presidents and other leaders to help shape a political agenda and successfully bring important policy ideas to fruition. These changes have also had the effect of bringing news and information to audiences with more and more speed and efficiency. The American media remain as important a political institution as any in our system of government. Americans' demand for information, the appetite of journalists to keep tabs on government performance, and political leaders' reliance on the media to communicate with citizens all serve to make the media stronger today than they have ever been.

Summary

12-1 The Media in American Politics

- The media serve a number of important functions in the political system, all of which promote the free flow of information to the public. These functions include providing objective coverage of events, facilitating public debate, and serving as government watchdog.

- Congress created the Federal Communications Commission (FCC) in 1934 to regulate the electronic media through licensing broadcasters and creating rules for broadcasters to follow. The FCC does not have authority to regulate the print media because the courts have consistently treated the right of print media to publish free from government regulation.

12-2 Historical Development of the Media

- From the nation's founding through the 1850s, news in America was largely provided by a partisan press, made up of newspapers supported by a particular political party. Over the past 150 years, however, the standards for news reporting have become less focused on serving political party interests and more focused on "objectivity."

- Technological change has greatly altered the news media. The invention of the rotary press in 1815 facilitated the mass printing of papers; the railroad system provided for speedy distribution of papers; the invention of the radio provided instantaneous coverage of events as they unfolded; and television brought taped and live footage of news events into people's homes.

12-3 The Mass Media Today

- Politics and political events, such as presidential campaigns, debates, and news conferences, are widely covered by media organizations. Today's mass media comprise large and varied types of news outlets, including radio, television, books, newspapers, and magazines. They also include the so-called new media facilitated by the internet, satellites, cell phones, broadband, and other newer technologies.

- Although the big-three television networks— ABC, CBS, and NBC—have dominated television viewership since the early 1950s, with the growing popularity of the Fox Network, as well as cable and satellite TV, additional networks have begun to offer stiff competition.

- Corporate ownership of news media outlets today is characterized by large nonmedia corporations such as Comcast and the Disney Corporation. Some argue that this concentration of large corporate ownership has stifled diversity in news content and blurred the line between what is news and what is entertainment.

12-4 Effects of the Media

- The effects of exposure to news on readers/viewers are the subject of much debate. A number of theories—including social learning, minimal effects, cultivation, and agenda-setting—seek to explain how the news media influence what people think about politics.

12-5 Criticisms of the News Media

- Media performance is often the subject of criticism. Some of the major sources of discontent with media performance include the concentration of corporate ownership of media outlets, sensationalized coverage of relatively unimportant events, and ideological bias in news reporting.

Key Terms

agenda-setting theory (p. 257)

blogs (p. 254)

citizen journalist (p. 254)

cultivation theory (p. 257)

digital divide (p. 254)

equal time rule (p. 243)

minimal effects theory (p. 257)

new media (p. 252)

objectivity (p. 244)

partisan press era (p. 246)

social learning theory (p. 257)

talk radio (p. 253)

13

POLITICAL PARTIES AND VOTING

Geo Images / Alamy Stock Photos

The Democratic and Republican Parties' symbols, the donkey and the elephant, respectively.

ALTHOUGH THEY MERIT NO mention at all in the Constitution, political parties have become the lifeblood of American politics. New laws are enacted through the debate and negotiation of party leaders in government, and individuals are recruited and promoted as political candidates through the political party structure. At the national, state, and local levels, the two major political parties set the tone for political debate, control the policy agenda, and run the government. The electoral successes and failures of the Democrats or the Republicans, and competition within the majority party to set the national agenda, define the nature of public policy. Further, political parties provide the framework through which citizens participate in American politics; they remain the primary cue that voters use to understand politics.

13-1 THE DEVELOPMENT OF POLITICAL PARTIES IN THE UNITED STATES

More than 70 years ago, the American Political Science Association (APSA) focused the scholarly community's attention on what it referred to as responsible party government.[1] The "responsible party government" model depicts the proper role of parties as organizations that offer clear programs and policy positions to voters. Voters make choices on the basis of those programs, and when victorious in elections, the party works toward achieving those programs and policies. At the time of the next election cycle, voters hold the party accountable for what it has accomplished.

The extent to which parties actually resemble the responsible party model has been the subject of much debate over the past half-century. Moreover, despite the large role parties play in the American political system, many observers argue that these parties are organizationally weak, particularly when compared to parties in other democracies around the world. Whereas most European parties have clearly defined constituencies based on social class and regional, ethnic, or religious divisions, American political parties are often ideologically vague, aligning with broader constituencies and gravitating toward more centrist positions on issues. Despite the prevalence of parties in U.S. politics, there are indications that their influence is on the decline.

The founders who drafted the Constitution designed a federal system without political parties. They envisioned a system that would be run by independent-minded people who served out of a sense of civic virtue. James Madison's famous Federalist No. 10 deplores "factions," as he calls them. Madison and his colleagues largely looked upon parties (the equivalent of extremely large factions) as tools of the politically ambitious that would tend to promote corruption and bias in the political system.

Despite the founders' disdain for political parties, they have become central to the American political system. E. E. Schattschneider, a well-regarded student of American politics, observed in 1942 that "democracy is unthinkable, save in terms of the parties."[2] The Democratic and Republican Parties not only have become important political institutions in their own right, but they play a central role in running government at all levels, and they organize and provide context to voters.

Political parties are organizations that seek to win elections for the purpose of influencing the outputs of government. They are typically guided by a political philosophy, rooted in particular values and an ideological approach to governing. The philosophy, values, and ideological approach generally lead to specific issue positions espoused by leaders of a party and the candidates who run for office under a party's label. Some minor parties focus less on the unrealistic assumption that they might win elections and more on articulating an ideological approach to governing and supporting particular issue positions. As in any organization, parties include leaders as well as citizens. In American politics, parties provide an important link between citizens and their leaders, playing a key role in recruiting citizens and relying on them for support at election time.

Even though the founders frowned on political parties and made no provision for them in the federal government they designed, not long after the first government under the new U.S. Constitution took office in 1791, some of the architects of the Constitution became strong advocates of particular parties.[3] Perhaps more than anything else, this contradiction serves to highlight not only the importance of political parties to the practice of democracy, but also the necessity of parties. In the United States, competition between the political parties has kept any one group or "faction" from becoming too powerful for too long. The Constitution provides various safeguards against the accumulation of power in the form of checks and balances. Paradoxically, although parties are not mentioned at all in the Constitution, competition between political parties has proven to be a significant check against tyranny.

THE FIRST PARTIES IN AMERICA

The history of political parties in the United States traces back to colonial America, when supporters of the English Crown aligned with the British Tory Party, and advocates of a new

> **political parties**
> Organizations that seek to win elections for the purpose of influencing the outputs of government.

independent American nation aligned themselves with the British Whig Party. The period following the war ushered in new challenges as leaders of the new American nation debated the relationship that should exist between the national government and the state governments. Ultimately, this debate created two new parties (or "factions," as many still called them in the eighteenth century). The U.S. Constitution that replaced the Articles of Confederation significantly enhanced the structure, power, and importance of the national government. The debate over ratification of the new Constitution pitted the Federalists, who supported a stronger federal government, against the Anti-Federalists, who opposed a strong federal government and supported state sovereignty.[4]

More formal, identifiable political parties emerged and began to assume the critical function of supporting candidates for elective office during the first administration of George Washington. Once again, the issue that spurred the emergence of parties as vehicles for nominating candidates was the distribution of power between the federal and state governments under the Constitution. The Federalists continued to support a stronger federal government and the policies of the Washington administration, which promoted the power of the national government. Most Federalists also favored maintaining close ties with Great Britain. President Washington did not consider himself a member of the Federalist Party; he despised parties and refused to endorse their presence in the politics of the new country. Yet many of Washington's supporters, led by Alexander Hamilton, organized the Federalist Party and used the organization to recruit candidates for office.

The Federalist Party was soon challenged by the Democratic-Republican Party, which asserted that the Washington administration was assuming greater powers than those the Constitution granted the federal government. It also criticized the federal government's favorable relations with Britain, preferring France as a closer European ally. As early as 1792, the Democratic-Republicans were organized and led by Thomas Jefferson and James Madison—the same Madison who, 10 years earlier, had authored in Federalist No. 10 perhaps the most eloquent argument *against* factions that has ever been written. In the congressional elections of 1792, Democratic-Republican candidates won a majority of seats in the House of Representatives.

Every presidential and congressional election since 1796 has featured some form of party competition. In this early period of American political parties, the Federalists drew most of their support from the northern states, whereas the Democratic-Republicans had greater support in the southern and mid-Atlantic states. Sectional differences in partisan support have characterized American politics for much of the nation's history. In the first competitive presidential election of 1796, the Federalists endorsed John Adams and the Democratic-Republicans endorsed Thomas Jefferson. Adams won 71 electoral votes and Jefferson won 68 votes, making Adams president and Jefferson vice president. Not anticipating political parties, the Constitution allowed for the election of a president and vice president who stood very far apart on critical issues of the day.

By the time of the election of 1800, the parties were highly organized. Each of the two political parties endorsed a slate of candidates for president and vice president to avoid the problem of having two separate parties occupy those offices. The party organization selected presidential electors, who dutifully cast their constitutionally granted two votes to their party's candidates. The Federalists nominated both John Adams and Charles Pinckney, whereas the Democratic-Republicans endorsed Thomas Jefferson and Aaron Burr. Jefferson and Burr each received 73 electoral votes, thus producing an Electoral College tie for the presidency. By the provisions of the Constitution, the election was then to be decided by the House of Representatives. After a fair amount of debate and politicking, the House eventually selected Jefferson on the 36th ballot. Clearly, the system of selecting the president needed to be modified from one that did not recognize the importance of political parties in the electoral process to one that did.

The Twelfth Amendment deferred to the reality of parties in presidential elections. Ratified prior to the election of 1804, this amendment formally separated the Electoral College vote for president and vice president. Rather than having electors cast two ballots for president, electors were now to cast separate votes for president and vice president. This modification in the electoral process helped avoid the problem that had occurred in 1796 of having

Hostility and Cynical Appeals Stoke Partisan Rancor Again . . . and Again

Many presidential candidates hope to run a positive campaign, appealing to the average voter's hopes and promises for a better future. The candidate hailing from the incumbent party in particular benefits from happy and contented voters who wish to keep their party in power. Just as often, however, the winning candidate appeals to voter discontent and frustration with the economy, the nation's foreign policy, or any of a host of problems afflicting the nation. And in some cases, the victor will actually seek to stoke the discontent of an angry electorate with the promise that everything will be better once we "kick the bums out" and "clean up Washington." Two of the many elections that fit the latter description are discussed here.

GOP presidential nominee Donald Trump addresses the Republican National Convention in July 2016 in Cleveland, Ohio.

Then

The 1968 presidential campaign was a tumultuous one. Not only were Americans seriously divided over continued U.S. involvement in the Vietnam War, but racial divisions produced riots across the country and unrest on the nation's college campuses. Richard Nixon, the Republican presidential nominee, ran a campaign based on a "Southern strategy": win over white Democratic voters in the South by promising to restore "law and order" to American communities. He also promised to redirect the military effort at winning the war. At campaign rallies Nixon spoke of returning to a "forgotten America," the label he gave to a nation of citizens who "obey the law, pay their taxes, go to church, send their children to school, love their country and demand new leadership." (A year later, he would popularize the term *silent majority* to describe these target voters.) Meanwhile, Hubert Humphrey, the Democratic candidate who was the sitting vice president, was forced with considerable difficulty to defend the status quo. Nixon effectively tapped into voter anger to gain a narrow win in the popular vote and a convincing 301–191 Electoral College victory that fall.

Now

In 2016, outsider candidate Donald Trump, a businessman who had never before held public office, proved the ideal messenger for millions of citizens who were angry with a federal government that seemingly did not care about them. Trump campaigned on the promise to "Make America Great Again," which appealed to the voters' sense that America was no longer great and that we should return to an earlier time when things were better. Critics of Trump's candidacy complained that his appeal harkened back to Nixon's "Southern strategy" by reaching out to poor and uneducated white voters who had suffered economic hardships under the Democrats. When polls in September showed him trailing significantly behind his Democratic opponent, former secretary of state Hillary Clinton, Trump spoke of his own "silent majority of voters" who would bring midwestern states back into the Republican fold. This strategy proved on the mark: on Election Day, Trump scored a startling upset victory thanks to millions of "silent" voters whom the pollsters had missed. Though Trump narrowly lost the popular vote, he managed to win a clear Electoral College victory thanks to stunning victories in Michigan, Wisconsin, and Pennsylvania, just as he had promised.

a president and vice president locked in partisan struggle, as well as the problem in the 1800 election that resulted in two candidates from the same party tied for the presidency.

The election of 1800 marked the beginning of the end for the Federalist Party. The Federalists would never again win a presidential election, and their strength in Congress diminished steadily over the next two decades. The Democratic-Republicans enjoyed party dominance to such an extent that the Federalists were virtually extinct after the election of 1820. Interestingly, this lack of competition from the Federalists during the first two decades of the nineteenth century had the effect of fragmenting the Democratic-Republicans. In 1824, the Democratic-Republican Party put forth several sectional candidates, but no candidate received a majority of electoral votes. Eventually, the House of Representatives decided in favor of John Quincy Adams. The result was a Democratic-Republican Party in disarray.

A SECOND PARTY SYSTEM EMERGES

Disillusioned by the outcome of the 1824 election, Andrew Jackson eventually formed a new political party, the Democratic Party, which remains one of the two major parties still competing in American politics today. Jackson's support in 1824 derived from many of the new states that had been added to the Union as a result of westward expansion. Many such states, including Jackson's home state of Tennessee, allowed voters to choose presidential electors directly, rather than following the traditional practice of authorizing the state's congressional delegation (known as the *congressional caucus*) to choose electors. Because he received more popular votes than John Quincy Adams in 1824, Jackson felt the presidency was rightfully his that year. However, Henry Clay, the fourth-place candidate, allied himself with Adams, thereby giving Adams enough votes for victory. When Adams became president, he appointed Clay as secretary of state. Jackson and his supporters accused Clay of making a "corrupt bargain" by trading his votes to Adams in exchange for his appointment as secretary of state. Those who remained loyal to John Quincy Adams began calling themselves the National Republicans. The next presidential election would be a contest essentially between two splinter groups (Democrats and National Republicans) of the now defunct Democratic-Republicans.[5]

Jackson took his case directly to the people and ran for president again in 1828, this time as a Democrat. He ran a populist campaign, arguing that the people should have a greater say in selecting the president, and developed his campaign theme around the Adams–Clay "corrupt bargain." Jackson's theme caught fire with the voters, and the nation's continuing westward expansion, along with voting reforms and increased suffrage in eastern states, suddenly expanded the role of voters in selecting presidential electors. In a campaign that was essentially decided by the people, puritanical John Quincy Adams proved no match for the flamboyant Jackson, still revered as the general who led American forces to victory in the Battle of New Orleans, the final military engagement of the War of 1812. And Jackson's newly established Democratic Party emerged as a national force to be reckoned with.

The election of 1828 also permanently changed the nature of campaigns, and, with them, the nature of parties. The precedent for a presidential election influenced by the masses was now set, and the era of congressional delegations selecting presidential electors was over. Parties quickly recognized the need to organize in states and localities to accommodate the new process of selecting presidential electors. Party organizations became larger and more powerful as they developed into critical instruments in campaigns. This era also established the tradition of holding national party conventions. These conventions drew together party delegates from across the states for several purposes. First, the delegates were responsible for choosing the party's presidential candidate and vice presidential candidate. Second, the delegates articulated their party platform, a document outlining the party's position on important policy issues. Third, the conventions coordinated the activities of parties across the states. National party conventions remain a central event both in the presidential selection process and in the organization of modern political parties in general.

The Democratic Party held its first national party convention in 1832, once again nominating Andrew Jackson for president. The National Republicans again nominated Henry Clay, who lost to Jackson in the November election. Several years later, a new political party, the Whigs, which was made up of a coalition of National Republicans and other groups,

national party convention
A large meeting that draws together party delegates from across the nation to choose (or formally affirm the selection of) the party's presidential and vice presidential candidates.

party platform
A document outlining the party's position on important policy issues.

emerged as a principal competitor to the Democrats. By the 1840s, the Democrats and Whigs dominated not only election contests but also leadership and committee assignments in Congress. Soon those two parties became the primary vehicles through which legislation was sponsored and then shepherded through the Congress.

From 1836 through 1856, the Whigs and the Democrats shared the presidency and the vast majority of seats in Congress. Both parties were truly national parties, with organizations in each of the states. The issue of slavery, however, soon became the principal issue on the American political agenda. The Civil War would transform American politics forever, and a product of this transformation was the demise of the Whig Party. Within the Whigs, there were strong differences of opinion over the slavery issue, which led to the decline of the Whigs as a national force by the late 1850s. New, smaller parties emerged, such as the Free Soil and Know-Nothing parties, but none of those parties was able to attract large numbers of voters over an extended period of time. By the late 1850s, a new Republican Party had emerged to absorb these smaller parties and replace the Whigs as the major opposition party to the Democrats.

THE MODERN PARTY SYSTEM IN AMERICA: DEMOCRATS VERSUS REPUBLICANS

The year 1856 marked the first presidential election when the precursors to the modern Democratic and Republican Parties faced off for office. Democratic nominee James Buchanan defeated Republican candidate John Fremont by 174 to 114 electoral votes. Since 1856, every presidential election but one has featured the Democrats and Republicans as the only two major political parties in serious contention for the White House.

In 1860, Democratic Party support for states' rights and Republican Party support for national power and preservation of the Union divided the parties over the issue of slavery. Republican Abraham Lincoln's successful campaign that year helped his party capture the presidency and a majority in both houses of Congress. It also precipitated the Civil War. With the eventual secession of 11 Democrat-heavy states in the South, the Republican Party came to dominate politics for the next decade.

Like the election of 1828, the election of 1860 is considered by many scholars to be a critical election. The theory of critical elections, developed by political scientist V. O. Key Jr., posits that certain elections can be characterized as producing sharp changes in patterns of party loyalty among voters.[6] This occurred in 1860 when voter support for parties realigned along the issue of slavery, based primarily on a North-versus-South division. Until 1860, the Democratic Party had enjoyed support from urban and industrial areas in both the North and the South and the demographic and social groups associated with those regions. The Civil War shifted these alignments to a North–South division, thus rendering the 1860 contest a critical election. The theory of critical elections suggests that every such election is accompanied by some type of electoral realignment,[7] a lasting reconfiguration of how certain groups of voters align with the parties.

When the last of the former Confederate states was readmitted to the Union in 1870, the Democratic Party once again began to assert itself in national politics. The Civil War had cemented a "solid South" stronghold for the Democratic Party that would continue for a century. Republicans remained the favored party in the northern and midwestern states, although some major cities in the North (including New York City) tended toward the Democratic Party. Republicans dominated the presidency for the remainder of the century, winning six of the next eight presidential contests.

A third realigning election occurred in 1896. That election did not result in a clear shifting of voter preferences from one party to another; rather, it marked the rise of the Republican Party to a near total consolidation of power and voter support in the northern and western states, as well as the continued Democratic Party dominance in southern states. Republican candidate William McKinley won the 1896 election and, with it, a realignment of new allegiances to the Republican Party. Indeed, the only Democrat to capture the presidency between 1896 and 1932 was Woodrow Wilson, and Wilson's initial success was more a consequence of Theodore Roosevelt's split with the Republican Party than it was a result of an

critical election
An election that produces sharp changes in patterns of party loyalty among voters.

expanded Democratic base. Roosevelt, a Republican president from 1901 to 1909, formed the Progressive "Bull Moose" Party and ran as its presidential candidate in 1912. He in effect split the Republican vote, handing Democrat Woodrow Wilson an Electoral College victory.

In 1912, the Republican Party's progressive and conservative wings split, giving the Democrats the White House and a majority in both houses of Congress. Within six years, however, Republicans regained control of Congress and were well positioned to retake the White House in 1920.

During the 62-year period from 1870 to 1932, the two major parties developed their party organizations and shored up their voting coalitions. They institutionalized their power in Congress by creating the party caucuses and electing party leaders. Also, during this period, the Democrats and Republicans developed party organizations so strong that the two-party Democrat–Republican system would become permanently institutionalized in American politics.

A fourth realigning election resulted from shifting party allegiances in the midst of the Great Depression. Republican Herbert Hoover was elected president in 1928, less than a year before the stock market crash of 1929 sent the economy into a tailspin. Hoover and the Republicans adopted some limited measures to deal with the economic disaster, but they maintained their party's traditional conservative faith in the dynamics of the market to solve economic problems. Franklin Delano Roosevelt, the Democratic candidate opposing Hoover in 1932, advocated a substantially larger and more activist role for government in dealing with the Depression. Roosevelt's pledge of a "New Deal" won the support of the urban working class, people of lower socioeconomic status, new immigrants, and many Catholics and Jews. The shift in allegiances from the Republican Party to the Democratic Party in 1932 (FDR carried 60 percent of the vote) had a lasting impact. Adding the "New Deal coalition" to the "solid Democratic South" resulted in Democratic Party domination of American politics for at least the next 36 years. The policies of Democratic presidents Roosevelt, Harry Truman, John F. Kennedy, and Lyndon Johnson during this era, supported by large Democratic majorities in Congress, were the product of the powerful New Deal coalition established in 1932.

Since 1968, however, both the New Deal coalition and the Democrats' solid grip on the South have all but disappeared.[8] At the same time, the century-long southern hostility toward the Republican Party of Abraham Lincoln has almost completely reversed, as many white conservatives in the South have become devotees to the Republican Party and its socially conservative agenda. Between 1969 and 2018, the Democrats controlled the White House for just 19 years, whereas the Republicans held the White House for 30 years. During that same period, the Democrats controlled both chambers of Congress for 24 years and the Republicans for 14 years, with 11 years of split majorities in the House and Senate. No clear critical elections appear to have occurred over this time frame, and few patterns in voter realignment are obvious. Indeed, some political scientists have argued that the term **dealignment**[9] best describes the behavior of voters since the 1960s. Dealignment refers to the decline in voter attachment to both parties.

Every federal election cycle between 2008 and 2018 produced new evidence of the electorate's diminished attachment to either of the two major political parties. After successive federal elections in which the Democratic Party took significant strides toward reestablishing itself as a lasting majority, many independents and

Drew Angerer/Getty Images

Democrats' perceived vulnerability of President Trump in his 2020 reelection bid led many to throw their hat in the ring for their party's presidential nomination. Taking part in the second night of the first Democratic presidential debate on June 27, 2019, in Miami, Florida, are (L-R) Marianne Williamson; former Colorado governor John Hickenlooper; former tech executive Andrew Yang; South Bend, Indiana, mayor Pete Buttigieg; former vice president Joe Biden; Sen. Bernie Sanders (I-VT); Sen. Kamala Harris (D-CA); Sen. Kirsten Gillibrand (D-NY); Sen. Michael Bennet (D-CO); and Rep. Eric Swalwell (D-CA).

disaffected Republicans who had voted for Democrats in 2006 and 2008 returned to the Republican fold in 2010. Four years later, in the 2014 midterm elections, the GOP secured control of the Senate once again. Whereas the GOP won the presidency and both houses of Congress in 2016, the Democrats recaptured control of the House in 2018. This much seems certain: neither party enjoys such a firm hold on the reins of government that they can afford to take any constituency for granted going forward.

As the Democrats and Republicans struggle with their long-term political identities, conflicting electoral outcomes will continue to hold their feet to the fire, threatening the long-term party attachments that had been so prevalent in the past.

13-2 THE FUNCTIONS OF POLITICAL PARTIES

Political parties serve a number of critical functions in the American political system at the national, state, and local levels of government. They give organizational coherence to both the operations of popular elections and the management of government. The functions that political parties serve have become inseparable from the principles that define how Americans choose leaders and how elected leaders formulate and administer public policies.

CONTESTING ELECTIONS

Free and open elections are the hallmark of the American republican form of government. With winning elections as their principal goal, political parties promote the prominence, competitiveness, and significance of elections in America. By winning elections and occupying seats in the government, members of the party can influence public policy. The larger the number of elective seats that a party controls, the greater will be the party's potential influence on policy outcomes. Thus, contesting elections lies at the core of a political party's functions.

To contest elections most effectively, the two major parties in the United States have developed a large set of party organizations. These organizations, which operate at the national, state, and local levels, are engaged in a number of activities directed toward winning elections. These activities include fund-raising, organizing events and meetings, providing funding to candidates who are running for office, recruiting and organizing volunteers who want to work for the election of candidates, and purchasing services (e.g., polling services, political advertisements, campaign materials such as bumper stickers, direct mail to homes) to promote the election of candidates. Many election contests feature a candidate from the party currently in office (the incumbent candidate) defending his or her record against an alternative candidate from the party out of power.

The fact that political parties are organized to contest elections and offer alternative proposals for making public policy promotes the responsiveness of elected officials to the voters: by offering voters alternative candidates more in line with public opinion, parties provide an effective mechanism for voters to remove leaders from office through elections. The alternative candidates offered by the Democratic and Republican Parties also serve to organize the process of competitive elections in the United States because the vast majority of elections feature a Democratic candidate and a Republican candidate running against each other. Some elections include independent or third-party candidates, and in some elections a Democratic candidate or a Republican candidate runs unchallenged. But most election contests feature some form of competition between candidates from the two major parties.

RECRUITING AND NOMINATING CANDIDATES

Political parties are the main vehicles through which candidates for office are recruited and screened. The fact that parties exist to win elections gives them the incentive to recruit candidates to run for office under the party label. Parties want to find candidates who will represent the party well, and thus they provide a "weeding-out" process that results in higher-quality candidates.

Most recruiting and promoting of candidates begins at the local party level. Individuals interested in politics often donate their time and efforts to working for political parties by, among other things, attending and participating in party meetings, distributing campaign literature, and driving candidates to campaign events. Local organizations tend to reward this service work with nominations for local offices, such as a seat on a local school board or a planning and zoning board. Successful candidates for these local offices often move up through the ranks of the local party organization to earn the endorsement and nomination of their party for higher office.

PROVIDING A FRAMEWORK FOR VOTERS TO MAKE CHOICES

Political parties also provide a useful framework for voters who must choose among candidates for elective office. Without even knowing the names of particular candidates for office, voters may be cued in to those candidates' political, ideological, and policy perspectives on the basis of a candidate's party. Most voters associate the political parties with at least broad approaches to governing, if not positions on specific policy issues. For example, on the role that government should play in fixing economic problems, most voters perceive the Democratic Party to be more likely to support an active role for government, whereas Republicans are perceived as having a more "hands-off" approach, preferring economic problems to correct themselves through the free market.

The organizational framework for voters to assess candidates is the political party. This framework helps voters more easily process and evaluate campaign information. Party labels thus offer voters an efficient shortcut mechanism for choosing among candidates. For instance, the Democratic Party and candidates running under that label are often regarded by voters as being more liberal or left of center in their position on issues, whereas candidates under the Republican Party label are viewed as being more conservative or right of center. Party identification is the psychological connection that voters have with a political party that influences other attitudes (such as one's position on gun control) as well as voting behavior. Party identification, an individual's feeling of attachment to a particular political party, is a political attitude that begins to form early in a person's life and generally remains quite stable throughout his or her lifetime. The authors of *The American Voter*,[10] a classic book on American voting behavior, described party identification as "generally a psychological identification which can persist without legal recognition or evidence of formal membership." Party identification serves an important role in forming attitudes on particular issues and making vote decisions.

Scientific surveys usually measure party identification by asking questions such as "Generally speaking, do you think of yourself as a Republican, a Democrat, an independent, or what?" Scholars began measuring party identification in the 1950s, and research on the concept has revealed several important findings. First, although the number of independents has grown slightly over the years, there are many more party identifiers than there are independents. Indeed, the majority of Americans today identify with a political party. Second, whereas the Democratic Party had more identifiers than the Republican Party from the mid-1940s to the 1980s, the number of Democrats and Republicans is nearly equal today. As a consequence, the two major parties enjoy pretty much equal amounts of support from the American public. Third, despite these shifts, party identification in the electorate is quite resistant to change. Thus, from one election to another, voting patterns remain remarkably stable and rarely deviate from either a Democratic or Republican victory. Fourth, party identification plays a very important role in helping voters make voting decisions: as shown in Figure 13-1, the vast majority of Republican identifiers vote for Republican candidates and the vast majority of Democratic identifiers vote for Democratic candidates.[11]

In addition to providing an important cue to voting habits, party identification also serves as an important influence on the policy positions that individuals hold. Party identification is also an important concept for candidates and party leaders in plotting campaign strategies and contesting elections. As political scientist Philip Converse has noted, a normal vote[12] can be expected for any given election contest. That is, a certain percentage of voters can be expected to cast a ballot for the Democrats, whereas another predictable percentage can be expected to

party identification The psychological attachment that an individual has to a particular party.

normal vote The percentage of voters that can be expected with reasonable certainty to cast a ballot for each of the two major political parties.

FIGURE 13-1

Party Identifiers Who Said They Would Support the Party Line in 2016

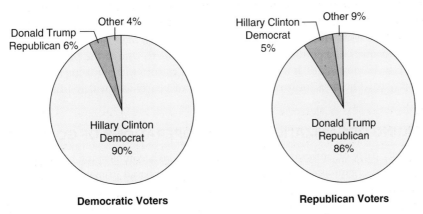

Democratic Voters   **Republican Voters**

Results of a preelection poll conducted by Quinnipiac University in September 2016.

vote for the Republicans. The strategy designed to win an election, and the chances that the strategy will result in a victory, largely depend on the normal vote distribution. The larger the margin is of one party's normal vote, the less competitive the race will be. The competitiveness of the race can also be influenced by the number of the nonpartisan voters.

An important caveat about the "normal vote" is that states vary widely in their distribution of Democrats and Republicans. In other words, what is normal for one state may be abnormal compared with another state. Figure 13-2 depicts the large variety in Democratic and Republican Party identifiers from state to state. For example, whereas in Rhode Island, Massachusetts, Hawaii, and Vermont Democratic Party identifiers largely outnumber Republicans, the opposite is true in Utah, Wyoming, Idaho, and Alaska.

FIGURE 13-2

Party Identification: The Most Democratic States and the Most Republican States Based on Party Registration

Top 10 Democratic States		Top 10 Republican States	
State	**Democratic advantage**	**State**	**Democratic advantage**
	Pct. pts.		Pct. pts.
District of Columbia	75	Utah	−23
Rhode Island	37	Wyoming	−20
Massachusetts	34	Idaho	−15
Hawaii	34	Alaska	−11
Vermont	33	Nebraska	−7
New York	27	Kansas	−2
Connecticut	26	Alabama	−1
Maryland	26	Arizona	0
Illinois	24	South Carolina	0
Delaware	23	Three tied at	1

Source: The Gallup Poll, www.gallup.com/poll/114016/state-states-political-party-affiliation.aspx.

Although party identification is defined as a psychological attachment that an individual has to a particular political party and is regarded by political scientists as an attitude, formal membership in a political party is generally associated with the process of voter registration. In addition to making a citizen eligible to vote, the voter registration process in many states includes registering as a member of a political party. In some states, membership in a political party is a necessary precondition for voting in that political party's primary elections to select the candidates who will represent the party in a general election. States with open primaries do not limit the nomination process to voters of one party. State laws govern how a citizen becomes a member of a political party and thus eligible to vote in the party's primary election contests. In most states, it is possible to register to vote without being a member of any particular party. The rules for becoming a member of a party vary widely from state to state.

PROVIDING ORGANIZATION FOR THE OPERATIONS OF GOVERNMENT

The majority party organizes its respective institution to accomplish the task of governing.[13] The leadership organization in the House and Senate is based primarily on majority-party leadership. The top leadership position in the House of Representatives is the Speaker of the House, who is always chosen by the majority-party caucus of the House. The chief leadership position in the Senate is the majority leader, who is selected by the majority-party caucus in the Senate. Members of the majority party chair committees in both houses of Congress. Leaders in Congress then try to implement the campaign pledges and platforms advocated by their party during the previous election campaigns. The executive branch, headed by the president, includes various departments and agencies that conduct the work of the federal government. Partisanship and loyalty to the president's political party are important factors that influence whom the president appoints to lead these agencies and departments.

The policy agenda and important policy decisions are largely the result of the political party organization and partisan leadership of these key branches of government. The greater a party's control is over the key governing institution, the more power that party has in influencing public policy. When the Democratic Party has a majority in both the House and the Senate and occupies the presidency, the Democratic Party has a great deal of control over what laws get passed. For example, the 1932 elections brought FDR, a Democrat, into the White House and resulted in increased Democratic majorities in both houses of Congress. The result of this dominance was passage of numerous laws promoting active government involvement in dealing with the Great Depression.

> **divided government**
> Split-party control of Congress and the presidency.

Democratic chair of the House Judiciary Committee Jerrold Nadler conducts a meeting in May 2019 in which subpoenas are issued to investigate portions of the Mueller report's findings regarding obstruction of justice activities of President Trump.

Tom Williams / Getty Images

Divided government, on the other hand, refers to split-party control of Congress and the presidency.[14] Because both houses of Congress are required for passing new laws, when the majority party in at least one house of Congress differs from the party occupying the presidency, a form of divided government exists. For example, the last six years of Democratic president Obama's term were characterized by GOP control of either one or both houses of Congress. This presence of divided government made it difficult for either party to advance its policy goals and objectives.

Whereas the first 150 years of the republic were mostly characterized by one party controlling both branches of government, the past half-century has been dominated by divided government. Eight of the last nine presidents have experienced at least some form of divided government during their term in office. Whereas President Trump and the GOP enjoyed united party government in 2017 and 2018, the Democrats won the House back in the 2018 midterm elections, ushering in yet another phase of divided government. Many observers of American politics question the rationality of an American electorate that so often sends one party to the presidency, yet keeps the opposite party in control of Congress. The stalemate or gridlock that may result from divided government is problematic to some. Still, many Americans believe that divided government has its benefits; certainly, divided control tends to intensify the checks and balances on power envisioned by the framers of the Constitution.

13-3 WHY A TWO-PARTY SYSTEM?

Political parties are an integral part of many of the world's democracies. Contemporary party systems are largely a product of the unique characteristics, history, issues, and social class structure of any given nation.

Although party systems in a democracy vary in numerous ways, they may generally be classified into one of two types: (1) two-party systems and (2) multiparty systems. The United States features a two-party system, dominated by the Democratic and Republican Parties.[15] The vast size and organizational structure of the two major parties, coupled with the fact that these two parties win the great majority of elections, appropriately classify the United States as a two-party system. Other democracies feature as many as 10 parties of relatively equal stature. The nations with multiparty systems typically include parties organized on the basis of political ideologies (such as the Socialist Party or Conservative Party), particular economic interests (such as the Agricultural Party or the Industrial Party), religion, geography, or positions on a single issue or set of issues.

In the United States, there is a wide range of ideological views, economic interests, religious orientations, ethnic groups, and geographic disparities. Other nations with such a wide diversity of interests typically rely on multiple parties to represent these different components of the population. However, in the United States, a two-party model has persisted now for more than two centuries.

REASONS FOR THE TWO-PARTY SYSTEM IN THE UNITED STATES

What are the factors that contribute to the American two-party model? A key factor is the Electoral College system for selecting the president of the United States. To win the presidency, a candidate must obtain a majority, not simply a plurality, of votes in the Electoral College. Naturally, this requirement encourages groups of voters to align with one of the major political parties, lest their votes be wasted. Minority groups, such as blue-collar union members, which have no chance of achieving a majority of votes as a single unified party, have found it in their best interest to support one of the two major parties in a presidential election. Being part of a winning coalition yields more influence than being in a smaller unified group with no chance of winning.

A second important factor that promotes the two-party system is the winner-take-all process that prevails in selecting members of Congress. In U.S. congressional elections, only the candidate with the most votes in a single district wins the seat. For example, in a race for a Senate seat, if the Democratic candidate receives 40 percent of the vote, the Republican 35 percent, the Reform Party 15 percent, and the Green Party 10 percent, the Democratic candidate with the 40 percent plurality is elected to Congress. By contrast, in other democracies, such as Israel, France, and Germany, forms of proportional representation are used. Under this system, the percentage of the vote that a party receives is reflected in the number of seats that that party occupies in the national legislature. In Israel, for example, a party that receives as little as 1.5 percent of the vote nationally is entitled to at least one seat in the 120-seat Knesset (the Israeli legislature). Whereas a proportional representation system gives minor parties representation in the legislature, the winner-take-all system does not. A third party must win the most votes in any given election contest to win a seat. The winner-take-all system promotes the two-party system and prevents smaller parties from achieving even minimal representation in the national legislature.

two-party system A political party system dominated by two major parties that win the vast majority of elections.

multiparty system A political system in which many different parties are organized on the basis of political ideologies, economic interests, religion, geography, or positions on a single issue or set of issues.

proportional representation A system of electing a national legislature in which the percentage of the vote that a party receives is reflected in the number of seats that the party occupies.

A third factor promoting the two-party system is the laws and regulations that govern campaigns in United States, which tend to benefit the major parties at the expense of third parties. For example, to qualify for matching federal funds for presidential campaigns and many state gubernatorial campaigns, candidates must demonstrate a minimum level of support in prior elections, primary elections, or both. Most minor parties, however, are eligible to receive such funds only after the election is over. They receive public funding in federal elections, for example, if (1) they receive 5 percent of the popular vote and (2) they appear on the ballot in at least 10 states. Because money to finance a campaign is necessary during, rather than after, the campaign, third parties are at a serious disadvantage. The lack of a history and lack of public interest in third-party primary elections precludes most from receiving federal or state funding in these elections. For a third party's candidate to appear on election ballots in the states, the party must meet a number of criteria, including petitions supporting the candidate and often significant fees.

MINOR AND THIRD PARTIES

Despite the dominance of the Republican and Democratic Parties over the past century and a half, third parties occasionally have contested elections in the United States. In 2016, two

TABLE 13-1
Third-Party Candidacies in Presidential Races

Third parties are by no means a new phenomenon in American politics. Despite their tendency to be short-lived and their relative lack of success in capturing elective office, third-party movements endure, often affecting which major-party candidate wins office. The following is a select list of third parties, their respective candidates, and the percentage of their vote totals in presidential elections.

Year	Party	Candidate	% of Popular Vote
1832	Anti-Masonic	William Wirt	8
1856	Know-Nothing	Millard Fillmore	22
1892	Populist	James Weaver	9
1912	Bull Moose	Theodore Roosevelt	27
1912	Socialist	Eugene V. Debs	6
1924	Progressive	Robert La Follette	17
1948	States' Rights	Strom Thurmond	2
1948	Progressive	Henry Wallace	2
1968	American Independent	George Wallace	14
1980	National Unity	John Anderson	7
1992	United We Stand America	Ross Perot	19
1996	Reform	Ross Perot	9
2000	Green	Ralph Nader*	3
2004	Independent	Ralph Nader	1
2016	Libertarian	Gary Johnson	3
2016	Green	Jill Stein	1

*Nader was technically the Green Party candidate for president in 1996 as well, but he was only on 22 state ballots that year and his candidacy labored under a self-imposed spending limit of $5,000. In the 2004 presidential election, the Green Party candidate was Texas attorney David Cobb; Nader ran as an independent in 2004.

third-party candidates (Libertarian Gary Johnson and the Green Party's Jill Stein) together received 4 percent of the vote. Most third-party candidates fail to register even one percentage point of the popular vote in presidential elections, and few third-party candidates are found in the U.S. Congress, in state legislatures or governorships, or in local government. For the past 160 years, not one president has been elected who did not run as either a Democrat or Republican.

Even the few-and-far-between third-party candidacies that have attracted a sizeable percentage of popular votes in presidential elections have experienced only short-lived success (see Table 13-1). The Progressive or "Bull Moose" Party of Theodore Roosevelt, for example, garnered 27 percent of the vote in 1912 but failed to establish itself as a permanent threat to the two major parties. Its success was largely based on Roosevelt's personal stature and popularity, and by 1916 Roosevelt had returned to the Republican fold. Likewise, Ross Perot, running as an independent in the 1992 presidential race, captured nearly 20 percent of the popular vote. But his attempt to match his 1992 success met with disappointment in his 1996 bid, when he took only 9 percent of the popular vote. By 2000, Perot's Reform Party showed up as barely a blip in the vote totals.[16]

Third parties face a number of obstacles in their attempt to become viable. First, their mostly negligible chance of winning at the outset leads many voters to sense that a vote for a third party would be wasted. The strong historical and cultural institutionalization of the American two-party system is another obstacle third parties face. The sizeable number of voters who identify themselves as either a Democrat or Republican inclines most voters to support major-party candidates in elections. In addition to the legal barriers already discussed, media coverage of campaigns also plays a role; the media tend to focus most of their coverage on the two major parties and give little attention to third-party candidacies.

Still, third parties persist. Despite their limited success in winning important government positions, they often have substantial influence on the outcome of elections. Third-party candidates in hotly contested presidential races have on occasion siphoned off enough votes from one of the major-party candidates to provide an Electoral College victory to the other major party. Twice since 1832, a third party has won more than 20 percent of the popular vote in a presidential race, and five times during this period a third party has won at least 10 percent of the popular vote.

13-4 PARTY ORGANIZATIONS

Political parties exist through party organizations at the national, state, and local levels. Although most elected government officials are members of the Democratic or the Republican Party, political parties also exist as organizations outside of the government. These party organizations, which often count millions of volunteers among their members, articulate positions on issues; enlist members from the public at large; recruit candidates who will run under the party label for elective office; raise money from individuals, corporations, and interest groups; and provide organizational and campaign services to candidates who are running for office.

Andrew Jackson is regarded as the father of the national party organization. Up until the election of 1828, a party's candidates for president and vice president were nominated by the party congressional caucus. Jackson changed this process by establishing a national party convention to be held several months before a presidential election. The convention brings together state and local party leaders to nominate the party's candidates for president and vice president. In addition to party leaders, the national conventions today include delegates from the states elected by members of the party in presidential primary elections.

Since the mid-nineteenth century, both Democratic and Republican national party organizations have been run by a national committee, which oversees the conduct of the presidential campaign and develops strategy for each party's congressional elections as well. The national committees, consisting of state and local party representatives, are run by a national committee chair chosen soon after the presidential election has concluded.

At the national level, the committees, chairs, and party organization largely provide a supportive role during the presidential campaign. Once providing a core advisory role to a presidential

national party organization The institution through which political parties exist at the national, state, and local levels, primarily focused on articulating policy positions, raising money, organizing volunteers, and providing services to candidates.

national committee The committee that oversees the conduct of a party's presidential campaign and develops strategy for congressional elections.

national committee chair The head of the national committee for one of the two major parties.

Bloomberg / Getty Images

Former secretary of labor Tom Perez is currently the chair of the Democratic National Committee.

candidate, the national organizations today are more involved in helping their candidate raise money and campaign for office. Strategy, planning, and advising are now handled mostly by the candidate's own campaign staff, which typically includes a media consultant, a pollster, a campaign manager, and various other campaign consultants. The modern-day national party organization is also less influential in determining who the nominee will be and more responsive to the victorious candidate's personal campaign staff. The national parties maintain greater influence in assisting state and local party efforts to win elections by providing polling and media consulting services, campaign management services, and financial resources.

In the modern era, state and local party organizations tend to be more influential in the nomination of candidates, in developing and organizing campaigns, and in providing a cue to voters about their vote selections. Voters pay less attention to campaigns in state and local elections and therefore depend more on partisan cues in their choice of candidates. State legislative and local election campaigns generally have limited resources to mount significant image-building campaigns for candidates. Candidates are thus more dependent on the resources of the state and local party organizations for financing. Local party organizations provide "get out the vote" services by funding phone banks to contact voters directly. State and local organizations also fund and make available polling services and media consulting services to candidates in less visible races. Because they benefit from these services, candidates for local and state offices may feel the need to be more responsive to the party organizations.

Local party organizations also provide the grassroots manpower for soliciting mass participation in political activities. These activities include implementing voter registration drives, organizing political fund-raisers and rallies, and staffing phone banks to make direct contact with voters urging them to vote for their party's candidates. Local organizations also provide the mechanism for identifying and recruiting talented citizens to become candidates for elective office. They provide the "farm team" for potential candidates for higher offices, such as governor, member of Congress, and senator.

13-5 VOTING

Political participation takes many forms in American politics. At the core of participation is the act of voting. Open and free elections held on a regular basis are the hallmark characteristic of a democratic government. Voting provides the critical linkage between citizens' preferences and governmental authority. The United States is not a direct democracy in which every citizen is invited to deliberate the issues and vote on public policy. Rather, the U.S. system is a representative democracy, sometimes referred to as an indirect democracy or republican form of government, in which citizens choose the individuals who are then responsible for making and enforcing public policy. The people do not directly rule, but they have the opportunity to exercise power vicariously by choosing as their leaders those whom they prefer.

The core principle underlying representative democracy is majoritarianism, or majority rule, which means that among the choices presented to voters, the choice that is supported by the most voters (i.e., receives the most votes) is the choice that prevails. When a majority makes its choice, the consent of the governed is satisfied. Given the diversity of opinions and interests among people in U.S. society, it is unrealistic to assume that all, or even most, voters will agree on one choice. But the will of the people is accomplished when the majority decides.

Voting in **elections** is the mechanism that ensures that the majority will rule. Times change, and so do people's opinions and preferences. Therefore, representative

elections The political mechanism that ensures that the majority will rule.

276 Chapter 13: Political Parties and Voting

democracy not only requires an election in the selection of leadership but also requires that elections occur on a regular basis so that the government's authority reflects changing majority views. Regular and periodic elections allow the majority of voters to continue to exercise ultimate control over the direction of public policy.

THE LEGAL STRUCTURE FOR VOTING IN THE UNITED STATES

The franchise, or suffrage, is the right to vote. When speaking about majority rule, it is important to ask, "majority of whom?" Article I, Section 4 of the U.S. Constitution assigns the system of voting, including the definition of who is granted suffrage, to the states. Voting registration, voter eligibility, methods of casting ballots, and the tallying of official results are all functions reserved for states. The original Constitution prescribes eligibility requirements for federal office-holders (representatives, senators, and the president) and lays out the system for selection of the president and vice president, but it says nothing about who can vote in the elections for these officials. Constitutional amendments have been ratified and federal laws have been passed that prevent states from discriminating in granting suffrage rights, but, technically, there exists no absolute constitutional right to vote in the first place.

TOWARD UNIVERSAL SUFFRAGE

The states have exercised significant authority in defining who is eligible to vote. For many years, states regularly denied minorities, women, young adults, Native Americans, and the poor the right to vote for office-holders at the local, state, and national levels of government. In addition, a number of states prescribed property ownership requirements that prevented many people from being eligible to vote. At various points in the nation's early history, some states sought to broaden the right of suffrage. New Jersey, for example, allowed women the right to vote in the early 1800s, and some northern states provided for black suffrage prior to the Civil War.[17] But the goal of universal suffrage—or the right of all citizens to vote—has been an elusive one throughout American history. Restrictions on voting rights have systematically denied the right of particular groups of people to participate in choosing their leaders.

Two centuries of government under the Constitution, however, have been marked by steady progress toward the goal of extending the franchise to all Americans. In the first federal elections in 1788, voting rights were limited to white men who owned property, whereas by the federal elections of 2018 all citizens of the United States aged 18 or older (who were not otherwise prohibited from voting due to a felony conviction or some similar offense) enjoyed the legal right to vote. Enfranchisement was not achieved quickly, nor did it happen as the result of one or two events. Rather, the process of extending the right to vote to all American adults occurred over centuries of time, and with much opposition.

The Civil War presented the first major challenge to the disenfranchisement of a particular class of people, namely, African Americans. Prior to the Civil War, African American slaves not only did not have the right to vote, they had no rights at all. In the infamous U.S. Supreme Court decision *Dred Scott v. Sandford* (1857),[18] the Court ruled that slaves were property, that they had no rights under the law, and that they were not and could never become legal citizens of the United States. Immediately after the surrender of Confederate forces in 1865, President Abraham Lincoln gave an address suggesting that freed slaves be given the franchise. The idea met with some resistance, even among the Northern states. However, the so-called Civil War amendments to the Constitution not only ended the institution of slavery (the Thirteenth Amendment) and granted citizenship to former slaves (the Fourteenth Amendment), but the Fifteenth Amendment, passed in 1870, guaranteed that "the right of citizens of the United States to vote shall not be denied or abridged by the United States or by any State on account of race, color, or previous condition of servitude." The Fifteenth Amendment was the first formal action granting the federal government the power to enforce voting rights over the states.

The Fifteenth Amendment, however, did not deter some officials from the former Confederate states from finding ways to deny African Americans their newly won voting rights after Reconstruction ended in 1877. Threats, beatings, destruction of property, and other

franchise The right to vote.

universal suffrage The idea that all citizens in a nation have the right to vote.

intimidation tactics, often ignored by local police, effectively kept blacks from coming to the polls on Election Day.[19] In addition, some states sought legal means to prevent blacks from voting. They passed laws instituting a poll tax that required individuals to pay a fee before being allowed to vote. They required potential voters to pass a literacy test to prove that they could read and write. Because most blacks were poor, they were often unable to pay the poll tax. Blacks also tended to have less education (in some states it had been illegal to teach slaves to read and write), so they frequently could not pass the literacy tests, which were often deliberately difficult and unfairly applied to minorities to prevent them from voting. From the late 1800s through the first half of the twentieth century, these methods posed a substantial barrier to black turnout in federal elections, which typically was about 10 percent. These laws also depressed turnout of poor people in general.

The civil rights movement of the 1960s addressed the problems associated with the disenfranchisement of blacks. Two important products of this movement were the Twenty-fourth

FIGURE 13-3

The Hispanic Vote in Presidential Elections, 1980–2016

The growing number of Hispanic voters, fully 25.2 million in 2012, has played to the advantage of Democratic Party presidential candidates. Latinos voted for Hillary Clinton over Donald Trump in 2016 by a margin of 66 percent to 28 percent.

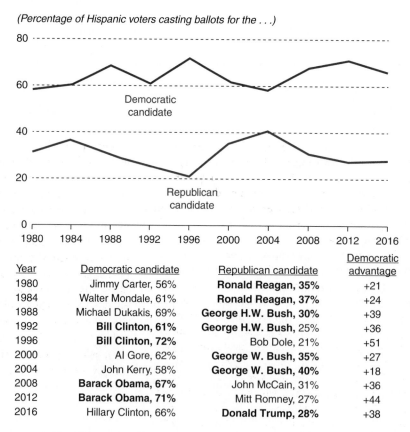

Year	Democratic candidate	Republican candidate	Democratic advantage
1980	Jimmy Carter, 56%	**Ronald Reagan, 35%**	+21
1984	Walter Mondale, 61%	**Ronald Reagan, 37%**	+24
1988	Michael Dukakis, 69%	**George H.W. Bush, 30%**	+39
1992	**Bill Clinton, 61%**	George H.W. Bush, 25%	+36
1996	**Bill Clinton, 72%**	Bob Dole, 21%	+51
2000	Al Gore, 62%	**George W. Bush, 35%**	+27
2004	John Kerry, 58%	**George W. Bush, 40%**	+18
2008	**Barack Obama, 67%**	John McCain, 31%	+36
2012	**Barack Obama, 71%**	Mitt Romney, 27%	+44
2016	Hillary Clinton, 66%	**Donald Trump, 28%**	+38

Notes: Winner in bold. Independent and other third-party candidates not shown. In 1992, the independent candidate Ross Perot received 14 percent of the Hispanic vote; "Democratic advantage" calculated after rounding.

Pew Hispanic Center analysis of national exit poll data, 1980–2016.

Source: "Latino Voters in the 2012 Election," Pew Research Center, Washington, DC, November 7, 2012, https://www.pewresearch.org/wp-content/uploads/sites/5/2012/11/2012_Latino_vote_exit_poll_analysis_final_11-09.pdf.

Amendment and the Voting Rights Act of 1965. The Twenty-fourth Amendment passed in 1964, outlawed poll taxes by making unconstitutional any law that made payment of a tax a voting eligibility requirement in federal elections.[20] The Voting Rights Act of 1965 denied states the right to use literacy tests as a requirement for voting; it also provided African Americans with protection from intimidating tactics that had been used to keep them away from the polls.

The past century also witnessed the enfranchisement of women. Although passage of the Fifteenth Amendment in 1870 granted African American men the legal right to vote, women would not receive the same constitutional guarantee until 1920 with the passage of the Nineteenth Amendment. In 1848, some 200 delegates—women and men—met in Seneca Falls, New York, to issue a call for women's rights, including the right to vote. The Civil War years diverted the nation's attention from women's rights to other pressing problems.[21] Attempts to include a women's right to vote in the Fifteenth Amendment proved unsuccessful, although women began voting in some states well before passage of the Fifteenth Amendment. By the late nineteenth century, some of the new western states, such as Utah, Wyoming, Colorado, Idaho, Washington, and California, enacted women's suffrage laws. Despite continued opposition from leaders, including President Woodrow Wilson, and many states in the Northeast, popular sentiment and a well-organized lobbying effort eventually led to the passage of the Nineteenth Amendment.

Three other groups have successfully won the right to vote through federal legislation and constitutional amendment. Until the early twentieth century, Native Americans had neither

DEBATES OVER DIVERSITY
Gender Trends in Party Support

The most recent presidential elections have demonstrated the huge electoral impact of specific groups, including racial/ethnic minorities and women. In particular, there was considerable attention paid to the "women's vote" in 2012 and 2016. Both parties focused on the critical gender gap in U.S. politics, defined as the difference between men's and women's support for the winning candidate. In the 2012 election, 55 percent of women supported Democratic candidate Barack Obama, which was 10 points higher than the male support he received. In 2016, 54 percent of women voters supported Democrat Hillary Clinton, a 13 point advantage.[22] This partisan gender gap has been evident in the United States since 1980, when women voters started to consistently support the Democratic presidential candidate by at least 7 to 10 points. The modern gender gap also includes women voting at higher rates than men, which in turn motivates both political parties to strategically appeal to the important "women's vote" through their policy stances and candidate selections.

Most of the focus on this modern gender gap is on the white majority population; however, the parties have also placed increasing importance on the gender gap among racial/ethnic minority voters as well. In terms of partisan identity and support, racial/ethnic minorities also provide a majority of their support to the Democratic Party. In fact, the modern partisan gender gap is now reinforced by the political behavior of racial/ethnic minority women. In 2012, black women and Latina voters overwhelmingly supported President Obama by 9 to 11 points, respectively, which was considerably greater than the support from their male counterparts. This partisan gender gap for black women and Latinas exceeded the gender gap for whites, which was 7 points. In 2016, the gender gap in support of Clinton was 14 points among blacks and 15 points among Latinos.[23] Meanwhile, the gender gap was 12 points among whites, with the majority of white women supporting Republican candidate Donald Trump.

For Critical Thinking and Discussion

1. Why do you think the Democratic Party has been more successful in attracting the majority of the women's vote in recent presidential elections?
2. What role do you think gender will play in influencing the outcome of the next presidential election?

citizenship nor voting rights, but federal laws passed in 1924 made it illegal for states to deny Native Americans the franchise. In 1961, the Twenty-third Amendment to the Constitution gave residents of the District of Columbia the right to vote in presidential elections. Because the district is not a state, its residents had not been allowed to participate in presidential elections. The Twenty-third Amendment allocates electoral votes to the District of Columbia using the same formula by which electoral votes are allocated to a state: the total number of representatives it would have in the House, if it were a state, plus two. Today, the District of Columbia has a total of three electoral votes. In 1971, in the midst of the Vietnam War when many young Americans were dying in battle, Congress passed and the states ratified the Twenty-sixth Amendment, which lowered the voting age to 18 in all local, state, and federal elections.

Although the administration of election and voting rules is largely controlled by the states, significant numbers of federal laws and constitutional amendments have extended voting rights in the United States. Collectively, these laws prevent states from discriminating against particular groups of citizens with respect to their right to vote. Unfortunately, racism and other forms of discrimination continue to exist and thus continue to affect voting rights in America. Subtle forms of discrimination, including intimidation tactics by groups such as the Ku Klux Klan, may scare individuals into not voting. But more overt discriminatory tactics, supported by some state and local laws, have largely been erased. As a society, the United States, over many years, has progressed toward the democratic ideal of universal suffrage. Today in the United States, the only adults legally disenfranchised are convicted felons in prison (47 states), on probation (29 states), and on parole (32 states).

VOTER REGISTRATION LAWS

Just as the extension of the franchise has evolved over the years, so has the system of voter registration. Most states today have voter registration systems in which individuals must qualify in order to become eligible to vote. The responsibility for qualifying lies with the individual. States do not compile and maintain a list of individuals who are eligible to vote. Rather, individuals must take it upon themselves to demonstrate their qualifications and file the appropriate paperwork to become eligible.

Massachusetts, in 1800, was the first state to require individuals to register to vote.[24] A handful of states followed Massachusetts's lead, but not until after the Civil War did most states adopt voter registration systems. Many of the voter registration systems that were adopted between the 1870s and the early 1900s made it harder for immigrants, the less educated, and those less familiar with the political system to vote. A leading force behind the institution of voter registration systems was the populist movement of the late nineteenth century, which largely included white, middle-class, native-born Americans. In the northern states, registration laws were intended to make it more difficult for new European immigrants to vote; in the West, the intention was to make voting by new Chinese and Japanese immigrants more difficult; in the South, registration was aimed at limiting the black vote; and the source of concern in the Southwest was Mexican immigrants. Most states today still rely on some form of self-initiated voter registration, which continues to present an obstacle to voting for some people.

A person must first find out how to register, remember to register in advance of Election Day, and then spend time registering. Many states require proof of age and citizenship, and many also impose a length-of-residence qualification, requiring a potential voter to prove that he or she has resided in the state for a specified period of time.[25]

Numerous organizations and public-interest groups have lobbied state legislatures and Congress to simplify and ease voter registration requirements in order to allow more people to vote on Election Day, including those who fail to register in advance of the election. North Dakota is the only state that does not currently require registration, and three states—Maine, Minnesota, and Wisconsin—permit voters to register on Election Day. The National Voter Registration Act of 1993, often called the Motor Voter law, mandates that when an individual applies for or renews a state driver's license, the state must also provide that individual with voter registration materials. The idea behind the law is that combining the process of

Twenty-third Amendment The constitutional amendment providing electoral votes to the District of Columbia, thus giving DC residents the right to vote in presidential elections.

Twenty-sixth Amendment The constitutional amendment that lowered the voting age to 18 in all local, state, and federal elections.

Motor Voter law The federal law mandating that when an individual applies for or renews a state driver's license, the state must also provide that individual with voter registration materials.

registering to vote with the more routine task of obtaining a driver's license makes voter registration easier. Research suggests that although this law has increased voter registration, it has not increased actual turnout.[26]

13-6 EXERCISING THE FRANCHISE

A number of factors explain why people decide to cast a ballot on Election Day. An individual's interest in politics is one important factor. People who are more interested in politics tend to follow news about campaigns to a much greater degree than those who are less interested, and those who are more interested are more likely to vote.

Interest in politics, however, is only one factor that leads people to vote. Another is a person's sense of "civic duty," or the belief that being a good citizen requires one to vote. Many people who are not very interested in politics show up to vote nonetheless because they have a sense of civic duty.[27] From a young age, most Americans are socialized to believe that participating in elections is characteristic of the good democratic citizen, and so they feel an obligation to cast a vote even though they may not be particularly interested in elections and campaigns.

Another factor that influences some people to vote is the perception that their vote can have an impact on the outcome of an election. Individuals who feel strongly about a particular issue, a set of issues, or a candidate may vote based on the theory that if the election is close, their vote might actually make a difference in the outcome. Indeed, the sense that one's vote can make a difference contributes to higher turnout in elections that are perceived to be close.

Finally, for some people, social group pressure can be a motivating factor in deciding to vote. Voting is often regarded as the "right" thing to do, and some people feel that casting a ballot is expected of them by others. This sense of social pressure to do what is acceptable by society's standards can increase the likelihood that a person will vote.

WHO TURNS OUT TO VOTE?

An individual's interest in politics and attentiveness to news about politics and campaigns, sense of civic duty, and sense of political efficacy (i.e., the belief that one's vote can make a difference) all lead to higher rates of voter turnout, which is the percentage of eligible voters who show up to vote on Election Day. In addition to these "political" factors that help to distinguish between citizens who are more or less likely to vote, there are a number of demographic characteristics that also help to explain turnout. A person's gender, age, race/ethnicity, and level of education are all related to the decision to vote (see Figure 13-4).

In many elections, younger people tend to pass up the opportunity to vote at greater rates than middle-aged and older people do. Youth nonvoting is often attributed to the more transient nature of younger people's lives.[28] At about age 18, many young people leave their parents' home to go to college, take a job, or start their careers. Younger Americans are less rooted in a community, have had less time to register to vote, and are experiencing major changes in their social and personal situations. Voting tends to be less of a priority under these changing circumstances. As people age, buy a home, have a family, and reside in a particular community for a period of time, they become more socially attached and are more likely to vote.

Two other demographic groups are substantially more likely to vote: better-educated Americans[29] and wealthier Americans.[30] These two factors are related because higher levels of education also lead to higher relative affluence and social status. The process of being educated sharpens a person's mind, improves the individual's ability to understand problems in society, and equips him or her to deal with complex information, such as the issues discussed in political campaigns. Education also enhances a person's appreciation for democracy and sense of civic duty. A better understanding of the issues and appreciation for the democratic process encourage higher levels of voter participation.

Racial and ethnic minority groups typically turn out to vote at lower rates compared to the white population, but the 2016 election marked the most diverse electorate in U.S. history. Thirty-one percent of eligible voters came from racial and ethnic minority groups, a

voter turnout The number of people who turn out to vote as a percentage of all those eligible to vote.

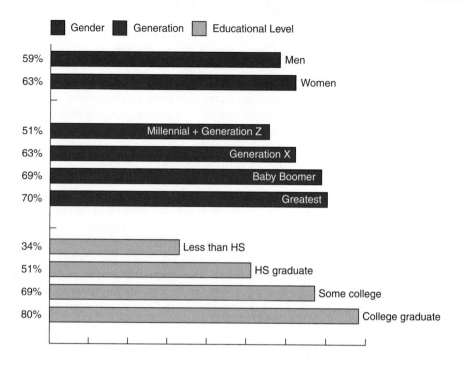

FIGURE 13-4

Differences in Voter Turnout among Demographic Groups in the 2016 Presidential Election

Legend: Gender | Generation | Educational Level

59%	Men
63%	Women
51%	Millennial + Generation Z
63%	Generation X
69%	Baby Boomer
70%	Greatest
34%	Less than HS
51%	HS graduate
69%	Some college
80%	College graduate

Source: U.S. Census Bureau.

net increase of 7.5 million voters.[31] In contrast, the share of the white non-Hispanic eligible voters hit an all-time low of 69 percent. The growing Latino population, in particular, has begun to wield major political influence.

As depicted in Figure 13-5, Hispanics nearly quadrupled in voting strength over the past 30 years to 27.3 million eligible voters, the largest increase of any racial/ethnic group.[32] Both major parties have sought the endorsement of this large and growing portion of the American electorate, but Democrats have proven more successful in capturing Latino interest, especially in national races. In the last two presidential elections, Democratic candidates won a substantial portion of the Latino vote: 71 percent in 2012 supported Barack Obama; 65 percent supported Hillary Clinton in 2016.[33] Hispanic voting dips, however, in midterm elections, such as in 2010 (when the GOP won back the House of Representatives) and 2014 (when Republicans won control of the Senate), muting the Democratic advantage provided by the Hispanic vote in presidential contests. Both parties know that the great untapped prize will come in the form of younger Hispanic voters aged 18 to 29, who make up a third of all eligible Hispanic voters but lag behind most other groups in turnout. And as the Hispanic population on the whole continues to grow, the next great ruling coalition in American politics may have Latino voters at its core.

Of course this modern surge in the size of the Hispanic electorate is hardly the first case of an immigration trend impacting the American political landscape. From 1880 through 1920, a surge in immigration from southern and eastern Europe occurred, as Italians, Hungarians, Poles, and Greeks (among others) left the economic and political strife of Europe seeking jobs and opportunities in America. This new immigrant population settled mostly in cities, which suffered disproportionately from the Great Depression. Neither party rushed to embrace America's newest citizens at the outset, yet it was the Democratic Party that was first to formulate policies aimed at these city dwellers. In 1932, Americans with eastern and southern European roots formed the core of Franklin D. Roosevelt's New Deal coalition, which came to dominate the American policy agenda for the next half-century.

FIGURE 13-5

A Record Number of Latinos Are Eligible to Vote

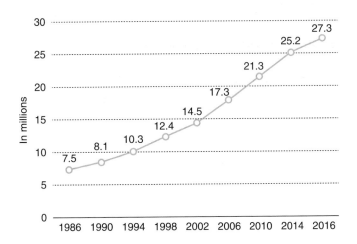

Note: Eligible voters are U.S. citizens ages 18 and older.

Source: "2016 Electorate Will Be the Most Diverse in U.S. History," Pew Research Center, Washington, DC, February 3, 2016, www.pewresearch.org/fact-tank/2016/02/03/2016-electorate-will-be-the-most-diverse-in-u-s-history/.

WHY DON'T MORE PEOPLE VOTE?

Despite the numerous factors that motivate people to vote, many in fact do not vote. Voter turnout is a measure of how engaged Americans are in voting in any given election contest. High turnout is considered a healthy sign for a democratic system. It implies that people are engaged in political issues, spend the time to contribute to the system, and take responsibility for selecting leaders. Lower turnout is often viewed as a by-product of alienation, mistrust, and lack of confidence in the political system.

Economist Anthony Downs originally offered an explanation for nonvoting based on a theory known as *rational choice*.[34] He argued that voters might decide not to vote because they reason that the costs of obtaining and understanding information about candidates and campaigns outweigh the benefits of making a vote choice. It is a rational choice, therefore, to decide not to vote, or to vote on the basis of certain "shortcuts" such as a candidate's political party.

Elections are plentiful in the United States and are held for many different offices at many different levels of government. Turnout varies from one type of election to another. Some elections draw much more media attention and thus engender more interest than others. Some feature much more political advertising and so provide more cues to voters. Some elections are inherently viewed as more important and so inspire a greater sense of civic duty among voters.

In 1966, political scientist Angus Campbell and his colleagues identified five factors that distinguish between "high-stimulus" elections (in which turnout tends to be higher) and "low-stimulus" elections (in which turnout is generally lower).[35] The factors that characterize a high-stimulus election are (1) greater levels of media coverage, (2) higher significance of the office, (3) campaigns in which voters assign high importance to an issue, (4) more desirable candidates, and (5) perceptions of a close race. Campbell and his colleagues argue that events external to voters may stimulate interest in elections and thus increase the likelihood that individuals will turn out to vote on Election Day. For example, when big issues such as war and peace are at stake, people are more likely to take an interest in the election and vote.

Presidential elections tend to produce the highest levels of turnout because (1) they are heavily covered by the media; (2) there is more spending on political advertisements, particularly on television, thus making the campaign more visible to voters; and (3) the presidency

FIGURE 13-6

Voter Turnout in U.S. Congressional and Presidential Elections 1789 to 2018

Trends in voter turnout for presidential year elections and midterm congressional elections.

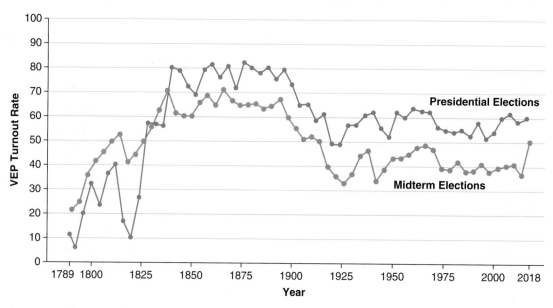

Source: Data from United States Election Project, http://www.electproject.org/national-1789-present.

is the most significant office in the U.S. political system. In presidential races where an issue important to many voters is at stake, such as problems with the Vietnam War in 1968, or the war with Iraq and terrorism in 2004, or immigration in 2016, turnout tends to be especially high. Races for higher office typically deal with bigger issues and feature candidates who are more attractive to voters. For these reasons, turnout in presidential races, and to a lesser extent in contests for U.S. senators and state governors, tends to be higher than turnout in elections for lower state offices and local races.

A well-documented trend from 1960 through 2000 was the declining rate of voter turnout in U.S. elections. Prior to 2004, turnout hovered around 50 percent for eight presidential elections. In fact, the election of 1996 marked the first time since 1908 that turnout dipped below the 50 percent mark, with only 49.1 percent of Americans of voting age going to the polls. More recently, however, voter turnout has trended upward (about 60 percent since 2004). Voter turnout is usually much lower in midterm congressional elections.

Figure 13-6 depicts the trend in voter turnout for presidential elections covering the past half-century. It shows that the downward trend in turnout from 1960 through 2000 has been reversed, with turnout in 2004 reaching the 60 percent level. It also shows how turnout is consistently higher in presidential elections compared to midterm congressional elections.

VOTING IN THE UNITED STATES COMPARED WITH OTHER DEMOCRACIES

Many observers of elections note that voter turnout rates are lower in the United States than they are in other democracies. Figure 13-7 shows turnout in other democracies around the world.[36]

Several explanations have been offered to account for both the lower turnout rates in the United States compared with turnout in other democracies as well as the trend toward declining rates of turnout in the United States over the past half-century.

FIGURE 13-7

Voter Turnout around the World

Voter turnout varies a great deal from one country to another. This figure depicts average voter turnout in recent elections in a number of the world's democracies. The turnout rates are expressed as the percentage of the voting-age population that actually voted in national elections. The data show that the United States tends to produce lower turnout compared with many other democracies around the world.

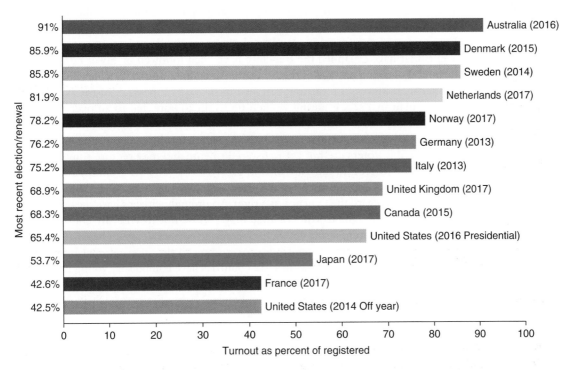

Source: Data from International Institute for Democracy and Electoral Assistance,
http://internationalcomparisons.org/political/voting.html.

1. **There are a large number of elections in America, making the opportunity to participate less of a novelty.** U.S. turnout rates may be lower than those in other democracies of the world simply because there are so many elections held in the United States.[37] The U.S. system of federalism produces several layers of government: national, state, and local. At the federal level, elections are held for president, the Senate, and the House of Representatives. At the state level, there are gubernatorial races as well as elections for other statewide offices. At the local level, there may be elections for mayor, city council, sheriff, local judges, and so on. The vast number of elections may help explain lower rates of voting in any one contest. Switzerland, which also has a large number of elections, also has relatively low turnout compared with other democracies.

2. **Tuesdays are workdays.** Traditionally, most elections in the United States have been held on Tuesdays. Most working people work on Tuesday, and so it may be inconvenient or difficult for many voters to find the time to vote on this day. In many other countries, elections are held on weekends or over a period of a number of days, making it easier for people to find the time to cast a vote. In May 2016, President Barack Obama called for Election Day to be a national holiday; Congress's determination to retain state control over the election process makes such a reform unlikely, at least in the short term.

3. **Voting in the United States usually requires advance registration.** As described earlier, voters in most U.S. states are required to register to vote prior to Election Day. In other countries, voter registration is often automatic; that is, citizens of legal age are automatically registered to vote. Thus, voters simply need to show up at the voting place on Election Day. In countries where registration is automatic, 100 percent of eligible

voters are thus registered; in the United States, where registration is usually a separate process, typically about 70 percent of eligible individuals have registered to vote.

4. **Over the past 50 years, perceptions both that participation can make a difference in what government does (i.e., voters' sense of "internal efficacy") and that government is responsive to the people ("external efficacy") have declined.** Many researchers have concluded that the decline in political efficacy,[38] which is accompanied by declines in political trust and in confidence in political institutions, has produced lower rates of voter turnout. As people come to feel that they are less able to influence the system and that the system is less responsive to them, they may become less likely to vote.

5. **Extensions of the franchise lead to short-term declines in turnout.** Ironically, events that have expanded the franchise have been followed by lower rates of voter turnout. Following passage of the Fifteenth Amendment in 1870, which enfranchised former male slaves, the turnout rate dropped in 1872; passage of the Nineteenth Amendment in 1920, granting women the right to vote, led to an overall drop in turnout; and passage of the Twenty-sixth Amendment in 1971 that lowered the voting age to 18 led to lower turnout rates. One explanation for this phenomenon is that many newly eligible voters are not yet registered to vote and may require some time and socialization to get into the habit of voting.

6. **Voting in the United States is not compulsory.** Some democracies, including the United States, regard the franchise as a right. Accordingly, citizens have the opportunity to exercise their right to vote, or they may choose not to vote. By contrast, some democracies have compulsory voting laws requiring citizens to vote. These nations assert that voting is a citizen's responsibility. According to the International Institute for Democracy and Electoral Assistance, 32 countries have compulsory voting laws on the books. Twenty-four countries enforce these laws to some degree, and of them, nine—Australia, Belgium, Cyprus, Fiji, Luxembourg, Nauru, Singapore, Switzerland, and Uruguay—have strict enforcement policies.

   Many arguments can be made in favor of or against compulsory voting laws, but one thing is certain: countries with compulsory voting laws have much higher turnout rates than countries without such laws. In Italy, for example, where lists of nonvoters are publicized, turnout has been around 90 percent. Though compulsory voting laws certainly increase turnout, many critics argue that the right to vote implicitly includes the right not to vote, just as the right to practice the religion of one's choice also includes the right not to practice a religion.

7. **The decline in "social capital."** Political scientist Robert Putnam has noted a general decline in social capital, which is the extent to which individuals are socially integrated into their community.[39] Over the past half-century, Americans have become less socially connected because they are not as likely to be members of organizations such as political parties, labor unions, civic groups, or even bowling leagues. As reasons for this decline, Putnam cites the increase of women in the workforce and corresponding reduction in the amount of time that women have available to spend on social and community activities. Other factors for the decline include the increase in residential mobility and technological innovations such as radio, television, and the internet. People today are more likely to stay home and watch TV or surf the internet and less likely to engage in social activities with other people. Voting is, in part, a social activity. The decline in social capital may be responsible, at least in part, for the general decline in voting.

social capital
The "social connectedness" of a community, or the extent to which individuals are socially integrated into their community.

13-7 PARTICIPATION BEYOND VOTING

Participation in American politics extends far beyond the act of voting. Many Americans volunteer to help out on political campaigns, contribute money to a candidate or party, try to influence others how to vote, and sign petitions endorsing a position on an issue. In addition, attending political rallies or participating in political protests are common ways of engaging in American politics.

Protesters rally in New York against the conduct of large corporations in the U.S. economy. These demonstrations have come to be known as the "Occupy Wall Street" movement.

One recent protest movement that gained a national following is the so-called Tea Party movement. Beginning in early 2009, a series of antitax protests emerged in response to the federal government's increase in spending to combat the economic recession. The Tea Party protests challenged the Barack Obama–Democratic Party policies of deficit spending and proposals to reform the nation's health care insurance system. The term *Tea Party* was chosen strategically to reference the Boston Tea Party, whose goal was to protest Britain's taxation policies toward the colonies during the American Revolutionary period. "TEA" is also used as an acronym for "taxed enough already." In addition to organizing protest rallies across the nation (annually on April 15, or "tax day," e.g.), Tea Party organizers were particularly active during the 2010 midterm elections and are credited with the large-scale GOP victories in the 2010 congressional contests.

Another protest movement that became popular in 2011 was the "Occupy Wall Street" protest movement. Beginning as a protest rally in New York City's financial district near Wall Street, many supporters of the movement organized rallies around the nation to voice their concerns about the growing division in economic equality between the top 1 percent of wealth and the remaining 99 percent. They blame the growing economic inequality on the greed and corruption of large financial institutions and demand reforms in public policy to reverse this inequality.

Protests can take one of three forms: legal protests in which citizens play by the "rules of the game" to speak out against a government policy, acts of nonviolent civil disobedience, and illegal protest activities that often include violence.

Marches, sit-ins, and rallies are forms of legal protests; such activities are designed to call attention to an issue that the protesters feel is not receiving adequate attention in the standard political process. Protesters are exercising their First Amendment right "peaceably to assemble, and to petition the Government for a redress of grievances." Many legal peaceful protests have raised awareness of an issue to a level that forces the normal legislative process to address it. A number of protest movements paved the way for substantial changes in public policy. Protests against the Vietnam War, for example, during the late 1960s and early 1970s led, in part, to American withdrawal from the Vietnam War. After World War I, protests among women's groups demanding the right of women to vote led to the adoption in 1920 of the Nineteenth Amendment granting women suffrage. Successful protests are often begun by small groups of individuals who feel strongly about an issue and are willing to spend the time and effort to make their case.

Youth Voting in 2012 and 2016 Made a Difference

Mitt Romney, the Republican nominee in 2012, decisively won middle-aged and senior voters (i.e., age 30 and older). His problem was the youth vote (voters aged 18 to 29), where he lost to Barack Obama by an overwhelming 60 percent to 37 percent. A study by the Center for Information and Research on Civic Learning and Engagement at Tufts University (CIRCLE) found that youth voting for Obama in four key battleground states (Florida, Pennsylvania, Ohio, and Virginia) tipped the outcome to an Obama win. Without the youth block in those states, Romney would have taken them and thus the election.

In response to the study, Heather Smith, president of Rock the Vote, was quoted in politico.com as saying, "I think we've now established a fairly decent pattern that this generation is different from their older brothers and sisters, and we can put those rumors of apathy to bed." On a conference call with reporters, Smith added, "This voting bloc can no longer be an afterthought to any party or campaign."[40]

In 2016, Hillary Clinton won the 18- to 29-year-old age group by an impressive margin of 55 percent to 37 percent over Donald Trump. Still, the youth vote for Clinton was not large enough to impact the Electoral College victory for Trump.

For Critical Thinking and Discussion

1. Why do you think that President Obama so handily won the youth vote in 2012, and Hillary Clinton did the same in 2016?
2. What issue positions and/or perspectives of young voters swayed them to these candidates?
3. What do you think about Heather Smith's comment regarding an established pattern that young voters today are different from their older cohorts? Was there a real difference in 2016?

Protests make for good television because they generally feature conflict, a grievance, and individuals who are outspoken about the particular cause. Well-organized groups that engage in protests on hot-button issues, such as environmental groups, pro-life or pro-choice groups, and anti–death penalty groups, have become adept at informing the news media about the protests ahead of time and engaging articulate speakers to make their case. The media attention often provides protesters an opportunity to ensure that their causes reach the policy agenda of governing institutions.

The second type of protest behavior, *civil disobedience*, involves protesters engaged in illegal but nonviolent activity. The goal of the protesters is to break laws that they feel are unjust, and the protesters willingly accept the consequences for breaking the law. Blacks protesting segregation laws in the southern states during the 1950s and 1960s would intentionally break those laws as a way of drawing attention to the problem of segregation.

Finally, a third type of protest behavior involves violent protests. In 1992, a number of rioters in south-central Los Angeles took to the streets after a jury acquitted several white police officers in a case where the officers had been caught on videotape brutally beating a black man they had stopped for a traffic violation. The rioters were protesting accusations of racial bias in the Los Angeles criminal justice system. The protesters looted businesses, stopped traffic, pulled a white truck driver out of his vehicle and severely beat him, and caused much damage to property.

The founders never intended for a two-party system to take hold in the republic they so carefully designed, and yet two-party systems have dominated U.S. politics for over two centuries, beginning with the rivalry between Federalists and the Democratic-Republicans in the 1790s and extending all the way to the present, in which Democrats and modern-day Republicans take turns controlling our government. Sometimes both major parties—despite all their built-in political advantages—lose touch with passionate strains of popular opinion. This is most likely to occur when the public grows increasingly skeptical about government as a whole. In such instances, an upstart political movement may suddenly arrive on the scene, connecting with the interests of a segment of the electorate that seeks a brand new means of influencing government. In the 1890s it was the "People's Party" (also known as the Populists) that made its voice heard; in 2010 and then again in 2014, the Tea Party movement lent its support to numerous antigovernment candidates and helped to shift party control of Congress in the process. In 2016 the victories of democratic socialists in the Democratic Party, such as Alexandria Ocasio-Cortez (D-NY) in the House of Representatives, began a far-left movement that is currently exerting its weight in Congress. If history is a guide, those movements tend to be short-lived, exerting significant influence in a series of election cycles before one or both of the major parties bring the movement's energetic set of followers into their own party's fold. Will the major political party that is most successful in this regard be willing to incorporate the upstart movement's ideas into its policy agenda as well? That was the dilemma that faced the Democratic Party in the 1890s and that faces both Republican and Democratic Parties today.

> **retrospective voting** A theory on voting behavior suggesting that voter evaluations of an incumbent's past performance provide important cues to voters in deciding whether to vote for that incumbent again.

TABLE 13-2
Making a Vote Choice

Political scientists and journalists attempt to explain why voters choose one candidate over another in an election. Research has identified a number of different factors that act as cues to individual voters in helping them make a vote decision. Collectively, these factors are referred to as *determinants of vote choice*.

Candidate Familiarity	The most basic voting cue is simple name recognition and familiarity with a candidate. Many voters pay little attention to politics and political campaigns. Recognizing the name of a candidate on a ballot, then, offers an important voting cue. High name recognition and voter familiarity propelled Hillary Clinton, former first lady, senator, and secretary of state, to frontrunner status early on in the race for the 2016 Democratic presidential nomination. In many congressional House races, incumbents tend to win reelection at rates in excess of 90 percent, in large part because voters recognize their names and are less familiar with the challengers.
Party Identification	Political parties play many important roles in the American political system. Often voters form a psychological attachment to a party, which helps them organize their political information and offers an important cue to vote choice. *Party identification* is the term for this psychological attachment. Party identification tends to be a long-term predisposition—once it is formed, it usually remains with an individual over the course of his or her life. Party identification, then, is an important determinant of vote choice.[41] Party identification is particularly powerful in influencing a vote decision in lower-profile political races.[42] It should be noted, however, that overall party identification and its impact on vote choice have been in a state of decline.[43]
Issue Voting	Voting on the basis of issues is more likely to occur in certain types of elections.[44] When a particular issue captures the attention of many people in the electorate, voters are more likely to use a candidate's position on that issue to form a vote decision. For example, in the 1968 presidential race, American involvement in the Vietnam War was a central concern for many voters, and many voted on the basis of the two candidates' positions on the war.[45] Issue voting occurs more often when an issue is of particular personal concern to a voter. Anthony Downs suggested that in making a vote choice,[46] voters examine the issue positions of the candidates and assess how close they are to the voters' own positions.
Retrospective Voting	Voters' past experience with a candidate or a political party also can be an important determinant of vote choice. Retrospective voting, a concept developed by political scientist Morris Fiorina, posits that evaluations of incumbents' past performance in office provide important cues for voters in deciding whether to vote for that incumbent.[47] Voters who believe that an incumbent has done a good job are likely to vote for the office-holder, whereas if they judge that an incumbent's job performance has been poor, they are likely to vote against the office-holder.
Candidate Image Voting	The image and personal traits of candidates can also influence the way people vote. Especially in higher-stimulus elections, where candidates make ample use of television advertisements to build an image, voter perceptions of candidates' qualities are important. Perceptions of candidate image include such characteristics as honesty, trustworthiness, leadership ability, concern for voters, integrity, intelligence, and sense of humor. Candidates for office who have more favorable images than their opponents among voters tend to fare much better in election contests. In 11 of the 13 presidential elections between 1952 and 2000, the candidate who had the higher "image score" from questions asked on the American National Election Survey won the election. In today's media age, candidates have found that image development is an efficient means of persuading swing voters how to vote.

Summary

13-1 The Development of Political Parties in the United States

- Despite the fact that the founders frowned on political parties and did not plan for them in the Constitution, every presidential and congressional election since 1796 has featured some form of party competition. National party conventions and national party organization originated during Andrew Jackson's presidency. The Democratic and Republican Parties have dominated since 1856.

- Certain elections, such as those of 1860, 1896, and 1932, are considered "critical elections" because they produced sharp and lasting changes in patterns of party loyalty among voters. Some political scientists have termed the era since 1968 as a period of dealignment, characterized by a decline in voter attachment to parties and in clarity of party coalitions.

13-2 The Functions of Political Parties

- There are four primary functions of political parties: recruiting and nominating candidates to run for office, providing organization and resources to help win elections, providing structure for voters as they make vote choices, and running the government.

13-3 Why a Two-Party System?

- The U.S. party system has been dominated by Democrats and Republicans since the election of 1856. This two-party system is perpetuated by several factors, including the need for a majority of Electoral College votes (not just a plurality) to win the presidency outright and a winner-take-all system that makes it especially hard for third parties to succeed to any degree.

- Third-party candidates rarely attract a significant percentage of popular votes in presidential elections because voters perceive that votes for such a candidate would be wasted and because various legal barriers make it hard for third-party candidates to receive government funding.

13-4 Party Organizations

- The two major political parties have organizations at the national level, at the state level in all 50 states, and at the local level in most cities and towns across the nation. These organizations are active in developing party platforms, recruiting candidates to run for office, and providing financial support and other resources to aid the candidates electorally.

13-5 Voting

- Traditionally, the states and not the federal government have had authority in running elections. However, state attempts to disenfranchise certain groups have been thwarted by constitutional amendments and federal laws. Although the goal of universal suffrage may not be fully realized today, over the centuries the United States has moved closer to this goal.

- The constitutional amendments that have limited states' ability to disenfranchise voters include the Fifteenth Amendment (guaranteeing African American men the franchise), Nineteenth Amendment (women's suffrage), Twenty-fourth Amendment (outlawing poll taxes), and Twenty-sixth Amendment (guaranteeing the vote to those 18 years of age).

- States are responsible for maintaining a system of voter registration, and the systems vary widely from state to state. Only one state (North Dakota) does not require voters to register to vote as a prequalification to voting. Through the Motor Voter law, the federal government has tried to encourage higher levels of voter registration.

13-6 Exercising the Franchise

- Among the factors that have been identified as relating to a citizen's propensity to vote are interest in politics, sense of civic duty, the perception that one's vote can make a difference, level of education, level of income, age, and social group pressure. The nature of the times and type of political campaign can also influence turnout. High-stimulus elections, in which the issues are very important or the campaigns are more visible, tend to produce higher voter turnout. Presidential elections generally promote the highest levels of turnout, and the less visible local races inspire the lowest levels of turnout.

- Although there has been a general declining trend in voter turnout in the United States over the past six or seven decades, recent presidential and midterm congressional elections have seen a modest increase in voting.

- Voter turnout in the United States tends to be lower than turnout in other democracies. Reasons that account for the lower U.S. turnout are the fact that there is no compulsory voting in the United States, the wide variation in states' voter registration requirements, the vast number of U.S. elections, and the tradition of holding elections on one weekday.

13-7 Participation beyond Voting

- Americans participate in politics in many ways beyond voting, including contributing time and money, participating in rallies and protests, and contacting their elected officials.

Key Terms

critical election (p. 267)
dealignment (p. 268)
divided government (p. 272)
elections (p. 276)
franchise (p. 277)
Motor Voter law (p. 280)
multiparty system (p. 273)
national committee (p. 275)
national committee chair (p. 275)
national party convention (p. 266)
national party organization (p. 275)
normal vote (p. 270)

party identification (p. 270)
party platform (p. 266)
political parties (p. 263)
proportional representation (p. 273)
retrospective voting (p. 289)
social capital (p. 286)
Twenty-sixth Amendment (p. 280)
Twenty-third Amendment (p. 280)
two-party system (p. 273)
universal suffrage (p. 277)
voter turnout (p. 281)

14

CAMPAIGNS AND ELECTIONS

Spencer Platt/Getty Images

Democratic presidential candidate and former vice president Joe Biden gives a speech on his foreign policy plan on July 11, 2019, in New York City.

THE U.S. CONSTITUTION CALLS for a presidential election every four years and congressional elections every two years. Without skipping a beat, the United States has met this constitutional requirement for more than two centuries. Through a Civil War, two world wars, and several major economic depressions, elections—the hallmark of American democracy—have taken place like clockwork. In designing this representative democracy, the founders intended a system that demanded accountability from elected officials. Elections for president and Congress provide this accountability. Regular and free elections are the linchpin underlying democracy in America. Every year Americans are invited to cast ballots in elections for many local, county, and statewide races, but no election receives more attention than the race for the presidency.

14-1 AMERICAN PRESIDENTIAL ELECTIONS IN HISTORICAL PERSPECTIVE

The U.S. Constitution says nothing about the process by which individuals become candidates for the presidency. The founders assumed that electors, chosen by the states (and heavily influenced by the House of Representatives), would identify and evaluate potential candidates, and then the Electoral College would select the chief executive.[1] The selection of president was intended to be the product of a select group of rational, wise men making choices at a lofty level above partisan politics.

Although their intentions for presidential selection were noble, the founders' expectations about how a president would actually be chosen proved to be quite naive. Political parties have provided the framework for every presidential election since George Washington. Each of the two major parties holds nomination contests in the 50 states to select the party's candidate in the general election; the party nominees then compete in the general election.

The modern presidential selection process is long and complex. The manner in which the 2020 selection process occurs is not based on some elaborate constitutional design. Rather, this complicated and quirky process is the result of more than 230 years of evolution. Over the years, two distinct phases of the presidential selection process have developed: the nomination phase and the general election phase.

THE NOMINATION PHASE

In the nomination phase, the political parties select specific people to run as the presidential and vice presidential candidates in the general election. This duo is referred to as the *party ticket*. The Constitution did not account for a nomination phase because the founders did not anticipate that a two-party system would emerge. The first two presidential elections did not even include political parties. Rather, the electors from the states all agreed that George Washington should be president in 1789 and again in 1792. Nevertheless, divisions within the federal government erupted and political alliances began to form during Washington's administration. These alliances resulted in the first two major political parties, the Federalists and their opponents, who eventually became known as the Democratic-Republicans. In 1796, when Washington decided not to seek a third term, each of these parties sought to win the presidency by recruiting and supporting candidates.[2]

The Federalists in Congress supported John Adams and the Democratic-Republicans threw their support to Thomas Jefferson. Electors, who were largely chosen by state legislatures, followed the cues of their partisan leadership in casting their electoral votes, and Adams, the Federalist-supported candidate, won the general election with 71 electoral votes, whereas Jefferson received 68 electoral votes. The nomination process in 1796 reflected a significant level of party discipline in the casting of ballots among electors. In the elections of 1800, 1804, and 1808, both the Federalists and the Democratic-Republicans used informal meetings and discussions to choose a party nominee. Democratic-Republicans dominated electoral politics from 1812 through 1828, as the Federalist Party eventually disappeared.

In 1824, however, a significant split occurred within the Democratic-Republican Party. Andrew Jackson, who had the support of many common people, challenged party favorite John Quincy Adams. Jackson won both the popular vote and a plurality of the electoral vote, but no candidate received a majority of electoral votes. By constitutional provision, the election was sent to the House of Representatives, which voted Adams the victor. Jackson then founded a new party, the Democratic Party,[3] which is, of course, one of the two major parties still in existence today. Jackson and his followers believed in the enfranchisement of all white men, rather than just the propertied class. During what became known as the Jacksonian era, white male suffrage was dramatically expanded throughout the country. Specifically, more and more state political parties adopted open caucuses, in which party members formally met to provide input as to who their party should nominate for elective office.

Electoral reforms during the Progressive Era of the early 1900s opened participation in the nomination process to a greater number of Americans. The direct primary gave voters an opportunity to cast a ballot for delegates, who would in turn be sent to a national convention for the purpose of choosing a presidential nominee. The state of Florida was the first to hold a direct primary in a presidential election, in 1900. Although direct primaries allowed greater numbers of people the opportunity to help select delegates, until the 1960s it was still the political elite of a party (governors, mayors, party chairs, and other officials) that selected most of the delegates and thus had the most input in choosing the party's presidential nominee.

The political unrest of the 1960s, spurred by anti–Vietnam War activism, led to further changes that gave voters in primaries even more weight in selecting party nominees. Benefiting from the increased percentage of convention delegates chosen through open primaries, Jimmy Carter, the little-known governor of Georgia, won the Democratic Party's nomination in 1976. A political outsider, Carter appealed directly to average voters. Carter not only won the nomination but also the presidency that year. His victory demonstrated to candidates in both the Democratic Party and the Republican Party that securing sufficient numbers of delegates to win the nomination requires direct appeals to voters, whether through party caucuses or, more likely, through party primary contests. Today this pattern persists: to win a party's nomination, a candidate must win a majority of delegates who are primarily chosen by voters in the state primaries and caucuses.

THE GENERAL ELECTION PHASE

The unanticipated emergence of political parties not only established a party nomination process but also forced a change in the founders' design for the Electoral College. The founders intended the state legislatures to pick well-qualified "electors," who would meet on a specified day in their state to decide who was the best choice to become president. At the end of the day, these electors would then cast votes for president. The states then sent their vote totals to the president of the U.S. Senate (the sitting vice president), who counted the votes before Congress. The candidate with a majority of votes became president and the second-place finisher became vice president. If no one candidate received a majority of the votes, the election was to be decided by the House of Representatives, with each state delegation having one vote to select the new president. The Senate was to select the vice president.

In the 1800 presidential race, nearly all of the Federalists voted for John Adams and Charles Pinckney (65 and 64 votes, respectively), and all of the Democratic-Republicans voted for Jefferson and Aaron Burr, each of whom received 73 votes. Although it was generally agreed that Jefferson was the leader of the Democratic-Republican ticket, Burr challenged Jefferson in the House. (Because the election was a tie, the House state delegations had to choose the new president.) Ultimately, the House decided in favor of Jefferson, who became president, with Burr then becoming vice president. It was clear that the presidential election system needed fixing.[4]

The Twelfth Amendment to the Constitution, passed in 1804, provided for separate balloting for president and vice president by requiring that electors designate one of their two votes for president and the second of their two votes for vice president. This amendment greatly reduced the possibility that future elections would end in a tie.

Several other amendments to the Constitution have altered the presidential selection process. The Twenty-second Amendment, ratified in 1951, limits presidents to two 4-year terms in office (or 10 years if a vice president serves out the term of a president). The Twenty-third Amendment, ratified in 1961, provides the District of Columbia with three electoral votes. Because the District of Columbia is not a state, it previously had no electoral votes.

14-2 THE NOMINATION CAMPAIGN

There are three distinct phases to the nomination campaign: the prenomination campaign, the primaries and caucus contests, and the national conventions.

THE PRENOMINATION CAMPAIGN

Although the presidential campaign officially begins with the first caucus contest in Iowa (held in early February 2020), the real campaign actually begins much earlier, soon after the previous presidential election has concluded. As part of the prenomination campaign,

prenomination campaign The political season in which candidates for president begin to explore the possibility of running by attempting to raise money and garner support.

behind-the-scenes candidates who are thinking about making a run often begin to "test the waters" by talking to party insiders, shoring up early commitments of support, lining up a campaign staff, beginning a fund-raising operation, traveling around the country making speeches and appearances, setting up "exploratory committees" to assess the feasibility of making a formal declaration of official candidacy, and then making the official announcement. Shortly after the 2016 election, for example, many candidates immediately began to plan for the 2020 Democratic nomination. By May 2019, 23 candidates had already thrown their hat into the ring. Table 14-1 lists the declared Democratic candidates as of October 2019 who had not yet dropped out of the race.

The prenomination campaign also marks the beginning of the "weeding-out" process. Early on, many would-be candidates find insufficient support from party insiders. Others cannot raise sufficient funds to be competitive. Some tire too quickly of the arduous and time-consuming schedule necessary for launching a run for the presidency. These and other obstacles begin the process of narrowing the field of candidates.

The **invisible primary** is the competition between candidates seeking the party nomination for frontrunner status. A candidate gains frontrunner status by winning broad support from important people within the party, raising more money than others, and

> **invisible primary** The competition among candidates seeking the party nomination for frontrunner status prior to the primaries and caucuses.

TABLE 14-1

Candidates for the 2020 Democratic Nomination for President, as of October 2019

Name	Candidate's Experience
Michael Bennet	**U.S. Senator from Colorado (2009–present)**
Joe Biden	**Vice President of the United States (2009–2017)** U.S. Senator from Delaware (1973–2009) Democratic candidate for President in 1988 and 2008
Cory Booker	**U.S. Senator from New Jersey (2013–present)** Mayor of Newark, New Jersey (2006–2013)
Steve Bullock	**Governor of Montana (2013–present)** Attorney General of Montana (2009–2013)
Pete Buttigieg	**Mayor of South Bend, Indiana (2012–present)** Democratic nominee for State Treasurer of Indiana in 2010
Julián Castro	**U.S. Secretary of Housing and Urban Development (2014–2017)** Mayor of San Antonio, Texas (2009–2014)
John Delaney	**U.S. Representative from MD-06 (2013–2019)**
Tulsi Gabbard	**U.S. Representative from HI-02 (2013–present)**
Kamala Harris	**U.S. Senator from California (2017–present)** Attorney General of California (2011–2017)
Amy Klobuchar	**U.S. Senator from Minnesota (2007–present)**
Wayne Messam	**Mayor of Miramar, Florida (2015–present)**
Beto O'Rourke	**U.S. Representative from TX-16 (2013–2019)** Democratic nominee for U.S. Senate from Texas in 2018
Bernie Sanders	**U.S. Senator from Vermont (2007–present)** U.S. Representative from VT-AL (1991–2007) Mayor of Burlington, Vermont (1981–1989) Democratic candidate for President in 2016
Joe Sestak	**U.S. Representative from PA-07 (2007-2011)** Democratic nominee for U.S. Senate from 2010 and 2016
Elizabeth Warren	**U.S. Senator from Massachusetts (2013–present)** Special Advisor for the Consumer Financial Protection Bureau (2010–2011)
Marianne Williamson	**Author, lecturer, and activist** Independent candidate for U.S. Representative from CA-33 in 2014
Andrew Yang	**Entrepreneur, philanthropist, and founder of Venture for America**

Democratic presidential candidates South Bend (Indiana) mayor Pete Buttigieg, former vice president Joe Biden, and Sen. Bernie Sanders (I-VT) take the stage for the second night of the first Democratic presidential debate on June 27, 2019, in Miami, Florida.

achieving the top position in the public polls conducted by leading news organizations. Frontrunners tend to receive more coverage in the news, thus promoting their name recognition and popularity as candidates.

In the campaign for the 2016 election, when there were 17 Republicans competing for the GOP nomination, the performance of the candidates in televised debates was an important part of the invisible primary. For the 2020 race, there will be at least 12 televised debates among the Democrats.

The invisible primary may go a long way toward winnowing the field down to a handful of realistic contenders for major-party nominations. Still, contenders for the party nomination must ultimately deliver victories in state primaries and caucuses or risk seeing their financial and volunteer support dry up in a hurry. Given the reduced importance of party conventions in influencing nomination decisions in the modern era, success in the early primaries and caucuses is crucial.

PRIMARIES AND CAUCUSES

The nomination of a candidate by a political party is the product of state-to-state contests in which delegates are committed to those candidates seeking the party's nomination. There are two basic methods by which states allocate delegates: presidential primary elections and caucuses.[5] A **presidential primary** is a statewide election to select delegates who will represent a state at the party's national convention.[6] In this election, voters choose among delegates who are committed to a particular candidate. The delegates who win go to the national convention and cast their vote for a party nominee to run in the general election. In 2016, 45 states used the presidential primary method of delegate selection. There are two types of primaries held by states. The less common approach is the **open primary**,[7] in which voters can show up at the voting booth on the primary Election Day and declare whether they want to vote in the Democratic Party primary or the Republican Party primary; they then cast their vote in the primary they have chosen. A **closed primary**[8] election, by contrast, requires voters to declare a party affiliation ahead of time. When the voters show up to vote in the primary, they are eligible to vote only for the party in which they are registered. Many states that use the closed primary have modified their requirements by allowing voters who have previously declared no party affiliation to show up at the polls on Election Day and declare a party and thus vote in that party's primary.

A handful of states, including Iowa, Nevada, and Maine, do not hold presidential primary elections; instead they use the caucus method to select delegates for the national party convention. In the **caucus** method, party members are invited to attend local meetings at which they choose delegates who make a commitment to a candidate for the party nomination. These delegates in turn attend more regionalized meetings and select delegates from that group. Depending on the size of the state and the number of regions, this process continues until a slate of delegates attends a statewide convention, or caucus. At this statewide caucus, attendees again vote for a slate of delegates, who are committed to a candidate, to send to the party's national convention.

presidential primary A statewide election to select delegates who will represent a state at the party's national convention.

open primary An election that allows voters to choose on the day of the primary election the party in which they want to vote.

closed primary An election that requires voters to declare their party affiliation ahead of time.

caucus A method of choosing party nominees in which party members attend local meetings at which they choose delegates committed to a particular candidate.

Role of Diversity in Vote Choice

An increasingly important campaign dynamic has been the role that descriptive characteristics of individual candidates have on voters' preferences. You may have noticed that certain candidates are more "familiar" to you, whether because their name or photo rings a bell. Many of us identify with candidates based on some shared descriptive characteristics such as gender, race, ethnicity, age, religion, or sexual orientation—we then vote based on that familiarity and disregard other factors such as ideology and policy position. Some political scientists have identified clear voter preferences for political candidates that share some of their own descriptive characteristics.

Voters may be assuming that if they share some of the same descriptive characteristics with the candidate, they might also share some of the same previous experiences, perspectives, and policy interests. Accordingly, these voter affinities may politically advantage some diverse candidates, while serving as a potential disadvantage for others due to the biases some of these voters hold. In the 2016 presidential campaign, gender became a focal point. Donald Trump accused Hillary Clinton of playing the "woman card," which he argued was the only reason she was doing well among voters. (You can see Clinton's campaign response in the tweeted image.) The 2020 presidential campaign also highlighted the influence of diverse candidate traits such as gender, race, ethnicity, and sexuality, which was evident with the crowded

Hillary Clinton ✔
@HillaryClinton

Lower wages! No paid family leave! Limited access to health care! Just some of the perks of your #WomanCard: hrc.io/1O1Jczr

9:25 PM · Apr 29, 2016 · TweetDeck

1.5K Retweets **3K** Likes

Twitter/Hillary Clinton

Screenshot of Hillary Clinton 2016 campaign tweet advertising an official "woman card."

Democratic field of candidates including Kamala Harris, Elizabeth Warren, Cory Booker, Pete Buttigieg, and Julián Castro.

For Critical Thinking and Discussion

1. Which candidates did you support in recent presidential elections, and do you think shared descriptive characteristics influenced your decision? Can you explain why?
2. If shared characteristics do indeed play a significant role in voter decision-making, racial/ethnic minority candidates may find it more difficult to win elections in majority white voter districts, while enjoying significant political advantages in districts with heavy racial/ethnic minority populations. Is this a healthy development for our democracy? Why or why not?

The first state contest for delegates, normally the Iowa caucus (scheduled for early February 2020) launches the process by which delegates from the states commit to candidates for the party nomination. One week after the Iowa caucus comes the New Hampshire primary,[9] which has traditionally been the first state primary election in which delegates commit to candidates.[10] Each of the 50 states (along with the District of Columbia, the U.S. Virgin Islands, American Samoa, and Guam) holds either a caucus or primary election, and in each of these contests delegates commit to candidates. The calendar of state caucuses and primaries, beginning in February and extending into June, is referred to as the nomination campaign. Table 14-2 lists the schedule of primaries and caucuses for the 2020 presidential campaign. Through the nomination campaign, a candidate attempts to win a majority of delegates in the caucus and primary contests to lay claim to be the winner of the party's nomination.

> **nomination campaign** The political season in which the two major parties hold primaries and caucuses in all the states to choose party delegates committed to specific candidates.

TABLE 14-2

Schedule of Primaries and Caucuses for 2020

- **February 3:** Iowa caucus
- **February 11:** New Hampshire primary
- **February 22:** Nevada caucus
- **February 29:** South Carolina primary
- **March 3:** Super Tuesday (Alabama, Arkansas, California, Colorado, Massachusetts, Minnesota, North Carolina, Oklahoma, Tennessee, Texas, Utah, Vermont, and Virginia primaries; Democrats Abroad preference vote through March 10)
- **March 7:** Louisiana primary
- **March 8:** Maine caucus (likely amended to a Tuesday-in-March primary if primary legislation passes)
- **March 10:** Idaho, Michigan, Mississippi, Missouri, Ohio, and Washington primaries; North Dakota firehouse caucus/primary
- **March 17:** Arizona, Florida, and Illinois primaries
- *To be determined:* Wyoming caucus (March, TBD)
- **April 4:** Alaska and Hawaii primaries
- **April 7:** Wisconsin primary
- **April 28:** Connecticut, Delaware, Maryland, Pennsylvania, and Rhode Island primaries
- **May 2:** Kansas primary
- **May 5:** Indiana primary
- **May 12:** West Virginia primary
- **May 19:** Kentucky and Oregon primaries
- **June 2:** Montana, New Jersey, New Mexico, and South Dakota primaries
- **June 7:** Puerto Rico primary
- **June 16:** District of Columbia primary

THE TRADITIONAL IMPORTANCE OF THE IOWA AND NEW HAMPSHIRE CONTESTS

Iowa and New Hampshire are small states with relatively few delegates. The Iowa caucus in 2016 had just 28 delegates at stake, and the 2016 New Hampshire primary had a mere 23 delegates at stake. To win the nomination campaign, the successful Republican candidate needed to amass support from at least 2,137 total delegates. In pure delegate count, larger states, such as California with 170 delegates and New York with 95, are, of course, much more important. Why, then, do Iowa and New Hampshire enjoy such disproportionately great influence in the nomination process? The answer is timing: Iowa and New Hampshire have traditionally been the first two contests held. The news media thus focus a tremendous amount of attention on these initial competitions. Winners of the Iowa and New Hampshire contests receive a great amount of attention in the news, whereas losers tend to get written off as "unelectable."

2020 Democratic nomination rivals Julián Castro, Cory Booker, and Elizabeth Warren joke with each other before a debate in 2019.

Joe Raedle/Getty Images

The importance of the early contests has led to a phenomenon known as frontloading,[11] a trend that has occurred over the past six or seven presidential elections in which states have moved their primary or caucus contests earlier in the year to attract greater attention from the candidates and the media. A state that holds its contest early makes itself more important in the nominee selection process. In 1988, the time between the Iowa caucus and the date by which most states had chosen their convention delegates was more than 20 weeks.

In 2020, most delegates from both parties will be selected within a six-week period, from early February to mid-March.

For the 2016 Democratic Party nomination, Hillary Clinton, Vermont senator Bernie Sanders, and three others threw their hats in the ring early on. All but Clinton and Sanders dropped out shortly after the primaries began. Sanders stayed in the race until the last of the primaries but fell short of Clinton by a final tally of 2,807 to 1,894 delegates.

On the GOP side, 17 candidates entered the race. By March 2016, five candidates had survived. Though dismissed by most pundits initially, Donald Trump campaigned furiously against the GOP establishment and appealed to frustrated Republican voters who had elected large majorities to Congress, only to be stymied by the Democratic president. Trump's message gained steam as the campaign wore on, and by June 2016 he had secured enough delegates to take the nomination.

THE NOMINATING CONVENTIONS

The national conventions for the Democratic and Republican Parties were once used to discuss the party platform and, most important, to choose the candidate who would represent the party in the general election. The images of the smoke-filled back rooms where deals were cut and delegates were lobbied to throw their support behind a particular candidate were very real. For most of our nation's history, the major parties selected candidates for the presidency in this way. Much of the brokering and deal-making took place by skilled political operators at the national conventions.

The 1968 Democratic National Convention, held in Chicago, was characterized by a great deal of divisiveness and discord, much of which was captured on national network television. Vietnam War protesters outside of the convention hall were beaten by Chicago police under the direction of Chicago mayor and "political boss" Richard J. Daley. Tension reigned inside the convention center as well, with antiwar supporters of Eugene McCarthy and George McGovern clashing with the party regulars supporting Hubert Humphrey. Television brought the negative images of the divided Democratic Party into American homes, seriously damaging the Democratic ticket. Four years later, television coverage again captured a disunited Democratic Party at the national convention in Miami, where delegates fought into the wee hours of the morning to nominate a party candidate (George McGovern finally won the nomination). The Democrats were not the only party to suffer discord and division. In 1976, grass-roots support for Ronald Reagan spoiled any momentum incumbent president Gerald Ford hoped to generate at the Republican National Convention.

By the mid-1980s, both major political parties, recognizing the influential role that television was playing in election politics, had begun to adjust their agenda for the national conventions. With the frontloading process allowing candidates to capture a majority of delegates prior to the national convention, the parties began to choreograph their conventions and use them as advertisements for the party ticket.

frontloading The recent trend of states moving their primaries and caucuses to earlier in the year to attract greater attention from the candidates and the media.

Hillary Clinton accepts the Democratic nomination for president at the party's 2016 national convention.

Bill Clark / Getty Images

Governor Mike Pence of Indiana (right) disagrees with Senator Tim Kaine of Virginia at the 2016 debate between the two major-party hopefuls for vice president. Vice presidents in the modern era have played increasingly influential roles as policy-makers in government.

Today's conventions tend to avoid airing any intraparty differences. Instead, they are "anointing" ceremonies for the party ticket. They feature popular members of the party endorsing the nominees and include prerecorded videos highlighting the nominees' record of public service and family values.[12]

Today's GOP and Democratic nominating conventions provide a week-long forum for the parties and their nominees to introduce themselves to voters and to formally kick off the general election campaign. With a very crowded candidate field on the Democratic side, it is possible that no one candidate will receive a majority of delegates by the end of the primaries. If that is the case, the Democratic Party convention will also be the event when a party nominee is selected through a brokered process.

At (or near) the conventions, the party nominee selects the vice presidential running mate. Significant amounts of thought and fanfare normally go into this selection. Vice presidential candidates are quite visible on the campaign trail and can provide a boost to the ticket. The choice of running mate often attempts to balance the ticket geographically. John Edwards, for example, was from the southern state of North Carolina, a factor deemed important by the 2004 Democratic nominee, John Kerry, who was from Massachusetts. Vice presidential candidates are often chosen on the basis of their ideological leanings. In 1980 Ronald Reagan selected George H. W. Bush as his running mate in part because Reagan was viewed as far to the political right and needed a running mate who was more moderate. By contrast, the more moderate Bob Dole chose the ideologically conservative Jack Kemp as his choice for vice president in 1996 to mobilize conservative Republican voters, as did Donald Trump with his selection of Indiana governor Mike Pence in 2016.

In 2016, Democrat presidential nominee Hillary Clinton selected as her running mate Senator Tim Kaine of Virginia. This choice was at least in part based on Kaine's reputation as a moderate Democrat (thus appealing to independent voters) and the fact that he was popular in the battleground state of Virginia, where he had once served as governor. Pence's popularity among social conservatives served as the basis for this choice, along with the fact that Pence had plenty of experience in elective office (something Trump lacked).

14-3 THE GENERAL ELECTION CAMPAIGN

A number of factors provide context for understanding general election campaigns in the American political system. These include whether an incumbent is running, the strategy for achieving a winning coalition of states, the presidential debates, political advertisements, and, finally, the vote in the Electoral College.

INCUMBENT RACE VERSUS OPEN ELECTION

incumbent race General election race pitting a person currently holding the office against a challenger.

General election campaigns for president are highly visible, very well funded, and among the most noteworthy of events in the American political system. Sometimes the contest is an incumbent race pitting a sitting president against a challenger. That was the case in 2020, as President Trump announced his reelection plans early on. In an incumbent race, the focus of the campaign tends to revolve around the performance of the incumbent over the past four years. In this sense, incumbent races are often viewed as a referendum on the performance of the current occupant of the White House.

In all, there have been 11 incumbents who lost bids for another term. Five of these incumbent losses occurred over the past 100 years: in 1912 Woodrow Wilson defeated President William Howard Taft; in 1932 Franklin Delano Roosevelt defeated President Herbert Hoover; in 1976 Jimmy Carter defeated President Gerald R. Ford; in 1980 Ronald Reagan beat President Carter; and in 1992 Bill Clinton defeated President George H. W. Bush.

In open elections, neither candidate is an incumbent. In 2016, for example, President Barack Obama was constitutionally prohibited from running for a third term. Former first lady, U.S. senator, and secretary of state Hillary Clinton was the Democratic Party's nominee, and billionaire businessman Donald Trump was the Republican Party's candidate in the general election. Clinton took credit for her work in the Obama administration, and Trump criticized Clinton's association with Obama. However, the focus of the race was more on the personality characteristics (and flaws) of these two candidates with far less discussion of President Obama's record.

GATHERING A WINNING COALITION OF STATES

A central feature of any general election campaign is each candidate's plan to put together a coalition of states sufficient to win a majority of electoral votes. At the outset of the campaign, states may be divided into three categories: reliably Republican states, reliably Democratic states, and the so-called battleground (or "swing") states, those that either candidate has a reasonable chance of winning. The map in Figure 14-1 depicts this categorization of states for the 2020 presidential campaign, based on the narrow margin of victory in 2016. The blue states were safely Democratic and the red were safely Republican; the gold states were close.

> **open election** General election race in which neither candidate is the incumbent. (Open elections for Congress are normally called *open-seat elections*.)
>
> **battleground states** States identified as offering either major-party candidate a reasonable chance for victory in the Electoral College.

FIGURE 14-1

Top Battleground States in 2020

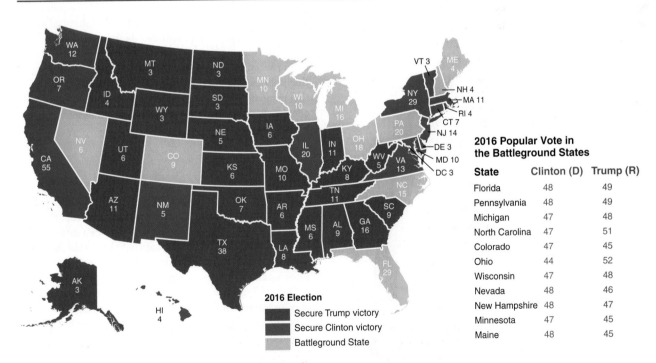

2016 Popular Vote in the Battleground States

State	Clinton (D)	Trump (R)
Florida	48	49
Pennsylvania	48	49
Michigan	47	48
North Carolina	47	51
Colorado	47	45
Ohio	44	52
Wisconsin	47	48
Nevada	48	46
New Hampshire	48	47
Minnesota	47	45
Maine	48	45

2016 Election

- Secure Trump victory
- Secure Clinton victory
- Battleground State

In the presidential campaign of 2016, the vast majority of states saw relatively little activity in terms of candidate appearances and television advertising. Instead, the candidates for both major parties targeted a few select states for concentrated activity. They spent most of their resources of time and money on these battleground states because, as each candidate knew well ahead of time, these were where the election outcome would be decided.

"It Was the Most Negative Campaign in the History of American Presidential Elections"

President Barack Obama famously proclaimed, "Elections have consequences." Certainly politicians of all stripes pour considerable time, effort, and money into presidential campaigns in hopes that those consequences will be favorable ones. Often the stakes in election outcomes are so high and the will to win so strong that campaigns take a negative tone. Living through a negative campaign can leave voters with the sense that "politics has never been so negative." However, the reality is that in the history of American presidential elections, campaigns are often quite negative.

Then

In 1828, incumbent John Quincy Adams, the sixth president of the United States, was embroiled in an intense rematch against Andrew Jackson, a general and war hero. Jackson had won a plurality of votes in the 1824 race and enjoyed a slight edge over Adams in the Electoral College count as well. Yet, because Jackson did not achieve a majority within the Electoral College, the race was thrown into the House of Representatives, where a questionable behind-the-scenes deal led to Adams winning the presidency. Four years later the stakes were high, as the United States economy was struggling. Debates over

U.S. president-elect Donald Trump arrives at his celebration party on November 8, 2016.

tariffs in international trade were especially intense, and the tone of the campaign turned negative. At one point Adams called Jackson's wife "a convicted adulteress" and his mother "a common prostitute." Jackson responded by accusing Adams of having premarital sex with his wife and acting as a pimp. Voters in 1828 were left with the feeling that politics could not get much worse. Many involved in that campaign were not around to see the highly negative campaign of 1800 waged between two of America's founding fathers.

Now

We all lived through the **2016** campaign—few of us will soon forget the negative, bitter tone that was reported by the media on a near daily basis. America's intense ideological divide over "Obamacare," taxes, immigration, and the war on terrorism fueled this negativity. At one point in the campaign Hillary Clinton referred to Donald Trump supporters as "a basket of deplorables," adding that they are "sexist, racist, homophobic, xenophobic, islamophobic" people. Trump, for his part, fueled the negativity with claims that "Bill Clinton has actually abused women and Hillary has bullied, attacked, shamed, and intimidated his victims." To be sure, the 2016 campaign was filled with vitriolic and personal attacks, but it was one of many such negative elections in American history.

"*Jackson is to be President. and you will be HANGED.*"

A cartoon during the 1828 campaign, accusing Andrew Jackson of lynching his opponents.

In 2020, President Trump and his Democratic challenger set their sights on these 11 battleground states: Colorado, Florida, Minnesota, Michigan, Nevada, New Hampshire, Maine, North Carolina, Ohio, Pennsylvania, and Wisconsin. In 2016, Trump won six of them and five went to Clinton. The six that went for Trump were the larger states and so his path to Electoral College victory included the large number of electoral votes in these swing states. Interestingly, in four of the six, Trump's margin of victory was 1 percent or less.

THE PRESIDENTIAL DEBATES

The media and the public have come to expect that a presidential campaign will feature debates between the presidential candidates and sometimes between the vice presidential candidates as well. Candidates may not believe it is in their strategic interest to debate their opponents. For example, a candidate who is ahead in the polls might prefer to play it safe and not run the risk of losing a debate and perhaps the lead in the campaign. Still, both major-party candidates usually agree to debate so that they aren't portrayed as being afraid to do so. The expectation of a set of debates, however, is a relatively recent phenomenon in presidential elections. The first debates that generated a high level of interest and scrutiny were those between John F. Kennedy and Richard M. Nixon in the 1960 election campaign. Some political scientists today credit Kennedy's victory as partly the result of his strong performance in the debates.[13]

The next set of presidential debates occurred in 1976, between Gerald Ford and Jimmy Carter. Each presidential campaign since then has included debates between the presidential candidates and sometimes also between the vice presidential candidates. (The presidential debates are discussed in further detail in Chapter 12.) The schedule of debates and the rules governing their conduct are the product of intense negotiation between the campaigns. In 2016, the detailed set of rules for the three presidential debates included instructions that the candidates could not cross over a line on the stage separating them and time limits on answering questions and offering rebuttals.

Despite the large amount of attention both the campaigns and the media pay to the debates, the impact that debates have on the election outcome is unclear. Many researchers have documented that those who tend to watch the debates already have moderate to strong convictions regarding who they want to win, and these convictions often shape how an individual voter evaluates the candidate's performance in the debates. Although polls sometimes show that the voters tend to identify a debate "winner," there is far less evidence to show that this has any impact on voter intentions. The first of the debates often gets the most attention, and yet many of the media-dubbed "winners" of first debates, whether Walter Mondale in 1984, Michael Dukakis in 1988, Ross Perot in 1992, or John Kerry in 2004, have ended up on the short side of the electoral vote count on Election Day. More evidence of this pattern emerged in the 2012 race, as Republican challenger Mitt Romney was widely regarded as the winner of the first debate against President Barack Obama. Yet it was Obama who secured the overall victory on Election Day. Some observers of elections indicate that although debates may not have a direct impact on vote intentions, they can change the dynamics of a campaign, which in turn may influence the outcome.[14]

THE ADVERTISING

Television advertisements have become a staple of presidential campaign strategies.[15] They are used to heighten name recognition, communicate core messages to voters,

Donald Trump and Hillary Clinton face off at their first presidential debate of the 2016 general election campaign. The event was watched by more than 100 million viewers.

and offer reasons why one should vote for (or against) a particular candidate. Television advertising uses a variety of different techniques to accomplish these goals. The most controversial of these techniques is the attack or "negative" ads that candidates often use to portray their opponents in a bad light.[16] Television ads can be very effective at convincing voters to support a candidate—particularly voters who are undecided on any particular candidate or who are politically independent rather than identifying themselves as a Democrat or a Republican. Whereas other forms of campaign communication (such as televised debates, political news columns, political talk shows on radio and TV, and news broadcasts) are provided in formats that appeal to voters who are interested in the campaign and have already made up their minds about who they will vote for, televised advertisements may be placed during certain shows or at certain times when independents and undecided voters are tuning in. The unsuspecting audience is captive to the short advertisement, which provides a unique opportunity for a campaign to attract votes.

THE ELECTORAL COLLEGE VOTE

Unlike elections for most public offices in the United States, the outcome of the popular vote does not determine who wins the presidential election. The winner of the presidential election is the candidate who receives a majority of the 538 votes in the Electoral College. Five times in American history the popular vote winner did not win in the Electoral College, most recently in 2016 when Trump won the electoral vote and Hillary Clinton won the popular vote.

How does the Electoral College work? The Constitution allocates to each state a certain number of electoral votes, based on the sum of the number of senators (2) plus representatives (currently anywhere from 1 to 53) that a state has in the U.S. Congress. The Twenty-third Amendment to the Constitution allocated three electoral votes to the District of Columbia. The number of seats a state has in the House of Representatives may change as a result of the official census conducted every 10 years. Thus, the number of electoral votes that a state has may change as well. The total number of electoral votes remains fixed at 538, and a candidate must receive a majority—270—to win the presidency (see Figure 14-1).

The minimum number of electoral votes allotted to any one state is three because the Constitution guarantees to each state exactly two senators and at least one House member. Vermont, Wyoming, North Dakota, South Dakota, Alaska, Montana, and Delaware all have three votes. California currently has the largest number of electoral votes with 55 (53 members of the House and 2 senators).

Even small states with as few as three electoral votes can influence the outcome of an election. In 2000, George Bush received 271 electoral votes, only one vote more than the 270 majority he needed to win. Had just one of the small states that gave Bush its three electoral votes voted for Gore, Bush would not have won the election.

Over the past 60 years the U.S. population has shifted, with the southern and western states gaining population and most of the northeastern and midwestern states losing population. Consequently, the number of electoral votes in states such as Florida, California, Texas, and Arizona has grown, and the number of votes allocated to states such as New York, Pennsylvania, Ohio, and Illinois has declined. Based on figures from the 2010 U.S. Census, the 2020 electoral vote count in Texas swelled from 34 to 38. Florida gained two electoral votes, and a number of states gained at least one electoral vote: Arizona, Georgia, Nevada, South Carolina, Utah, and Washington. By contrast, each of the following states lost at least one electoral vote: Illinois, Iowa, Louisiana, Massachusetts, Michigan, New Jersey, and Pennsylvania. Ohio and New York lost two each. As a result of this trend, the southern and southwestern states have become more influential in the presidential selection process. The results of the 2020 Census are likely to continue these trends, though the 2020 Census will not impact the Electoral College until the 2024 presidential election.

Article II of the Constitution gives each state legislature the authority to appoint electors, one for each electoral vote that a state has been allocated. During the first few presidential elections, most states used the state legislature to select the individuals who would be the state's electors.[17] By 1860, however, states gradually shifted to using the popular vote outcome

Electoral College The constitutional mechanism by which presidents are chosen. Each state is allocated Electoral College votes based on the sum of that state's U.S. senators and House members.

electors Individuals appointed to represent a state's presidential vote in the Electoral College; in practice, voters in presidential elections vote for a slate of electors committed to a particular candidate, rather than voting directly for the candidate.

in the state to allocate electors, or the so-called unit rule. The unit rule (or "winner-take-all" system) means that the candidate who receives the most votes among the popular votes cast for president in a state will receive all the electoral votes from that state. At present, only two states, Maine and Nebraska, do not use the unit rule. Rather, in those states the popular vote winner in each congressional district receives the electoral vote from that district, and the two votes that derive from the state's Senate seats are awarded to the statewide popular vote winner.

In practice, the voters in a presidential election vote not for the actual candidate but for the slate of electors who commit to the candidate for whom the voters cast their ballots. Interestingly, the electors who pledge themselves to a candidate are under no legal obligation to actually cast their electoral vote for that candidate. In fact, electors sometimes break their pledge; these are dubbed "faithless electors." In 8 of the last 16 presidential elections, there was at least one "faithless elector."

In 2016, there were a record seven faithless electors (five switched from Clinton and two switched from Trump), not surprising given the negativity of the campaigns and the confusion surrounding the unexpected victory of Donald Trump. A movement to find a Republican alternative to Trump was the basis for this large number of faithless electors. The previous election with a faithless elector occurred in 2004, when a Minnesota elector who had initially pledged to vote for John Kerry cast his presidential vote for "John Ewards" [sic] instead. That vote may have been an accident. By contrast, in 2000, Washington, DC, elector Barbara Lett-Simmons, while pledged to vote for Democrats Al Gore and Joe Lieberman, intentionally cast no electoral votes as a protest against the District of Columbia's lack of statehood. To date, however, these faithless electors have not had an impact on an election outcome.[18]

The significance of the unit rule is illustrated by the outcome of the 2000 presidential election. In Florida, which had 25 electoral votes, the popular vote distribution between Bush and Gore was very close. For nearly one month after Election Day in 2000, controversies surrounding the vote count and the ballot in Florida left uncertain which candidate won the most popular votes in the state. What loomed in the balance was all of Florida's 25 electoral votes—and the election victory. Without Florida, Gore had 267 electoral votes—just 3 votes shy of victory, whereas Bush had 246. Because the unit rule applied to Florida's 25 votes, all 25 would be allocated on the basis of which candidate received the most popular votes.

· The founders' original intent in creating the Electoral College was to keep the presidential selection process out of the direct hands of the people. They felt that the people were best represented by the House of Representatives, whose members were elected directly by voters. But the founders questioned the ability of the general public to select the chief executive. Rather, they believed that the more knowledgeable, wise, and politically thoughtful members of each state's legislature should be empowered with the authority to appoint electors who would choose from the best of the best.

But as the meaning of democracy changed and as American politics opened up to greater popular participation, states began to use the popular vote as a means of allocating their electoral votes. Further, public opinion polls strongly endorse presidential selection based on the national popular vote rather than the electoral vote. For example, a Politico Poll conducted in March 2019 favored the popular vote over the electoral vote system by a margin of 50 to 34 percent.

If Americans strongly prefer the selection of a president based on the total national popular vote rather than by the electoral vote, why, then, do we continue to use this rather complicated, indirect system for voters to choose their president? Why not simply use the sum total of the popular vote to choose a winner? The most basic answer is explained by politics, not necessarily logic. The Electoral College system benefits smaller states. For example, Wyoming's population of approximately 650,000 represents 0.17 percent of the potential popular vote. But its three electoral votes constitute 0.56 percent of the electoral vote total. Because every state starts off with two electoral votes (for its two U.S. senators), smaller states end up with disproportionately more voting power in the Electoral College than in the popular vote. In recent years, the states that benefit from the Electoral College system have tended to be dominated by Republican legislatures. Because changing the Electoral College system requires a constitutional amendment, and because amendment procedures require approval

unit rule The system in 48 states by which the candidate who wins the most votes among popular votes cast for president in a state receives all the electoral votes from that state; also known as the "winner-take-all" system.

by three-fourths of the state legislatures, any attempt to change the system is unlikely to win the support of a sufficient number of state legislatures, enough of which are small enough to benefit from the Electoral College. Despite the many proposals that have been offered to reform or eliminate the Electoral College, it seems likely, at least for the foreseeable future, that the Electoral College is here to stay.

14-4 CAMPAIGN FUNDING

Waging a political campaign, particularly a presidential campaign, is becoming increasingly expensive.[19] Figure 14-2 shows the total fund-raising by presidential candidates over the past 11 elections. In 2016 the Clinton campaign spent $770 million and the Trump team spent $400 million.

Campaign financing, then, is one of the most important functions of a political campaign. Hiring a professional staff to develop and implement a successful campaign, producing and airing TV commercials and radio spots, renting campaign headquarters office space, conducting polls to monitor the course of the campaign, and producing buttons, bumper stickers, and signs all cost money. Good candidates have demonstrated a high capacity for raising money to wage a campaign.

SOURCES OF FUNDING

Where do campaigns find financial support? They find money from individual citizens, from interest groups and political action committees, and from political parties. Companies, groups, and individuals all have vested interests in the political system, and each may provide support (including monetary contributions) to promote candidates who advocate their own positions on issues. The U.S. system of politics encourages people and groups to participate in the political process, and this participation includes financial contributions to campaigns. Indeed, giving money to candidates may be seen as a healthy sign that people are engaged in the political process and want to participate in making a difference.

Beginning in the 1970s, parties and candidates turned to political action committees (PACs) to address the new realities of political campaigns, particularly regarding fund-raising and limits on individual contributions. PACs are the arms of interest groups that raise and give

FIGURE 14-2

Total Fund-Raising by Presidential Candidates, 1976–2016

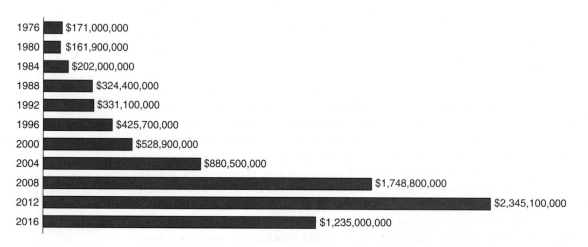

1976	$171,000,000
1980	$161,900,000
1984	$202,000,000
1988	$324,400,000
1992	$331,100,000
1996	$425,700,000
2000	$528,900,000
2004	$880,500,000
2008	$1,748,800,000
2012	$2,345,100,000
2016	$1,235,000,000

Source: Based on data from www.opensecrets.org.

FIGURE 14-3
The Growth of Political Action Committees

The federal campaign finance legislation of the 1970s was the first vigorous attempt to monitor and regulate the money that was raised and spent on political campaigns. These laws applied to the regulation of hard money, which was money raised directly by and spent by the political candidates. They influenced the creation of political action committees (PACs), which raise and spend soft money—funds for political campaigning independent of the political candidates. In 1974, there were only 608 PACs registered with the federal government; by 2002, 4,027 PACs were registered. This figure shows the total amount of receipts and expenditures of all PACs registered with the federal government from the 1975–1976 election cycle to the 2011–2012 election cycle.

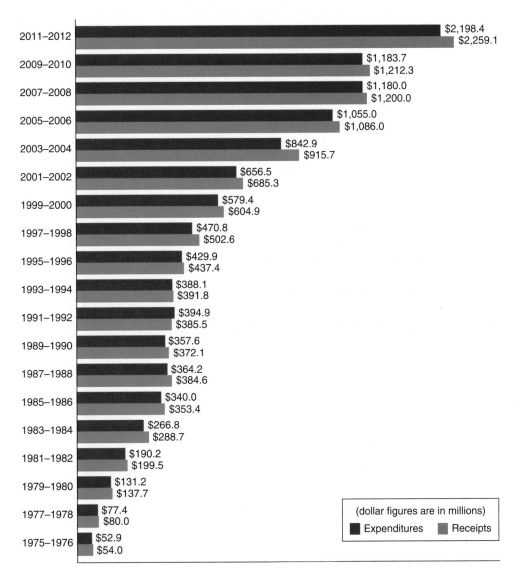

Source: Harold W. Stanley and Richard G. Niemi, Vital Statistics on American Politics 2004–2005, 103 (Washington, DC: CQ Press, 2006). Data for 2005–2012 are from www.fec.gov/press/press2009/20090415pac/20090424pac.shtml.

money to political candidates. Any group that wishes to participate in financing campaigns must create a PAC and register it with the Federal Elections Commission (FEC). There are more than 4,000 PACs currently registered with the federal government (see Figure 14-3). Of the $1 billion raised by House and Senate campaigns in 2004, about 30 percent came from the fund-raising efforts of PACs.

In addition to individual and PAC contributions, the political parties play an important role in financing political campaigns. Both major parties have national and statewide committees, which raise money to fund campaigns. In 2000, each of the national party committees collected and spent about $200 million to help fund their candidates. Typically, the parties support House and Senate candidates, particularly those who have a competitive chance of winning.

Another important source of campaign funding comes from the individual candidates' House and Senate campaigns. Members of Congress who hold safe seats are very effective at raising money for their own campaigns. These campaigns, because they are for safe seats, tend not to need a great deal of funding. So the incumbents use their campaign war chests to help fund the campaigns of their colleagues in more competitive races. Often they do so through the formation of a PAC.

Although not the norm, some federal candidates for office use their own personal wealth to fund their campaigns. In 2016, billionaire Donald Trump spent $66 million of his own money on the campaign. In that same year, GOP senate candidate from Florida, Rick Scott, spent $64 million of his personal wealth in a successful campaign bid.

The federal government and a handful of state governments (including those of Arizona, Connecticut, North Carolina, and Maine) maintain some form of public campaign financing as well. Although candidates cannot be forced to participate in public financing schemes, which restrict their expenditures, the government may entice their participation by offering them significant public funds in return for their agreement to abide by personal campaign spending limits. The federal government's presidential election financing system allows major-party candidates to draw on funds received when taxpayers check a box on their tax returns agreeing to donate to the fund. In 2004, presidential candidates were eligible to receive approximately $70 million each if they agreed to limit their campaign expenditures. Yet neither of the two major-party candidates in 2004, George W. Bush and John Kerry, elected to participate in the federal financing scheme. By rejecting the use of such public financing, they were able to freely spend throughout the primaries and general election campaign without regard to any federally imposed limits. In 2008, John McCain accepted the $85 million he qualified for in public financing to fund his general election campaign. Barack Obama, however, declined public financing and continued to privately raise funds through the general election—a decision based on his widespread success in raising campaign money during the primaries. The 2012 general election between Barack Obama and Mitt Romney marked the first time that *both* major candidates turned down public financing so they could continue unlimited fund-raising activities after their respective conventions. Similarly in 2016, neither major-party candidate accepted public financing, opting to raise and spend much more than public financing normally provides.

In recent presidential election cycles, candidates have been able to take advantage of the internet as yet another means of fund-raising. In 2000, Bill Bradley raised more than $2 million via the internet for his campaign for the Democratic presidential nomination. (He ended up losing his bid for the nomination to Al Gore.) Then, in the 2004 race for the Democratic presidential nomination, a little-known former governor from the small state of Vermont, Howard Dean, waged an impressive campaign by tapping into the vast potential of the internet and online fund-raising. His followers, who came to be known as "Deaniacs," tended to be younger Americans, a group much more inclined to use the internet, to IM (instant message), and to blog. The Dean campaign translated this orientation of his followers into the most successful internet fund-raising campaign that American politics had ever seen before.

Dean raised an unprecedented $40 million in his campaign for the nomination. This amount exceeded that of all his competitors for the nomination, and the vast bulk of his campaign war chest was derived from small, individual donations solicited through the internet. Although Dean's campaign collapsed after the candidate suffered unexpected losses in Iowa and New Hampshire and although most of his $40 million war chest was depleted by the first primary contest, Dean's success at internet fund-raising was nonetheless impressive. Then, in 2008, Barack Obama's campaign substantially raised the stakes in fund-raising through the internet by raising over $200 million through that medium, and in 2012 the Obama reelection campaign proved groundbreaking in this regard, leveraging micro-donations by raising money online from over 3 million separate donors. His appeal to voters through the internet represents a significant achievement in the use of this technology in campaign politics. Today, political parties as well as individual candidates use the internet as a fund-raising tool. As Americans increasingly come to rely on the internet, it is likely that more and more political candidates will follow Dean's and Obama's examples and harness this technology for fund-raising and other campaigning.

REGULATING CAMPAIGN FINANCING

Congress and the states have passed many and varied laws to regulate the conduct of campaign contributions. These laws are not intended to prevent individuals or groups from giving money. Rather, they attempt to prevent a "quid pro quo," or a donation in return for an elected official voting or acting in a certain way in direct response to accepting the campaign gift.

The first significant piece of federal legislation aimed at regulating campaign financing was the Federal Election Campaign Act (FECA), passed in 1971 and amended in 1974. The law required that all federal candidates accurately disclose campaign contributions and document all campaign expenditures. Subsequent amendments to FECA imposed legal limits on campaign contributions by individuals ($1,000 to each candidate per election cycle, $5,000 to PACs per year, and $20,000 to national party committees per year). Additionally, FECA imposed an outright ban on certain campaign contributions by corporations, unions, national banks, and foreign nationals, among others.

All of these provisions targeted so-called hard money, contributions that go directly to candidates and their campaign committees. Although the Supreme Court in 2014 struck down attempts to limit the *total amount* an individual can contribute to federal candidates as a whole in a two-year cycle, the federal government still imposes limits on how much an individual can contribute to a single candidate in primaries and general elections. Meanwhile, FECA did little to stem the influx of soft money funds to political parties and political advocacy groups that are not contributed directly to candidate campaigns and that do not expressly advocate the election of a particular candidate. In the four decades following FECA, the two major political parties have strategically spent soft money on administrative and party-building activities, as well as on issue ads that do not specifically promote an individual candidate but that nevertheless attempt to affect the election outcome.

The Federal Election Commission (FEC) was established in 1974 to enforce all campaign financing rules and regulations, including limits on campaign contributions. Today, the FEC is the federal agency in charge of enforcing election laws. Provisions for public funding of presidential campaigns were subsequently passed in 1976 and 1979.

Critics have voiced a number of complaints about the system of campaign finance regulations. For one thing, the original limits on individual contributions— fixed by legislation in the 1970s—were never indexed to inflation. This oversight was addressed in legislation in 2002 mandating that limits be indexed for inflation every two years. For example, in 2005– 2006 individuals were able to give up to $2,100 to candidates and up to $26,700 to national party committees.

Another complaint concerns the failure of the system to adapt to modern campaign

Federal Election Campaign Act (FECA) The federal legislation passed in 1971 that established disclosure requirements and restricted individual campaign contributions.

hard money Donations made directly to political candidates and their campaigns that must be declared with the name of the donor (which then becomes public knowledge).

soft money Money not donated directly to a candidate's campaign but rather to a political advocacy group or a political party for "party-building" activities.

Federal Election Commission (FEC) The agency created in 1974 to enforce federal election laws.

Screenshot of Senator Bernie Sanders's 2016 campaign web page.

dynamics. As a result of frontloading, presidential primary elections are now bunched up earlier and earlier in the general election campaign; yet the strict limits on expenditures imposed on those who accept public financing do not really account for these new campaign realities, which compel candidates to spend a considerable amount of their money during a relatively short period of time.

In recent years, advocates of campaign finance reform have focused their greatest criticism on soft money in the form of independent campaign expenditures. These are monies that PACs or individuals spend to support political campaigns but that do not directly contribute to them. FECA banned the unlimited use of independent expenditures to directly support the election of one candidate or the defeat of another candidate, but those funds could still be used to build the party as a whole. For example, a PAC can produce and support a political advertisement that endorses a party's position on an issue and pay for the airtime to broadcast that ad on television. The money for the ad is not donated to a campaign per se but instead is spent on services that support the campaign; thus, the money spent is considered an "independent" expenditure. The U.S. Supreme Court in *Buckley v. Valeo* (1976)[20] ruled that Congress could limit campaign contributions consistent with the First Amendment, but that it could not limit independent campaign expenditures or personal money spent by candidates on behalf of their own campaigns. Nearly 30 years later, in *McConnell v. F.E.C.* (2003),[21] the Court extended that ruling to apply to spending by political parties as well. Thus, political parties themselves often sponsor television ads that talk more generally about issues facing the country without mentioning any individual candidate or race; of course, most political experts acknowledge that these ads may have a significant impact on individual campaigns.

The most recent reform attempts have focused on soft money and independent campaign expenditures. Loopholes in campaign financing have allowed soft money to go unregulated by the FEC. Legislation designed to better regulate the way campaigns are financed and how the money is spent was passed by Congress in 2002. The Bipartisan Campaign Reform Act (BCRA) of 2002 prohibited national parties and candidates for federal office from accepting soft money (i.e., that which is not subject to regulation by the FEC). The BCRA also raised limits on contributions to a particular candidate for federal office from $1,000 to $2,000. The U.S. Supreme Court, in the highly controversial decision of *Citizens United v. FEC* (2010),[22] struck down as unconstitutional several other provisions of the BCRA, including certain limits on corporate and union funding of broadcast ads right before an election.

14-5 CONGRESSIONAL CAMPAIGNS AND ELECTIONS

Although presidential elections typically receive the most attention from the media and the public, many other elections also occur regularly, including those that send members to the two houses of Congress. In each presidential election year, all 435 seats in the House of Representatives are contested, as are one-third of the seats in the Senate. Midway between successive presidential elections are the midterm congressional elections, in which all 435 House seats are contested again and another one-third of the Senate seats are voted on (senators serve six-year terms, and the 100 Senate elections are staggered so that about one-third of the seats are contested every two years).

Midterm elections for Congress differ from presidential-year elections in important ways.[23] First, voter turnout tends to be lower in the midterm contests. Without the large-scale attention the presidential race receives, voter interest and engagement in the midterm elections are lower, and thus turnout tends to suffer. Even in the highly charged midterm elections of 2018, voter turnout was just 47 percent, almost 13 percentage points below voter turnout figures for the preceding presidential election.

Second, midterm elections fail to offer congressional candidates what has come to be known as the coattail effect. In a presidential election year, the names of candidates for Congress typically are listed below the name of their party's candidate for president on the ballot. Thus, voters' selection of congressional candidates may be influenced by their choice for president. The congressional candidates, in effect, ride the coattails of the presidential candidate.[24] For the coattail effect to be apparent, the outcome of the presidential race typically

independent campaign expenditures Political donations that PACs or individuals spend to support campaigns but do not directly contribute to the campaigns.

Buckley v. Valeo (1976) The 1976 Supreme Court opinion that held that spending money to influence elections is protected First Amendment speech and that prohibited limitations on independent expenditures or personal money spent by candidates on their own campaigns.

Bipartisan Campaign Reform Act (BCRA) of 2002 Also called the McCain-Feingold Act, the federal legislation that (1) restricted soft money spent by political parties, (2) regulated expenditures on ads that refer to specific candidates immediately before an election, and (3) increased limits on hard money donated directly to candidates and their campaigns.

Citizens United v. FEC (2010) The 2010 Supreme Court opinion that held that government restrictions on independent political spending by corporations, unions, and other associations violate the First Amendment. Critics of the decision predicted the ruling would bring about a new era of corporate influence in politics. In fact, the bulk of large expenditures has come from so-called super PACs dominated by a small group of billionaires; this development more than anything else has shifted significant power away from the political parties and toward the donors themselves.

midterm congressional elections Congressional elections held midway between successive presidential elections.

needs to be a landslide victory for the winner, such as in 1984 when President Ronald Reagan soundly defeated Democrat Walter Mondale. For the first time in decades, the 1984 elections ushered in a Republican majority to the U.S. Senate. By contrast, George W. Bush's narrow victory in 2004 did not appear to produce a coattail effect.

Third, midterm elections show a discernible trend—although often not very strong—that favors congressional candidates in the party opposite the president's party. When a president wins, especially by a large margin, the coattail effect distorts what would normally occur in any given congressional race. Yet in midterm elections, without the president's name at the top of the ballot, the absence of the coattail gives the advantage to the opposing party. In the modern era, the party in opposition to the president has managed to regain control of Congress only in the midterm elections when the president's popularity is waning. Thus, in 1946 and then in 1994, the Republicans wrestled both houses of Congress back from the Democrats at midterm elections during the presidencies of Democrats Harry Truman and Bill Clinton, respectively. True to form, the 2010 midterm elections once again offered a rebuke to the political party holding the White House. Running on a platform that opposed Democratic spending initiatives and promised to rein in the size of government, Republican House candidates transformed a 178-seat minority into a 240-seat majority. By taking more than 60 seats away from the Democrats, Republicans enjoyed a level of midterm election success not seen by either party in decades. Similarly, the 2018 midterms rebuked Trump and the GOP by shifting more than 30 House seats to the Democrats and giving them majority control of that chamber.

More important than presidential coattails or any other factor in congressional elections, however, is the **power of incumbency**. Incumbent members of Congress, particularly those in the House, are returned to office by voters at amazingly high rates. In a normal year of House races, an incumbent who is running for reelection stands a better than 90 percent chance of being returned to office.[25] What accounts for such a high return rate? First, name

coattail effect The potential benefit that successful presidential candidates offer to congressional candidates of the same political party during presidential election years.

power of incumbency The phenomenon by which incumbent members of Congress running for reelection are returned to office at an extremely high rate.

FROM YOUR PERSPECTIVE
Getting Involved in Political Campaigns

Politics is very much on the minds of college-age Americans today. In 2008, a record 35.6 percent of first-year college students said that they had frequently discussed politics in the past year.[26] (The previous high was 33.6 percent in 1968, at the height of the Vietnam War.) In the

Iowa State University students at a Bernie Sanders campaign stop in Ames, Iowa.

NurPhoto / Getty Images

2012 and 2016 presidential campaigns, college students were more interested and more active than ever before. Students who work on election campaigns may find themselves performing such simple tasks as stuffing envelopes or walking door to door to distribute leaflets. Those who are technologically savvy may assist campaigns in other ways—for example, by helping to create Facebook profiles or fan pages on the internet. About 11 percent of first-year college students in 2008 said they were active in election campaigns. (This figure was up by about 3 percentage points from 2004.) More first-year college students also report that they are likely to engage in a political protest (6.1 percent in 2008, as compared to 4.9 percent in 1966).

For Critical Thinking and Discussion

1. Why do you think your peers were so energized about the recent presidential elections? What do you think about youth energy for future elections—will the trend toward greater interest in politics continue to rise?
2. Do you think college students' participation made a difference in the election outcome in 2016 and 2020?

recognition of the candidate is a significant factor in lower-profile congressional races, and incumbents, because they have been in office, tend to have higher name recognition than do challengers. Second, the vast majority of congressional districts—and thus the vast majority of seats in Congress—are dominated by either the Republican Party or the Democratic Party. Congressional seats from districts that include either a high percentage of Democratic voters or a high percentage of Republican voters are dominated by their respective majority party and are referred to, as noted earlier, as safe seats. A far smaller number of districts tend to have similar numbers of Democratic and Republican voters and are known as marginal seats. In the redistricting of congressional districts that periodically takes place, the political parties try to configure districts to their own partisan advantage. This maneuvering tends to create a large number of safe seats and often very few marginal seats.

Finally, incumbent members of Congress enjoy financial advantages, such as the franking privilege, which allows members to mail materials to their constituents without paying postage.

Elections and campaigns are central features of the republican form of government in the United States. The number of elections is many; the cost of campaigns is high; and the process for selecting the nation's chief office-holder, the president of the United States, is long and complex. U.S. presidential elections evoke a great deal of passion, engage the interest of millions of voters, persuade vast numbers of citizens and groups to contribute large amounts of money, and focus attention on the great issues of the day. Thus, campaigns and elections duly serve their purpose in providing an important connection between Americans and their government.

> **safe seat** A congressional seat from a district that includes a high percentage of voters from one of the major parties.
>
> **marginal seat** A seat in a congressional district that has relatively similar numbers of Democratic and Republican voters.
>
> **franking privilege** The traditional right of members of Congress to mail materials to their constituents without paying postage.

Summary

14-1 American Presidential Elections in Historical Perspective

- From 1796 up through the 1830s, the presidential nomination process was dominated by officials of the two major parties who chose party nominees based on informal discussions; by the twentieth century, electoral reforms such as the direct primary gave voters in many states a formal opportunity to cast a ballot for delegates, who would in turn choose their party's nominees at a national convention. For the general election, the Electoral College began as a mechanism for the political elite to select the chief executive and has evolved into a complex system where voters select the president.

14-2 The Nomination Campaign

- Nomination campaigns focus on attaining victories in presidential primaries and caucuses. The Iowa caucus and the New Hampshire primary have traditionally come at the beginning of the nomination calendar, and so they tend to disproportionately influence final outcomes. In recent elections, many states have attempted to move their primaries and caucuses up on the calendar in a process known as frontloading.

- National party conventions used to play an important role in helping choose party nominees; today they are mostly made-for-television affairs, anointing the party ticket with speeches offering testimonials to the nominees.

14-3 The General Election Campaign

- General election races may be either incumbent races (pitting a sitting president against a challenger) or open elections (with no incumbent in the race). In the former, the election often amounts to a referendum on the performance of the president over the previous four years.

- Presidential candidates choose their running mates (the vice presidential candidates) strategically to address specific weaknesses of the presidential candidate or to boost the ticket's prospects in certain geographical areas.

- To win the presidency, a candidate must put together a coalition of states sufficient to win a majority of the 538 Electoral College votes, which are allocated to each state based on the sum of the number of their senators and their representatives. The candidate who does well in battleground states will normally win the 270 votes necessary to secure a majority.

14-4 Campaign Funding

- Campaign funding is critical to the success of individual candidates. Election laws since 1974 have limited the amount individuals or organizations can give to candidates (hard money). The Bipartisan Campaign Reform Act (BCRA) of 2002 went a step further, restricting expenditures to political parties or advocacy groups that are theoretically independent of specific candidates or campaigns (soft money). The Federal Election Commission enforces all such limitations that have been upheld as constitutional by the U.S. Supreme Court.

14-5 Congressional Campaigns and Elections

- In congressional elections, the power of incumbency is more important than any other factor. Unlike midterm elections, congressional elections that coincide with presidential elections tend to garner greater voter turnout, and members of the successful presidential candidate's party sometimes benefit from the coattail effect.

Key Terms

battleground states (p. 301)
Bipartisan Campaign Reform Act (BCRA) of 2002 (p. 310)
Buckley v. Valeo (1976) (p. 310)
caucus (p. 296)
Citizens United v. FEC (2010) (p. 310)
closed primary (p. 296)
coattail effect (p. 310)
Electoral College (p. 304)
electors (p. 304)
Federal Election Campaign Act (FECA) (p. 309)
Federal Election Commission (FEC) (p. 309)
franking privilege (p. 312)
frontloading (p. 299)
hard money (p. 309)

incumbent race (p. 300)
independent campaign expenditures (p. 310)
invisible primary (p. 295)
marginal seat (p. 312)
midterm congressional elections (p. 310)
nomination campaign (p. 297)
open election (p. 301)
open primary (p. 296)
power of incumbency (p. 311)
prenomination campaign (p. 294)
presidential primary (p. 296)
safe seat (p. 312)
soft money (p. 309)
unit rule (p. 305)

Part IV
PUBLIC POLICY

Chapter 15: American Public Policy

15
AMERICAN PUBLIC POLICY

Bloomberg / Getty Images

A pedestrian passes the National Debt Clock in New York City on January 11, 2019.

IN THE 1950s, Yale Professor Charles E. Lindblom described U.S. domestic policy-making as the "science of muddling through."[1] Lindblom's view challenged what had been the prevailing model of policy-making: a rational and comprehensive process in which decision-makers utilized scientific analysis and logic to develop public policy. By contrast, Lindblom introduced the human element and expressly partisan factors into the process. Today we view public policy—whether in the form of small, incremental shifts or in the form of landmark, sweeping legislation—as the product of reluctant compromises entered into between the president, Congress, and other political actors based on the immediate political environment. Indeed, the very term "public policy" in the United States has come to be associated today with the coordinated response of public institutions to immediate events and conditions, a nod to the often messy reality of modern policy-making. Whether the government is enacting economic policy, social policy, or foreign policy, imperfect solutions to significant problems are a given, and the final outcome rarely garners widespread satisfaction. So long as the political (and often highly partisan) branches of government engage in some form of conflict, such "muddling through" to landmark legislation may offer the best policy process to which we can realistically aspire.

Learning Objectives

15-1   An Overview of the Policy-Making Process

- Describe the stages of the public policy-making process and the various players involved.

15-2   Theories and Practice in Economic Policy

- Recognize the theories of economic policy, distinguish between fiscal and monetary policy, define different categories of spending, and trace the budget-making process.

15-3   The Welfare State and Programs for the Poor

- Contrast the U.S. welfare state model to those found in other Western democracies.

15-4   The Social Security System and Health Care Policy

- Assess both the state of the Social Security system (including its prospects and reforms), and assess America's health care system, comparing it to European systems that feature universal care.

15-5   Foreign Policy

- Discuss the actors and institutions that conduct foreign policy under the Constitution, and trace the history and theories of U.S. foreign policy from its roots to the present day.

States as "Laboratories of Democracy" that Point the Way for National Domestic Policy

State governments that sponsor innovative new programs may—if the programs are successful—start a movement of similar initiatives in other states. They may also offer a model for the federal government to enact a program on a national scale. In this way, state governments can fulfill an even greater purpose in a democracy: as Supreme Court justice Louis Brandeis stated in 1932, states provide the nation as a whole with true "laboratories for democracy." Consider two such laboratories in action:

Then

In 1930 during the Great Depression, New York governor Franklin Delano Roosevelt signed the Old Age Pension Act into law. By 1935, 30 states had passed some form of elderly assistance legislation. Thus, when President Franklin Delano Roosevelt proposed the national system of Social Security legislation in 1935, he was able to borrow from states' experiences, including his own. Unlike failed programs in other states, California and Massachusetts did not require counties to "opt in" to the program to participate; all counties were enrolled automatically. Roosevelt also learned that many of the failed state programs had trouble enrolling older citizens who were reluctant to "go on welfare"; the more successful state policies billed themselves instead as variations on employee savings programs. Accordingly, the national Social Security program passed in 1935 was mandatory, and it too would be financed by payroll taxes, distinguishing it further from more traditional welfare programs. The state governments had performed a valuable service with their experimental policies, pointing the way to a national program that survives nearly 85 years later.

Now

In 2019, a bipartisan group of federal law-makers proposed legislation that would allow states to legalize marijuana. Their sponsorship of the STATES (Strengthening the Tenth Amendment Through Entrusting States) Act was empowered by a decade of policy activity in a number of states aimed at legalizing marijuana. In 2012, Colorado and Washington became the first two states to legalize the recreational use of marijuana. By early 2019, ten states and the District of Columbia had legalized all marijuana use, with another 23 states allowing its use for medical purposes only. Though federal law prohibiting the use of marijuana remains the controlling authority on the subject, state experimentation with legalization shifted the burden onto the federal government to aggressively enforce such laws. A 2009 Department of Justice memo had advised U.S. attorneys to only prosecute medical cannabis providers who violated state law or engaged in other illegal activity. Though the Trump administration rescinded that memo in 2018, it remained unclear whether its enforcement practices would actually change. Seeking to head off a new wave of enforcement, Congress in early 2019 started debating laws like the STATES Act. Clearly, states' experimentation with marijuana legalization has influenced how the federal government treats the use of the drug throughout the nation.

For Critical Thinking and Discussion

1. Are some states so unique or different in culture and character from most other states that they make poor "laboratories" for experimentation? In considering national legislation, can we really learn much from states such as Hawaii, Alaska, or Wyoming, to name just a few places?
2. How can the federal government do more to encourage state-level policy innovations?

A road sign along a Maine highway advertises legalized marijuana for sale at a roadside shack in that state.

AP Photo / NewsBase

15-1 AN OVERVIEW OF THE POLICY-MAKING PROCESS

Public policy refers to the set of laws, regulations, and rules that affect the whole of society. Because the responsibilities and interests of private and public institutions often overlap, some battles that are waged primarily among private parties may still fall under the general subject of public policy—after all, government may seek to enact laws or regulations aimed at monitoring such disputes. There are many different types of social policy, and this chapter will review most of the major ones: economic policy, social policy, and foreign policy.

Although the policy-making process tends to vary considerably from one subject area to another, most policies unfold in five separate stages:

- The recognition/definition stage, in which objectives to be fulfilled and goals to be pursued through policy are first identified and defined according to how the problem fits within existing policy categories, and *then* prioritized;
- The formulation stage, in which various alternative courses for this policy are considered, and a preferred course is selected;
- The adoption (or legitimation) stage, in which the policy under consideration assumes the authority of law through ratification by Congress, regulations issued by the relevant administrative agencies or in some cases (especially in foreign policy) by unilateral executive action;
- The implementation stage, in which an executive or executive agency translates law into action through the adoption of administrative regulations and/or the dedication of resources to carry out the policy; and
- The evaluation stage, in which the policy is assessed for its worth and effectiveness in meeting its original objectives and goals.

Numerous actors and institutions are involved in making policy in the United States. Bureaucrats in administrative agencies often play a key role at every stage of the policy-making process, helping to define the problem and identify the possible options, proposing alternatives and implementing the preferred course, and assisting in collecting information necessary to evaluate the policy.[2] The Department of Commerce, for example, in addition to the secretary of commerce, employs at least six undersecretaries responsible for overseeing the formulation of numerous policy initiatives on behalf of the agency. Just one of those commerce officials, the undersecretary for the National Oceanic and Atmospheric Administration, oversees a $5.5 billion bureaucracy that supervises the National Marine Fisheries Service, the National Ocean Service, and the National Weather Service, among other ocean-related agencies.

Congress and the president are most directly involved in the recognition, formulation, and adoption stages of policy-making, when media attention is most intense; their influence over the other stages is limited by the practical need to delegate administrative details to agencies with the resources and expertise to handle such matters. The courts may play a role in ensuring that all proper procedures are followed in the formulation of policy and in interpreting rules, regulations, and policies that emerge from the policy-making process.[3]

Interest groups and think tanks (policy research institutes) tend to focus on influencing program choices and decisions, where they have the opportunity to make significant gains on behalf of their members.[4] For example, the Sierra Club lobbies bureaucrats at the EPA and members of Congress on environmental committees to ensure that the Clean Air Act is successfully updated to meet new challenges. The specialized committee structure of Congress encourages interest groups to focus their resources on those legislators and members of legislative staffs who have authority over relevant issue areas. Think tanks are organizations that do intensive research and problem solving, either on behalf of other entities or on their own (see Table 15-1). Normally, a think tank staffed by researchers and policy analysts will produce an elaborate report detailing the implications of the problem it has studied; as with interest groups, it then seeks to publicize its findings, whether by holding a press conference, sponsoring a symposium or panel discussion, or some other means.

public policy The set of laws, regulations, and rules that affect the whole of society.

TABLE 15-1

Influential Policy Think Tanks

Institute	Date Established	Philosophy/Goals
American Enterprise Institute	1943	A conservative think tank dedicated to preserving "limited government, private enterprise . . . and a strong foreign policy and national defense."
The Brookings Institution	Roots trace back to 1916	A more liberal policy institute (once targeted by the Nixon administration) that aims to improve "the performance of American institutions and the quality of public policy" through the use of social science.
The Cato Institute	1977	Mostly libertarian; seeks to broaden the parameters of public policy debate to allow consideration of "the traditional American principles of limited government, individual liberty, free markets, and peace."
The Heritage Foundation	1973	Seeks "to formulate and promote conservative public policies based on the principles of free enterprise, limited government, individual freedom, traditional American values, and a strong national defense."
The Progressive Policy Institute	1989	Affiliated with the Democratic Leadership Council; maintains as its mission the definition and promotion of a new progressive politics in America. Its work rests on three ideals: equal opportunity, mutual responsibility, and self-governing citizens and communities.
The RAND Corporation	1945	Seeks to provide policy analysis and solutions that address challenges facing the nation and the world, including education, poverty, crime, and the environment, as well as a range of national security issues.

15-2 THEORIES AND PRACTICE IN ECONOMIC POLICY

Economic policy-making encompasses all the legislative and rule-making initiatives that affect the management of wealth and resources within this country. For much of its history, the United States maintained one of the world's most entrepreneurially free economies, with minimal government regulation. Today the government's role in managing the economy is significant—elections are often decided by voter perceptions of success or failure in this area. Overseeing the economy includes two distinct forms of policy-making: fiscal policy-making and monetary policy-making.

Fiscal policy is concerned with how to raise revenue through taxation and how to spend the revenue generated. Many economists believe that the nation's fiscal policy has direct implications for unemployment, measured as the percentage of the workforce that wants to work and is not currently employed, and inflation, or consistent increases in the prices of goods and services. The primary instrument by which the federal government manages fiscal policy is the *federal budget*, a comprehensive plan laying out what the government will spend for its various programs during the coming fiscal years and how it expects to raise the money to pay for them.

Fiscal policy can be thought of as lying on a spectrum. At one end of the spectrum is the policy of minimal government interference in the economy, in which the government exercises little or no budget-making power by authorizing only minimal spending, taxation, and regulation of private business practices. At the opposite end of the spectrum is the policy of considerable government intervention in the economy, perhaps by taxing citizens or by offering subsidies to farmers in return for their agreement not to overproduce certain commodities.

Various economic theories explain the decision to craft fiscal policy at a given point along the fiscal policy spectrum. For example, the economic doctrine known as laissez-faire (a French phrase meaning literally "leave us alone") economics guided the fiscal policy

fiscal policy Decisions by the federal government that relate to raising revenue through taxation and spending the revenue that is thereby generated.

inflation The overall general upward price movement of goods and services in an economy, normally measured by the consumer price index (CPI).

laissez-faire economics Fiscal policy theory that favors minimal intervention in the nation's economy.

that prevailed for much of the eighteenth and nineteenth centuries in the United States.[5] Laissez-faire favors less intervention in the economy, allowing businesses to conduct their affairs more or less free from governmental regulation. The theory came under attack toward the end of the 1800s, when increasing industrialization led to more frequent financial panics, bouts of severe unemployment, corrupt business practices, and the abuse of workers, especially in big cities. Government's involvement in the economy gradually increased, and in the 1930s widespread public support for President Franklin Delano Roosevelt's New Deal programs, enacted to address the problems of the Great Depression, effectively spelled the end of laissez-faire theory as the guiding principle for the nation's fiscal policy.

Many of FDR's New Deal policies were based on **Keynesian economic theory**, named for the British economist John Maynard Keynes. Keynesian theory argues that the government should increase spending when economic times are bad as a way of raising total demand. Total demand for goods and services, according to this theory, is the key determinant of whether the economy is performing well.[6] The economic recovery that occurred during World War II, when federal military spending increased significantly, is often used to support the validity of Keynesian theory. Administrations that attempted to draw on the theory quickly learned that although government spending may forestall or even end a **recession**—defined as an economic slowdown characterized by higher unemployment, reduced productivity, or some other negative economic indicators—it may also bring about other economic problems such as inflation and chronically high deficits. Barack Obama's administration also adopted a Keynesian approach to addressing the financial crisis of 2007–2010.

Supply-side economics is an alternative to Keynesian economics, arguing that rather than increasing government spending, cutting taxes (and cutting the government spending such taxes help to fund) is the preferred way to increase economic productivity and spur the economy. According to supply-side theory, high taxes take money out of the economy that would otherwise be invested in goods and services; thus, by decreasing taxes, money flows back into the economy, stimulating business, new jobs, and overall productivity. While campaigning for the presidency in 1980, Ronald Reagan seized on this theory to propose that a program of implementing tax cuts and spending cuts and balancing the budget was the best means to promote economic growth. Donald Trump did the same while campaigning in 2016. During their respective first terms as president, both Trump and Reagan signed into law significant tax cuts that they hoped would boost economic growth.

ASSESSING THE ECONOMY'S PERFORMANCE

Different measures are used to assess whether the nation's fiscal policy has been a success. Following are several economic measures regarded as especially significant indicators of general economic performance:

- **Gross domestic product (GDP)** is an estimate of the total money value of all the goods and services produced in the United States in a given one-year period. When GDP improves, workers are producing more in fewer hours, allowing employers in turn to increase wages without raising prices.
- The consumer price index (CPI) is an index of prices for goods and services regularly traded in the U.S. economy. A sustained rise over time in the CPI indicates that inflation is on the rise and consumers' buying power is on the decline.
- The unemployment rate measures the percentage of people unemployed and actively looking for work in the U.S. labor market. In April 2019, the unemployment rate hit what was then a 50-year low of 3.6 percent.
- The **budget deficit** is the amount of money spent by the U.S. government over and above what it collects in taxes and other revenue in a single year. A **budget surplus**, on the other hand, is the amount by which the U.S. government's revenue exceeds its spending in a given fiscal year. The federal government has posted annual budget surpluses just 11 times since 1931. According to the Congressional Budget Office, the deficit forecast for fiscal year 2020 will exceed $900 billion.
- The **national debt** is the total sum of the outstanding debt obligations of the U.S. government, largely generated through the sale of interest-bearing U.S. savings bonds,

Keynesian economic theory Fiscal policy theory that favors government taxation and spending during difficult economic times.

recession An economic slowdown characterized by high unemployment, reduced productivity, or other negative economic indicators.

supply-side economics Economic theory that favors cutting taxes as a way of increasing economic productivity.

gross domestic product (GDP) An estimate of the total money value of all the goods and services produced in the United States in a one-year period.

budget deficit The amount of money spent by the U.S. government beyond that which it collects in taxes and other revenue in a single year.

budget surplus The amount by which the U.S. government's revenue exceeds its spending in a given fiscal year.

national debt The total sum of the federal government's outstanding debt obligations.

U.S. treasury notes, and U.S. treasury bills to individuals or organizations. In February 2019, the debt reached the $22-trillion mark; it will likely continue to escalate by at least $1 trillion per year for the foreseeable future. Consequently, the government must pay in excess of $390 billion per year in interest costs alone.

- The Dow Jones Industrial Average is perhaps the most widely used indicator of the overall condition of the stock market, where publicly owned companies are actively traded each business day. "The Dow" is an index of 30 actively traded "blue-chip" stocks (that is, very large companies); its prominence in the news testifies to the important status it holds in the minds of consumers. Other stock market indexes include the Standard & Poor's 500 Index, which encompasses a broader range of large company stocks, and the NASDAQ, an index of high-tech company stocks.

- Housing starts are a measure of the number of U.S. residential building construction projects begun during a specific period of time. Many experts believe that a decline in housing starts is one of the first signs of an approaching economic downturn, and thus it is one of the first indicators consulted by those trying to assess the overall direction of the economy.

- The consumer confidence index (CCI) measures the public's evaluation of the economy by asking a representative sample of Americans how they feel about the current condition of the economy, their personal financial situation, and their prediction about the future of the economy.

- Balance-of-trade figures (also called net exports) measure the sum of the money gained by a given economy by selling exports, minus the cost of buying imports. When a country exports more than it imports, the country has a trade surplus, whereas the reverse situation denotes a trade deficit. The United States has posted an annual trade deficit dating back to the 1970s.

Although most observers agree that presidents actually exert only a marginal impact on the economy, economic performance can still be a crucial factor in determining which party wins a presidential election.[7] The U.S. economy normally runs in cycles. The onset of a recession tends to deliver a "one-two punch" against the economy: first, federal revenues decline as profits decrease and fewer people work; then federal expenditures increase as people claim more and more *entitlements* (guaranteed government benefits such as food stamps and welfare) to get them through the jobless period. A recession is eventually followed by an economic recovery, marked by an upswing of positive economic indicators.

THE FEDERAL BUDGET-MAKING PROCESS

With passage of the Employment Act of 1946, Congress permanently committed the federal government to use the budgetary process to promote maximum employment, production, and purchasing power. The budget process begins when federal agencies formulate their budget requests and pass them on to the Office of Management and Budget (OMB). A part of the Executive Office of the President, the OMB determines whether the agency's budget proposals are in accord with the president's program and then uses those proposals to prepare an overall budget for the coming fiscal year, setting guidelines for estimating revenue and allotting spending.[8]

After receiving the president's proposals, Congress offers its own budget resolution for the fiscal year, based on its own projections for revenue. The appropriations committees of the House and the Senate are primarily responsible for such budget formulation. Each of the two committees plans overview hearings during which the OMB director and representatives of federal agencies discuss the president's budget priorities. Each of the appropriations committees must eventually pass appropriations bills to keep the government running.

All appropriations bills originate in the House; after the full House has passed each measure, the Senate Appropriations Committee takes its turn revising the House version. After Senate subcommittee work has been completed on the House bills, the Senate Appropriations Committee marks up its own versions of the bills and reports them to the Senate for floor action.

Eventually the House and Senate must reconcile their competing versions of the budget and secure additional votes from their members for approval of the final budget bill, which is then presented to the president for signature. All these legislative obstacles must be navigated over a period of eight months, extending from the first Monday in February (when the president's budget proposal is delivered to Congress) through October 1, when the new fiscal year begins. If Congress and the president cannot agree on a final budget over this period of time, Congress may be forced to pass *continuing resolutions* to allow the government to keep running while final budget negotiations continue.[9]

Occasionally, Congress and the president are at such loggerheads that a budget showdown becomes inevitable. President Donald Trump and leaders of the recently elected Democratic House of Representatives, for example, battled over how much funding would be provided for a southern border wall in fulfillment of the president's 2016 campaign promise that he would "build a wall" between the United States and Mexico. Unable to reach an agreement, the government shutdown beginning December 22, 2018, lasted 35 days, making it the longest shutdown in American history.

Some within and outside Congress have attempted to introduce bolder budgetary reforms in response to the escalating deficits of recent decades. The Gramm-Rudman-Hollings Act of 1985 set annual targets for reducing the deficit and required the General Accounting Office to determine whether automatic spending cuts would take effect if Congress passed budgets that missed the established deficit target. (In 1986, the Supreme Court struck down the act as unconstitutional because the GAO, accountable only to Congress, could not legally perform such "executive" acts.) The Budget Enforcement Act of 1990 set deficit targets that could be adjusted due to unforeseen economic changes; however, the act did not compensate for unexpected spending increases by requiring offsetting cuts elsewhere.

Unfortunately, the central problem of the budget process—that it allows the federal government to spend more money than it takes in—remained in place even with such reforms. Thus, as shown in Figure 15-1, the total U.S. debt continues to grow by leaps and bounds, with little end in sight. In recent years, Congress has debated passing a balanced budget amendment to the Constitution, which would at least require that annual federal spending be

FIGURE 15-1

Total U.S. Debt by Fiscal Year

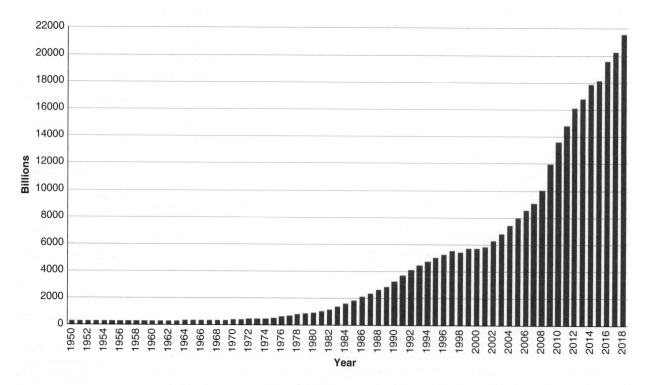

Source: U.S. Department of the Treasury, Bureau of Fiscal Service.

kept at or below revenue collected during the year. Proponents of the amendment argue that it would force free-spending law-makers to become accountable: just as many taxpayers must live off their income (or even considerably less), the government should be expected to do likewise. Opponents of the amendment counter that the government might—in accordance with Keynesian principles—want to engage in deficit spending during times of recession as a method of economic stimulation. They also note that the federal government must be able to spend freely to defend the national security of the United States, even if that means running up large deficits. The Balanced Budget Amendment has been passed in one house but defeated in the other on at least five separate occasions since 1982.

TAXATION POLICY

Americans commonly complain about the high taxes they pay, and politicians do not like to be perceived as favoring tax increases. Yet all governments need revenue to pay the salaries of government workers and to fund various activities. Taxation policies tend to fall into one of two general categories. Redistributive tax policies aim to provide a social safety net to meet the minimum physical needs of citizens. Such policies accomplish this end by following Robin Hood's principle of "taking from the rich and giving to the poor." For example, taxes that are channeled directly into public assistance programs are redistributive. Distributive tax policies, on the other hand, are intended to promote the interests of all economic classes equally. Taxes that are directed toward the maintenance of national parks or the national highway system theoretically benefit all citizens.

In July 1789, just four months after the creation of the new government, Congress passed its first revenue-raising bill: specifically, it levied tariffs, which are taxes on imported foreign goods. Up until the Civil War, tariffs provided approximately 90 percent of the federal government's revenue. Eventually it started to draw more heavily on internal sources of revenue, including payroll taxes, corporate income taxes, and individual income taxes. Eventually, the Sixteenth Amendment to the U.S. Constitution authorized Congress to tax an individual's increase in wealth, whether that wealth comes from wages, benefits, bonuses, or any other form of income. The fairness of individual income taxes, which now provide nearly half of all revenue that flows into the U.S. treasury, remains a subject of contentious debate. The federal government has traditionally imposed a progressive tax on incomes. With a progressive tax, the tax rate on an individual's income increases as the amount of income gets larger. Conversely, a tax that charges all individuals the same amount, regardless of income, is called a regressive tax because it exacts a larger percentage of income from the lower-wage earner than it does from the high-income earner. Most state sales taxes are regressive because they apply equally to every purchaser: for example, both a poor person and a wealthy person pay the same amount of sales tax for a gallon of gasoline, but that amount constitutes a higher percentage of the poor person's income. (Some people confuse regressive taxes with flat taxes, which tax all entities at the same rate *as a proportion of income*. Thus, with a flat tax, a rich person may pay far more in total taxes than a poor person, although the two are still being taxed at the same percentage rate.

During the past century Congress has also imposed corporate income taxes, which today make up more than 10 percent of the government's revenues. Other important revenue sources include federal taxes on gasoline, communications services, estates, large financial gifts, and customs duties. And if these revenue sources fall short of projected expenditures in the form of a deficit, the federal government must make up the difference by borrowing money in the form of issuing U.S. savings bonds, treasury bills, and the like.

SPENDING POLICIES—DIVIDING THE PIE

Budget surpluses are a rarity in modern American politics because the federal government has demonstrated time and again its capacity to spend taxpayer money—U.S. government spending topped $3.9 trillion in fiscal year 2017 alone. Although the president is legally responsible for proposing budgets and has the power to veto spending decisions, Article I of the Constitution grants the Congress exclusive power to lay and collect duties "to pay the Debts and provide for the common Defence and general Welfare of the United States." In

redistributive tax policies Taxation policies that aim to provide a social safety net to meet the minimum physical needs of citizens.

distributive tax policies Taxation policies intended to promote the interests of all classes equally.

progressive tax A tax whose effective rate on an individual's income increases as the person's income rises.

regressive tax A tax that charges individuals the same amount, regardless of income.

flat tax A tax that draws money from all entities at the same proportion of their income.

reality, Congress allots funds from the U.S. treasury to federal departments and agencies and then gives them **budget authority**, which allows them to incur obligations to spend or lend that money. Budget authority for a fiscal year is essentially like the permission for an agency to enter a contract; it is not the same thing as how much the agency will spend in that fiscal year—that amount is called **outlays**.

Where does taxpayer money go? The truth about government spending might surprise you. Spending tends to fall into two general categories. **Mandatory spending** refers to spending not controlled by annual budget decisions—these funds are automatically obligated by virtue of previously enacted laws and may not be modified by annual budget decisions (although they can be modified by repeal or modification of the original legislation). Most mandatory spending occurs in the form of entitlements: government spending such as Social Security, Medicare (national health insurance for seniors), and veterans benefits that must be paid to anyone meeting specific eligibility requirements. President Franklin Delano Roosevelt's New Deal programs and President Lyndon Johnson's Great Society programs substantially expanded the number of entitlements, forcing future law-makers to grapple with those entitlements when they considered reforms of their own. Since 1995, nearly two-thirds of all government spending has been mandatory, almost double the percentage of mandatory spending outlays of the early 1960s (see Figure 15-2).

Discretionary spending encompasses all those spending categories that Congress does have the power to modify or eliminate in a given year. Budgeting is normally a give-and-take process between Congress and the president concerning the most appropriate levels of discretionary spending. Most federal spending on education, the environment, and national defense is based on discretionary spending outlays. When an administration's critics accuse the president of not being fiscally conservative enough with government spending, their criticisms usually focus on government spending as a whole; in fairness, however, only discretionary spending really lies within the president's immediate influence.

budget authority
The power of federal departments and agencies to incur obligations to spend or lend money.

outlays The amount of money a government agency will actually spend during a fiscal year.

mandatory spending Federal government spending that is not controlled by annual budget decisions; includes entitlements such as Medicare and Social Security.

discretionary spending Forms of federal government spending that Congress can modify or eliminate in any given year, including spending on education, the environment, and national defense.

FIGURE 15-2
Where Do Federal Tax Dollars Come from and Where Do They Go?

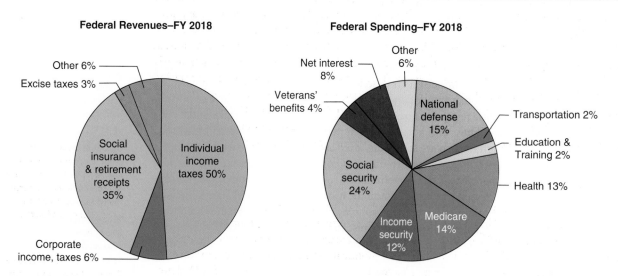

Mandatory spending (required by law) represents such a large percentage of the budget (approximately two-thirds of all government spending) that law-makers often complain that their hands are tied as they wrestle with ways to cut costs. Unlike most spending on our national defense, which Congress authorizes each year at its discretion, entitlements such as Social Security, Medicare, and the food stamp program are examples of mandatory spending categories. The two pie charts shown here illustrate sources of federal revenues and the allocation of federal spending in fiscal year 2018.

Source: Based on data from Office of Management and Budget, Budget of the U.S. Government Fiscal Year 2018, Historical Tables.

America's increasingly diverse population has brought a new set of challenges and opportunities to its various educational systems. Indeed, the demographic makeup of the nation's classrooms has been transformed. The 2014–2015 academic school year marked the first time in U.S. history that a majority of students (50.2 percent) in pre-kindergarten through 12th grade were nonwhite. The National Center for Education Statistics (NCES) projects that by 2023, our country's schools will include about 45 percent white and 55 percent nonwhite students.[10] The NCES also provides evidence that this population diversity is not likely to be reflected in the makeup of our school teachers and administration, as at least 80 percent of classroom teachers are currently non-Hispanic white.[11] This teacher-to-student disparity has significant ramifications for students' sense of well-being in schools, and even for various measures of academic achievement. In addition, this changing demographic picture has raised critical questions concerning educational policy, such as (1) How should the government encourage schools to incorporate more diverse curricula and recruit more teachers from a variety of backgrounds? (2) Can state educational policy effectively address academic achievement gaps among different racial/ethnic groups? (3) How do schools address the high incidence of racial and income-related school segregation across the country? The next decade will present significant challenges to educational reformers charged with addressing the needs of our changing American population.

For Critical Thinking and Discussion

1. Can state and local government effectively address this changing demographic picture with policy reforms? If so, how?
2. What opportunities do the challenges of a changing student population offer to incoming new teachers?

Year in and year out, one particular mandatory spending category—Social Security spending—tops all the other categories. In the fiscal year 2017, the federal government for the first time spent over $1 trillion on the program, as approximately 88 percent of the American population aged 65 and over received benefits. Among the discretionary program outlays, national defense has traditionally constituted the largest part of the budget. In 1962, the federal government allotted $52.4 billion to defense, almost 10 times the amount earmarked to any other discretionary program category. More than a half-century later, nearly $600 billion was allotted to national defense. The growth in discretionary spending during the past 20 years can be attributed in part to the George W. Bush administration's desire to increase spending on defense and homeland security in the wake of the terrorist attacks of September 11, 2001, as well as to subsequent administrations' willingness to continue most of those same defense policies as well as to increase military spending in Afghanistan.

MONETARY POLICY

Monetary policy is the means by which the government controls the supply and price of money in the economy. Although this may seem like a nonpolitical, technical function, the exercise of monetary policy can have profound implications on unemployment rates and inflation, and thus is the focus of considerable political interest. With few exceptions, the Federal Reserve System, which is headed by the Federal Reserve Board ("the Fed"), determines monetary policy in the United States. Since 1913, this independent agency has acted as the nation's central bank, supervising and regulating all of the nation's banks and providing financial information to the public.

Perhaps the single most important responsibility of the Federal Reserve is to set the discount rate that all member banks and other depository institutions will be charged to borrow short-term funds. A high discount rate makes it more expensive for member banks to borrow money from the Federal Reserve Banks, but more profitable for banks to lend money

> **monetary policy** Regulation of the money supply and interest rates by a central bank, such as the U.S. Federal Reserve Board, in order to control inflation and stabilize the currency.
>
> **Federal Reserve Board** The Federal Reserve System's board of governors, which votes on monetary policy in the United States, supervises the nation's banks by setting rules for the 12 Federal Reserve Banks, and engages in open market operations.

Federal Reserve chairman Jerome Powell testifies before Congress in February 2019.

(because they'll secure a greater interest on their investment). A second important function of the Federal Reserve is its engagement in open market operations, in which it buys and sells government securities as a means of controlling the national money supply—buying bonds increases the amount of money in circulation, whereas selling has the opposite effect. Finally, the Federal Reserve sets the reserve requirements of member banks, determining the minimum liquid assets each bank must keep on hand to back customer loans. Any of these actions has the effect of either tightening or loosening the overall money supply.

Few federal agencies in history faced a more daunting challenge than the Federal Reserve in late 2008, when the U.S. economy collapsed into what many economists called "the great recession." The Fed approached the crisis by proposing initiatives designed to save the world economy rather than simply to shape U.S. monetary policy. Under its leadership, the Federal Reserve Bank used its powers to ratchet interest rates down to zero; lent money to mutual funds, hedge funds, foreign banks, investment banks, manufacturers, insurers, and other borrowers; and jump-started stalled credit markets and revolutionized housing finance in the United States by purchasing mortgage bonds in bulk.

15-3 THE WELFARE STATE AND PROGRAMS FOR THE POOR

The term welfare state refers to a social system in which the state assumes a considerable degree of responsibility for citizens in matters of health care, employment, education, and retirement income. In its ideal form, a welfare state is expected to do more than merely guarantee a minimum level of subsistence in these matters; thus, welfare states do not simply ensure a "safety net" for their citizens. (Naturally, these welfare states require higher levels of taxation than do more strictly capitalist systems.) The actual amount of welfare provided varies widely from nation to nation. Nearly all modern welfare states sit somewhere on a spectrum between pure capitalism (an economic system in which all or most of the means of production are privately owned under competitive conditions) and socialism (an economic system in which all or most of the means of production are owned by the community as a whole). Most welfare states have this much in common: they ensure that whatever welfare is provided is done so in universal fashion—in short, they tend to cover every person who meets welfare standards as a matter of right, rather than discretion.

Fiercely protective of its capitalist origins, the U.S. government vigorously resisted assuming broad welfare state functions up until the 1930s, when the Great Depression exposed the harsh realities that unfettered capitalism can occasionally impose on the masses. Although Franklin Delano Roosevelt's New Deal is accurately credited with establishing the modern welfare state in America with its provisions for assisting the poor, his program actually featured few express provisions that directly ensured better education or health care for the masses, to name just two examples.[12]

Poverty has always been a problem in the United States, but until the middle part of the twentieth century, true welfare programs—defined as those programs that maintain the economic and physical well-being of society's poorest members—were primarily the responsibility of local communities and private organizations, including churches. Once again it was the Great Depression that created a significant change in attitudes about welfare programs and led directly to broader government involvement. New Deal programs such as the Works

welfare state Social system in which the state assumes a considerable degree of responsibility for citizens in matters of health care, employment, education, and retirement income.

capitalism Economic system in which all or most of the means of production are privately owned under competitive conditions.

socialism Economic system in which all or most of the means of production are owned by the community as a whole.

Progress Administration and the Federal Emergency Relief Administration provided public jobs and emergency aid. Aid to Dependent Children (later called Aid to Families with Dependent Children, or AFDC) supplemented existing state programs by providing money to poor single mothers unable to work and partake in federal jobs programs.[13] More a public charity than an entitlement, AFDC money went to the extremely poor, and its benefits were often below prevailing minimum wages.

President Lyndon Johnson's Great Society program of the mid-1960s substantially expanded federal welfare programs. As part of his administration's "war on poverty," a federal food stamps program was initiated in 1964; the federal government also gave money to community service programs such as Legal Aid, medical clinics in poor neighborhoods, and the Head Start preschool education program for disadvantaged children. The Medicare program was created to provide health insurance for the elderly in general, whereas Medicaid became the first federal program to provide limited health care services to the poor.[14] Mismanagement slowed the progress of the war on poverty; the outbreak of riots and crimes in the inner cities—where much of the antipoverty legislation was targeted—further doomed legislative support for the expansion of such programs.

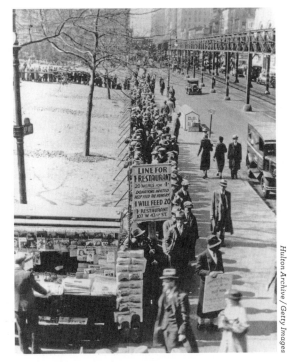

Long lines of people in New York City waiting patiently for handouts during the Great Depression.

As a presidential candidate in 1992, Bill Clinton promised to "end welfare as we know it"; four years later, with the Republicans firmly in control of Congress, President Clinton was presented with legislation that held him to those very words. In 1996, Congress passed and Clinton signed into law the Personal Responsibility and Work Opportunity Reconciliation Act, which replaced AFDC with the Temporary Assistance to Needy Families (TANF) program. TANF devolved much of the former AFDC program back to the states, scaled back the food stamps program, and required welfare recipients to work, or at least actively look for work. Because "last-hired" individuals tend to be the first ones fired during more difficult times, many have returned to welfare in the last 15 years, increasing caseloads for state governments to manage.

15-4 THE SOCIAL SECURITY SYSTEM AND HEALTH CARE POLICY

Even working individuals who make a reasonable living require a "safety net" to guard against sudden and tragic events that threaten to ruin them financially. Significant fluctuations in the market and/or a failure to adequately save enough money for retirement in the first place can leave society's most senior citizens on the brink of poverty. Additionally, a family member's unexpected illness can cripple an individual's financial outlook with exorbitant and continuous medical bills. In the modern economy, government efforts to provide retirement insurance (in the form of Social Security) and to manage health care costs are as compelling as they are controversial.

Social Security has frequently been called the "third rail" of American politics—any politician who touches it is sure to get shocked into submission.[15] The specter of millions of older Americans living in poverty as a result of the Great Depression led to the establishment of Social Security in 1935 as a sort of national pension system. The system was originally intended to be a self-sufficient, "pay-as-you-go" system: workers and their employers would pay dedicated Social Security taxes, and these funds would then be disbursed in the form of pension payments to current retirees. During its early years, the Social Security system often ran surpluses because the ratio of workers to beneficiaries remained high. In the 1950s, Congress even broadened the system's coverage and raised minimum benefits to lower-income contributors.

Medicare Federal program that provides health insurance for the elderly.

Medicaid Federal program that provides limited health care services to the poor.

Unfortunately, the severe economic strains of the 1970s, including high inflation, substantially eroded the Social Security trust fund, which contains securities redeemable to make payments to retirees whenever contributions are not sufficient to pay benefits. Some experts predict that by the year 2035, when all baby boomers are eligible, the Social Security fund will be broke. Social Security thus represents a conundrum for politicians: many recognize the need for large-scale reform of the system, but public opinion and interest groups that favor the current system have proven just as stubborn. This broad political support may be based on the premise that the system is not simply another form of welfare; although lower-income contributors do receive some breaks, rich and poor employees alike pay into the system and receive its benefits.

Because of the concern over the long-run solvency of the Social Security system, many future retirees have been forced to adjust their savings strategies to plan for a future without any guarantee of Social Security. Through the use of tax incentives, the federal government encourages people to put aside extra savings for retirement. As a result, millions today directly invest a substantial portion of their savings in the stock market through the use of tax-favored retirement vehicles such as individual retirement accounts (IRAs) and 401(k) plans. Not only do such vehicles help provide an extra retirement cushion, they also have helped to ensure that a stream of investment capital continues to flow into publicly traded companies on the stock market, which in turn contributes to the well-being of the economy.

As for health care, the U.S. system differs in important ways from the public-run systems found in other modern industrial nations. France, Great Britain, and other European democracies have all adopted systems of universal health care, in which full access to health care is provided to citizens at government expense. In the United States, health care has remained a privately-operated activity, in which patients secure health care insurance and enter into relationships with physicians largely outside of government control. The **Patient Protection and Affordable Care Act of 2010 ("PPACA," also known as "Obamacare")** and subsequent legislation passed by Congress (most notably the Health Care and Education Reconciliation Act of 2010) featured an "individual mandate" that penalized most citizens who do not obtain health care insurance by 2014. Seeking to undermine Obamacare, the Trump Administration and the GOP Congress eliminated the individual mandate portion of Obamacare when it passed the Tax Cuts and Jobs Act of 2017.

Criticism of the PPACA is not limited to the individual mandate. Because insurers are required to charge the same premiums to individuals regardless of health status, they are often incentivized to leave the best doctors and the best hospitals out of their networks to keep costs down. Additionally, provisions of the PPACA that mandate preventive care without any deductible or copayment make it impossible to give enrollees financial incentives to use non-doctor services, which would in turn expand the supply of care without sacrificing quality. Finally, some low-income families have not qualified for subsidies under the law because the definition of "affordable" employer-based coverage only takes into account the cost of individual plans and not family plans. (Critics call this the "family glitch.") Accordingly, even the most ardent supporters of Obamacare have called for improvements to the controversial legislation.

Significant criticisms of the American health care system as a whole persist as well. Most of those who do have health insurance receive it through group plans offered by their employers, and the 2010 legislation did little to reverse that reality. Thus, when employees change jobs, their health insurance coverage is normally disrupted. Additionally, health insurance is not the same as actual health care. Many continue to be hindered by a lack of access to primary care: more than 20 million people in the United States live in rural areas or inner-city neighborhoods that have a shortage of physicians to meet their basic health care needs.[16] Rural residents are particularly disadvantaged; according to the U.S. Department of Health and Human Services, residents of rural areas maintain the highest death rates for unintentional injuries generally and for motor-vehicle injuries specifically, due in large part to the shortage of physicians in such areas. Thus, health care delivery practices will continue to be a problem, no matter how far government extends the scope of health care insurance coverage.

Patient Protection and Affordable Care Act of 2010 (PPACA, aka "Obamacare") The main federal legislation passed in 2010 that overhauled the health care system by expanding Medicaid and guaranteeing health care coverage for select groups of citizens.

15-5 FOREIGN POLICY

Article I of the Constitution gives Congress the exclusive power to declare war, raise armies, punish maritime crimes, and regulate foreign commerce. Under Article II, the president is empowered as commander in chief to conduct the course of war. The founders' intent in separating the power to command from the power to fund the military was to check the war power from being abused. Perhaps the most basic elements of foreign policy during the eighteenth and nineteenth centuries were the treaties the United States entered into with foreign nations. Because the Senate alone was vested with the authority to ratify such treaties (by a two-thirds vote), many expected that this small legislative body (there were just 26 senators at the outset) would exert a strong influence over the nation's foreign policy.

Within the next two centuries, control over foreign affairs, including the power to make war, would shift from Congress to the White House. Fundamental changes in America's role in world affairs during the twentieth century spurred this transfer of power. America's ascendancy to superpower status in the early part of the twentieth century led to U.S. involvement in world affairs. The presidency was well suited to respond to these new demands on America's attention; the single chief executive is best positioned to respond to sudden changes in circumstances around the globe in a quick and forceful manner.

Although the Constitution appears to give Congress primary authority over foreign and military affairs, the large and often unwieldy Congress has proven no match for modern presidents on the world stage. Political scientist Aaron Wildavsky's **two presidencies theory** suggests the existence of a more powerful presidency in foreign affairs and a more limited presidency in the domestic sphere.[17] Of course, the president's dominance over foreign affairs hasn't stopped Congress from at least trying to reassert its authority in this realm. In 1973, with public opinion shifting against military involvement around the globe, Congress passed the **War Powers Resolution**. The resolution theoretically restricted the president's power to engage in war to instances in which Congress had declared war or specifically granted the president permission to use armed forces, or to cases where the nation was under attack. Every president since Nixon has either evaded or ignored the War Powers Resolution, arguing that it unconstitutionally infringes on the president's war powers.

THE ROOTS OF AMERICAN FOREIGN POLICY

As a new nation with a limited military, the United States was at first heavily dependent on maintaining good foreign relations to avoid disadvantageous military engagements. Fortunately, the great distance that separated America from Western European superpowers provided a measure of protection from frequent threats and incursions.

During the nation's early years, the United States maintained a foreign policy marked by **isolationism**, defined as opposition to both (1) interventions in distant wars (that is, outside the Western hemisphere) and (2) involvement in permanent military alliances. The policy of isolationism dominated America's foreign affairs for nearly a century and a half, preserving America's freedom to refuse to act until the very last minute, and in most cases allowing it to forgo intervention altogether. America's brand of military isolationism never applied to the Western hemisphere. On December 2, 1823, President James Monroe declared the nation's commitment to a foreign policy that would eventually become known as the **Monroe Doctrine**. Specifically, Monroe proclaimed that both North and South America should not be considered "as subjects for future colonization by any European power," and that the United States would consider any efforts by Europeans to colonize these areas "as dangerous to our peace and safety."

Though seen as a defining moment in American foreign policy, the Monroe doctrine was rarely tested in its first half-century that changed with the rise of European imperialism at the end of the nineteenth century. In 1895, the United States intervened in a dispute between Great Britain and Venezuela over the boundaries between Venezuela and British Guiana (present-day Guyana). In the early twentieth century, the United States prevented European nations from interfering in the affairs of debt-ridden Latin American countries by taking over the struggling economies of the Dominican Republic (1907) and Nicaragua

two presidencies theory Theory articulated by political scientist Aaron Wildavsky that posits the existence of a more powerful presidency in foreign affairs and a more limited presidency in the domestic sphere.

War Powers Resolution Largely ignored congressional policy that restricts the president's power to engage in war except (1) when Congress has declared war, (2) when Congress has specifically granted the president permission to use armed forces, or (3) when the nation is under attack. The resolution further requires the president to report to Congress whenever American forces are entered into hostilities.

isolationism Foreign policy doctrine that opposes intervention in distant wars and involvement in permanent military alliances.

Monroe Doctrine U.S. foreign policy that proclaimed North and South America unavailable for future colonization by any European power and that declared that any such colonization would be viewed as an act of war on the United States.

Universal History Archive / Getty Images

A cartoon satirizing President Theodore Roosevelt's approach to foreign policy: "Speak softly and carry a big stick."

(1911). The United States also actively encouraged the revolt of Latin American nations against Spain in the early part of the twentieth century, even though Spanish possession of these territories predated the Monroe Doctrine.

U.S. opposition to further European colonization in the Western hemisphere helped the nation to establish itself as the preeminent power in the Americas. Meanwhile, the United States practiced a policy of expansionism on the North American continent. **Expansionism** is the doctrine of expanding the territory or economic influence of one's own country. The policy began as a systematic effort to pursue what many American officials viewed as the nation's defining ideology: its **manifest destiny** to acquire lands and occupy the entire continent from the Atlantic to the Pacific Ocean.

America's increasing willingness to intervene militarily in foreign affairs signaled a potential shift in the traditional balance of powers, as the United States increasingly found itself a major player on the world stage. Nevertheless, up until World War I, the United States remained primarily separate from the rest of the world militarily. Only when American efforts to settle the war failed, and Germany began to relentlessly attack U.S. vessels in 1917, did America enter the war on the side of the Allies—Great Britain, France, Italy, and Russia. The war's victors (including U.S. president Woodrow Wilson) hoped a newly established League of Nations would help avoid future wars. Yet preferences for a policy of isolationism still ran strong throughout America, and the U.S. Senate balked at the risk that the League of Nations might force the U.S. to engage in unwarranted military action. After the Senate voted against U.S. membership in the League, American isolationism prevailed once again.

U.S. involvement in World War II more than two decades later proved critical to the final outcome: American manpower and resources were an important component in the success of the D-Day invasion of France and much of Western Europe in 1944. The United States detonated two atomic bombs over Japan in August 1945, forcing the Japanese to surrender. After the war, the European victors looked to the United States again to help keep international peace. This time they were not disappointed, as the United States promptly joined the newly created **United Nations (UN)**, an international organization formed to promote and maintain international security and peace.

Since World War II, America's prevailing foreign policy has shifted from one marked by isolationism to one featuring **internationalism**—the United States actively participated in a process that collectively secured the political independence and territorial boundaries of other countries by a system of economic and military sanctions against aggressor nations. In fact, America went even further than other nations in this regard. The Marshall Plan (formally the European Recovery Program), introduced by Secretary of State George Marshall in 1947, provided $13 billion in loans to Western European countries whose economies had been ravaged by World War II.

Out of the wreckage of World War II there emerged two global military and political superpowers, the United States and the Soviet Union, locked in what would become a half-century-long struggle called the **Cold War**.[18] This conflict over ideological differences (the promotion of democracy by the United States versus the promotion of communism by the Soviet Union) lasted from 1945 until the dissolution of the Soviet Union in 1991 and was carried on by a variety of methods, including economic warfare, arms build-ups, and tense diplomacy. Formally created in 1949, the **North Atlantic Treaty Organization (NATO)** bound the United States to the military defense of Western Europe. President Harry Truman also articulated the **Truman Doctrine**, which provided money and resources to sustaining noncommunist governments in areas strategically vital to the United States, such as the Mediterranean and the Middle East. American foreign policy during the Cold War generally adhered to a policy of **containment**

expansionism Doctrine that favors a country expanding its own territory and influence.

manifest destiny U.S. policy of the mid-nineteenth century that advocated acquiring lands and occupying the entire American continent from one ocean to the other.

United Nations (UN) International organization formed after World War II to promote and maintain international security and peace.

internationalism Doctrine that favors active participation of the nation in collective arrangements that secure the political independence and territorial boundaries of other countries.

Cold War The nearly half-century struggle over ideological differences between the United States and the Soviet Union. Waged through economic warfare, arms build-ups, and tense diplomatic talks, the Cold War never broke out into a sustained military engagement between the two nations and ended with the dissolution of the Soviet Union in 1991.

—restricting Soviet power to its current geographical sphere and resisting any efforts to expand communist influence.

Most U.S. presidents during the Cold War subscribed to some version of the domino theory, which posited that communist takeovers of these Southeast Asian countries would be followed by takeovers of Taiwan, India, Iran, and possibly other nations as well. The American military failure in the Vietnam War in particular led officials at every level of the American government to revisit some of the most fundamental premises of U.S. foreign policy, including the theory of containment.[19] The American phase of that war, extending from 1964 until 1973, proved longer-lasting and more divisive than any other war involving the United States up to that point.[20] The conflict eventually left 58,000 Americans dead or missing and cost the U.S. government more than $167 billion.

U.S. responsibilities around the world have not decreased much in the aftermath of the Cold War. In his January 1991 State of the Union speech, President George H. W. Bush spoke of the onset of a new world order, in which numerous nations would work together for the purpose of securing collective peace, security, freedom, and the rule of law.[21] Maintaining this new world order has been a challenge for American political leaders ever since. With the U.S. economy increasingly intertwined with the global economy, economic relations with East Asia, Europe, and other countries in the Western hemisphere continue to be a central factor in American foreign policy. Of course, economic concerns do not eliminate other interests—tragic human rights abuses in Somalia and Bosnia put pressure on the U.S. to intervene on humanitarian grounds in those countries. Most modern presidents have been willing to provide limited aid but no military assistance, prompted criticisms that they have failed to wield America's superpower status in the most appropriate fashion.[22]

Militarily, the greatest threats to U.S. security during the first decade of the twenty-first century remain in the Middle East. U.S. support for Israel has assured the United States of a friendly ally in the Middle East, yet it has also at times run counter to fundamental principles of self-determination, as U.S. officials have been forced to confront another dilemma—what to do with the tens of thousands of Palestinian refugees uprooted from their homes in the years following Israel's occupation of former Palestinian territory. The Trump administration in particular has come out strongly in favor of Israel's hardline approach to the conflict.

The events of September 11, 2001, refocused the U.S. government's foreign policy energies toward a global war on terrorism. After initiating wars in Afghanistan and Iraq to expel the Al Qaeda and ISIS terrorist networks, the U.S. has more recently set its focus on the Iranian government's long-time support for terrorism by ramping up its economic sanctions on that nation in an attempt to break its economy and inspire an overthrow of the government.

Additionally, North Korea has emerged as a potential nuclear threat in the past decade. Since 2006, the North Korean government has conducted at least four underground nuclear tests, drawing sanctions from the United Nations Security Council. Critics charge that the end of the Cold War has in fact ushered in a "new world disorder," featuring ever-shifting alliances and grave terrorist threats from entities not formally associated with any specific nation. Certainly, the Trump administration has charted its own course with North Korea. On one hand, it has tried to use economic sanctions as a tool to alter North Korea's quest for its

A napalm strike erupting in a fireball near U.S. soldiers in Vietnam in 1966.

The September 11, 2001, terrorist attacks on the World Trade Center towers shifted the focus of American foreign policy to fighting terrorism in the Middle East and elsewhere.

North Atlantic Treaty Organization (NATO) A military, political, and economic alliance of nations formally bound to protect self-determination and open trade in Western Europe.

North Korean leader Kim Jong-un (left) greets President Donald Trump at the start of their historic U.S.-North Korea summit in Singapore on June 12, 2018.

own nuclear arsenal. Meanwhile, in 2018 President Trump met in person with North Korean Chairman Kim Jong-un in Singapore, marking the first-ever summit between leaders of North Korea and the U.S. Still, at the time this book went to press no agreement had yet been reached between the two nations, raising the question of whether the Trump Administration's more conciliatory approach was likely to continue.

Within this constantly shifting international terrain, America continues to search for its role and identity in the twenty-first-century world. In *Colossus: The Rise and Fall of the American Empire*, British-born Harvard University Professor Niall Ferguson argues that like the great British empire of old, the United States needs to embrace its imperial character and commit to more securely establishing the types of democratic institutions around the world that foster long-term prosperity.[23] In another influential book, *Soft Power: The Means to Success in World Politics*, Joseph Nye argues that rather than relying on unilateralism and military power, the United States should endeavor to win the voluntary cooperation of foreign governments.[24] Is the United States an empire? Does it want to be? In light of the difficulties U.S. military forces are facing in many regions of the world, these questions will continue to be debated in the years ahead.

THE STRUCTURE OF AMERICAN FOREIGN POLICY-MAKING

Many actors and institutions attempt either formally or informally to influence American foreign policy. The president of the United States sits squarely at the center of foreign policy-making—within the federal government, the president often dictates its terms with little interference from the other branches.[25] On the positive side, presidential dominance of foreign policy allows the U.S. government to act immediately and decisively in response to developments abroad. The quick reactions to the bombing of Pearl Harbor, the threat of nuclear missiles in Cuba, and the 9/11 terrorist attacks might not have been possible had the principal decision-makers been a legislative body or council. At the same time, more controversial foreign policy forays such as America's involvement in the Vietnam War, the trading of arms for hostages with Iran in the 1980s, and military intervention in Iraq without proof of weapons of mass destruction might well have been avoided had so much power not been vested in one individual. Although the president is at the center of foreign policy-making, other executive branch departments and agencies help formulate and implement foreign policy.

The **Department of State**, headed by the secretary of state, maintains primary responsibility for many foreign policy programs. State Department programs include diplomatic missions to other countries, foreign aid to developing nations, and contributions to **international organizations** (official entities of international scope or character, usually established by treaty, such as the World Bank and the International Monetary Fund). During the latter half of the twentieth century, the secretary of state emerged as a principal spokesperson for the U.S. government on all foreign policy matters.

Military power is an important factor in U.S. foreign relations. The **Department of Defense** plays a critical role in helping formulate and implement U.S. foreign policy by managing the nation's military. The secretary of defense is the principal civilian adviser to the president on military matters. On the military side, the president is advised by the **Joint Chiefs of Staff (JCS)**, which consists of the chief officers of the four branches of the armed forces (U.S. Army, Navy, Air Force, and Marines) as well as the JCS chair and vice chair. The JCS delivers the president's orders to the military commands involved in a particular operation.

Truman Doctrine Doctrine articulated by President Harry Truman in the late 1940s by which money and resources were provided to support and sustain noncommunist governments in areas strategically vital to the United States.

containment U.S. foreign policy that sought to restrict Soviet power (and communist influence) to its existing geographical sphere.

domino theory The theory that held that communist takeovers of countries in Southeast Asia and elsewhere would be followed by subsequent communist takeovers of nearby countries.

new world order President George H. W. Bush's description of the post–Cold War world, in which nations would work together for the purpose of securing collective peace, security, freedom, and the rule of law.

Department of State Executive branch agency that is primarily responsible for most foreign policy programs within the executive branch, including diplomatic missions, foreign aid, and contributions to international organizations.

Is the American Military Draft a Thing of the Past?

The U.S. government discontinued use of compulsory military service in 1973, much to the relief of a generation of young Americans that had grown increasingly hostile to America's military involvement in Vietnam. Since then, Americans have marveled at the degree to which America's comparative advantage in military technology has helped to reduce (although certainly not eliminate) casualties of U.S. military incursions. Yet is the move to an all-voluntary military force permanent? Critics of the Bush administration's invasion of Iraq argue that America's active military force of nearly 1.5 million soldiers was stretched far too thin between 2003 and 2008. Several high-profile members of Congress at the time, including Charles Rangel (D-NY), even called for the draft to be reinstated as a means of ensuring that service would be spread equally between the rich and the poor (those from poor families are more apt than those from wealthier families to voluntarily enlist for military service). President Barack Obama's decision to upgrade the nation's military presence in Afghanistan reopened those same questions yet again.

Should college-age students anticipate that the draft might come again in the near future? On one hand, the political platforms of both parties have consistently opposed reinstatement of the draft. On the other hand, since 1980 all male U.S. citizens age 18 or older have been required by law to register with the selective service, in case emergency manpower needs in a time of national crisis require conscription (recruitment) once again.

Agence France Presse / Getty Images

An official at Selective Service Headquarters in Washington, DC, drawing labeled ping-pong balls to determine the rank order of birthdates in the first nationally televised draft lottery on December 2, 1969. All 19-year-old male citizens with birthdays chosen early in the process would become the first draftees in the Vietnam War.

For Critical Thinking and Discussion

1. Do you believe America's selective service system—the agency that maintains information on those who may be subject to a military draft—is unfair? Should it apply only to male U.S. citizens, or to others as well?
2. Given the advanced state of military technology, can involuntary conscription still be justified in the twenty-first century?

In 1947, the National Security Act established the **National Security Council (NSC)** as an advisory body to the president, coordinating information about foreign, military, and economic policies that affect national security. By law, the NSC must include the president, vice president, and the secretaries of state and defense. But recent presidents have also appointed a national security adviser to supervise the council and monitor the implementation of national security decisions made by the president. Dating back to the 1960s, the national security adviser has served as both a key adviser and policy-maker for most modern presidents.[26]

With a number of executive branch officials in a position to advise the president on foreign policy, some conflicts are inevitable. For example, when the George W. Bush administration turned its attention to a possible war in Iraq in 2003, sharp divisions among senior officials emerged. Although such terms may be oversimplified, the administration's **hawks**—who called for aggressive military action wherever hostile forces might be found—were led by the secretary of defense, the national security advisor, and the vice president. On the other side

international organization Entity of international scope or character, usually established by treaty, such as the World Bank or the International Monetary Fund.

Department of Defense Executive branch agency that is responsible for managing the nation's military and advising the president on all military matters.

of this divide were the realists, led by the secretary of state, who counseled diplomacy as the primary means of protecting U.S. interests abroad. Ultimately, the hawks won the day.

Although not directly responsible for formulating the administration's overall foreign policy direction, other agencies and executive branch officials also influence aspects of foreign policy. In the aftermath of the 9/11 terrorist attacks, the Bush administration sought to create a unified security structure to coordinate the protection of U.S. citizens against terrorist threats within the nation's own borders. Accordingly, Congress in 2002 established the Department of Homeland Security (DHS). Various governmental divisions responsible for U.S. security have been brought under DHS control, including border and transportation security, infrastructure protection, the U.S. Coast Guard, the U.S. Secret Service, the Federal Emergency Management Agency (FEMA), and the Bureau of Citizenship and Immigration Services. The National Security Act of 1947 created the Central Intelligence Agency (CIA) to correlate, evaluate, and disseminate intelligence information from throughout the world that affects national security. Unlike the NSC, the CIA is also responsible for disseminating propaganda or performing public relations functions on behalf of the U.S. government and for engaging in overt or covert activities at the direction of the president.

OTHER FOREIGN POLICY ACTORS AND INTERESTS

Congress possesses various constitutional powers that give it some stake in crafting U.S. foreign policy. Although presidents have committed troops to battle more than a hundred times in our nation's history without a formal declaration of war from Congress—including most notably in Korea and Vietnam—modern chief executives have learned that there may be some political benefits to asking for a congressional resolution to support military action. Congressional approval of such actions can help rally public support and possibly provide some political cover should those military operations fail. In October 2002, for example, Congress passed a resolution backing the use of military force in Iraq. In the months that followed the invasion when guerrilla warfare continued to threaten American soldiers, many Democratic senators who voted for the resolution were hard-pressed to criticize the president's decision to invade.

Most Americans seeking to influence foreign policy organize themselves into special interest or "pressure" groups for the purpose of doing so. The power that the so-called pro-Israel lobby wields in Congress is well known: the American-Israel Public Affairs Committee (AIPAC) has influenced important appropriation decisions on Capitol Hill during the past 30 years, helping to ensure the continuation of American aid to Israel. AIPAC's tactics have included letter-writing campaigns and active involvement in election campaigns to assist members of Congress who it believes are sympathetic to Israel.

The term military-industrial complex refers to the vast network of defense industries in America, such as manufacturers of weapons, missiles, aircraft, submarines, and so forth, and their bureaucratic allies. The complex as a whole maintains a keen interest in foreign policy-making that is concerned with defense and national security. These industries expanded during the Cold War as U.S. defense budgets rose to as much as 40 percent of annual federal spending. In the late 1990s, defense spending amounted to just 15 percent of the budget, generating ever-more-feverish efforts by members of the military-industrial complex to either increase that allotment or shift the focus of defense spending to weapons and resources that meet their own areas of expertise. One of the by-products of the terrorist attacks of 9/11 was a renewed commitment to military and national security spending; 10 years after the tragedy, America's military spending had leveled to approximately 20 percent of the overall U.S. budget.

ADDITIONAL FOREIGN POLICY CHALLENGES

Some foreign policy dilemmas of the twenty-first century, such as North Korea's current attempts to build a nuclear capability, represent new versions of old challenges that the U.S. government has faced. Others represent unforeseen obstacles produced by circumstances unique to the modern era, such as Iran's support for terrorist groups. Regardless, American

---

Joint Chiefs of Staff (JCS) Group of chief officers of the four branches of the armed forces as well as a JCS chair and vice chair, which advises the president on military matters and delivers the president's orders to the military.

National Security Council (NSC) Advisory body to the president charged with coordinating information about foreign, military, and economic policies that affect national security.

hawks Members of the president's administration who call for aggressive military actions wherever hostile forces may be found.

realists Members of the president's administration who advocate diplomacy as the primary means of protecting U.S. interests abroad.

Department of Homeland Security (DHS) Executive branch agency established in 2002 to coordinate government entities in protecting U.S. citizens against terrorism within the nation's borders.

Central Intelligence Agency (CIA) Federal agency charged with evaluating and disseminating intelligence information, performing public relations functions that affect international perceptions of the United States, and engaging in overt and covert operations at the direction of the president.

military-industrial complex The vast network of defense industries in America (including manufacturers of weapons, missiles, aircraft, and so forth) and their allies in the federal bureaucracy.

officials must always be on the lookout for foreign policy challenges that arise with little or no warning. Consider just a few such challenges:

- **Russia.** The fall of the Soviet Union in 1990 did not eliminate threats to the United States from that part of the globe. The Russian Federation headed by Vladimir Putin maintains one of the world's most powerful military threats because most of the nuclear capabilities of the former Soviet Union were passed on to Russia (see Table 15-2 for a rundown of the nations that currently maintain some form of nuclear capability). Concerns have been raised about Russia's continued use of military force in the smaller Republic of Chechnya; additionally, allegations that Putin's intelligence service interfered with the 2016 U.S. Presidential election were confirmed by most U.S. intelligence agencies.
- **China.** In addition to maintaining its own nuclear threat, the People's Republic of China has been accused by international human rights organizations of organizing and sanctioning human rights abuses within that country. Chinese trade policies have also put U.S. patent holders at a disadvantage in Chinese markets. All this puts the U.S. government in something of a quandary: though it may wish to impose financial sanctions on China, American business interests want access to China's one-billion-person consumer market. In 2018 and 2019, the Trump administration imposed tariffs on a broad range of Chinese products, including consumer goods such as internet modems, routers, and circuit boards; the Beijing government responded by imposing retaliatory tariffs of its own on more than $60 billion in American goods. While many claim that these tariffs are necessary to force China to trade fairly, others fear that a trade war will hurt the U.S. economy.

TABLE 15-2
Who Is in the Nuclear Club?

The list of states that have successfully detonated nuclear weapons—often termed the "nuclear club"—continues to grow in the post-Cold War era. Only five members of the club are considered "nuclear weapon states" under the terms of the Nuclear Non-Proliferation Treaty (NPT), a landmark international treaty first established in 1970 between states that possess such weapons and 190 nations that do not. Four other states in the club do not subscribe to the NPT, but they are known or believed to possess nuclear weapons. Just one state (South Africa) has actually dropped out of the club, dissembling its arsenal before joining the NPT. The current list of states in the nuclear club is as follows:

Recognized Nuclear Weapon States Under the Terms of the NPT	Year of First Test
1. The United States	1945
2. Russia (successor state to the Soviet Union)	1949
3. United Kingdom	1952
4. France	1960
5. China	1964
Other States Believed to Have Nuclear Weapons (non-signatories to the NPT)	
6. India	1974
7. Pakistan	1998
8. North Korea	2006
9. Israel	1979*

* Year is disputed; Israel neither confirms nor denies that it has conducted nuclear tests.
Based on data from National Resources Defense Council Archive of Nuclear Data, www.nrdc.org/nuclear/nudb/datainx.asp.

Spencer Platt / Getty Images

President Donald Trump addresses the United Nations General Assembly in September 2018 in New York City.

• **Foreign aid.** Critics of foreign aid charge that much of the money provided by America goes to elites in the recipient nations, rather than to those who need help. The United States continues to be a leading contributor to such international aid institutions as the World Bank, which since 1945 has extended credit to nations for building and economic development. America also contributes substantially to the International Monetary Fund, which helps to maintain the value of foreign currencies during times of crisis. But the heyday of foreign aid—when it served as a critical instrument of U.S. foreign relations—appears to be a thing of the past.

• **United Nations.** The United States dominated the UN on all security issues during its first 40 years, but as U.S. influence over the body has declined, calls have increased within Congress to reduce American aid to the organization and to ignore its dictates whenever American security interests are at issue. In 2003, America went to war in Iraq even though the UN Security Council was unwilling to offer advance authorization for any such military action. Yet immediately after the war with Iraq had concluded, the UN began relief and reconstruction activities in the war-torn nation and began pushing for a resolution that would broaden international control over the region. Thus, in the twenty-first century, the UN seems destined to play at least a limited role in international affairs, asserting its authority most strongly during peacekeeping and relief missions that follow military action.

Regardless of what new foreign policy challenges may arise, U.S. officials must be prepared to justify their actions according to some theory or well-articulated rationale, lest they be accused of conducting foreign policy "on the fly." Those officials who offer no persuasive reason for endangering American resources—and possibly putting American troops in harm's way—may find themselves on the politically endangered list in relatively short order.

Public policy in the United States has been a source of continued frustration for many. This nation's status as one of the richest nations in the world over the past century might imply a responsibility on the part of the government to spread around those riches so that each person is assured at least a minimum level of subsistence and welfare. At the same time, the U.S. capitalist system tends to foster a culture of "pull yourself up by your bootstraps," which is at odds with policy efforts leading to the systematic provision of goods and services to needy people.

The course of public policy is rarely a smooth one, and frustrations can weigh down even the most well-intentioned policy initiatives. Clearly, Charles Lindblom's "science of muddling through" is a policy-making process for the patient and determined only, even in the case of policy reforms that are considered groundbreaking in many respects.

Summary

15-1 An Overview of the Policy-Making Process

- The policy-making process generally unfolds in five stages: a recognition/definition stage, a formulation stage, an adoption stage, an implementation stage, and an evaluation stage. Bureaucrats in administrative agencies, interest groups (including think tanks), Congress, and the president are all actively involved throughout the process.

15-2 Theories and Practice in Economic Policy

- Fiscal policy is concerned with the raising of revenue through taxation and the spending of whatever revenue has been generated. Laissez-faire capitalism, which favors minimal government interference in the economy, dominated the U.S. economy for much of the eighteenth and nineteenth centuries; in the 1930s, the government began to apply the principles of Keynesian economic theory, which favors government spending during difficult economic times. Finally, during the past quarter century, some presidents have turned to supply-side economics, whereas others have returned to Keynesian economic theory once again.

- The federal budget, which lays out a comprehensive plan of government spending, is the primary means by which government carries out fiscal policy. Today's budget-making process is dominated by the president, who proposes an initial budget that will serve as the framework for all budget negotiations. Congress responds initially through its appropriations and budget committees, which in turn formulate budget proposals based on their own projections for future revenue.

- Taxation policies may be redistributive (benefiting the poor at the expense of the rich) or distributive (promoting the interests of all economic classes equally). A large percentage of taxpayer funds goes to mandatory spending (usually in the form of entitlements such as Medicare and Social Security) that is unaffected by annual budget decisions.

- The Federal Reserve supervises the nation's monetary policy by setting the discount rate that its Federal Reserve Banks may charge member banks to receive loans and by determining the minimum assets banks must keep on hand, called the reserve requirements. When the Federal Reserve lowers the discount rate, it may stimulate economic investment, but it risks setting off higher inflation rates.

15-3 The Welfare State and Programs for the Poor

- The welfare state is a social system in which the state assumes a considerable degree of responsibility for citizens in matters of health care, employment, education, and retirement income. The actual amount of welfare provided varies widely from nation to nation. Most Western democracies feature welfare systems that sit on the end of the spectrum closer to pure socialism, whereas the U.S. welfare state mixes elements of socialism and capitalism in its regulatory schemes that protect citizens.

15-4 The Social Security System and Health Care Policy

- Social Security has provided retirement income for millions of retirees since 1935. Although many economists predict that the system will eventually be forced to pay out significantly more than it brings in, to date the U.S. Congress has enacted no major policy changes, putting off all discussion of privatization for the time being. The U.S. government encourages private retirement investing through tax-free investment vehicles such as IRAs and 401(k) plans.

- The U.S. health care system contrasts sharply with systems found in other Western democracies that feature universal health care. The controversial 2010 federal legislation, entitled the Patient Protection and Affordable Care Act, addressed various inequities in the insurance industry, but it did not guarantee universal health care for all, and it failed to address these access-to-care issues.

15-5 Foreign Policy

- The president is the commander in chief and has the power to negotiate treaties and appoint and receive ambassadors; Congress has the power to declare war, raise armies, and regulate foreign commerce, among its other functions. The United States adhered to a policy of isolationism from the time of its founding until the late nineteenth century, generally forgoing intervention in foreign wars during that period. With its entry into World War I and World War II, the United States rose to the status of a world superpower emphasizing internationalism, by which it participated in a system of collective security.

- The Cold War, pitting the United States against the Soviet Union from 1945 until 1991, was waged through economic warfare, arms build-ups, and moments of tense diplomacy that fell short of direct military engagements between the two superpowers. The U.S. military overthrew the governments of Afghanistan and Iraq in 2001 and 2003, respectively, as part of the war on terrorism.

- In formulating foreign policy, the president is assisted by the secretary of state, the secretary of defense, the Joint Chiefs of Staff, the national security adviser, and the Director of National Intelligence. The Department of Homeland Security, created by an act of Congress in 2002, is responsible for border and transportation security, intelligence analysis, infrastructure protection, and all activities that protect against terrorist threats in the United States.

- U.S. foreign policy today is further complicated by the determination of what role (if any) the United States should play in supporting the United Nations, questions as to whether the United States should increase or decrease foreign aid in general, and increasingly tense relations between the United States and nuclear powers Russia and China.

Key Terms

budget authority (p. 324)
budget deficit (p. 320)
budget surplus (p. 320)
capitalism (p. 326)
Central Intelligence Agency (CIA) (p. 334)
Cold War (p. 330)
containment (p. 330)
Department of Defense (p. 332)
Department of Homeland Security (DHS) (p. 334)
Department of State (p. 332)
discretionary spending (p. 324)
distributive tax policies (p. 323)
domino theory (p. 331)
expansionism (p. 330)
Federal Reserve Board (p. 325)
fiscal policy (p. 319)
flat tax (p. 323)
gross domestic product (GDP) (p. 320)
hawks (p. 333)
inflation (p. 319)
international organization (p. 332)
internationalism (p. 330)
isolationism (p. 329)
Joint Chiefs of Staff (JCS) (p. 332)
Keynesian economic theory (p. 320)
laissez-faire economics (p. 319)
mandatory spending (p. 324)

manifest destiny (p. 330)
Medicaid (p. 327)
Medicare (p. 327)
military-industrial complex (p. 334)
monetary policy (p. 325)
Monroe Doctrine (p. 329)
national debt (p. 320)
National Security Council (NSC) (p. 333)
new world order (p. 331)
North Atlantic Treaty Organization (NATO) (p. 330)
outlays (p. 324)
Patient Protection and Affordable Care Act of 2010 (PPACA) (p. 328)
progressive tax (p. 323)
public policy (p. 318)
realists (p. 334)
recession (p. 320)
redistributive tax policies (p. 323)
regressive tax (p. 323)
socialism (p. 326)
supply-side economics (p. 320)
Truman Doctrine (p. 330)
two presidencies theory (p. 329)
United Nations (UN) (p. 330)
War Powers Resolution (p. 329)
welfare state (p. 326)

APPENDIX
Declaration of Independence

In Congress, July 4, 1776.

A DECLARATION

By the Representatives of the United States of America,

In General Congress Assembled.

When in the Course of human Events, it becomes necessary for one People to dissolve the Political Bands which have connected them with another, and to assume among the Powers of the Earth, the separate and equal Station to which the Laws of Nature and of Nature's God entitle them, a decent Respect to the Opinions of Mankind requires that they should declare the causes which impel them to the Separation.

We hold these Truths to be self-evident, that all Men are created equal, that they are endowed by their Creator with certain unalienable Rights, that among these are Life, Liberty, and the Pursuit of Happiness—That to secure these Rights, Governments are instituted among Men, deriving their just Powers from the Consent of the Governed, that whenever any Form of Government becomes destructive of these Ends, it is the Right of the People to alter or abolish it, and to institute new Government, laying its Foundation on such Principles, and organizing its Powers in such Form, as to them shall seem most likely to effect their Safety and Happiness. Prudence, indeed, will dictate that Governments long established should not be changed for light and transient Causes; and accordingly all Experience hath shewn, that Mankind are more disposed to suffer, while Evils are sufferable, than to right themselves by abolishing the Forms to which they are accustomed. But when a long Train of Abuses and Usurpations, pursuing invariably the same Object, evinces a Design to reduce them under absolute Despotism, it is their Right, it is their Duty, to throw off such Government, and to provide new Guards for their future Security. Such has been the patient Sufferance of these Colonies; and such is now the Necessity which constrains them to alter their former Systems of Government. The History of the present King of Great Britain is a History of repeated Injuries and Usurpations, all having in direct Object the Establishment of an absolute Tyranny over these States. To prove this, let Facts be submitted to a candid World.

He has refused his Assent to Laws, the most wholesome and necessary for public good.

He has forbidden his Governors to pass Laws of immediate and pressing importance, unless suspended in their Operation till his Assent should be obtained; and when so suspended, he has utterly neglected to attend to them.

He has refused to pass other Laws for the Accommodation of large Districts of People, unless those People would relinquish the Right of Representation in the Legislature, a Right inestimable to them, and formidable to Tyrants only.

He has called together Legislative Bodies at Places unusual, uncomfortable, and distant from the Depository of their public records, for the sole Purpose of fatiguing them into Compliance with his Measures.

He has dissolved Representative Houses repeatedly, for opposing with manly Firmness his Invasions on the Rights of the People.

He has refused for a long Time, after such Dissolutions, to cause others to be elected; whereby the Legislative Powers, incapable of Annihilation, have returned to the People at large for their exercise; the State remaining in the mean time exposed to all the Dangers of Invasion from without, and Convulsions within.

He has endeavoured to prevent the Population of these States; for that Purpose obstructing the Laws for Naturalization of Foreigners; refusing to pass others to encourage their Migrations hither, and raising the Conditions of new Appropriations of Lands.

He has obstructed the Administration of Justice, by refusing his Assent to Laws for establishing Judiciary Powers.

He has made Judges dependent on his Will alone, for the Tenure of their Offices, and the Amount and Payment of their Salaries.

He has erected a Multitude of new Offices, and sent hither Swarms of Officers to harass our People, and eat out their Substance.

He has kept among us, in Times of Peace, Standing Armies, without the consent of our Legislatures.

He has affected to render the Military independent of and superior to the Civil Power.

He has combined with others to subject us to a Jurisdiction foreign to our Constitution, and unacknowledged by our Laws; giving his Assent to their Acts of pretended Legislation:

For quartering large Bodies of Armed Troops among us:

For protecting them, by a mock Trial, from Punishment for any Murders which they should commit on the Inhabitants of these States:

For cutting off our Trade with all Parts of the World:

For imposing Taxes on us without our Consent: For depriving us, in many Cases, of the Benefits of Trial by Jury:

For transporting us beyond Seas to be tried for pretended Offences:

For abolishing the free System of English Laws in a neighbouring Province, establishing therein an arbitrary Government, and enlarging its Boundaries, so as to render it at once an Example and fit Instrument for introducing the same absolute Rule into these Colonies:

For taking away our Charters, abolishing our most valuable Laws, and altering fundamentally the Forms of our Governments:

For suspending our own Legislatures, and declaring themselves invested with Power to legislate for us in all Cases whatsoever.

He has abdicated Government here, by declaring us out of his Protection and waging War against us.

He has plundered our Seas, ravaged our Coasts, burnt our Towns, and destroyed the Lives of our People.

He is, at this Time, transporting large Armies of foreign Mercenaries to compleat the Works of Death, Desolation, and Tyranny, already begun with circumstances of Cruelty and Perfidy, scarcely paralleled in the most barbarous Ages, and totally unworthy the Head of a civilized Nation.

He has constrained our fellow Citizens taken Captive on the high Seas to bear Arms against their Country, to become the Executioners of their Friends and Brethren, or to fall themselves by their Hands.

He has excited domestic Insurrections amongst us, and has endeavoured to bring on the Inhabitants of our Frontiers, the merciless Indian Savages, whose known Rule of Warfare, is an undistinguished Destruction, of all Ages, Sexes and Conditions.

In every stage of these Oppressions we have Petitioned for Redress in the most humble Terms: Our repeated Petitions have been answered only by repeated Injury. A Prince, whose Character is thus marked by every act which may define a Tyrant, is unfit to be the Ruler of a free People.

Nor have we been wanting in Attentions to our British Brethren. We have warned them from Time to Time of Attempts by their Legislature to extend an unwarrantable Jurisdiction over us. We have reminded them of the Circumstances of our Emigration and Settlement here. We have appealed to their native Justice and Magnanimity, and we have conjured them by the Ties of our common Kindred to disavow these Usurpations, which, would inevitably interrupt our Connections and Correspondence. They too have been deaf to the Voice of Justice and of Consanguinity. We must, therefore, acquiesce in the Necessity, which denounces our Separation, and hold them, as we hold the rest of Mankind, Enemies in War, in Peace, Friends.

We, therefore, the Representatives of the UNITED STATES OF AMERICA, in GENERAL CONGRESS, Assembled, appealing to the Supreme Judge of the World for the Rectitude of our Intentions, do, in the Name, and by Authority of the good People of these Colonies, solemnly Publish and Declare, That these United Colonies are, and of Right ought to be, FREE AND INDEPENDENT STATES; that they are absolved from all Allegiance to the British Crown, and that all political Connection between them and the State of Great Britain, is and ought to be totally dissolved; and that as FREE AND INDEPENDENT STATES, they have full Power to levy War, conclude Peace, contract Alliances, establish Commerce, and to do all other Acts and Things which INDEPENDENT STATES may of right do. And for the support of this Declaration, with a firm Reliance on the Protection of divine Providence, we mutually pledge to each other our Lives, our Fortunes, and our sacred Honor.

THE CONSTITUTION OF THE UNITED STATES OF AMERICA

We the people of the United States, in order to form a more perfect union, establish justice, insure domestic tranquility, provide for the common defense, promote the general welfare, and secure the blessings of liberty to ourselves and our posterity, do ordain and establish this Constitution for the United States of America.

As a statement containing the essential reasons for drafting the Constitution and the purposes of the new central government, the Preamble theoretically does not confer any actual power on government. Nevertheless, on numerous occasions the Supreme Court has cited the preamble to illustrate the origin, scope, and purposes of the Constitution, as well as to help discern the meaning of certain constitutional provisions that follow it. Most notably in McCulloch v. Maryland *(1819), Chief Justice John Marshall quoted from the Preamble at length to confirm that the Constitution comes directly from the people, and not from the states.*

ARTICLE I

Section 1. All legislative powers herein granted shall be vested in a Congress of the United States, which shall consist of a Senate and House of Representatives.

The placement of provisions for congressional power in Article I confirms what the founders undoubtedly assumed to be true: that Congress would be the preeminent branch of the new central government. Section 1 established two important principles. First, by specifying "powers herein granted," it declared that the national government is one of enumerated powers. Despite the broadening of powers implied by the necessary and proper clause of Section 8, this statement of Section 1 still means that Congress theoretically cannot do whatever it wants to do. Rather, it must ground its exercise of power (whether explicitly stated or implied) in a specific provision of Article I. Second, Section 1 established the principle of bicameralism—the presence of two separate but equally powerful legislative bodies—as a further safeguard against government tyranny.

Section 2. The House of Representatives shall be composed of members chosen every second year by the people of the several states, and the electors in each state shall have the qualifications requisite for electors of the most numerous branch of the state legislature.

No person shall be a Representative who shall not have attained to the age of twenty five years, and been seven years a citizen of the United States, and who shall not, when elected, be an inhabitant of that state in which he shall be chosen.

Representatives and direct taxes shall be apportioned among the several states which may be included within this union, according to their respective numbers, which shall be determined by adding to the whole number of free persons, including those bound to service for a term of years, and excluding Indians not taxed, three fifths of all other Persons. The actual Enumeration shall be made within three years after the first meeting of the Congress of the United States, and within every subsequent term of ten years, in such manner as they shall by law direct. The number of Representatives shall not exceed one for every thirty thousand, but each state shall have at least one Representative; and until such enumeration shall be made, the state of New Hampshire shall be entitled to chuse three, Massachusetts eight, Rhode Island and Providence Plantations one, Connecticut five, New York six, New Jersey four, Pennsylvania eight, Delaware one, Maryland six, Virginia ten, North Carolina five, South Carolina five, and Georgia three.

When vacancies happen in the Representation from any state, the executive authority thereof shall issue writs of election to fill such vacancies.

The House of Representatives shall choose their speaker and other officers; and shall have the sole power of impeachment.

Section 2 of Article I establishes a House of Representatives as the lower House of the Congress. The membership of the U.S. House of Representatives is apportioned according to each state's population; the so-called Three-Fifths Compromise (only three-fifths of the population of slaves would be counted for enumeration purposes) helped resolve an impasse at the Convention between Southern states, which wanted slaves to count as more, and Northern states, which wanted them to count as less. Although the number of House members has grown with the population, since 1911 it has been fixed by statute at 435. As constituted, the House is as powerful as the U.S. Senate, and in one respect is even more powerful: the House has the sole power to originate revenue bills. Section 2 also lays out the two-year-term rule and qualifications for each House member, as well as providing procedures for apportionment and filling vacancies. Finally, it authorizes the House to choose top officials, including the Speaker.

Section 3. The Senate of the United States shall be composed of two Senators from each state, chosen by the legislature thereof, for six years; and each Senator shall have one vote.

Immediately after they shall be assembled in consequence of the first election, they shall be divided as equally as may be into three classes. The seats of the Senators of the first class shall be vacated at the expiration of the second year, of the second class at the expiration of the fourth year, and the third class at the expiration of the sixth year, so that one third may be chosen every second year; and if vacancies happen by resignation, or otherwise, during the recess of the legislature of any state, the executive thereof may make temporary appointments until the next meeting of the legislature, which shall then fill such vacancies.

No person shall be a Senator who shall not have attained to the age of thirty years, and been nine years a citizen of the United States and who shall not, when elected, be an inhabitant of that state for which he shall be chosen.

The Vice President of the United States shall be President of the Senate, but shall have no vote, unless they be equally divided.

The Senate shall choose their other officers, and also a President pro tempore, in the absence of the Vice President, or when he shall exercise the office of President of the United States.

The Senate shall have the sole power to try all impeachments. When sitting for that purpose, they shall be on oath or affirmation. When the President of the United States is tried, the Chief Justice shall preside: And no person shall be convicted without the concurrence of two thirds of the members present.

Judgment in cases of impeachment shall not extend further than to removal from office, and disqualification to hold and enjoy any office of honor, trust or profit under the United States: but the party convicted shall nevertheless be liable and subject to indictment, trial, judgment and punishment, according to law.

Just as Section 2 does for the House of Representatives, Section 3 establishes various powers and procedures for the U.S. Senate. Individual senators may be more powerful than their counterparts in the House because of the longer length of their terms (six years) and because there are far fewer members in the body; however, there is no constitutional basis for the claim that the Senate is a superior chamber. Although the vice president theoretically presides over the Senate as its president, and the president pro tempore serves in the vice president's absence, in actual practice the president pro tempore usually deputizes a more junior senator to preside over most Senate business. The provisions of Clause 1 and Clause 2 that state legislatures choose senators have been overturned by the Seventeenth Amendment, which now provides that senators are chosen by popular election.

Section 4. The times, places and manner of holding elections for Senators and Representatives, shall be prescribed in each state by the legislature thereof; but the Congress may at any time by law make or alter such regulations, except as to the places of choosing Senators.

The Congress shall assemble at least once in every year, and such meeting shall be on the first Monday in December, unless they shall by law appoint a different day.

According to Article I, Section 4, states can regulate the time, place, and manner of all federal elections, but Congress can still establish a single uniform date for federal elections (and it has done so on the first Tuesday following the first Monday in November).

Section 5. Each House shall be the judge of the elections, returns and qualifications of its own members, and a majority of each shall constitute a quorum to do business; but a smaller number may adjourn from day to day, and may be authorized to compel the attendance of absent members, in such manner, and under such penalties as each House may provide.

Each House may determine the rules of its proceedings, punish its members for disorderly behavior, and, with the concurrence of two thirds, expel a member.

Each House shall keep a journal of its proceedings, and from time to time publish the same, excepting such parts as may in their judgment require secrecy; and the yeas and nays of the members of either House on any question shall, at the desire of one fifth of those present, be entered on the journal.

Neither House, during the session of Congress, shall, without the consent of the other, adjourn for more than three days, nor to any other place than that in which the two Houses shall be sitting.

Section 6. The Senators and Representatives shall receive a compensation for their services, to be ascertained by law, and paid out of the treasury of the United States. They shall in all cases, except treason, felony and breach of the peace, be privileged from arrest during their attendance at the session of their respective Houses, and in going to and returning from the same; and for any speech or debate in either House, they shall not be questioned in any other place.

No Senator or Representative shall, during the time for which he was elected, be appointed to any civil office under the authority of the United States, which shall have been created, or the emoluments whereof shall have been increased during such time: and no person holding any office under the United States, shall be a member of either House during his continuance in office.

Article I, Section 6 extends to members of Congress various immunities. The speech and debate clause of Section 6 prevents House members or senators from being sued for slander during congressional debates, committee hearings, or most other official congressional business. In deference to the principle of separation of powers, Clause 2 ensures that members of Congress cannot hold another civil office while retaining their legislative seats.

Section 7. All bills for raising revenue shall originate in the House of Representatives; but the Senate may propose or concur with amendments as on other Bills.

Every bill which shall have passed the House of Representatives and the Senate, shall, before it become a law, be presented to the President of the United States; if he approve he shall sign it, but if not he shall return it, with his objections to that House in which it shall have originated, who shall enter the objections at large on their journal, and proceed to reconsider it. If after such reconsideration two thirds of that House shall agree to pass the bill, it shall be sent, together with the objections, to the other House, by which it shall likewise be reconsidered, and if approved by two thirds of that House, it shall become a law. But in all such cases the votes of both Houses shall be determined by yeas and nays, and the names of the persons voting for and against the bill shall be entered on the journal of each House respectively. If any bill shall not be returned by the President within ten days (Sundays excepted) after it shall have been presented to him, the same shall be a law, in like manner as if he had signed it, unless the Congress by their adjournment prevent its return, in which case it shall not be a law.

Every order, resolution, or vote to which the concurrence of the Senate and House of Representatives may be necessary (except on a question of adjournment) shall be presented to the President of the United States; and before the same shall take effect, shall be approved by him, or being disapproved by him, shall be repassed by two thirds of the Senate and House of Representatives, according to the rules and limitations prescribed in the case of a bill.

Article I, Section 7 is often referred to as the presentment clause. It establishes the procedures by which Congress presents bills to the president for approval; it also lays out the process by which the president may veto legislation, either by refusing to sign it and sending it back, or by keeping the bill for a period of 10 days without signing it while Congress has adjourned in the interim (referred to as a pocket veto). In 1996, Congress passed the Line Item Veto Act, which allowed the president to veto specific expenditures at the time of signing; the Supreme Court declared the Line Item Veto Act unconstitutional in Clinton v. City of New York *(1998) because it gave the president the power to repeal parts of duly enacted statutes in a manner different from the "finely wrought and exhaustively considered procedure" described in this section.*

Section 8. The Congress shall have power to lay and collect taxes, duties, imposts and excises, to pay the debts and provide for the common defense and general welfare of the United States; but all duties, imposts and excises shall be uniform throughout the United States;

To borrow money on the credit of the United States;

To regulate commerce with foreign nations, and among the several states, and with the Indian tribes;

To establish a uniform rule of naturalization, and uniform laws on the subject of bankruptcies throughout the United States;

To coin money, regulate the value thereof, and of foreign coin, and fix the standard of weights and measures;

To provide for the punishment of counterfeiting the securities and current coin of the United States;

To establish post offices and post roads;

To promote the progress of science and useful arts, by securing for limited times to authors and inventors the exclusive right to their respective writings and discoveries;

To constitute tribunals inferior to the Supreme Court;

To define and punish piracies and felonies committed on the high seas, and offenses against the law of nations;

To declare war, grant letters of marque and reprisal, and make rules concerning captures on land and water;

To raise and support armies, but no appropriation of money to that use shall be for a longer term than two years;

To provide and maintain a navy;

To make rules for the government and regulation of the land and naval forces;

To provide for calling forth the militia to execute the laws of the union, suppress insurrections and repel invasions;

To provide for organizing, arming, and disciplining, the militia, and for governing such part of them as may be employed in the service of the United States, reserving to the states respectively, the appointment of the officers, and the authority of training the militia according to the discipline prescribed by Congress;

To exercise exclusive legislation in all cases whatsoever, over such District (not exceeding ten miles square) as may, by cession of particular states, and the acceptance of Congress, become the seat of the government of the United States, and to exercise like authority over all places purchased by the consent of the legislature of the state in which the same shall be, for the erection of forts, magazines, arsenals, dockyards, and other needful buildings;—And

To make all laws which shall be necessary and proper for carrying into execution the foregoing powers, and all other powers vested by this Constitution in the government of the United States, or in any department or officer thereof.

Article I, Section 8 may be the most heavily cited clause in the original Constitution, as it lays out all the enumerated powers of Congress. The 18th clause listed, the necessary and proper

clause, was the source of significant controversy in the early republic. In McCulloch v. Maryland *(1819), Chief Justice John Marshall interpreted the clause as essentially aiding Congress in carrying out its expressed powers. Combining the powers granted by the 18th clause with other powers allows Congress to exercise implied powers not explicitly listed in the Constitution, so long as those powers offer a theoretical means of achieving the enumerated powers. Thus, Congress successfully incorporated a bank of the United States because it was deemed necessary and proper to achieve the power to coin money and regulate its value (Clause 5), as well as other powers. No wonder the necessary and proper clause has also been called the elastic clause: it gives Congress the power to enact laws on almost any subject it desires. The power to regulate interstate commerce under Clause 3 has been especially useful in this regard. Citing the commerce clause, Congress since 1937 has regulated minimum wages of state employees, outlawed loan sharking, and passed numerous civil rights laws, among other legislation. The modern limits to that practice were outlined by the Supreme Court in* United States v. Lopez *(1995),* United States v. Morrison *(2000), and* NFIB v. Sebelius *(2012)—the law in question must regulate affirmative activities that are directly economic in nature. By comparison, the Supreme Court recently held that Congress may regulate even inactivity (e.g., a refusal to purchase health insurance) under its power to collect taxes in Clause 1.*

Section 9. The migration or importation of such persons as any of the states now existing shall think proper to admit, shall not be prohibited by the Congress prior to the year one thousand eight hundred and eight, but a tax or duty may be imposed on such importation, not exceeding ten dollars for each person.

The privilege of the writ of habeas corpus shall not be suspended, unless when in cases of rebellion or invasion the public safety may require it.

No bill of attainder or ex post facto Law shall be passed.

No capitation, or other direct, tax shall be laid, unless in proportion to the census or enumeration herein before directed to be taken.

No tax or duty shall be laid on articles exported from any state.

No preference shall be given by any regulation of commerce or revenue to the ports of one state over those of another: nor shall vessels bound to, or from, one state, be obliged to enter, clear or pay duties in another.

No money shall be drawn from the treasury, but in consequence of appropriations made by law; and a regular statement and account of receipts and expenditures of all public money shall be published from time to time.

No title of nobility shall be granted by the United States: and no person holding any office of profit or trust under them, shall, without the consent of the Congress, accept of any present, emolument, office, or title, of any kind whatever, from any king, prince, or foreign state.

Section 9 places some explicit limits on congressional power, including restrictions on the power to ban the import of slaves (at least through 1808), the power to bestow titles of nobility, and the power to lay direct taxes not apportioned to the states' populations. This last restriction was effectively removed by ratification of the Sixteenth Amendment in 1913. It also prohibits Congress from issuing bills of attainder (legislative acts that inflict punishment without a judicial trial) and from passing ex post facto laws (criminal laws that apply retroactively to acts committed in the past).

Section 10. No state shall enter into any treaty, alliance, or confederation; grant letters of marque and reprisal; coin money; emit bills of credit; make anything but gold and silver coin a tender in payment of debts; pass any bill of attainder, ex post facto law, or law impairing the obligation of contracts, or grant any title of nobility.

No state shall, without the consent of the Congress, lay any imposts or duties on imports or exports, except what may be absolutely necessary for executing its inspection laws: and the net produce of all duties and imposts, laid by any state on imports or exports, shall be for the use of the treasury of the United States; and all such laws shall be subject to the revision and control of the Congress.

No state shall, without the consent of Congress, lay any duty of tonnage, keep troops, or ships of war in time of peace, enter into any agreement or compact with another state, or with a foreign power, or engage in war, unless actually invaded, or in such imminent danger as will not admit of delay.

The final section of Article I limits states from exercising powers reserved exclusively to the federal government. Most controversial of these clauses was the contracts clause, which prohibits states from impairing the obligation of contracts. Added to the Constitution largely to prevent state laws that undermined the collection of valid debts, it was later used to protect certain franchises or special privileges that corporations had received from state legislatures. Thus, the Supreme Court held in Trustees of Dartmouth College v. Woodward *(1819) that the charter given to Dartmouth by a colonial legislature in 1769 could not be changed without Dartmouth's consent. State legislatures complained that the contracts clause unduly restricted their ability to legislate; thus, the Supreme Court over the course of two centuries has narrowed the meaning of the clause to allow states greater freedom to operate, relying on the theory that such contracts are by implication the laws of the state and thus may be modified by the state. The Court has also upheld state bankruptcy laws when the laws are applied to debts incurred after passage of the law.*

ARTICLE II

Section 1. The executive power shall be vested in a President of the United States of America. He shall hold his office during the term of four years, and, together with the Vice President, chosen for the same term, be elected, as follows:

Each state shall appoint, in such manner as the Legislature thereof may direct, a number of electors, equal to the whole number of Senators and Representatives to which the State may be entitled in the Congress: but no Senator or Representative, or person holding an office of trust or profit under the United States, shall be appointed an elector.

The electors shall meet in their respective states, and vote by ballot for two persons, of whom one at least shall not be an inhabitant of the same state with themselves. And they shall make a list of all the persons voted for, and of the number of votes for each; which list they shall sign and certify, and transmit sealed to the seat of the government of the United States, directed to the President of the Senate. The President of the Senate shall, in the presence of the Senate and House of Representatives, open all the certificates, and the votes shall then be counted. The person having the greatest number of votes shall be the President, if such number be a majority of the whole number of electors appointed; and if there be more than one who have such majority, and have an equal number of votes, then the House of Representatives shall immediately choose by ballot one of them for President; and if no person have a majority, then from the five highest on the list the said House shall in like manner choose the President. But in choosing the President, the votes shall be taken by States, the representation from each state having one vote; a quorum for this purpose shall consist of a member or members from two thirds of the states, and a majority of all the states shall be necessary to a choice. In every case, after the choice of the President, the person having the greatest number of votes of the electors shall be the Vice President. But if there should remain two or more who have equal votes, the Senate shall choose from them by ballot the Vice President.

The Congress may determine the time of choosing the electors, and the day on which they shall give their votes; which day shall be the same throughout the United States.

No person except a natural born citizen, or a citizen of the United States, at the time of the adoption of this Constitution, shall be eligible to the office of President; neither shall any person be eligible to that office who shall not have attained to the age of thirty five years, and been fourteen Years a resident within the United States.

In case of the removal of the President from office, or of his death, resignation, or inability to discharge the powers and duties of the said office, the same shall devolve on the Vice President, and the Congress may by law provide for the case of removal, death, resignation or inability, both of the President and Vice President, declaring what officer shall then act as President, and such officer shall act accordingly, until the disability be removed, or a President shall be elected.

The President shall, at stated times, receive for his services, a compensation, which shall neither be increased nor diminished during the period for which he shall have been elected, and he shall not receive within that period any other emolument from the United States, or any of them.

Before he enter on the execution of his office, he shall take the following oath or affirmation:—'I do solemnly swear (or affirm) that I will faithfully execute the office of President of the United States, and will to the best of my ability, preserve, protect and defend the Constitution of the United States.'

Article II, Section 1 lays out the manner by which the president and vice president are selected, the qualifications for those two offices, and the means for removal and succession. (Clause 2 on presidential elections has been replaced by the Twelfth Amendment.) Section 1 begins with the vague declaration that the "executive power shall be vested in a president of the United States of America." Does this clause serve as a source of independent power for the chief executive? Beginning in the twentieth century, the Supreme Court has held that the president possesses broad "inherent powers" to exercise certain powers not specifically enumerated in the Constitution. These vast executive powers included, for example, Franklin Roosevelt's various executive agreements extending the scope of the federal government during the 1930s. On the other hand, the Supreme Court ruled in Youngstown Sheet and Tune Co. v. Sawyer *(1951) that a president's inherent powers did not include President Truman's attempt to seize the steel mills to avert a strike without congressional approval; similarly, in* United States v. Nixon *(1974), the Court held that the chief executive's inherent powers did not encompass President Richard Nixon's refusal to turn over important documents in a criminal matter.*

Section 2. The President shall be commander in chief of the Army and Navy of the United States, and of the militia of the several states, when called into the actual service of the United States; he may require the opinion, in writing, of the principal officer in each of the executive departments, upon any subject relating to the duties of their respective offices, and he shall have power to grant reprieves and pardons for offenses against the United States, except in cases of impeachment.

He shall have power, by and with the advice and consent of the Senate, to make treaties, provided two thirds of the Senators present concur; and he shall nominate, and by and with the advice and consent of the Senate, shall appoint ambassadors, other public ministers and consuls, judges of the Supreme Court, and all other officers of the United States, whose appointments are not herein otherwise provided for, and which shall be established by law: but the Congress may by law vest the appointment of such inferior officers, as they think proper, in the President alone, in the courts of law, or in the heads of departments.

The President shall have power to fill up all vacancies that may happen during the recess of the Senate, by granting commissions which shall expire at the end of their next session.

Article II, Section 2 is striking for how few expressed powers are granted to the president, as compared to the long list of powers granted to Congress in Article I, Section 8. In the twentieth century the powers granted to the president expanded to create a far more powerful presidency than the founders envisioned. Thus, invoking their power as commander in chief, modern presidents have deployed troops around the world in military battles even without a formal declaration of war by Congress. Recent presidents have occasionally terminated treaties without the consent of the Senate. Presidents have also asserted the power to terminate officers of the United States without cause. The combined Supreme Court precedents of Myers v. United States *(1926) and* Humphrey's Executor v. United States *(1935) authorize them to do so in the case of purely executive officers but not in the case of independent agency heads.*

Section 3. He shall from time to time give to the Congress information of the state of the union, and recommend to their consideration such measures as he shall judge necessary and expedient; he may, on extraordinary occasions, convene both Houses, or either of them, and in case of disagreement between them, with respect to the time of adjournment, he may adjourn them to such time as he shall think proper; he shall receive ambassadors and other public ministers; he shall take care that the laws be faithfully executed, and shall commission all the officers of the United States.

Article II, Section 3 lists numerous presidential responsibilities, including the obligation to give a report on the "state of the union" to Congress (today this occurs in the form of a yearly address) and the duty to "take care that laws be faithfully executed." Citing this latter phrase, presidents have asserted the power to impound money appropriated by Congress and to suspend the writ of habeas corpus. Although reluctant to afford the chief executive such unbridled authority, the Supreme Court has upheld nearly all efforts by the president to call upon the military to assist in faithfully executing the law. President Eisenhower, for example, exercised this power when he used federal troops to enforce desegregation decrees in Arkansas and Mississippi in the late 1950s.

Section 4. The President, Vice President and all civil officers of the United States, shall be removed from office on impeachment for, and conviction of, treason, bribery, or other high crimes and misdemeanors.

Article II, Section 4 lays out the process of impeachment and conviction of civil officers, but the phrase "high crimes and misdemeanors" is vague and subject to conflicting interpretations. Regardless, the House of Representatives has asserted its authority to decide on its own how to define the term. Only two chief executives have ever been formally impeached under this section: Andrew Johnson in 1868 and Bill Clinton in 1998. However, in both cases, the U.S. Senate failed to provide the required two-thirds vote necessary for conviction.

ARTICLE III

Section 1. The judicial power of the United States, shall be vested in one Supreme Court, and in such inferior courts as the Congress may from time to time ordain and establish. The judges, both of the supreme and inferior courts, shall hold their offices during good behaviour, and shall, at stated times, receive for their services, a compensation, which shall not be diminished during their continuance in office.

Section 2. The judicial power shall extend to all cases, in law and equity, arising under this Constitution, the laws of the United States, and treaties made, or which shall be made, under their authority;—to all cases affecting ambassadors, other public ministers and consuls;—to all cases of admiralty and maritime jurisdiction;—to controversies to which the United States shall be a party;—to controversies between two or more states;—between a state and citizens of another state;—between citizens of different states;—between citizens of the same state claiming lands under grants of different states, and between a state, or the citizens thereof, and foreign states, citizens or subjects.

In all cases affecting ambassadors, other public ministers and consuls, and those in which a state shall be party, the Supreme Court shall have original jurisdiction. In all the other cases before mentioned, the Supreme Court shall have appellate jurisdiction, both as to law and fact, with such exceptions, and under such regulations as the Congress shall make.

The trial of all crimes, except in cases of impeachment, shall be by jury; and such trial shall be held in the state where the said crimes shall have been committed; but when not committed within any state, the trial shall be at such place or places as the Congress may by law have directed.

Section 3. Treason against the United States, shall consist only in levying war against them, or in adhering to their enemies, giving them aid and comfort. No person shall be convicted of treason unless on the testimony of two witnesses to the same overt act, or on confession in open court.

The Congress shall have power to declare the punishment of treason, but no attainder of treason shall work corruption of blood, or forfeiture except during the life of the person attainted.

Article III establishes a U.S. Supreme Court, spells out the terms of office of its members, and lists the various cases to which its judicial power extends. Just as important, it provides the basis for a more elaborate judicial system featuring numerous levels of courts, which Congress may establish at its discretion. Note how vague and general this article is compared to Articles I and II: only one court (the Supreme Court) is specifically mentioned, and there are no provisions that specify the size or composition of the court. Congress subsequently established that federal judges on the courts of appeals and the district courts, like justices of the Supreme Court, be appointed by the president and confirmed by the Senate. They too serve for indefinite terms on good behavior, which provides the equivalent of life tenure to federal judges on those three levels of courts. Article III does not specifically grant the Supreme Court the power of judicial review, that is, the power to review the actions of other branches for their constitutionality. The Supreme Court seized that power for itself in Marbury v. Madison *(1803), and it remains a fundamental precept of the federal judicial system today.*

ARTICLE IV

Section 1. Full faith and credit shall be given in each state to the public acts, records, and judicial proceedings of every other state. And the Congress may by general laws prescribe the manner in which such acts, records, and proceedings shall be proved, and the effect thereof.
Section 2. The citizens of each state shall be entitled to all privileges and immunities of citizens in the several states.

A person charged in any state with treason, felony, or other crime, who shall flee from justice, and be found in another state, shall on demand of the executive authority of the state from which he fled, be delivered up, to be removed to the state having jurisdiction of the crime.

No person held to service or labor in one state, under the laws thereof, escaping into another, shall, in consequence of any law or regulation therein, be discharged from such service or labor, but shall be delivered up on claim of the party to whom such service or labor may be due.
Section 3. New states may be admitted by the Congress into this union; but no new states shall be formed or erected within the jurisdiction of any other state; nor any state be formed by the junction of two or more states, or parts of states, without the consent of the legislatures of the states concerned as well as of the Congress.

The Congress shall have power to dispose of and make all needful rules and regulations respecting the territory or other property belonging to the United States; and nothing in this Constitution shall be so construed as to prejudice any claims of the United States, or of any particular state.
Section 4. The United States shall guarantee to every state in this union a republican form of government, and shall protect each of them against invasion; and on application of the legislature, or of the executive (when the legislature cannot be convened) against domestic violence.

Article IV describes the responsibilities states have to one another under the Constitution and the obligations of the federal government to the states. It also provides the procedures for admitting new states to the union. (No state has been admitted since the entry of Alaska and Hawaii in 1959.) In recent decades, the most controversial aspect of Article IV has been the full faith and credit clause of Section 1, which theoretically binds states to respect the public acts and proceedings of other states, including child custody rulings and the granting of drivers' licenses. Initially that clause did not deter the federal government (through the Defense of Marriage Act) and various states from seeking to evade the recognition of gay marriages sanctioned elsewhere through legislation. However, the Supreme Court rendered the controversy moot when it upheld the right of same-sex couples to marry in all 50 states. See Obergefell v. Hodges *(2015).*

The ambiguous privileges and immunities clause of Article IV, Section 2 requires that states not discriminate against citizens of other states in favor of their own citizens, although the Supreme Court has allowed states to establish more favorable terms for in-state residents when distributing certain recreational rights such as amateur fishing licenses or permits to use state parks; taxes on commuters, by contrast, may be unconstitutional if they penalize out-of-state residents who work or do business in the state. The requirement in Section 4 that the United States guarantee to every state a republican form of government was invoked in the 1840s when President John Tyler threatened the use of federal troops after a rebellion occurred in Rhode Island. Today that provision is obscure and seldom used.

ARTICLE V

The Congress, whenever two thirds of both houses shall deem it necessary, shall propose amendments to this Constitution, or, on the application of the legislatures of two thirds of the several states, shall call a convention for proposing amendments, which, in either case, shall be valid to all intents and purposes, as part of this Constitution, when ratified by the legislatures of three-fourths of the several states, or by conventions in three-fourths thereof, as the one or the other mode of ratification may be proposed by the Congress; provided that no amendment which may be made prior to the year one thousand eight hundred and eight shall in any manner affect the first and fourth clauses in the ninth section of the first article; and that no state, without its consent, shall be deprived of its equal suffrage in the Senate.

Article V spells out the process for amending the Constitution. By far the most common form of constitutional amendment has been by congressional proposal, with state legislatures ratifying the proposal. Twenty-six of the 27 amendments have been adopted in this way. The sole exception was the Twenty-first Amendment, which was ratified by specially chosen state ratifying conventions to ensure that farmer-dominated state legislatures would not undermine the effort to repeal Prohibition. The procedure by which the requisite number of state legislatures (two-thirds) applies to Congress to call a convention for proposing amendments has never been used. Article V does not provide a deadline for considering proposed amendments, although Congress has the power to set such deadlines in the language of the proposed amendment. Congress did not do so in the case of the Twenty-seventh Amendment, which received the approval of the required three-fourths of states necessary for ratification in 1992—fully 203 years after the amendment was first proposed.

ARTICLE VI

All debts contracted and engagements entered into, before the adoption of this Constitution, shall be as valid against the United States under this Constitution, as under the Confederation.

This Constitution, and the laws of the United States which shall be made in pursuance thereof; and all treaties made, or which shall be made, under the authority of the United States, shall be the supreme law of the land; and the judges in every state shall be bound thereby, anything in the Constitution or laws of any State to the contrary notwithstanding.

The Senators and Representatives before mentioned, and the members of the several state legislatures, and all executive and judicial officers, both of the United States and of the several states, shall be bound by oath or affirmation, to support this Constitution; but no religious test shall ever be required as a qualification to any office or public trust under the United States.

Article VI establishes that the Constitution, laws, and treaties are to be the supreme law of the land. In interpreting this supremacy clause, the U.S. Supreme Court has countenanced little resistance. Thus, the Supreme Court has consistently struck down attempts by states to control federal institutions, and it has reminded state governments that even state constitutions are subordinate to federal statutes. Even more important, in Cooper v. Aaron *(1957), the U.S. Supreme Court stated in no uncertain terms that its own rulings are to be treated as if they are the words of the Constitution itself, heading off attempts by some state governments to resist Supreme Court rulings on desegregation by offering their own interpretations of the federal Constitution as authority.*

ARTICLE VII

The ratification of the conventions of nine states, shall be sufficient for the establishment of this Constitution between the states so ratifying the same. Done in convention by the unanimous consent of the states present the seventeenth day of September in the year of our Lord one thousand seven hundred and eighty seven and of the independence of the United States of America the twelfth. In witness whereof We have hereunto subscribed our Names,

AMENDMENTS TO THE CONSTITUTION OF THE UNITED STATES

The Bill of Rights, ratified in 1791, consists of the first 10 amendments to the Constitution. Since that time, 17 additional amendments have been ratified by the states. Originally the Bill of Rights applied only to the federal government and not to the state governments; however, through a process known as incorporation, the Supreme Court has ruled that the Fourteenth Amendment (adopted in 1868) made most of the provisions found in the Bill of Rights applicable to the states as well. Subsequent amendments have extended the franchise, established (and repealed) Prohibition, and clarified important procedures that the federal government must follow.

AMENDMENT I (1791)

Congress shall make no law respecting an establishment of religion, or prohibiting the free exercise thereof; or abridging the freedom of speech, or of the press; or the right of the people peaceably to assemble, and to petition the government for a redress of grievances.

Although many provisions of the original Bill of Rights are based on aspects of English law, the extensive guarantees found in the First Amendment have no true English equivalent. The First Amendment offered one of the first written guarantees of religious freedom, and it formed the basis for extensive free speech and free press protection as well. Yet its unqualified language notwithstanding, the First Amendment has never conveyed absolute freedom to Americans. Whether it was the Alien and Sedition Acts of 1798, the aggressive application of the Espionage Act during World War I, or the "red scare" of the late 1940s, government has often found ways to evade the First Amendment, especially during times of crisis. The Supreme Court has also specifically exempted obscenity, libel, fighting words, and incitement from free speech protections. Nor has the separate and independent provision for the freedom of the press been interpreted to give members of the press any more protection than is afforded to ordinary citizens. Finally, as noted, although the first word of the amendment implies that its protections apply only against actions of the federal government, today the First Amendment offers protection against the state governments as well.

AMENDMENT II (1791)

A well regulated militia, being necessary to the security of a free state, the right of the people to keep and bear arms, shall not be infringed.

The Second Amendment originated as a compromise in the debate between those who feared mob rule by the people and those committed to give the people everything they need to fight governmental tyranny. In 2008, the U.S. Supreme Court ruled for the first time that certain gun-control laws may violate an individual's Second Amendment right to "bear arms." Two years later it went a step further, applying those protections against all 50 state governments and their subdivisions. See District of Columbia v. Heller, 554 U.S. 570 (2008); and McDonald v. Chicago, 561 U.S. 742 (2010).

AMENDMENT III (1791)

No soldier shall, in time of peace be quartered in any house, without the consent of the owner, nor in time of war, but in a manner to be prescribed by law.

The Third Amendment has been all but lost to history. The Quartering Act, which required the American colonists to provide shelter and supplies for British troops, was one of the grievances that provoked the Declaration of Independence and ultimately the Revolution. Many colonists resented having to house British soldiers in private homes. The Third Amendment aimed to protect private citizens from such intrusions.

AMENDMENT IV (1791)

The right of the people to be secure in their persons, houses, papers, and effects, against unreasonable searches and seizures, shall not be violated, and no warrants shall issue, but upon probable cause, supported by oath or affirmation, and particularly describing the place to be searched, and the persons or things to be seized.

Like the First Amendment, the Fourth Amendment is a uniquely American right. It arose out of colonists' anger over the warrantless searches and so-called General Warrants by which British authorities would conduct raids of colonists' homes virtually at their own discretion. The Fourth Amendment guarantees that with certain carefully specified exceptions (consent of the owner, urgent circumstances, etc.), government authorities can conduct searches only when they possess a reasonably specific warrant demonstrating probable cause. Enforcement of the Fourth Amendment occurs primarily through application of the controversial exclusionary rule, which excludes from trial all evidence seized in violation of a defendant's constitutional rights.

AMENDMENT V (1791)

No person shall be held to answer for a capital, or otherwise infamous crime, unless on a presentment or indictment of a grand jury, except in cases arising in the land or naval forces, or in the militia, when in actual service in time of war or public danger; nor shall any person be subject for the same offense to be twice put in jeopardy of life or limb; nor shall be compelled in any criminal case to be a witness against himself, nor be deprived of life, liberty, or property, without due process of law; nor shall private property be taken for public use, without just compensation.

The Fifth Amendment is a collection of various rights, most of which are important primarily to those accused of a crime. Those who "take the Fifth" under oath are normally invoking the privilege against self-incrimination; under current precedents they can invoke that privilege in other contexts as well, such as whenever they are being questioned by police or other authorities. The grand jury requirement has never been incorporated to apply against state governments. The requirement against double jeopardy prevents defendants who have been acquitted from being retried for the same offense by the same government. The due process clause of the Fifth Amendment was later duplicated in the Fourteenth Amendment and applied to states as well. Finally, the takings clause limits the traditional power of eminent domain by requiring that the government must pay compensation whenever it takes private property for public use.

AMENDMENT VI (1791)

In all criminal prosecutions, the accused shall enjoy the right to a speedy and public trial, by an impartial jury of the state and district wherein the crime shall have been committed, which district shall have been previously ascertained by law, and to be informed of the nature and cause of the accusation; to be confronted with the witnesses against him; to have compulsory process for obtaining witnesses in his favor, and to have the assistance of counsel for his defense.

The Sixth Amendment offers the accused numerous constitutional protections. The need for a speedy and public trial dates back to concerns raised by imprisoned enemies of the British Crown who were detained indefinitely and without notice. The right to a jury trial—considered a sacred aspect of the American political culture—is not all-encompassing either: it applies only to non-petty offenses (punishable by more than six months of prison).

AMENDMENT VII (1791)

In suits at common law, where the value in controversy shall exceed twenty dollars, the right of trial by jury shall be preserved, and no fact tried by a jury, shall be otherwise reexamined in any court of the United States, than according to the rules of the common law.

The Seventh Amendment is the only amendment in the Bill of Rights that focuses on elements of civil trials exclusively. It preserves the distinction the English system draws between courts of common law (in which juries grant monetary relief) and courts of equity (in which a judge grants nonmonetary relief, such as an injunction).

AMENDMENT VIII (1791)

Excessive bail shall not be required, nor excessive fines imposed, nor cruel and unusual punishments inflicted.

The Eighth Amendment offers protections that come directly from the English Bill of Rights. The prohibition against excessive bail was established to prevent judges from keeping the accused indefinitely imprisoned while waiting for trials on minor offenses; it has subsequently been interpreted to allow judges to deny bail in instances where the charges are sufficiently serious, or where preventative detention is warranted for the safety of the community. The prohibition against cruel and unusual punishment forbids some punishments entirely (drawing and quartering, burning alive, and other forms of torture), while forbidding other punishments only when they are excessive compared to the crime. Aside from the four-year period from 1972 through 1976, the Supreme Court has consistently held that with proper safeguards, capital punishment is not cruel and unusual punishment. However, consistent with this clause, it may not be imposed for rape or crimes lesser than murder, and it may not be imposed against mentally handicapped or juvenile offenders.

AMENDMENT IX (1791)

The enumeration in the Constitution, of certain rights, shall not be construed to deny or disparage others retained by the people.

The Ninth Amendment has been nicknamed "the Madison Amendment" in deference to James Madison's general concerns about the Bill of Rights. During debates over ratification of the Constitution, Anti-Federalists called for a Bill of Rights to protect the people against a potentially abusive new central government. In correspondence with Thomas Jefferson, Madison expressed the fear that by listing exceptions to congressional powers, such a Bill of Rights would effectively deny the existence of rights that did not happen to appear on the list. Eventually, as a member of the House of Representatives in the First Congress, Madison sponsored passage of the Bill of Rights, but he included this amendment as a way to ensure that the listing of certain rights did not mean that other rights were denied. As interpreted, the Ninth Amendment has not had much impact on the constitutional landscape. Likened by some to an "inkblot," it has been most commonly viewed not as a source of rights but rather as a loose guideline on how to interpret the Constitution.

AMENDMENT X (1791)

The powers not delegated to the United States by the Constitution, nor prohibited by it to the states, are reserved to the states respectively, or to the people.

The Tenth Amendment lays out in explicit terms that the federal government is limited only to the powers granted to it in the Constitution. For most of the twentieth century, the Supreme Court regarded this amendment largely as a redundant truism, adding little to the Constitution as it was originally ratified. In the early 1990s, the Supreme Court began to put teeth into the amendment, interpreting it as a prohibition on attempts by Congress to force states to participate in federal programs.

AMENDMENT XI (1798)

The judicial power of the United States shall not be construed to extend to any suit in law or equity, commenced or prosecuted against one of the United States by citizens of another state, or by citizens or subjects of any foreign state.

The Eleventh Amendment was ratified to modify the Supreme Court's controversial decision in Chisholm v. Georgia *(1793), which upheld the authority of federal courts to hear lawsuits brought by citizens of one state against another state. The Supreme Court has ruled that the Eleventh Amendment provides states with some form of sovereign immunity, which means that it generally protects states from civil or criminal prosecution. The Supreme Court has also determined that under the Eleventh Amendment, a state cannot be sued by one of its own citizens.*

AMENDMENT XII (1804)

The electors shall meet in their respective states and vote by ballot for President and Vice-President, one of whom, at least, shall not be an inhabitant of the same state with themselves; they shall name in their ballots the person voted for as President, and in distinct ballots the person voted for as Vice-President, and they shall make distinct lists of all persons voted for as President, and of all persons voted for as Vice-President, and of the number of votes for each, which lists they shall sign and certify, and transmit sealed to the seat of the government of the United States, directed to the President of the Senate;—The President of the Senate shall, in the presence of the Senate and House of Representatives, open all the certificates and the votes shall then be counted;—the person having the greatest number of votes for President, shall be the President, if such number be a majority of the whole number of electors appointed; and if no person have such majority, then from the persons having the highest numbers not exceeding three on the list of those voted for as President, the House of Representatives shall choose immediately, by ballot, the President. But in choosing the President, the votes shall be taken by states, the representation from each state having one vote; a quorum for this purpose shall consist of a member or members from two-thirds of the states, and a majority of all the states shall be necessary to a choice. And if the House of Representatives shall not choose a President whenever the right of choice shall devolve upon them, before the fourth day of March next following, then the Vice-President shall act as President, as in the case of the death or other constitutional disability of the President. The person having the greatest number of votes as Vice-President, shall be the Vice-President, if such number be a majority of the whole number of electors appointed, and if no person have a majority, then from the two highest numbers on the list, the Senate shall choose the Vice-President; a quorum for the purpose shall consist of two-thirds of the whole number of Senators, and a majority of the whole number shall be necessary to a choice. But no person constitutionally ineligible to the office of President shall be eligible to that of Vice-President of the United States.

The Twelfth Amendment altered the Constitution's original procedures for holding presidential elections. Under Article II, the winner of a majority of Electoral College votes would become president, and the runner-up would become vice president. The election of 1800 exposed the peculiarity that if every member of the Electoral College voted for both members of a party ticket, each member of the most popular ticket would receive the same number of votes, resulting in a deadlock. The Twelfth Amendment cured that flaw by requiring electors to cast separate votes for president and vice president, and by ensuring that if a deadlock occurred anyway and the House of Representatives failed to choose a president, then the candidate who received the highest number of votes on the vice presidential ballot would act as president (thus, all vice presidents must be constitutionally eligible to serve as president).

AMENDMENT XIII (1865)

Section 1. Neither slavery nor involuntary servitude, except as a punishment for crime whereof the party shall have been duly convicted, shall exist within the United States, or any place subject to their jurisdiction.

Section 2. Congress shall have power to enforce this article by appropriate legislation.

The Thirteenth Amendment was the first of the three Civil War Amendments. It officially prohibited slavery in all states and, with certain exceptions (such as in the case of convicts), involuntary servitude. Immediately prior to its ratification in December 1865, slavery remained legal in only two states, Kentucky and Delaware. (Slavery in the former confederate states had been outlawed by the Emancipation Proclamation of 1863.)

AMENDMENT XIV (1868)

Section 1. All persons born or naturalized in the United States, and subject to the jurisdiction thereof, are citizens of the United States and of the state wherein they reside. No state shall make or enforce any law which shall abridge the privileges or immunities of citizens of the United States; nor shall any state deprive any person of life, liberty, or property, without due process of law; nor deny to any person within its jurisdiction the equal protection of the laws.

Section 2. Representatives shall be apportioned among the several states according to their respective numbers, counting the whole number of persons in each state, excluding Indians not taxed. But when the right to vote at any election for the choice of electors for President and Vice President of the United States, Representatives in Congress, the executive and judicial officers of a state, or the members of the legislature thereof, is denied to any of the male inhabitants of such state, being twenty-one years of age, and citizens of the United States, or in any way abridged, except for participation in rebellion, or other crime, the basis of representation therein shall be reduced in the proportion which the number of such male citizens shall bear to the whole number of male citizens twenty-one years of age in such state.

Section 3. No person shall be a Senator or Representative in Congress, or elector of President and Vice President, or hold any office, civil or military, under the United States, or under any state, who, having previously taken an oath, as a member of Congress, or as an officer of the United States, or as a member of any state legislature, or as an executive or judicial officer of any state, to support the Constitution of the United States, shall have engaged in insurrection or rebellion against the same, or given aid or comfort to the enemies thereof. But Congress may by a vote of two-thirds of each House, remove such disability.

Section 4. The validity of the public debt of the United States, authorized by law, including debts incurred for payment of pensions and bounties for services in suppressing insurrection or rebellion, shall not be questioned. But neither the United States nor any state shall assume or pay any debt or obligation incurred in aid of insurrection or rebellion against the United States, or any claim for the loss or emancipation of any slave; but all such debts, obligations and claims shall be held illegal and void.

Section 5. The Congress shall have power to enforce, by appropriate legislation, the provisions of this article.

The Fourteenth Amendment was ratified in an attempt to secure rights for freed slaves by broadening the definition of national citizenship and offering all persons equal protection of the law as well as due process of law from state governments. In the Slaughterhouse Cases (1873), the Supreme Court held that the privileges and immunities of national citizenship are actually quite limited: they include visiting the seat of government, petitioning Congress, using the nation's navigable waters, and other narrow privileges. By contrast, beginning in the twentieth century, the equal protection clause provided the basis for dismantling legally enforced segregation in Brown v. Board of Education (1954) and other cases. It has been used to extend equal protection to African Americans and other racial and ethnic minorities, women, and most recently, gays and lesbians. Of equal significance, the Supreme Court has also interpreted the equal protection clause to require states to apportion their congressional districts and state legislative seats on a "one-person, one-vote" basis.

The due process clause has been interpreted to provide procedural safeguards before the government deprives a person of life, liberty, or property. More controversially, in the early part of the twentieth century, the Supreme Court in Lochner v. New York (1905) interpreted the clause as providing substantive protection to private contracts and other economic agreements. In later rulings, the clause sparked considerable controversy when the Court used it as the basis for protecting substantive privacy rights not explicitly spelled out in the Constitution, such as that of a woman's right to an abortion (in the Court's 1973 Roe v. Wade decision), and of homosexual sodomy (in its 2003 ruling in Lawrence v. Texas).

AMENDMENT XV (1870)

Section 1. The right of citizens of the United States to vote shall not be denied or abridged by the United States or by any state on account of race, color, or previous condition of servitude.
Section 2. The Congress shall have power to enforce this article by appropriate legislation.

The Fifteenth Amendment was ratified in order to enfranchise all the former male slaves. (As was the case with all women, former female slaves would have to wait for passage of the Nineteenth Amendment to gain the franchise.) Unfortunately, the promise of the franchise was subsequently undermined in many states by the proliferation of rigorous voter qualification laws, including literacy tests and poll taxes. Not until passage of the Voting Rights Act of 1965 and the elimination of poll taxes did the franchise become a reality for African American voters in many parts of the South.

AMENDMENT XVI (1913)

The Congress shall have power to lay and collect taxes on incomes, from whatever source derived, without apportionment among the several states, and without regard to any census of enumeration.

The Sixteenth Amendment was ratified in response to the Supreme Court's controversial decision in Pollack v. Farmer's Loan & Trust Co. *(1895), which held that a tax on incomes derived from property was a "direct tax." Prior to the* Pollack *case, income taxes had been considered "indirect" taxes and thus well within the powers given to Congress by the Constitution. "Direct taxes," by contrast, could be imposed only if they were apportioned among the states according to each state's population (Article I, Section 9). The effect of the* Pollack *decision was to make an income tax all but impractical; the Sixteenth Amendment remedied the situation by placing income taxes back in the category of "indirect taxes."*

AMENDMENT XVII (1913)

The Senate of the United States shall be composed of two Senators from each state, elected by the people thereof, for six years; and each Senator shall have one vote. The electors in each state shall have the qualifications requisite for electors of the most numerous branch of the state legislatures.

When vacancies happen in the representation of any state in the Senate, the executive authority of such state shall issue writs of election to fill such vacancies: Provided, that the legislature of any state may empower the executive thereof to make temporary appointments until the people fill the vacancies by election as the legislature may direct.

This amendment shall not be so construed as to affect the election or term of any Senator chosen before it becomes valid as part of the Constitution.

The Seventeenth Amendment changed the method by which U.S. senators were elected, overturning the provisions in Article I, Section 3. The amendment was the culmination of an extended effort of Progressive Era reformers at the beginning of the twentieth century, who frequently targeted institutions marked by economic privilege and corrupt politics. Eventually they demanded that U.S. senators should be more responsive to the public will—the best way to accomplish that goal was to require that senators should be chosen by popular election rather than by state legislatures. Prior to the amendment's ratification, many states had already amended their primary laws to allow a popular vote for party nominees, and a handful of states had bound their respective legislatures to select the candidate who received the highest number of popular votes in the general election. The Seventeenth Amendment soon followed, receiving the approval of the required number of states (three-fourths) less than a year after it was first introduced.

AMENDMENT XVIII (1919)

Section 1. After one year from the ratification of this article the manufacture, sale, or transportation of intoxicating liquors within, the importation thereof into, or the exportation thereof from the United States and all territory subject to the jurisdiction thereof for beverage purposes is hereby prohibited.

Section 2. The Congress and the several states shall have concurrent power to enforce this article by appropriate legislation.

Section 3. This article shall be inoperative unless it shall have been ratified as an amendment to the Constitution by the legislatures of the several states, as provided in the Constitution, within seven years from the date of the submission hereof to the states by the Congress.

The Eighteenth Amendment slipped into the Constitution on the strength of efforts by the Anti-Saloon League and members of other groups who believed that intoxicating liquors were harmful and sinful. The amendment was proposed immediately after the end of World War I, and the Prohibition era began a year after its formal ratification on January 16, 1919.

AMENDMENT XIX (1920)

The right of citizens of the United States to vote shall not be denied or abridged by the United States or by any state on account of sex.

Congress shall have power to enforce this article by appropriate legislation.

The Nineteenth Amendment was a reform spurred by the Progressive movement. Although women had been fighting for their right to vote since before the Civil War, the drive for woman suffrage started achieving success only with the entry of western states such as Wyoming, which extended the right to vote to women upon its admission to the Union in 1890. (Five other western states followed suit in subsequent decades.) By concentrating their efforts on a federal constitutional amendment guaranteeing women the right to vote, woman suffrage activists brought immediate pressure to bear on Congress and the president to support the movement. With momentum clearly on its side, the Nineteenth Amendment was ratified less than 15 months after it was first proposed.

AMENDMENT XX (1933)

Section 1. The terms of the President and Vice President shall end at noon on the 20th day of January, and the terms of Senators and Representatives at noon on the 3d day of January, of the years in which such terms would have ended if this article had not been ratified; and the terms of their successors shall then begin.

Section 2. The Congress shall assemble at least once in every year, and such meeting shall begin at noon on the 3d day of January, unless they shall by law appoint a different day.

Section 3. If, at the time fixed for the beginning of the term of the President, the President elect shall have died, the Vice President elect shall become President. If a President shall not have been chosen before the time fixed for the beginning of his term, or if the President elect shall have failed to qualify, then the Vice President elect shall act as President until a President shall have qualified; and the Congress may by law provide for the case wherein neither a President elect nor a Vice President elect shall have qualified, declaring who shall then act as President, or the manner in which one who is to act shall be selected, and such person shall act accordingly until a President or Vice President shall have qualified.

Section 4. The Congress may by law provide for the case of the death of any of the persons from whom the House of Representatives may choose a President whenever the right of choice shall have devolved upon them, and for the case of the death of any of the persons from whom the Senate may choose a Vice President whenever the right of choice shall have devolved upon them.

Section 5. Sections 1 and 2 shall take effect on the 15th day of October following the ratification of this article.

Section 6. This article shall be inoperative unless it shall have been ratified as an amendment to the Constitution by the legislatures of three-fourths of the several states within seven years from the date of its submission.

The Twentieth Amendment brought an end to the excessively long period of time between the November election and the March inauguration of a new president. Given advances in transportation and communications systems over the previous century, such a delay in the president taking office—with the outgoing president reluctant to act even during times of crisis—could no longer be justified. The amendment also limited Congress's lame-duck sessions that followed the November elections: newly elected members of Congress could now begin their service to constituents in early January, rather than waiting 13 months until the following December. Finally, the amendment authorized Congress to provide for a line of succession in the event that neither a president-elect nor a vice president–elect qualified to serve by the January 20th date.

AMENDMENT XXI (1933)

Section 1. The eighteenth article of amendment to the Constitution of the United States is hereby repealed.

Section 2. The transportation or importation into any state, territory, or possession of the United States for delivery or use therein of intoxicating liquors, in violation of the laws thereof, is hereby prohibited.

Section 3. This article shall be inoperative unless it shall have been ratified as an amendment to the Constitution by conventions in the several states, as provided in the Constitution, within seven years from the date of the submission hereof to the states by the Congress.

The Twenty-first Amendment repealed Prohibition. The enforcement of the Eighteenth Amendment had proven too difficult and expensive, as thousands of illegal sources arose to meet the continuing public demand for alcohol. Crime gangs involved in the illegal liquor trade spread violence and bloodshed throughout the nation, which pressured politicians to end Prohibition. Finally, when both political parties came out in favor of repeal during the 1932 election, Prohibition's days were clearly numbered. After the Twenty-first Amendment was ratified on December 5, 1933, states would thereafter have the exclusive power to prevent the import and use of liquor in their respective jurisdictions.

AMENDMENT XXII (1951)

Section 1. No person shall be elected to the office of the President more than twice, and no person who has held the office of President, or acted as President, for more than two years of a term to which some other person was elected President shall be elected to the office of the President more than once. But this article shall not apply to any person holding the office of President when this article was proposed by the Congress, and shall not prevent any person who may be holding the office of President, or acting as President, during the term within which this article becomes operative from holding the office of President or acting as President during the remainder of such term.

Section 2. This article shall be inoperative unless it shall have been ratified as an amendment to the Constitution by the legislatures of three-fourths of the several states within seven years from the date of its submission to the states by the Congress.

Franklin Roosevelt's election to a record fourth term as president in 1944 sent politicians clamoring for a means of restoring the unwritten two-term tradition originally established by George Washington. Within two years of FDR's death, Congress proposed the Twenty-second Amendment, and it was adopted soon thereafter. In addition to setting a limit on the number of terms (two) to which a president may be elected, the amendment also sets a maximum of 10 years less one day for a president to serve in the event he or she also succeeds to a part of another president's term. The amendment was worded so as not to apply to the then-sitting president, Harry S. Truman, but it has applied to Dwight Eisenhower and all other presidents since that time.

AMENDMENT XXIII (1961)

Section 1. The District constituting the seat of government of the United States shall appoint in such manner as the Congress may direct:

A number of electors of President and Vice President equal to the whole number of Senators and Representatives in Congress to which the District would be entitled if it were a state, but in no event more than the least populous state; they shall be in addition to those appointed by the states, but they shall be considered, for the purposes of the election of President and Vice President, to be electors appointed by a state; and they shall meet in the District and perform such duties as provided by the twelfth article of amendment.

Section 2. The Congress shall have power to enforce this article by appropriate legislation.

The Twenty-third Amendment cured the anomaly of U.S. citizens being denied the right to vote for federal officials (including president of the United States) so long as they remained permanent residents of the District of Columbia. Since ratification of the amendment in 1961, DC residents have been entitled to vote for presidential and vice presidential candidates, but the amendment did not authorize residents of DC to elect members to either branch of Congress. Nor did it provide DC residents with home rule or the power to run their own local government. Since 1973, Congress has authorized the DC government to be run primarily by locally elected officials, subject to the oversight and supervision of Congress.

AMENDMENT XXIV (1964)

Section 1. The right of citizens of the United States to vote in any primary or other election for President or Vice President, for electors for President or Vice President, or for Senator or Representative in Congress, shall not be denied or abridged by the United States or any state by reason of failure to pay any poll tax or other tax.

Section 2. The Congress shall have power to enforce this article by appropriate legislation.

The Twenty-fourth Amendment eliminated yet another vestige of legally enforced racism in the South and elsewhere. Many states had already eliminated the requirement that voters pay a tax before voting, a restriction that created an undue hardship on lower economic classes, including disproportionate numbers of racial/ethnic minorities. Still, as late as 1964, five states (Alabama, Arkansas, Mississippi, Texas, and Virginia) continued to tie a poll tax to the voting privilege. In 1966 the Supreme Court ruled in Harper v. Board of Education *that poll taxes also violated the equal protection clause of the Fourteenth Amendment.*

AMENDMENT XXV (1967)

Section 1. In case of the removal of the President from office or of his death or resignation, the Vice President shall become President.

Section 2. Whenever there is a vacancy in the office of the Vice President, the President shall nominate a Vice President who shall take office upon confirmation by a majority vote of both Houses of Congress.

Section 3. Whenever the President transmits to the President pro tempore of the Senate and the Speaker of the House of Representatives his written declaration that he is unable to discharge the powers and duties of his office, and until he transmits to them a written declaration to the contrary, such powers and duties shall be discharged by the Vice President as Acting President.

Section 4. Whenever the Vice President and a majority of either the principal officers of the executive departments or of such other body as Congress may by law provide, transmit to the President pro tempore of the Senate and the Speaker of the House of Representatives their written declaration that the President is unable to discharge the powers and duties of his office, the Vice President shall immediately assume the powers and duties of the office as Acting President.

Thereafter, when the President transmits to the President pro tempore of the Senate and the Speaker of the House of Representatives his written declaration that no inability exists, he shall resume the powers and duties of his office unless the Vice President and a majority of either the principal officers of the executive department or of such other body as Congress may by law provide, transmit within four days to the President pro tempore of the Senate and the Speaker of the House of Representatives their written declaration that the President is unable to discharge the powers and duties of his office. Thereupon Congress shall decide the issue, assembling within forty-eight hours for that purpose if not in session. If the Congress, within twenty-one days after receipt of the latter written declaration, or, if Congress is not in session, within twenty-one days after Congress is required to assemble, determines by two-thirds vote of both Houses that the President is unable to discharge the powers and duties of his office, the Vice President shall continue to discharge the same as Acting President; otherwise, the President shall resume the powers and duties of his office.

The Twenty-fifth Amendment clarified several ambiguous aspects of presidential succession. At the outset, it formalized an unwritten precedent first established by John Tyler, who succeeded to the presidency upon the death of William Henry Harrison in 1841: If the office of president becomes vacant because of the president's death or resignation, the vice president becomes president and assumes all powers and duties of the office. If the vice presidency is vacant, the amendment establishes new procedures for filling the position between elections: the president nominates a successor, to be confirmed by a majority vote of both houses of Congress. Since its adoption in 1967, two vice presidents have been selected in this manner: Gerald Ford in 1973 and Nelson Rockefeller in 1974. When Gerald Ford succeeded to the presidency upon the resignation of Richard Nixon in 1974, he became the first—and to date, the only—president in American history to hold that office without being formally elected to either the presidency or the vice presidency.

The amendment also addresses the vexing problem of presidential disabilities. In the early twentieth century, Woodrow Wilson was an invalid for more than a year of his presidency; in the 1950s, Dwight Eisenhower suffered a stroke once during each of his two terms in office. The Twenty-fifth Amendment addresses the problem of presidential disability by providing procedures for the president to temporarily discharge the duties and powers of the office to the officer next in line (normally the vice president), who then becomes "acting president." This has happened only twice: in 1985, when Vice President George H. W. Bush received a transmission of power temporarily while President Ronald Reagan underwent a minor medical procedure, and in 2002, when President George W. Bush temporarily transferred his powers to Vice President Dick Cheney while he underwent a colonoscopy. The amendment further authorizes the vice president and certain members of the executive branch to declare the president disabled or incapacitated, subject (within 27 days) to Congress upholding the finding of incapacity. This final provision has never been invoked.

AMENDMENT XXVI (1971)

Section 1. The right of citizens of the United States, who are 18 years of age or older, to vote, shall not be denied or abridged by the United States or any state on account of age.
Section 2. The Congress shall have the power to enforce this article by appropriate legislation.

The Twenty-sixth Amendment extended suffrage to those age 18 and older. At the time of its passage, soldiers under the age of 21 were fighting in Vietnam, creating intense pressure on Congress and state legislatures to extend the vote to all those who were old enough to fight. The amendment does not apply to the denial of rights other than voting to those who are between 18 and 21 years of age. Thus, the National Minimum Drinking Age Act of 1984 obliges states to establish a 21-year-old drinking age or risk the loss of federal highway funds. Additionally, Utah and Alaska have established 19 as the minimum age for tobacco use.

AMENDMENT XXVII (1992)

No law, varying the compensation for the services of the Senators and Representatives, shall take effect, until an election of Representatives shall have intervened.

The Twenty-seventh Amendment was intended to serve as a restraint on the power of Congress to raise its own pay—it may only do so if the raise takes effect after a subsequent general election. Although the Supreme Court has never ruled on the issue, lower courts have held that this amendment does not prevent Congress from receiving cost-of-living adjustments immediately.

FEDERALIST NO. 10

November 23, 1787

TO THE PEOPLE OF THE STATE OF NEW YORK

Among the numerous advantages promised by a well-constructed Union, none deserves to be more accurately developed than its tendency to break and control the violence of faction. The friend of popular governments never finds himself so much alarmed for their character and fate, as when he contemplates their propensity to this dangerous vice. He will not fail, therefore, to set a due value on any plan which, without violating the principles to which he is attached, provides a proper cure for it. The instability, injustice, and confusion introduced into the public councils, have, in truth, been the mortal diseases under which popular governments have everywhere perished; as they continue to be the favorite and fruitful topics from which the adversaries to liberty derive their most specious declamations. The valuable improvements made by the American constitutions on the popular models, both ancient and modern, cannot certainly be too much admired; but it would be an unwarrantable partiality, to contend that they have as effectually obviated the danger on this side, as was wished and expected. Complaints are everywhere heard from our most considerate and virtuous citizens, equally the friends of public and private faith, and of public and personal liberty, that our governments are too unstable, that the public good is disregarded in the conflicts of rival parties, and that measures are too often decided, not according to the rules of justice and the rights of the minor party, but by the superior force on an interested and overbearing majority. However anxiously we may wish that these complaints had no foundation, the evidence of known facts will not permit us to deny that they are in some degree true. It will be found, indeed, on a candid review of our situation, that some of the distresses under which we labor have been erroneously charged on the operation of our governments; but it will be found, at the same time, that other causes will not alone account for many of our heaviest misfortunes; and, particularly, for that prevailing and increasing distrust of public engagements, and alarm for private rights, which are echoed from one end of the continent to the other. These must be chiefly, if not wholly, effects of the unsteadiness and injustice with which a factious spirit has tainted our public administrations.

By a faction, I understand a number of citizens, whether amounting to a majority or a minority of the whole, who are united and actuated by some common impulse of passion, or of interest, adversed to the rights of other citizens, or to the permanent and aggregate interests of the community.

There are two methods of curing the mischiefs of faction: the one, by removing its causes; the other, by controlling its effects.

There are again two methods of removing the causes of faction: the one, by destroying the liberty which is essential to its existence; the other, by giving to every citizen the same opinions, the same passions, and the same interests.

It could never be more truly said than of the first remedy, that it was worse than the disease. Liberty is to faction what air is to fire, an aliment without which it instantly expires. But it could not be less folly to abolish liberty, which is essential to political life, because it nourishes faction, than it would be to wish the annihilation of air, which is essential to animal life, because it imparts to fire its destructive tendency.

The second expedient is as impracticable as the first would be unwise. As long as the reason of man continues fallible, and he is at liberty to exercise it, different opinions will be formed. As long as the connection subsists between his reason and his self-love, his opinions and his passions will have a reciprocal influence on each other; and the former will be objects to which the latter will attach themselves. The diversity in the faculties of men, from which the rights of property originate, is not less an insuperable obstacle to a uniformity of interests. The protection of these faculties is the first object of government. From the protection of different and unequal faculties of acquiring property, the possession of different degrees and kinds of property immediately results; and from the influence of these on the sentiments and views of the respective proprietors, ensues a division of the society into different interests and parties.

The latent causes of faction are thus sown in the nature of man; and we see them everywhere brought into different degrees of activity, according to the different circumstances of civil society. A zeal for different opinions concerning religion, concerning government, and many other points, as well of speculation as of practice; an attachment to different leaders ambitiously contending for pre-eminence and power; or to persons of other descriptions whose fortunes have been interesting to the human passions, have, in turn, divided mankind into parties, inflamed them with mutual animosity, and rendered them much more disposed to vex and oppress each other than to co-operate for their common good. So strong is this propensity of mankind to fall into mutual animosities, that where no substantial occasion presents itself, the most frivolous and fanciful distinctions have been sufficient to kindle their unfriendly passions and excite their most violent conflicts. But the most common and durable source of factions has been the various and unequal distribution of property. Those who hold and those who are without property have ever formed distinct interests in society. Those who are creditors, and those who are debtors, fall under a like discrimination. A landed interest, a manufacturing interest, a mercantile interest, a moneyed interest, with many lesser interests, grow up of necessity in civilized nations, and divide them into different classes, actuated by different sentiments and views. The regulation of these various and interfering interests forms the principal task of modern legislation, and involves the spirit of party and faction in the necessary and ordinary operations of the government.

No man is allowed to be a judge in his own case, because his interest would certainly bias his judgment, and, not improbably, corrupt his integrity. With equal, nay with greater reason, a body of men are unfit to be both judges and parties at the same time; yet what are many of the most important acts of legislation, but so many judicial determinations, not indeed concerning the rights of single persons, but concerning the rights of large bodies of citizens? And what are the different classes of legislators but advocates and parties to the causes which they determine? Is a law proposed concerning private debts? It is a question to which the creditors are parties on one side and the debtors on the other. Justice ought to hold the balance between them. Yet the parties are, and must be, themselves the judges; and the most numerous party, or, in other words, the most powerful action must be expected to prevail. Shall domestic manufactures be encouraged, and in what degree, by restrictions on foreign manufactures? are questions which would be differently decided by the landed and the manufacturing classes, and probably by neither with a sole regard to justice and the public good. The apportionment of taxes on the various descriptions of property is an act which seems to require the most exact impartiality; yet there is, perhaps, no legislative act in which greater opportunity and temptation are given to a predominant party to trample on the rules of justice. Every shilling with which they overburden the inferior number, is a shilling saved to their own pockets.

It is in vain to say that enlightened statesmen will be able to adjust these clashing interests, and render them all subservient to the public good. Enlightened statesmen will not always be at the helm. Nor, in many cases, can such an adjustment be made at all without taking into view indirect and remote considerations, which will rarely prevail over the immediate interest which one party may find in disregarding the rights of another or the good of the whole.

The inference to which we are brought is, that the *causes* of faction cannot be removed, and that relief is only to be sought in the means of controlling its *effects*.

If a faction consists of less than a majority, relief is supplied by the republican principle, which enables the majority to defeat its sinister views by regular vote. It may clog the administration, it may convulse the society; but it will be unable to execute and mask its violence under the forms of the Constitution. When a majority is included in a faction, the form of popular government, on the other hand, enables it to sacrifice to its ruling passion or interest both the public good and the rights of other citizens. To secure the public good and private rights against the danger of such a faction, and at the same time to preserve the spirit and form of popular government, is then the great object to which our inquiries are directed. Let me add that it is the great desideratum by which this form of government can be rescued from the opprobrium under which it has so long labored, and be recommended to the esteem and adoption of mankind.

By what means is this object attainable? Evidently by one of two only. Either the existence of the same passion or interest in a majority at the same time must be prevented, or the majority, having such coexistent passion or interest, must be rendered, by their number and local situation, unable to concert and carry into effect schemes of oppression. If the impulse and the opportunity be suffered to coincide, we well know that neither moral nor religious motives can be relied on as an adequate control. They are not found to be such on the injustice and violence of individuals, and lose their efficacy in proportion to the number combined together, that is, in proportion as their efficacy becomes needful.

From this view of the subject it may be concluded that a pure democracy, by which I mean a society consisting of a small number of citizens, who assemble and administer the government in person, can admit of no cure for the mischiefs of faction. A common passion or interest will, in almost every case, be felt by a majority of the whole; a communication and concert result from the form of government itself; and there is nothing to check the inducements to sacrifice the weaker party or an obnoxious individual. Hence it is that such democracies have ever been spectacles of turbulence and contention; have ever been found incompatible with personal security or the rights of property; and have in general been as short in their lives as they have been violent in their deaths. Theoretic politicians, who have patronized this species of government, have erroneously supposed that by reducing mankind to a perfect equality in their political rights, they would, at the same time, be perfectly equalized and assimilated in their possessions, their opinions, and their passions.

A republic, by which I mean a government in which the scheme of representation takes place, opens a different prospect, and promises the cure for which we are seeking. Let us examine the points in which it varies from pure democracy, and we shall comprehend both the nature of the cure and the efficacy which it must derive from the Union.

The two great points of difference between a democracy and a republic are: first, the delegation of the government, in the latter, to a small number of citizens elected by the rest; secondly, the greater number of citizens, and greater sphere of country, over which the latter may be extended.

The effect of the first difference is, on the one hand, to refine and enlarge the public views, by passing them through the medium of a chosen body of citizens, whose wisdom may best discern the true interest of their country, and whose patriotism and love of justice will be least likely to sacrifice it to temporary or partial considerations. Under such a regulation, it may well happen that the public voice, pronounced by the representatives of the people, will be more consonant to the public good than if pronounced by the people themselves, convened for the purpose. On the other hand, the effect may be inverted. Men of factious tempers, of local prejudices, or of sinister designs, may, by intrigue, by corruption, or by other means, first obtain the suffrages, and then betray the interests, of the people. The question resulting is, whether small or extensive republics are more favorable to the election of proper guardians of the public weal; and it is clearly decided in favor of the latter by two obvious considerations.

In the first place, it is to be remarked that, however small the republic may be, the representatives must be raised to a certain number, in order to guard against the cabals of a few; and that, however large it may be, they must be limited to a certain number, in order to guard against the confusion of a multitude. Hence, the number of representatives in the two cases not being in proportion to that of the two constituents, and being proportionally greater in the small republic, it follows that, if the proportion of fit characters be not less in the large than in the small republic, the former will present a greater option, and consequently a greater probability of a fit choice.

In the next place, as each representative will be chosen by a greater number of citizens in the large than in the small republic, it will be more difficult for unworthy candidates to practice with success the vicious arts by which elections are too often carried; and the suffrages of the people being more free, will be more likely to centre in men who possess the most attractive merit and the most diffusive and established characters.

It must be confessed that in this, as in most other cases, there is a mean, on both sides of which inconveniences will be found to lie. By enlarging too much the number of electors, you render the representatives too little acquainted with all their local circumstances and lesser interests; as by reducing it too much, you render him unduly attached to these, and too little fit to comprehend and pursue great and national objects. The federal Constitution forms a happy combination in this respect; the great and aggregate interests being referred to the national, the local and particular to the State legislatures.

The other point of difference is, the greater number of citizens and extent of territory which may be brought within the compass of republican than of democratic government; and it is this circumstance principally which renders factious combinations less to be dreaded in the former than in the latter. The smaller the society, the fewer probably will be the distinct parties and interests composing it; the fewer the distinct parties and interests, the more frequently will a majority be found of the same party; and the smaller the number of individuals composing a majority, and the smaller the compass within which they are placed, the more easily will they concert and execute their plans of oppression. Extend the sphere, and you take in a greater variety of parties and interests; you make it less probable that a majority of the whole will have a common motive to invade the rights of other citizens; or if such a common motive exists, it will be more difficult for all who feel it to discover their own strength, and to act in unison with each other. Besides other impediments, it may be remarked that, where there is a consciousness of unjust or dishonorable purposes, communication is always checked by distrust in proportion to the number whose concurrence is necessary.

Hence, it clearly appears, that the same advantage which a republic has over a democracy, in controlling the effects of faction, is enjoyed by a large over a small republic,—and is enjoyed by the Union over the States composing it. Does the advantage consist in the substitution of representatives whose enlightened views and virtuous sentiments render them superior to local prejudices and schemes of injustice? It will not be denied that the representation of the Union will be most likely to possess these requisite endowments. Does it consist in the greater security afforded by a greater variety of parties, against the event of any one party being able to outnumber and oppress the rest? In an equal degree does the increased variety of parties comprised within the Union, increase this security? Does it, in fine, consist in the greater obstacles opposed to the concert and accomplishment of the secret wishes of an unjust and interested majority? Here, again, the extent of the Union gives it the most palpable advantage.

The influence of factious leaders may kindle a flame within their particular States, but will be unable to spread a general conflagration through the other States. A religious sect may degenerate into a political faction in a part of the Confederacy; but the variety of sects dispersed over the entire face of it must secure the national councils against any danger from that source. A rage for paper money, for an abolition of debts, for an equal division of property, or for any other improper or wicked project, will be less apt to pervade the whole body of the Union than a particular member of it; in the same proportion as such a malady is more likely to taint a particular county or district, than an entire State.

In the extent and proper structure of the Union, therefore, we behold a republican remedy for the diseases most incident to republican government. And according to the degree of pleasure and pride we feel in being republicans, ought to be our zeal in cherishing the spirit and supporting the character of Federalists.

FEDERALIST NO. 51

February 8, 1788

TO THE PEOPLE OF THE STATE OF NEW YORK

TO WHAT expedient, then, shall we finally resort, for maintaining in practice the necessary partition of power among the several departments, as laid down in the Constitution? The only answer that can be given is, that as all these exterior provisions are found to be inadequate, the defect must be supplied, by so contriving the interior structure of the government as that its several constituent parts may, by their mutual relations, be the means of keeping each other in their proper places. Without presuming to undertake a full development of the important idea, I will hazard a few general observations, which may perhaps place it in a clearer light, and enable us to form a more correct judgment of the principles and structure of the government planned by the convention.

In order to lay a due foundation for that separate and distinct exercise of the different powers of government, which to a certain extent is admitted on all hands to be essential to the preservation of liberty, it is evident that each department should have a will of its own; and consequently should be so constituted that the members of each should have as little agency as possible in the appointment of the members of the others. Were this principle rigorously adhered to, it would require that all the appointments for the supreme executive, legislative, and judiciary magistracies should be drawn from the same fountain of authority, the people, through channels having no communication whatever with one another. Perhaps such a plan of constructing the several departments would be less difficult in practice than it may in contemplation appear. Some difficulties, however, and some additional expense would attend the execution of it. Some deviations, therefore, from the principle must be admitted. In the constitution of the judiciary department in particular, it might be inexpedient to insist rigorously on the principle: first, because peculiar qualifications being essential in the members, the primary consideration ought to be to select that mode of choice which best secures these qualifications; secondly, because the permanent tenure by which the appointments are held in that department, must soon destroy all sense of dependence on the authority conferring them.

It is equally evident, that the members of each department should be as little dependent as possible on those of the others, for the emoluments annexed to their offices. Were the executive magistrate, or the judges, not independent of the legislature in this particular, their independence in every other would be merely nominal.

But the great security against a gradual concentration of the several powers in the same department, consists in giving to those who administer each department the necessary constitutional means and personal motives to resist encroachments of the others. The provision for defense must in this, as in all other cases, be made commensurate to the danger of attack. Ambition must be made to counteract ambition. The interest of the man must be connected with the constitutional rights of the place. It may be a reflection on human nature, that such devices should be necessary to control the abuses of government. But what is government itself, but the greatest of all reflections on human nature? If men were angels, no government would be necessary. If angels were to govern men, neither external nor internal controls on government would be necessary. In framing a government which is to be administered by men over men, the great difficulty lies in this: you must first enable the government to control the governed; and in the next place oblige it to control itself. A dependence on the people is, no doubt, the primary control on the government; but experience has taught mankind the necessity of auxiliary precautions.

This policy of supplying, by opposite and rival interests, the defect of better motives, might be traced through the whole system of human affairs, private as well as public. We see it particularly displayed in all the subordinate distributions of power, where the constant aim is to divide and arrange the several offices in such a manner as that each may be a check on the other—that the private interest of every individual may be a sentinel over the public rights. These inventions of prudence cannot be less requisite in the distribution of the supreme powers of the State.

But it is not possible to give to each department an equal power of self-defense. In republican government, the legislative authority necessarily predominates. The remedy for this inconveniency is to divide the legislature into different branches; and to render them, by different modes of election and different principles of action, as little connected with each other as the nature of their common functions and their common dependence on the society will admit. It may even be necessary to guard against dangerous encroachments by still further precautions. As the weight of the legislative authority requires that it should be thus divided, the weakness of the executive may require, on the other hand, that it should be fortified. An absolute negative on the legislature appears, at first view, to be the natural defense with which the executive magistrate should be armed. But perhaps it would be neither altogether safe nor alone sufficient. On ordinary occasions it might not be exerted with the requisite firmness, and on extraordinary occasions it might be perfidiously abused. May not this defect of an absolute negative be supplied by some qualified connection between this weaker department and the weaker branch of the stronger department, by which the latter may be led to support the constitutional rights of the former, without being too much detached from the rights of its own department?

If the principles on which these observations are founded be just, as I persuade myself they are, and they be applied as a criterion to the several State constitutions, and to the federal Constitution it will be found that if the latter does not perfectly correspond with them, the former are infinitely less able to bear such a test.

There are, moreover, two considerations particularly applicable to the federal system of America, which place that system in a very interesting point of view.

First. In a single republic, all the power surrendered by the people is submitted to the administration of a single government; and the usurpations are guarded against by a division of the government into distinct and separate departments. In the compound republic of America, the power surrendered by the people is first divided between two distinct governments, and then the portion allotted to each subdivided among distinct and separate departments. Hence a double security arises to the rights of the people. The different governments will control each other, at the same time that each will be controlled by itself.

Second. It is of great importance in a republic not only to guard the society against the oppression of its rulers, but to guard one part of the society against the injustice of the other part. Different interests necessarily exist in different classes of citizens. If a majority be united by a common interest, the rights of the minority will be insecure. There are but two methods of providing against this evil: the one by creating a will in the community independent of the majority that is, of the society itself; the other, by comprehending in the society so many separate descriptions of citizens as will render an unjust combination of a majority of the whole very improbable, if not impracticable. The first method prevails in all governments possessing an hereditary or self-appointed authority. This, at best, is but a precarious security; because a power independent of society may as well espouse the unjust views of the major as the rightful interests of the minor party, and may possibly be turned against both parties. The second method will be exemplified in the federal republic of the United States. Whilst all authority in it will be derived from and dependent on the society, the society itself will be broken into so many parts, interests, and classes of citizens, that the rights of individuals, or of the minority, will be in little danger from interested combinations of the majority. In a free government the security for civil rights must be the same as that for religious rights. It consists in the one case in the multiplicity of interests, and in the other in the multiplicity of sects. The degree of security in both cases will depend on the number of interests and sects; and this may be presumed to depend on the extent of country and number of people comprehended under the same government. This view of the subject must particularly recommend a proper federal system to all the sincere and considerate friends of republican government, since it shows that in exact proportion as the territory of the Union may be formed into more circumscribed Confederacies, or States oppressive combinations of a majority will be facilitated: the best security, under republican forms, for the rights of every class of citizens, will be diminished; and consequently the stability and independence of some member of the government, the only other security, must be proportionately increased. Justice is the end of government. It is the end of civil society. It ever has been and ever will be pursued until it be obtained, or until liberty be lost in the pursuit. In a society under the forms of which the stronger faction can readily unite and oppress the weaker, anarchy may as truly be said to reign as in a state of nature, where the weaker individual is not secured against the violence of the stronger; and as, in the latter state, even the stronger individuals are prompted, by the uncertainty of their condition, to submit to a government which may protect the weak as well as the more powerful. It can be little doubted that if the State of Rhode Island was separated from the Confederacy and left to itself, the insecurity of rights under the popular form of government within such narrow limits would be displayed by such reiterated oppressions of factious majorities that some power altogether independent of the people would soon be called for by the voice of the very factions whose misrule had proved the necessity of it. In the extended republic of the United States, and among the great variety of interests, parties, and sects which it embraces, a coalition of a majority of the whole society could seldom take place on any other principles than those of justice and the general good; whilst there being thus less danger to a minor from the will of a major party, there must be less pretext, also, to provide for the security of the former, by introducing into the government a will not dependent on the latter, or, in other words, a will independent of the society itself. It is no less certain than it is important, notwithstanding the contrary opinions which have been entertained, that the larger the society, provided it lie within a practical sphere, the more duly capable it will be of self-government. And happily for the *republican cause*, the practicable sphere may be carried to a very great extent, by a judicious modification of mixture of the *federal principle*.

Presidents of the United States

Name of President	Dates of Service	Political Party Affiliation	Vice President(s)	Major Party Candidate(s) Defeated in General Election
George Washington	1789–97		Adams	
John Adams	1797–1801	Federalist	Jefferson	Jefferson
Thomas Jefferson	1801–9	Democratic-Republican	Burr/Clinton	Adams, Pinckney
James Madison	1809–17	Democratic-Republican	Clinton/Gerry	Pinckney, D. Clinton
James Monroe	1817–25	Democratic-Republican	Tompkins	King
John Quincy Adams	1825–29	Democratic-Republican/ Democratic	Calhoun	Jackson
Andrew Jackson	1829–37	Democratic	Van Buren	J. Q. Adams, Clay
Martin Van Buren	1837–41	Democratic	Johnson	Harrison
William Harrison	1841	Whig	Tyler	Van Buren
John Tyler	1841–45	Whig	vacant	
James Polk	1845–49	Democratic	Dallas	Clay
Zachary Taylor	1849–50	Whig	Fillmore	Cass
Millard Fillmore	1850–53	Whig	vacant	
Franklin Pierce	1853–57	Democratic	King/vacant	Scott
James Buchanan	1857–61	Democratic	Breckinridge	Fremont
Abraham Lincoln	1861–65	Republican	Hamlin/Johnson	Breckinridge, Douglas, McClellan
Andrew Johnson	1865–69	Democratic	vacant	
Ulysses S. Grant	1869–77	Republican	Colfax/Wilson/vacant	Seymour, Greeley
Rutherford B. Hayes	1877–81	Republican	Wheeler	Tilden
James Garfield	1881	Republican	Arthur	Hancock
Chester Arthur	1881–85	Republican	vacant	
Grover Cleveland	1885–89	Democratic	Hendricks/vacant	Blaine
Benjamin Harrison	1889–93	Republican	Morton	Cleveland
Grover Cleveland	1893–97	Democratic	Stevenson	Harrison
William McKinley	1897–1901	Republican	Hobart	Bryan
Theodore Roosevelt	1901–9	Republican	vacant/Fairbanks	Parker
William Taft	1909–13	Republican	Sherman/vacant	Bryan

Name of President	Dates of Service	Political Party Affiliation	Vice President(s)	Major Party Candidate(s) Defeated in General Election
Woodrow Wilson	1913–21	Democratic	Marshall	T. Roosevelt, Taft, Hughes
Warren G. Harding	1921–23	Republican	Coolidge	Cox
Calvin Coolidge	1923–29	Republican	vacant/Dawes	Davis
Herbert Hoover	1929–33	Republican	Curtis	Smith
Franklin D. Roosevelt	1933–45	Democratic	Garner/Wallace/Truman	Hoover, Landon, Wilkie, Dewey
Harry Truman	1945–53	Democratic	vacant/Barkley	Dewey
Dwight Eisenhower	1953–61	Republican	Nixon	Stevenson
John F. Kennedy	1961–63	Democratic	Johnson	Nixon
Lyndon Johnson	1963–69	Democratic	vacant/Humphrey	Goldwater
Richard Nixon	1969–74	Republican	Agnew/vacant/Ford	Humphrey, McGovern
Gerald Ford	1974–77	Republican	vacant/Rockefeller	
Jimmy Carter	1977–81	Democratic	Mondale	Ford
Ronald Reagan	1981–89	Republican	G. H. W. Bush	Carter, Mondale
George H. W. Bush	1989–93	Republican	Quayle	Dukakis
William Clinton	1993–2001	Democratic	Gore	G. H. W. Bush, Dole
George W. Bush	2001–09	Republican	Cheney	Gore, Kerry
Barack Obama	2009–17	Democratic	Biden	McCain, Romney
Donald Trump	2017–present	Republican	Pence	H. Clinton

Electoral College Results, 2000–2016

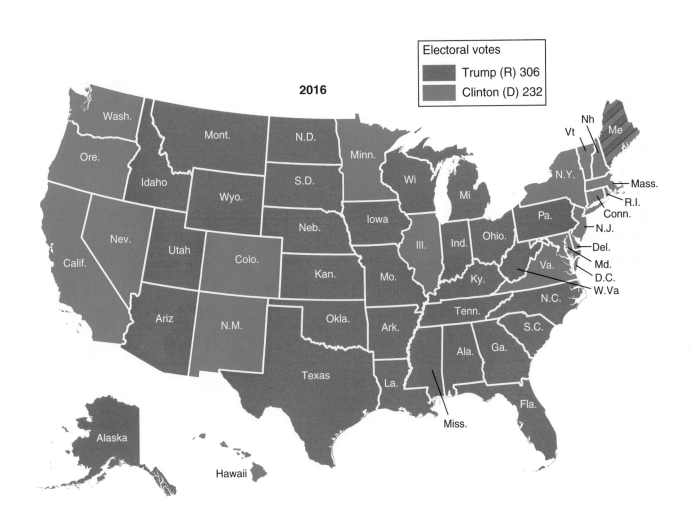

2016

Electoral votes

Trump (R) 306
Clinton (D) 232

Wash.

Ore.

Mont.

Idaho

Wyo.

N.D.

S.D.

Minn.

Wi

Mi

Nev.

Utah

Colo.

Neb.

Iowa

Ill.

Ind.

Ohio

Pa.

N.Y.

Vt

Nh

Me

Calif.

Ariz

N.M.

Kan.

Okla.

Mo.

Ky.

W.Va

Va.

N.C.

Mass.

R.I.

Conn.

N.J.

Del.

Md.

D.C.

Texas

La.

Ark.

Tenn.

Miss.

Ala.

Ga.

S.C.

Fla.

Alaska

Hawaii

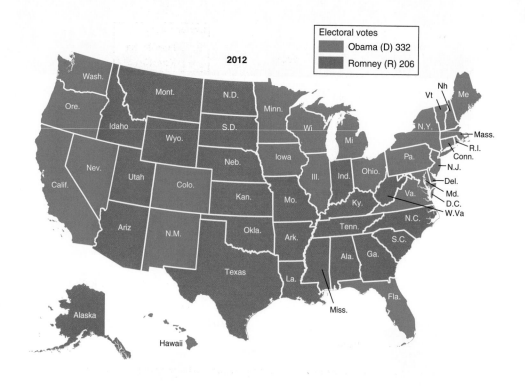

2012

Electoral votes
Obama (D) 332
Romney (R) 206

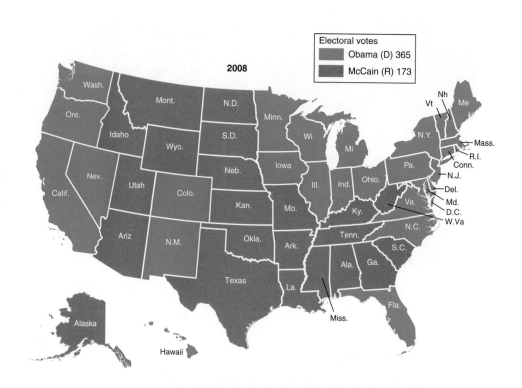

2008

Electoral votes
Obama (D) 365
McCain (R) 173

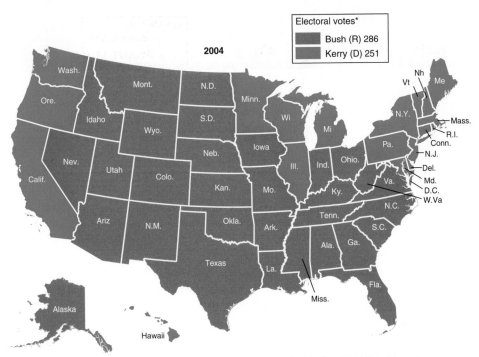

2004

Electoral votes*

Bush (R) 286
Kerry (D) 251

* A Minnesota elector who was pledged to Kerry cast a ballot instead for John Ewards [sic] (John Edwards).

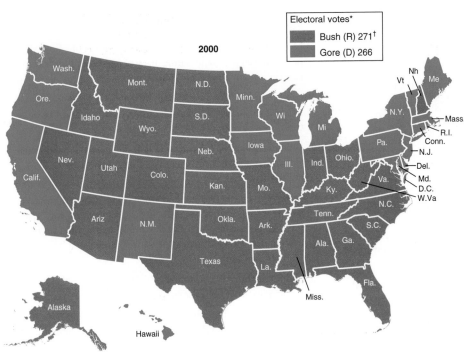

2000

Electoral votes*

Bush (R) 271[†]
Gore (D) 266

* A District of Columbia elector who was pledged to Gore cast no ballot as a protest against the District of Columbia's lack of representation in the U.S. Congress.

[†] The state of Florida certified Bush the winner on November 26, a result that Gore contested unsuccessfully in court.

GLOSSARY

administrative discretion The freedom of agencies to decide how to implement a vague or ambiguous law passed by Congress.

administrative law A law that relates to the authority of administrative agencies and the rules promulgated by those agencies.

adversarial system A system of justice in which opposing groups contend against each other; the judge is not actively involved in investigating the facts of the case.

affirmative action Programs, laws, or practices designed to remedy past discriminatory hiring practices, government contracting, and school admissions.

agenda-setting theory The theory holding that although the effects of television exposure may be minimal or difficult to gauge, the media are quite influential in telling the public what to think about.

agents of political socialization Factors that have a significant impact on an individual's socialization to politics.

amendments Modifications or additions to the U.S. Constitution passed in accordance with the amendment procedures laid out in Article V.

amicus curiae briefs Written documents filed by outside parties in the case with an interest in the outcome of the litigation expressing their own views on how the Court should decide a particular case.

anarchy A state of lawlessness and discord in the political system caused by lack of government.

Anti-Federalists Those who opposed ratification of the proposed constitution of the United States between 1787 and 1789.

appellate jurisdiction The authority of a court to review decisions handed down by another court.

Articles of Confederation The document creating a "league of friendship" governing the 13 states during and immediately after the war for independence; hampered by the limited power the document vested in the legislature to collect revenue or regulate commerce, the Articles eventually proved unworkable for the new nation.

authoritarian A form of government in which one political party, group, or person maintains such complete control over the nation that it may refuse to recognize and may even suppress all other political parties and interests.

authority The ability of public institutions and the officials within them to make laws, independent of the power to execute them.

bail An amount of money determined by a judge that the accused must pay to a court as security against his or her freedom before trial.

battleground states States identified as offering either major-party candidate a reasonable chance for victory in the Electoral College.

bicameral legislature A legislature composed of two separate chambers.

bill A proposed law presented for consideration to a legislative body.

bill of attainder An act of a legislature declaring a person (or group) guilty of some crime, and then carrying out punishment without a trial. The Constitution denies Congress the ability to issue a bill of attainder.

Bill of Rights The first 10 amendments to the U.S. Constitution, which protect various rights of the people against the new federal government.

Bipartisan Campaign Reform Act (BCRA) of 2002 Also called the McCain-Feingold Act, the federal legislation that (1) restricted soft money spent by political parties, (2) regulated expenditures on ads that refer to specific candidates immediately before an election, and (3) increased limits on hard money donated directly to candidates and their campaigns.

block grants Grants from the federal government to the states that may be used at the discretion of states to pursue more generalized aims.

blogs Internet sites that include a combination of editorial page, personal web page, and online diary of personal observations in real time about news events and issues.

briefs Written documents filed by parties in an appealed case arguing why constitutional or statutory law weighs in favor of their respective positions.

Brown v. Board of Education (1954) The 1954 U.S. Supreme Court decision that declared school segregation to be unconstitutional.

Buckley v. Valeo (1976) The 1976 Supreme Court opinion that held that spending money to influence elections is protected First Amendment speech and that prohibited limitations on independent expenditures or personal money spent by candidates on their own campaigns.

budget authority The power of federal departments and agencies to incur obligations to spend or lend money.

budget deficit The amount of money spent by the U.S. government beyond that which it collects in taxes and other revenue in a single year.

budget surplus The amount by which the U.S. government's revenue exceeds its spending in a given fiscal year.

bureaucracy An organization set up in a logical and rational manner for the purpose of accomplishing specific functions.

bureaucratic adjudicating Determining the rights and duties of particular parties within the scope of an agency's rules or regulations.

cabinet The collection of the principal officers in each of the executive departments of the federal government who serve as key advisers to the president.

cabinet departments Those federal agencies that qualify as the major administrative organizations of the executive branch.

capitalism Economic system in which all or most of the means of production are privately owned under competitive conditions.

casework The direct assistance that a member of Congress provides to a constituent, community group, or local or state official.

caucus A method of choosing party nominees in which party members attend local meetings at which they choose delegates committed to a particular candidate.

Central Intelligence Agency (CIA) Federal agency charged with evaluating and disseminating intelligence information, performing public relations functions that affect international perceptions of the United States, and engaging in overt and covert operations at the direction of the president.

checks and balances A system of limits imposed by the Constitution that gives each branch of government the limited right to change or cancel the acts of other branches.

citizen journalist A member of the general public who collects, disseminates, and analyzes news and information, especially by means of the internet.

Citizens United v. FEC **(2010)** The 2010 Supreme Court opinion that held that government restrictions on independent political spending by corporations, unions, and other associations violate the First Amendment. Critics of the decision predicted the ruling would bring about a new era of corporate influence in politics. In fact, the bulk of large expenditures has come from so-called super PACs dominated by a small group of billionaires; this development more than anything else has shifted significant power away from the political parties and toward the donors themselves.

civil law This term has two meanings: (1) legislative codes, laws, or sets of rules enacted by duly authorized law-making bodies such as Congress, state and local legislatures, or any executive authority entrusted with the power to make laws; (2) the body of noncriminal laws of a nation or state that deal with the rights of private citizens.

civil liberties Those specific individual rights that are guaranteed by the Constitution and cannot be denied to citizens by government. Most of these rights are in the first 10 amendments to the Constitution, known as the Bill of Rights.

civil rights Those positive rights, whether political, social, or economic, conferred by the government on individuals or groups.

Civil Rights Act of 1964 The federal law that banned racial discrimination in all public accommodations, including those that were privately owned; prohibited discrimination by employers and created the Equal Employment Opportunity Commission to investigate complaints of discrimination; and denied public funds to schools that continued to discriminate on the basis of race.

Civil Rights Act of 1968 The federal law that banned race discrimination in housing and made interference with a citizen's civil rights a federal crime.

civil service The system whereby workers in the federal bureaucracy are supposed to be immune from partisan political maneuvering.

Civil Service Reform Act of 1978 The federal act that replaced the Civil Service Commission (the agency that oversaw federal hiring and firing practices) with the Office of Personnel Management (OPM) and the Merit Systems Protection Board (MSPB).

class action lawsuits Lawsuits filed by a large group of people with clearly defined common interests.

closed primary An election that requires voters to declare their party affiliation ahead of time.

closed rule A rule of procedure adopted by the House Rules Committee that severely limits the ability of members of Congress to amend a bill.

closed shop The law that requires employees to become members of the union as a condition of employment in unionized workplaces.

cloture A Senate debate procedure that permits that body to end debate and force a vote on a bill by a vote of 60 senators.

coattail effect The potential benefit that successful presidential candidates offer to congressional candidates of the same political party during presidential election years.

Cold War The nearly half-century struggle over ideological differences between the United States and the Soviet Union. Waged through economic warfare, arms build-ups, and tense diplomatic talks, the Cold War never broke out into a sustained military engagement between the two nations and ended with the dissolution of the Soviet Union in 1991.

common law Judge-made law handed down through judicial opinions, which over time establish precedents.

complaint A document written by the plaintiff arguing why the court is empowered to hear the case and explaining why the plaintiff is entitled to some form of relief under the current law.

concurrent powers Those powers shared by the federal and state governments under the Constitution.

concurring opinion The opinion of one or more justices that agrees with the end result reached by the majority but disagrees with the reasons offered for the decision.

confederation A system of government (or "league") in which two or more independent states unite to achieve certain specified common aims.

conference committee A joint committee of Congress appointed by the House of Representatives and the Senate to resolve differences on a particular bill.

congressional agencies Government bodies formed by and relied on by Congress to support members of Congress in performing their functions.

congressional committee staff A group of workers assigned to congressional committees to support each committee's legislative work.

congressional district A geographic region (either a state itself or a region located entirely within one state) whose residents select one member to represent it in the House of Representatives.

congressional oversight Congress's exercise of its authority to monitor the activities of agencies and administrators.

congressional personal staff A group of workers who assist an individual member of Congress in performing his or her responsibilities.

conservative ideology A political orientation that generally favors government activism in defense of more traditional values on social issues but favors government restraint in economic redistribution.

Constitutional Convention Meeting of delegates from 12 states in Philadelphia during the summer of 1787, at which was drafted an entirely new system to govern the United States.

containment U.S. foreign policy that sought to restrict Soviet power (and communist influence) to its existing geographical sphere.

continuity (in public opinion) A tendency for political preferences to remain generally stable over time.

cooperative federalism The doctrine of federalism that affords Congress nearly unlimited authority to exercise its powers through means that often coerce states into administering and/or enforcing federal policies.

critical election An election that produces sharp changes in patterns of party loyalty among voters.

cultivation theory The theory of media effects that suggests that heavy television exposure helps develop an individual's overall view of the world.

dealignment A decline in voter attachment to parties and in clarity of party coalitions.

Declaration of Independence Formal document listing colonists' grievances and articulating the colonists' intention to seek independence; formally adopted by the Second Continental Congress on July 4, 1776.

defendant The target of a plaintiff's complaint.

delegated congressional power Congress's transferring of its law-making authority to the executive branch of government.

democracy Form of government in which the people, either directly or through elected representatives, hold power and authority. The word *democracy* is derived from the Greek *demos kratos*, meaning "rule by the people."

Department of Defense Executive branch agency that is responsible for managing the nation's military and advising the president on all military matters.

Department of Homeland Security (DHS) Executive branch agency established in 2002 to coordinate government entities in protecting U.S. citizens against terrorism within the nation's borders.

Department of State Executive branch agency that is primarily responsible for most foreign policy programs within the executive branch, including diplomatic missions, foreign aid, and contributions to international organizations.

deregulation The elimination of government oversight and government regulation of certain activities.

devolution The transfer of power and responsibilities for certain regulatory programs from the federal government back to the states.

digital divide The large differences in usage of the internet between older and younger people, lower- and middle-/upper-class people, lesser and better educated people, and minority groups and nonminority groups.

direct democracy A system of government in which all citizens participate in making policy, rules, and governing decisions.

direction (of public opinion) A tendency toward a particular preference, usually (though not always) characterized as either positive or negative.

discovery A stage of pretrial litigation in which the plaintiff and defendant have the right to learn what information the other side has about the case by requesting documents or materials, access to property, and/or examinations, or by offering answers to questions about the litigation either in written form or verbally at a deposition.

discretionary spending Forms of federal government spending that Congress can modify or eliminate in any given year, including spending on education, the environment, and national defense.

dissenting opinion The opinion of one or more justices who disagree with the result reached by the majority.

distributive tax policies Taxation policies intended to promote the interests of all classes equally.

divided government Split-party control of Congress and the presidency.

domino theory The theory that held that communist takeovers of countries in Southeast Asia and elsewhere would be followed by subsequent communist takeovers of nearby countries.

double jeopardy clause The constitutional protection that those accused of a crime cannot be tried twice for the same crime.

dual federalism The doctrine of federalism that holds that state authority acts as a significant limit on congressional power under the Constitution.

economic equality May be defined as providing all groups the equality of opportunity for economic success, or as the equality of results. In the United States, the latter has been the more common understanding of economic equality.

economic interest group An organized group that exists to promote favorable economic conditions and economic opportunities for its members.

elections The political mechanism that ensures that the majority will rule.

Electoral College The constitutional mechanism by which presidents are chosen. Each state is allocated Electoral College votes based on the sum of that state's U.S. senators and House members.

electors Individuals appointed to represent a state's presidential vote in the Electoral College; in practice, voters in presidential elections vote for a slate of electors committed to a particular candidate, rather than voting directly for the candidate.

enumerated powers Those powers granted to Congress that are listed in the Constitution, including exclusive federal powers as well as concurrent powers shared with the states.

equal time rule The FCC mandate that radio and TV broadcast stations offer equal amounts of airtime to all political candidates who want to broadcast advertisements.

establishment clause The clause in the First Amendment that prohibits government from enacting any law "respecting an establishment of religion." Separationist interpretations of this clause affirm that government should not support any religious activity. Accommodationists say that support for a religion is legal provided that all religions are equally supported.

ex post facto law A law that punishes someone for an act that took place in the past, at a time when the act was not illegal. The Constitution denies government the ability to write laws ex post facto.

exclusionary rule The legal rule requiring that all evidence illegally obtained by police in violation of the Bill of Rights must be "excluded" from admission in a court of law, where it might have assisted in convicting those accused of committing crimes.

executive agreement A pact reached between the president and a foreign government that does not require the consent of Congress.

Executive Office of the President The staffers who help the president of the United States manage the rest of the federal bureaucracy.

executive orders Rules or regulations issued by the chief executive that have the force of law and do not require the consent of Congress.

expansionism Doctrine that favors a country expanding its own territory and influence.

Federal Election Campaign Act (FECA) The federal legislation passed in 1971 that established disclosure requirements and restricted individual campaign contributions.

Federal Election Commission (FEC) The agency created in 1974 to enforce federal election laws.

Federal Register The journal that publishes regulations that implement federal programs.

Federal Reserve Board The Federal Reserve System's board of governors, which votes on monetary policy in the United States, supervises the nation's banks by setting rules for the 12 Federal Reserve Banks, and engages in open market operations.

federalism The doctrine underlying a system of government in which power is divided between a central government and constituent political subunits.

Federalist Papers A series of articles authored by Alexander Hamilton, James Madison, and John Jay that argued in favor of ratifying the proposed constitution of the United States; the Federalist Papers outlined the philosophy and motivation of the document.

Federalists Those who supported ratification of the proposed constitution of the United States between 1787 and 1789.

Fifteenth Amendment The 1870 amendment to the Constitution that guaranteed the franchise regardless of race, color, or previous condition of servitude.

filibuster The action by a single senator or a minority of senators to block a bill from passage by refusing to end discussion. Under modern Senate rules, not all legislation or presidential appointments are subject to the filibuster.

fiscal policy Decisions by the federal government that relate to raising revenue through taxation and spending the revenue that is thereby generated.

flat tax A tax that draws money from all entities at the same proportion of their income.

Fourteenth Amendment The 1868 amendment that granted full U.S. and state citizenship to all people born or naturalized in the United States and guaranteed to each person "the equal protection of the laws."

franchise The right to vote.

franking privilege The traditional right of members of Congress to mail materials to their constituents without paying postage.

free exercise clause The religious freedom clause in the First Amendment that denies government the ability to prohibit the free exercise of religion. Debate over the clause has largely focused on whether government laws can force adherents of a certain religion to engage in activities that are prohibited by their religious beliefs or prevent them from performing acts that are compelled by their religious beliefs.

free rider An individual who does not join or contribute to an interest group that is representing his or her interests.

frontloading The recent trend of states moving their primaries and caucuses to earlier in the year to attract greater attention from the candidates and the media.

full faith and credit clause The provision in Article IV, Section 1 of the Constitution that forces states to abide by the official acts and proceedings of all other states.

gerrymandering The drawing of House district boundaries to the benefit of one political party over another. The term is named for Elbridge Gerry, a Massachusetts delegate to the Constitutional Convention, who (as governor) redrew districts in this fashion to favor the Democratic-Republicans.

Gibbons v. Ogden (1824) The Supreme Court case that held that under the Constitution, a federal license to operate steamboats overrides a state-granted monopoly of New York water rights.

good faith exception An exception to the exclusionary rule stating that if a search warrant is invalid through no fault of the police, evidence obtained under that warrant may still be admitted into court.

government The collection of public institutions in a nation that establish and enforce the rules by which the members of that nation must live.

government corporations Units in the federal bureaucracy set up to run like private companies that depend on revenue from citizens to provide their services.

grand jury A jury whose duty it is to hear the evidence offered by a prosecutor and determine whether a trial is justified.

grandfather clause requirement Need for proof that one's grandfather had previously voted in order to be eligible to vote.

grants-in-aid Grants from the federal government to states that allow state governments to pursue specific federal policies, such as highway construction.

grassroots lobbying Communications by interest groups with government officials through the mobilization of public opinion to exert influence on government action.

Great Compromise A proposal also known as the "Connecticut Compromise" that provided for a bicameral legislature featuring an upper house based on equal representation among the states and a lower house whose membership was based on each state's population; approved by a 5–4 vote of the state delegations.

Great Society A set of aggressive federal domestic policies proposed by President Lyndon Johnson and passed by Congress in the 1960s that further enhanced the role of the presidency.

gross domestic product (GDP) An estimate of the total money value of all the goods and services produced in the United States in a one-year period.

hard money Donations made directly to political candidates and their campaigns that must be declared with the name of the donor (which then becomes public knowledge).

hawks Members of the president's administration who call for aggressive military actions wherever hostile forces may be found.

impeachment The first step in a two-step process outlined in Article II, Section 4, of the U.S. Constitution to remove a president or other high official from office. The House of Representatives, by majority vote, may impeach if the official has committed "Treason, Bribery, or other high Crimes and Misdemeanors." The second step requires a conviction in the Senate by a two-thirds vote.

incorporation The process by which the U.S. Supreme Court used the due process clause of the Fourteenth Amendment to make most of the individual rights guaranteed by the Bill of Rights also applicable to the states. Incorporation provided that state and local governments, as well as the federal government, could not deny these rights to citizens.

incumbent race General election race pitting a person currently holding the office against a challenger.

independent agencies Departments that focus on a narrower set of issues than do higher-status cabinet departments.

independent campaign expenditures Political donations that PACs or individuals spend to support campaigns but do not directly contribute to the campaigns.

indictment A decision by a grand jury authorizing the government to proceed to trial against the defendant.

individualism The value that individuals are primarily responsible for their own lot in life and that promotes and rewards individual initiative and responsibility. This value underlies America's reliance on a capitalist economy and free market system.

inflation The overall general upward price movement of goods and services in an economy, normally measured by the consumer price index (CPI).

inquisitorial system A system of justice in which the court (in the form of one or more judges) is actively involved in investigating the facts of the case.

intensity (of public opinion) The degree of strength or commitment the public feels about the opinion it holds.

interest group An organization of people with shared goals that tries to influence public policy through a variety of activities.

intergovernmental lobby Any interest group that represents the collective interests of states, cities, and other governments.

international organization Entity of international scope or character, usually established by treaty, such as the World Bank or the International Monetary Fund.

internationalism Doctrine that favors active participation of the nation in collective arrangements that secure the political independence and territorial boundaries of other countries.

invisible primary The competition among candidates seeking the party nomination for frontrunner status prior to the primaries and caucuses.

iron triangle A three-sided network of policy-making that includes congressional committees (and subcommittees) in a specific policy area, executive agencies with authority over that area, and private interest groups focused on influencing that area.

isolationism Foreign policy doctrine that opposes intervention in distant wars and involvement in permanent military alliances.

issue and ideological group An organized group that focuses on specific issues and ideological perspectives.

issue network The broad array of actors (beyond just the iron triangle) that try to collectively influence a policy area in which they maintain a vested interest.

Jim Crow laws Laws used by some southern states that required segregation of nonwhites and whites in public schools, railroads, buses, restaurants, hotels, theaters, and other public facilities. The laws excluded nonwhites from militias and denied them certain education and welfare services.

Joint Chiefs of Staff (JCS) Group of chief officers of the four branches of the armed forces as well as a JCS chair and vice chair, which advises the president on military matters and delivers the president's orders to the military.

joint committee A committee composed of members of both the House and the Senate that is investigative in nature.

judicial review The power of a court to declare acts of the other branches of government or of a subordinate government to be unconstitutional and thus invalid.

***Katz* test** The legal standard that requires the government to attain a warrant demonstrating "probable cause" for any "search" that violates a person's actual and reasonable expectation of privacy.

Keynesian economic theory Fiscal policy theory that favors government taxation and spending during difficult economic times.

laissez-faire economics Fiscal policy theory that favors minimal intervention in the nation's economy.

layer-cake federalism Description of federalism as maintaining that the authority of state and federal governments exists in distinct and separate spheres.

legitimacy The extent to which the people afford the government the authority and right to exercise power.

Lemon test The legal test that determines if a government statute aiding public or private schools is an unconstitutional violation of the establishment clause. The statute is unconstitutional if the statute has no secular purpose, if its principal or primary effect advances or inhibits religion, or if it fosters "an excessive government entanglement with religion."

libel Printing or disseminating false statements that harm someone.

liberal ideology A political orientation that favors a more assertive role in the redistribution of economic resources but emphasizes individual freedom on a range of social issues.

limited government The value that promotes the idea that government power should be as restricted as possible.

literacy test The requirement that individuals prove that they can read and write before being allowed to vote.

litigation Any judicial contest, including all the events that lead up to a possible court event.

lobbying The means by which interest groups attempt to influence government officials to make decisions favorable to their goals.

logrolling The trading of influence or votes among legislators to achieve passage of projects that are of interest to one another.

loose construction Constitutional interpretation that gives constitutional provisions broad and open-ended meanings.

majoritarianism The theory that public policy is a product of what majorities of citizens prefer.

majority caucus The members of the party that has the majority of seats in a particular chamber.

majority leader In the Senate, the controlling party's main spokesperson who leads his or her party in proposing new laws and crafting the party's platform. The Senate majority leader also enjoys the power to make committee assignments. In the House, the majority leader is the controlling party's second in command, who helps the Speaker to oversee the development of the party platform.

majority opinion The opinion of a majority of members of the U.S. Supreme Court, which carries the force of law.

majority rule The notion that the will of the majority should guide decisions made by American government.

majority-minority district A congressional district drawn with geographic boundaries that promote the chances of electing a minority member to represent that district.

mandatory spending Federal government spending that is not controlled by annual budget decisions; includes entitlements such as Medicare and Social Security.

manifest destiny U.S. policy of the mid-nineteenth century that advocated acquiring lands and occupying the entire American continent from one ocean to the other.

marble-cake federalism Description of federalism as intertwining state and federal authority in an inseparable mixture.

marginal seat A seat in a congressional district that has relatively similar numbers of Democratic and Republican voters.

Martin v. Hunter's Lessee (1816) The Supreme Court case that established that state governments and state courts must abide by the U.S. Supreme Court's interpretation of the federal Constitution.

material benefits (of group membership) The specific, tangible benefits individuals receive from interest-group membership, such as economic concessions, discounts on products, and so forth.

McCulloch v. Maryland (1819) The Supreme Court case that established that Congress enjoys broad and extensive authority to make all laws that are "necessary and proper" to carry out its constitutionally delegated powers.

Medicaid Federal program that provides limited health care services to the poor.

Medicare Federal program that provides health insurance for the elderly.

Mendez v. Westminster (1947) The federal court decision that ended the segregation of Mexican Americans in California primary schools.

merit system A system of appointing and promoting civil service personnel based on merit rather than political affiliation or loyalty.

midterm congressional elections Congressional elections held midway between successive presidential elections.

military-industrial complex The vast network of defense industries in America (including manufacturers of weapons, missiles, aircraft, and so forth) and their allies in the federal bureaucracy.

minimal effects theory The theory that deep-seated, long-term political attitudes have much greater influence on an individual's vote decisions than does news media coverage.

minority caucus The members of the party that has a minority of seats in a particular chamber.

minority leader The leader of the minority party in each chamber.

Miranda warning The U.S. Supreme Court's requirement that an individual who is arrested must be read a statement that explains the person's right to remain silent and the right to an attorney.

monarchy A form of government in which one person, usually a member of a royal family or a royal designate, exercises supreme authority.

monetary policy Regulation of the money supply and interest rates by a central bank, such as the U.S. Federal Reserve Board, in order to control inflation and stabilize the currency.

Monroe Doctrine U.S. foreign policy that proclaimed North and South America unavailable for future colonization by any European power and that declared that any such colonization would be viewed as an act of war on the United States.

Motor Voter law The federal law mandating that when an individual applies for or renews a state driver's license, the state must also provide that individual with voter registration materials.

multiparty system A political system in which many different parties are organized on the basis of political ideologies, economic interests, religion, geography, or positions on a single issue or set of issues.

national committee The committee that oversees the conduct of a party's presidential campaign and develops strategy for congressional elections.

national committee chair The head of the national committee for one of the two major parties.

national debt The total sum of the federal government's outstanding debt obligations.

national party convention A large meeting that draws together party delegates from across the nation to choose (or formally affirm the selection of) the party's presidential and vice presidential candidates.

national party organization The institution through which political parties exist at the national, state, and local levels, primarily focused on articulating policy positions, raising money, organizing volunteers, and providing services to candidates.

National Security Council (NSC) Advisory body to the president charged with coordinating information about foreign, military, and economic policies that affect national security.

national supremacy doctrine Chief Justice John Marshall's interpretation of federalism as holding that states have extremely limited sovereign authority, whereas Congress is supreme within its own sphere of constitutional authority.

natural law According to John Locke, the most fundamental type of law, which supersedes any law that is made by government. Citizens are born with certain natural rights (including life, liberty, and property) that derive from this law and that government cannot take away.

necessary and proper clause The clause in Article I, Section 8 of the Constitution that affords Congress the power to make laws that serve as a means to achieving its expressly delegated powers.

New Deal A set of aggressive federal domestic policies proposed by President Franklin Delano Roosevelt in the 1930s and passed by Congress as a response to the Great Depression; it ultimately transformed the presidency into an institution marked by permanent bureaucracies and well-established repositories of power.

New Jersey Plan A proposal known also as the "small states plan" that would have retained the Articles of Confederation's principle of a legislature where states enjoyed equal representation.

new media Media outlets that rely on relatively newer technologies for communicating, such as the internet, DVDs, fax machines, cell phones, satellites, cable TV, and broadband.

new world order President George H. W. Bush's description of the post–Cold War world, in which nations would work together for the purpose of securing collective peace, security, freedom, and the rule of law.

NFIB v. Sebelius (2012) The Supreme Court case that upheld as constitutional the bulk of the Patient Protection and Affordable Care Act (aka Obamacare), including the requirement that certain individuals pay a financial penalty for not obtaining health insurance.

Nineteenth Amendment The constitutional amendment that guarantees women equal voting rights.

nomination campaign The political season in which the two major parties hold primaries and caucuses in all the states to choose party delegates committed to specific candidates.

noneconomic interest group An organized group that advocates for reasons other than its membership's commercial and financial interests.

normal vote The percentage of voters that can be expected with reasonable certainty to cast a ballot for each of the two major political parties.

North Atlantic Treaty Organization (NATO) A military, political, and economic alliance of nations formally bound to protect self-determination and open trade in Western Europe.

objectivity The journalistic standard that news reporting of events must be factual, accurate, fair, and equitable.

oligarchy A form of government in which a small exclusive class, which may or may not attempt to rule on behalf of the people as a whole, holds supreme power.

open election General election race in which neither candidate is the incumbent. (Open elections for Congress are normally called *open-seat elections.*)

open primary An election that allows voters to choose on the day of the primary election the party in which they want to vote.

open rule A rule of procedure adopted by the House Rules Committee that permits amendments to a bill.

open shop The law that allows employees the option of joining or not joining the certified union at a unionized workplace.

original jurisdiction The authority of a court to be the initial court in which a legal decision is rendered.

outlays The amount of money a government agency will actually spend during a fiscal year.

overriding (a veto) The power of the Congress to enact legislation despite a president's veto of that legislation; requires a two-thirds vote of both houses of Congress.

pardon The president's constitutional authority to relieve an individual of both the punishment and the guilt of violating the law.

partisan press era The period from the late 1700s to the mid-1800s when newspapers typically supported a particular political party.

party identification The psychological attachment that an individual has to a particular party.

party platform A document outlining the party's position on important policy issues.

Patient Protection and Affordable Care Act of 2010 (PPACA, aka "Obamacare") The main federal legislation passed in 2010 that overhauled the health care system by expanding Medicaid and guaranteeing health care coverage for select groups of citizens.

patronage The act of appointing people to government positions in return for their partisan and/or political support.

Pendleton Civil Service Reform Act The 1883 law that created a merit system for hiring many federal workers, protected them from being fired for partisan reasons, and set up a Civil Service Commission to oversee the hiring and firing process.

plaintiff The party that chooses to initiate formal legal proceedings in a civil case.

plea bargain A pretrial negotiated resolution in a criminal case in which the defendants seek to reduce their jail sentences by pleading guilty and in return prosecutors are willing to trade down the severity of the punishment.

Plessy v. Ferguson (1896) The Supreme Court case that upheld a Louisiana segregation law on the theory that as long as the accommodations between the racially segregated facilities were equal, the equal protection clause was not violated. The Court's ruling effectively established the constitutionality of racial segregation and the notion of "separate but equal."

pluralism The theory that public policy largely results from a variety of interest groups competing with one another to promote laws that benefit members of their respective groups.

pocket veto The indirect veto of a bill received by the president within 10 days of the adjournment of Congress, effected by the president's retaining the bill unsigned until Congress adjourns.

policy implementation The process of carrying out laws, and the specific programs or services outlined in those laws.

political action committee (PAC) The political arm of an interest group that promotes candidates in election campaigns primarily through financial contributions.

political culture The values and beliefs about government, its purpose, and its operations and institutions that are widely held among citizens in a society; it defines the essence of how a society thinks politically and is transmitted from one generation to the next.

political equality A condition in which members of different groups possess substantially the same rights to participate actively in the political system. In the United States, these rights include voting, running for office, petitioning the government for redress of grievances, free speech, free press, and the access to an education.

political ideology A philosophical guide that people use to help translate their values and beliefs into political preferences.

political orientations The translation of values and beliefs into a systematic way of assessing the political environment.

political parties Organizations that seek to win elections for the purpose of influencing the outputs of government.

political preferences The attitudes people maintain regarding the performance of political leaders and institutions, their candidate preferences in elections, and specific policy issues.

political socialization The process by which an individual acquires values, beliefs, and opinions about politics.

politics The way in which the institutions of government are organized to make laws, rules, and policies, and how those institutions are influenced.

poll tax Fee a voter had to pay before being allowed to vote.

popular sovereignty The idea that the ultimate source of power in the nation is held by the people.

pork-barrel legislation A government project or appropriation that yields jobs or other benefits to a specific locale and patronage opportunities to its political representative.

power The ability to get individuals to do something that they may not otherwise do, such as pay taxes, stop for red lights, or submit to a search before boarding an airplane.

power of appointment The president's constitutional power to hire and fire those charged with administrative authority to help execute federal laws, such as ambassadors; federal judges, including those on the Supreme Court; and all other federal officers under the president's charge. Most of these appointments require the consent of the Senate.

power of incumbency The phenomenon by which incumbent members of Congress running for reelection are returned to office at an extremely high rate.

preemption The constitutional doctrine that holds that when Congress acts affirmatively in the exercise of its own granted power, federal laws supersede all state laws on the matter.

prenomination campaign The political season in which candidates for president begin to explore the possibility of running by attempting to raise money and garner support.

president pro tempore In the absence of the vice president, the senator who presides over the Senate session. By tradition, this is usually the senator from the majority caucus who has served the longest number of consecutive years in the Senate.

presidential primary A statewide election to select delegates who will represent a state at the party's national convention.

primacy tendency The theory that impressions acquired while an individual is younger are likely to be more influential and longer lasting.

prior restraint The government's requirement that material be approved by government before it can be published.

privatization The process of replacing government-provided services with services provided by the private sector.

progressive tax A tax whose effective rate on an individual's income increases as the person's income rises.

property requirements Need for some form of property-owning and residency documentation to be eligible to vote.

proportional representation A system of electing a national legislature in which the percentage of the vote that a party receives is reflected in the number of seats that the party occupies.

pseudo-poll Phone calls from members of political campaigns or PACs who present themselves as pollsters for the purpose of planting messages with voters rather than measuring public opinion.

public opinion The summation of individual opinions on any particular issue or topic.

public opinion poll A method of measuring the opinions of a large group of people by asking questions of a subset of the larger group and then generalizing the findings to the larger group.

public policy The set of laws, regulations, and rules that affect the whole of society.

public-interest group An organized group that promotes the broad, collective good of citizens and consumers.

purposive benefits (of group membership) Rewards that do not directly benefit the individual member, but benefit society as a whole.

racial profiling The law enforcement practice of taking race into account when identifying possible suspects of crimes.

random-digit dialing (RDD) A probability technique for scientific telephone polling that randomly assigns the last four digits to known information about telephone area codes and exchanges.

realists Members of the president's administration who advocate diplomacy as the primary means of protecting U.S. interests abroad.

reapportionment The allocation of a fixed number of House seats to the states.

recession An economic slowdown characterized by high unemployment, reduced productivity, or other negative economic indicators.

redistributive tax policies Taxation policies that aim to provide a social safety net to meet the minimum physical needs of citizens.

redistricting The act of redrawing congressional boundaries to achieve equal representation in each of the congressional districts.

regressive tax A tax that charges individuals the same amount, regardless of income.

regulations Rules or other directives issued by government agencies.

regulatory agencies Government bodies responsible for the control and supervision of specified activities or areas of public interest.

reporting legislation The exclusive power of standing committees to forward legislation to the full House or Senate. Neither chamber can vote on a bill unless the committee votes to approve it first.

representative democracy A form of government designed by the U.S. Constitution: Free, open, and regular elections allow voters to choose those who govern on their behalf; it is also referred to as *indirect democracy* or a *republican* form of government.

reprieve The president's constitutional authority to reduce the severity of a punishment without removing the guilt for those who have violated the law.

reserved powers Those powers expressly retained by the state governments under the Constitution.

retrospective voting A theory on voting behavior suggesting that voter evaluations of an incumbent's past performance provide important cues to voters in deciding whether to vote for that incumbent again.

Rules Committee A committee in the House of Representatives that determines the rules by which bills will come to the floor, be debated, and so on.

safe seat A congressional seat from a district that includes a high percentage of voters from one of the major parties.

sampling error The amount of error in a poll that results from interviewing a sample of people rather than the whole population under study; the larger the sample, the less the sampling error.

scientific sample A randomly selected subgroup drawn from a population using probability theory.

select committee A committee established by a resolution in either the House or the Senate for a specific purpose and, usually, for a limited time.

Senior Executive Service (SES) Since the late 1970s, a defined group of approximately 7,500 career professionals in the federal bureaucracy who provide continuity in the operations of the bureaucracy from one presidential administration to the next.

separation of powers The principle that each branch of government enjoys separate and independent powers and areas of responsibility.

Shays's Rebellion Armed uprising by debt-ridden Massachusetts farmers frustrated with the state government.

SLAPS test A standard that courts established to determine if material is obscene based in part on whether the material has serious literary, artistic, political, or scientific value. If it does, then the material is not obscene.

social capital The "social connectedness" of a community, or the extent to which individuals are socially integrated into their community.

social contract From the philosophy of Jean-Jacques Rousseau, an agreement people make with one another to form a government and abide by its rules and laws, and, in return, the government promises to protect the people's rights and welfare and promote their best interests.

social equality Equality and fair treatment of all groups within the various institutions in society, both public and private, that serve the public at large, including in stores, theaters, restaurants, hotels, and public transportation facilities, among many other operations open to the public.

social learning theory The theory that viewers imitate what they view on television through observational learning.

social movements A large informal grouping of individuals and/or organizations focused on specific political or social issues.

socialism Economic system in which all or most of the means of production are owned by the community as a whole.

soft money Money not donated directly to a candidate's campaign but rather to a political advocacy group or a political party for "party-building" activities.

solicitor general The lawyer representing the U.S. government before the U.S. Supreme Court.

solidary benefits (of group membership) Satisfaction that individuals receive from interacting with like-minded individuals for a cause.

sovereignty The supreme political power of a government to regulate its affairs without outside interference.

Speaker of the House The leader of the House of Representatives, responsible for assigning new bills to committees, recognizing members to speak in the House chamber, and assigning chairs of committees.

spoils system The postelection practice of rewarding loyal supporters of the winning candidates and party with appointive public offices.

standing The requirement that a party must be uniquely or singularly affected by a controversy in order to be eligible to file a lawsuit.

standing committee A permanent committee that exists in both the House and Senate; most standing committees focus on a particular substantive area of public policy, such as transportation, labor, foreign affairs, and the federal budget.

stare decisis A Latin term meaning "stand by the decision" that has already been settled by the court.

State of the Union address An annual speech that the president delivers to Congress laying out the status of the nation and offering suggestions for new legislation.

straw poll An unscientific poll that gathers the opinions of people who are conveniently available in a gathering place, such as a shopping center.

strict construction Constitutional interpretation that limits the government to only those powers explicitly stated in the Constitution.

strict scrutiny A legal standard set in *Brown v. Board of Education* for cases related to racial discrimination that tends to invalidate almost all state laws that segregate racial groups.

supply-side economics Economic theory that favors cutting taxes as a way of increasing economic productivity.

supremacy clause The provision in Article VI, Clause 2 of the Constitution that provides that the Constitution and federal laws override any conflicting provisions in state constitutions or state laws.

symbolic speech Nonspoken forms of speech that might be protected by the First Amendment, such as flag-burning, wearing armbands at school to protest a war, or camping out in public parks to protest the plight of the homeless.

talk radio A specialized form of radio programming in which one or more hosts provide commentary and often invite listeners to call in to the show and offer their own opinions.

theocracy A form of government in which a particular religion or faith plays a dominant role in the government.

Thirteenth Amendment (ratified in 1865) Banished slavery from all states and U.S. territories.

Three-Fifths Compromise A compromise proposal in which five slaves would be counted as the equivalent of three free people for purposes of taxes and representation.

Title IX The section of the Federal Educational Amendments Law of 1972 that prohibits the exclusion of women from an educational program or activity receiving financial assistance from the federal government. Courts have interpreted those provisions to force colleges and universities to provide as many athletic teams for women as they do for men.

trade association A business association that focuses on one particular industry, with membership drawn exclusively from that industry.

Truman Doctrine Doctrine articulated by President Harry Truman in the late 1940s by which money and resources were provided to support and sustain noncommunist governments in areas strategically vital to the United States.

Twenty-fourth Amendment A 1964 constitutional amendment that banned poll taxes in federal elections.

Twenty-second Amendment Passed in 1951, this constitutional amendment restricts any one person from being elected to the presidency "more than twice," or from acting as president for longer than two and a half terms.

Twenty-sixth Amendment The constitutional amendment that lowered the voting age to 18 in all local, state, and federal elections.

Twenty-third Amendment The constitutional amendment providing electoral votes to the District of Columbia, thus giving DC residents the right to vote in presidential elections.

two presidencies theory Theory articulated by political scientist Aaron Wildavsky that posits the existence of a more powerful presidency in foreign affairs and a more limited presidency in the domestic sphere.

two-party system A political party system dominated by two major parties that win the vast majority of elections.

union shop The law that requires that employees in unionized workplaces either join the union or pay the equivalent of union dues to it after a set period of time.

unit rule The system in 48 states by which the candidate who wins the most votes among popular votes cast for president in a state receives all the electoral votes from that state; also known as the "winner-take-all" system.

unitary system of government A system of government in which the constituent states are strictly subordinated to the goals of the central government as a whole.

United Nations (UN) International organization formed after World War II to promote and maintain international security and peace.

universal suffrage The idea that all citizens in a nation have the right to vote.

unscientific poll A poll in which the sample of people interviewed is not representative of any group beyond those who register their opinion.

values and beliefs The broad principles underlying the American political culture that citizens support and adhere to.

veto The constitutional procedure by which the president refuses to approve a bill or joint resolution and thus prevents its enactment into law.

Virginia Plan A proposal known also as the "large states plan" that empowered three separate branches of government, including a legislature with membership proportional to population.

voter turnout The number of people who turn out to vote as a percentage of all those eligible to vote.

Voting Rights Act of 1965 The federal law that invalidated literacy tests and property requirements and required select states and cities to apply for permission to the Justice Department to change their voting laws. As a consequence, millions of African Americans were effectively re-enfranchised in the South.

War Powers Resolution Largely ignored congressional policy that restricts the president's power to engage in war except (1) when Congress has declared war, (2) when Congress has specifically granted the president permission to use armed forces, or (3) when the nation is under attack. The resolution further requires the president to report to Congress whenever American forces are entered into hostilities.

warrant A document issued by a judge or magistrate that allows law enforcement to search or seize items at a home, business, or anywhere else that might be specified.

welfare state Social system in which the state assumes a considerable degree of responsibility for citizens in matters of health care, employment, education, and retirement income.

whips (majority and minority) Member of Congress elected by his or her party to count potential votes and promote party unity in voting.

White House chief of staff The manager of the White House staff, which serves the president's organizational needs, including speechwriting, advance work for presidential appearances, scheduling, congressional relations, public relations, and communications.

White House Office of Legislative Affairs A presidential office that serves as a liaison between the president and Congress. This office helps the president develop the strategy used to promote passage of the president's legislative agenda.

White House press secretary The person on the White House staff who plays an especially important role in briefing the press, organizing news conferences, and even briefing the president on questions that may be asked.

white-only primaries Restricted political party primaries that did not allow African Americans and other people of color to participate in choosing nominees for the general election.

writ of certiorari The formal term for an order by which the Supreme Court acts in its discretion to review a case from a lower court.

NOTES

CHAPTER 1

1. See Thomas Hobbes, *Leviathan* (London, UK: A. Crooke, 1651).
2. For a collection of Rousseau's work, see Jean-Jacques Rousseau, *The Social Contract and Discourses*, translation and commentary by G. D. H. Cole (London, UK: Guernsey Press, 1983).
3. Harold Lasswell, *Politics: Who Gets What, When and How* (New York, NY: McGraw-Hill, 1936).
4. John Locke, *Two Treatises of Government*, ed. Peter Laslett (Cambridge, UK: Cambridge University Press, 1960).
5. Alexis de Tocqueville, *Democracy in America*, 1835, ed. Richard Hefner (New York, NY: Penguin Books, 1956).
6. Craig K. Elwell, Marc Labonte, and Wayne M. Morrison, "Is China a Threat to the U.S. Economy?" *Congressional Research Service Report*, no. RL33604, January 23, 2007, www.fas.org/sgp/crs/row/RL33604.pdf.
7. Ruchir Sharma, "China Slows Down, and Grows Up," *New York Times*, April 26, 2012.

CHAPTER 2

1. Fred Anderson, *The War That Made America: A Short History of the French-Indian War* (New York, NY: Viking, 2005).
2. Robert Middlekauff, *The Glorious Cause* (New York, NY: Oxford University Press, 1982).
3. *The Political Writings of Thomas Paine, Vol. 1* (Boston, MA: J. P. Mendum Investigator Office, 1870).
4. Pauline Maier, *American Scripture: Making the Declaration of Independence* (New York, NY: Vintage, 1998).
5. Merrill Jensen, *The Articles of Confederation: An Interpretation of the Social-Constitutional History of the American Revolution, 1774–1781* (Madison: University of Wisconsin Press, 1959).
6. For an account of Massachusetts public policy during this period, see Van Beck Hall, *Politics without Parties: Massachusetts 1780–1791* (Pittsburgh: University of Pittsburgh Press, 1972).
7. Robert Gross, ed., *In Debt to Shays* (Charlottesville: University of Virginia Press, 1993).
8. Christopher Collier, *Decision in Philadelphia: The Constitutional Convention of 1787* (New York, NY: Ballantine Books, 2007).
9. For a discussion of the Founders' silence on slavery, see Joseph Ellis, *Founding Brothers* (New York, NY: Knopf, 2000), 81–119.
10. Jacob E. Cooke, ed., *The Federalist* (Middletown, CT: Wesleyan University Press, 1961).
11. Saul Cornell, *The Other Founders: Anti-Federalism and the Dissenting Tradition in America 1788–1828* (Chapel Hill: University of North Carolina Press, 1999).
12. Henry Mayer, *A Son of Thunder: Patrick Henry and the American Republic* (Charlottesville: University of Virginia Press, 1992).
13. Paul Murphy, *The Historic Background of the Bill of Rights* (New York, NY: Taylor & Francis, 1990).
14. See Jefferson–Madison correspondence republished in Philip Kurland, ed., *The Founders' Constitution* (Indianapolis, IN: Liberty Fund, 2000).
15. There may be numerous legal problems implicated by the holding of such a convention, as noted in Russell Caplan, *Constitutional Brinksmanship: Amending the Constitution by National Convention* (New York, NY: Oxford University Press, 1988). See also John R. Vile, *The Alternate Article V Mechanism for Proposing Amendments to the U.S. Constitution* (Athens: University of Georgia Press, 2016).
16. One of the better works on Marshall's tenure at the Court is R. Kent Newmyer, *John Marshall and the Heroic Age of the Supreme Court* (Baton Rouge: Louisiana State University Press, 2002).
17. 17 U.S. 316 (1819).
18. Justice Antonin Scalia, interview with *60 Minutes* (episode aired April 27, 2008), www.cbsnews.com/news/justice-scalia-on-the-record/.
19. Lawrence Tribe, *Constitutional Choices* (Cambridge, MA: Harvard University Press, 2004).
20. John Hart Ely, *Democracy and Distrust* (Cambridge, MA: Harvard University Press, 1980).
21. Obergefell v. Hodges, 576 U.S. _____ (2015).
22. 5 U.S. 137 (1803).

CHAPTER 3

1. 372 U.S. 335 (1963).
2. 567 U.S. 519 (2012).
3. Stanley R. Sloan, *NATO, The European Union and the Atlantic Community: The Transatlantic Bargain Reconsidered* (New York, NY: Rowman & Littlefield, 2002).
4. See McCulloch v. Maryland, 17 U.S. 316 (1819).
5. 14 U.S. 304 (1816).
6. 576 U.S. _____, 135 S. Ct. 2584 (2015).
7. For example, in Supreme Court of New Hampshire v. Piper, 470 U.S. 274 (1985), the Supreme Court interpreted the privileges and immunities clause of Article IV to forbid states from excluding nonresidents from admission to the practice of law.
8. See New Jersey v. New York, 523 U.S. 767 (1998).
9. Stanley Elkins and Eric McKitrick, *The Age of Federalism: The Early American Republic 1788–1800* (New York, NY: Oxford University Press, 1995).
10. 17 U.S. 316 (1819).
11. 22 U.S. 1 (1824).
12. H. W. Brands, *Andrew Jackson: His Life and Times* (New York, NY: Doubleday, 2005).
13. Railroad Retirement Board v. Alton Railroad Co., 295 U.S. 330 (1935); Carter v. Carter Coal Co., 298 U.S. 238 (1936).

14. William E. Leuchtenburg, *The Supreme Court Reborn: The Constitutional Revolution in the Age of Roosevelt* (New York, NY: Oxford University Press, 1995).
15. Heart of Atlanta Motel v. United States, 379 U.S. 241 (1964); Katzenbach v. McClung, 379 U.S. 294 (1964).
16. 483 U.S. 203 (1987).
17. For an application of the term to welfare policy, see Pamela Winston, *Welfare Policymaking in the States: The Devil in Devolution* (Washington, DC: Georgetown University Press, 2002).
18. 514 U.S. 549 (1995).
19. 529 U.S. 598 (2000).
20. National Federation of Independent Business v. Sebelius, 567 U.S. _____, 132 S. CT. 2566 (2012).
21. John T. Noonan Jr., *Narrowing the Nation's Power: The Supreme Court Sides with the States* (Berkeley: University of California Press, 2003).
22. New State Ice Co. v. Liebmann, 285 U.S. 262, 311 (1932).
23. See Gloria G. Guzman, "Household Income: 2017," *American Community Survey Briefs*, no. 17-01, U.S. Census Bureau, September 2018, https://www.census.gov/content/dam/Census/library/publications/2018/acs/acsbr17-01.pdf

CHAPTER 4

1. Antonin Scalia, "Law and the Winds of Change." Remarks made at the 24th Australian Legal Convention, Perth, West Australia, September 21, 1987.
2. Alexander Hamilton, James Madison, and John Jay, *The Federalist Papers*, ed. Clinton Rossiter (New York, NY: New American Library, 1971).
3. Jefferson–Madison correspondence in Philip Kurland, ed., *The Founders' Constitution* (Indianapolis: Liberty Fund, 2000).
4. 32 U.S. 243 (1833).
5. Thomas Jefferson first coined that phrase in a letter he wrote as president to the Baptists of Danbury, Connecticut, in 1802. George Seldes, ed., *The Great Quotations* (Secaucus, NJ: Citadel Press, 1983), 369.
6. 319 U.S. 624 (1943).
7. 374 U.S. 398 (1963).
8. 406 U.S. 205 (1972).
9. 98 U.S. 145 (1878).
10. 494 U.S. 872 (1990).
11. Carolyn N. Long, *Religious Freedom and Indian Rights: The Case of Oregon v. Smith* (Lawrence: University Press of Kansas, 2000).
12. Noah Feldman, *Divided by God* (New York, NY: Farrar, Straus and Giroux, 2005).
13. 482 U.S. 578 (1987).
14. 370 U.S. 421 (1962).
15. 374 U.S. 203 (1963).
16. 472 U.S. 38 (1985).
17. 536 U.S. 639 (2002).
18. 403 U.S. 602 (1971).
19. 505 U.S. 577 (1992).
20. 530 U.S. 290 (2000).
21. 249 U.S. 247 (1919).
22. 304 U.S. 144 (1938).
23. 395 U.S. 444 (1969).
24. Harry Kalven, *A Worthy Tradition: Freedom of Speech in America* (New York, NY: Harper & Row, 1988).
25. 376 U.S. 254 (1964).
26. Anthony Lewis, *Make No Law: The Sullivan Case and the First Amendment* (New York, NY: Vintage Books, 1992).
27. 403 U.S. 713 (1971).
28. 413 U.S. 15 (1973).
29. 521 U.S. 844 (1997).
30. John W. Johnson, *The Struggle for Students' Rights: Tinker v. Des Moines and the 1960s* (Lawrence: University Press of Kansas, 1997).
31. Tinker v. Des Moines, 393 U.S. 503 (1969).
32. 391 U.S. 367 (1968).
33. 491 U.S. 397 (1989).
34. Robert Justin Goldstein, *Flag Burning and Free Speech: The Case of Texas v. Johnson* (Lawrence: University Press of Kansas, 2000).
35. Philippa Strum, *When the Nazis Came to Skokie: Freedom for Speech We Hate* (Lawrence: University Press of Kansas, 1999).
36. 528 U.S. 343 (2003).
37. Milton Heumann and Thomas W. Church, eds., *Hate Speech on Campus* (Boston: Northeastern University Press, 1997).
38. 554 U.S. 570 (2008).
39. 561 U.S. 742 (2010).
40. Lucas A. Powe Jr., *The Warren Court and American Politics* (Cambridge, MA: Belknap Press of Harvard University, 2002).
41. 389 U.S. 347 (1967).
42. 367 U.S. 643 (1961).
43. Kyllo v. United States, 533 U.S. 27 (2001).
44. It should be noted, however, that a majority of states have chosen to use grand juries, even without being compelled to do so by the U.S. Constitution.
45. 384 U.S. 436 (1966).
46. Dickerson v. United States, 530 U.S. 428 (2000).
47. Gary Stuart, *Miranda: The Story of America's Right to Remain Silent* (Tucson: University of Arizona Press, 2004).
48. 372 U.S. 335 (1963).
49. 536 U.S. 304 (2002).
50. Austin Sarat, *When the State Kills* (Princeton, NJ: Princeton University Press, 2002).
51. 381 U.S. 479 (1965).
52. John W. Johnson, *Griswold v. Connecticut: Birth Control and the Constitutional Right of Privacy* (Lawrence: University Press of Kansas, 2005).
53. 410 U.S. 113 (1973).
54. N. E. H. Hull and Peter Charles Hoffer, *Roe v. Wade: The Abortion Rights Controversy in American History* (Lawrence: University Press of Kansas, 2001).
55. 505 U.S. 833 (1992).
56. 550 U.S. 124 (2007).
57. 539 U.S. 558 (2003).
58. Jade Wood and Justin McCarthy, "Majority of Americans Remain Supportive of Euthanasia," Gallup.com, June 12, 2017, https://news.gallup.com/poll/211928/majority-americans-remain-supportive-euthanasia.aspx.

CHAPTER 5

1. Louis R. Harlan, *Booker T. Washington: The Making of a Black Leader* (New York, NY: Oxford University Press, 1975).
2. David Levering Lewis, *W. E. B. DuBois, 1868–1919: Biography of a Race* (New York, NY: Owl Books, 1994).

3. 347 U.S. 483 (1954).

4. 60 U.S. 393 (1857).

5. Eric Foner, *Reconstruction: America's Unfinished Revolution* (New York, NY: Harper, 2000).

6. 83 U.S. 36 (1873).

7. 109 U.S. 3 (1883).

8. 163 U.S. 537 (1896).

9. For a comprehensive account of the NAACP's strategy, see Richard Kluger, *Simple Justice* (New York, NY: Vintage Books, 1975).

10. 161 F.2d 774 (9th Cir. 1947).

11. 358 U.S. 1 (1958).

12. Jennifer Hochschild, *The New American Dilemma: Liberal Democracy and School Desegregation* (New Haven, CT: Yale University Press, 1984).

13. A. W. Geiger, "Many Minority Students Go to Schools Where at Least Half of Their Peers Are Their Race of Ethnicity," Pew Research Center, October 25, 2017, http://www.pewresearch.org/fact-tank/2017/10/25/many-minority-students-go-to-schools-where-at-least-half-of-their-peers-are-their-race-or-ethnicity/

14. 347 U.S. 475 (1954).

15. See Taylor Branch, *Pillar of Fire: America in the King Years, 1963–65* (New York, NY: Simon & Schuster, 1999).

16. For two excellent accounts of the passage of the Civil Rights Act of 1964, see Todd Purdum, *An Idea Whose Time Has Come* (New York, NY: Henry Holt & Co., 2014); Clay Risen, *The Bill of the Century: The Epic Battle for the Civil Rights Act* (New York, NY: Bloomsbury, 2014).

17. Wendy Underhill, "Voter Identification Requirements," National Conference of State Legislatures, January 17, 2019, www.ncsl.org/research/elections-and-campaigns/voter-id.aspx.

18. 208 U.S. 412 (1908).

19. 335 U.S. 464 (1948).

20. 368 U.S. 57, 61 (1961).

21. 404 U.S. 71 (1971).

22. 411 U.S. 677 (1973).

23. 429 U.S. 190 (1976).

24. "State of the Gender Pay Gap 2019," Payscale.com, https://www.payscale.com/data/gender-pay-gap.

25. Robert Jackson and Meredith Newman, "Sexual Harassment in the Federal Workplace Revisited: Influences on Sexual Harassment by Gender," *Public Administration Review* 64 (2004): 705–17.

26. 517 U.S. 620 (1996).

27. 539 U.S. 558 (2003).

28. 135 S. Ct. 2584 (2015).

29. 438 U.S. 265 (1978).

30. Howard Ball, *The Bakke Case: Race, Education and Affirmative Action* (Lawrence: University Press of Kansas, 2000).

31. 515 U.S. 200 (1995).

32. 539 U.S. 306 (2003).

33. 539 U.S. 244 (2003).

34. Michael Jones and Eileen Poe-Yamagata, *And Justice for Some* (Washington, DC: Building Blocks for Youth Press, 2000).

CHAPTER 6

1. Woodrow Wilson, *Congressional Government* (Baltimore, MD: Johns Hopkins University Press, 1981; originally published in 1885).

2. For a good discussion of the Constitutional Convention and issues related to Congress, see Charles Stewart III, "Congress and the Constitutional System," in *Institutions of American Democracy: The Legislative Branch*, eds. Paul J. Quirk and Sarah A. Binder (New York, NY: Oxford University Press, 2005).

3. See Reflective Democracy Campaign website, www.WhoLeads.us.

4. Alexander Hamilton, James Madison, and John Jay, *The Federalist Papers* (Chicago, IL: The New American Library of World Literature; reprinted in 1961).

5. Thomas Mann, *Unsafe at Any Margin: Interpreting Congressional Elections* (Washington, DC: Brookings Institution Press, 1978).

6. Paul Finkelman and Peter Wallenstein, *The Encyclopedia of American Political History* (Washington, DC: CQ Press, 2001), 55–56.

7. See, for example, Baker v. Carr, 369 U.S. 186 (1962); Reynolds v. Sims, 377 U.S. 533 (1964); Wesberry v. Sanders, 376 U.S. 1 (1964).

8. See James Madison, Federalist No. 63.

9. For a discussion of leadership in Congress, see Burdett A. Loomis, *The Contemporary Congress*, 3rd ed. (Boston: Bedford St. Martin's, 2000), chap. 6.

10. See Eric Schickler, "Institutional Development of Congress," in *Institutions of American Democracy: The Legislative Branch*, eds. Paul J. Quirk and Sarah A. Binder (New York, NY: Oxford University Press, 2005), chap. 2.

11. A classic work on congressional committees is Richard F. Fenno Jr., *Congressmen in Committees* (Boston: Little, Brown, 1973).

12. See Stephen S. Smith and Christopher Deering, *Committees in Congress*, 2nd ed. (Washington, DC: CQ Press, 1990).

13. See Scott A. Frisch and Sean Q. Kelly, *Committee Assignment Politics in the U.S. House of Representatives* (Norman, OK: University of Oklahoma Press, 2006).

14. See John Manley, "Wilbur Mills: A Study of Congressional Influence," *American Political Science Review* 63 (1969): 442–64.

15. Eric Redman, *The Dance of Legislation* (Seattle: University of Washington Press, 1974).

16. For a discussion of the motivations for senators to filibuster, see Sarah A. Binder and Stephen S. Smith, *Politics or Principles? Filibustering in the United States Senate* (Washington, DC: Brookings Institution Press, 1997).

17. Morris P. Fiorina, *Congress: Keystone of the Washington Establishment*, 2nd ed. (New Haven, CT: Yale University Press, 1989).

18. For an excellent discussion of the executive appointment process, see David E. Lewis, *The Politics of Presidential Appointments: Political Control and Bureaucratic Performance* (Princeton, NJ: Princeton University Press, 2008).

19. Richard F. Fenno Jr., *Home Style: House Members in Their Districts* (Boston: Little, Brown, 1978).

CHAPTER 7

1. Justin McCarthy, "In U.S., Socialist Presidential Candidates Least Appealing," Gallup.com, June 22, 2015, https://news.gallup.com/poll/183713/socialist-presidential-candidates-least-appealing.aspx.

2. Joseph Ellis, *His Excellency: George Washington* (New York, NY: Knopf, 2004).

3. Dates provided after a president's name refer to year(s) of service as president of the United States.

4. H. W. Brands, *Andrew Jackson: His Life and Times* (New York, NY: Random House, 2005).

5. See Ex Parte Merryman, 17 Fed. Cas. 144 (1961).

6. See Clinton Rossiter, *The American Presidency* (Baltimore, MD: Johns Hopkins University Press, 1987).

7. See John Locke, *Two Treatises of Government and a Letter Concerning Toleration*, ed. Peter Laslett (Cambridge, UK: Cambridge University Press, 1963).

8. Baron de Montesquieu, *The Spirit of the Laws*, eds. Anne M. Cohler et al. (Cambridge, UK: Cambridge University Press, 1989).

9. Michael J. Gerhardt, *The Federal Appointments Process: A Constitutional and Historical Analysis* (Durham, NC: Duke University Press, 2003).

10. 272 U.S. 52 (1926).

11. Robert F. Kennedy Jr., *Thirteen Days: A Memoir of the Cuban Missile Crisis* (New York, NY: W. W. Norton, 1999).

12. Mark Peterson, *Legislating Together: The White House and Capitol Hill from Eisenhower to Reagan* (Cambridge, MA: Harvard University Press, 1990).

13. Paul Light, *The President's Agenda: Domestic Policy Choice from Kennedy to Clinton* (Baltimore, MD: Johns Hopkins University Press, 1999).

14. Lee Hamilton and Jordan Tama, *A Creative Tension: The Foreign Policy Roles of the President and Congress* (Washington, DC: Woodrow Wilson Press, 2003).

15. Kenneth Mayer, *With the Stroke of a Pen: Executive Orders and Presidential Power* (Princeton, NJ: Princeton University Press, 2001).

16. The most recent version of this work is Richard Neustadt, *Presidential Power and the Modern Presidents: The Politics of Leadership from Roosevelt to Reagan* (New York, NY: Free Press, 1991).

17. Jules Witcover, *Crapshoot: Rolling the Dice on the Vice Presidency* (New York, NY: Crown, 1991).

18. Bob Woodward, *Plan of Attack* (New York, NY: Simon & Schuster, 2004).

19. For a comprehensive discussion of the various ways that modern presidents have organized the White House, see Stephen Hess, *Organizing the Presidency* (Washington, DC: Brookings Institution Press, 1988).

20. Bill Adler, *America's First Ladies* (New York, NY: Taylor, 2002).

21. Samuel Kernell, *Going Public: New Strategies of Presidential Leadership* (Washington, DC: CQ Press, 1992).

22. Elizabeth Drew, *On the Edge: The Clinton Presidency* (New York, NY: Touchstone, 1995).

23. See Kathleen Hall Jamieson and Paul Waldman, *The Press Effect: Politicians, Journalists, and the Stories That Shape the Political World* (New York, NY: Oxford University Press, 2002).

24. John A. Maltese, *Spin Control: The White House Office of Communications and the Management of Presidential News* (Chapel Hill: University of North Carolina Press, 1992).

CHAPTER 8

1. See *Washington Monthly*, a periodical that regularly reports on the excesses and waste in the federal bureaucracy.

2. For a comprehensive discussion of the virtues of modern bureaucracy, see Charles T. Goodsell, *The Case for Bureaucracy* (Chatham, NJ: Chatham House Publishers, 1994).

3. Max Weber, *Economy and Society*, eds. Guenther Roth and Claus Wittich (New York, NY: Bedminster Press, 1968), chaps. 11 and 12.

4. For a good discussion of organizational issues in the federal bureaucracy, see James Q. Wilson, *Bureaucracy: What Government Agencies Do and Why They Do It* (New York, NY: Basic Books, 1989).

5. See Joel Aberbach, *Keeping a Watchful Eye: The Politics of Congressional Oversight* (Washington, DC: Brookings Institution Press, 1990).

6. Beverly Cigler, "The Paradox of Professionalization," in *Democracy, Bureaucracy and the Study of Administration*, ed. Camilla Stivers (Boulder, CO: Westview Press, 2001).

7. For a good discussion of the growth of the federal bureaucracy during the New Deal era, see Brian J. Cook, "Serving the Liberal State," in *Bureaucracy and Self-Government: Reconsidering the Role of Public Administration in American Politics* (Baltimore, MD: Johns Hopkins University Press, 1996), chap. 5.

8. David Osborne and Ted Gaebler, *Reinventing Government: How the Entrepreneurial Spirit Is Transforming the Public Sector* (New York, NY: Penguin Books, 1993).

9. Harold S. Stanley and Richard G. Niemi, *Vital Statistics on American Politics, 2005–2006* (Washington, DC: CQ Press, 2006), 266.

10. "Obama Ups Diversity in Appointees," *Washington Post*, September 20, 2015, https://www.washingtonpost.com/politics/obama-ups-diversity-in-appointees/2015/09/20/5b042aac-5ffb-11e5-8e9e-dce8a2a2a679_graphic.html?noredirect=on.

11. Robert H. Wiebe, *The Search for Order: 1877–1920* (New York, NY: Hill and Wang, 1967).

12. Jasmine C. Lee, "Trump's Cabinet So Far Is More White and Male Than Any First Cabinet since Reagan's," *New York Times*, March 10, 2017, https://www.nytimes.com/interactive/2017/01/13/us/politics/trump-cabinet-women-minorities.html?_r=1

13. "Size of the Federal Bureaucracy," Boundless.com, http://oer2go.org/mods/en-boundless/www.boundless.com/political-science/textbooks/boundless-political-science-textbook/bureaucracy-13/bureaucracy-86/size-of-the-federal-bureaucracy-472-8009/index.html.

14. "American Government: Who Are the Bureaucrats?" USHistory.org, www.ushistory.org/gov/8c.asp.

15. See Ari Hoogenboom, *Outlawing the Spoils: A History of the Civil Service Reform Movement, 1865–1883* (Champaign: University of Illinois Press, 1961).

CHAPTER 9

1. For an account of the ways in which the Supreme Court's methods contribute to its image and status as an institution, see John Brigham, *The Cult of the Court* (Philadelphia: Temple University Press, 1987).

2. John Merryman, *The Civil Law Tradition* (Palo Alto, CA: Stanford University Press, 1985).

3. G. Alan Tarr and Mary Cornelia Porter, *State Supreme Courts in State and Nation* (New Haven, CT: Yale University Press, 1988).

4. 5 U.S. 137 (1803).

5. Arthur Hellman, *Restructuring Justice: The Innovations of the Ninth Circuit and the Future of the Federal Courts* (Ithaca, NY: Cornell University Press, 1991).

6. One rare exception to the strict use of the adversarial approach in the American legal system comes in the form of "structural reform litigation," a term that describes certain types of lawsuits brought against bureaucracies such as prisons, school systems, or welfare systems. Judges in these types of cases often assume a more active managerial approach in the process, overseeing the implementation of remedies and occasionally taking a proactive role to ensure that the lawyers are properly representing their clients' interests. For comprehensive analysis of one example of structural reform litigation in action, see Malcolm Feeley and Edward Rubin, *Judicial Policymaking and the Modern State: How the Court Reformed America's Prisons* (Cambridge, UK: Cambridge University Press, 2000). Of course, the more traditional adversarial system still tends to predominate in most other forms of civil litigation.

7. See George Fisher, *Plea Bargaining's Triumph: A History of Plea Bargaining in America* (Palo Alto, CA: Stanford University Press, 2003); Milton Heumann, *Plea Bargaining: The Experiences of Prosecutors, Judges, and Defense Attorneys* (Chicago, IL: University of Chicago Press, 1981).

8. James Eisenstein, Roy Flemming, and Peter Nardulli, *The Contours of Justice* (New York, NY: Addison-Wesley Publishing, 1988).

9. For an excellent analysis of the case, see R. Kent Newmyer, *The Supreme Court Under Marshall and Taney* (Arlington Heights, IL: Harlan Davison, 1968).

10. 17 U.S. 316 (1819).

11. 1 Wheat (14 U.S.) 304 (1816).

12. 358 U.S. 1 (1958).

13. 60 U.S. 393 (1857).

14. 347 U.S. 483 (1954).

15. 418 U.S. 683 (1974).

16. 6 Pet. (31 U.S.) 515 (1832).

17. 347 U.S. 483 (1954).

18. 370 U.S. 421 (1962).

19. Robert Dahl, "Decision-Making in a Democracy: The Supreme Court as a National Policy-Maker," *Journal of Public Law* 6 (1957): 279–95.

20. Philip DuBois, *From Ballot to Bench: Judicial Elections and the Quest for Accountability* (Austin: University of Texas Press, 1980).

21. Sheldon Goldman, *Picking Federal Judges* (New Haven, CT: Yale University Press, 1997).

22. Barbara Perry, *A Representative Supreme Court* (Westport, CT: Greenwood Press, 1991).

23. See "ABA Mission and Goals" on its website, https://www.americanbar.org/about_the_aba/aba-mission-goals/.

24. Ciara Torres-Spelliscy, Monique Chase, Emma Greenman, and Susan M. Liss, "Improving Judicial Diversity," Brennan Center for Justice, March 3, 2010, www.brennancenter.org/publication/improving-judicial-diversity.

25. John Maltese, *The Selling of Supreme Court Nominees* (Baltimore, MD: Johns Hopkins University Press, 1995).

26. Richard Davis, *Justices and Journalists: The U.S. Supreme Court and the Media* (Cambridge, UK: Cambridge University Press, 2011), 100.

27. Ethan Bronner, *Battle for Justice: How the Bork Nomination Shook America* (New York, NY: W. W. Norton, 1989).

28. 410 U.S. 113 (1973).

29. Richard Pacelle, *Between Law and Politics: The Solicitor General and the Structuring of Race, Gender, and Reproductive Rights Litigation* (College Station: Texas A&M University Press, 2003).

30. 478 U.S. 186 (1986).

31. 539 U.S. 558 (2003).

32. 384 U.S. 436 (1966).

33. Jeffrey Segal and Harold Spaeth, *The Supreme Court and the Attitudinal Model* (Cambridge, UK: Cambridge University Press, 1993), 246.

34. See, for example, Sheldon M. Novick, *Honorable Justice: The Life of Oliver Wendell Holmes, Jr.* (Boston, MA: Little, Brown & Co., 1989).

35. 567 U.S. 519 (2012).

36. 558 U.S. 310 (2010).

37. 531 U.S. 98 (2000).

38. Justice Antonin Scalia, interview with CNBC, October 10, 2005.

CHAPTER 10

1. Vincent Price, *Public Opinion* (Newbury Park, CA: SAGE, 1992), 5–22.

2. E. E. Schattschneider, *The Semisovereign People: A Realist's View of Democracy in America* (New York, NY: Holt, Rinehart and Winston, 1960).

3. V. O. Key Jr., *Public Opinion and American Democracy* (New York, NY: Knopf, 1961).

4. Samuel P. Huntington, *American Politics: The Promise of Disharmony* (Cambridge, MA: Harvard University Press, 1981).

5. For a good discussion of the value of individualism in the American culture, see Herbert McClosky and John Zaller, *The American Ethos* (Cambridge, MA: Harvard University Press, 1984).

6. The concept of partisanship and controversies surrounding it over the years are presented in Warren E. Miller and Merrill Shanks, *The New American Voter* (Cambridge, MA: Harvard University Press, 1996).

7. See M. Kent Jennings and Richard G. Niemi, *Generations and Politics: A Panel Study of Young Adults and Their Parents* (Princeton, NJ: Princeton University Press, 1981).

8. James Madison, Alexander Hamilton, and John Jay, Federalist No. 51, in *The Federalist Papers* (New York, NY: Doubleday, 1966; originally published in 1788).

9. Walter Lippmann, *Public Opinion* (New York, NY: Harcourt Brace Jovanovich, 1922).

10. Angus Campbell, Philip E. Converse, Warren E. Miller, and Donald E. Stokes, *The American Voter* (New York, NY: John Wiley and Sons, 1960).

11. Chris Cillizza, "Americans Know Literally Nothing about the Constitution," CNN Politics, September 13, 2017, https://www.cnn.com/2017/09/13/politics/poll-constitution/index.html.

12. V. O. Key Jr., *The Responsible Electorate* (Cambridge, MA: Belknap Harvard, 1966).

13. Benjamin I. Page and Robert Y. Shapiro, *The Rational Public: Fifty Years of Trends in Americans' Policy Preferences* (Chicago, IL: University of Chicago Press, 1992).

14. Samuel Kernell, *Going Public: New Strategies of Presidential Leadership* (Washington, DC: CQ Press, 1997).

15. Jack Dennis, ed., *Socialization to Politics* (New York, NY: John Wiley and Sons, 1973).

16. See, generally, David Easton, *A Systems Analysis of Political Life* (New York, NY: John Wiley and Sons, 1965).

17. Michael X. Delli Carpini and Scott Keeter, *What Americans Know About Politics and Why It Matters* (New Haven, CT: Yale University Press, 1996).

18. Michael Xenos, Ariadne Vromen, and Brian D. Loader, "The Great Equalizer? Patterns of Social Media Use and Youth Political Engagement in Three Advanced Democracies," *Information, Communication & Society*, 17 (2014): 151–67.

19. Pew Global Attitudes Project, "Social Networking Popular across the Globe," December 12, 2012, www.pewglobal .org/2012/12/12/social-networking-popular-across-globe/.

20. Herb Asher, *Polling and the Public*, 6th ed. (Washington, DC: CQ Press, 2004).

21. Charles W. Roll and Albert H. Cantril, *Polls: Their Use and Misuse in Politics* (New York, NY: Basic Books, 1972).

22. Gary Segura, "How the Exit Polls Misrepresent Latino Voters, and Badly," Latino Decisions blog, November 1, 2012, https://latinodecisions.com/blog/ how-the-exit-polls-misrepresent-latino-voters-and-badly.

23. For a more detailed discussion of these concepts, see W. Lance Bennett, *Public Opinion in American Politics* (New York, NY: Harcourt Brace Jovanovich, 1980).

CHAPTER 11

1. James Madison, Federalist No. 10, in *The Federalist Papers* (reprinted by Mentor Books, 1961), 77.

2. Alexis de Tocqueville, *Democracy in America* (New York, NY: Mentor Books, reprint edition, 1956).

3. Robert Dahl, *A Preface to Democratic Theory* (Cambridge, UK: Cambridge University Press, 1956).

4. David B. Truman, *The Governmental Process* (New York, NY: Alfred Knopf, 1951).

5. C. Wright Mills, *The Power Elite* (New York, NY: Oxford University Press, 1956).

6. John P. Heinz, Edward O. Laumann, Robert L. Nelson, and Robert H. Salisbury, *The Hollow Core* (Cambridge, MA: Harvard University Press, 1993).

7. See www.uspirg.org/about-us.

8. See www.opensecrets.org/lobbyists/index.asp.

9. Unitedwedream.org.

10. Blacklivesmatter.com.

11. 558 U.S. 310 (2010).

12. See Theodore J. Lowi, *The End of Liberalism* (New York, NY: W. W. Norton, 1979).

13. See William Gormley, "Regulatory Issue Networks in a Federal System," *Polity* 18 (1986): 595–620.

14. See www.uschamber.com.

15. Mancur Olson, *The Logic of Collective Action: Public Goods and the Theory of Groups* (Cambridge, MA: Harvard University Press, 1971), 22–35.

16. Robert Salisbury, "An Exchange Theory of Interest Groups," *Midwest Journal of Political Science* 13 (1969): 1–32.

17. Peter B. Clark and James Q. Wilson, "Incentives Systems: A Theory of Organization," *Administrative Science Quarterly* 6 (1961): 129–66.

18. For a good discussion of the influence of group member dedication to group effectiveness, see Olson, *The Logic of Collective Action: Public Goods and the Theory of Groups*, op. cit.

19. 410 U.S. 113 (1973).

20. Olson, *The Logic of Collective Action: Public Goods and the Theory of Groups*, op. cit.

21. See www.commoncause.org.

22. Ralph Nader, *Unsafe at Any Speed: The Designed-in Dangers of the American Automobile* (New York, NY: Grossman, 1965).

23. David Lowery and Holly Brasher, *Organized Interests and American Government* (New York, NY: McGraw-Hill, 2004), 247.

CHAPTER 12

1. 250 U.S. 616 (1919).

2. 438 U.S. 726 (1978).

3. "Divided 2019: The Media Gender Gap," Women's Media Center, January 31, 2019, http://www.womensmediacenter .com/reports/divided-2019-the-media-gender-gap.

4. See Philip Meyer, *Precision Journalism: A Reporter's Introduction to Social Science Methods* (Lanham, MD: Rowman & Littlefield, 2002).

5. The word *muckrakers* is derived from the idea that this group was "raking up the mud" from scandals and corruption of government and industry. For a descriptive history of the role the muckrakers played in progressive policy-making during the early nineteenth century, see Doris Kearns Goodwin, *The Bully Pulpit: Theodore Roosevelt, William Howard Taft and the Golden Age of Journalism* (New York, NY: Simon & Schuster, 2013).

6. For a chronicle of the Watergate story, see Bob Woodward and Carl Bernstein, *All the President's Men* (New York, NY: Simon & Schuster, 1974).

7. For a thorough review of the history of news, see Mitchell Stephens, *A History of News: From the Drum to the Satellite* (New York, NY: Viking, 1989).

8. Kurt Lang and Gladys Lang, *Television and Politics* (Edison, NJ: Transaction Publishers, 2001).

9. Marshall McLuhan, *Understanding Media: The Extensions of Man* (New York, NY: McGraw-Hill, 1964).

10. For a good review of the process and impact of presidential debates, see Alan Schroeder, *Presidential Debates* (New York, NY: Columbia University Press, 2000).

11. See Doris Graber, *Processing Politics: Learning from Television in the Internet Age* (Chicago, IL: University of Chicago Press, 2001).

12. Kenneth Dautrich, David Yalof, and Mark Hugo-Lopez, *The Future of the First Amendment* (New York, NY: Rowman & Littlefield, 2008).

13. Robert Bond et al., "A 61-Million-Person Experiment in Social Influence and Political Mobilization," *Nature*, vol. 489 (September 13, 2012): 295–98.

14. "U.S. Public Libraries Provide Access to Computers, the Internet, and Technology Training," Press Release, Bill and Linda Gates Foundation, 2005, https://www.gates-foundation.org/Media-Center/Press-Releases/2005/06/ Support-Needed-for-Library-Technology.

15. Mass communications researcher Joseph Klapper was a pioneer of the minimal effects (or limited effects) theory. He introduced the theory in a book titled *The Effects of Mass Communication* (New York, NY: Free Press, 1960).

16. For a good discussion of selection retention, see D. Sears and J. Freeman, "Selective Exposure to Information: A Critical

Review," in *The Process and Effects of Mass Communication*, ed. Wilbur Lang Schramm (Chicago: University of Illinois Press, 1972).

17. To learn more about social learning theory, see Albert Bandura, *Social Foundations of Thought and Action* (Englewood Cliffs, NJ: Prentice-Hall, 1986).

18. See L. Berkowitz, "Some Effects of Thought on Anti- and Pro-Social Influences of Media Effects," *Psychological Bulletin* 95 (1984): 410–27.

19. A pioneer in developing cultivation theory was George Gerbner. See George Gerbner et al., "Growing Up with Television: The Cultivation Perspective," in *Media Effects: Advances in Theory and Research*, eds. Jennings Bryant and Dolf Zillman (Hillsdale, NJ: Lawrence Erlbaum, 1994), 17–41.

20. A number of studies have demonstrated the agenda-setting power of the media, including Maxwell E. McCombs, "The Agenda-Setting Approach," in *Handbook of Political Communication*, eds. Dan D. Nimmo and Keith Sanders (Thousand Oaks, CA: SAGE, 1981), 121–140; and Shanto Iyengar and Donald R. Kinder, *News That Matters* (Chicago, IL: University of Chicago Press, 1987).

21. Doris A. Graber, *Mass Media and American Politics* (Washington, DC: CQ Press, 2002), 207.

22. Kenneth Dautrich and Thomas H. Hartley, *How the News Media Fail American Voters* (New York, NY: Columbia University Press, 1999), 92–95.

CHAPTER 13

1. "Toward a More Responsible Party System: A Report of the Committee on Political Parties, American Political Science Association," *American Political Science Review* 44, no. 3 (September 1950).

2. E. E. Schattschneider, *Party Government* (New York, NY: Farrar and Rinehart, 1942).

3. See John F. Bibby, *Politics, Parties and Elections in America*, 5th ed. (Belmont, CA: Wadsworth, 2002), chap. 2.

4. See Paul Finkelman and John Moore, "Political Parties," in *The Encyclopedia of American Political History*, eds. Peter Wallenstein and Paul Finkelman (Washington, DC: CQ Press, 2001).

5. See Bibby, *Politics, Parties and Elections in America*, op. cit.

6. V. O. Key Jr., "A Theory of Critical Elections," *Journal of Politics* 16, no. 1 (1955): 13–18.

7. See Walter Dean Burnham, *Critical Elections and the Mainsprings of American Politics* (New York, NY: W. W. Norton, 1970).

8. For a thorough analysis of how the American party system has changed since the New Deal, see Sidney M. Milkus, *The President and the Parties: The Transformation of the American Party System since the New Deal* (New York, NY: Oxford University Press, 1993).

9. Paul Allen Beck, "The Dealignment Era in America," in *Electoral Change in Advanced Industrial Democracies: Realignment or Dealignment*, eds. M. N. Dalton, T. T. Flanagan, and H. Beck (Princeton, NJ: Princeton University Press, 1984).

10. Angus Campbell, Philip E. Converse, Warren E. Miller, and Donald E. Stokes, *The American Voter* (New York, NY: Wiley, 1960), 121.

11. For a thorough discussion of the concept of party identification, see Warren E. Miller and J. Merrill Shanks, *The New American Voter* (Cambridge, MA: Harvard University Press, 1996).

12. Philip E. Converse, "The Concept of the Normal Vote," in *Elections and the Political Order*, eds. Angus Campbell, Philip E. Converse, Warren E. Miller, and Donald E. Stokes (New York, NY: John Wiley and Sons, 1966).

13. For a discussion of governance and the parties, see John H. Aldrich, *Why Parties? The Origin and Transformation of Political Parties in America* (Chicago, IL: University of Chicago Press, 1995), chap. 7.

14. See Richard S. Conley, *The Presidency, Congress and Divided Government* (College Station: Texas A&M University Press, 2002).

15. For a good discussion of the rationale for America's two-party system, see Frank J. Sorauf, *Party Politics in America*, 5th ed. (Boston, MA: Little, Brown, 1984).

16. To learn more about nineteenth- and twentieth-century third-party candidacies, see Steven J. Rosenstone, Roy L. Behr, and Edward H. Lazarus, *Third Parties in America*, 2nd ed. (Princeton, NJ: Princeton University Press, 1996).

17. For a discussion of the struggle for suffrage, see William H. Flanigan and Nancy H. Zingale, *Political Behavior of the American Electorate* (Washington, DC: CQ Press, 1998), chap. 2.

18. 60 U.S. 393 (1857).

19. See Margaret M. Conway, *Political Participation in the United States* (Washington, DC: CQ Press, 2000), chap. 5.

20. Some southern states continued to use the poll tax in state elections after passage of the Twenty-fourth Amendment. In 1966, the U.S. Supreme Court in *Harper v. Virginia Board of Elections* 383 U.S. 663 (1966) outlawed the use of the poll tax in state elections as well as federal elections.

21. See Nancy McGlen and Karen O'Connor, *Women, Politics and American Society*, 2nd ed. (Upper Saddle River, NJ: Prentice Hall, 1998).

22. "Election 2016 Presidential Results," CNN Politics, www.cnn.com/election/results/president.

23. "2016 National Election Eve Poll," Latino Decisions, www.latinodecisions.com/files/8614/7866/3919/National_2016__Xtabs.pdf.

24. A thorough discussion of the development of states' voter registration systems can be found in Joseph P. Harris, *Registration of Voters in the United States* (Washington, DC: Brookings Institution Press, 1929).

25. A federal statute requires that the waiting period from becoming a state resident to being eligible to vote may not exceed 30 days.

26. Michael D. Martinez and David B. Hill, "Did Motor Voter Work?" *American Politics Quarterly* 27 (1999): 296–315.

27. See Lee Sigelman et al., "Voting and Non-voting: A Multi-Election Perspective," *American Journal of Political Science* 29 (November 1985): 749–65.

28. See Raymond E. Wolfinger and Steven J. Rosenstone, *Who Votes?* (New Haven, CT: Yale University Press, 1980), 44–46.

29. Norman H. Nie, Jane Junn, and Kenneth Stehlik-Barry, *Education and Democratic Citizenship in America* (Chicago, IL: University of Chicago Press, 1996).

30. Todd G. Shields and Robert K. Goidel, "Participation Rates, Socioeconomic Class Biases and Congressional Elections: A Cross Validation," *American Journal of Political Science* 41 (1997): 683–91.

31. Jens Manuel Krogstad, "2016 Electorate Will Be the Most Diverse in U.S. History," Pew Research Center, February 3,

2016, www.pewresearch.org/fact-tank/2016/02/03/2016-electorate-will-be-the-most-diverse-in-u-s-history

32. Jens Manuel Krogstad and Mark Hugo Lopez, "Hillary Clinton Won Latino Vote but Fell below 2012 Support for Obama," Pew Research Center, November 29, 2016, www.pewresearch.org/fact-tank/2016/11/09/hillary-clinton-wins-latino-vote-but-falls-below-2012-support-for-obama

33. Holly K. Sonneland and Nicki Fleischner, "Chart: How U.S. Latinos Voted in the 2016 Presidential Election," Americas Society/Council of the Americas, November 20, 2016, https://www.as-coa.org/articles/chart-how-us-latinos-voted-2016-presidential-election

34. Anthony Downs, *An Economic Theory of Democracy* (New York, NY: Harper and Brothers, 1957).

35. Angus Campbell, Philip E. Converse, Warren E. Miller, and Donald E. Stokes, *Elections and the Political Order* (New York, NY: Wiley, 1966).

36. For a comprehensive examination of the trends in voter turnout, see Thomas E. Patterson, *The Vanishing American Voter: Public Involvement in an Age of Uncertainty* (New York, NY: Alfred A. Knopf, 2002).

37. See Ivor Crewe, "As the World Turns Out," *Public Opinion* 4 (February–March 1981).

38. For a discussion of trends in political efficacy, see also M. Margaret Conway, *Political Participation in the United States*, 3rd ed. (Washington, DC: CQ Press, 2000), 51–53.

39. Robert Putnam, *Bowling Alone* (New York, NY: Simon & Schuster, 2000).

40. Kevin Robillard, "Youth Vote Was Decisive," Politico.com, November 7, 2012, www.politico.com/story/2012/11/study-youth-vote-was-decisive-083510

41. The psychological concept of party identification is developed in Angus Campbell, Philip E. Converse, Warren E. Miller, and Donald E. Stokes, *The American Voter* (New York, NY: Wiley, 1960).

42. For discussion of the role of party identification in forming vote choices, see Warren E. Miller and J. Merrill Shanks, *The New American Voter* (Cambridge, MA: Harvard University Press, 1996); and William H. Flanagan and Nancy H. Zingale, *Political Behavior of the American Electorate*, 9th ed. (Washington, DC: CQ Press, 1998).

43. See Martin P. Wattenberg, *The Decline of Political Parties 1952–1996* (Cambridge, MA: Harvard University Press, 1998).

44. Miller and Shanks, *The New American Voter*, op. cit., chap. 12.

45. See Norman Nie, Sidney Verba, and John Petrocik, *The Changing American Voter* (Cambridge, MA: Harvard University Press, 1979).

46. Anthony Downs, *An Economic Theory of Democracy* (New York, NY: Harper and Brothers, 1957).

47. Morris P. Fiorina, *Retrospective Voting in American National Elections* (New Haven, CT: Yale University Press, 1981).

CHAPTER 14

1. See Lawrence D. Longley and Neal R. Peirce, *The Electoral College Primer* (New Haven, CT: Yale University Press, 1996).

2. For a good discussion of the development of parties in the early republic, see Stanley Elkins and Eric McKitrick, *The Age of Federalism: The Early American Republic 1788–1800* (New York, NY: Oxford University Press, 1993).

3. See Paul Finkelman and John Moore, "The Democratic Party," in *The Encyclopedia of American Political History*, eds. Peter Wallenstein and Paul Finkelman (Washington, DC: CQ Press, 2001).

4. See Tadahisa Kuroda, *The Origins of the Twelfth Amendment: The Electoral College in the Early Republic 1787–1804* (Westport, CT: Greenwood Press, 1994).

5. A thorough discussion of the nomination process as well as other aspects of the presidential campaign can be found in Stephen Wayne, *The Road to the White House 2008*, 8th ed. (Boston: Wadsworth Press, 2008).

6. Larry M. Bartels, *Presidential Primaries and the Dynamics of Public Choice* (Princeton, NJ: Princeton University Press, 1988).

7. See John F. Bibby, *Politics, Parties and Elections in America* (Chicago, IL: Nelson-Hall, 1992), chap. 6.

8. Ibid.

9. For a good discussion of the relevance of the New Hampshire primary, see Dante J. Scala, *Stormy Weather: The New Hampshire Primary and Presidential Politics* (New York, NY: Palgrave Macmillan, 2003).

10. Nevada disrupted this traditional order in 2008 when it scheduled its Republican and Democratic caucuses for January 19, three days before the New Hampshire primary. New Hampshire then moved its primary to January 8.

11. See William G. Mayer and Andrew Busch, *The Frontloading Problem in Presidential Nominations* (Washington, DC: Brookings Institution Press, 2003).

12. For a history of party conventions, see CQ Press's *National Party Conventions 1831–2004* (2005).

13. See, for example, James Druckman, "The Power of Television Images: The First Kennedy-Nixon Debate Revisited," *Journal of Politics* 65, no. 2 (2003): 559–571.

14. See Alan Schroeder, *Presidential Debates: 50 Years of High Risk TV* (New York, NY: Columbia University Press, 2008).

15. See Darrell M. West, *Television Advertising in Election Campaigns 1952–1996* (Washington, DC: CQ Press, 1997).

16. For an analysis of the effects of negative ads on voters, see Richard R. Lau and Gerald M. Pomper, *Negative Campaigning: An Analysis of U.S. Senate Elections* (Lanham, MD: Rowman & Littlefield, 2004).

17. For a discussion of why the Electoral College was created and how it has changed, see Lawrence D. Longley and Neal R. Peirce, *The Electoral College Primer 2000* (New Haven, CT: Yale University Press, 1999), chap. 2.

18. Ibid., chap. 4.

19. See David B. Magleby and Candice J. Nelson, *The Money Chase* (Washington, DC: Brookings Institution Press, 1990).

20. 424 U.S. 1 (1976).

21. 540 U.S. 93 (2003).

22. 558 U.S. 310 (2010).

23. For a thorough discussion of congressional elections, see Paul S. Herrnson, *Congressional Elections: Campaigning at Home and in Washington* (Washington, DC: CQ Press, 2011).

24. For a complete discussion of the coattail effect, see Gary C. Jacobson, *Electoral Origins of Divided Government 1946–1988* (Boulder, CO: Westview Press, 1990).

25. See Gary C. Jacobson, *The Politics of Congressional Elections* (New York, NY: Pearson, 2012), chap. 3.

26. Mary Beth Marklein, "*Presidential Race Raised Student Political Involvement,*" *USA Today*, January 22, 2009.

CHAPTER 15

1. Charles Lindblom, "The Science of Muddling Through," *Public Administration Review* 19 (Spring 1959): 79–88.

2. Carl E. Van Horn, Donald Baumer, and William T. Gormley Jr., *Politics and Public Policy*, 3rd ed. (Washington, DC: CQ Press, 2001).

3. Ibid., 193–230.

4. William T. Gormley Jr., "Interest Group Interventions in the Administrative Process," in *The Interest Group Connection*, eds. Paul S. Herrnson, Ronald G. Shaiko, and Clyde Wilcox (Chatham, NJ: Chatham House, 1998), 213–223.

5. See Adam Smith, *The Wealth of Nations* (reprinted by New York, NY: Modern Library, 1994).

6. John Maynard Keynes's most famous work is *The General Theory of Employment, Interest, and Money* (New York, NY: Harcourt Brace Jovanovich, 1936).

7. For a more detailed discussion of this argument, see the work of Michael Lewis-Beck, including- *Economics and Elections: The Major Western Democracies* (Ann Arbor: University of Michigan Press, 1990).

8. Shelley Lynne Tomkin, *Inside OMB: Politics and Process in the President's Budget Office* (Armonk, NY: M. E. Sharpe, 1998).

9. See Allen Schick and Felix Lostracco, *The Federal Budget: Politics, Policy, Process* (Washington, DC: Brookings Institution Press, 2000).

10. nces.ed.gov/programs/digest/d13/tables/dt13_203.60 .asp?current=yes.

11. nces.ed.gov/fastfacts/display.asp? id=55.

12. William Leuchtenberg, *Franklin Roosevelt and the New Deal* (New York, NY: HarperCollins, 1963).

13. Kristen Lindenmeyer, *A Right to Childhood: The U.S. Children's Bureau and Child Welfare* (Urbana: University of Illinois Press, 1997).

14. Jonathan Oberlander, *The Political Life of Medicare* (Chicago, IL: University of Chicago Press, 2003).

15. Robert Hudson, ed., *The New Politics of Old Age Policy* (Baltimore, MD: Johns Hopkins University Press, 2005).

16. William Gesler and Thomas Ricketts, eds., *Health Care in Rural North America: The Geography of Health Care Services in North America* (Newark, NJ: Rutgers University Press, 1992).

17. Aaron Wildavsky, "The Two Presidencies," *Trans-action* 4, no. 2 (December 1966): 7–14.

18. D. F. Flemming, *The Cold War and Its Origins: 1917–1960* (New York, NY: Doubleday, 1961).

19. David DiLeo, *George Ball, Vietnam and the Rethinking of Containment* (Chapel Hill: University of North Carolina Press, 1991).

20. Stanley Karnow, *Vietnam: A History* (New York, NY: Penguin, 1997).

21. One of the key architects of this new understanding was Bush's secretary of state, James A. Baker III. See James A. Baker III, *The Politics of Diplomacy* (New York, NY: Putnam, 1995).

22. Many of these criticisms are discussed in Samantha Power's award-winning book *A Problem from Hell: America and the Age of Genocide* (New York, NY: Harper Perennial, 2003).

23. Niall Ferguson, *Colossus: The Rise and Fall of the American Empire* (New York, NY: Penguin Books, 2005).

24. Joseph Nye, *Soft Power: The Means to Success in World Politics* (New York, NY: Public Affairs, 2005).

25. Louis Fisher, "Without Restraint: Presidential Military Initiatives from Korea to Bosnia," in *Domestic Sources of American Foreign Policy*, 3rd ed., eds. Eugene Wittkopf and James McCormick (Lanham, MD: Rowman & Littlefield, 1999), 141–155.

26. Geoffrey Kemp, "Presidential Management of the Executive Bureaucracy," in *United States Foreign Policy: The Search for a New Role*, eds. Robert J. Art and Seyom Brown (Upper Saddle River, NJ: Prentice Hall, 1993).

INDEX

foreign affairs, 140–141

Great Depression, 164, 268

issue of Court size, 179

New Deal, 140, 282, 324

permanent bureaucracies of 140

presidency of, 140

ranking of, 140

relations with the media, 155

Social Security legislation, 317

vetoes by, *147*

Roosevelt, Theodore, 135, 137, 139, *147, 369*

Roper Organization, 217

Rousseau, Jean-Jacques, 6, 19

Rules Committee, 125, *125*

safe seat, 312, *312*

sampling error, 216, *216*

Sanders, Bernie, 3, 16, *145, 241, 249, 268, 299*

Santa Fe Independent School District v. Doe (2000), 66

Schenck v. United States (1919), 67

Schumer, Chuck, *15, 118, 143*

scientific sample, 213, *213*

Second Amendment, 72–73, 352

Second Treatise of Government (Locke), 143

Sedition Act, 69

select committee, 120, *120*

Senate, 115–116, 118. *See also* Congress

Senior Executive Service (SES), 172, *172*

separation of powers, 29, *29*

September 11, 2001, terrorist attacks, 142, 149, 331

Sestak, Joe, *295*

Seventeenth Amendment, 357

Seventh Amendment, 353–354

Shays's Rebellion, 26, *26*

Shelby County v. Holder (2013), 93

Sherbert v. Verner (1963), 62

signing statements, *148*

Sipuel v. Board of Regents of University of Oklahoma (1948), *89*

Sixteenth Amendment, 357

Sixth Amendment, 77, 353

SLAPS test, 70, *70*

Slaughterhouse Cases (1873), 356

slavery issue, 28–29, *28*

social capital, 286, *286*

social contract, 6, *6*

social equality, 84, 8i4

socialism, 326, *326*

Socialist Party, 273, 274

social learning theory, 257, *257*

social media, *220, 251, 258, 259*

social movements, 96, *96*

Social Security Act (1935), 160

soft money, 309, *309*

solicitor general, 194, *194*

solidary benefits (of group membership), 231, *231*

sovereignty, 44, *44*

Speaker of the House, 117, *117*

spoils system, 173, *173*

Stamp Act (1765), 22

standing, 186, *186*

standing committees, 119, *119, 120*

stare decisis, 195, *195*

state legal systems and state courts, 178

STATES (Strengthening the Tenth Amendment Through Entrusting States) Act, 317

states, relations between, 47–49

State of the Union address, 146, *146*

straw poll, 212, *212*

strict construction, 38, *38*

strict scrutiny, 90, *90*

Sugar Act of 1764, 22

SUGing (selling under the guise of polling), 214

supply-side economics, 320, *320*

supremacy clause, 47, *47*

Swalwell, Eric, *268*

Sweatt v. Painter (1950), *89*

symbolic speech, 71, *71*

Taft, William, *369*

Taft-Hartley Act, 234

talk radio, 253, *253*

Tax Cuts and Jobs Act (2017), 128, 328

Taylor, Zachary, 135, *369*

Tea Act (1773), 23

Telecommunications Act (1996), 243, 257

Temporary Assistance to Needy Families (TANF), 327

Tenth Amendment, 354

Texas v. Johnson (1989), 71

theocracy, 6, *6*

Think tanks, *319*

Third Amendment, 352

Thirteenth Amendment, 87, *87,* 355–356

Three-Fifths Compromise, 29, *29*

Title IX, 98, *98*

Tory Party, 263

Townshend Acts, 23

trade association, 232, *232*

Truman, Harry, 135, 137, *370*

firing of Douglas MacArthur by, 144

New Deal coalition and, 268

polls projecting defeat, *213*

presidential approval, 214

ranking of, 140

troops sent to Korea by, 149

Truman Doctrine, 141, 330, *332*

vetoes by, *147*

Truman Doctrine, 141, 330, *332*

Trump, Donald, 9, *15,* 135, *143, 190, 265, 302, 303, 336, 370*

claim during 2016 campaign, *302*

election of 2016, 2, *111*

election of 2020, 3

executive orders of, 21, 150

presidency of, 142

presidential honeymoon, *214*

Twitter targets, 156, 247

vetoes by, *147*

Trump, Melania, *152*

Trump v. Hawaii (2018), 103

Trustees of Dartmouth College v. Woodward (1819), 347

Twelfth Amendment, 355

Twentieth Amendment, 358–359

Twenty-fifth Amendment, 360–361

Twenty-first Amendment, 359